ASSESSMENT

FIFTH EDITION

JOHN SALVIA
The Pennsylvania State University

JAMES E. YSSELDYKE
University of Minnesota

HOUGHTON MIFFLIN COMPANY **BOSTON**
Dallas   Geneva, Illinois   Palo Alto   Princeton, New Jersey

Part-opening photo credits: Part 1, p. xviii, Elizabeth Crewes; Part 2, p. 64, Susan Lapides; Part 3, p. 158, Nita Winter/The Image Works; Part 4, p. 334, Meri Houtchens-Kitchens/The Picture Cube; Part 5, p. 518, Susan Lapides.

Figure photo credits: Figure 10.2, p. 207, Photo courtesy Stoetling Company; Figure 12.1, p. 238, Courtesy Titmus Optical; Figure 12.2, p. 244, Courtesy Maico Hearing Instruments, Inc.; Figure 12.5, p. 251, Welch Allyn, Inc., Skaneateles Falls, NY; Figure 16.2, Peabody Individual Achievement Test–Revised (PIAT-R) by Frederick C. Markwardt, Jr., © 1989, American Guidance Service, Inc., Circle Pines, MN 55014-1796. All rights reserved.

Excerpt on p. 186 from *The Random House Dictionary of the English Language,* 1967. Used by permission of the publisher.

Printed in the U.S.A.

Library of Congress Catalog Card Number: 90-83040

ISBN: 0-395-54451-3

ABCDEFGHIJ–D–9543210

CONTENTS

PREFACE

Audience for This Book

Assessment, Fifth Edition, is intended for a first course in assessment for those whose careers require understanding and informed use of assessment data. The primary audience comprises those who are or will be teachers in special education at the elementary or secondary level. The secondary audience is the large support system for special educators: school psychologists, child development specialists, counselors, educational administrators, nurses, preschool educators, reading specialists, social workers, speech and language specialists, and specialists in therapeutic recreation. In writing for those who are taking their first course in assessment, we have assumed no prior knowledge of measurement and statistical concepts.

Purpose

Students have the right to an appropriate education in the least restrictive educational environment. Decisions regarding the most appropriate environment and the most appropriate program for an individual should be data-based decisions. Assessment is one part of the process of collecting the data necessary for educational decision making, and the administration of tests is one part of assessment. To date, tests have sometimes been used to restrict educational opportunities; many assessment practices have not been in the best interests of students. Those who assess have a tremendous responsibility; assessment results are used to make decisions that directly and significantly affect students' lives. Those who assess are responsible for knowing the devices they use and for understanding the limitations of those devices and the procedures they require.

Teachers are confronted with the results of tests, checklists, scales, and batteries on an almost daily basis. This information is intended to be useful to them in understanding and making educational plans for their students. But the intended use and actual use of assessment information have often differed. However good the intentions of test designers, misuse and misunderstanding of tests may well occur unless teachers are informed consumers and users of tests. To be an informed consumer and user of tests, a teacher must bring to the task certain domains of knowledge, including knowledge of the basic uses of tests, the important attributes of good tests, and the kinds of behaviors sampled by particular tests. This text aims at helping education professionals acquire that knowledge.

The New Edition

The fifth edition continues in the tradition of the style, content, and organization of the first four editions. It offers evenhanded, documented evaluations of standardized tests in each domain; straightforward and clear coverage of basic assumptions and assessment concepts; and case applications reinforcing the decision-making process.

We also have made a significant effort to produce a text that is even more applied than its predecessors. In addition to its strong coverage of tests and basic concepts, the fifth edition features an extensively revised chapter on assessment of toddlers, infants, and preschool children (Chapter 21) and two entirely new chapters — Chapter 23, "Assessing Behavior through Observation," and Chapter 24, "Teacher-Made Tests of Achievement." Also significantly revised are Chapter 13, "Assessment of Oral Language," and Chapter 15, "Assessment of Personality."

Test information has been updated, and new reviews added. The following new or revised tests are reviewed in this fifth edition of *Assessment:*

Peabody Individual Achievement Test – Revised

KeyMath Revised: A Diagnostic Inventory of Essential Mathematics

Test of Written Language – 2 (TOWL-2)

Woodcock-Johnson Psycho-Educational Battery – Revised

Wechsler Preschool and Primary Scale of Intelligence – Revised (WPPSI-R)

Otis-Lennon School Ability Test (OLSAT)

Battelle Developmental Inventory (BDI)

The new text, in five parts, is an introduction to psychoeducational assessment in special education. Parts 1 and 2 provide a general overview of and orientation to assessment. In Part 1, testing is placed in the broader context of assessment, assessment is described as a multifaceted process, the kinds of decisions made using assessment data are delineated, and basic terminology and concepts are introduced. Chapter 3, "Legal and Ethical Considerations in Assessment," covers issues in current practice that are dictated in the courtroom and mandated by legislation and includes guidelines on collection, maintenance, and dissemination of pupil records. In Part 2, we introduce students to the basic concepts of measurement, giving readers an understanding of the measurement principles needed not only to comprehend the content in Parts 3 and 4 but also to apply and use information obtained from tests they may administer.

In Parts 3 and 4, we review the most commonly used formal assessment devices. In order to distinguish more clearly between tests that measure processes (such as intelligence, sensory acuity, and personality) and those that assess skills (for example, reading, mathematics, and adaptive behavior), we have divided the chapters that evaluate tests into two parts—Assessment of Processes and Assessment of Skills.

Each chapter that includes test evaluations follows a similar format. Initially, we describe the kinds of behaviors typically sampled by tests in the domain under discussion. Representative tests are then reviewed. For each test, we describe its general format, the kinds of behaviors it samples, the kinds of scores it provides, the nature of the sample on whom it was standardized, and evidence for its reliability and validity. The technical adequacy of the tests is evaluated in light of the standards set forth by three professional associations (American Psychological Association, American Educational Research Association, and National Council on Measurement in Education) in their document entitled *Standards for Educational and Psychological Tests*.

Part 4 concludes with two new chapters. Chapter 23, "Assessing Behavior Through Observation," is a comprehensive overview of observation filled with practical advice on defining, sampling, targeting, and evaluating student behavior. It provides students with a general overview of good practices to make decisions about academic and social instruction. Chapter 24, "Teacher-Made Tests of Achievement," provides an overview of the advantages of teacher-made tests, testing formats, direct performance measures, assessment in core achievement areas, and potential sources of difficulty in teacher-made tests.

In Part 5, we examine the ways in which assessment data are used in educational settings to make decisions about students. We do this not only by considering the various procedures that are involved in educational decision making but also by including case studies that apply the procedures to students at various grade levels with a range of learning difficulties. Part 5 is organized according to three different kinds of decisions: referral, classification, and instructional planning. In Chapter 25, we describe the ways in which assessment information is used to make referral decisions, and we include specific coverage of the very important process of prereferral intervention. We also discuss the ways in which teachers and related services personnel can gather information on instructional effectiveness and how such information can be used to make referral decisions. In Chapter 26, we describe the use of assessment information in making classification decisions about students who have been referred for special services. Chapter 27 examines the process of using assessment information to plan instructional programs for students who have been classified. The case studies in the chapters follow this same decision-making process, continuing throughout Part 5 to illustrate the activities that correspond to each stage.

A summary of chapter content, additional readings, and study questions appear at the end of each chapter in the text to help readers expand their knowledge and apply the fundamental concepts developed. Chapters in Part 2 also include problems related to the measurement concepts discussed in the text;

answers are provided to give students immediate feedback. Appendixes at the end of the text include comparative features of major cognitive batteries, two tables of statistical data, a list of equations used in the text, a list of tests reviewed, a directory of test publishers, and suggestions for how to review a test. Complete bibliographical references for in-text citations follow the appendixes.

Assessment is a controversial topic; we have attempted to be objective and evenhanded in our review and portrayal of current assessment practices.

Acknowledgments

Many people have been of assistance in our efforts. We wish to express our sincere appreciation to the following individuals who have provided constructive criticism and helpful suggestions during the development of this text:

Candace Burns, University of Arkansas (Little Rock)

William Callahan, University of Nebraska (Omaha)

Mary S. Kelly, Teachers College, Columbia University

Jeffrey Messerer, Northeastern Illinois University

Kay Norlander, University of Connecticut (Storrs)

Linda Christie Peterson, University of Mary (Bismarck)

Kay Stevens, University of Kentucky

Sherri Strawser, University of Utah

We especially appreciate the contributions of Tom Frank, The Pennsylvania State University, who revised the section on assessment of hearing difficulties in Chapter 12, and Stephen Camarata, Vanderbilt University, who revised Chapter 13 on the assessment of oral language.

The text represents a collaborative effort, and we believe we have produced an integrated text that speaks for both of us.

John Salvia
James E. Ysseldyke

PART 1

ASSESSMENT: AN OVERVIEW

School personnel regularly use assessment information to make important decisions about students. Part 1 of this text is a description of basic considerations in psychological and educational assessment of students.

Chapter 1 is a description of assessment and includes a delineation of the factors that must be considered in assessment, the various kinds of assessment information school personnel collect, and a description of the steps in the assessment process. In Chapter 2, assessment is more specifically defined, the purposes of assessing students are described, and fundamental assumptions underlying assessment are discussed. Chapter 3 is a description of fundamental legal and ethical considerations in assessment.

The concepts and principles introduced in Part 1 constitute a foundation for informed and critical use of tests and the information they provide.

C·H·A·P·T·E·R 1

THE ASSESSMENT OF STUDENTS

All of us have taken tests during our lives. In elementary and secondary school, tests were given to measure our scholastic aptitude or intelligence or to evaluate the extent to which we had profited from instruction. We may have taken personality tests, interest tests, or tests that would assist us in vocational selection and career planning. As part of applying for a job, we may have taken civil service examinations or tests of specific skills like typing or manual dexterity. Enlisting in the armed forces meant taking a number of tests. Enrolling in college meant undergoing entrance examinations. Those of us who decided to go on to graduate school usually had to take an aptitude test; many of those who became teachers had to take a national teacher examination. Physicians, lawyers, psychologists, real estate agents, and many others were required to take tests to demonstrate their competence before being licensed to practice their profession or trade. It is estimated that students attending America's public schools take more than 250 million standardized tests each year. We witness today a situation in which school districts increasingly are being held accountable for the performance of their pupils. District personnel use tests to document student achievement. At the time we prepared this edition some states (such as Kentucky) were proposing to base the magnitude of teacher pay increases on the magnitude of student achievement.

Throughout their professional careers, teachers, guidance counselors, school social workers, school psychologists, and school administrators will be required to give, score, and interpret a wide variety of tests. Because professional school personnel routinely receive test information from their colleagues within the schools and from community agencies outside the schools, they need a working knowledge of important aspects of testing.

According to the joint committee of the American Psychological Association (APA), the American Educational Research Association (AERA), and the National Council on Measurement in Education (NCME), a test "may be thought of as a set of tasks or questions intended to elicit particular types of behaviors when presented under standardized conditions and to yield scores that have desirable psychometric properties" (1974, p. 2). *Testing*, then, means exposing a person to a particular set of questions in order to obtain a score. That score is the end product of testing.

Testing may be part of a larger process known as *assessment;* however, testing and assessment are not synonymous. Assessment in educational settings is a multifaceted process that involves far more than the administration of a test. When we assess students, we consider the way they perform a variety of tasks in a variety of settings or contexts, the meaning of their performances in terms of the total functioning of the individual, and the likely explanations for those performances. Good assessment procedures take into consideration the fact that anyone's performance on any task is influenced by the demands of the task itself, by the history and characteristics the individual brings to the task, and by the factors inherent in the setting in which the assessment is carried out.

Assessment is the process of collecting information. Some of the information that is collected may be test data; much of it will likely be other forms of information. However, assessment is more than just the collection of information; it is collection with a purpose. *Assessment is the process of collecting data for the purposes of (1) specifying and verifying problems and (2) making decisions about students.* As shown in Figure 1.1, five[1] general types of decisions are made: referral, screening, classification, instructional planning, and pupil progress evaluation. Also, as shown in Figure 1.1, in the schools we specify and verify problems in three areas: academic, behavior, and physical.

TYPES OF DECISIONS

The decisions required in special education assessment are varied and complex. Figure 1.2 shows the nature and relationship of the major types of decisions. Figure 1.3 shows how teachers are involved in decisions.

Referral Decisions

Referral decisions are decisions about the need to seek additional assistance from other school personnel. Although anyone can refer students (for example, parents, the students themselves, or other individuals), teachers are generally the ones who make referrals. Teachers regularly refer students to other professionals in the school and sometimes to professionals or agencies outside the school. Recent surveys show that 3 to 5 percent of the students in public schools are referred each year for psychological and educational assessment.

---

1. Actually, there are at least three more reasons for assessment. Individuals may be assessed because they are curious about themselves, because they are participants in research studies, or because a school district is evaluating educational programs.

About 92 percent of those students who are referred are tested, and about 73 percent of those who are tested are placed in special education (Algozzine, Christenson, & Ysseldyke, 1982).

Whom do teachers refer for evaluation? That question can be answered simply: they refer students who bother them. Although the question can be answered simply, it is not easy to predict whether a student will be referred. Different teachers are bothered by different behaviors, although some behaviors and characteristics would probably bother most, if not all, teachers.

Screening Decisions

Since there is some variability in teachers' tolerances for and awareness of various problems, there may be students in classrooms who are exceptional and who are not having their needs met. School districts want to find these students and provide special services to them, so screening programs are started. Thus, screening decisions are essentially administrative in nature. All students in particular schools or school districts are given cursory examinations to ascertain whether any of the students who are evaluated need further, more intensive assessment. Tests may be administered to identify students who differ significantly from their agemates (in either a positive or a negative sense) and who therefore require special education services. Just as vision and hearing tests are routinely given to identify pupils with vision or hearing problems, intelligence tests are administered to identify students who may

FIGURE 1.1   Assessment Is the Collection of Data to Specify and Verify Problems and to Aid in Decision Making

Problem Area	Referral	Type of Decision			
		Screening	Classification	Instructional Planning	Evaluating Pupil Progress
Academic					
Behavior					
Physical					

need special attention, either because of limited intellectual capacity or because of highly superior intellectual ability. Achievement tests, measures of what has been taught to and learned by students, are routinely given to identify students who are experiencing academic difficulty and for whom further assessment may be appropriate.

FIGURE 1.2   Educational Assessment and Decision Making

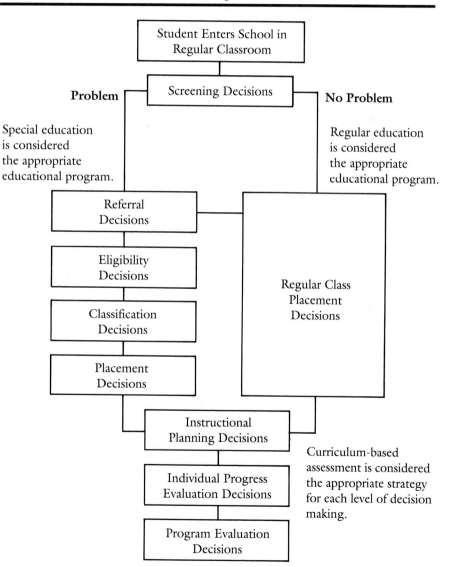

SOURCE: James E. Ysseldyke and Bob Algozzine, *Introduction to Special Education*, 2nd ed. (Boston: Houghton Mifflin, 1990), p. 310. Reprinted by permission.

FIGURE 1.3   How Teachers Participate in Decision-Making Activities

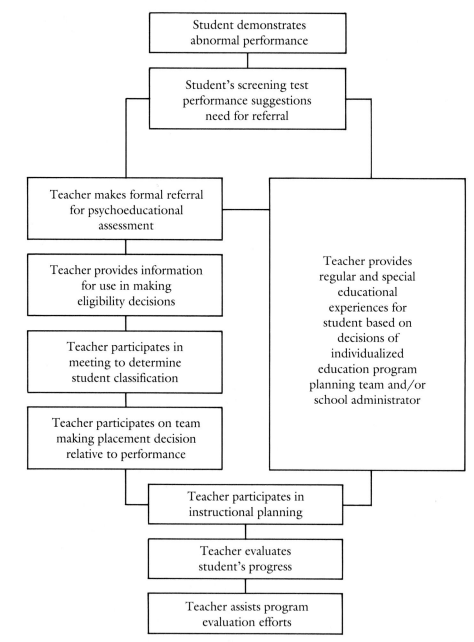

SOURCE: James E. Ysseldyke and Bob Algozzine, *Introduction to Special Education,* 2nd ed. (Boston: Houghton Mifflin, 1990), p. 312. Reprinted by permission.

Screening is an initial stage during which those who may evidence a particular problem, disorder, disability, or disease are sorted out from among the general population. Screening has its origins in medicine and uses terminology from medical screening practices. We speak of individuals who perform poorly on screening measures as being "at risk"; we describe individuals as "false positives" when they perform poorly on screening measures but later do well on follow-up assessments. Sometimes students show no problems at the time of screening and are screened "normal." Later, these same students may evidence the very problems for which screening was conducted; these students are said to be "false negatives." Finally, when we talk about the accuracy of screening decisions, we often speak of the "hit rate" (proportion of accurate positive decisions) for screening.

Classification Decisions

Classification decisions take several forms. In the schools, classification decisions concern a pupil's eligibility for special services: special education services, remedial education services, speech services, and so forth. In this book, we are primarily concerned with eligibility for special education services. Thus, we are interested in whether a pupil is exceptional. Usually, special services are much more costly than the services provided to students in general education. Moreover, these extra costs (sometimes called excess costs) are paid in part by federal and state governments. Governments want to ensure that tax money goes to programs for individuals who have been specially targeted for services, those who are *eligible* for services at government expense. Students who are eligible for services are those who are shown to meet specified state or federal criteria.

In addition to the classification system employed by the federal government, every state has an education code that specifies the kinds of students considered handicapped. In Table 1.1 we show the categories of exceptionality used in each of the states. States have different names for the same handicap. For example, in California some students are called deaf or hard of hearing; in other states, such as Colorado, the same kinds of students are called hearing impaired. Different states have different standards for classification of the same handicap. In Pennsylvania, the maximum IQ for mentally retarded individuals is 80; in Minnesota, the maximum IQ is 70; in California, a black student cannot be tested with an individual intelligence test for classification as mentally retarded. Some states consider gifted students as exceptional and entitled to special education services; other states do not. In some states, brain-damaged students are considered exceptional; in others, there are no provisions for a category of students termed brain injured. Each state has its own criteria for each type of handicap for which special education is provided.

TABLE 1.1   Categories of Exceptionality Used in the United States

Categories	Alabama	Alaska	Arizona	Arkansas	California	Colorado	Connecticut	Delaware	District of Columbia	Florida	Georgia	Hawaii	Idaho	Illinois	Indiana	Iowa	Kansas	Kentucky	Louisiana
Autistic c			X				X	X	X		X								X
DEAF a		X		X	X		X				X			X					X
DEAF-BLIND a	X			X	X	X	X	X	X		X						X	X	X
EARLY CHILDHOOD SPECIAL EDUCATION b		X		X									d	X	X				d
Gifted/Talented c	X	X		X			X		X			X						X	X
HARD OF HEARING a		X		X			X	X				X							X
Hearing Impaired/Disordered/Handicapped	X		X	X	X				X		X			X	X	X	X	X	
Homebound/Hospitalized c		X									X								X
MENTALLY RETARDED a		X		X											X				
Mentally Impaired/ Disabled/Handicapped c			X				X	X				X				X	X		
Educable (Mild) c	X	X			X				X	X	X			X				X	X
Trainable (Moderate) c	X	X			X				X	X	X			X				X	X
Severe/ Profound c	X	X			d				X	X	X			X				X	X
MULTIHANDICAPPED a	X			X															X
Multiply Impaired/Handicapped c		X	X	X	X			X						X	X			X	
Severely/Profoundly (Multiply) Impaired/Handicapped c												X				X	X		
ORTHOPEDICALLY IMPAIRED a	X	X	d	X			X		d		X								d
Physically Impaired/Disabled/Handicapped c					d		X	X						X	X	X	X	X	
OTHER HEALTH IMPAIRED a	X	X		X	X		X	X	X		X	X	d	X			X	X	X
SERIOUSLY EMOTIONALLY DISTURBED a	d	X	X	X	X	d	d	d	X	d	d				X			X	X
Behaviorally Impaired/Disordered c							d					X		X			X	X	X
Emotionally Disturbed/Handicapped c	d								d	X		d							
SPECIFIC LEARNING DISABILITIES a	X			X	X				X	X	X	X					X		
Learning Disabled/Impaired/Handicapped c		X	X				X	X						X	X	X		X	X
SPEECH-LANGUAGE IMPAIRED a	X	X	X	X	X		d		X	X	X	X	X				X	X	
Speech-Language Disabled/Disordered/Handicapped c					X						X								d
Communication Disorder/Handicap c					X									X					
VISUALLY HANDICAPPED a			X		X	X	X					d		X				X	d
Visually Impaired c	X	X		X					X	X	X		X	X		X	X		

a PL 94-142 category
b PL 99–457 category
c Nonfederal category
d Category reported but not the same as PL 142 category, PL 99-457 category, or nonfederal categories reported

State/Territory

The following matrix indicates, by state/territory, the terminology used. Three vertical section labels run through the matrix columns: **Children in need of special services** (in the Massachusetts column), **Children in need of special assistance/prolonged assistance** (in the South Dakota column), and **Special needs students** (in the Off. of Indian Progs. column). Entries are marked "X" (used) or "d" (defined/other designation).

	ME	MD	MA	MI	MN	MS	MO	MT	NE	NV	NH	NJ	NM	NY	NC	ND	OH	OK	OR	PA	RI	SC	SD	TN	TX	UT	VT	VA	WA	WV	WI	WY	OIP	AS	GU	PW	PR	SP	VI
1				X	X		X								X	X			X					X	X	X		X											
2	X	X						X			X			X			X		X	X						X		X	X			X		X			X	X	X
3	X	X		X	X	X	X	X			X			X			X	X	X	X				X	X			X	X			X		X			X	X	X
4				d	X			d			d	d	d			d	d					X					X	d	d					X				X	X
5					X						X			X			X	X		X	X	X		X					X					X					
6	X	X						X		d		X	d		X			X						d	X		X	X				X		X	X	X		X	
7				X	X	X	X		X					X			X	X	X			X	X	X	X	X		X		X	X	X		X					X
8																					X												X					
9	X			X							X			X		X		d	X							d						X	X					X	X
10		X				X	X			X			X										X	X				X	X	X	X		X	X	X				
11				X		X			X				X				X			X	X	X	X			d		X	X					X					
12				X		X			X				X				X			X	X	X	X			d		X	X					X					
13				X		X			X				d				X			X	X	X				d		X	X					X					
14	X	X				X	X	X	X			X					X					X		X		X		X	X			X		X	X	X	X	X	
15											X		X	X	X	X			X						X						X								
16				X															X					X															
17	X	X					X	X			X	X		X	X	X	X	X	X		X	X				X	X	X	X			X	X		X	X	X	X	X	
18				X	X	X	X			X			X					X						X	X	X		X	X										
19	X	X		X	X		X	X	X		X	d		X	X	X	X	X	X		X		X		X	X	X	X		X	X		X	X	X	X	X	X	
20		X						X					X			X		X	X					X			X	X	d		X					X	X	X	
21	X					X		X			X		d			d					X						X		X		X	X							
22				d	d	X		X		X		X	X	X			d					X		X				X		X	X		X	X		X	X		
23		X		X	X			X			X		X	d			X	X	X					X		X	X	X	X		X	X		X	X	X				
24	X				X	X	X		X			X	X				X					X					X				X			X					X
25	X	X		X	X		X	X		X			X	X	X			X	X	X				X			X	X			X			X	X	X	X	X	X
26						X	X			X			X					X	X					X			X	X			X	X							
27						X	X			X				X	X							X		X			X		X	X	X			X	X				X
28	X			X		X	X	X	X	X			X				X				X			X	X		X	X	X	d		X		X	X			X	X
29	X			X	X		X			X				X	X	X	X	X	X					X			X	X				X		X	X	X	X	X	X

In most states, students must be evaluated by certified diagnostic specialists before they are eligible for special education services. Public Law 94-142, the Education for All Handicapped Children Act of 1975, specifies that eligibility, classification, and/or placement decisions are to be made by teams of professionals with the concurrence of the pupil's parents.

In assessment for classification, those persons responsible for determining a pupil's eligibility develop a plan to clarify and verify that the student is handicapped. Data are then gathered (that is, tests are administered, systematic observations made, interviews conducted, and so forth) to clarify and specify the extent to which students meet the eligibility requirements for services for handicapped persons. Although there are many problems apparent in the use of tests to make classification decisions, most federal and state regulations require that decisions be test based. This requirement is designed to protect students. If teachers, diagnosticians, and administrators were allowed to make classification and eligibility decisions on the basis of subjective impressions, classification could be haphazard and capricious.

Instructional Planning Decisions

Assessment data are often used to clarify and specify how and where a pupil is to be taught. Thus, tests are administered in an effort to assist teachers and administrators in planning education programs for individuals or groups of students. Test information might be used to decide placement in reading groups or assignment of students to specific compensatory or remedial programs. Observations and interviews may be used to decide whether special services will be delivered in the regular classroom or in a special education environment. Test results are also used in deciding what goals to stress, what objectives to teach, and how to teach, for individuals as well as for groups.

With the increase in the attention given to learning disabilities and with federal and state requirements for individualized education programs for exceptional students, we have seen an expansion in the use of curriculum-based assessment procedures in planning instructional efforts. The merits and limitations in the use of tests in planning specific education programs are discussed in several chapters in Parts 3 and 4 of this text. Chapter 27 is in large part devoted to a discussion and illustration of this purpose of testing.

Pupil Progress Decisions

Finally, assessment data are used to verify that a pupil has made progress and to specify the particular objectives that have (and have not) been attained in the prescribed educational curriculum. Various kinds of assessment data are used to monitor a pupil's day-to-day progress so that teachers can fine-tune education programs. Other kinds of assessment data are used to tell teachers, parents, and the students themselves the extent to which progress has been made during longer periods of time (for example, over the semester). Grades on teacher-constructed tests and scores on standardized achievement tests are the usual indicators of academic progress. Some tests tell teachers and parents what specific educational objectives have or have not been achieved. Evaluation of pupil progress is intimately related to the particular program in which a student is enrolled. It is absolutely essential that the content of the assessment parallel the curriculum exactly. Should this not be the case, the decisions about progress will quite likely be incorrect. Thus, we must distinguish between attainment and achievement. *Attainment* is what an individual has learned, regardless of where it has been learned. *Achievement* is what has been learned as a result of instruction in the schools. Any test of factual information measures attainment; however, a test of factual information is an achievement test only if it measures what has been directly taught. Only achievement tests can be used to monitor pupil progress. It would be pointless to use a test that did not assess what a teacher had covered.

PROBLEM AREAS FOR SPECIFICATION AND VERIFICATION

Assessment is the process of collecting data for the purposes of (1) specifying and verifying problems and (2) making decisions about students. We just described the kinds of decisions that are made in educational settings. We now describe three kinds of problems with which assessment is usually concerned: academic problems, behavior problems, and physical problems. In doing so, we describe the specification and verification of problems for the purpose of making different kinds of decisions.

Academic Problems

The most common reason students are referred for psychological or educational assessment is that a teacher or parent believes they are not performing as well as could be expected academically. Teachers usually make that decision on the basis of their observations of pupil performance in academic content areas: reading, mathematics, spelling, science, social studies, and so forth. When students are referred for assessment, it is necessary that teachers specify their concerns. Teachers who refer students for assessment because of "reading problems" provide diagnostic personnel with limited information. To the extent that teachers describe and specify the nature of a student's problems (for example, "Richy is the poorest reader in the class and consistently has difficulty associating letters with sounds"), they help diagnostic personnel. Some very effective teachers regularly gather information on pupil progress in academic content areas and use those data to make referral decisions.

Academic performance is nearly always assessed in making classification decisions. For example, a student referred for reading problems may be given a reading test to provide a comparison of the development of reading skills relative to other students in the school or even the nation. The results of the test would be used to verify the existence of a problem.

Academic performance is nearly always assessed in making instructional decisions. In deciding what to teach a student it is necessary to specify those skills that the student does and does not already have.

Behavior Problems

Students are often referred for psychological or educational assessment because they demonstrate behavior problems. Students for whom severe behavior problems can be specified and verified are often declared eligible for special education services.

Behavior problems include failure to get along with peers, delinquent activities, and excessive withdrawal, as well as disruptive and noncompliant behavior. For example, Ms. Swanson may be troubled because Larry is so quiet and withdrawn. She might begin to verify that this is actually the problem by counting the frequency of Larry's interactions with his peers. A low count would not, by itself, indicate a problem. Therefore, Ms. Swanson might select another boy whose behavior she judged to be appropriate and count the frequency of his interactions with his peers. She could then verify that Larry interacted much less frequently than a boy who had no problems interacting.

Ms. Swanson might plan a behavior-modification program for Larry to increase the number of positive interactions that he had with his classmates. She could systematically collect data on the effectiveness of this new program and reach some decisions about Larry's progress.

Physical Problems

Physical problems include sensory handicaps (vision and hearing), problems of physical structure (for example, spina bifida or cerebral palsy), and chronic health problems (diabetes or asthma).

Severe physical problems are often first brought to the attention of parents by physicians before a child enters school. When a child with a severe physical problem enters school, the parents might supply specific information from physicians that confirm and specify the physical nature of the child's problem.

Milder, but nonetheless important, problems that have not been noticed by the parents are often discovered during routine screening. For example, White Haven Area Schools might require that the school nurse (Ms. Slique) regularly conduct hearing tests (for example, a puretone audiometric test for hearing within the speech range). When the first-grade students are screened, Ms. Slique notes that Jane has a 65 decibel loss in her better ear. A hearing loss of such magnitude, if confirmed, would have serious educational implications and would necessitate substantial educational modifications so that Jane could profit from her education. However, the screening assessment was conducted in the nurse's room, which had not been soundproofed, and with equipment that had not been checked recently for accuracy. Therefore, Ms. Slique decides that it would be best to have an audiologist see Jane and diagnose her hearing problem.

ASSESSMENT AND SOCIETY

The students we teach in assessment classes often enter the class with questions about the role that testing plays in social decision making. Their concerns are formulated in such questions as "Is it fair to place students in special education on the basis of their performance on a test?" "What do tests say about a person?" and "Should an employer decide whether to hire a person on the basis of how that person does on a test?" Our students also question the use of tests in making decisions about college entrance or admission to graduate school. Throughout this text, when appropriate, we address these and other issues on the use of tests in schools. The joint committee of three professional associations that developed a set of standards for test construction and use addressed the kinds of issues our students often raise:

> *Educational and psychological testing represents one of the most important contributions of behavioral science to our society. It has provided fundamental and significant improvements over previous practices in industry, government, and education. It has provided a tool for broader and more equitable access to education and employment. Although not all tests are well-developed, nor are all testing practices wise and beneficial, available evidence supports the judgment that the proper use of well-constructed and validated tests provides a better basis for making some important decisions about individuals and programs than would otherwise be available.*
>
> *Educational and psychological testing has also been the target of extensive scrutiny, criticism, and debate both outside and within the professional testing community. The most frequent criticisms are that tests play too great a role in the lives of students and employees and that tests are biased and exclusionary. Individuals and institutions benefit when testing helps them achieve their goals. Society, in turn, benefits when the achievement of individual and institutional*

goals contributes to the general good. (American Educational Research Associ-
ation, American Psychological Association, and National Council on Measure-
ment in Education, 1985, p.1)

SUMMARY

Testing is part of a larger concept—assessment. In assessment, information is gathered for two reasons. First, assessment data are used to clarify and verify the existence of educational problems in the areas of academic functioning, behavioral and social adaptation, and physical development. Second, assessment provides data to facilitate decision making. Five types of decisions are especially pertinent in special education assessment: referral, screening, classification, instructional planning, and evaluation of pupil progress. There are many complex social, political, and ethical issues that arise when tests are used to make important decisions about individuals. Assessment is an important activity, and it is critical that it be done right. Throughout the text we address issues in the appropriate and inappropriate use of tests.

STUDY QUESTIONS

1. Differentiate between testing and assessment.
2. Read the Eaves and McLaughlin paper listed in Additional Reading and identify the three levels of assessment that the authors describe.
3. Differentiate between specification and verification.
4. If you were to make an assessment for the purpose of planning an instructional program for a student with reading problems, of what would your assessment consist?
5. If you were to make an assessment for the purpose of deciding whether to refer a student with behavior problems, what form would your assessment take?
6. All of us have taken achievement tests such as the Iowa Tests of Basic Skills or the Stanford Achievement Tests. Think back to two or three instances in which you took such tests. To what use(s), if any, did you expect the results of these assessments to be put?

ADDITIONAL READING

Cronbach, L. J. (1984). *Essentials of psychological testing.* New York: Harper & Row. (Chapter 2: Varieties of tests and test interpretations, pp. 26–48.)

Eaves, R. C., & McLaughlin, P. (1977). A systems approach to the assessment of the child and his environment: Getting back to basics. *Journal of Special Education, 11,* 99–111.

McCutcheon, G. (1981). On the interpretation of classroom observations. *Educational Researcher, 10,* 5–10.

Poland, S. F., Thurlow, M. L., Ysseldyke, J. E., & Mirkin, P. K. (1982). Current psychoeducational assessment and decision-making practices as reported by directors of special education. *Journal of School Psychology, 20,* 171–179.

Ysseldyke, J. E. (1983). Current practices in making psychoeducation decisions about learning disabled students. *Journal of Learning Disabilities, 16,* 226–233.

Ysseldyke, J. E. (1986). The use of assessment information to make decisions about students. In R. J. Morris & B. Blatt (Eds.), *Special education: Research and trends.* Elmsford, NY: Pergamon Press.

Ysseldyke, J. E., & Algozzine, B. (1990). *Introduction to special education* (2nd ed). Boston: Houghton Mifflin. (Chapter 9: Assessment practices in special education, pp. 307–354.)

C·H·A·P·T·E·R 2

Basic Considerations in Assessment

Assessment is a process of collecting data for two purposes: (1) specifying and verifying problems and (2) making decisions for or about students. Assessment data are used in making many different kinds of decisions about students, as described in the first chapter.

Those who assess students must be aware of several assumptions inherent in assessment and of how failure to meet those assumptions directly affects the validity of obtained results. They must consider many factors in assessment, going beyond the student to gather additional kinds of information. In this chapter we describe factors to be considered and the various kinds of information collected in the process of assessment, and we differentiate between formal and informal assessment.

Those who assess students need to identify a starting point for assessment and decide the specific kinds of data that will be collected. We address several questions commonly asked in deciding how students will be assessed. We end the chapter with a set of guidelines for teacher administration of standardized tests.

ASSUMPTIONS UNDERLYING ASSESSMENT

A number of assumptions underlie the valid assessment of students. To the extent that these assumptions are not met, test results and interpretations lack validity. Newland (1973) has identified and discussed the following five assumptions underlying assessment.

The Person Giving the Test Is Skilled

When pupils are tested, we assume that the person doing the testing has adequate training for the purpose of testing. We also assume that the tester knows how to—and indeed does—establish rapport with pupils; students generally perform best in an atmosphere of trust and security. We further assume that the tester knows how to administer the test correctly. Testing consists of a standardized presentation of stimuli. To the extent that the person giving the test does not correctly present the questions or materials, the obtained scores lose validity.

We also assume that the person who administers a test knows how to score the test. Correct scoring is a prerequisite to the attainment of a meaningful picture of a student. Finally, we assume that accurate interpretation can and will be made.

Test administration, scoring, and interpretation require different degrees of training and expertise depending on the kind of test being administered and the degree of interpretation required to draw meaning from the test taker's performance. Although most teachers can readily administer or learn to administer group intelligence and achievement tests, a person must have considerable training to score and interpret most individual intelligence and personality tests. Most states now require that a person be certified or licensed as a psychologist in order to administer these types of tests. Licensing or certification, in turn, is often contingent on the demonstration of competence.

Obviously, a terribly important point is implicit in this first assumption. Professionals should administer only the tests they are qualified to administer. Too often, unfortunately, we hear of people with no training in individual intelligence testing who nonetheless administer individual intelligence tests; or we see people with no formal training in personality test administration or interpretation giving personality tests. Such tests may *look* easy enough to give; however, the correct administration, scoring, and interpretation are complex. Because tests are so often used to make decisions that will affect a child's future, this assumption of a skilled observer or tester is especially important.

Error Will Be Present

No psychological or educational measurement is free from error. A certain amount of error is always present when we test. Although measurement error is dealt with extensively in Chapter 7, a few points are appropriate here. Nunnally (1978) differentiates between two kinds of error in any measurement effort: *systematic error*, or bias, and *random error*. He illustrates systematic error by the example of a chemist who uses an inaccurate thermometer, one that always reads 2 degrees higher than the actual temperature of a liquid. All of the readings the chemist takes will be biased, but they will be biased systematically; that is, all readings will be in error by 2 degrees.

In the measurement process, random error occurs in two ways. First, the measurer may be inconsistent. Nunnally's illustration of this is a nearsighted chemist who reads an accurate thermometer inaccurately. The readings will be in error, but the amount and direction of error will be random. In some cases, the chemist may read the thermometer 5 degrees high, in others 4 degrees low. An indeterminate amount of error, then, affects obtained measurements. Second, measurement devices may produce inconsistent results. For example, an elastic rubber ruler produces inconsistent measures of length.

Reliability concerns the extent to which a measurement device is free from random error. A test with very little random error, an accurate test, is said to be reliable, while one with considerable random error, an inaccurate test, is said to be unreliable. Tests differ considerably in degree of reliability. To the extent that unreliable devices (devices with considerable random error) are used to make decisions about students, those decisions may, in fact, be erroneous. Factors that contribute to lack of reliability in testing are discussed in Chapter 7.

Acculturation Is Comparable

Every schoolchild has a particular set of background experiences in educational, social, and cultural environments. When we test students using a standardized device and compare them to a set of norms to gain an index of their relative standing, we assume that the students we test are similar to those on whom the test was standardized; that is, we assume their acculturation is comparable, but not necessarily identical, to that of the students who made up the normative sample for the test.

When a child's general background experiences differ from those of the children on whom a test was standardized, then the use of the norms of that test as an index for evaluating that child's current performance or for predicting future performances may be inappropriate. Incorrect educational decisions may well be made. It must be pointed out that acculturation is a matter of experiential background rather than of gender, skin color, race, or ethnic background. When we say that a child's acculturation differs from that of the group used as a norm, we are saying that the *experiential background* differs, not simply that the child is of different ethnic origin, for example, from the children on whom the test was standardized.

Unfortunately, many psychologists, counselors, remedial specialists, and others who select tests to be administered to students often do so with little regard to the characteristics of the students who constitute the normative samples. Many school administrators routinely purchase tests with more concern for price than for the technical adequacy and appropriateness of those tests.

The Quick Test, for example, was standardized on white children in Missoula, Montana; yet it is used daily to measure the "intelligence" of black ghetto children, children whose educational, social, and cultural background *may* differ extensively from that of the children on whom the test was standardized.

The performance section of the Wechsler Intelligence Scale for Children-Revised (WISC-R) consists of a variety of tests (mostly manipulative, like putting puzzle pieces together to form objects) that require no verbal response by the child. The fact that the child does not have to speak has encouraged psychologists to use the test in an effort to test deaf children. Levine (1974), in a survey of testing practices used by psychologists who work with the deaf, reported that the test most frequently used to measure the intelligence of deaf children is the WISC performance section: norms based entirely on the performance of youngsters who can hear are used to interpret the performances of deaf children! Appropriate application of the norms presumes that the child evaluated can *hear* the directions and has had acculturation comparable to that of the children on whom the test was standardized. Several nonverbal subtests of the Wechsler scales (for example, Picture Completion and Picture Arrangement) require verbal competence.

Behavior Sampling Is Adequate

A fourth assumption underlying psychoeducational assessment is that the behavior sampling is adequate in amount and representative in area. Any test is a sample of behavior. If we want information about a student's math skills, we give the student a sample of math problems to solve. Similarly, if we want to know about spelling skills, we ask the student to spell a representative number of words. When we administer a math or spelling test, we assume that we have a large enough sample of items to enable us to make statements regarding a student's overall skill development in that area. Few teachers would ask a student to solve only two arithmetic problems and presume that the results would tell much at all about that student's skill development in arithmetic. Testing requires an adequate sampling of behavior to assist in decision-making processes.

Not only do we assume that the behavior sampling is adequate in amount, but we assume that the test measures what its authors claim it measures. We assume that an intelligence test measures intelligence and that a spelling test measures spelling skills. A test of addition would be a poor measure of overall skill in math, because math entails much more than addition. Similarly, a measure of a student's skill in addition of single-digit numbers provides only one part of a test of that student's skill in addition. We cannot rely on a test's name as we attempt to define the behaviors sampled by the test. Many tests, for example, are called "reading" tests. Yet reading has several subcomponents, such as recognition, comprehension, and phonetic analysis. As we shall show in Chapter 17, no reading test samples reading per se. Each test samples one or more reading behaviors. The user of reading tests—or any tests, for that matter—must go beyond test names in an effort to ascertain the behaviors that the tests measure.

To the extent that tests used to measure students' performances are incomplete or fail to measure what they claim to measure, decisions based on students' scores on those tests may well be wrong.

Present Behavior Is Observed; Future Behavior Is Inferred

When we give a test, we observe only the test taker's performance on one sampling of behavior, at a particular time, under particular testing conditions, and in a particular situation. We observe what a person *does;* we may or may not observe what that person is capable of doing. We sample a limited number of behaviors and generalize the individual's performance to other, similar behaviors. For example, because Heathcote correctly works ten of ten problems in single-digit addition, we infer that he could add any two single digits correctly. Moreover, judgments or predictions about an individual's behavior at some future time may be made. These predictions are inferences in which we may place varying degrees of confidence. We may better trust the inferences we make about future performance if we have seen to it that the other assumptions about assessment have been satisfied. If we have administered a test that is adequate in its behavior sampling and representative in area, that is relatively free from error, and that was accurately administered, scored, and interpreted, using as norms students of background comparable to the background of those we tested, then we may put a reasonable amount of faith in the adequacy of observed data. Data obtained from such an administration may be used with greater assurance in making predictions than data obtained under conditions in which any of the assumptions were not met. Human behavior is extremely complex, and we must remember that any prediction about future behavior is an inference.

FACTORS CONSIDERED IN ASSESSMENT
Current Life Circumstances

An individual's performance on any task must be understood in light of that individual's current circumstances. We must understand current circumstances to be aware of what a person brings to a task.

In educational assessment, health is a significant current life circumstance. Health and nutritional status can play an important role in children's performances on a wide variety of tasks. Sick or malnourished children are apt to be lethargic, inattentive, perhaps irritable.

Children's attitudes and values also should contribute to our evaluation of their performance. Willingness to cooperate with a relatively unfamiliar adult, willingness to give substantial effort to tasks, and belief in the worth of the task or of schooling have their influence on performance.

Finally, the level of acculturation children bring to a task is of utmost importance. A child's knowledge and acceptance of societally sanctioned mores and values, use of standard English, and fund of general and specific cultural information all influence performance on school-related tasks.

Developmental History

A person's current life circumstances are shaped by the events that make up his or her history of development. Deleterious events in particular may have profound effects on physical and psychological development. Physical and sensory limitations may restrict a student's opportunity to acquire various skills and abilities. A history of poor health or poor nutrition may result in missed opportunities to acquire various skills and abilities. An individual's history of reward and punishment shapes what that person will achieve and how that person will react to others. In short, it is not enough to assess a student's current level of performance; those who assess must also understand what has shaped that current performance.

Extrapersonal Factors

In addition to the skills, characteristics, and abilities a pupil brings to any task, other factors affect the assessment process. How another person interprets or reacts to various behaviors or characteristics can even determine whether an individual will be assessed. For example, some teachers do not understand that a certain amount of physical aggression is typical of young children or that verbal aggression is typical of older students. Such teachers may refer "normally" aggressive children for assessment because they have interpreted aggression as a symptom of some underlying problem.

The theoretical orientation of the diagnostician (the person responsible for performing the assessment) also plays an important part in the assessment process. Diagnosticians' backgrounds and training may predispose them to look for certain types of pathologies. Just as Freudians may look for unresolved conflicts while behaviorists may look for antecedents and consequences of particular behaviors, diagnosticians may let their theoretical orientation influence their interpretation of particular information.

Finally, the conditions under which a student is observed or the conditions under which particular behaviors are elicited can influence that student's performance. For example, the level of language used in a question or the presence of competing stimuli in the immediate environment can affect a pupil's responses.

Interpretation of Performance

After an individual's behavior and characteristics have been considered in light of current life circumstances, developmental history, and extrapersonal factors that may influence performance, the information is summarized. This often results in classification and labeling of the individual being assessed. The assessor arrives at the judgment that when all things are considered, the child "fits" a particular category. For example, a child may be judged mentally retarded, emotionally disturbed, learning disabled, educationally handicapped, culturally or socially disadvantaged, backward, normal, gifted, or a member of the Red Birds reading group.

Assessors, especially when they have assigned negative labels, often attempt to impute a cause for an individual's status. Classification according to cause *(etiology)* is common in medicine but less common in education and psychology. In some cases the cause of the condition is highly probable. For example, Kevin may be developing quite normally until he sustains a severe head injury, after which his performance and development are measurably retarded. However, in most instances the causes are elusive and speculative.

Prognosis

All assessments and classifications of students contain an explicit or implicit *prognosis,* a prediction of future performance. A prognosis may be offered for students both in their current environment and life circumstances and in some therapeutic or remedial environment. For example, "If Rachel is left in her current educational placement, she can be expected to fall further and further behind the other children and to develop problem behaviors. If she is placed in an environment where she will receive more individual attention, she should make more progress academically and socially." Such prognoses are made, it is hoped, on the basis of sound data rather than speculation.

KINDS OF ASSESSMENT INFORMATION

Although this book is concerned primarily with tests and testing, it is well to remember that a test is only one of several assessment techniques or procedures available for gathering information. Figure 2.1 shows that there are six general classes of diagnostic-information sources; the classification shown in the figure depends on the time at which the information is collected (current or historical) and on how the information is collected (from observation, tests, or judgments).

FIGURE 2.1   Sources of Diagnostic Information Classified According to Type of Information and Time at Which the Information Is Collected.

| | **Time At Which Information Is Gathered** | |
	Current	Historical
Observations	Frequency counts of occurrence of a particular behavior	Birth weight
		Anecdotal records
	Antecedents of behavior	Observations by last year's teacher
	Critical incidents	
Tests	Results of an intelligence test administered during the assessment	Results of a standardized achievement-test battery given at the end of last year
	Results of this week's spelling test given by the teacher	
Judgments	Parent's evaluations of how well the child gets along in family, neighborhood, etc.	Previous medical, psychological, or educational diagnoses
	Rating scales completed by teachers, social workers, etc.	Previous report cards
	Teacher's reason for referral	Parents' recall of developmental history, of undiagnosed childhood illnesses, etc.

(Type of Information — row label)

Current vs. Historical Information

Diagnostic information can be categorized according to the currentness of the information: information that describes how a person is functioning now and information that describes how that person has functioned in the past. Obviously, the distinction between current and historical information blurs, and the point at which current information becomes historical information depends in part on the particular fact or bit of information. For example, if Johnny had his appendix removed *three years ago,* we know he currently has no appendix. On the other hand, if 9-year-old Jane weighed 56 pounds *three years ago,* we could not conclude that she weighs the same today.

There are several advantages in having and using current information. The first is the most obvious. Current information describes a person's current behavior and characteristics. It offers two more subtle advantages as well: (1)

the diagnostician can select the information to be collected, and (2) the information can be verified. However, current information alone cannot provide a complete picture of a person's present level of functioning, because the antecedents of this functioning are not considered. This is the advantage of historical information. School diagnosticians cannot go back in time to observe previous characteristics, behaviors, and situations. A diagnostician who wishes to incorporate a student's history into the assessment procedure must rely on previously collected information or the memory of individuals who knew the student.

Historical information has four limitations of which diagnosticians must be aware. First, a diagnostician cannot control what information was collected in the past; crucial bits of information may never have been collected. Second, past information is difficult and sometimes impossible to verify. Third, the conditions under which the information was collected are often difficult to evaluate. Fourth, remembered observations may not be as reliable as current observations.

Types of Information

Diagnostic information can also be categorized according to the type of information: observations, tests, and judgments. Each of the three types of information has advantages as well as disadvantages. Each type can be collected by a diagnostician (in which case the data become *direct information*) or by another person *(indirect information)*. Diagnosticians do not have the time, competence, or opportunity to collect all possible types of information. In cases where specialized information is needed, they must rely on the observations, tests, and judgments of others. If a behavior occurs infrequently or is demonstrated only outside school, the diagnostician may have to rely on the observations and judgments of others who have more opportunity to collect the information—parents, perhaps, or ward attendants in institutional settings. For example, bed wetting does not occur at school, but few diagnosticians would question the accuracy of parents' reports of bed wetting. Moreover, if a child is an intermittent bed wetter, a diagnostician might have to spend several nights at the child's home in order to observe the behavior directly. In such cases indirect information is usually adequate.

Observations can provide highly accurate, detailed, verifiable information not only about the person being assessed but also about the contexts in which the observations are being made. There are two types of observation: nonsystematic and systematic. In nonsystematic observation, the observer simply watches an individual in his or her environment and takes note of the behaviors, characteristics, and personal interactions that seem of significance. Nonsystematic observation tends to be anecdotal and subjective. In systematic observation, the observer sets out to observe one or more behaviors. The observer specifies or defines the behaviors to be observed and then typically counts or otherwise measures the frequency, duration, magnitude, or latency of the behaviors. The major disadvantage of *systematic observation* is that it may allow other important behaviors and characteristics to be ignored.

There are two major difficulties in collecting systematic and nonsystematic observational data. The first is that observation is very time consuming; a diagnostician pays for the highly accurate, specific information that observation provides by not being able to collect other information. The second problem is that the very presence of an observer may distort or otherwise alter the situation to such a degree that the behavior of the individual being observed also is altered.

Tests are a predetermined set of questions or tasks to which predetermined types of behavioral responses are sought. Tests are particularly useful because they permit tasks and questions to be presented in exactly the same way to each person tested. Because a tester elicits and scores behavior in a predetermined and consistent manner, the performances of several different test takers can be compared no matter who does the testing. Hence, tests tend to make many extrapersonal factors in assessment consistent for all those tested. Basically, two types of information, quantitative and qualitative, result from the administration of a test. *Quantitative* data are the actual scores achieved on the test. Examples of quantitative data include such statements as "Lee earned a score of 80 on her math test," or "Henry scored at the 83rd percentile on a measure of scholastic aptitude." *Qualitative* information consists of nonsystematic observations made while a child is tested and tells us how the child achieved the score. For example, in earning a score of 80 on her math test, Lee may have solved all of the addition and subtraction problems with the exception of those that required regrouping. Henry may have performed best on measures of his ability to define words, while demonstrating a weakness in comprehending verbal statements. When tests are used in assessment, it is not enough simply to know the scores a student earned on a given test; it is important to know how the student earned those scores.

The *judgments* and assessments made by others can play an important role in assessment. In instances where a diagnostician lacks competence to render a judgment, the judgments of those who possess the necessary competence are essential. Diagnosticians seek out other professionals to complement their own skills and background. Thus, referring a student to various specialists (hearing specialists, vision specialists, reading teachers, and so on) is a common and desirable practice in assessment. Judgments by teachers, counselors, psychologists, and practically any other school employees may be useful in particular circumstances. Expertise in making judgments is often a function of familiarity with the student being assessed. Teachers regularly express professional judgments; for example, report-card grades represent the teacher's judgment of a student's academic progress during the marking period; referrals for psychological evaluation represent a different type of judgment based on experience with many students and observations of the particular student. Judgments represent both the best and the worst of assessment data. Judgments made by conscientious, capable, and objective individuals can be an invaluable aid in the assessment process. Inaccurate, biased, subjective judgments can be misleading at best and harmful at worst. Finally, assessment ultimately requires judgment.

Integration of Assessment Information

To see how the various types of information can come into play in an assessment, consider the following example. Mary, who is 6 years old, is falling behind in reading, her teacher reports (a current judgment). The teacher also reports that Mary does not listen or pay attention and does not associate sounds with letters (current observations). An inspection of Mary's kindergarten records indicates that she was absent thirty-one days in January and February (past observation). Mary's scores on the reading readiness test administered in June of her kindergarten year were sufficiently high that her teacher recommended her promotion to the first grade (past judgment). An interview with Mary's parents revealed that Mary has a history of treated middle-ear infections (past observations and judgments) during the winters. According to her parents, she currently has an ear infection that is being treated by the family doctor (current observation). Pulling together all this information, the school authorities hypothesize that Mary is having hearing difficulties. They obtain a hearing examination (current test), which indicates that Mary is currently suffering from a moderate hearing loss of sufficient magnitude to affect her progress in phonics adversely (current judgment). With background and current information, it is now possible to assess (understand and interpret) Mary's classroom behavior. With medical treatment for her ear problem and some classroom intervention by the teacher, Mary can be expected to do better in school.

Formal vs. Informal Assessment

Increasingly, educators are advocating informal over formal assessment, especially in instructional decision making and in evaluating pupil progress. When such a distinction is made, any assessment that involves collection of data by anything other than a norm-referenced (standardized) test is generally considered informal assessment. Collection of information by means of *observation* is often thought of as informal assessment, as is information gathering by *interviewing* and by means of *teacher-constructed tests*.

Over the past decade there has been a significant increase in curriculum-based assessment. Curriculum-based assessment includes (1) direct observation and analysis of the learning environment, (2) analysis of the processes used by students in approaching tasks, (3) examination of pupil products, and (4) control and arrangement of tasks for students. Focus is on assessment of a student's ongoing performance in the existing curriculum.

Observation of the learning environment involves looking at the kinds of instructional materials being used with students as well as at the basis for selection of the materials. Specific observation techniques include systematic analysis of the way in which instruction is organized and sequenced, with specific attention to potential pitfalls in instructional organization; looking at and examining the adequacy of the ways in which instruction is being presented (lecture, workbook, programmed instruction, and so on); and examination of the extent to which sufficient time is allocated to instruction and the extent to which the student is actively engaged in responding to academic content.

Evaluation of the ways in which students approach tasks, student demeanor, student attention to tasks, and the extent to which students read and follow instructions are also part of curriculum-based assessment. Teachers who follow curriculum-based assessment attend carefully to the products students produce in an effort to analyze the specific kinds of errors students make. For example, teachers may examine errors on math worksheets in order to spot patterns of difficulties. Curriculum-based assessment is often called diagnostic teaching because teachers or diagnostic specialists have an opportunity to modify several aspects of instruction and to study the impact of such adaptations on pupil performance.

Increasingly, school personnel are using the kinds of informal assessment strategies noted above. In this text, we choose to concentrate on formal assessment. In our opinion, the topic of informal assessment requires adequate treatment in a separate book.

APPROACHES TO ASSESSMENT

There are three different approaches to assessing students that differ primarily in what is assessed and where the assessor begins assessment. Each approach is described below.

Assessing the Learner

Most often, when students are referred for evaluation because they are experiencing academic or behavior problems, school personnel use an approach in which they assess the learner. This type of assessment addresses the question "What is wrong with the student?" Tests are administered in an effort to identify within-student deficits or disabilities, or efforts are made to find strengths and weaknesses in the development of specific skills.

As noted, assessment of the learner is the most frequently used approach, and it is the approach most often taught in college and university courses. This approach is based on several assumptions. Students who experience academic difficulties are assumed to suffer from internal conditions (called *deficits, disorders, disabilities,* or *dysfunctions*) that cause their academic difficulties. It is assumed that tests can and should be used to identify the students' deficits, that the deficits can be reliably and validly identified, and that instructional approaches can be selected based on pupil performance on tests. Thus, we see school personnel engaged in assessment of perceptual, perceptual-motor, psycholinguistic, and other kinds of abilities and in attempts to remediate those abilities.

The approach that begins assessment by diagnosing the learner has been criticized repeatedly and strongly. It has been shown that the assumptions underlying the approach are not met (Ysseldyke & Salvia, 1974), that the approach is technically inadequate (Ysseldyke & Marston, 1982), and that the approach seldom leads to effective instruction (Arter & Jenkins, 1979; Engelmann, Granzin, & Severson, 1979).

Diagnosing Instruction

Engelmann, Granzin, and Severson (1979) recommend that assessment begin with instructional diagnosis, the purpose of which is "to determine aspects of instruction that are inadequate, to find out precisely how they are inadequate, and to imply what must be done to correct their inadequacy" (p. 361). In such an approach, emphasis is on initiating assessment by asking, "To what extent are the student's problems caused by poor instruction?"

Instructional diagnosis consists of systematic analysis of the instruction and of the appropriateness of instruction to the learner. It includes engaging in activities described earlier in the discussion on curriculum-based assessment: observation of the learning environment, evaluation of the ways in which students approach tasks, evaluation of the products of instruction, and diagnostic teaching.

Assessing the Instructional Environment

Until recently, most assessment activities in school settings consisted of efforts to assess the learner or to diagnose instruction. Yet school personnel often have difficulty developing instructional recommendations solely on the basis of information about the characteristics of students. It is also clear that instruction involves more than curriculum. Instruction is a complex activity, and instructional outcomes depend on a complex interaction of many factors, only some of which relate to student characteristics or are specific to instructional tasks. Recognition of this fact has led to efforts to assess the qualitative nature of students' instructional environments (Christenson & Ysseldyke, 1989; Ysseldyke & Christenson, 1987a; 1987b).

Assessment of the instructional environment consists of systematically analyzing the extent to which those factors known to make a difference in pupils' learning are present in the instruction that students receive. For example, there is consensus that ample amounts of two kinds of practice—controlled (guided) and independent (seatwork)—need to be present for optimal student achievement. Also, it is clear that students learn more when they receive corrective feedback on their work. Researchers who gather data on the quality of students' academic environments look at such factors as the extent to which students are given adequate opportunity to practice with appropriate materials, the extent to which drill and practice are continued until skills become automatic, the extent to which students receive immediate and specific information about their performance or behavior, and whether or not students are provided with corrective feedback when they make mistakes.

CONSIDERATIONS IN TEST SELECTION AND ADMINISTRATION

Who Is to Be Tested?

In answering the question "Who is to be tested?" we must address two issues. First, we must decide whether we want to test a single student or a group of students. Second, we must determine to what extent the single student (or any student in the group) demonstrates special limitations that must be taken into account in testing.

Group vs. Individual Tests

The distinction between a group test and an individual test is both obvious and subtle. Group tests can be given to one person or to several people simultaneously; individual tests must be administered to only one person at a time. Any group test can be administered to an individual; no individual test should be administered to more than one person at the same time. This is the obvious distinction. There are several subtle distinctions, however.

In an individual test, the questions and demands usually are given orally by a tester who also observes the individual's responses directly and in many cases records these responses. The tester is able to control the tempo and pace of the testing and often can rephrase or clarify questions as well as probe responses to elicit the best performance. If a student undergoing testing be-comes fatigued, the tester can interrupt or terminate the test. If a student loses his or her place on the test, the tester can help; if the student dawdles, the tester can urge; if the student lacks confidence, the tester can reinforce effort. Individual tests usually allow the tester to encourage a test taker's best efforts and to gather a considerable amount of qualitative information. Thus, the examiner can infer strengths and weaknesses in terms of both quantitative and qualitative information.

With a group test, the examiner may provide oral directions for younger children, but for children beyond the fourth grade, the directions usually are written. The pupils write or mark their own responses, and the examiner must monitor the progress of several test takers simultaneously. The examiner typi-cally cannot rephrase, probe, or prompt responses. Even when a group test is given to a single student, qualitative information is very difficult, if not im-possible, to obtain.

The choice between an individual and a group test is determined in part by the decision to be made and the efficiency with which that purpose can be achieved. Basically, when we test for program evaluation, screening, and some types of program planning (for example, tracking students into ability groups), group tests can be appropriately used. Individual tests could be used, but the time and expense would not be justified in terms of the information desired. When we plan individual programs, individual tests are more appro-priate. Typically, when a student is to be placed in a special education pro-gram, an individually administered test is required by law.

Special Limitations and Considerations

A particular student may have special limitations that make a group test inappropriate. As previously discussed, most group-administered tests are lim-ited in their applicability because of the way the questions are presented (that is, they require that test takers be able to read) and the way responses are to be made (generally, by writing or marking). Common sense tells us that if a student cannot read the directions or write the responses, a test requiring these abilities is inappropriate. In such cases, the test measures inability in reading directions or writing answers rather than skill or ability in the con-tent of the test. A child without arms may know the content of the test but may not answer any questions correctly because she cannot write. Similarly, children without speech or with severe speech impediments may know the answers to the questions a test asks but be unable (or unwilling) to respond to even the most sensitively administered individual test that requires oral an-swers. Children with physical or sensory handicaps may perform more slowly than nonhandicapped children simply because of their handicaps. A test that awards "points" for the speed as well as the accuracy of response would not be a valid test of such children's mastery of content.

A related concern is the relationship between a person's functional level and social maturity. Often, older individuals with relatively low levels of skill development are assessed. In such cases, the tester must be careful to select test materials that reflect the test taker's social maturity. An adolescent who is just learning to read may well resent test materials geared to 6-year-old children. The use of test materials that are inappropriate in terms of the older individual's social maturity may reduce or eliminate rapport and thereby jeopardize the accuracy of the test results.

What Behaviors Are to Be Tested?

Any test is a sample of behavior. In deciding what behaviors to test, an examiner must take into account three subquestions: What stimulus and response demands will be made? What domain (content) will be measured? How many domains will be tested?

Stimulus and Response Demands

A test or an individual test item measures an individual's ability to receive a stimulus and then express a response. These demands are present in all tests. Skill in the content of a test cannot be measured accurately if the stimulus and response demands of a question are beyond the capabilities of the test taker. As noted earlier, tests can be administered orally or visually: an examiner can show written materials to a student while simultaneously reading them. There is little reason why a test could not be tactilely administered, too, so that specially limited students could understand its basic stimulus demands.

Response demands can also vary. Test instructions may call for an oral *yes* or *no* response or for oral definition or elaboration. Tests may also require written responses that can range from a simple yes-no, true-false, or multiple-choice response to an elaborate, written essay.

A tester should be sensitive to any limitations a student may have. Such limitations are especially important in relation to the stimulus and response demands of testing. The tester should also have quite specific intentions to measure a particular skill or trait. How to measure should be considered as well as what to measure. For example, all spelling tests are not the same. Writing words from dictation is a different kind of spelling test from recognizing a correctly or incorrectly spelled word in a multiple-choice format.

The Domain

The content domain that is tested is generally what we think of as the "kind" of test. There are many kinds of tests, many traits or characteristics that can be measured: intelligence, personality, aptitude, interest, perceptual-motor development, linguistic ability, and so on. Most general traits or characteristics can be further subdivided. For example, intelligence can be divided into performance abilities and verbal abilities or fractionated into as many as 120 separate abilities (Guilford, 1967). There are also many skills and knowledge areas that can be measured: reading, mathematics, social studies, and anatomy are only a few. Some tests are designed to measure skill development in one specific content area (for example, reading) whereas other tests measure skill development in several different areas. The former are known as *single-skill tests* while the latter are *multiple-skill batteries.*

Often, a test item readily lends itself to only one domain. We would have trouble using the question "Do you like yourself?" on other than a personality test. Generally, however, particular test items are identified with particular domains as a function of a student's age or experience. For instance, the question "What is 3 and 5?" can be used to measure several different domains, depending on the particular student. If a child has just received systematic instruction in the addition of single-digit numbers, the question would be appropriate in an achievement test. If the question were asked of a child who had not received formal instruction in addition (a four-year-old, for instance), the question would be appropriate in an intelligence test. If the same question were given to a child who had received several years of systematic instruction, it would be appropriate in a math aptitude test. In short, the type of test in which an item is placed depends more on the characteristics of the person to be tested or on the intended use of the test than on the content of the particular item.

What Interpretative Data Are Desired?

The process of deciding what interpretative data the examiner wants to obtain necessarily includes answering several subquestions: (1) Is the examiner interested in the student's actual level of mastery or in an index of the student's relative standing? In other words, will the examiner use criterion-referenced or norm-referenced assessment? (2) Is the examiner interested in the student's maximum performance or in the level of performance the student can attain in a given amount of time? In other words, will the examiner use *power tests* (untimed tests) or *speed tests* (timed tests)?

Norm-Referenced vs. Criterion-Referenced Tests

Most noneducational tests are *norm-referenced devices,* which compare an individual's performance to the performance of his or her peers. In norm-referenced assessment, learning of particular content or skills is important only to the extent that differential learning allows the tester to rank individuals in order, from those who have learned many skills to those who have learned few. The emphasis is on the relative standing of individuals rather than on absolute mastery of content.

Norm-referenced tests are of two types: point scales and age scales. These differ in their construction. Age scales are less common today than in the past because of both statistical and conceptual limitations. Age scales are developed by scaling test items in terms of the percentages of children of different ages responding correctly to each test item. For example, an item would be placed at the 6-year level if 25 percent of five-year-olds responded to it correctly, 50 percent of six-year-olds responded to it correctly, and 75 percent of seven-year-olds responded to it correctly. When a test question is correctly placed in an age scale, younger children fail the item while older children pass it. The statistical and conceptual limitations of age scales are discussed in Chapter 5 in the sections dealing with developmental scores and quotients. The reader is cautioned that some tests, such as the 1972 revision of the Stanford-Binet, appear to be age scales but are more correctly considered point scales (compare Salvia, Ysseldyke, & Lee, 1975).

A point scale is constructed by selecting and ordering items of different levels of difficulty. The levels of difficulty are not associated with ages. In point scales, the correct responses (that is, points) are summed, and the total raw score is transformed to various derived scales (see Chapter 5).

Norm-referenced devices typically are designed to do only one thing: to separate the performances of individuals so that there is a distribution of scores. They allow the tester to discriminate among the performances of a number of individuals and to interpret how one person's performance compares to that of other individuals with similar characteristics. In norm-referenced testing, a person's performance on a test is measured relative to or in reference to the performances of others who are presumably like that person. Norm-referenced tests are standardized on groups of individuals, and typical performances for students of certain ages or in certain grades are obtained. The raw score that an individual student earns on a test is compared to the scores earned by other students, and a transformed score (for example, a percentile rank) is used to express the given student's standing in the group.

All norm-referenced and criterion-referenced tests are objective. Objective tests are tests that have predetermined answers and standards for scoring a response. They are objective in the sense that attitudes, opinions, and idiosyncrasies of the examiner do not affect scoring; any two examiners would score a response in the same way.[1]

Objective scoring does not imply "fair" or justifiable scoring; it implies only predetermined criteria and standardized scoring procedures. Suppose a tester shows a child pictures of a ship, an automobile, the car of a passenger train, and a bus and then asks the child, "Which one is different?" The keyed

---

1. A subjective test, by contrast, is a test for which a predetermined answer does not exist. Therefore, the examiner's subjective judgments, attitudes, and opinions can affect the scoring. Many people erroneously define an essay test as a subjective test. Such a test would be objective if there were predetermined, explicit criteria for correct responses; then the "same" response would be assigned the same score by two or more examiners.

response (the objective answer) is *ship;* the ship is the only water transport. If the child reasons that only an automobile is private transportation and gives the response *car,* the response would be scored as an incorrect answer. Similarly, if the child reasons that the car on the passenger train is the only vehicle that is not self-propelled—or the only one that requires tracks—and responds accordingly, the response is scored incorrect. "Being fair" has nothing to do with scoring objectively.

Norm-referenced devices have an advantage over criterion-referenced devices when the purpose of testing is screening or program evaluation: they provide a means of comparing a student's performance to the performance obtained by others. Placement decisions, too, are most often made following the administration of norm-referenced devices, which enable the placement team to see where a student stands relative to other students. In fact, in most states evaluation with norm-referenced tests *must* play a part in any placement decision. In addition, norm-referenced tests are helpful in screening entire classes of students to identify those who demonstrate particular kinds of difficulties. Yet norm-referenced tests have many limitations.

Criterion-referenced tests are a relatively recent development in education and behavioral psychology. Rather than indicating a person's relative standing in skill development, criterion-referenced tests measure a person's development of particular skills in terms of absolute levels of mastery. Thus, criterion-referenced tests provide answers to specific questions such as "Does Maureen spell the word *dog* correctly?"

When tests are administered for the purpose of assisting the classroom teacher in planning appropriate programs for children, criterion-referenced devices are recommended. When planning a program for an individual student, a teacher obviously should be more concerned with identifying the specific skills that the student does or does not have than with knowing how the student compares to others. In criterion-referenced measurement, the emphasis is on assessing specific and relevant behaviors that have been mastered. Criterion-referenced tests treat the student as an individual rather than simply providing numerical indexes of where the student stands on a variety of subtest continua.

Items on criterion-referenced tests are often linked directly to specific instructional objectives and therefore facilitate the writing of objectives. Test items sample sequential skills, enabling a teacher not only to know the specific point at which to begin instruction but also to plan those instructional aspects that follow directly in the curricular sequence.

It is important to recognize that school personnel use many different terms or labels to refer to assessment activities that are parts of or derivatives of criterion-referenced assessment: "curriculum-based assessment," "objective-referenced assessment," "direct and frequent measurement," "curriculum-based measurement," "direct assessment," and "formative evaluation of student progress." Curriculum-based assessment is defined as "a procedure for determining the instructional needs of a student based on the student's ongoing performance within existing course content" (Tucker, 1985, p. 200). In curriculum-based assessment, school personnel evaluate the extent to which the student is profiting from instruction by measuring whether or not specific instructional objectives have been accomplished. In objective-referenced assessment, tests are referenced to specific instructional objectives rather than to the performance of a peer group or norm group. Pupil performance is evaluated by measuring whether or not the student has met specific objectives. Direct and frequent measurement is simply the direct and frequent assessment of specific skills. Direct assessment means directly evaluating pupil progress through the curriculum. The word *direct* is used to differentiate such approaches from more indirect and inferential approaches such as intelligence testing and personality assessment. Finally, *formative evaluation* refers to ongoing assessment activities that are designed to monitor or keep track of pupil progress. Formative evaluation activities are designed to provide teachers with information they can use to make changes in the ways in which they teach students. Summative evaluation activities are designed to help teachers determine whether or not the student has learned the content of instruction, after instruction has occurred.

Will a Commercially Prepared Test Be Used?

The preceding three sections can be applied to teacher-made and commercially prepared tests. Teacher-made tests are often termed "informal" tests. Yet teachers can prepare group or individually administered tests that measure single or multiple skills and that require speed or power. Such tests can be criterion-referenced or, if the teacher has a little statistical background, norm-referenced.[2] The only type of informal test we have not seen is an age scale.

Commercially prepared, or formal, tests may offer several advantages. They are often carefully constructed. The procedures for administering and scoring are standardized so that the test can be administered in a variety of settings. A description of the technical characteristics of the test (reliability, validity, norms) is often available. Finally, commercially prepared tests save the tester the time and effort required to develop a test.

In deciding whether to use a commercially prepared test as opposed to a homemade device, the domain of behaviors to be sampled is of prime concern. Informal achievement tests have one major advantage over commercially prepared achievement tests: teacher-made tests can correspond very closely to the content being taught and can therefore be superior for measuring the content of specific classroom experiences. Commercially prepared achieve-

2. Such norm-referenced devices would employ local norms. See Chapter 6.

ment tests may be useful in screening, program evaluation, and individual program planning. Moreover, because most people within the profession are familiar with standardized achievement tests, the results based on such tests are rapidly communicated to other professionals. In personality assessment, in cases when the test materials are used mainly as a device for eliciting a person's responses, either informal or standardized procedures can probably be used with equal effectiveness.

In areas other than achievement and personality testing, commercially prepared devices are usually superior to informal tests. In these areas (intelligence, readiness, and so on), a great deal of experimental work is necessary in order to develop accurate tests, and this is better done by the professional test maker.

The Social Validity of the Measure

The term *social validity* refers to the consumer's reaction to a change or intervention. The concept can be applied to assessment. Social validity plays a major role in determining the extent to which a particular approach to assessment or a specific test will be used. If, for any reason, school personnel find a particular test or approach undesirable, it is highly unlikely that the approach will be used. Many relatively worthwhile tests stay on the shelf because they are very difficult to administer. Others are not used because school personnel do not like the test items, format, or whatever. Still others are not used because school personnel believe the measures provide meaningless or useless information.

CONSIDERATIONS SPECIFIC TO ASSESSMENT OF HANDICAPPED STUDENTS

Most commercially available standardized tests were developed for use with nonphysically and nonsensorily handicapped students. Later in this text we describe a number of tests designed specifically for use with handicapped students, but in this chapter on test selection we need to consider briefly some of the major problems encountered when professionals modify tests designed for use with nonhandicapped students and administer them to handicapped students.

Two kinds of test modifications are regularly made in assessment of handicapped students: modification of the stimulus demands and modification of the response requirements. Quite often, examiners modify *both* stimulus demands and response requirements. Very often diagnostic personnel change the way in which items are administered in an effort to accommodate the student's physical or sensory limitations. Verbal directions are often signed or pantomimed to hearing-impaired or deaf students; written items are read to visually impaired or blind students. Similarly, examiners often modify response requirements, such as by requiring multiple-choice pointing responses for students who evidence severe language disabilities and elimination of time requirements for motorically disabled students.

Modification of tests to facilitate their use with the handicapped has both good and bad points. By modifying stimulus demands and/or response requirements, examiners are able to obtain samples of behavior. However, the test is no longer a "standardized" test, since the conditions under which it was normed have been altered. Consequently, it is no longer appropriate for test users to attempt to make norm-referenced interpretations of the "scores" handicapped students earn. The norms are no longer relevant.

Suggestions for Teacher Administration of Standardized Tests

When administering standardized tests to children, teachers must take a number of factors into consideration.

Group Size

Generally, when group tests are administered, the smaller the group the better. The optimal group size depends on the ages or grades of the test takers. For young children (kindergarten through grade 3), group size should not exceed fifteen. Young handicapped children should be tested in even smaller groups. When as many as fifteen children are tested at one time, it is advisable to have a monitor (another teacher, a teacher's aide, or some other informed adult) present to insure that directions are followed, broken pencils are replaced, and children do not dawdle or lose their place. Group size may be increased for older students, but, again, the presence of at least one additional monitor is advised. When handicapped children are tested, group size should probably not exceed five.

Adherence to Standardized Procedures

The examiner must at all times administer tests *exactly* according to directions. Standardized tests were meant to be given in exactly the same way each time. Departure from standardized procedures destroys the meaning of test scores by rendering the norms useless. Test users must not coach children on test items before administering the test; they must not alter time limits.

Length of Sittings

The length of testing sessions will vary with the age of the test takers and the extent of their handicaps. As a general rule, a testing session should not exceed 30 minutes in the primary grades, 40 to 60 minutes in the intermediate grades, and 90 minutes in junior and senior high school. However, the tester must exercise common sense. If children become restless, unruly, distracted, or uninterested, testing can be interrupted, the children given a brief break, and the testing resumed. If the test is timed, administration should be interrupted only *between* subtests and never during a subtest.

Elimination of Distractions

Tests should not be administered at times when children are regularly engaged in particularly pleasurable activities. Tests should not be administered at times when children regularly go to assembly, recess, gym, lunch, or art class. Care should be taken to avoid testing at times when other classes are having lunch, recess, and so on. Furthermore, it is usually not advisable to administer tests just before or after a long vacation, a special event, or a holiday.

While administering a group test, the tester should be as unobtrusive as possible. The tester should not move around the room and ask children how they are doing or make small talk. Likewise, conversations between the tester and the monitors should be minimized. Finally, the teacher should avoid publicly preparing an interesting activity to follow the test. Children will attend to the movie projector that is being set up, the novel apparatus for a lab experiment, the elephant that has just been brought into the classroom.

Providing Encouragement

Testers can use discretion in encouraging children taking tests. If a tester sees a child watching a bird building a nest outside the window, the child can be encouraged to pay attention to the test now and watch the bird later; the tester can also draw the window shades. The tester must use common sense so that the standard administration procedures are not violated.

Knowledge of the Tests

The tester should carefully study the manuals provided with the tests. The joint committee of the American Psychological Association, the American Educational Research Association, and the National Council on Measurement in Education stated that "it is appropriate to ask that any test manual provide the information necessary for a test user to decide whether the consistency, relevance, or standardization of a test makes it suitable for [the user's] purpose" (1974, p. 5). Users must study the actual content of a test carefully to make sure that the test adequately assesses the curricular content being taught and that the child has the skills necessary to take the test.

Using the Services of the Buros Institute of Mental Measurements

In addition to inspecting test manuals, all test users should be familiar with the resources available from the Buros Institute of Mental Measurements, now located at the University of Nebraska. The Buros Institute was founded by Oscar Krisen Buros and has one of the richest sources of data on tests in the world.

The institute provides three references that may be of use to educators and psychologists. First, the institute publishes *Tests in Print*. This reference work contains a listing of every test that is registered with the institute. *Tests in Print* is cumulative, so it contains not only the most recent test but also tests from each of the previous *Tests in Print* as well as each volume of the *Mental Measurements Yearbooks*, which are also published by the institute. The Buros Institute attempts to acquire every commercially available test published in English throughout the world. *Tests in Print* simply lists all these tests and provides a short description of each.

The second and most notable reference work published by the Buros Institute is the *Mental Measurements Yearbook*. There are eleven *Mental Measurements Yearbooks*. Unlike *Tests in Print*, the *Mental Measurements Yearbooks* are not cumulative; instead, information in each yearbook pertains only to those tests that are new or revised at the time each volume is published. A listing of new or revised tests is typically accompanied by evaluative reviews written by qualified professionals.

Both *Tests in Print* and the *Mental Measurements Yearbooks* contain references. The institute has an ongoing policy of monitoring most major journals in psychology, business, and various other fields to find articles that reference tests. If a journal article does reference a test, the reference for the journal article is listed along with the test entry in *Tests in Print* and the *Mental Measurements Yearbooks*.

The third service provided by the institute is a computerized data base that is associated with bibliographic retrieval services and can be accessed through most major libraries. The data base is essentially a replication of the *Mental Measurements Yearbooks*. Currently, the entire *Eleventh Mental Measurements Yearbook* has been read into the data base, and the institute provides monthly updates whereby all new information that will appear in the *Twelfth Mental Measurements Yearbook* is blended into the data base. The major advantage of the data base is that it can be searched by means of the computer. The following questions could be answered easily using the computerized data base: (1) How many intelligence tests are designed for 3½-year-old children? (2) What tests are available that assess both reading recognition and reading comprehension for eighth-grade students? (3) Are there any behavior-rating scales available for assessing hyperactivity?

Tests in Print and the *Mental Measurements Yearbooks* are available in the reference departments of most libraries. Information about the data base or any institute services may be obtained from the Buros Institute of Mental Measurements, 135 Bancroft Hall, University of Nebraska, Lincoln, Nebraska 68588-0348.

SUMMARY

Assessment is a complex process, and assessment data are used to make important decisions about individuals. Much can go wrong in the process of assessing students, and when things go wrong students and their life opportunities can be adversely affected. Several assumptions are inherent in assessing students. It is assumed that the person who gives tests is skilled in doing so, that error is always present, that the students we assess are like those to whom we compare them, that behavior sampling is adequate, and that only present behavior is observed. To the extent assumptions are not met or recognized, assessment is invalid.

Many factors must be considered in assessment. They include the student's current life circumstances, developmental history, and extrapersonal factors. Many different kinds of assessment information are typically collected on students, both formal and informal assessments.

There are three fundamentally different approaches to assessment. Many assessors focus their assessment efforts on finding out what is wrong with students, while others focus on diagnosing instruction. In yet a third approach, efforts are made to assess opportunity to learn.

In selecting and administering tests, users must evaluate the kinds of behaviors to be tested, the kinds of interpretative data they want, and the extent to which a commercially prepared test ought to be used. To effectively use and interpret standardized tests, teachers must consider group size, follow standardized procedures, limit length of sittings, eliminate distractions, provide encouragements, and know the test.

STUDY QUESTIONS

1. It is assumed that people who give tests to students are adequately trained to do so. What broad skills can you expect a qualified assessor to have? What happens when people who do not have these competencies assess students?
2. Differentiate between random error and systematic bias.
3. How might you evaluate the extent to which the students you assess have comparable acculturation to those in a test's norm group?
4. Differentiate between an observation and an inference and give two examples of each.
5. Identify three different ways to begin an assessment. Describe an optimal sequence of activities for assessing a student.
6. When and why might you want to administer a group test individually?
7. Differentiate between norm-referenced and criterion-referenced tests and give an advantage of each.
8. Identify two advantages and three disadvantages of informal (teacher-made) tests.
9. Lupe's parents are migrant workers who have just moved into the area. Lupe is enrolled in second grade a few weeks before the annual standardized achievement tests are administered. The decision is made to let her take the tests in Mr. Peno's room, although he is not her teacher, since he speaks Spanish (the language that Lupe speaks at home). Is this sufficient to ensure test validity for Lupe? Defend your answer.

ADDITIONAL READING

Boehm, A., & Weinberg, R. A. (1987). *The classroom observer: A guide for developing observation skills.* New York: Teachers College Press.

Christenson, S. L., & Ysseldyke, J. E. (1989). Assessing student performance: An important change is needed. *Journal of School Psychology, 27,* 409–426.

Deno, S. L. (1985). Curriculum-based measurement: The emerging alternative. *Exceptional Children, 52*(3), 219–232.

Deno, S. L. (1986). Formative evaluation of individual school programs: A new role for school psychologists. *School Psychology Review, 15*(3), 358–374.

Fuchs, L. S., & Fuchs, D. (1986). Linking assessment to instructional interventions: An overview. *School Psychology Review, 15*(3), 318–323.

Germann, G., & Tindal, G. (1985). An application of curriculum-based assessment: The use of direct and repeated measurement. *Exceptional Children, 52*(3), 244–265.

Howell, K. W. (1986). Direct assessment of academic performance. *School Psychology Review, 15* (3), 324–335.

Lentz, F. E., & Shapiro, E. S. (1986). Functional assessment of the academic environment. *School Psychology Review, 15*(3), 346–357.

Marston, D., & Magnusson, D. (1985). Implementing curriculum-based measurement in special and regular education settings. *Exceptional Children, 52*(3), 266–276.

Newland, T. E. (1973). Assumptions underlying psychological testing. *Journal of School Psychology, 11,* 316–322.

Newland, T. E. (1980). Psychological assessment of exceptional children and youth. In W. Cruickshank (Ed.), *Psychology of exceptional children and youth.* Englewood Cliffs, NJ: Prentice-Hall.

Semmell, M. I., & Thiagarajan, S. (1973). Observation systems and the special education teacher. *Focus on Exceptional Children, 5,* 1–12.

Shapiro, E. S. (1987) *Behavioral assessment in school psychology.* Hillsdale, NJ: Erlbaum.

Shapiro, E. S. (1989). Academic skills problems: Direct assessment and intervention. New York: Guilford Press.

Shapiro, E. S., & Kratochwill, T. R. (Eds.). (1988). *Behavioral assessment in schools: Conceptual foundations and practical applications.* New York: Guilford Press.

Ysseldyke, J. E., & Christenson, S. L. (1987). Evaluating students' instructional environments. *Remedial and Special Education, 8,* 17–24.

Ysseldyke, J. E., & Shinn, M. (1981). Psychoeducational evaluation: Procedures, considerations, and limitations. In D. Hallahan & J. Kauffman (Eds.), *The handbook of special education.* Englewood Cliffs, NJ: Prentice-Hall.

C•H•A•P•T•E•R 3

LEGAL AND ETHICAL CONSIDERATIONS IN ASSESSMENT

Much of the practice of assessing students is the direct result of legislation, guidelines, and court cases. If you were to interview directors of special education in your area and ask them why students are assessed, they might initially tell you that students are assessed to provide information on how best to teach them. Pressed harder, these directors would probably tell you that students are assessed because assessment is required by law. They might also tell you that specific kinds of students (for example, minority students) are *not* assessed because such assessments have been forbidden by the courts. Federal laws mandate that students must be assessed before they are declared eligible for special education services. Such laws also mandate that there must be an individualized education plan for every handicapped student and that instructional objectives for each of those students must be derived from a comprehensive individualized assessment.

In this chapter we review Public Law 94-142 and Public Law 99-457, guidelines, and major court cases in which specific kinds of assessment activities have been prescribed. We then describe some of the ethical standards on assessment that have been developed by professional associations. We close the chapter by reviewing guidelines for the collection, maintenance, and dissemination of pupil records.

PUBLIC LAW 94-142

Education is a responsibility of state rather than federal government. No provision of the U.S. Constitution mandates education. Yet every state has compulsory education laws, laws that say that students must attend school. In 1975, the U.S. Congress passed a compulsory special education law, the Education for All Handicapped Children Act. Ballard and Zettel (1977) described that law (often known by its congressional number—Public Law 94-142) as designed to meet four major purposes:

1. To guarantee that special education services are available to children who need them

2. To insure that decisions about providing services to handicapped students are made in fair and appropriate ways
3. To set clear management and auditing requirements and procedures for special education at all levels of government
4. To provide federal funds to help states educate handicapped students

Much of what happens in assessment is directly mandated by one of the four provisions of Public Law 94-142. These provisions are described in the following sections.

Individualized Education Plan (IEP) Provisions

Public Law 94-142 specifies that all handicapped students have the right to a free, appropriate public education and that for each handicapped student schools must have an individualized education plan (IEP). In that document, school personnel must specify the long-term and short-term goals of the instructional program. IEPs must be based on a comprehensive assessment by a multidisciplinary team. The team must specify not only goals and objectives but also plans for implementing the instructional program. They must specify how and when progress toward accomplishment of objectives will be evaluated.

IEPs are to be formulated by a multidisciplinary team meeting with the parents. Parents have the right to agree to the contents of the plan. We stress here the fact that assessment data are collected for the purpose of helping team members specify the components of the IEP. Figure 3.1 is an example of an IEP for a student in a Minnesota school district. Note that specific assessment activities that form the basis for the plan are listed, as are specific instructional goals or objectives.

Protection in Evaluation Procedures (PEP) Provisions

Congress included a number of specific requirements in Public Law 94-142. These requirements were designed to protect students and help insure that assessment procedures and activities would be fair, equitable, and nondiscriminatory. Specifically, Congress mandated eight provisions.

1. Tests are to be selected and administered in such a way as to be racially and culturally nondiscriminatory.
2. To the extent feasible, students are to be assessed in their native language or primary mode of communication.
3. Tests must have been validated for the specific purpose for which they are used.

4. Tests must be administered by trained personnel in conformance with the instructions provided by the test producer.
5. Tests used with students must include those designed to provide information about specific educational needs, and not just a general intelligence quotient.
6. Decisions about students are to be based on more than performance on a single test.
7. Evaluations are to be made by a multidisciplinary team that includes at least one teacher or other specialist with knowledge in the area of suspected disability.
8. Children must be assessed in all areas related to a specific disability, including—where appropriate—health, vision, hearing, social and emotional status, general intelligence, academic performance, communicative skills, and motor skills.

Least Restrictive Environment (LRE) Provisions

In writing the Education for All Handicapped Children Act, Congress wanted to insure that, to the greatest extent appropriate, handicapped students would be placed in settings that would maximize their opportunities to interact with nonhandicapped students. Section 612(5)(B) states,

> *To the maximum extent appropriate, handicapped children . . . are educated with children who are not handicapped, and that special classes, separate schooling, or other removal of handicapped children from the regular educational environment occurs only when the nature or the severity of the handicap is such that education in regular classes with the use of supplementary aids and services cannot be achieved satisfactorily.*

The least restrictive environment provisions arose out of court cases in which state and federal courts had ruled that when two equally appropriate placements were available for a handicapped student, the most normal placement was preferred.

Due Process Provisions

In Section 615 of Public Law 94-142, Congress specified the procedures that schools and school personnel would have to follow to insure due process in decision making. Specifically, when a decision affecting a student's educational environment is to be made, the student's parents or guardians must be

FIGURE 3.1 Example of Individualized Education Program

INDIVIDUAL EDUCATIONAL PLAN

DATE: 11/11/87

STUDENT: Last Name ____ First ____ Middle ____

School of Attendance ____ Home School ____ Grade Level: 5.3 Birthdate/Age: 8-4-76

School Address ____ School Telephone Number ____

Child Study Team Members

Case Manager: LD Teacher

Name	Title	Name	Title
	Homeroom		Parents
	Facilitator		
	Speech		

Summary of Assessment results

IDENTIFIED STUDENT NEEDS: Reading from last half of DISTAR II - present performance level

LONG TERM GOALS: To improve reading achievement level by at least one year's gain. To improve math achievement to grade level. To improve language skills by one years' gain.

SHORT TERM GOALS: Master ~~grade~~-level 4 vocabulary and reading skills. master math skills in basic curriculum. Master spelling words from Level 3 list. Complete units 1-9 from ~~grade~~-level 3 curriculum.

MAINSTREAM MODIFICATIONS ____

White Copy - Cumulative Folder
Pink Copy - Special Teacher
Golden Rod - Case Manager
Yellow Copy - Parent

Description of Services to be Provided

Type of Service	Teacher	Starting Date	Amt. of time per day	OBJECTIVES AND CRITERIA FOR ATTAINMENT
SLD Level III	LD teacher	11-11-87	2½ hrs.	Reading: will know all vocabulary through the "Honeycomb" level. Will master skills as presented through Distar II. Will know 123 sound-symbols presented in "Sound Way to Reading"
				Math: will pass all tests at Basic 4 level.
				Spelling: 5 words each week from Level 3 list.
				Language: will complete Units 1-9 of the 4th grade language program. Will also complete supplemental units from Language Step by Step.

Mainstream Classes	Teacher	Amt of time per day	OBJECTIVES AND CRITERIA FOR ATTAINMENT
		3½ hrs.	Out of seat behavior: sit attentively and listen during mainstream class discussions. A simple management plan will be implemented if he does not meet this expectation.
			Mainstream modifications of Social Studies: will keep a folder in which he expresses through drawing the topics his class will cover. Modified district social studies curriculum. No formal testing will be made. An oral reader will read text to him, and oral questions will be asked.

The following equipment, and other changes in personnel, transportation, curriculum, methods, and educational services will be made:

Distar II Reading Program, Spelling Level 3, "Sound Way to Reading" Program, Vocabulary tapes

Substantiation of least restrictive alternatives: The planning team has determined   academic needs are best met with direct SLD support in reading, math, language, and spelling.

ANTICIPATED LENGTH OF PLAN 1 yr.   The next periodic review will be held: May 1988,
DATE/TIME/PLACE

☒ I approve this program placement and the above IEP
☐ I do not approve this placement and/or the IEP
☐ I request a conciliation conference

_____
PARENT/GUARDIAN

_____
Principal or Designee

given the opportunity to be heard and the right to have an impartial due process hearing to resolve conflicting opinions.

Schools must provide opportunities for parents to inspect the records that are kept on children and to challenge material that they believe should not be included in those records. Parents have the right to have their child evaluated by an independent party and to have the results of that evaluation considered when psychoeducational decisions are made. In addition, parents must receive written notification before any education agency can begin an evaluation that might result in changes in the placement of students.

PUBLIC LAW 99-457

In 1986 Congress passed a major set of amendments to the Education for All Handicapped Children Act, extending all rights and protections of the law to preschoolers who are handicapped. The provisions of this set of amendments, called Public Law 99-457, require states to provide a free appropriate public education to children ages 3 through 5 by school year 1990–91. In addition, these amendments provide grants to states so that they can offer interdisciplinary educational services to handicapped infants and toddlers and their families. Thus, states now have a significant incentive to serve handicapped children from birth through age 2. This bill also expands PL 94-142 by requiring that noneducational federal, state, and local resources and services be made available to all handicapped children. Agencies other than schools can no longer argue that they cannot provide services to children if the services can be provided by schools.

Public Law 99-457 specifies that each school district use a multidisciplinary assessment to develop an individualized family service plan for each child. The IFSP must include

- A statement of the child's present level of cognitive, social, speech and language, and self-help development
- A statement of the family's strengths and needs related to enhancing the child's development
- A statement of the major outcomes expected for the child and family
- Criteria, procedures, and timelines for measuring progress
- A statement of the specific early intervention services necessary to meet the unique needs of the child and family, including methods, frequency, and intensity of service
- Projected dates for initiation and expected duration of services
- The name of the person who will manage the case
- Procedures for transition from early intervention into a preschool program

LITIGATION

Several major court cases preceded passage of Public Law 94-142, and it has been argued that the court cases led Congress to pass that law (Bersoff, 1979). Many issues were contested. In the mid-1960s, a suit was brought against the Washington, D.C., schools on behalf of black students, who were assigned in disproportionate numbers to lower-ability groups or tracks. The chief issue was the fairness of using ability and achievement tests to assign students to groups or tracks. Judge Skelly Wright ruled against tests:

> *The evidence shows that the method by which track assignments are made depends essentially on standardized aptitude tests which, although given on a system-wide basis, are completely inappropriate for use with a large segment of the student body. Because these tests are standardized primarily on and are relevant to a white middle-class group of students, they produce inaccurate and misleading test scores when given to lower-class and Negro students. (Hansen v. Hobson, 1967, p. 514)*

After the ruling in *Hansen* v. *Hobson*, both ability grouping and standardized testing came under intense judicial scrutiny. Repeatedly, plaintiffs have argued that the use of standardized ability and achievement tests results in disproportionate placement of poor and minority students both in lower educational tracks and in special education. Judges have most often, although not always, ruled in favor of plaintiffs.

Another important court case, *Tinker* v. *Des Moines Independent Community School District*, set the stage for legislation and later litigation. This case had nothing to do with assessment. The issue it addressed was whether students had the right to wear black armbands to protest U.S. involvement in the Vietnam War. The court ruled that children are persons under the Constitution, have civil rights independent of their parents, and do not lose those civil rights when they attend school.

In 1972, in *Mills* v. *Board of Education*, the court asserted the rights of students to a due process hearing prior to exclusion from school, the right of handicapped students to an appropriate education, and the unconstitutionality of the exclusion of handicapped students from said education. Three other points are important:

1. Exclusion of students labeled as behavior problems, mentally retarded, emotionally disturbed, or hyperactive is unconstitutional.
2. Any handicapped child has the right to a "constructive education" including appropriate specialized instruction.

3. Due process of law requires a hearing prior to exclusion, termination, or classification into a special program.

Two major court cases addressed misclassification of students as handicapped. In both cases a consent agreement was reached: the cases were settled out of court when schools agreed to a number of actions. In *Diana* v. *State Board of Education* (1970), the California Department of Education agreed (1) to test all children whose primary language was not English in both their primary language and English, (2) to eliminate unfair verbal items from tests, (3) to reevaluate all Mexican-American and Chinese students enrolled in classes for the educable mentally retarded, using only nonverbal items and testing them in their native language, and (4) to develop IQ tests that reflect Mexican-American culture and are standardized only on Mexican-Americans. In *Covarrubias* v. *San Diego Unified School District* (1971) plaintiffs won the right to monetary damages as a result of being misclassified as handicapped.

In 1971, the Pennsylvania Association for Retarded Children sued the Commonwealth of Pennsylvania for excluding mentally retarded students from public school programs. The state agreed to engage in extensive efforts to locate and assess all mentally retarded students in the state; all students placed in public school classes for the mentally retarded were also reevaluated.

The best known court decision after passage of PL 94-142 was a 1979 decision in response to a case that began in 1971, *Larry P.* v. *Riles*. The result of that case was threefold:

1. The state of California was forced to stop using, permitting the use of, or approving the use of any standardized intelligence test for identification of black educable mentally retarded children, or to stop placing them in special classes for the educable mentally retarded.
2. Defendants were ordered to monitor or eliminate disproportionate placement of black students in such classes in California.
3. Defendants were ordered to reevaluate every black child currently identified as an educable mentally retarded pupil without using standardized intelligence tests.

The issue of bias in assessment was not settled in the *Larry P.* case; it continues to be debated in the nation's courtrooms. *PASE* v. *Hannon* (1980) was a class action suit brought by Parents in Action on Special Education on behalf of "all black children who have been or will be placed in special classes for the educable mentally handicapped in the Chicago school system" (p. 2). Plaintiffs observed that while 62 percent of the enrollment of the Chicago public schools was black, black students comprised 82 percent of the enrollment in classes for the educable mentally handicapped.

The judge ruled in favor of the defendants, stating that he could find little evidence that the tests were, in fact, biased. The ruling was clearly contrary to *Larry P.* Judge Grady addressed this fact:

As is by now obvious, the witnesses and the arguments which persuaded Judge Peckham [the judge in the Larry P. *case] have not persuaded me. Moreover, I believe the issue in the case cannot properly be analyzed without a detailed examination of the items on the tests. It is clear that this was not undertaken in the* Larry P. *case. (p. 108)*

Judge Grady found only eight items on the WISC-R and one item on the Stanford-Binet to be biased against black children. He further stated that poor performance on these items alone was not sufficient to result in the misclassification of black students as educable mentally handicapped.

One other court case, in Mississippi, also addressed assessment practices with minority students. In February 1979, U.S. District Judge Orma Smith approved a consent decree settling the four-year-old case *Mattie T. v. Holladay* (Civil Action No. DC-75-31-S, N.D. Miss.). The case was filed on behalf of all schoolage children classified as handicapped in Mississippi and charged the Mississippi Department of Education with failure to meet the requirements of PL 94-142. Under this decree the following agreements were reached:

1. Specific criteria were established for determining when a school district can place handicapped children in classes and buildings separate from regular education programs.
2. The state must hire outside experts to evaluate and revamp the entire state procedure for classifying and placing handicapped students.
3. A timetable was set for the assessment process.
4. Each school district had to identify children misclassified as mentally retarded and give them an opportunity to enroll in a compensatory education program.
5. School districts were prohibited from removing students from school for more than three days.
6. The Mississippi Department of Education was required to monitor local school districts' compliance with the law.

The most far-reaching requirement in this case was the one mandating a reworking of assessment procedures and timelines.

Clearly, courts can keep school personnel from testing students, or at least from giving specific kinds of tests to specific kinds of students. Moreover, the inverse is true: courts can require school systems to administer tests. This was one of the outcomes of the *Pennsylvania Association for Retarded Children (PARC) v. Commonwealth of Pennsylvania* case, as school personnel were required to engage in massive child-find activities. It also was an outcome of *Frederick L. v. Thomas* (1976, 1977). In that action, the Philadelphia public schools were charged with failure to provide an appropriate education to learning disabled students and with serving too few learning disabled students. The Philadelphia schools were required to engage in massive screening and follow-up individual psychoeducational evaluations to identify all learning disabled students in the system.

In a recent court case in Louisiana (*Luke S. & Han S. v. Nix et al.*, 1981),[1] attorneys sued the Louisiana Department of Education for failure to evaluate referred children in a timely fashion. In a consent decree, the state agreed to increase the number of assessment personnel statewide and to assess larger percentages of students in accord with state assessment criteria and in a timely manner. In July 1983 a supplemental agreement was reached. It was found that students were being assessed in a timely manner, but state criteria for appropriate assessment were not being followed. The state agreed to implement statewide training of all assessment personnel.

ETHICAL CONSIDERATIONS

Professionals who assess students have the responsibility to engage in ethical behavior. Many professional associations have put together sets of ethical standards to guide the practice of their members; many of these standards relate directly to assessment practices. Here we cite a number of important ethical considerations, borrowing heavily from the *Ethical Standards of Psychologists* (American Psychological Association, 1979). The standards are not cited per se, but we have distilled from them a number of specific ethical considerations.

Responsibility for the Consequences of One's Work

The assessment of students is a social act that has specific social and educational consequences. Those who assess students use assessment data to make decisions about the students, and the decisions can significantly affect an individual's life opportunities. Those who assess students must accept responsibility for the consequences of their work, and they must make every effort to be certain that their services are used appropriately.

For the individual who assesses students, this ethical standard means sometimes refusing to engage in assessment activities that are desired by a school system but that are clearly inappropriate. It means very careful decision making and assumption of responsibility for the decisions that are made.

---

1. The names Luke S. and Han S. represent Luke Skywalker and Han Solo, characters from *Star Wars*. The attorneys for the plaintiffs selected these names because they felt they were taking on the Empire (the Louisiana Department of Education).

Recognizing the Boundaries of One's Competence

Those who are entrusted with responsibility for assessing and making decisions about students have differing degrees of competence. Not only must professionals regularly engage in self-assessment to be aware of their limitations, but they should recognize the limitations of the techniques they use. For the individual this sometimes means refusing to engage in activities in areas in which one is not competent. It also means using techniques that meet recognized standards.

Confidentiality of Information

Those who assess students regularly obtain a considerable amount of very personal information about those students. It is expected that that information will be held in strict confidence. A general ethical principle held by most professional organizations is that confidentiality is broken only when there is clear and imminent danger to an individual or society. Results of pupil performance on tests must not be discussed informally with school staff. Formal reports of pupil performance on tests must be released only with the permission of the persons tested or their parents or guardians.

Adherence to Professional Standards on Assessment

A joint committee of the American Psychological Association, American Educational Research Association, and National Council on Measurement in Education publishes a document entitled *Standards for Educational and Psychological Tests*. These standards specify a set of requirements for test development and use. It is imperative that those who develop tests behave in accord with the standards and that those who assess students use instruments and techniques that meet the standards. In Parts 3 and 4 of this text we review commonly used tests and talk about the extent to which those tests meet the standards. We provide information to help test users make informed judgments about the technical adequacy of specific tests. There is no federal or state agency that acts to limit the publication or use of technically inadequate tests. Only by refusing to use technically inadequate tests will users force developers to improve inadequate tests. Think about this. If you were a test developer, would you spend considerable time and effort developing a test that few people purchased and used? Would you make changes in a technically inadequate test that people did buy and use and that yielded a large annual profit to you or your firm?

Test Security

Those who assess students are expected to maintain test security. It is expected that assessors will not reveal to others the content of specific tests or test items. At the same time, assessors must be willing and able to back up decisions that may adversely affect individuals with data on which those decisions are based.

PUPIL RECORDS: COLLECTION, MAINTENANCE, AND DISSEMINATION

Policies and standards for the collection, maintenance, and dissemination of information about children must balance two sometimes conflicting needs. Parents and children have a basic right to privacy; schools need to collect and use information about children (and sometimes parents) in order to plan appropriate educational programs. Schools and parents have a common goal: to promote the welfare of children. In theory schools and parents should agree on what constitutes and promotes a child's welfare, and in practice schools and parents generally do work cooperatively.

On the other hand, there have been situations where cooperation has been absent or schools have operated against the best interests and basic rights of children and parents. School personnel have often flagrantly disregarded the rights to privacy of parents and children. Educationally irrelevant information about the personal lives of parents as well as subjective, impressionistic, unverified information about parents and children has been amassed by the schools. Parents and children have been denied access to pupil records, and therefore they have effectively been denied the opportunity to challenge, correct, or supplement those records. At the same time, schools have on occasion irresponsibly released pupil information to public and private agencies that had no legitimate need for or right to the information. Worse yet, parents and children were often not even informed that the information had been accumulated or released.

Abuses in the collection, maintenance, and dissemination of pupil information were of sufficient magnitude that the Russell Sage Foundation convened a conference in 1969 to deal with the problem. Professors of education, school administrators, sociologists, psychologists, professors of law, and a juvenile court judge participated in the conference to develop voluntary guidelines for the proper collection, maintenance, and dissemination of pupil data. Since then, the guidelines (Goslin, 1969) that were developed at the Russell Sage Foundation Conference have been widely accepted and implemented.

In 1974, many of the recommended guidelines became federal law when the Family Educational Rights and Privacy Act (PL 93-380, commonly called the Buckley amendment) was enacted. The basic provisions of the act are quite simple. Any educational agency that accepts federal money (preschools, elementary and secondary schools, community colleges, and colleges and universities) must give parents the opportunity to inspect, challenge, and correct their children's records. (Students aged 18 or older are given the same rights in regard to their own records.) Also, educational agencies must not release identifiable data without the parents' written consent. Violators of the provisions of the Family Educational Rights and Privacy Act are subject to punishment; no federal funds are given to agencies found to be in violation of the law.

The remainder of this chapter deals with specific issues and principles in the collection, maintenance, and dissemination of pupil information. Our discussion draws on the issues raised by and the recommendations of the Russell Sage Foundation Conference Guidelines (hereafter referred to as RSFCG)(Goslin, 1969). The Buckley amendment is considered as it applies, as are specific provisions of Public Law 94-142.

Collection of Pupil Information

Schools collect massive amounts of information about individual pupils and their parents. As we said in Chapter 1, information can be put to several legitimate educational uses: referral, screening, and placement decisions, instructional planning decisions, and pupil guidance. A considerable amount of data must be collected if a school system is to function effectively in delivering educational services to children and in reporting the results of its educational programs to the various community, state, and federal agencies to which it may be responsible.

Classes of Information

The RSFCG delineated three classes of information that schools typically collect. The first class of information (category A) includes the basic, minimum information schools need to collect in order to operate an educational program. Category A data include identifying information (the child's and parents' name and address, the student's age, and so forth) as well as the student's educational progress (grades completed, achievement evaluations, attendance).

Category B data are test results and other verified information useful to the school in planning a student's educational program or maintaining a student "safely" in school. Some of the data that pertain to maintaining a student safely in school can be considered absolutely necessary. For example, available records of medical and pharmacological information about severe allergic reactions such as a sensitivity to bee stings, special diets for children with certain chronic diseases such as diabetes, and unusual medical conditions such as hemophilia may mean the difference between life and death. Other category B data may not be absolutely necessary, but they are nonetheless clearly important in providing an appropriate educational program for a student. Intelligence test data are clearly relevant if the school places a student in a special program for the mentally retarded. Certain types of aptitude or ability data may be necessary if the school district attempts to differentiate instruction on the basis of differences in abilities. Systematic observations, counselor ratings, and various standardized test scores may be useful in cases where a student has problems that are thought to "interfere" with school progress. Certain types of information about a family's background may be important in selecting and interpreting tests used for guidance and placement or in individualizing instruction.

Category C data include information that may be *potentially* useful. When we are gathering information, we often do not know whether a particular bit of information is important or should be followed up. Category C can be considered as the repository for unevaluated but potentially useful information until it can be considered category B information or until it is removed from the student's records.

Consent

According to the RSFCG, no data should be collected without the consent of parents or their agents. The RSFCG accept the notion of representational consent for the collection of category A information and certain types of category B data (for example, intelligence or aptitude tests). *Representational consent* means that consent to collect data is given by appropriately elected officials, such as the state legislature.

The RSFCG recommend that individual informed consent be obtained for the collection of information *not* directly relevant and essential to the education of particular children. Individual informed consent should be obtained in writing prior to the collection of category C data. Informed consent means that the parent (or pupil) is "reasonably competent to understand the nature and consequences of his decision" (Goslin, 1969, p. 17). Individual consent usually should be required for the collection of family information (religion, income, occupation, and so on), personality data, and other noneducational information.

Public Law 94-142, in its section on procedural safeguards, mandates that written prior notice be given to the parents or guardians of a child whenever an educational agency proposes to initiate or change, or refuses to initiate or change, the identification, evaluation, or educational placement of the child or the provision of a free and appropriate education to the child. It is further required that the notice fully inform the parent, in the parent's native language, of all appeal procedures available. Thus, schools must inform parents of their right to present any and all complaints regarding the identification, evaluation, or placement of their child, their right to an impartial due process hearing, and their right to appeal decisions reached at a due process hearing, if necessary by bringing civil action against a school district.

The collection of research data requires individual informed consent of parents. Various professional groups, such as the American Psychological Association, consider the collection of data without informed consent to be unethical; according to the Buckley amendment, it is *illegal* to experiment with children without prior informed consent. Typically, informed consent for research-related data collection requires that the pupil or parents understand (1) the purpose and procedures involved in the investigations, (2) any risks involved in participation in the research, (3) the fact that all participants will remain anonymous, and (4) the option given any participant to withdraw from the research at any time.

Verification

While information is being collected, some distinctions must be made in terms of the quality of the information. Verification is a key concept. *Verifying information* means ascertaining or confirming the information's truth, accuracy, or correctness. Depending on the type of information, verification may take several forms. For observations or ratings, verification means confirmation by another individual. For standardized test data, verification can be equated with reliable and valid assessment.

Information that is not verified cannot be considered category A or B data. Unverified information can be collected, but every attempt should be made to verify such information before it is retained. For example, serious misconduct or extremely withdrawn behavior is of direct concern to the schools. Initial reports of such behavior by a teacher or counselor are typically based on unverified observations. The unverified information provides hints, hypotheses, and starting points for diagnosis. However, if the data are not confirmable, they should not be collected and must not be retained. Similarly, data from unreliable tests (for example, the Illinois Test of Psycholinguistic Abilities or the Developmental Test of Visual Perception) should, we believe, be considered unverified information unless other data are presented to confirm the results.

Maintenance of Pupil Information

Keeping test results and other information, once they are collected, should be governed by three principles. First of all, the information should be retained only as long as there is a continuing need for it. In any event, only category A and category B data—that is, verified data of clear educational value—should be retained. A pupil's school records should be periodically examined, and information that is no longer educationally relevant or no longer accurate should be removed. Natural transition points (for example, promotion from elementary school to junior high) should always be used to remove material from students' files.

The second major principle in the maintenance of pupil information is that parents have the right to inspect, challenge, and supplement student records. The Russell Sage Foundation Conference Guidelines recommended that "formal procedures should be established whereby a student or his parents might challenge the validity of any information contained in Categories 'A' or 'B'" (Goslin, 1969, p. 23). This recommendation presupposes that parents have access to the data.

Parents of exceptional children have had the right to inspect, challenge, and supplement their children's school records for some time. The landmark right-to-education case *(Pennsylvania Association for Retarded Children* v. *Commonwealth of Pennsylvania)* not only won the guarantee of a free, public, appropriate educational program for *all* retarded children in Pennsylvania but also guaranteed parents the right to inspect and challenge the contents of their children's school records. The consent agreement that terminated this suit, in addition to guaranteeing the right to education of all mentally retarded children in Pennsylvania, specified the right of parents to a due process hearing:

> *The notice of the due process hearing shall inform the parent or guardian of his right . . . to examine before the hearing his child's school records including any tests or reports upon which the proposed action may be based, of his right to present evidence of his own. (71-42, Sec. 2f)*

In Pennsylvania, the right to education and the right to a due process hearing before changes in educational placement have been extended to all exceptional individuals, including the gifted. After 1972, several other right-to-education suits were brought against state departments of education.

Parents of all children won the right to inspect, challenge, and supplement their children's school records in 1974. The Buckley amendment brought the force of federal law to the RSFCG recommendations and the various right-to-education cases. No educational agencies receiving federal support may prevent parents (or persons 18 years of age or older) from (1) inspecting all official files and data related to their children or themselves, (2) challenging the content of such files, and (3) correcting or deleting inaccurate, misleading, or inappropriate information contained in the records.

In Public Law 94-142 the provisions of the Buckley amendment are again reiterated. Parents or guardians must be given the opportunity to examine all relevant records with respect to the identification, evaluation, and educational placement of the child and the free and appropriate public education of the child; and to obtain an independent evaluation of the child. Again, if parents have complaints, they may request an impartial due process hearing to challenge either the records or the school's decision regarding their child. The law specifies further that parents have the right to (1) be accompanied and advised by counsel and by individuals with special knowledge or training with respect to the problems of handicapped children, (2) present evidence and confront, cross-examine, and compel the attendance of witnesses, (3) a written or electronic verbatim record of such hearing, and (4) written findings of facts and decisions.

The third major principle in the maintenance of pupil records is that the records should be protected from snoopers, both inside and outside the school system. In the past, secretaries, custodians, and even other students have had access, at least potentially, to pupil records. "Curious" teachers and administrators who had no legitimate educational interest had access. Individuals outside the schools, such as credit bureaus, have often found it easy to obtain information about former or current students. To make sure that only individuals with a legitimate need have access to the information contained in a pupil's records, the RSFCG recommend that pupil records be kept under lock and key. Adequate security mechanisms are necessary to insure that the information in a pupil's records is not available to unauthorized personnel.

Dissemination of Pupil Information

Both access to information by officials and dissemination of information to individuals and agencies outside the school need to be considered. In both cases, the guiding principles are (1) the protection of pupils' and parents' rights of privacy and (2) the legitimate need to know of the person or agency to whom the information is disseminated.

Access Within the Schools

The Russell Sage Foundation Conference recommended that category A and category B data may be released within the school district to school officials with a legitimate educational interest. Those desiring access to pupil records should sign a form stating why they need to inspect the records; a list of people who have had access to their child's files and the reasons why access was sought should be available to parents (Goslin, 1969). The provisions of the Buckley amendment correspond to the Russell Sage Foundation Conference Guidelines (Goslin, 1969):

All persons, agencies, or organizations desiring access to the records of a student shall be required to sign a written form which shall be kept permanently with the file of the student, but only for inspection by the parents or student, indicating specifically the legitimate educational or other interest that each person, agency, or organization has in seeking this information. (Sec. 438, 4A)

When a pupil transfers from one school district to another, a pupil's records are also transferred. The Buckley amendment is very specific here as to the conditions of transfer. When a pupil's file is transferred to another school or school system in which the pupil plans to enroll, the school must (1) notify the pupil's parents that the records have been transferred, (2) send the parents a copy of the transferred records if the parents so desire, and (3) provide the parents with an opportunity to challenge the content of the transferred data.

Access to Individuals and Agencies Outside the Schools

School personnel collect information about pupils enrolled in the school system for educationally relevant purposes. There is an implicit agreement between the schools and parents that the *only* justification for collecting and keeping any pupil data is educational relevance. However, because the schools have so much information about pupils, they are often asked for pupil data by potential employers, credit agencies, insurance companies, police, the armed services, the courts, and various social agencies. To divulge information to any of these sources is a violation of this implicit trust, unless the pupil (if over 18) or the parents request that the information be released.

First, we must recognize the fact that the courts and various administrative agencies have the power to subpoena pupil records from schools. In such cases, the Buckley amendment requires that the parents be notified that the records will be turned over in compliance with the subpoena.

Except in the case of the subpoena of records or their transfer to another school district, the RSFCG recommend that no school personnel release *any* pupil information without the written consent of the parents. The Buckley amendment takes a similar position when it states that no educational agency may release pupil information unless "there is written consent from the student's parents specifying records to be released, the reasons for such release, and to whom, and with a copy of the records to be released to the student's parents and the student if desired by the parents" (Sec. 438, b2A). Although the Buckley amendment lists exceptions, such as applications for financial aid, the thrust of the law and of the Russell Sage Foundation Conference Guidelines is to control the dissemination of personal pupil information.

SUMMARY

The practice of assessing students takes place in a social, political, and legal context. Much of assessment takes place because it is mandated by law. School personnel are required to assess students before declaring them eligible for special education services. The major piece of legislation that currently serves as a guide for assessment activities is the Education for All Handicapped Children Act (Public Law 94-142). The law includes provisions specifying that schools must have individualized education plans for students, that students must be educated in least restrictive environments, and that students who are assessed have due process rights. The law also specifies a number of ways in which students who are evaluated are to be protected.

Public Law 99-457, a set of amendments to the Education for All Handicapped Children Act, was enacted in 1986 to extend the right to an education to handicapped preschoolers and to extend the right to noneducational federal, state, and local resources and services to all handicapped children.

The practice of assessing students changes as courts define and set limits on that practice. We showed how assessment practices have changed as a function of specific court cases.

Those who assess students have certain ethical responsibilities. They are responsible for the consequences of their actions and for recognizing the limits of their competence. There are specific requirements for confidentiality of information obtained in assessment and for keeping the content of tests secure. Those who assess students should adhere to the professional standards outlined in *Standards for Educational and Psychological Tests.*

Schools are entrusted with the lives of children. Every day decisions are made that are intended to be in the children's best interests. These decisions are based on both objective information and professional interpretation of that information. The schools must exercise their power over the lives of children very carefully. When school personnel collect data, they must make sure that the data are educationally relevant; their authority does not include the power to snoop and pry needlessly. The schools need latitude in deciding what information is educationally relevant, but the parents must have the right to check and halt the school's attempts to collect some types of information. Parents' informed consent to the collection of information about their children is basic to the family's right to privacy.

The schools should periodically examine all pupil records and destroy all information that is not of immediate or long-term utility or that has not been verified. The information that is retained must be guarded. Parents, and students over 18, must be given the opportunity to examine records, to correct or delete information, and to supplement the data contained in files.

Sometimes the release of information that has been gathered could be damaging or embarrassing to children and their families. Schools must not release data to outside agencies except under subpoena or with the written consent of parents or a pupil who is over 18. As in all areas of testing and data maintenance, common sense and common decency are required.

STUDY QUESTIONS

1. What were the major purposes of Public Law 94-142, the Education for All Handicapped Children Act of 1975?
2. What four things must be specified in an individualized education plan (IEP)?
3. How might you go about deciding the extent to which a test was fair for use in making decisions about a specific student?
4. Identify two major court cases and describe the effect they have had on the practice of assessing students.
5. Describe differences in the conclusions judges Peckham and Grady reached in *Larry P. v. Riles* and *PASE v. Hannon*.
6. Under what circumstances is it ethically appropriate to divulge the scores that a client earned on a test?
7. What kinds of information on a student can one school send to another school? For which of these must the permission of the student or the student's parent or guardian first be obtained?

ADDITIONAL READING

Abeson, A., & Zettel, J. (1977). The end of the quiet revolution: The Education for All Handicapped Children Act of 1975. *Exceptional Children, 44,* 115–128.

American Educational Research Association, American Psychological Association, and National Council on Measurement in Education. (1985). *Standards for educational and psychological testing.* Washington, DC: American Psychological Association.

Ballard, J., & Zettel, J. (1977). Public Law 94-142 and Section 504: What they say about rights and protections. *Exceptional Children, 44,* 177–185.

Bersoff, D. (1979). Regarding psychologists testily: Legal regulation of psychological assessment in the public schools. *Maryland Law Review, 39,* 27–120.

Clearinghouse on the Handicapped, Office of Special Education and Rehabilitative Services, U.S. Department of Education. (1988). *Summary of existing legislation affecting persons with disabilities.* Washington, DC: U.S. Government Printing Office.

"Litigation and special education." (1986). *Exceptional Children, 52*(4). (This special issue describes ten court cases in the field of special education, several of which are significant tests of policy and practice in the assessment of handicapped and potentially handicapped students.)

Smith, B. (Ed.). (1988). *Mapping the future for children with special needs: PL 99-457.* Iowa City: University of Iowa.

Ysseldyke, J. E., & Algozzine, B. (1990). *Introduction to special education.* Boston: Houghton Mifflin. (Chapter 2: The legal basis for special education)

PART 2

BASIC CONCEPTS OF MEASUREMENT

Part 2 begins with a chapter on basic measurement concepts. Chapter 4, designed for the person who has no background in descriptive statistics, presents the major concepts necessary for understanding the remaining chapters in this part and later parts of the book. In Chapter 5 we discuss the scores typically used in norm-referenced assessment. Especially important is the section dealing with development scores, because these scores are so often misinterpreted and misused. The principal scores used in norm-referenced assessment compare a student to other students who make up the test norms. Chapter 6 gives a detailed description of how normative samples are obtained and the important characteristics of individuals in these samples. Chapter 7, on reliability, is often the most difficult chapter. It deals with the important concept that test scores are fallible and

with the amount of error associated with test scores. In Chapter 8, the last chapter in this part of the text, we examine the concept of test validity. Validity is *the* most important and inclusive aspect of a test's technical adequacy.

Basic statistics and psychometric theory are the foundation of test development and use. Neither subject is easy to master, but both are important. The development and use of tests by people who lack understanding of either statistics or theory have caused many abuses in educational evaluation and decision making. This is the rationale for including Part 2. We realize that numbers and formulas often scare both beginning students and seasoned veterans. Yet they lie at the heart of testing. Everyone who uses tests must understand both in order to evaluate students fairly and intelligently.

Throughout Part 2 we emphasize the basic technical information that a consumer needs to understand in order to interpret tests adequately. However, many nuances and subtleties are not discussed, and no derivations or proofs are presented. We *do* include equations and computational examples to show how particular numbers are obtained as well as to provide material for the logical understanding of basic measurement concepts that is crucial to an understanding of tests and testing.

C·H·A·P·T·E·R 4

Descriptive Statistics

We use descriptive statistics to describe or summarize data. In testing, the data are scores: several scores on one individual, one score on several individuals, or several scores on several individuals. Descriptive statistics are calculated with the basic mathematical operations of addition, subtraction, multiplication, and division as well as simple exponential operations (squares and square roots). Advanced knowledge of mathematics is not required, although many calculations are repetitive and tedious. Calculators and computers facilitate these calculations, and for many applications test authors provide tables of all of the pertinent descriptive statistics. This chapter deals with the basic concepts needed for an understanding of descriptive statistics. Specifically, it discusses scales of measurement, distributions, measures of central tendency, measures of dispersion, and measures of relationship.

SCALES OF MEASUREMENT

The ways in which data can be summarized depend on some characteristics of the scores that are to be described. We can use all of the basic mathematical operations with some types of scores; with other types of scores, none of the basic mathematical operations can be used. The scale on which performances are measured determines how we can describe those performances. There are four scales of measurement: nominal, ordinal, ratio, and equal interval.[1]

Ordinal and equal-interval scales are the most frequently used scales in norm-referenced measurement. Nominal and ratio scales are seldom used. The four scales are distinguished primarily on the basis of the relationship between adjacent or consecutive values on the measurement continuum. An *adjacent value* in this case means a potential or possible value rather than an obtained or measured value. In Figure 4.1, which depicts a portion of a yardstick, the possible values are any points between 2 inches and 6 inches,

---

1. For a more complete discussion, see "Mathematics, Measurement, and Psychophysics" (p. 23) by S. S. Stevens, in *Handbook of Experimental Psychology*, edited by S. S. Stevens, 1951, New York: Wiley.

measured in intervals of eighths of an inch. Any two consecutive points (for instance, 3⅛ inches and 3¼ inches) are adjacent values. Any two points on the scale that have intervening values (for instance, 3⅛ inches and 4¼ inches) are *not* adjacent points. We could, of course, think of adjacent intervals larger than ⅛ of an inch. For example, adjacent 1-inch intervals could be considered, and the adjacent "points" would then be 1 inch, 2 inches, and so on.

Nominal Scales

On nominal scales, adjacent values have no inherent relationship. Nominal scales name values on the scale. For example, at the local ice cream shop, ice cream flavor is a variable. The specific values that this variable can take are names: chocolate, strawberry, tutti-frutti, mocha almond fudge, and others. The first flavor listed is not better than the second flavor listed. Banana sherbet is not better than orange sherbet (although many may prefer one or the other). In education and psychology, we occasionally use nominal scales to describe attributes (for example, sex and eye color), geographic region in which a person resides (for example, the Pacific Northwest), educational classification (for example, learning disabled and emotionally disturbed), and so forth. However, few if any test scores are nominal.

Because values on a nominal scale represent names, the various mathematical operations cannot be performed. For example, we cannot average banana and orange sherbet. Mathematically, all we can do with nominal scales is determine the frequency of each value (for example, how many customers bought orange sherbet).

An occasionally confusing aspect of nominal scales is that numbers may be used as names. For example, numbers on athletic shirts refer only to individual players, in the same way that social security numbers identify people.

FIGURE 4.1   Adjacent and Nonadjacent Values

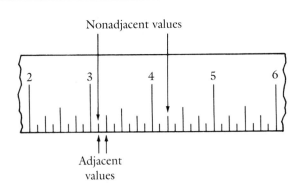

When numbers are used to name people or objects and when these numbers have no inherent relationship to one another in terms of their adjacent values, the scale of measurement is a *nominal scale*. An obvious illustration of a nominal scale is the assignment of numbers to football players. A number is used simply to identify an individual player. The player who wears the number 80 is not necessarily a better player than 70 or 77; 80 is just a different player. Numbers 68 and 69, which are typically thought of as adjacent values, have no relationship to each other on a nominal scale; there is no implied rank ordering in the numbers worn on the shirts. It would not make any sense to add up shirt numbers or to compute the players' average social security number to determine which athletic team is the best.

Ordinal Scales

Ordinal scales order things from best to worst or from worst to best. Several examples of ordinal scales are familiar from everyday life. Some ordinal scales may use names for the values of the variable; however, the names always imply a quantitative relationship. All comparisons of adjectives are ordinal: good, better, best; tall, taller, tallest; poor, worse, worst; and so forth. Ordinal scales also use numbers. Ordinal numbers—first, second, third, and so on —are, of course, an ordinal scale. Other examples include standing in the graduating class, the AP and UPI sports poll of the top twenty football or basketball teams, the winner and finalists in the Miss America contest, and so forth.

Ordinal scales order or rank information or scores on some kind of continuum. Adjacent numbers on an ordinal scale indicate higher or lower value. A simple example of an ordinal scale is a ranking of persons from first to last for some trait or characteristic, such as weights or test scores. Suppose Ms. Smith administers a test to her arithmetic class, in which twenty-five students are enrolled. The test results are reported in Table 4.1. Column 1 gives the name of each student, while column 2 contains each child's raw score. Column 3 contains the ranking of the twenty-five students; the children are listed in decreasing rank order from the student with the "best" performance to the student with the "worst" performance. It is important to note that the difference in raw-score points between adjacent ranks is not the same at each point on the rank (or order) continuum. For example, the difference between the "best" student and the next best student is not the same as the difference between the second-best and the third-best students. Column 4 contains the difference between each student's raw score and the raw score of the immediately preceding student. From this column, it is apparent that differences in adjacent *ranks* do not reflect the magnitude of differences in raw scores. The difficult concept to keep in mind is that although the difference between rank scores (first, second, third, and so on) is 1 everywhere on the scale, the differences between the raw scores that correspond to the ranks are not equal.

TABLE 4.1   Ranking of Students in Ms. Smith's Arithmetic Class

Student	Raw-Score Total	Rank	Difference Between Score and Next Higher Score
Bob	27	1	0
Lucy	26	2	1
Sam	22	3	4
Mary	20	4	2
Luis	18	5	2
Barbara	17	6	1
Carmen	16		
Jane	16	8	1
Charles J.	16		
Hector	14		
Virginia	14		
Manuel	14		
Sean	14	13	2
Joanne	14		
Jim	14		
John	14		
Charles B.	12		
Jing-Jen	12	18	2
Ron	12		
Carole	11	20	1
Bernice	10	21	1
Hugh	8	22	2
Lance	6	23	2
Ludwig	2	24	4
Harpo	1	25	1

In education we often use ordinal scales. As we shall see in Chapter 5, many test scores are ordinal: age equivalents, grade equivalents, and percentiles. Thus, ordinal scales have some interpretative value; however, they are not suitable for more complex interpretations that require some mathematical comparison (for example, calculating averages or differences between achievement in mathematics and reading).

Ratio Scales

Ratio scales have all the characteristics of ordinal scales, but they have two additional characteristics. First, the magnitude of the difference between any two adjacent points on the scale is the same. For example, weight in pounds is measured on a ratio scale; the difference between 15 and 16 pounds is the same as the difference between 124 and 125 pounds. In Table 4.1, if we assume that each raw-score point that makes up the student's total score is of the same value, then the total test score is a ratio scale. This assumption requires that we accept the notion that the difference between 18 and 17 correct is the same as the difference between 11 and 10 correct (or between any other pair of adjacent scores).

The second additional characteristic is that ratio scales have an absolute and logical zero. For instance, temperature on the Kelvin scale is a ratio scale. Absolute zero on that scale indicates the complete cessation of molecular action, or the absence of heat. The absolute zero of a ratio scale, then, allows one to construct ratios with scores. For example, if John weighs 200 pounds and Shawn weighs 100 pounds, John weighs twice as much as Shawn. Few, if any, educational or psychological tests give this type of score.

When ratio scales are used, all mathematical operations can be performed. We can add scores, square scores, create ratios of and differences between scores, etc. Thus, ratio scales are potentially very useful. In education and psychology, ratio scales are associated almost exclusively with the measurement of physical characteristics (for example, height and weight) and some time-based measures (for example, times in a 100-meter dash).

Equal-Interval Scales

Equal-interval scales are ratio scales without an absolute and logical zero. Fahrenheit and Celsius temperature scales are equal-interval not ratio scales— neither zero Fahrenheit nor zero Celsius indicate an absolute absence of heat. Because equal-interval scales lack an absolute zero, we cannot construct ratios with data measured on this scale. Consider the information in Figure 4.2. The differences among lines A, B, C, and D are readily measured.

We can start measuring from any point, such as from the point where line S intersects lines A, B, C, and D. Measured from S, line A is ½ inch long; line B is 1 inch long; line C is 1¼ inches long; and line D is 1¾ inches long. The lines are measured on an equal-interval scale, and the *differences* among the lines would be the same no matter where the starting point, S, was located. However, because S is not a logical and absolute zero, we cannot make ratio comparisons among the lines. Although we have begun measuring from S and found line A to measure ½ inch and found line B to measure 1 inch, the whole line B is obviously not twice as long as line A. In the same way that line B is not twice as long as line A, an IQ of 100 is not twice as large as an IQ of 50; IQ is not measured on a ratio scale.

In education and psychology, we often used equal interval scales. As we shall see in Chapter 5, all standard scores are equal interval. Because we can add, subtract, multiply, and divide data measured on an equal interval scale, these scales can be very useful when complex interpretations of test scores are made.

DISTRIBUTIONS

Distributions of scores may be graphed to demonstrate visually the relations among the scores in the group or set. In such graphs, the horizontal axis *(abscissa)* is the continuum on which the individuals are measured; the vertical axis *(ordinate)* is the frequency (or the number) of individuals earning any given score shown on the abscissa. Three types of graphs of distributions are common in education and psychology: *histograms, polygrams,* and *curves.* To illustrate these, let us graph the examination scores already presented in Table 4.1. The scores earned on Ms. Smith's arithmetic examination can be grouped in three-point intervals (that is, 1 to 3, 4 to 6, . . . , 25 to 27). The grouped scores are presented as a histogram in the first part of Figure 4.3. In the second part of that figure, the same data are presented as a polygram; note that the midpoints of the intervals used in the histogram are connected in constructing the polygram. The third part of Figure 4.3 contains a smoothed curve.

Distributions are defined by four characteristics: mean, variance, skew, and kurtosis. The *mean* is the arithmetic average of the scores and is the balance point of the distribution. The *variance* describes the "spread" or clustering of scores in a distribution. Both of these characteristics are discussed in greater detail in later sections.

Skew refers to the symmetry of a distribution. The distribution of scores from Ms. Smith's exam is not skewed; the distribution is *symmetrical.* How-

FIGURE 4.2   The Measurement of Lines as a Function of the Starting Point

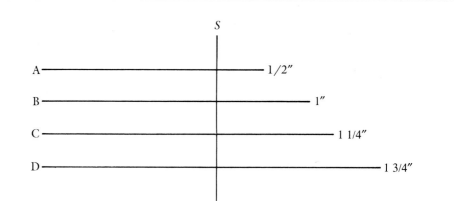

FIGURE 4.3   Distribution of Ms. Smith's Pupils on a Histogram, Polygram, and Curve

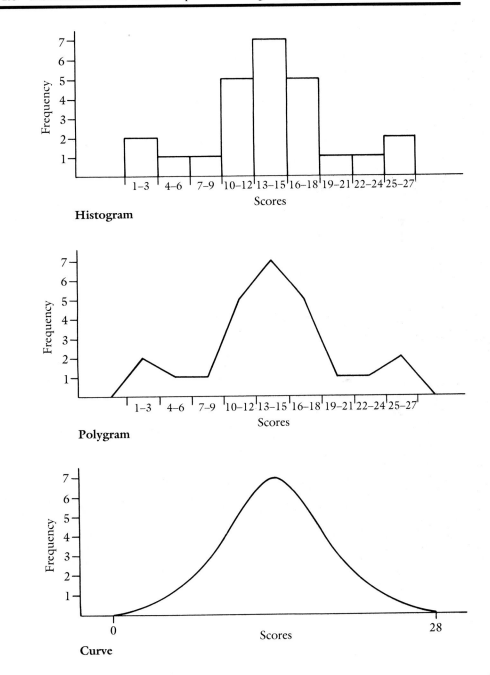

ever, if Ms. Smith had given a very easy test on which many students earned very high scores while only a few students earned fairly low scores, the distribution would have been skewed. In such a case, the distribution would have "tailed off" to the low end and would be called a *negatively skewed* distribution. On the other hand, if she had given a very hard test on which most of her students earned low scores and relatively few earned high scores, the distribution of scores would have tailed off to the higher end of the continuum. Such a distribution is called a *positively skewed* distribution. Figure 4.4 contains an example of a positively skewed curve and a negatively skewed curve. The label assigned to a skewed distribution is determined by the direction of the tail of the distribution. Skewed distributions in which the tail is in the upper (higher-score) end are positively skewed, while those in which the tail slopes toward the lower end are negatively skewed.

Kurtosis, the fourth characteristic of curves, describes the "peakedness" of a curve or the rate at which a curve rises. Distributions that are flat and slow

FIGURE 4.4   Positive and Negative Skews

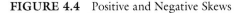

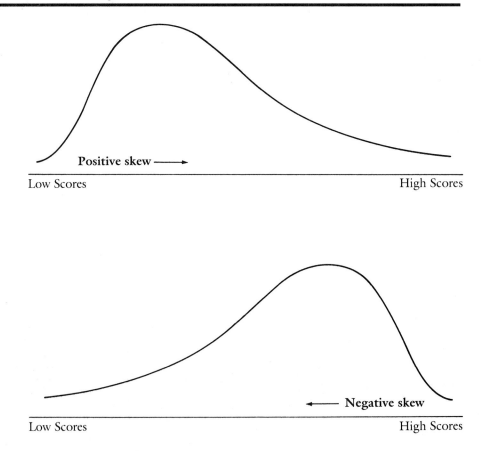

rising, such as the distribution formed by the scores on Ms. Smith's test, are called *platykurtic curves*. (*Platy*kurtic curves are flat, just as a plate or a plateau is flat.) Fast-rising curves are called *leptokurtic curves*. Tests that do not "spread out" (or discriminate among) those taking the test are typically leptokurtic. Figure 4.5 illustrates a platykurtic and a leptokurtic curve.

The normal curve is a particular symmetrical curve. Many variables are distributed normally in nature; many are not. The *only* value of the normal curve lies in the fact that it is known exactly how many cases fall between any two points on the horizontal axis of the curve.

BASIC NOTATION

A number of symbols are used in statistics, and different authors use different symbols. The symbols that we will use in this book are given in Table 4.2. The summation sign Σ means "add the following," while X denotes any score. The number of scores in a distribution is symbolized by N, while f is used to denote the frequency of occurrence of a particular score. The arith-

FIGURE 4.5   A Platykurtic and a Leptokurtic Curve

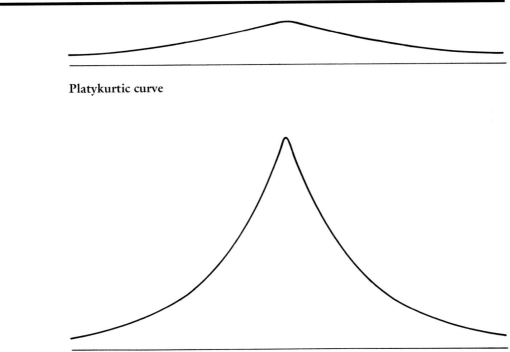

Platykurtic curve

Leptokurtic curve

TABLE 4.2   Commonly Used Statistical Symbols

Symbol	Meaning
Σ	Summation sign
X	Any score
N	Number of cases
f	Frequency
$\overline{X}$	Mean
S^2	Variance
S	Standard deviation

metic average (mean) of a distribution is denoted by $\overline{X}$. The variance of a distribution is symbolized by S^2, and the standard deviation by S.

MEASURES OF CENTRAL TENDENCY

A set of scores can be described by their average (for example, the average score on this week's spelling test was 92 percent correct). This information gives us a general description of how the group as a whole performed. Actually there are three different averages that are used: mode, median, and mean. The *mode* is defined as the score most frequently obtained. A mode (if there is one) can be found for data on a nominal, ordinal, ratio, or equal-interval scale. Distributions may have two modes (if they do, they are called *bimodal* distributions), or they may have more than two. The mode of the distribution of raw scores obtained by Ms. Smith's class on the arithmetic test is readily apparent from an inspection of the data in Table 4.1 and the graphs in Figure 4.3. The mode of this distribution is 14; seven children earned this score.

A *median* is the score that divides the top 50 percent of test takers from the bottom 50 percent. It is that point on a scale above which 50 percent of the cases (people *not* scores) occur and below which 50 percent of the cases occur. Medians can be found for data that are ordinal, equal-interval, and ratio; they should not be used with nominal scales. The median score may or may not actually be earned by a student. Given a set of scores (4, 5, 7, and 8), the median is 6 although no one earned a score of 6. Given a different set of scores (4, 5, 6, 7, and 8), the median is 6, and someone earned that score.

The *mean* is the arithmetic average of the scores in a distribution. It is the sum of the scores divided by the number of scores. Means should be computed only on ratio and equal-interval scales. The formula for computing the mean, using statistical notation, is given in equation 4.1.

$$\overline{X} = \frac{\Sigma X}{N} \tag{4.1}$$

Using the scores obtained from Ms. Smith's arithmetic examination (Table 4.1), we find that the sum of the scores is 350 and that the number of scores is 25. The mean (arithmetic average), then, is 14. The mean was earned by seven children in the class. The mean, like the median, may or may not be earned by a child in the distribution.

The mode, median, and mean have particular relationships depending on the symmetry (skew) of a distribution. As Figure 4.6 shows, in symmetrical unimodal distributions the mode, median, and mean are at the same point. In positively skewed distributions, the median and mean are displaced toward the positive tail of the curve; the mode is a lower value than the median, and the median is a lower value than the mean. In negatively skewed distributions, the median and mean are displaced toward the negative tail of the curve; the mode is a higher value than the median, and the median is a higher value than the mean.

MEASURES OF DISPERSION

Although a mean tells us about a group's average performance, it does not tell us how close to the average people scored. For example, did everyone earn 92 percent correct on the weekly spelling test, or were the scores spread out from 0 to 100 percent? To describe how scores spread out, we use three indexes of dispersion: range, variance, and standard deviation. All three measures can be computed when the scale of measurement is ratio or equal interval, and none of the three can be computed when the scale of measurement is nominal. Range can be calculated with ordinal data.

The *range* is the distance between the extremes of a distribution, including those extremes; it is the highest score less the lowest score plus one. On Ms. Smith's test (Table 4.1), it is 27 (27 = 27 − 1 + 1). The range is a relatively crude measure of dispersion, since it is based on only two bits of information.

The variance and the standard deviation are the most important indices of dispersion. The *variance* is a numerical index describing the dispersion of a set of scores around the mean of the distribution. Specifically, the variance (S^2) is the average squared-distance of the scores from the mean. Since the variance is an average, it is not affected by the number of cases in the set or distribution. Large sets of scores may have large or small variances; small sets of scores may have large or small variances. Also, since the variance is measured in terms of distance from the mean, it is not related to the actual value of the mean. Distributions with large means may have large or small variances; distributions with small means may have large or small variances. The variance of a distribution may be computed with equation 4.2. The *variance* (S^2)

FIGURE 4.6   Relationships Among Mode, Median, and Mean for Symmetrical and Asymmetrical Distributions

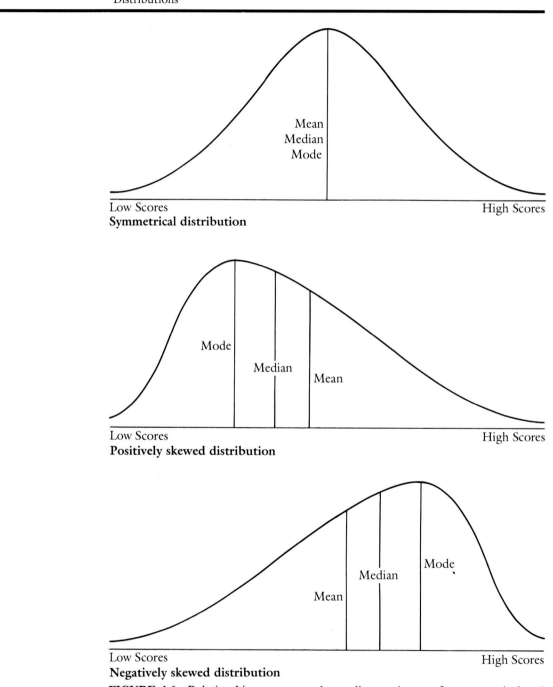

Mean
Median
Mode

Low Scores   High Scores
Symmetrical distribution

Mode

Median

Mean

Low Scores   High Scores
Positively skewed distribution

Mode

Median

Mean

Low Scores   High Scores
Negatively skewed distribution

FIGURE 4.6   Relationships among mode, median, and mean for symmetrical and asymmetrical distributions equals the sum (Σ) of the square of each score less the mean $[(X - \overline{X})^2]$, divided by the number of scores (N).

$$S^2 = \frac{\Sigma(X - \overline{X})^2}{N} \tag{4.2}$$

The scores from Ms. Smith's arithmetic test are reproduced in Table 4.3. The second column contains the score earned by each student. The first step in computing the variance is to find the mean. Therefore, the scores are added and the sum is divided by the number of scores. The mean in this example is 14. The next step is to subtract the mean from each score; this is done in column 3 of Table 4.3, which is labeled $X - \overline{X}$. Note that the scores above the mean are positive, the scores at the mean are zero, and the scores below the mean are negative. The differences (column 3) are then squared (multiplied by themselves); the squared differences are in column 4, labeled $(X - \overline{X})^2$. Note that all numbers in this column are positive. The squared differences are then summed; in this example, the sum of all the squared distances of scores from the mean of the distribution is 900. The variance equals the sum of all the squared distances of scores from the mean divided by the number of scores; in this case, the variance equals 900/25, or 36.

The variance is very important in psychometric theory but has very limited application in score interpretation. However, its calculation is necessary for the computation of the standard deviation (S), which is *very* important in the interpretation of test scores. The standard deviation is the positive square root ($\sqrt{}$) of the variance.[2]

Thus, in our example, since the variance is 36, the standard deviation is 6. In later chapters, the standard deviation will be used in other computations such as standard scores and the standard error of measurement.

The standard deviation is used as a *unit of measurement* in much the same way an inch or ton is used as a unit of measurement. When scores are equal-interval, they can be measured in terms of standard deviation units from the mean. The advantage of measuring in standard deviations is that when the distribution is normal, we know exactly how many cases occur between the mean and the particular standard deviation. As shown in Figure 4.7, approximately 34 percent of the cases in a normal distribution always occur between the mean and one standard deviation (S) either above or below the mean. Thus, approximately 68 percent of all cases occur between one standard deviation below and one standard deviation above the mean (34% + 34% = 68%). Approximately 14 percent of the cases occur between one and two standard deviations below the mean *or* between one and two standard deviations above the mean. Thus, about 48 percent of all cases occur between the mean and two standard deviations either above or below the mean (34% +

2. The square root of a particular number is the number that when multiplied by itself produces the particular number. For example: $\sqrt{144} = 12, \sqrt{25} = 5, \sqrt{4} = 2$. Appendix 1 contains a table of square roots for numbers between 1 and 100.

TABLE 4.3   Computation of the Variance of Ms. Smith's Arithmetic Test

Student	Test Score	$X - \overline{X}$	$(X - \overline{X})^2$
Bob	27	13	169
Lucy	26	12	144
Sam	22	8	64
Mary	20	6	36
Luis	18	4	16
Barbara	17	3	9
Carmen	16	2	4
Jane	16	2	4
Charles J.	16	2	4
Hector	14	0	0
Virginia	14	0	0
Manuel	14	0	0
Sean	14	0	0
Joanne	14	0	0
Jim	14	0	0
John	14	0	0
Charles B.	12	−2	4
Jing-Jen	12	−2	4
Ron	12	−2	4
Carole	11	−3	9
Bernice	10	−4	16
Hugh	8	−6	36
Lance	6	−8	64
Ludwig	2	−12	144
Harpo	1	−13	169
SUM	350	0	900

14% = 48%). About 96 percent of all cases occur between two standard deviations above and two standard deviations below the mean. Appendix 2 lists the proportion of cases in a normal distribution occurring between the mean and any standard deviation above or below the mean. If we enter Appendix 2 at .44 (that is, .4 and .04), we find the number .1700. This number means that 1,700/10,000 (17 percent) of the cases in the normal curve occur between the mean and .44 standard deviation from the mean, either below or above the mean. Thirty-three percent of the cases fall below .44 standard deviation below the mean. (Half of the cases, 50 percent, fall below the mean; 17 percent fall between −0.44 S and the mean; 50 percent less 17 percent equals 33 percent.)

As shown by the positions and values for scales A, B, and C in Figure 4.7, it does not matter what the values of the mean or standard deviation are. The relationship holds for various obtained values of the mean and the standard deviation. For scale A, where the mean is 25 and the standard deviation is 5, 34 percent of the scores occur between the mean (25) and one standard deviation below the mean (20) *or* between the mean and one standard deviation above the mean (30). Similarly, for scale B, where the mean is 50 and the standard deviation is 10, 34 percent of the cases occur between the mean (50) and one standard deviation below the mean (40) *or* one standard deviation above the mean (60).

It is extremely important that those who use tests to make decisions about students be aware of the means and standard deviations of the tests they use. Some intelligence tests, for example, have a mean of 100 and a standard deviation of 16. If scores on those tests are normally distributed, we would expect approximately 68 percent of the school population to have IQs between 84 and 116. Another intelligence test may have a mean of 100 and a standard deviation of 24. We would expect approximately 68 percent of the school population to have IQs between 76 and 124 if scores on that test are normally distributed. The meaning of a score in a distribution depends on the mean, the standard deviation, and the shape of that distribution. This is an obvious point, yet it is often overlooked. For example, some states use an absolute score in the school code for the placement and retention of mentally retarded children in special education programs; Pennsylvania uses a score of 79 for maintaining eligibility for placement. On the Stanford-Binet Intelligence Scale, a score of 79 is 1.31 standard deviations below the mean [(79 − 100)/16]; on the Wechsler Intelligence Scale for Children-Revised, a score of 79 is 1.40 standard deviations below the mean [(79 − 100)/15]. If a single absolute score is specified, several *different* levels of eligibility for special education classes are written into the school code unintentionally.

FIGURE 4.7   Scores on Three Scales, Expressed in Standard Deviation Units

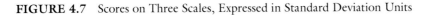

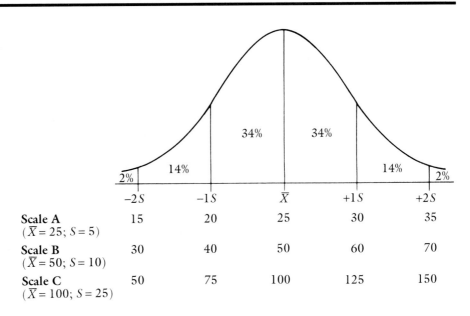

CORRELATION

Correlations quantify relationships between variables. *Correlation coefficients* are numerical indices of these relationships. They tell us the extent to which any two variables go together, the extent to which changes in one variable are reflected by changes in the second variable. These coefficients are used in measurement to estimate both the reliability and the validity of a test. Correlation coefficients can range in value from .00 to *either* +1.00 or −1.00. The sign (+ or −) indicates the direction of the relationship while the number indicates the magnitude of the relationship. A correlation coefficient of .00 between two variables means that there is no relationship between the variables. The variables are independent; changes in one variable are not related to changes in the second variable. A correlation coefficient of either +1.00 or −1.00 indicates a perfect relationship between two variables. Thus, if you know a person's score on one variable, you can predict that person's score on the second variable exactly. Correlation coefficients between .00 and 1.00 offer some prediction, and the greater the coefficient, the greater is its predictive power.

Correlation coefficients are very important in assessment. As we shall see in Chapter 7, they are used to estimate the amount of error associated with measurement. In Chapter 8, we shall learn that correlation coefficients are also used to estimate a test's validity.

The Pearson Product-Moment Correlation Coefficient

The most commonly used correlation coefficient is the Pearson product-moment correlation coefficient (r). This is an index of the straight-line (linear) relationship between two variables measured on an equal-interval scale. Suppose Ms. Smith administered a second exam to her arithmetic class. The results of the first exam (the data from Table 4.1) are reproduced in column 2 of Table 4.4, while the results of the second exam are presented in column 3. (For the sake of simplicity, the example has been constructed so that the second test has the same mean and the same standard deviation— that is, 14 and 6—as the first test.) The two scores for each student are plotted on a graph (called a *scattergram* or *scatterplot*) in Figure 4.8. The scatterplot contains twenty-five points—one for each child. Inspection of the figure indicates that there is a pronounced tendency for high scores on the first test to be associated with high scores on the second test. There is a *positive* relationship (correlation) between the first and second tests. The line drawn through the scatterplot in Figure 4.8 is called a *regression line*. When the points corresponding to each pair of scores cluster closely around the

TABLE 4.4 Scores Earned on Two Tests Administered by Ms. Smith to Her Arithmetic Class

Student	Raw Score, Test 1	Raw Score, Test 2
Bob	27	26
Lucy	26	22
Sam	22	20
Mary	20	27
Luis	18	14
Barbara	17	18
Carmen	16	16
Jane	16	17
Charles J.	16	16
Hector	14	14
Virginia	14	14
Manuel	14	16
Sean	14	14
Joanne	14	12
Jim	14	14
John	14	12
Charles B.	12	14
Jing-Jen	12	11
Ron	12	12
Carole	11	10
Bernice	10	14
Hugh	8	6
Lance	6	1
Ludwig	2	2
Harpo	1	8

regression line, there is a high degree of relationship. The points from Table 4.4 do cluster closely around the regression line; there is a high correlation (specifically, .89) between the first and second tests.[3] If all the points fell on the regression line, there would be a perfect correlation (1.00).

Figure 4.9 contains six scatterplots of different degrees of relationship. In parts a and b, all points fall on the regression line so that the correlation between the variables is perfect. Part a has a correlation coefficient of +1.00; high scores on one test are associated with high scores on the other test. Part b has a correlation of –1.00; high scores on one test are associated with low

3. The correlation coefficient can be computed with the following formula:

$$r = \frac{N\sum XY-(\sum X)(\sum Y)}{\sqrt{N\sum X^2-(\sum X)^2}\sqrt{N\sum Y^2-(\sum Y)^2}}$$

scores on the other test (this negative correlation is called an *inverse* relationship). Parts c and d show a high degree of positive and negative relationship, respectively. Note that the departures from the regression lines are associated with lower degrees of relationship. Parts e and f show scatterplots with a low degree of relationship. Note the wide departures from the regression lines.

Zero correlations can occur in three ways, as shown in Figure 4.10. First, if the scatterplot is essentially circular (part a), the correlation is approximately .00. Second, if either or both variables are constant (part b), the correlation is .00. And third, if the two variables are related in a nonlinear way, the correlation may be .00. In part c, for example, there is a very strong curvilinear relationship where all points fall close to a curved line, but the *linear* regression line would parallel one of the axes. Thus, while there is a curvilinear relationship, the coefficient of linear correlation is approximately .00.

FIGURE 4.8   Scatterplot of the Two Tests Administered by Ms. Smith

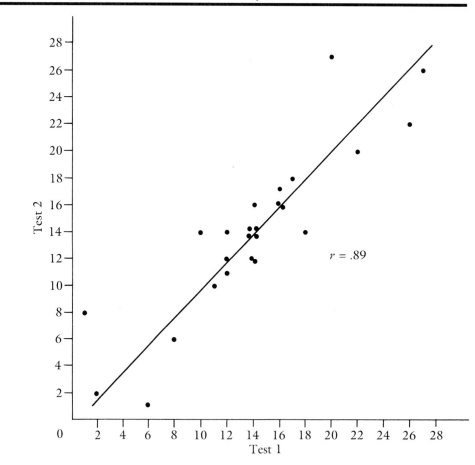

FIGURE 4.9   Six Scatterplots of Different Degrees and Directions of Relationship

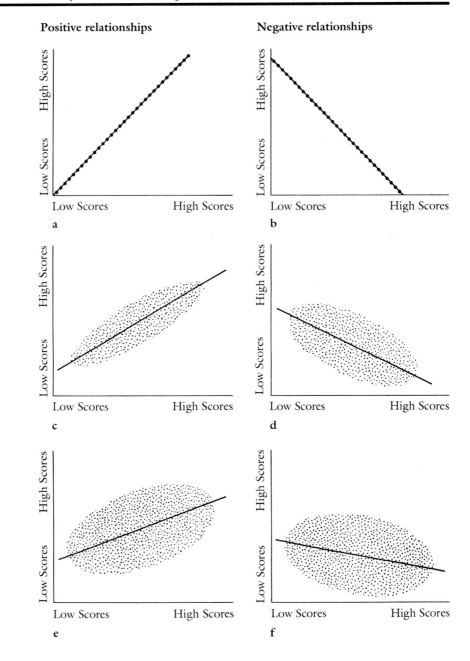

FIGURE 4.10 Three Zero-Order, Linear Correlations

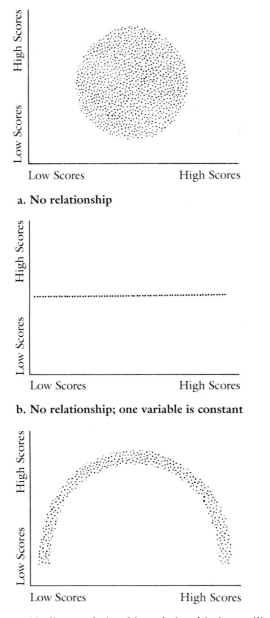

a. No relationship

b. No relationship; one variable is constant

c. No linear relationship; relationship is curvilinear

Variant Correlation Coefficients

Six variations of linear correlation are commonly found in test manuals and research literature dealing with reliability and validity. Four are members of the Pearson family of correlation coefficients, which means that they are computed by the same (or by a computationally equivalent) formula (see footnote 4). Two variations are not members of the Pearson family of coefficients and are calculated differently. These six coefficients are used in different situations.

Pearson-Family Coefficients

Different names are typically given to the Pearson product-moment correlation coefficient depending on the scale of measurement used. The first member of the family of correlation coefficients is called the *Pearson product-moment* correlation coefficient and is symbolized by the letter *r*. This name or symbol is used when the variables to be correlated are measured on an equal-interval (or ratio) scale. The second member of the Pearson family is called the *Spearman rho* (ρ). This coefficient is used when both variables are measured on an ordinal scale. The third and fourth members of the Pearson family are used when either or both of the variables to be correlated are naturally occurring dichotomous variables (for example, male/female). When a naturally occurring dichotomous variable such as sex is correlated with a continuous, equal-interval variable (height measured in inches, for example), the correlation coefficient is called a *point biserial* correlation coefficient ($r_{pt.bis}$). When two sets of naturally occurring dichotomous variables (for example, male/female and dead/alive) are correlated, the correlation coefficient is called a *phi* coefficient (φ).

Non-Pearson-Family Coefficients

A continuous variable can be forced into a dichotomy. For example, the entire range of intelligence can be dichotomized into smart and dull at some arbitrary point on the continuum. If a variable that has been forced into an arbitrary dichotomy (for example, smart/dull) is correlated with a continuous equal-interval variable (for example, grade-point average), the resulting coefficient is called a *biserial* correlation coefficient (r_{bis}). If two arbitrarily dichotomized variables (for example, tall/short, smart/dull) are correlated, the coefficient is called a *tetrachoric* correlation coefficient (r_{tet}). These two correlation coefficients are computed differently from the way the Pearson-family coefficients are computed.

Relationship Among Correlation Coefficients

Figure 4.11 illustrates the different correlation coefficients commonly used in measurement that we have discussed.

In test manuals you will often see correlations between individual test items or between each test item and the total test score. Test authors typically report phi and point biserial correlation coefficients rather than tetrachoric and biserial coefficients in such cases. In selecting particular coefficients, an author assumes the nature of correct or incorrect response. An author who selects phi and point biserial correlations assumes that each response is either correct or incorrect; there are no "in-betweens." The author who reports tetrachoric and biserial correlations assumes that each test item represents a continuum ranging from totally correct to totally incorrect, even though the individual items are scored only as right or wrong. The differences between Pearson-family and non-Pearson-family coefficients should not cause a test administrator any difficulty. Modern tests rely almost exclusively on Pearson-family coefficients. But occasionally one sees r_{tet} or r_{bis}.

Causality

No discussion of correlation is complete without mentioning causality. Correlation is a necessary but insufficient condition for determining causality. Two

FIGURE 4.11   Different kinds of correlation coefficients are used, depending on the scales of measurement for each variable. There are coefficients for some of the blanks in this figure (for example, biserial phi and rank biserial), but test users are not likely to encounter them in test manuals.

	Characteristics of Variable 1			**Non-Pearson family**
	Pearson family			
	Ordinal	Equal interval	Natural dichotomy	Forced dichotomy
Ordinal	Spearman's rho (ρ)			
Equal interval		Pearson product-moment (r)	Point biserial ($r_{pt.bis}$)	Biserial (r_{bis})
Natural dichotomy			Phi (ϕ)	
Forced dichotomy				Tetrachoric (r_{tet})

Characteristics of Variable 2

variables cannot be causally related unless they are correlated. However, the mere presence of a correlation does not imply causality. For any correlation between two variables (A and B), *three* causal interpretations are possible: A causes B; B causes A; or a third variable, C, causes both A and B. For example, firefighters (A) are often present at fires (B). Firefighters do not cause fires (A does not cause B).[4] Fires cause firefighters to be present (B causes A). As a second example, in a sample of children ranging from 6 months to 8 years of age, we might find a positive relationship between shoe size and mental age. Big feet do not cause intelligence (A does not cause B). Moreover, intelligence does not cause big feet (B does not cause A). More likely, as children grow older (C) they tend to increase in both shoe size and mental age; C causes both A and B.

Although the above examples illustrate fairly obvious instances of inappropriate reasoning, in testing situations the errors or potential errors are not so clear. For example, scores on intelligence tests and scores on achievement tests are correlated. Some argue that intelligence causes achievement; others argue that achievement causes intelligence. Since there are at least three possible interpretations of correlational data—and since correlational data do not tell us which interpretation is true—we must never draw causal conclusions from such data.

SUMMARY

Descriptive statistics provide summary information about groups of individuals. Data can be obtained on one of four scales of measurement: *nominal, ordinal, ratio,* and *equal-interval* scales. Collections of scores are called *distributions.* Distributions are defined by four characteristics: *mean, variance, skew,* and *kurtosis.* Depending on the scale of measurement, three indices may be used to indicate a distribution's central tendency: the *mode* (the most frequent score), the *median* (the score that separates the top 50 percent from the bottom 50 percent), and the *mean* (the arithmetic average). Depending on the scale of measurement, the dispersion of a distribution can be described by three indices: the *range* of scores, the *variance,* and the *standard deviation.* The quantification of the relationship between two variables is called *correlation.* When there is no relation between variables, the correlation is zero. When there is a perfect relationship between variables, the correlation is 1. A plus or a minus sign indicates the type of relationship, not the magnitude of relationship. A positive correlation indicates that high scores on one variable are associated with high scores on the second variable. A negative correlation indicates an inverse relationship: high scores on one variable are associated

4. Exceptions have been reported by Bradbury (1953).

with low scores on the other variable. There are several types of correlations that are often used in tests.

STUDY QUESTIONS

1. All third-grade pupils in a particular state took an achievement test. The superintendent of public instruction reviewed the test results and in a news conference reported concern for the quality of education in the state. The superintendent reported, "Half the third-grade children in this state performed below the state average." What is foolish about that statement?
2. What is the relationship among the mode, median, and mean in a normal distribution?
3. The following statements about test A and test B are known to be true:
   Tests A and B measure the same behavior.
   Tests A and B have means of 100.
   Test A has a standard deviation of 15.
   Test B has a standard deviation of 5.
   a. Following classroom instruction, the pupils in Mr. Radley's room earn an average score of 130 on test A. Pupils in Ms. Purple's room earn an average score on test B of 110. On this basis, the local principal concludes that Mr. Radley is a better teacher than Ms. Purple. Why is this inappropriate?
   b. Assuming the pupils were equal prior to instruction, what conclusions could the principal legitimately make?
4. On the Stanford-Binet Intelligence Scale, Harry earns an IQ of 52 and Ralph earns an IQ of 104. Their teacher concludes that Ralph is twice as smart as Harry. To what extent is this conclusion warranted?

PROBLEMS

1. Ms. Robbins administers a test to ten children in her class. The children earn the following scores: 14, 28, 49, 49, 49, 77, 84, 84, 91, 105. For this distribution of scores, find the following:
   a. Mode
   b. Mean
   c. Range
   d. Variance and standard deviation
2. Mr. Garcia administers the same test to six children in his class. The children earn the following scores: 21, 27, 30, 54, 39, and 63. For these scores, find the following:
   a. Mean

   b. Range

   c. Variance and standard deviation

3. Ms. Shumway administers a test to six children in her nursery school program. The children earn the following scores: 23, 33, 38, 53, 78, and 93. Find the mean and standard deviation of these six scores.

4. Using Appendix 2, find the proportion of cases that

   a. occur between the mean and the following standard deviation units: −1.5, +.37, +.08, +2.75.

   b. occur between + and −1.7S, between + and −.55S, and between + and −2.1S.

   c. occur above −.7S, +1.3S, and +1.9S.

   d. occur below −.7S, +1.3S, and +1.9S.

Answers

1. (a) 49; (b) 63; (c) 92; (d) 784 and 28.
2. (a) 39; (b) 43; (c) 225 and 15.
3. Mean = 53; standard deviation = 25.
4. (a) .4332, .1443, .0319, .4970; (b) .9108, .4176, .9642; (c) .7580, .0968, .0287; (d) .2420, .9032, .9713.

ADDITIONAL READING

Psychological Corporation. (1966). *Test Service Bulletin* No. 148: *The Normal Curve*. New York: Psychological Corporation.

Psychological Corporation. (1965). *Test Service Bulletin* No. 13: *Glossary of Measurement Terms*. New York: Psychological Corporation.

C·H·A·P·T·E·R 5

QUANTIFICATION OF TEST PERFORMANCE

Most behaviors occur without systematic observation, quantification, and evaluation; the vast majority of behaviors do not occur in situations specifically structured to quantify and evaluate them. A test is an exception. A test is a structured, standardized situation in which standardized materials are presented to an individual in a predetermined manner in order to evaluate that individual's responses using predetermined criteria.

How the individual's responses are quantified depends on the test materials, the intent of the test author, and the tester's intent in choosing the test. If we were interested only in determining if a student had learned a specific fact or concept (for example, What is 3 + 5?), we would make explicit the criteria for what constitutes a correct response and would classify the student's response as right or wrong. Although we would have no need to quantify the test results, keeping track of a student's mastery of all specific facts and concepts can be a recordkeeping nightmare, even with a computer in every classroom. Therefore, this approach is generally restricted to the most essential information that each and every student must master. When we were interested in determining if a student had learned a finite set of facts (for example, the addition of all combinations of single-digit numbers), we could readily quantify a student's performance as the number of facts known or the percentage of facts known.

More often, though, the information that we wish to assess is not finite, and it is impractical or impossible to assess all the facts and relationships that might be tested. For example, it seems unlikely that anyone could make up a test to assess every aspect of all Shakespeare's plays; however, even if it were possible, it would be virtually impossible to administer all the possible questions to a student in one or even several settings. Even when we cannot test all the possible information on a topic, we still would want to estimate how much of the information that students had learned. To do so, testers are forced to ask a few questions and base their inferences about all the information (called the *domain*) on student responses to the sample of questions. When we sample knowledge of a domain with a smaller number of items, we assume that a student's performance on all the items in the domain can be accurately inferred from the performance on the sample of items. Particular items are only important as representatives of the domain and tend to lose their individual importance. Moreover, we generally cannot infer the percent correct on the entire domain directly from test unless items are very carefully selected in terms of their difficulty, a condition that is never known on an *a priori* basis.

When a large domain is assessed, a student's performance is typically interpreted by comparing it to the performances of a group of subjects of known demographic characteristics (age, sex, grade in school, and so on). This group is called a *normative sample* or *norm group*. These comparison scores are called *derived scores* and are of two types: developmental scores and scores of relative standing.

DEVELOPMENTAL SCORES
Developmental Levels

Developmental scores are one method of transforming raw scores. The most common types of developmental scores are age equivalents (mental ages, for example) and grade equivalents. Suppose the average performance of 10-year-old children on an intelligence test was twenty-seven correct answers. Further, suppose that Horace answered twenty-seven questions correctly. Horace would have answered as many questions correctly as the average of 10-year-old children. He would have earned a mental age of 10 years. An *age equivalent* means that a child's raw score is the average (the median or mean) performance for that age group. Age equivalents are expressed in years and months; a hyphen is used in age scores (for example, 7-1). A *grade equivalent* means that a child's raw score is the average (the median or mean) performance for a particular grade. Grade equivalents are expressed in grades and tenths of grades; a decimal point is used in grade scores (for example, 7.1). Age-equivalent and grade-equivalent scores are interpreted as a performance equal to the average of X-year-old's and average of Xth grader's performance, respectively.

Suppose we gave a test to 1,000 children, 100 at each age (within two weeks of their birthdays) from 5 to 14 years. For each 100 children at each age, there is a distribution with a mean. These hypothetical means are connected in Figure 5.1. As the figure shows, a raw score of 16 corresponds exactly to the average score earned by children in the 6-year-old distribution. Thus, the child who earns a score of 16 has an age equivalent of 6 years, 0 months, or 6-0. A score of 36, by contrast, falls *between* the average of the 11-year-old distribution and the average of the 12-year-old distribution. A raw score of 36 would be estimated (*interpolated*) as an age score of 11-6; it would be awarded a score between 11 and 12, despite the fact that no children between 11 and 12 years of age were tested. A score of 4 would fall below the average of the lowest age group, the five-year-olds. If a child earned a raw score of 4, that child's age equivalent would be estimated (*extrapolated*) by continuing the curve in Figure 5.1. A raw score of 4 could be extrapolated to be the equivalent of an age score of 3-6 although *no* children that young are included in the sample. Similarly, a score greater than the average performance of the oldest children could also be extrapolated.

The interpretation of age and grade equivalents requires great care. Five problems occur in the use of developmental scores. The first problem is systematic misinterpretation. Students who earn an age equivalent of 12-0 have merely answered correctly as many questions as the average of children 12 years of age. They have not necessarily "performed as" a 12-year-old child would; they may well have attacked the problems in a different way or demonstrated a different performance pattern from many 12-year-old students. Similarly, a second grader and a ninth grader may both earn grade equivalents of 4.0. They probably have not performed identically. Thorndike and Hagen (1978) have suggested that it is more likely that the younger child has performed lower-level work with greater accuracy (for instance, successfully

FIGURE 5.1   Mean Number Correct for Eleven Age Groups: An Example of Arriving at Age-Equivalent Scores

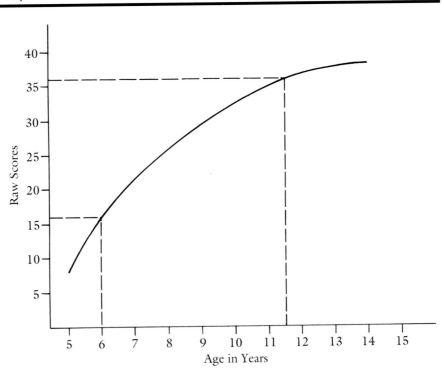

answered thirty-eight of the forty-five problems attempted), while the older child has attempted more problems with less accuracy (for instance, successfully answered thirty-eight of the seventy-eight problems attempted).

The second problem inherent in the use of developmental scores is interpolation and extrapolation. Average age and grade scores are estimated for groups of children who are never tested. Consequently, a child can earn a grade equivalent of 3.2 when only children in the first and middle of third grade have ever been tested; or a child can earn a grade equivalent of 8.0 even though no children above the sixth grade have been tested.

The third problem is that the use of developmental scores promotes typological thinking. The average 12-0 child is a statistical abstraction surrounded by a family with 1.2 other children, 0.8 dogs, and 2.3 automobiles; in other words, the average child does not exist. Average 12-0 *children* more accurately represent a range of performances, typically the middle 50 percent.

The fourth problem is that equivalent scores imply a false standard of performance. One expects a third grader to perform at a third-grade level or a nine-year-old to perform at a 9-year-old level. However, the way equivalent scores are constructed insures that 50 percent of any age or grade group will perform below age or grade level because half of the test takers earn scores below the median.

The fifth problem with developmental scores is that such scales tend to be ordinal, not equal-interval. The line relating the number correct to the various ages is typically curved, with a flattening of the curve at higher ages or grades. Figure 5.1 is a typical developmental curve. Because they are ordinal and not based on equal-interval units, they should not be added or multiplied in any computation.

Developmental Quotients

Before we try to interpret a developmental score, we must know the age of the person being evaluated. Knowing developmental age as well as chronological age (CA) allows us to judge an individual's relative performance. Suppose Horace earns a mental age (MA) of 120 months. If Horace is 8 years (96 months) old, his performance is above average. If he is 35 years old, however, it's below average. The relationship between developmental age and chronological age is often quantified as a developmental quotient. For example, a *ratio IQ* is

$$IQ = \frac{\text{MA (in months)} \times 100}{\text{CA (in months)}}$$

The developmental age is often interpreted as the level of functioning, whereas the quotient is interpreted as the rate of development. In any such scheme, a third variable, chronological age, is always involved. Of the three variables, only chronological age and the developmental quotient are independent of each other (that is, uncorrelated). The developmental age is related to both of the other two variables. In the case of intelligence, the developmental age is far more closely associated with chronological age than it is with the quotient (Kappauf, 1973). Developmental levels do not provide independent information. They only summarize data for age (or grade) and relative standing.

All the problems that apply to developmental levels also apply to developmental quotients. There is one additional problem that is particularly bothersome. The variance of age scores within different chronological age groups is not constant. As a result, the same quotient may mean different things at different ages. For example, a developmental quotient of 120 at age 5 may mean that Billy performs better than 55 percent of five-year-olds. However, a developmental quotient of 120 at age 11 may mean that Billy performs better than 80 percent of eleven-year-olds. A related problem is that different quotients at different ages can mean the same thing. For example, a developmental quotient of 120 at age 5 may mean that Sally performs better than 55 percent of five-year-olds, but a developmental quotient of 110 at age 10 may mean that Sally performs better than 55 percent of ten-year-olds. This problem engenders a great deal of unnecessary confusion.

SCORES OF RELATIVE STANDING

Unlike developmental scores, scores of relative standing use more than the mean or median to interpret a person's test score. Moreover, when the same type of relative-standing score is used, the units of measurement are exactly the same. Thus, we can compare the performances of different people even when they differ in age, and we can compare one person's scores on several different tests. This specificity of meaning is very useful. For example, it is not particularly helpful to know that George is 70 inches tall; Bill is 6 feet, 3 inches tall; Bruce is 1.93 meters tall; and Alan is 177.8 centimeters tall. To compare their heights, it is necessary to transform the heights into comparable units. In feet and inches, the four heights are George, 5 feet, 10 inches; Bill, 6 feet, 3 inches; Bruce, 6 feet, 4 inches; and Alan, 5 feet, 10 inches. Scores of relative standing put raw scores into comparable units.

Percentile Family

Percentile ranks (%iles) can be used when the scale of measurement is ordinal or equal-interval scales. They are derived scores that indicate the percentage of people or scores that occur *at or below* a given raw score. The percentage correct is not the same as the percentage of people scoring below. Percentiles corresponding to particular scores can be computed by a four-step sequence.

1. Arrange the scores from the highest to the lowest (that is, best to worst).
2. Compute the percentage of cases occurring *below* the score to which you wish to assign a percentile rank.
3. Compute the percentage of cases occurring *at* the score to which you wish to assign a percentile rank.
4. Add the percentage of cases occurring below the score to one-half the percentage of cases occurring at the score to obtain the percentile rank.

In Table 5.1, a numerical example is provided. Mr. Greenberg gave a test to his developmental reading class, which has an enrollment of twenty-five children. The scores are presented in column 1, and the number of children obtaining each score (the *frequency*) is shown in column 2. Column 3 gives the percentage of all twenty-five scores that each score obtained represents. Column 4 contains the percentage of all twenty-five scores that occurred below that particular score. In the last group of columns, the percentile rank is computed. Only one child scored 24; the one score is 1/25, or 4 percent. No one scored lower than 24 so there is 0 percent (0/25) below 24. The child who scored 24 received a percentile rank of 2—that is, 0 plus one-half of 4. The next score obtained is 38, and again only one child received this score. Four percent of the total (1/25) scored at 38, and 4 percent of the total scored below 38. Therefore, the percentile rank corresponding to a score of 38 is 6—that is, 4 + (1/2)(4). Two children earned a score of 40, and two children have scored below 40. Therefore, the percentile rank for a score of 40 is 12—that is, 8 + (1/2)(8). The same procedure is followed for every score a child obtains. The best score in the class, 50, was obtained by two students. The percentile rank corresponding to the highest score in the class is 96.

The interpretation of percentile ranks is based on the percent of *people*. The data from Table 5.1 provide a specific example. All students who score 48 on the test have a percentile rank of 84. These four students have *scored as well as or better than* 84 percent of their classmates on the test. Similarly, an individual who obtains a percentile rank of 21 on an intelligence test has scored as well as or better than 21 percent of the people in the norm sample.

Because the percentile rank is computed using one-half of the percentage of those obtaining a particular score, it is not possible to have percentile ranks of either 0 or 100. Generally, percentile ranks may contain decimals, so it is possible for a score to receive a percentile rank of 99.9 or 0.1. The fiftieth percentile rank is the median.

Deciles are bands of percentiles that are 10 percentile ranks in width; each decile contains 10 percent of the norm group. The first decile contains percentile ranks from .1 to 9.9; the second decile contains percentile ranks from 10 to 19.9; the tenth decile contains percentile ranks from 90 to 99.9.

Quartiles are bands of percentiles that are 25 percentile ranks in width; each quartile contains 25 percent of the norm group. The first quartile contains percentile ranks from .1 to 24.9; the fourth quartile contains the ranks 75 to 99.9.

Standard Scores

A standardized distribution is a set of scores that have been transformed so that the mean and standard deviation of the set take predetermined (standard) values. The most basic standardized distribution is the z distribution. A z distribution has a predetermined mean of zero and a predetermined standard deviation of 1. To transform raw scores (for example, the number correct on a test) to z-scores, the mean of the distribution is subtracted from each raw score; this operation sets the mean to zero. Next, the difference between the raw score and the mean is divided by the standard deviation; this operation sets the standard deviation to 1.

Standard score is the general name for any derived score that has been standardized. Although a distribution of scores can be standardized to produce

TABLE 5.1   Computing Percentile Ranks for a Hypothetical Class of Twenty-five

				Percentile Rank			
Score	Frequency	Percent at the Score	Percent Below the Score	Percent Below the Score	+	½ of Percent at the Score	= Percentile
50	2	8	92	92	+	(½)(8)	= 96
49	0						
48	4	16	76	76	+	(½)(16)	= 84
47	0						
46	5	20	56	56	+	(½)(20)	= 66
45	5	20	36	36	+	(½)(20)	= 46
44	3	12	24	24	+	(½)(12)	= 30
43	2	8	16	16	+	(½)(8)	= 20
42	0	—	—				
41	0	—	—				
40	2	8	8	8	+	(½)(8)	= 12
39	0	—	—				
38	1	4	4	4	+	(½)(4)	= 6
⋮							
24	1	4	0	0	+	(½)(4)	= 2

any predetermined mean and standard deviation, there are five commonly used standard-score distributions.

z-Scores

As just indicated, *z-scores* are standard scores the distribution of which has a mean of zero and a standard deviation of 1. Any raw score can be converted to a *z*-score by using equation 5.1

$$z = \frac{X - \overline{X}}{S} \tag{5.1}$$

A *z*-score equals the raw score less the mean of the distribution, divided by the standard deviation of the distribution. The *z*-scores are interpreted as standard deviation units. Thus, a *z*-score of +1.5 means that the score is 1.5 standard deviations *above* the mean of the group. A *z*-score of −.6 means that the score is .6 standard deviation *below* the mean. A *z*-score of 0 is the mean performance.

Since + and − signs have a tendency to "get lost" and decimals may be awkward in practical situations, *z*-scores often are transformed to other standard scores. The general formula for changing a *z*-score into a different standard score is given by equation 5.2. In the equation, *SS* stands for any standard score, as does the subscript *ss*. Thus, any standard score equals the mean of the distribution of standard scores ($\overline{X}_{ss}$) plus the product of the standard deviation of the distribution of standard scores (S_{ss}) multiplied by the *z*-score.

$$SS = \overline{X}_{ss} + (S_{ss})(z) \tag{5.2}$$

T-Scores

A *T-score* is a standard score with a mean of 50 and a standard deviation of 10. In Table 5.2, five *z*-scores are converted to *T*-scores. A *T*-score of 60 is 10 points above the mean (50). Since the standard deviation is 10, a *T*-score of 60 is one standard deviation above the mean.

TABLE 5.2 Converting *z*-Scores to *T*-Scores

	T-Score = 50 + (10)(z)
$z = +1.0$	$60 = 50 + (10)(+1.0)$
$z = -1.5$	$35 = 50 + (10)(-1.5)$
$z = -2.1$	$29 = 50 + (10)(-2.1)$
$z = +3.6$	$86 = 50 + (10)(+3.6)$
$z = \ \ .0$	$50 = 50 + (10)(\ \ .0)$

Deviation IQs

When the IQ was first introduced, it was defined as the ratio of mental age (MA) to chronological age (CA) multiplied by 100. Soon statisticians found that MA has different variances and standard deviations at different chronological ages. Consequently, the same IQ has different meanings at different ages; the same IQ corresponds to different *z*-scores at different ages. To remedy that situation, MAs are converted to *z*-scores for each age group, and *z*-scores are converted to deviation IQs. *Deviation IQs* are standard scores with a mean of 100 and a standard deviation of 15 or 16 (depending on the test). A *z*-score can be converted to a deviation IQ by equation 5.2. In Table 5.3, five *z*-scores are converted to deviation IQs with standard deviations of 15 (column 2) and 16 (column 3).

Normal-Curve Equivalents

Normal-curve equivalents are standard scores with a mean equal to 50 and a standard deviation equal to 21.06. Although the standard deviation may at first appear a bit strange, this scale divides the normal curve into 100 equal intervals.

Stanines

Stanines are standard-score bands that divide a distribution into nine parts. The first stanine includes all scores that are 1.75 standard deviations or more below the mean, and the ninth stanine includes all scores 1.75 or more standard deviations above the mean. The second through eighth stanines are each .5 standard deviation in width, with the fifth stanine ranging from .25 standard deviation below the mean to .25 standard deviation above the mean.

Except for ease of interpretation, standardizing scores offers all the advantages of converting raw scores to percentiles. However, standardizing scores has two additional advantages. First, when equal-interval data are standardized, the standardized scores remain on an equal-interval scale. Second, standardization of scores allows test users to combine (for example, add or average) test scores precisely. A major difficulty occurs when teachers or psychologists combine the results of several tests. The combined score is

TABLE 5.3   Converting *z*-Scores to Deviation IQs ($\overline{X} = 100$)

z-Score	IQ ($S = 15$)	IQ ($S = 16$)
−2.00	70	68
−1.00	85	84
.00	100	100
+1.00	115	116
+2.00	130	132

known technically as a *composite,* and the elements in a composite (for example, eighteen scores from weekly spelling tests that are averaged to obtain a semester average) do not count the same (that is, they do not carry the same weight) *unless* they have equal variances. Tests that have larger variances contribute more to the composite than tests with smaller variances. When each of the elements have been standardized into the same scores (for example, when each of the weekly spelling tests have been standardized as z-scores), the elements will carry exactly the same weight when they are combined. Moreover, the only way that a teacher can weight tests differentially is standardize all the tests and then multiply, by the weight, the tests to be weighted. For example, if a teacher wished to count the second test as three times the first test, both tests would have to be standardized and the second test scores then multiplied by 3.

CONCLUDING COMMENTS ON DERIVED SCORES

The test author provides the tables to convert raw scores into derived scores. Thus, test users do not have to calculate derived scores. However, test users may wish to convert raw scores to standard scores for which no conversion tables are provided. Because all standard scores are based on z-scores, standard scores have the same relationship to each other regardless of a distribution's shape. Therefore, standard scores can be transformed into other standard scores readily with the formulas provided earlier in this chapter. Standard scores can be converted to percentiles without conversion tables only when the distribution of scores is normal. In normal distributions, the relationship between percentiles and standard scores is known. Figure 5.2 compares various of standard scores and percentiles for normal distributions. In all other instances, conversion tables are required. These conversion tables are test specific so that they can only be provided by a test author. Thus, when the distribution of scores is not normal, conversion tables are necessary to convert percentiles to standard scores (or vice versa). Moreover, conversion tables are always required to convert developmental scores to scores of relative standing even when the distribution of test scores is normal. If the only derived score available on a test is an age equivalent, then there is no way for a test user to convert raw scores to percentiles or standard scores.

The selection of the particular type of score to use and to report depends on the purpose of testing and the sophistication of the consumer. In our opinion, *developmental scores should never be used.* These scores are readily misinterpreted by both lay and professional people. In order to understand the precise meaning of developmental scores, one must generally know both the mean and standard deviation and then *convert* the developmental score to a more meaningful score, a score of relative standing. Various professional organizations (for example, the International Reading Association, the American Psychological Association, the National Council on Measurement in Education, and the Council for Exceptional Children) also hold very negative official opinions about developmental scores and quotients.

Standard scores are convenient for test authors. Their use allows the author to give equal weight to various test components or subtests. Their utility for the consumer is twofold. First, *if* the score distribution is normal, the consumer can readily *convert* standard scores to percentile ranks. Second, because standard scores are equal-interval scores, they are useful in analyzing strengths and weakness of individual students and in research.

We favor the use of percentiles. These unpretentious scores require the fewest assumptions for accurate interpretation. The scale of measurement need only be ordinal, although it is very appropriate to compute percentiles on equal-interval or ratio data. The distribution of scores need not be normal; percentiles can be computed for any shape of distribution. They are readily understood by professionals, parents, and students. Most important, however, is the fact that percentiles tell us nothing more than what any norm-referenced derived score can tell us—namely, an individual's relative standing

FIGURE 5.2   Relationship Among Selected Standard Scores, Percentiles, and *One* Age Score and the Normal Curve

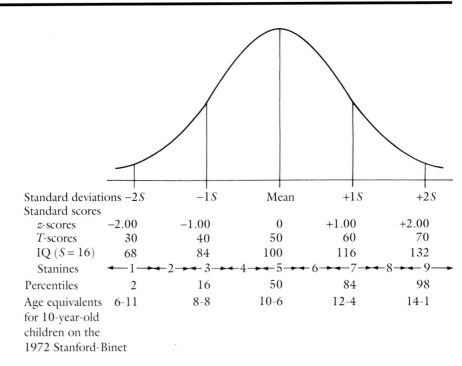

Standard deviations	−2*S*	−1*S*	Mean	+1*S*	+2*S*
Standard scores					
z-scores	−2.00	−1.00	0	+1.00	+2.00
T-scores	30	40	50	60	70
IQ (*S* = 16)	68	84	100	116	132
Stanines	←1→◄2→◄3→	◄4→◄5→◄6→	◄7→◄8→◄9→		
Percentiles	2	16	50	84	98
Age equivalents for 10-year-old children on the 1972 Stanford-Binet	6-11	8-8	10-6	12-4	14-1

in a group. Reporting scores in percentiles may remove some of the aura sur-rounding test scores, but it permits test results to be presented in terms users can understand.

SUMMARY

The number of correct answers or the number of errors a student makes on a test provides the examiner with relatively little information. One method of interpreting such raw scores is to compare them to the raw scores of a group of students of known characteristics called a norm group.

Two types of comparisons can be made—across ages and within ages. *Developmental scores* (that is, age and grade equivalents) compare students' performances across age or grade groups. Within a group, comparisons can be made using several different types of scores that have different characteristics. A *developmental quotient* (an age or grade equivalent divided by chronological age or actual grade placement, respectively) is the least desirable within-age comparison. Of greater value are *standard scores* (for example, z-scores, T-scores, and deviation IQs). Such scores have a predetermined mean and standard deviation that define them. The best derived scores for general use are percentile ranks.

STUDY QUESTIONS

1. Eleanore and Audrey take an intelligence test. Eleanore obtains an MA of 3-5 and Audrey obtains an MA of 12-2. The test had been standardized on fifty boys and girls at each of the following ages: 3-0 to 3-1, 4-0 to 4-1, 5-0 to 5-1, 6-0 to 6-1, and 7-0 to 7-1. The psychologist reports that Eleanore functions like a child aged 3 years and 5 months, while Audrey has the mental age of a 12-year-old child. Identify five problems inherent in these interpretations.
2. Differentiate between a *ratio IQ* (developmental quotient) and a *deviation IQ*. Why is a deviation IQ preferable?
3. Sam earned a percentile rank of 83 on a kindergarten admission test. What is the statistical meaning of his score? To what *decile* does the score correspond? To what *quartile* does the score correspond?
4. Marietta takes a battery of standardized tests. The results are as follows:
   Test A: Mental age = 8-6
   Test B: Reading grade equivalent = 3.1
   Test C: Developmental age = 8-4
   Test D: Developmental quotient = 103
   Test E: Percentile rank = 56

What must the teacher do in order to interpret Marietta's performances on these five scales and compare the performances to each other?

5. Andrew earns a stanine of 1 on an intelligence test. To what *z-scores, percentile ranks,* and *T-scores* does his stanine score correspond?

PROBLEMS

Turn back to Table 4.4, which shows the results of the two tests Ms. Smith gave to her arithmetic class. For test 1, make the following computations.

1. Compute the percentile rank for each student.
2. Compute each student's z-score.
3. Convert Bob's, Sam's, Sean's, and Carole's z-scores to T-scores.
4. Convert Lucy's, Carmen's, John's, and Ludwig's z-scores to deviation IQs with a mean of 100 and a standard deviation of 15.

Answers

1. 98, 94, 90, 86, 82, 78, 70, 70, 70, 50, 50, 50, 50, 50, 50, 50, 30, 30, 30, 22, 18, 14, 10, 6, 2
2. 2.17, 2.00, 1.33, 1.00, .67, .5, .33, .33, .33, 0, 0, 0, 0, 0, 0, 0, −.33, −.33, −.33, −.5, −.67, −1.00, −1.33, −2.00, −2.17
3. 72, 63, 50, 45
4. 130, 105, 100, 70

C·H·A·P·T·E·R 6

NORMS

It is seldom possible to test everyone in a particular population, because the membership of the population is constantly changing. Some children who are in the 6-year-old population today will be 7 years old tomorrow. Grade populations change at least once a year. However, testing an entire population is not only virtually impossible but also unnecessary. The characteristics of a population can be accurately estimated from the characteristics of a representative subset of the population (called a *sample*); inferences based on what one has learned from a sample can be extended to a population at large. Thus, the normative samples used in norm-referenced assessment are intended to allow inferences to be made about a population.

In norm-referenced assessment, norms are important for two reasons. First, the normative sample is often used to obtain the various statistics on which the final selection of test items is based. For example, Wechsler (1974, p. iii) states that "the final selection of test items and scoring procedures was fixed only after all the standardization data had been analyzed and evaluated." Consequently, measures of internal consistency, item-total correlations, and indices of item difficulties (p-values), as well as item selection and item-scoring procedures, are all affected by the adequacy of the standardization sample.

The second reason that norms are important is more obvious. In norm-referenced assessment, an individual's performance is evaluated in terms of other people's performances. All the derived scores that were described in Chapter 5—percentiles, standard scores, and the rest—are based on the performance of the individuals in the normative sample. When we test individuals, we compare their performances to the performances of the individuals in the norm group. Even if a test is otherwise satisfactory, test scores may be misleading if the norms are inadequate. The adequacy of a test's norms depends on three factors: the representativeness of the norm sample, the number of cases in the norm sample, and the relevance of the norms in terms of the purpose of testing.

REPRESENTATIVENESS

In evaluating representativeness, particular attention must be paid to demographic variables because of their relationship—either theoretical or empirical—to what the test is intended to measure. Which demographic variables are significant for a particular test depends on the content of the test and/or the construct being measured. Representativeness hinges on two questions. The first is, Does the norm sample contain the same *kinds* of people as the population that the norms are intended to represent? "Kinds" of people usually refers to relative levels of maturation, levels of skill development, and degrees of acculturation. The second question of representativeness is, Are the various kinds of people present in the same proportion in the sample as they are in the population of reference?

When we compare a child's performance to a norm sample in order to predict future behavior, we assume that the child has had an opportunity to acquire skills, concepts, or experiences comparable to the opportunities of the children in the norm sample. When we compare a child's performance to a norm sample in order to understand better that child's current level of functioning, we need assume only that the norm sample is representative of the population. The distinction between understanding current level of functioning and predicting future behavior is part of the controversy over culture-free (or culture-fair) testing. If a 10-year-old child has had no opportunity to learn to read (and consequently has not acquired the skills), the tester who notes that the child *currently* lacks skill is not being unfair or biased. If the child being tested and the children in the normative sample have not had comparable opportunities to acquire the behaviors sampled in the test, it may be misleading to use the child's test score to predict *future* behavior. When we predict future behavior, we assume that children have learned what they *can* learn. Children who have had no chance to learn have not been able to demonstrate what they *can* learn. Not knowing how well such children *will* learn given the opportunity, we cannot use their test scores to make predictions.

Kinds of People

Several factors are usually considered in the development of norms for psychoeducational tests. Following is a brief discussion of the most commonly considered factors, together with a rationale for the importance of each.

Age

A child's age is an excellent general indicator of several important factors. Physiological maturation is an important variable in motor and perceptual-motor tests, and age is directly related to maturation. It would be foolish to say that a 6-year-old child lacks physical stamina because that child can run for only as long a period of time as 2 percent of all ten-year-olds. Six-year-old children are not as big and strong as 10-year-old children. Consequently, we would not want to compare children of different ages on tests where there are physical, developmental effects.

A child's amount of experience with practically everything is a function of age. Indeed, age is an excellent indicator of the opportunity to acquire skills, information, and concepts. Mental growth (as measured by mental ages) and chronological ages are very highly correlated; Kappauf (1973) has empirically estimated the correlation to be in excess of .90. Again, it would usually be inappropriate to compare a six-year-old's fund of general information with that of a twelve-year-old. The six-year-old simply has not been around as long and therefore has not had the opportunity to acquire as much information.

There is a tendency for test authors to assume that some psychological traits stop developing after 16 or 18 years of age—and many traits do. In such instances, all individuals over a given age are treated as adults. For example, test users may be required to use 16 years in computation of the ratio IQ. The assumption of no growth after 16 may be tenable with supporting data. Yet Wechsler (1981) provides adult norms that clearly indicate age is an important variable in interpreting IQ beyond 16. As shown in Figure 6.1, verbal ability continues to grow until 25 to 34 years of age; after 35 it slowly declines. Scores on the performance scale, however, peak between 20 and 24 years and then rapidly decline. Different abilities may be expected to have different growth curves (see Guilford, 1967, pp. 417–426).

Grade

All achievement tests and some intelligence tests measure the results of systematic academic instruction. Children of different ages are present in most grades. Consequently, grade norms are more appropriate than age norms for such tests when used with children of school age. Grade in school bears a more direct relationship to what is taught in school than does age. Some 7-year-old children may not be enrolled in school; some may be in kindergarten, some in first grade, some in second grade, and some even in third grade. The academic proficiency of seven-year-olds can be expected to be more closely related to what they have been taught than to their age.

Sex

Sex also plays an important role in a child's development. There are pronounced differences in typical patterns of physical development around puberty (Tanner, 1970). Personality differences have also been observed: boys tend to be more aggressive than girls; girls tend to be more dependent and socially passive (Mischel, 1970).

Sex differences have also been reported in intellectual development. For example, Roberts (1971) reported that boys scored higher than girls on the Vocabulary and Block Design subtests of the Wechsler Intelligence Scale for Children. But the magnitude of sex differences on ability, achievement, and aptitude measures is nearly always very small; the male and female distributions overlap a great deal.

Although sex-role expectations seem to be changing, gender still may systematically limit the types of activities in which a child engages. This may result from such influences as modeling, peer pressure, or responsiveness to the attitudes of significant adults. For whatever reasons boys and girls differ systematically on tests, children of both sexes should be represented in the norm sample. Appropriate representation is especially important for behaviors on which there are known sex differences.

FIGURE 6.1   Sums of Scaled Scores on the WAIS for Performance IQs and Verbal IQs of 100, by Ages

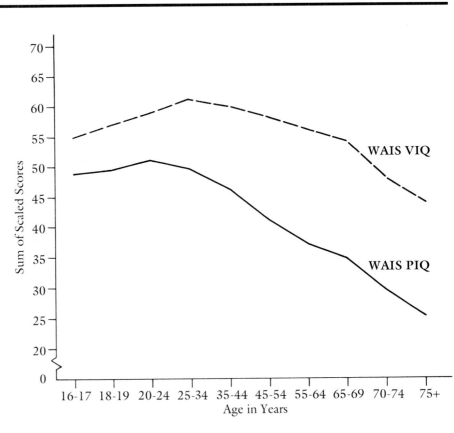

Acculturation of Parents

The level of acculturation of a child's parents or guardians has a direct impact on the child's performance on intellectual and academic tests. One can consider the academic or occupational attainment (*socioeconomic status*) of the parents as an indication of the child's acculturation as well as the level of acculturation in the home. There is a consistent relationship between these indices of acculturation and the performance of the child on various psychoeducational measures. Parental occupation and income have been consistently reported to be related to school achievement (for example, Schaie & Roberts, 1971) and intelligence (for example, Burt, 1959; Roberts, 1971). The causes of these consistent social-class differences have been debated for years, and the debate continues today (see Gottesman, 1968). However, the causes of such differences are beyond the scope of this text. Whether one subscribes to a genetic interpretation, an environmentalist interpretation, or an interactionist interpretation, the fact of social-class differences is undeniable. For this reason, test standardizations should include children of all social classes.

Geographic Factors

Different geographic regions of the United States differ in values and mores, and various psychoeducational tests reflect these regional differences. Children in the Midwest typically score better than children in the South on achievement tests (for example, Schaie & Roberts, 1971). During World War II rates of rejection for military service because of mental deficiency varied according to geographic region (Ginzberg & Bray, 1953); these differences reflected both intellectual and achievement differences. Community size is also related to academic and intellectual development; urban children typically score higher on achievement tests than rural children do (Schaie & Roberts, 1971).

Race and Ethnic Cultural Differences

Race is a particularly sensitive issue, especially since the scientific community has often been insensitive to the issue and has even on occasion been blatantly racist (for example, Down, 1866/1969). With few exceptions, children of minority races score lower than white children on intellectual measures (for example, Roberts, 1971) and academic achievement (for example, Coleman et al., 1966).

Most explanations for racial differences are beyond the scope of this text. Two are not. First, there has been a tendency to systematically *exclude* nonwhite children from standardization samples. For example, until the 1972 edition of the Stanford-Binet Intelligence Test, no blacks were included in the standardization sample. To the extent that children of different races undergo cultural experiences that differ even within social class and geographic region, norm samples that exclude them are biased. Also, to the extent that nonwhite children score lower than white children of equal social standing and from the same geographic region, test-score distributions that exclude nonwhites are unrepresentative of the total population.

The second argument deals with item selection. If nonwhites differ in acculturation and are excluded from the field tests of the test items, item difficulty estimates (p-values) and point biserial (item-total) correlations may be inaccurate. Hence, the test scaling may be in error. We believe that both these arguments have merit. It is important to include children of all racial and ethnic groups both in field tests of items and in the standardization of a test.

Intelligence

A representative sample of individuals, in terms of their level of intellectual functioning, is essential for standardizing an intelligence test—or any other kind of test. Intelligence is related to a number of variables that are considered in psychoeducational assessment. It is certainly related to achievement, since most intelligence tests were actually developed to predict school success. Correlations ranging between .60 and .80 are typical (for example, Hieronymus, Hoover, & Lindquist, 1986). Since language development and facility are often considered an indication of intellectual development, intelligence tests are often verbally oriented. Consequently, one would also expect to find substantial correlations between scores on tests of intelligence and scores on tests of linguistic or psycholinguistic ability. Items thought to reflect perceptual ability appear on intelligence tests, and Thurstone (1944) found various perceptual tasks to be a factor in intelligence. Koppitz (1975) reports substantial correlations between scores on the Bender Visual Motor Gestalt Test and scores on intelligence tests. Thus, intelligence should be considered in the development of norms for perceptual and perceptual-motor tests.

In the development of norms for intelligence tests per se, it is essential to test the full range of intellectual ability. Limiting the sample to children enrolled in and attending school (usually regular classes) restricts the norms. Failure to consider the individuals classified as mentally retarded in standardization procedures introduces systematic bias into test norms. It has been estimated that 3 percent of the school-age population may be mentally retarded (Robinson & Robinson, 1976; Farber, 1968, pp. 46, 58). Dingman and Tarjan (1960) estimated that there is an excess frequency at the lower end of the intelligence distribution, probably as a result of pathological genetic conditions. They estimated that the mean IQ of this group was approximately 32, with a standard deviation approximately the same as that in the intellectually normal population. Exclusion of such a large portion of the schoolage population seriously biases the estimate of the population mean and standard deviation. For example, let us assume that a test is standardized excluding mentally retarded children and that the scores of the children in the normative sample are converted to deviation IQs with a mean of 100 and a standard deviation of 16. Increasing the sample by including 3 percent more subjects whose scores have a mean IQ of 32 and a standard deviation of 16 would have the same effect as including the mentally retarded children who were excluded. The mean would be lowered from 100 to 98.[1] The standard deviation would be increased from 16 to 19.7.[2]

A score that fell two standard deviations below the mean would be 68 without the retarded; it would be 59 if the retarded were included. Representative sampling would substantially reduce the ranks of students labelled mentally retarded because test means and standard deviations would more accurately reflect the performance of the entire population. (However, it would not reduce the number of students having problems in school.)

Age of Norms

An often overlooked consideration in assuring representativeness is when the norms were developed. We live in an age of rapidly expanding knowledge and rapidly expanding communication of knowledge. Children of today know more than did the children of the 1930s or the 1940s. Children of today probably know less than will the children of tomorrow. For a norm sample to be representative, it must be *current*. Moreover, during the late 1960s and 1970s the social fabric of the United States changed substantially. The civil rights and right-to-education movements brought much-needed reform to the U.S. education system. Thus, comparing a 9-year-old student's performance today with the performance of 1960 nine-year-olds appears unwise. The

1. If the number of subjects in the norm group is 1,000 and the mean is 100, the sum of all scores is 100,000. If 30 children (3 percent of 1,000) whose mean is 32 are added to the 1,000 children, the sum of all scores is increased by 960 (30 × 32). The mean of the 1,030 children is 98 (100,960/1,030).

2. The variance is computationally equal to $\Sigma X^2/N - (\Sigma X/N)^2$. If the number of subjects (N) is 1,000 and the mean is 100, the sum of all scores is 100,000; if the standard deviation is 16, the variance is 256. By substituting these figures into the preceding formula, we obtain the sum of the squared scores, which is 10,256,000:

$$256 = \frac{\Sigma X^2}{1,000} - \left(\frac{100,000}{1,000}\right)^2$$

If we increase the sample by 30 children whose scores have a mean of 32 and standard deviation of 16, we increase the sum of the squared scores by 38,400:

$$256 = \frac{\Sigma X^2}{30} - \left(\frac{960}{30}\right)^2$$

The variance of the 1,030 children is 386.76:

$$386.76 = \frac{10,256,000 + 38,400}{1,030} - \left(\frac{100,000 + 960}{1,030}\right)^2$$

The standard deviation (the square root of the variance) is 19.67.

point at which norms become outdated is more judgmental than empirical and will depend in part on the ability or skill being assessed. With these cautions, it seems to us that fifteen years is about the maximum useful life for norm samples. Some states (for example, Texas) are recommending much shorter norm life.

Special Population Characteristics

Some characteristics of the sample and of the population are important only for particular types of tests. For example, test authors often caution test users to make sure the content of achievement tests reflects the content of the test user's classroom curriculum. However, the test author must also make sure that the content is appropriate for the norm sample. Thus, for reading diagnostic tests, which often measure specific skills such as syllabication and sound blending, the author should specify the curriculum followed by the children in the norm sample. If a visual, sight-vocabulary orientation is used by children in the norm sample, the derived scores of children taught by a phonics method may be inflated; the children taught by the phonics method may earn relatively high scores when compared to the less skilled children in the norm group.

Tests used to identify children with particular problems should include such children in their standardization sample. For example, the Illinois Test of Psycholinguistic Abilities is often used to identify children with psycholinguistic dysfunctions that presumably underlie academic difficulties. Yet the norm sample included "only those children demonstrating average intellectual functioning, average school achievement, average characteristics of personal-social adjustment, sensory-motor integrity, and coming from predominantly English-speaking families" (Paraskevopoulos & Kirk, 1969, pp. 51-52). How can a test be used to identify children whose academic difficulties are caused by psycholinguistic dysfunction when such children are *excluded* from the normative sample? A child who earns the same score as any child in the norm sample has earned a score associated with school success.

Proportion of the Kinds of People

Implicit in the foregoing discussion of characteristics of the representative normative sample was the notion that the various kinds of people should be included in the *same proportion* in the sample as in the population. The development of systematic norms requires systematic data collection, which is both time-consuming and expensive. It is incumbent on the author of a test to demonstrate that its norms are in fact representative. Samples that are convenient, such as samples consisting of volunteers, are not necessarily representative; in fact, they are probably unrepresentative. Large numbers of subjects do not guarantee a representative sample. Roosevelt was reelected president of the United States, even though predictions based on a large sample had proclaimed that Alf Landon would be the next president; the sample had been unrepresentative.

Because representative samples require careful selection, test authors or publishers usually develop sampling plans to try to obtain subjects in the correct proportions. Sampling plans usually involve the selection of communities of specific sizes within geographic regions. Cluster sampling and selection of representative communities (or some combination of the two) are two common methods of choosing these communities. In cluster sampling, urban areas and the surrounding suburban and rural communities are selected. Such sampling plans have the advantage of requiring fewer testers and less travel. When a sampling plan calls for the selection of representative communities, "representative" is usually defined by its residents' mean on important demographic characteristics (such as, educational level and income) being approximately the same as the national or regional average. For example, in the 1980 U.S. Census about 53 percent of the population was female; 19 percent had attended college for at least four years, while about 30 percent had not completed high school; and so forth. A representative community would thus be one in which about 53 percent of the population was female, about 19 percent had attended college for four years, and so forth.

However, neither cluster sampling nor selection of representative communities guarantees that the subjects within the norms are, as a group, representative of the population: The sample selected may not be representative of the representative community. Consequently, test authors often tinker with norms to make them representative on important characteristics. One method of adjusting norms is systematically oversample subjects (that is, select many more subjects than are needed) and then drop subjects until a representative sample has been achieved. Another method is to weight subjects within the normative sample differentially. Subjects with underrepresented characteristics may be counted as more than one subject while subjects with overrepresented characteristics may be counted as fractions of persons. In such ways, norms samples can be manipulated to conform with population characteristics.

Test authors should demonstrate that their norms are representative by presenting data that show the correspondence of their sample to the population. Preferably this correspondence should be shown for each age or grade group. Because of the constraints placed on the space in a technical manual, however, one generally sees these data for only the total sample.

SMOOTHING NORMS

After the norms sample has been finalized, norm tables are prepared. Because of minor sampling errors, even well-selected norm groups will show minor fluctuations in distribution shape. Minor smoothing is believed to result in better estimates of derived scores, means, and standard deviations. For example, there might be a few outliers (that is, scores at the extremes of a distribution that are not contiguous to the distribution—scores several points beyond what would be considered the highest or lowest score in a distribution). A test author might drop outliers. Similarly, the progression of group means from age to age may not be consistent, or group variances may differ slightly from age to age for no apparent reason. As a result, test developers will often smooth these values to conform to a theoretical or empirically generated model of performance (for example, using predicted means rather than obtained means).

Smoothing is also done to remove unwanted fluctuations in the shapes of age or grade distributions by adjusting the relationship between standard scores and percentiles. Even when normal test distributions are expected on the basis of theory, the obtained distributions of scores are never completely normal. For example, several models of intelligence posit a normal distribution of scores; in practice, the distribution-test scores are skewed because of an excess of low-scoring individuals. Thus, standard scores do not correspond to the percentile ranks that are expected in a normal distribution. In such cases, a test author may force standard scores into a normal distribution by assigning them to percentile ranks on the basis of the relationship between standard scores and percentiles found in normal distributions. For example, a raw score corresponding to the 84th percentile will be assigned a T-score of 60, regardless of the calculated value. The process, called *area transformation* or *normalizing a distribution*, is discussed in detail in advanced measurement texts (for example, Ghiselli, 1964). When normal distributions are not expected, a test developer may remove minor inconsistencies in distribution shapes from age to age or grade to grade. To smooth out minor inconsistencies, test authors may average the percentile ranks associated with specific standard scores. For example, a T-score of 60 might be associated with percentile ranks of 72, 74, 73, and 73 in 6-, 7-, 8-, and 9-year-old groups. These percentiles could be averaged, and T-scores of 60 in each age group would be assigned a percentile rank of 73.

NUMBER OF SUBJECTS

The number of subjects in a norm sample is important for several reasons. First, the number of subjects should be large enough to guarantee stability. "If the number of cases is small we cannot put much dependence on the norms, since another group consisting of the same number of persons might give quite different results. The larger the number of cases the more stable will be the norms" (Ghiselli, 1964, p. 49). Next, the number of cases should be large enough so that infrequent elements in the population can be represented. Finally, there should be enough subjects that the sizes of interpolations and extrapolations are relatively small. In a normally distributed array of scores, 100 subjects is the minimum number for which a full range of percentiles can be computed and for which standard scores between ±2.3 standard deviations can be computed without extrapolation. Consequently, we believe that 100 should be the minimum number of persons in any norm sample. If the test spans a number of ages or grades, the norm sample should contain at least 100 subjects per age or grade.

RELEVANCE OF THE NORMS

The major question regarding relevance of norms concerns the extent to which people in the norm sample will provide comparisons that are relevant in terms of the purpose for which the test was administered. For some purposes, national norms are the most appropriate. If we are interested in knowing how a particular child is developing intellectually, perceptually, linguistically, or physically, national norms would be the most appropriate.

In other circumstances, norms developed on a particular portion of the population may be meaningful. For example, if we wished to ascertain the degree to which a student had profited from his twelve years of schooling, norms developed for the particular school district he had been served by might be appropriate. Suppose the school district is providing such poor educational services that, as a district, it falls well below the national average. If this is the case, our twelfth grader could earn a percentile rank of 75 based on district norms and a percentile rank of only 35 based on representative national norms. Still, despite the fact that his score looks low in comparison to scores made nationwide, it's clear that our student has made comparatively good use of the inadequate services he has been getting. The same relationship between scores based on national and scores based on local norms might also be obtained if the school district were teaching materials not covered by the achievement test.

Local norms may be more useful in retrospective interpretations of a student's performance than in predictive interpretations. Thus, in the preceding example, if the content of the local achievement test was appropriate in terms of what the schools were actually attempting to teach, we could conclude that the student had profited from instruction but nonetheless would probably be at a disadvantage if he entered college.

In addition, norms based on particular groups may be more relevant than those based on the population as a whole. Some devices are standardized on special populations: the Nebraska Test of Learning Aptitude is standardized on the deaf, the AAMD Adaptive Behavior Scale on institutionalized retardates, and the Blind Learning Aptitude Test on blind children. Aptitude tests are often standardized on individuals in specific trades or professions. The utility of special population norms is similar to the utility of local norms: they are likely to be more useful in retrospective comparisons than in future predictions. Without knowing how the special population corresponds to the general population, inferences may not be appropriate. Suppose a deaf child earns a learning quotient of 115 derived from norms based on deaf children. One knows only that the child scored better than the average deaf child. The basic question that must be addressed is, Does the score based on special population norms lead to correct interpretations? Thus, the test user must know how the change in norms affects prediction.

There are, however, specific instances in which special population norms have been misused. When a person's performance is similar to that of a special population, it does *not* mean the person belongs to or should belong to that population. Because Mary earns the same score as a typical lawyer on a test of legal aptitude does not mean Mary is or should become a lawyer. The argument that she should contains a logical fallacy, an undistributed middle term. (Clearly, if dogs eat meat and university professors eat meat, dogs are not university professors.)

Reasoning of this sort is often inferred when criterion groups are used in test standardization. Such inferences are valid if it can be demonstrated that *only* members of a particular group score in a particular manner. If some people who are not members of the particular group earn the same scores as members of that group, the relationship between group membership and scores should be quantified. For example, let us assume that 90 percent of brain-injured children make unusual—perhaps rotated, distorted, or simplified—reproductions of geometric designs. Let us also assume that 3 percent of the population is brain injured. If *only* non-brain-injured children made normal drawings, we could say with certainty that any child who makes normal drawings is not brain injured. However, since 10 percent of brain-injured children make normal reproductions, we cannot be so sure: .31 percent of the children who make normal drawings *are* brain injured.

In some instances, the "normal" population makes deviant responses. Assume that 20 percent of the normal population and all brain-injured children make unusual drawings. If 3 percent of the population is brain injured, 22.4 percent of the population will perform as brain injured (100% of 3% + 20% of 97% = 22.4%). A deviant performance on the test would mean only a 13 percent (.03/.224) chance that the child is brain injured.

USING NORMS CORRECTLY

The manuals accompanying commercially prepared tests usually contain a table that allows a tester to convert raw scores to various derived scores, such as percentile ranks, without laborious calculations. Occasionally, the tester is even confronted with several tables for converting raw scores. For example, it is not uncommon for the same manual to contain one set of tables for converting raw scores to percentile ranks on the basis of the age of the person tested and another set of tables for converting raw scores to percentile ranks on the basis of the school grade of the person tested. The tester must select tables based either on age or on grade. To select the appropriate table, the tester must determine the population to which the performance of the sample is inferred. This can be learned by examining how the norm group was selected. If the test author sampled by grades in school, then the population of reference is students in a particular grade; consequently, the grade tables should be used for converting raw scores to derived scores. Conversely, if the test author sampled by age, the age tables should be used, since the population of reference is a particular age group.

Tests often lose their power to discriminate near the extremes of the distribution. For example, an intelligence test might be constructed in such a way that even if a person failed every item, it might be impossible for that person to earn an IQ of less than 50. Since complete failure on a test provides little or no information about what a person *can* do, testers often administer tests based on a norm sample of people younger than the test taker. While such a procedure may provide useful *qualitative* information, norm-referenced interpretations are unjustified because the ages of the individuals in the norm group and the age of the person being tested are not the same. Another serious error is committed when the tester uses a person's mental age to obtain derived scores from conversion tables set up on the basis of chronological age. The reasoning behind such practices, we suppose, is that if the person functions as an 8-year-old child intellectually, the use of conversion tables based on the performances of 8-year-old children is appropriate. Such practices are incorrect, since the norms were not established by sampling persons of a particular mental age. When assessing the reading skill of an adolescent or adult who performs below the first percentile, a tester has little need for further or more precise norm-referenced comparisons. The tester already knows the person is not a good reader. If the examiner wants to ascertain which reading skills a person has or lacks, a criterion-referenced (norm-free) device would be more suitable. Sometimes the most appropriate use of norms is no use at all.

To use norms effectively, the tester must be sure that the norm sample is appropriate both for the purpose of testing and for the person being tested.

Concluding Comment: *Caveat Emptor*

If the test author recognizes that the test norms are inadequate, the test user should be explicitly cautioned (AERA et al., 1985). The inadequacies do not, however, disappear on the inclusion of a cautionary note; the test is still inadequate. It is occasionally argued that inadequate norms are better than no norms at all. This argument is analogous to the argument that even a broken clock is correct twice a day. With 86,400 seconds in a day, remarking that a clock is right twice a day is an overly optimistic way of saying that the clock is wrong 99.99 percent of the time. Inadequate norms do not allow meaningful and accurate inferences about the population. If poor norms are used, misinterpretations follow. The difficulty is that the test user seldom knows whether a particular test has an inflated or deflated mean or variance.

A joint committee of the American Educational Research Association, (AERA), the American Psychological Association, and the National Council on Measurement in Education (1985) has prepared a pamphlet, *Standards for Educational and Psychological Testings,* which outlines the standards to which test authors should adhere: "*Norms that are presented should refer to clearly described groups. These groups should be the ones with whom users of the test will ordinarily wish to compare the people who are tested*" (p. 33). The pamphlet states that the test author should report how the sample was selected and whether any bias was present in the sample. The author should also describe the sampling techniques and the resultant sample in sufficient detail for the test user to judge the utility of the norms. "Reports of norming studies should include the year in which normative data were collected, provide descriptive statistics, and describe the sampling design and participation rates in sufficient detail so that the study can be evaluated for appropriateness" (p. 33).

In the marketplace of testing, let the buyer beware.

SUMMARY

The normative sample is important because it is the group of individuals with whom a tested person is compared. Norms should be representative of the population to which comparisons are made. A number of variables are typically considered important: age, grade, sex, acculturation of the persons tested and of their parents, geographic factors, race, intelligence, the date of the norms, and special population characteristics. The norm sample should contain the same types of people in the same proportion as are found in the population of reference. The norm sample should be large enough to be stable and to provide a full range of derived scores. The norms should be relevant in terms of the purposes of testing, and they should be used correctly.

STUDY QUESTIONS

1. Identify two fundamental reasons that norms are important.
2. Willy Smith has only one leg. His teacher concludes that he cannot be tested in reading because no test demonstrates inclusion of one-legged children in its normative group. To what extent is the teacher's conclusion warranted?

3. Test X is standardized on fifty boys and fifty girls at each grade level from kindergarten through sixth grade. The children who made up the norm group were white, middle-class children living in Mount Pleasant, Michigan. Separate norm tables are provided for boys and girls in each grade. Danny, a third-grade black child residing in Oakland, California, is tested with test X, and the norm tables are used to interpret his score.

    a. To how many children is Danny being compared?

    b. To whose performance is Danny's performance being compared?

    c. What assumptions are being made about the relationship between Danny's acculturation and the acculturation of the normative sample?

4. Many tests were initially developed to discriminate between brain-injured and non-brain-injured adults. These same tests are now used to identify brain-injured children. Why is such a use inappropriate?

5. Under what conditions are local norms useful?

6. How might the author of a test demonstrate that its normative sample is representative of the population of children attending school in the United States?

ADDITIONAL READING

American Educational Research Association, American Psychological Association, & National Council on Measurement in Education. (1985). *Standards for educational and psychological testing*. Washington, DC: American Psychological Association, pp. 31–34.

C·H·A·P·T·E·R 7

RELIABILITY

When we test, we are interested in *generalizing* what we see today under one set of conditions to other occasions. For example, if we cannot generalize Billy's reading skills that are observed during testing to the classroom situation, then the test data are of little or no value. To the extent that we can generalize from a particular set of observations (a test, for example), those observations are reliable.

Reliability is a major consideration in evaluating a test or scale. For example, when we give a person an individually administered test, we would like to be able to generalize the results in three different ways. We would like to assume that if another tester were to score the exam, the results would be the same; we would not usually be confident about a student's test score if different examiners evaluated the same response differently. We would also like to assume that the behavior we see today would be seen tomorrow (or next week) if we were to test again; behaviors that are stable are generally of interest in educational settings. Finally, we would like to assume that similar but different test questions would give us similar results; we would like to be able to generalize to other similar test items. Thus, there are three kinds of reliability. Reliability for generalizing to different scorers is called *interrater* or *interscorer reliability*. Reliability for generalizing to different times is called *stability* or *test-retest reliability*. Reliability for generalizing to other test items is called *alternate-form* or *internal-consistency reliability*.

It is useful to describe specifically what we mean by generalization. Suppose that Ms. Amig wanted to assess her kindergartners' recognition of upper- and lower-case letters of the English alphabet. She could assess the *domain*—all fifty-two upper- and lower-case letters—*or* she could sample from the domain. For example, she could ask each of her students to name the following letters: *A, h, j, L, q, r, R, u, V, w*. She would like to assume that another sample of letters (say, *b, E, k, m, s, T, U, v, w, z*) would lead to the same scores by her students. Moreover, she would like to assume that each student would earn the same derived score on any sample from the domain or on all the items in the domain. Thus, she wants to *generalize* from a sample of items to all the other items in the domain from which the sample was drawn. However, Ms. Amig wants more than that. Suppose that she tests her pupils on

Monday morning at 9:30. She would like to assume that the students would earn the same scores if they were tested Tuesday at 1:45 P.M. There is a domain of times as well as a domain of items. Any one occasion is a sample from the time domain—all times. Ms. Amig would like to generalize the results found on one sample of time to the domain. Her pupils' knowledge of the alphabet would not be very useful if they knew the letters only on Monday at 9:30 A.M.

An easy way to think of reliability is to think of any obtained score as consisting of two parts: *true score* and *error*. By definition, error is uncorrelated with true score and is essentially random. Error is best thought of as lack of generalizability that results from the failure to get a representative sample from the domain. For example, a sample of alphabet letters that consisted of A, B, C, D, and E would probably be much easier than other samples of letters. A systematically easier sample would inflate the scores earned by Ms. Amig's students. Similarly, a sample made up of the most difficult letters would probably deflate the scores earned by her students. Thus, error— failure to select a representative sample of items—can raise or lower scores. The average (mean) of error in the long run is equal to zero. In the long run, the samples that raise scores are balanced by samples that lower scores. If Ms. Amig made up and administered all the possible four-letter tests, a student's mean performance would be that student's true score. There would be no error associated with that score. However, there would be a distribution of test scores around that mean; it would be a distribution of obtained test scores centered on the true score.

Another way to think of a true score is that it is the score that a student would earn if the entire domain of items were assessed. On achievement tests dealing with beginning material and with certain types of behavioral observations, it is occasionally possible to assess an entire domain (for example, reading and writing the letters of the alphabet or knowing all the addition, subtraction, multiplication, and division facts). In such cases, the obtained score is a student's true score, and there is no need to estimate the test's item reliability. The potential for assessing an entire domain is very limited, even in the primary grades. It is often impossible to assess an entire achievement domain in more advanced curricula. Moreover, it is never possible to assess the entire domain when a hypothetical construct (such as intelligence or visual perception) is being assessed. Therefore, in these cases item reliability should always be estimated.

As you may recall from the discussion of the assumptions underlying psychological assessment, error of measurement is always present. The important question is, How much error is attached to a particular score? Unfortunately, a direct answer to this question is not readily available. To estimate both the amount of error attached to a test score in general, two statistics are needed: (1) a reliability coefficient for the particular generalization, and (2) the standard error of measurement of the test.

The Reliability Coefficient

The symbol used to denote a reliability coefficient is r with two identical subscripts (for example, r_{xx} or r_{aa}). The *reliability coefficient* is generally defined as the square of the correlation between obtained scores and true scores on a measure (r_{xt}^2). As it turns out, this quantity is identical to the ratio of the variance of true scores to the variance of obtained scores for a distribution. (The variance of obtained scores equals the variance of true scores plus the variance of error.) Accordingly, a reliability coefficient indicates the *proportion* of variability in a set of scores that reflects true differences among individuals. In the special case where two equivalent forms of a test exist, the Pearson product-moment correlation coefficient between scores from the two forms is equal to the reliability coefficient for either form. These relationships are summarized in equation 7.1, where x and x' are parallel measures, and S^2 is, of course, the variance.

$$r_{xx'} = r_{xt}^2 = \frac{S^2 \text{ true scores}}{S^2 \text{ obtained scores}} = r_{xx'} \tag{7.1}$$

If there is relatively little error, the ratio of true-score variance to obtained-score variance approaches a reliability index of 1.00 (*perfect reliability*); if there is a relatively large amount of error, the ratio of true-score variance to obtained-score variance approaches .00 (*total unreliability*).[1] Thus, a test with a reliability coefficient of .90 has relatively less error of measurement and is more reliable than a test with a reliability coefficient of .50.

There are different methods of estimating a reliability coefficient that depend on what generalization one wishes to make. Test authors should always report the extent to which one can generalize to different times and the degree to which one can generalize to different samples of questions or items. If a test is difficult to score, the test author should also report the extent to which one can generalize to different scorers.

Generalizing to Different Times

Test-retest reliability is an index of *stability*. Educators are interested in many human traits and characteristics that, theoretically, change very little over time. For example, children diagnosed as colorblind at age 5 are expected to be diagnosed as colorblind at any time in their lives. Colorblindness is an inherited trait that cannot be corrected. Consequently, the trait should be

---

1. Although it is mathematically possible to obtain a negative reliability estimate, such an obtained coefficient is theoretically meaningless.

perfectly stable. When a test identifies a child as colorblind on one occasion and not colorblind on a later occasion, the test is unreliable.

Other traits are less stable than color vision over a long period of time; they are developmental. A person's height will increase from birth through adulthood. The increase is relatively slow and predictable. Consequently, measurement with a reliable ruler should indicate little change in height over a one-month period. Radical changes in height (especially decreases) over short periods of time would cause us to question the reliability of the measurement device. Most educational and psychological characteristics are conceptualized much as height is. For example, we expect reading achievement to increase with length of schooling but to be relatively stable over short periods of time, such as two weeks. Devices used to assess traits and characteristics must produce sufficiently consistent and stable results if those results are to have practical meaning for making educational decisions.

The procedure for obtaining a stability coefficient is fairly simple. A large number of students are tested. A short time later (preferably two weeks, but the time interval can vary from one day to several months) they are retested with the same device. The students' scores from the two administrations are then correlated. The obtained correlation coefficient is the *stability coefficient*.

Estimates of the amount of error derived from stability coefficients tend to be inflated. Any change in the students' true scores attributable to maturation or learning is added to the error variance unless every student in the sample changes in the same way. Thus, if there is a "maturational spurt" between the two test administrations for only a few students, the change in the true score is incorporated into the error term. Similarly, if some of the students cannot answer some of the questions on the first administration of the test but learn the answers by the second administration, the learning (change in true score) is interpreted as error. The experience of taking the test once may also make answering the same questions the second time easier; the first test may sensitize the student to the second administration of the test. Generally, the closer together in time the test and retest are, the higher the reliability is, since within a shorter time span there is less chance of true scores changing.

Generalizing to Different Item Samples

There are two main approaches for estimating the extent to which we can generalize to different samples of items. The first approach requires that test authors develop two (or more) similar tests, called *alternate forms;* the second approach does not.

Alternate forms of a test are defined as two tests that measure the same trait or skill to the same extent and are standardized on the same population. Alternate forms offer essentially equivalent tests; sometimes, in fact, they're called *equivalent forms.* Let's look at a nonpsychometric example. At a local variety store counter, where several 12-inch rulers are sold, any ruler is thought to be the equivalent (or alternate form) of any other ruler. If one purchased a red ruler and a green ruler and measured several objects with both, one would expect a high correlation between the green measurements and the red measurements. This example is analogous to alternate-form reliability. There is one important difference, however. Alternate forms of tests do not contain the same items. Still, while the items are different, the means and variances for the two tests are assumed to be (or should be) the same. In the absence of error of measurement, any subject would be expected to earn the same score on both forms.

To estimate the reliability coefficient by two alternate forms (A and B), a large sample of students is tested with both forms. Half the subjects receive form A, then form B; the other half receive form B, then form A. Scores from the two forms are correlated. The correlation coefficient is a reliability coefficient.

Estimates of reliability based on alternate forms are subject to one of the same constraints as stability coefficients: the more time between the administration of the two (or more) forms, the greater the likelihood of change in true scores. Unlike stability coefficients, alternate-form reliability estimates are not subject to a sensitization effect since the subjects are not tested with the same items twice.

The second approach does not require that the authors develop more than one form of the test. This method of estimating a test's reliability, called *internal consistency,* is a little different.

Suppose we wanted to use this second method to estimate the reliability of a ten-item test. After the test was constructed, we would administer it to a sample of students (for example, twenty students). The results of this hypothetical test are presented in Table 7.1. If the ten individual test items all measure the same trait or characteristic, we can divide the test into two 5-item tests, each measuring that same trait or characteristic. Thus, *after* the test is administered, we can create two alternate forms of the test, each containing one-half of the total number of test items, or five items. We can then correlate the two sets of scores and obtain an estimate of the reliability of each of the two halves in the same way we would estimate the reliability of two alternate forms of a test. This procedure for estimating a test's reliability is called a *split-half reliability estimate.*

It should be apparent that there are many ways to divide a test into two equal-length tests. The ten-item test in Table 7.1 can be divided into over 100 different pairs of five-item tests. If the ten items in our full test are arranged in order of increasing difficulty, both halves should contain items from the beginning of the test (that is, easier items) and items from the end of the test (harder items). There are many ways of dividing such a test (for example, 1, 4, 5, 8, 9, and 2, 3, 6, 7, 10). The most common way to divide a

TABLE 7.1   Hypothetical Performance of Twenty Children on a Ten-Item Test

	Items										Totals		
Child	1	2	3	4	5	6	7	8	9	10	Total Test	Evens Correct	Odds Correct
1	+	+	+	−	+	−	−	−	+	−	5	1	4
2	+	+	+	+	−	+	+	+	−	+	8	5	3
3	+	+	−	+	+	+	+	−	+	+	8	4	4
4	+	+	+	+	+	+	+	+	−	+	9	5	4
5	+	+	+	+	+	+	+	+	+	−	9	4	5
6	+	+	−	+	−	+	+	+	+	+	8	5	3
7	+	+	+	+	+	−	+	−	+	+	8	3	5
8	+	+	+	−	+	+	+	+	+	+	9	4	5
9	+	+	+	+	+	+	−	+	+	+	9	5	4
10	+	+	+	+	+	−	+	+	+	+	9	4	5
11	+	+	+	+	+	−	+	−	−	−	6	2	4
12	+	+	−	+	+	+	+	+	+	+	9	5	4
13	+	+	+	−	−	+	−	+	−	−	5	3	2
14	+	+	+	+	+	+	+	−	+	+	9	4	5
15	+	+	−	+	+	−	−	−	−	−	4	2	2
16	+	+	+	+	+	+	+	+	+	+	10	5	5
17	+	−	+	−	−	−	−	−	−	−	2	0	2
18	+	−	+	+	+	+	+	+	+	+	9	4	5
19	+	+	+	+	−	+	+	+	+	+	9	5	4
20	+	−	−	−	−	+	−	+	−	−	3	2	1

test is by odd–numbered and even–numbered items (see the columns labeled "Evens Correct" and "Odds Correct" in Table 7.1).

While odd-even divisions and subsequent correlation of the two halves of a test are a common method for estimating a test's internal-consistency reliability, it does not necessarily offer the best method. A more generalizable method of estimating internal consistency has been developed by Cronbach (1951) and is called *coefficient alpha*. Coefficient alpha is the average split-half correlation based on all possible divisions of a test into two parts. In practice there is no need to compute all possible correlation coefficients; coefficient alpha can be computed from the variances of individual test items and the variance of the total test score as shown in equation 7.2 where k is the number of items in the test.

$$r_{aa} = \frac{k}{k-1}\left(1 - \frac{\sum S^2_{items}}{S^2_{test}}\right) \tag{7.2}$$

Coefficient alpha can be used when test items are scored pass-fail or when more than one point of credit is awarded for a correct response. An earlier, more restricted method of estimating a test's reliability, based on the average correlation between all possible split halves, was developed by Kuder and Richardson. This procedure is called *KR-20* and *is* coefficient alpha for dichotomously scored test items (that is, items that can be scored only right or wrong). Equation 7.2 can be used with dichotomous data; however, in this case the resulting estimate of reliability is usually called a KR-20 estimate rather than coefficient alpha.[2]

There are two major considerations in the use of internal-consistency estimates. First, this method should not be used for timed tests or tests that are not completed by all those being tested. Second, it provides no estimate of stability over time.

Generalizing to Different Scorers

There are two very different approaches to estimating the extent to which we can generalize to different scorers. The first way is similar to the ways of estimating generalizability that we have just discussed. Two testers score a set of tests independently. Scores obtained by each tester for the set are then correlated. The resulting correlation coefficient is a reliability coefficient for scorers. For example, suppose that a psychologist (Ms. Hawthorne) was interested in the distortion of body image in emotionally disturbed schoolchildren. Further suppose she decided to assess distortion by evaluating the human-figure drawings of such children. Even with explicit criteria for what constitutes distorted image, scoring of human-figure drawings is difficult. Would another, equally trained, tester—Mr. Torrance—arrive at the same conclusions as Ms. Hawthorne? Can Ms. Hawthorne's judgments be generalized to other testers and scorers? To quantify the extent to which this type of generalization is possible, the two testers could evaluate the human-figure drawings made by a class of emotionally disturbed pupils. As shown in Table 7.2, there would be two ratings of distortion of body image for each drawing, and these two scores could be correlated. The resulting correlation coefficient (phi = .41) would be an estimate of interscorer reliability or agreement.

The second approach to estimating generalizability to different scorers is prevalent in behavioral assessment. Instead of correlating the two scorers' ratings, percentage of agreement between raters is computed. Four indexes of percent agreement are used. *Simple agreement* is calculated by dividing the smaller number of occurrences by the larger number of occurrences and multiplying the quotient by 100. In this example, Ms. Hawthorne observed eight distorted drawings and Mr. Torrance observed ten distorted drawings. Their simple agreement is 80 percent; that is, $(8/10)(100)$. This index may be quite misleading, however, because agreement for each observation is not considered. Thus, it is possible (although not very likely) for two scorers to observe the same number of distorted drawings but completely disagree with each

---

2. Sometimes a test author will estimate KR-20 with a formula called KR-21. However, this is usually not a desirable shortcut.

TABLE 7.2   Judgment of Distorted Body Image in a Class of Emotionally Disturbed Children

Child Number	Ms. Hawthorne	Mr. Torrance
1	normal	normal
2	distorted	distorted
3	distorted	normal
4	normal	normal
5	normal	normal
6	distorted	distorted
7	distorted	distorted
8	distorted	normal
9	normal	normal
10	normal	distorted
11	distorted	distorted
12	normal	normal
13	normal	normal
14	normal	normal
15	distorted	distorted
16	normal	distorted
17	normal	normal
18	distorted	distorted
19	normal	distorted
20	normal	distorted

other on which drawings are distorted. Therefore, the use of simple agreement should be restricted to those circumstances where it is the only index that can be computed (for example, in assessing the latency of a response or the frequency of behavior under continuous observation). A more precise way of computing percentage of agreement is to consider agreement for each data point. The computation of *point-to-point agreement* takes this relationship into consideration (see equation 7.3). The data from Table 7.2 are summarized in Table 7.3. The point-to-point agreement is computed by adding the frequency of agreement for the occurrence (in this example, of distorted drawings, $n = 6$) and frequency of agreement for nonoccurrence (in this example, normal drawings, $n = 8$), dividing this sum by the total number of agreements and disagreements, and multiplying the quotient by 100. Point-to-point agreement for the data in Table 7.3 is .70 [that is, $(14/20)$ (100)]. When the occurrences and nonoccurrences of a behavior differ substantially, point-to-point agreement overestimates the accuracy of the set of observations. In such cases, a more precise way of computing the percentage of agreement is to compute the *percentage of agreement for the occurrence of the target behavior* (see equation 7.4). In this example, since Ms. Hawthorne is interested in the occurrences of distorted body image, it might make better sense to look only at how well the two raters agree on the occurrence. The eight nonoccurrences where both Ms. Hawthorne and Mr. Torrance agree are

TABLE 7.3   Summary of Agreements and Disagreements from Table 7.2

		Ms. Hawthorne	
		Distorted	Normal
Mr. Torrance	Normal	2	8
	Distorted	6	4

not of interest and are ignored. Using the data in Table 7.3, the percentage of agreement for occurrence is 50 percent; that is, $(100) * (6)/(20 - 8)$.

% point-to-point agreement =

$$\frac{(100) \, (\text{number of agreements on occurrence and nonoccurrence})}{\text{number of observations}} \qquad (7.3)$$

% agreement occurrence =

$$\frac{(100) \, (\text{number of agreements on occurrence})}{\text{number of observations} - \text{number of agreements on nonoccurrence}} \qquad (7.4)$$

Both point-to-point agreement and agreement of occurrence indexes can be affected systematically by chance agreement. Thus, both indexes tend to overestimate agreement. Cohen (1960) developed a coefficient of agreement, called *kappa*, that adjusts the proportion of agreement by removing the proportion of agreement that one would find by chance. Kappa values range from −1.00 (total disagreement) to +1.00 (total agreement); a value of zero indicates chance agreement. Thus, a positive index of agreement indicates agreement above what one would expect to find by chance. The computation of kappa is more complicated than other agreement indexes (see equation 7.5, where P equals proportion).

$$\text{Kappa} = \frac{P_{\text{occurrence}} - P_{\text{expected}}}{1 - P_{\text{expected}}} \qquad (7.5)$$

Because kappa is more readily calculated using proportions rather than frequencies, the frequencies displayed in Table 7.3 are displayed in Table 7.4 as proportions (that is, the frequency divided by the number of observations); the marginal frequencies (that is, Ms. Hawthorne's and Mr. Torrance's proportions of normal and distorted drawings) have been added in parentheses.

The expected proportion of occurrence (that is, distorted) equals the product of the proportions of occurrence for each observer (in this example, .50 and .40); the expected proportion of nonoccurrence (that is, normal) equals the product of the proportions of nonoccurrence for each observer (in this example, .50 and .60). The expected proportion of agreement equals the sum of the expected proportion of agreement for occurrence and the expected proportion of agreement for nonoccurrence; in this example, .50 = .20 (that is, .50 * .40) + .30 (that is, .50 * .60). Substituting these values into equation

TABLE 7.4 Proportions for the Agreement-Disagreement Data from Table 7.3

		Ms. Hawthorne	
		Distorted	Normal
Mr. Torrance	Normal	.10	.40 (.50)
	Distorted	.30	.20 (.50)
		(.40)	(.60)

7.5, Kappa equals .40; that is, $(.40 + .30 - .20 - .30) / (1 - .20 - .30)$. Thus, the ratings of drawings by Ms. Hawthorne and Mr. Torrance demonstrate some agreement beyond what one would expect by chance; however, we should not have great confidence in their scoring.

Factors Affecting Reliability

Several factors that affect a test's reliability can inflate or deflate reliability estimates.

Test Length

As a general rule, the more items in a test, the more reliable the test. Thus, long tests tend to be more reliable than short tests. This fact is especially important in an internal-consistency estimate of reliability, because in this kind of estimate the number of test items is reduced by 50 percent. Internal-consistency estimates of reliability actually estimate the reliability of half the test. Therefore, such estimates are usually corrected by a formula developed by Spearman and Brown. As shown in equation 7.6 the reliability of the total test is equal to twice the reliability as estimated by internal consistency divided by the sum of 1 plus the reliability estimate.

$$r_{xx} = \frac{2r_{(1/2)(1/2)}}{1 + r_{(1/2)(1/2)}} \tag{7.6}$$

For example, if coefficient alpha were computed on a test and found to be .80, the corrected estimated reliability would be .89:

$$.89 = \frac{(2)(.80)}{1 + .80} = \frac{1.60}{1.80}$$

A related issue is the number of effective items for each test taker. Tests are generally more reliable in the middle ranges of scores (for example, $\pm 1.5S$). For a test to be effective at the extremes of a distribution, there must be a sufficient number of difficult items for very superior pupils as well as a sufficient number of easy items for deficient pupils. Often there are not enough very easy and very hard items on a test. Therefore, extremely high or extremely low scores tend to be less reliable than scores in the middle of a distribution.

Test-Retest Interval

A person's true abilities can and do change between two administrations of a test. The greater the amount of time between the two administrations, the more likely the possibility that true scores will change. Thus, when employing stability or alternate-form estimates of reliability, one must pay close attention to the interval between tests. Generally, the shorter the interval, the higher the estimated reliability.

Constriction of Range

Constriction of range refers to the range of ability of the people whose performances are used to estimate a test's reliability. When the range of ability of these people is less than the range of ability in population, a test's reliability will be underestimated. The more constricted is the range of ability, the more biased (underestimated) will be the reliability coefficient.

As Figure 7.1 shows, alternative forms of a test produce a strong positive correlation when the entire range of the test is used. However, within any restricted range of the test, as illustrated by the dark rectangular outline, the correlation may be very low. (Although it is possible to correct a correlation coefficient for restriction in range, it is generally unwise to do so.)

FIGURE 7.1   Constricting the Range of Test Scores Reduces the Estimate of a Test's Reliability

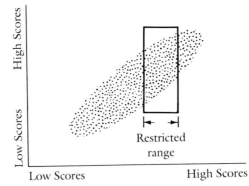

SOURCE: From *Psychological Testing* (p. 115) by A. Anastasi, 1954 (New York: Macmillan). Copyright 1954 by The Macmillan Company. Copyright renewed 1982 by Anne Anastasi. Adapted by permission of the publisher.

A related problem is that *extension* of range seriously *overestimates* a test's reliability. Figure 7.2 contains alternate-form correlations of first, third, and fifth grades. The scatterplot for each grade, considered separately, indicates poor reliability. However, spelling-test scores increase as a function of schooling; students in higher grades earn higher scores. When test authors combine the scores for several grades (or from several ages), poor correlations may be combined to produce a spuriously high correlation.

Guessing

Guessing is responding randomly to items. Even if a guess results in a correct response, it introduces error into a test score and into our interpretation of that score.

Variation Within the Testing Situation

The amount of error that variation in the testing situation introduces into the results of testing can vary considerably. Children can misread or misunderstand the directions for a test, get a headache halfway through testing, lose their place on the answer sheet, break the point on their pencil, or choose to watch a squirrel eat nuts on the windowsill of the classroom rather than taking the test. All such situational variations introduce an indeterminate amount of error in testing and, in doing so, lower reliability.

FIGURE 7.2   Extending the Range of Test Scores May Spuriously Increase the Estimate of a Test's Reliability

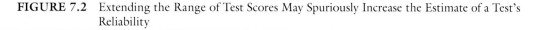

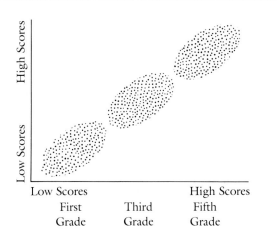

What Method Should Be Used?

The first consideration is the type of generalization one wishes to make. One must select the method that goes with the generalization. For example, if one were interested in generalizing about the stability of a score or observation, the appropriate method would be test-retest correlations. It would be inappropriate to use interscorer agreement as an estimate of the extent to which one can generalize to different times. Additional considerations in selecting the method to be used include the following:

1. When estimating stability, the convention is to retest after two weeks. There is nothing special about two weeks. (If all test authors used the same interval, it would be easier to compare relative stability of tests.)
2. When estimating the extent to which we can generalize to similar test items, we subscribe to Nunnally's (1967, p. 217) hierarchy for estimating reliability. The first choice is to use alternate-form reliability with a two-week interval. (Again, there is nothing special about two weeks; it is just a convention.) If alternate forms are not available, divide the test into equivalent halves and administer the halves with a two-week interval, correcting the correlation by the Spearman-Brown formula given in equation 7.6. When alternate forms are not available and subjects cannot be tested more than once, use coefficient alpha.
3. When estimating the extent to which we can generalize among different scorers, we prefer computing correlation coefficients to percentages of agreement. Correlation coefficients bear a direct relationship to other indicators of reliability and other uses of reliability coefficients; percentages of agreement do not. We also realize that current practice is to report percentages of agreement and not to bother with the other uses of the reliability coefficient. If one uses percent agreement to estimate interscorer reliability, Kappa should be used when possible.

Standard Error of Measurement

The standard error of measurement (SEM) is another index of test error. The SEM allows one to *estimate* the amount of each type of error associated with true scores. One can compute standard errors of measurement for scorers, times, and item samples. However, SEMs are usually computed only on stability and item samples.

Earlier we discussed the generalization of performance on one sample of items to the domain. This provides a convenient example for the interpretation of the standard error of measurement. Consider the alphabet-recognition task again. There are so many samples of ten-letter tests that could be developed. If we constructed one hundred of these tests and tested one kindergartner, we would probably find that the distribution of scores for that kinder-gartner was approximately normal. The mean of that distribution would be the student's true score. The distribution around the true score would be the result of imperfect samples of letters; some letter samples would overestimate the pupil's ability, and others would underestimate it. Thus, the distribution would be the result of error. The standard deviation of that distribution is the standard deviation of errors attributable to sampling and is called the *standard error of measurement (SEM)*.

When students are assessed with norm-referenced tests, they are typically tested only once. Therefore, we cannot generate a distribution similar to the one shown in Figure 7.3. Consequently, we do not know the test taker's true score or the variance of the measurement error that forms the distribution around that person's true score. By using what we know about the test's standard deviation and its reliability for items, we can *estimate* what that error distribution would be. However, when estimating the error distribution for one student, test users should understand two things. First, the standard error of measurement is an average; some standard errors will be greater than that average and some will be less. Second, there is a tendency for the distributions of error around true scores close to the mean to be smaller than the distributions of error around true scores that are farther from the mean. For example, there is generally less measurement error associated with an IQ of 105 than with an IQ of 135.

Equation 7.7 is the general formula for finding the standard error of measurement. The standard error of measurement (SEM) equals the standard deviation of the obtained scores (S) multiplied by the square root of 1 minus the

FIGURE 7.3   The Standard Error of Measurement Is the Standard Deviation of the Error Distribution Around a True Score for One Subject

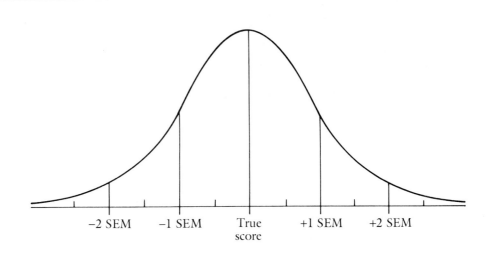

−2 SEM   −1 SEM   True   +1 SEM   +2 SEM
score

TABLE 7.5 Relationship Between Reliability Coefficient and SEM (Part A) and Relationship Between Standard Deviation and SEM (Part B)

Part A			Part B		
S	r_{xx}	SEM	S	r_{xx}	SEM
10	.96	2	5	.91	1.5
10	.84	4	10	.91	3.0
10	.75	5	15	.91	4.5
10	.64	6	20	.91	6.0
10	.36	8	25	.91	7.5

reliability coefficient ($\sqrt{1-r_{xx}}$). The type of unit (IQ, raw score, and the like) in which the standard deviation is expressed is the unit in which the SEM is expressed. Thus, if the test scores have been converted to *T*-scores, the standard deviation is in *T*-score units and is 10; the SEM is also in *T*-score units. Similarly, if the reliability coefficient is based on stability, then the SEM is for times of testing. If the reliability coefficient is based on different scorers, then the SEM is for testers/observers.

$$SEM = S\sqrt{1-r_{xx}} \tag{7.7}$$

From equation 7.7 it is apparent that as the standard deviation increases, the SEM increases; and as the reliability coefficient decreases, the SEM increases. In Part A of Table 7.5 the same standard deviation (10) is used with different reliability coefficients. As reliability coefficients decrease, SEMs increase. When the reliability coefficient is .96, the SEM is 2; when the reliability is .64, the SEM is 6. In Part B of Table 7.5, different standard deviations are used with the same reliability coefficient (r_{xx} = .91). As the standard deviation increases, the SEM increases.

Because of the presence of measurement error, there is always some uncertainty about an individual's true score. The standard error of measurement provides information about the certainty or confidence with which a test score can be interpreted. When the SEM is relatively large, the uncertainty is large; we cannot be very sure of the individual's score. When the SEM is relatively small, the uncertainty is small; we can be more certain of the score.

ESTIMATED TRUE SCORES

Unfortunately, we never know a subject's true score. Moreover, the obtained score on a test is not the best estimate of the true score. As mentioned in the previous discussion, true scores and errors are uncorrelated. However, obtained scores and errors *are* correlated. Scores above the test mean have more "lucky" error (error that raises the obtained score above the true score), while scores below the mean have more "unlucky" error (error that lowers the obtained score below the true score). An easy way to understand this effect is to think of a test on which a student guesses on half the test items. If all the guesses are correct, the student has been very lucky and earns a high grade. However, if all guesses are incorrect, the student has been unlucky and earns a low grade. Thus, obtained scores above or below the mean are often more discrepant than true scores. As can be seen from Figure 7.4, the less reliable the test, the greater the discrepancy between obtained scores and true scores. Nunnally (1967, p. 220) has provided an equation (equation 7.8) for determining the estimated true score (X'). The estimated true score equals the test mean plus the product of the reliability coefficient and the difference between the obtained score and the group mean.

$$X' = \overline{X} + (r_{xx})(x - \overline{x}) \tag{7.8}$$

The particular mean that one uses is the subject of some controversy. We believe the preferred mean is the mean of the demographic group that best represents the particular child. Thus, if the child is Asian and resides in a lower-class urban area, the most appropriate mean would be the mean of same-age Asian children from lower socioeconomic backgrounds who live in urban areas. In the absence of means for particular children of particular backgrounds, one is forced to use the overall mean for the child's age. As has been the case throughout this chapter, the choice of reliability coefficient depends on the type of generalization one wishes to make.

The discrepancy between obtained scores and estimated true scores is a function of both the reliability of the obtained score and the difference between the obtained score and the mean. In Table 7.6, a general case is illustrated where the mean in each example is 100; the obtained scores are 90, 75, and 50. The reliability coefficients are .90, .70, and .50. When the obtained score is 90 and the estimated reliability is .90, the estimated true score is 91 [91 = 100 + (.90)(90 − 100)]. However, when the obtained score is 50 and the reliability coefficient is .90, the estimated true score is 55 [100 + (.90)(50 − 100)]. Even when the reliability coefficient is constant, the farther an obtained score is from the mean, the greater will be the discrepancy between the obtained score and the estimated true score.

When the obtained score is 75 and the reliability coefficient is .90, the estimated true score is 77.5 [100 + (.90)(75 − 100)]. However, when the reliability coefficient drops to .50 and the obtained score doesn't change, the estimated true score rises to 87 [100 + (.50)(75 − 100)].

When the obtained score is below the test mean and the reliability coefficient is less than 1.00, the estimated true score is *always* higher than the obtained score. Conversely, when the obtained score is above the test mean and the reliability coefficient is less than 1.00, the estimated true score is *always* less than the obtained score. Note that the equation does not give the *true score*, only the *estimated true score*.

CONFIDENCE INTERVALS

Although we can never know a person's true score, we can *estimate* the likelihood that a person's true score might be found within a specified range of scores. This range is called a *confidence interval*. A 50 percent confidence interval is a range of values within which the true score will be found about 50 percent of the time. Of course, about 50 percent of the time the true score

FIGURE 7.4   Relationship Between True-Score Distribution and Obtained-Score Distribution for Reliable and Unreliable Tests

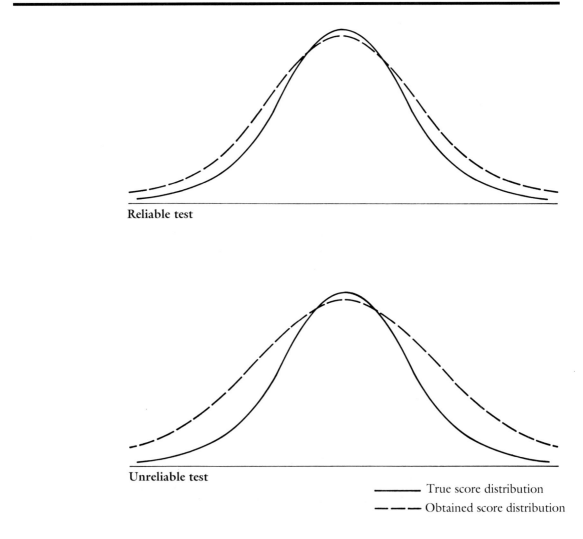

Reliable test

Unreliable test

——— True score distribution

– – – Obtained score distribution

TABLE 7.6   Estimated True Scores for Different Obtained Scores on Tests with Different Reliability Coefficients

Test Mean ($\overline{X}$)	Reliability Coefficient (r_{xx})	Obtained Score (X)	Estimated True Score (X')	Difference Between Obtained Score and Estimated True Score
100	.90	90	91.0	1.0
100	.90	75	77.5	2.5
100	.90	50	55.0	5.0
100	.70	90	93.0	3.0
100	.70	75	82.5	7.5
100	.70	50	65.0	15.0
100	.50	90	95.0	5.0
100	.50	75	87.5	12.5
100	.50	50	75.0	25.0

will be outside the interval. A larger range—a greater confidence interval—could make us feel more certain that we have included the true score within the range. For example, 90 percent, 95 percent, and 99 percent confidence intervals can be constructed; with confidence intervals as certain as these, chances of the true score falling outside of the confidence interval are about 10 percent, 5 percent, and 1 percent, respectively.

There is some disagreement over how to construct confidence intervals (see Schulte & Borich, 1988) or even whether or not to construct confidence intervals (see Sabers, Feldt, & Reschly, 1988). In the following sections, we use the statistics recommended by Nunnally (1978): estimated true score and standard error of measurement. Others (for example, Schulte & Borich, 1988) prefer to use the estimated true score and the standard error of estimation[3] (which is the average standard deviation of true scores around an obtained score) rather than the standard error of measurement. When test reliability is high, the difference in the two procedures is negligible.

Establishing Confidence Intervals for True Scores

The characteristics of a normal curve have already been discussed. We can apply the relationship between z-scores and areas under the normal curve to the normal distribution of error around a true score. We can use equation 7.8 to estimate the mean of the distribution (the true score) and equation 7.7 to estimate the standard deviation of the distribution (the standard error of

---

3. The standard error of estimation equals the product of the standard deviation and square root of the product of the reliability coefficient multiplied by 1 minus the reliability coefficient: $S\sqrt{r_{xx}(1-r_{xx})}$.

TABLE 7.7 Commonly Used z-Scores, Extreme Areas, and Area Included Between + and − z-Score Values

z–Score	Extreme Area	Area Between + and −
.67	25.0%	50%
1.00	16.0%	68%
1.64	5.0%	90%
1.96	2.5%	95%
2.33	1.0%	98%
2.57	.5%	99%

measurement). With these two estimates, we can construct a confidence interval for the *true score*. Since 68 percent of all elements in a normal distribution fall within one standard deviation of the mean, there is about a 68 percent chance that the true score is within one SEM of the estimated true score. We can construct an interval with almost any degree of confidence except 100 percent confidence. Table 7.7 contains the extreme area for the z-scores most commonly used in constructing confidence intervals. The general formula for a confidence interval is given in equation 7.9. The lower limit of the confidence interval equals the estimated true score less the product of the z-score associated with that level of confidence and the standard error of measurement. The upper limit of the confidence interval is the estimated true score plus the product of the z-score and the SEM.

Lower limit of c.i. = $X' - (z\text{-score})(\text{SEM})$
Upper limit of c.i. = $X' + (z\text{-score})(\text{SEM})$ (7.9)

To construct a symmetrical confidence interval for a true score, a simple procedure is followed.

1. Select the degree of confidence; for example, 95 percent.
2. Find the z-score associated with that degree of confidence (for example, a 95 percent confidence interval is between z-scores of −1.96 and +1.96).
3. Multiply each z-score associated with the confidence interval (for example, 1.96 for 95 percent confidence) by the SEM.
4. Find the estimated true score.
5. Take the product of the z-score and the SEM, and both add it to and subtract it from the estimated true score.

For example, assume that a person's estimated true score is 75 and that the SEM is 5. Further assume that you wish to be about 68 percent sure of constructing an interval that will contain the true score. About 68 percent of the time, the true score will be contained in the interval of 70 to 80 [75 − (1)(5) to 75 + (1)(5)]; there is about a 16 percent chance that the true score is less than 70 and about a 16 percent chance that the true score is greater than 80.

If you are unwilling to be wrong about 32 percent of the time, you must increase the width of the confidence interval. Thus, with the same true score (75) and SEM (5), if you wish 95 percent confidence, the size of the interval must be increased; it would have to range from 65 to 85 [75 − (1.96)(5) to 75 + (1.96)(5)]. About 95 percent of the time the true score will be contained within that interval; there is about a 2.5 percent chance that the true score is less than 65, and there is about a 2.5 percent chance that it is greater than 85.

DIFFERENCE SCORES

In many applied settings, we are interested in differences between two scores. For example, we might wish to know if a student's reading achievement is commensurate to her intellectual ability, or we might want to know if the achievement score obtained after instruction (that is, a post-test) is greater than the achievement score obtained prior to instruction (that is, a pretest). In many definitions of educational disorders (for example, learning disabilities), a "significant" discrepancy is a defining characteristic of the disorder. In other disorders (for example, mental retardation), significant discrepancies are not expected.

Because significant differences are used so frequently in special and remedial education, it is important for users of test information to understand the meaning of a "significant discrepancy." Salvia and Good (1982) have discussed three different meanings of the term *significant difference*. The first meaning, a *reliable* difference, is the most pertinent to our discussion of reliability, although it is not the most important consideration in general. A difference is considered reliable when it is unlikely to have occurred by chance. Because every norm-referenced test score has some error associated with it, two test scores could appear discrepant by chance or because of the measurement error associated with each test score. However, Salvia and Good point out that the fact that a difference is real does not mean that it is rare. A large proportion of students may show reliable discrepancies. Moreover, even if a difference is reliable and rare, it may not have educational implications. Educators and psychologists are interested in meaningful differences. One can be sure that unreliable differences are not meaningful. (These differences are chance.) Probably because because only reliable differences can be meaningful and too little emphasis has been placed on rarity and meaningfulness of a difference, diagnosticians have relied heavily on a difference's reliability for interpretation.

Difference scores are usually less reliable than the scores on which the differences are based. The reliability of a difference between two scores (A and B) is a function of three things: (1) the reliability of test A, (2) the reliability of test B, and (3) the correlation between tests A and B. In addition, differences in norm groups can produce differences in obtained scores. For example, suppose that June was absolutely average in reading and intellectual ability. Further suppose that she was tested with an intelligence test normed on a sample of students somewhat lower in ability than the general population. June would earn an IQ that was above the mean. Suppose that the test to measure reading was normed on a sample of students whose achievement was somewhat higher than the general population. June would earn a reading score somewhat lower than the mean. If the disparity in norms were sufficiently large, June might appear to have a significant discrepancy between her intellectual ability and her reading achievement. However, that discrepancy would be an artifact of inaccurate norms.

There are several approaches to evaluating the reliability of a difference. The following two methods are particularly useful but rest on different assumptions and combine the data in different ways (that is, use different formulas).

One method uses a regression model and was originally described by Thorndike (1963). Within this model, one score is presumed to cause the second score. For example, intelligence is believed to cause achievement. Therefore, intelligence is identified as an independent (or predictor) variable, and achievement is identified as the dependent (or predicted) variable. When the predicted score (for example, the predicted achievement score) differs from the achievement score that is actually obtained, a deficit exists. The reliability of a predicted difference is given by equation 7.10. The reliability of a predicted difference ($\hat{D}$) is equal to the reliability of the dependent variable (r_{bb}) plus the product of the reliability of the independent variable (r_{aa}) and the square of the correlation between the independent variable and the dependent variable ($r_{aa}\, r^2_{ab}$) less twice the squared correlation of the independent and dependent variable ($-2r_{ab}$). This combination is divided by 1 minus the squared correlation between independent and dependent variables ($1 - r^2_{ab}$). The standard deviation of predicted differences (S), also called the standard error of estimate, is given in equation 7.11. The standard deviation of predicted differences is equal to the standard deviation of the dependent variable (S_b) multiplied by the square root of 1 minus the squared correlation between independent and dependent variables $\left(\sqrt{1 - r^2_{ab}}\right)$.

$$\hat{D} = \frac{r_{bb} + (r_{aa})(r^2_{ab}) - 2r_{ab}}{1 - r^2_{ab}} \tag{7.10}$$

$$S_{\text{dif}} = S_b \sqrt{1 - r^2_{ab}} \tag{7.11}$$

The second method was proposed by Stake and Wardrop (1971). In this method, one variable is not assumed to be the cause of the other; neither variable is identified as the independent variable. However, this method does require that both measures be in the same unit of measurement (for example,

T-scores or IQs). The reliability of a difference in *obtained scores* is given in equation 7.12.

$$r_{\text{dif}} = \frac{\frac{1}{2}(r_{aa} + r_{bb}) - r_{ab}}{1 - r_{ab}} \quad (7.12)$$

The reliability of an obtained difference equals the average reliability of the two tests $[\frac{1}{2}(r_{aa} + r_{bb})]$ less the correlation between the two tests $(- r_{ab})$; this difference is divided by 1 minus the correlation between the two tests $(1 - r_{ab})$. The standard deviation for obtained differences is given in equation 7.13.

$$S_{\text{dif}} = \sqrt{S_a^2 + S_b^2 - 2r_{ab}S_a S_b} \quad (7.13)$$

The standard deviation of an obtained difference is equal to the square root of the sum of the variances of tests A and B $(S_a^2 + S_b^2)$ less twice the product of the correlation of A and B multiplied by the standard deviations of A and B $(- 2r_{ab}S_a S_b)$. The reliability of a difference and the standard deviation are combined in the same manner for a difference score as for a single score. Substituting in equation 7.7, equation 7.14 is generated.

$$\text{SEM}_{\text{dif}} = \sqrt{S_a^2 + S_b^2 - 2r_{ab}S_a S_b} \sqrt{1 - \frac{1/2(r_{aa} + r_{bb}) - r_{ab}}{1 - r_{ab}}} \quad (7.14)$$

The standard error of measurement of a difference describes the distribution of differences between *obtained* scores. To evaluate difference scores, the simplest method is to establish a level of confidence (for example, 95 percent) and find the z-score associated with that level of confidence (1.96). We then divide the obtained difference by the SEM of difference. If the quotient exceeds the z-score associated with the level of confidence selected (1.96), the obtained difference is reliable. When a difference is assumed reliable at a particular level of confidence, we can estimate the true difference in the same manner as we estimate a true score on one test. In general, we assume that the group mean difference is .00. Thus, the formula for estimating the true difference for a particular student simplifies to equation 7.15.

Estimated true difference = (obtained difference)$(r_{xx(\text{dif})})$ \quad (7.15)

DESIRABLE STANDARDS

It is important for test authors to present sufficient information in test manuals for the test user to interpret test results accurately. Test results must be generalizable before they are useful. Whether a test measures what it purports to measure is a question of validity, the topic of the next chapter.

However, for a test to be valid (to measure what its authors claim it measures), it must be reliable. Although not the only condition that must be met, reliability is a necessary condition for validity. No test can measure what it purports to measure unless it's reliable. No score is interpretable unless it's reliable. Therefore, test authors and publishers must present sufficient reliability data to allow the user to interpret test results accurately. Reliability indexes for each type of score (for example, raw scores, grade equivalents, and standard scores) must be reported. These should be reported for each age and grade. Furthermore, these indexes should be presented clearly in tabular form in one place. Test authors should not play hide and seek with reliability data. Test authors who recommend computing difference scores should provide, whenever possible, the reliability of the difference and the SEM of the difference. Once test users have access to reliability data, they must judge the adequacy of the test.

How high must a test's reliability be before it can be used in applied settings? The answer depends on the use to which test data are put. A simple answer is to use the most reliable test available. However, such a response is misleading, for the "best" test may be too unreliable for any application (for example, .45). We recommend that two standards of reliability be used in applied settings.

1. *Group Data*   If test scores are to be used for administrative purposes and are reported for groups of individuals, a reliability of .60 should probably be the minimum.
2. *Individual Data*   If a test score is used to make a decision for an individual student, a much higher standard of reliability is demanded. When important educational decisions, such as tracking and placement in a special class, are to be made for a student, the minimum standard should be .90. When the decision being made is a screening decision, such as a recommendation that a child receive further assessment, there is still need for high reliability. For screening devices, we recommend a .80 standard.

Finally, when reporting test performance, we strongly recommend that confidence intervals be used.

SUMMARY

The term *reliability* refers to the ability to generalize from a sample to a domain. The domains to which we usually want to generalize are other times (stability or test-retest reliability), other scorers (interrater or interscorer reliability), and other items (alternate-form or internal-consistency reliability). Reliability coefficients may range from .00 (total lack of reliability) to 1.00 (total reliability); .90 is recommended as the minimum standard for tests used to make important educational decisions for students. In diagnostic work, the reliability coefficient has three major uses: It allows the user (1) to estimate the test's relative freedom from measurement error, (2) to estimate an individual subject's true score, and (3) to find the standard error of measurement. Knowledge of the standard error of measurement and the estimated true score allows the test user to estimate confidence intervals for a subject's true score.

The discussion of estimated true scores, standard error of measurement, and confidence intervals can be extended to difference or discrepancy scores. The reliability of a difference score is affected by the reliability of the tests and by the correlation between the tests on which the difference is based. Differences in norm samples also affect difference scores, but this effect cannot be evaluated. Provided the two tests are correlated, difference scores are less reliable than the average of the reliabilities of the tests on which the difference is based.

There are several factors that affect reliability: the method used to calculate the reliability coefficient, test length, the test-retest interval, constriction of range, guessing, and variation within the testing situation.

STUDY QUESTIONS

1. Why is it necessary that a test be reliable?
2. Test A and test B have identical means and standard deviations. Test A has a standard error of measurement of 4.8; test B has a standard error of measurement of 16.3. Which test is more reliable, and why?
3. What is the greatest limitation of reliability estimates based on test-retest correlation?
4. List and explain five factors that affect the estimated reliability of a test.
5. The standard error of measurement is the standard deviation of what? Illustrate your answer with a drawing.

PROBLEMS

1. Mr. Treacher administers an intelligence test ($\overline{X} = 100$, $S = 16$, $r_{rx} = .75$) to his class. Five children earn the following scores: 68, 124, 84, 100, and 148. What are the estimated true scores for these children?
2. What is the standard error of measurement for the intelligence test in problem 1?
3. What are the upper and lower boundaries of a symmetrical confidence interval of 95 percent for the first child?
4. What are the upper and lower boundaries of a symmetrical confidence interval of 50 percent for the child who earns a score of 100?

5. Test A and test B have reliabilities of .90 and .80; the correlation between tests A and B is .50. What is the reliability of a difference between scores on test A and test B?

Answers

1. 76, 118, 88, 100, 136
2. 8
3. 92, 60
4. 105, 95
5. .70

ADDITIONAL READING

American Educational Research Association, American Psychological Association, & National Council on Measurement in Education. (1985). *Standards for educational and psychological testing.* Washington, DC: American Psychological Association.

Coates, T., & Thoresen, C. (1978). Using generalization theory in behavioral observation. *Behavior Therapy, 9*, 605–613.

Cronbach, L., Gleser, G., Nanda, H., & Rajaratnam, N. (1972). *The dependability of behavioral measurement: Theory of generalizability of scores and profiles.* New York: Wiley.

Ghiselli, E. E. (1964). *Theory of psychological measurement.* New York: McGraw-Hill. (Chapter 8, pp. 207–253.)

Kazdin, A. (1982). *Single-case research designs.* New York: Oxford University Press. (Chapter 3: Interobserver agreement.)

Salvia, J., & Good, R. (1982). Significant discrepancies in the classification of pupils: Differentiating the concept. In J. T. Neisworth (Ed.), *Assessment in special education.* Rockville, MD: Aspen Systems.

C·H·A·P·T·E·R 8

Validity

Validity refers to the extent to which a test measures what its authors or users claim it measures. Specifically, test validity concerns the appropriateness of the inferences that can be made on the basis of test results. A test's validity is not measured; rather, a test's validity for various uses is judged on a wide array of information, including its reliability and the adequacy of its norms. The process of gathering information about the appropriateness of test-based inferences is called *validation*. Three interrelated types of validity are usually considered in the validation of tests: content validity, criterion-related validity, and construct validity.

The valid use of tests is the responsibility of both the test author and the test user.

> *Evidence of validity should be presented for the major types of inferences for which the use of a test is recommended. A rationale should be provided to support the particular mix of evidence presented for the intended uses. . . . If validity for some common interpretation has not been investigated, that fact should be made clear, and potential users should be cautioned about making such interpretations. (AERA et al., 1985, p. 13)*

To evaluate a test's validity, test users must have a clear understanding of what is to be measured. One must define what is to be measured before deciding how the measuring is to be done. Test authors should not start with a series of test items and then decide what those items might measure. Rather, they should first define what a trait (or characteristic or skill) is and what it is not, and then select items to measure it. Selection of test items depends on a test author's own definition of and assumptions about the domain to be measured.

METHODS OF TEST VALIDATION

This section treats content, criterion-related, and construct validity separately. However, it is important to note that these three aspects of validity are not separable in the real world; they are interdependent.

Content Validity

Content validity is especially important in the measurement of products such as achievement and adaptive behavior. It is evaluated by a careful examination of the content of a test. Such an examination is judgmental in nature and requires a clear definition of what the content should be. Content validity is established by evaluating three factors: the appropriateness of the types of items included, the completeness of the item sample, and the way in which the items assess the content.

The first factor to examine in determining content validity is the appropriateness of the items included in the test. We must ask, "Is this an appropriate test question?" and "Does this test item really measure the domain?" Consider the four test items from a hypothetical elementary (kindergarten through grade 3) arithmetic achievement test presented in Figure 8.1. The first item requires the student to read and add two single-digit numbers whose sum is less than 10. This seems to be an appropriate item for an elementary arithmetic achievement test. The second item requires the student to complete a geometric progression. While this item is mathematical, the skills and knowledge required to complete the question correctly have not been taught in any elementary school curriculum by the third grade. Therefore, the question should be rejected as an invalid item for an arithmetic achievement test to be used with children in kindergarten through the third grade.

The third item also requires the student to read and add two single-digit numbers whose sum is less than 10. However, the question is written in Spanish. Although the content of the question is suitable (this is an elementary addition problem), the methods of presentation require other skills. Failure to complete the item correctly could be attributed to the fact that the child does not know Spanish and/or to the fact that the child does not know "2 + 3 = 5." One should conclude that the item is not valid for an arithmetic test for children who do not read Spanish. The fourth item requires that the student select the correct form of the Latin verb *amare* ("to love"). Clearly, this is an inappropriate item for an elementary arithmetic test and should be rejected as invalid.

In addition to judgments about how appropriately an item fits within a domain, test developers often rely on point biserial correlations between individual test items and total score to make decisions about item appropriateness. Items that do not correlate positively and at least moderately (that is, .25 or .30 or more) with the total score are dropped. Retaining only items that have positive correlations with the total score insures homogeneous test items and internally consistent (reliable) tests. Moreover, when test items are homogeneous, they are likely to be measuring the same skill or trait. Therefore, to obtain reliable tests, test developers are likely to drop items that do not belong in the domain.

The second factor to examine in determining content validity is the completeness of the item sample. The validity of any elementary arithmetic test would be questioned if it included *only* problems requiring the addition of single-digit numbers whose sum was less than 10. One would reasonably expect an arithmetic test to include a far broader sample of tasks (for example, addition of two- and three-digit numbers, subtraction, and so forth).

The third factor to examine is how the test items assess the content—that is, the level of mastery at which the content is assessed. In the previous example, the child was expected to add two single-digit numbers whose sum was less than 10. However, one could evaluate a child's arithmetic skills in a variety of ways. The child might be required to recognize the correct answer in a multiple-choice array, supply the correct answer, apply the proper addition facts in a word problem, or analyze the condition under which the mathematical relationship obtains.

One way to insure content validity of a test is to construct a test that measures the desired content in the desired way. Bloom, Hastings, and Madaus (1971) have devoted several hundred pages to this topic in their book *Handbook of Formative and Summative Evaluation of Student Learning.* They have recommended that authors of achievement tests develop a *table of specifica-*

FIGURE 8.1   Sample Multiple-choice Questions for an Elementary-level (K–3) Arithmetic Achievement Test

1. Three and six are _____.
   a. 4
   b. 7
   c. 8
   d. 9
2. What number follows in this series? 1, 2.5, 6.25, ____
   a. 10
   b. 12.5
   c. 15.625
   d. 18.50
3. Cuánto son tres y dos?
   a. 3
   b. 4
   c. 5
   d. 6
4. Ille puer puellas _____.
   a. amo
   b. amat
   c. amamus
   d. amant

tions for the content to be tested. Such a table can be readily generalized to other types of tests. A table of specifications formally enumerates the particular contents of a test and the processes (or behaviors) it assesses. *Content* refers to the particular domains or subdomains the test author wishes to assess. The task of the test author is to specify the content as precisely as possible in order to convey clearly to both himself or herself and the test user what is being measured. The next step is to specify how the particular content objectives will be measured (the process by which the measurement will occur). Several levels of measurement are possible; they range from knowledge objectives to evaluation objectives. The definitions used by Bloom (1956) and Bloom, Hastings, and Madaus (1971) follow:

1. *Knowledge* is the "recall or recognition of specific elements in a subject area" (Bloom et al., p. 41).
2. *Comprehension* consists of three types of measurement: translation, interpretation, and extrapolation. *Translation* refers to rewording information or putting it into one's own words. Interpretation is evidenced "when a student can go beyond recognizing the separate parts of a communication . . . and can see the interrelationships among the parts" (Bloom et al., p. 149). Interpretation also is evidenced when a student can differentiate the essentials of a message from unimportant elements. *Extrapolation* refers to the student's ability to go beyond literal comprehension and to make inferences about what the anticipated outcome of an action is or what will happen next.
3. *Application* is "the use of abstractions in particular and concrete situations. The abstractions may be in the form of general ideas, rules of procedures, or generalized methods. The abstractions may also be technical principles, ideas, and theories which must be remembered and applied" (Bloom, 1956, p. 205).
4. *Analysis* is "the breakdown of a communication into its constituent elements or parts such that the relative hierarchy of ideas is made clear and/or the relations between ideas expressed are made explicit. Such analyses are intended to clarify the communication, to indicate how the communication is organized, and the way in which it manages to convey its effects, as well as its basis and arrangements" (Bloom, 1956, p. 205).
5. *Synthesis* refers to "the putting together of elements and parts so as to form a whole. This involves the process of working with pieces, parts, elements, etc., and arranging and combining them in such a way as to constitute a pattern or structure not clearly there before" (Bloom, 1956, p. 206).
6. *Evaluation* means "the making of judgments about the value, for some purpose, of ideas, works, solutions, methods, material, etc. It involves the use of criteria as well as standards for appraising the extent to which particulars are accurate, effective, economical, or satisfying. The judg-

TABLE 8.1   Table of Specifications for a Hypothetical Reliability Test

Processes	Contents				
	Reliability Coefficient	Standard Error of Measurement	Estimated True Scores	Confidence Intervals	Difference Scores
Knowledge	3 questions	2 questions	1 question	1 question	1 question
Comprehension	5 questions	2 questions	1 question	3 questions	1 question
Application	Not tested	2 questions	1 question	5 questions	Not tested
Analysis	Not tested	Not tested	Not tested	Not tested	Not tested
Synthesis	Not tested	Not tested	Not tested	Not tested	Not tested
Evaluation	Not tested	Not tested	Not tested	Not tested	Not tested

ments may be quantitative or qualitative, and the criteria may be either those determined by the student or those which are given to him" (Bloom, 1956, p. 185).

To illustrate how a table of specifications can be used, let us assume that we wish to develop a test to assess the understanding of reliability demonstrated by beginning students of psychoeducational assessment. The first step is to enumerate the *content areas* of the domain. Using Chapter 7 as a guide, we could assess the following areas: the reliability coefficient (meaning, methods of estimating it, and factors affecting it), standard error of measurement (meaning and computation), estimated true scores, confidence intervals (meaning and computation), and difference scores. One might reasonably expect a test user to have a better understanding of the meaning of the reliability coefficient and the construction and interpretation of confidence intervals. Therefore, these content areas could be stressed. The next step is to specify the *processes* by which the content areas are to be measured. One might expect beginning students to demonstrate understanding at the *knowledge, comprehension,* and *application* levels only. Therefore, the test might not contain items assessing analysis, synthesis, or evaluation. A table of specifications for this hypothetical test would resemble Table 8.1.

The number of questions used to assess each cell also is given in the table. The table of specifications shows that, of the twenty-eight questions in the test, eight deal with the reliability coefficient and nine deal with confidence intervals; eight questions assess knowledge, twelve questions assess comprehension, and eight assess application. Thus, while the hypothetical test assesses a student's understanding of reliability, it does so by emphasizing comprehension of the reliability coefficient and applications of confidence intervals.

Content validity is a major component of the validation process for any educational and psychological test. It is hard to imagine a valid test that lacks content validity.

In developing a test, it is important that a test developer consider the purposes for which a test is going to be used and then specify adequately the universe of content that a test is intended to represent. For instructional decisions, it is important to demonstrate agreement between the test and the specific instructional or curricular areas it is meant to cover. It is also necessary to make sure that the format and response properties of the sample of items or tasks that make up a test are representative of the universe of possible item and response types for the particular area being assessed.

When content-related evidence serves as a significant demonstration of validity for a particular test use, a clear definition of the universe represented, its relevance to the proposed test use, and the procedures followed in generating test content to represent that universe should be described. (AERA et al., 1985, p. 14)

Criterion-Related Validity

A test's *criterion-related validity* is the extent to which a person's score on a criterion measure can be estimated from that person's test score. This is usually expressed as a correlation between the test and the criterion. The correlation coefficient is called a *validity coefficient*.

Concurrent validity and predictive validity denote the time when a person's score on the criterion measure is obtained. *Concurrent* criterion-related validity refers to how accurately a person's current test score can be used to estimate the *current* criterion score. *Predictive* criterion-related validity refers to how accurately a person's current test score can be used to estimate what the criterion score will be *at a later time.* Thus, concurrent and predictive criterion-related validity of a test refer to the temporal sequence by which a person's score on some criterion measure is estimated on the basis of that person's current test score; concurrent and predictive validity differ as a function of the time at which scores on the criterion measure are obtained.

The nature of the criterion measure is extremely important. The criterion itself must be valid if it is to be used to establish the validity of another measure. Let's investigate this point by looking briefly at two examples of criterion-related validation, the first concurrent and the second predictive.

Concurrent Criterion-Related Validity

The basic concurrent criterion-related validity question is, Does knowledge of a person's test score allow the accurate estimation of that person's performance on a criterion measure? For example, if the Acme Ruler Company manufactures yardsticks, how do we know that a person's height as measured by the yardstick is that person's true height? How do we know that the "Acme foot" is really a foot? The first step is to find a valid criterion measure.

The National Bureau of Standards maintains *the* foot (.3048 meter), and *the* foot is the logical choice for a criterion measure. We can take the Acme foot to the Bureau and compare Acme measurements with measurements made with *the* foot. If the two sets of measurements correspond closely (that is, are highly correlated and have very similar means and standard deviations), we can conclude that the Acme foot is a valid measure of length.

Similarly, if we are developing a test of achievement, we can ask, "How does knowledge of a person's score on our achievement test allow the estimation of that person's score on a criterion measure?" How do we know that our new test really measures achievement? Again, the first step is to find a valid criterion measure. However, there is no National Bureau of Standards for Educational Tests. Therefore, we must turn to a less-than-perfect criterion. There are two basic choices: other achievement tests that are presumed to be valid and teacher judgments of achievement. We can, of course, use both. If our new test presents evidence of content validity and elicits test scores corresponding closely (correlating significantly) to teacher judgments and scores from other achievement tests presumed to be valid, we can conclude that our new test is a valid measure of achievement.

Predictive Criterion-Related Validity

The basic predictive criterion-related validity question is, Does knowledge of a person's test score allow an accurate estimation of that person's score on a criterion measure administered some time in the future? For example, if Acme Ruler Company decides to diversify and manufacture tests of color vision, how do we know that a diagnosis of colorblindness made on the basis of the Acme test is accurate? How do we know that the Acme-based diagnoses will correspond to next month's diagnosis made by an ophthalmologist? We can test several children with the Acme test, schedule an appointment with an ophthalmologist, and compare the Acme-based diagnoses with the ophthalmologist's diagnoses. If the Acme test accurately predicts the ophthalmologist's diagnoses, we can conclude that the Acme test is a valid measure of color vision.

Similarly, if we are developing a test to assess reading readiness, we can ask, "Does knowledge of a child's score on our reading readiness test allow an accurate estimation of the child's actual readiness for subsequent instruction?" How do we know that our test really assesses reading readiness? Again, the first step is to find a valid criterion measure. In this case, the child's initial progress in reading can be used. Reading progress can be assessed by a reading achievement test (presumed to be valid) or by teacher judgments of reading ability or reading readiness at the time reading instruction was actually begun. If our reading readiness test has content validity and corresponds closely with either later teacher judgments of readiness or validly assessed reading skill, we can conclude that ours is a valid test of reading readiness.

Three aspects of criterion-related validity are extremely important. First, "All criterion measures should be described accurately, and the rationale for choosing them as relevant criteria should be made explicit" (AERA et al., 1985, p. 16). Obviously, because the validity of the test is established by its relationship to a criterion, the criterion itself must be valid. Test authors need to present sufficient information to allow test users to judge the adequacy of the criterion. Second, "A report of a criterion-related validity study should provide a description of the sample and the statistical analysis used to determine the degree of predictive accuracy. Basic statistics should include numbers of cases (and the reasons for eliminating any cases), measures of central tendency and variability, relationships, and a description of any marked tendency toward nonnormality of distribution" (AERA et al., 1985, p. 16). You will see in later sections of this book that many of the validity studies for tests we review are based on small samples, samples of convenience, or very restrictive (one location or one private school) samples. It is important that test authors show that their test is valid not only for the recommended purposes of the test but also for the kinds of people who will be tested. Third, test authors must provide information on the limits of generalizability of validity information.

Construct Validity

Construct validity refers to the extent to which a test measures a theoretical trait or characteristic. Construct validity is especially important for measures of process such as intelligence. To validate a test of a construct, the test author must rely on indirect evidence and inference. The definition of the construct and the theory from which the construct is derived allow us to make certain predictions that can be confirmed or disconfirmed. In a real sense, one does not validate a test; one conducts experiments to demonstrate that the test *is not* a valid measure of the trait or construct. Continued inability to disconfirm the validity of a test, in effect, validates the test. For example, intellectual ability is generally believed to be developmental. One would hypothesize that, if we were to conduct an experiment, a test of intelligence would be correlated with chronological age. If a test of intelligence did not correlate with chronological age, it would cast serious doubt on the test as a measure of intelligence. (The experiment would disconfirm the test as a measure of intelligence.) However, the presence of a substantial correlation between chronological age and scores on the test does not confirm that the test is a measure of intelligence. Indeed, many test developers use a positive correlation between age or grade and passing an item as a criterion for item inclusion. Some test developers use even more sophisticated methods—for example, item-characteristic curves (Thorndike, 1982)—to insure that test scores are correlated with chronological age. Moreover, many other abilities correlate with chronological age (for example, achievement, perceptual abilities, and language skills). Gradually, one accumulates evidence that the test continues to act in the way that it would if it were a valid measure of the construct. As the research evidence accumulates, some claim to construct validity can be made.

Several types of evidence are generally brought to bear in research on construct validity. Correlation of test scores with chronological age is used with several types of tests. When tests claim to measure several different factors, factor-analytic research is often conducted to learn if the test is really composed of different factors. Often we expect differences in the behavior of individuals with different levels of the trait or characteristic. For example, a test to assess learning ability should be able to differentiate between fast and slow learners. One can predict, therefore, that the individuals who learn more in a given amount of time have more learning ability; that is, they would have higher scores on a measure of learning ability. If children with IQs of 125 on test X learn more material in one week than do children with IQs of 100 on test X, there would be a failure to disconfirm the test as a valid measure of learning ability. In that sense, there would be some evidence for the validity of the test. Other possible examples of this type of research are numerous. We would expect tests of intelligence to predict school achievement; the correlation between test X and school achievement does not mean that test X measures achievement. (Test X *could* measure achievement.) We would expect readiness tests to predict school achievement. If test Y does not predict school achievement, it probably is not a measure of readiness; if it does predict school achievement, it may be measuring any number of abilities or traits.

Nonvalidity Data

Information intended to document validity is often presented in test manuals and advertisements, but some of these data do not really establish the validity of the test. The following are examples of "nonvalidity" data—data that sound impressive but are not true indications of validity.

1. *Cash Validity* Just because a test is a "big seller" does not imply that it is valid. The only thing that large sales guarantee is cash for the authors and publishers. Good tests may or may not sell well; poor tests may or may not sell well.
2. *Clinical Utility* Unevaluated, uncontrolled clinical reports are simply testimonials. Testimonials about the practical utility of a test are not validity data. Only controlled experiments and evaluated investigations should be considered potentially useful in assessing a test's validity.
3. *Internal Consistency* The internal consistency of a test (interitem or item-total correlations) is reliability information, not validity data. A high

degree of internal consistency insures only that the test items are drawn from the same domain. That domain may or may not be the one the test is intended to measure. A reliable test may or may not be valid.

Factors Affecting Validity

Whenever a test fails to measure what it purports to measure, validity is threatened. Consequently, any factor that results in measuring "something else" affects a test's validity. Unsystematic error (unreliability) and systematic error (bias) threaten validity.

Reliability

Reliability is a necessary but not a sufficient condition for valid measurement. *All valid tests are reliable; no unreliable tests may be valid; reliable tests may or may not be valid.* Finally, the validity of a particular test can never exceed the reliability of that test. Unreliable tests measure error; valid tests measure the traits they are designed to measure. The relationship between the reliability and validity of any test is expressed in equation 8.1. The empirically determined validity coefficient (r_{xy}) equals the correlation between true scores on the two variables ($r_{x(t)y(t)}$) multiplied by the square root of the product of the reliability coefficients of test X and test Y ($r_{xx}r_{yy}$). Hence, the reliability of the test limits its potential validity.

$$r_{xy} = r_{x(t)y(t)} \sqrt{r_{xx}r_{yy}} \tag{8.1}$$

Systematic Bias

Method of Measurement

The method used to measure a skill or trait often determines what score a child will receive. A true score can be considered a composite of trait variance and method-of-measurement variance (Campbell & Fiske, 1959). To take just one example: Werner and Strauss (1941) conducted a series of experiments to study the figure-background perception of brain-injured and non-brain-injured retarded persons. They presented stimulus items tachistoscopically for a fraction of a second and asked their subjects to name what they saw. They found that brain-injured retarded persons responded more often to the background stimuli than did the non-brain-injured retarded persons. They concluded that brain injury results in figure-ground dysfunction. However, the method of testing (tachistoscopic presentation) and the trait to be tested (figure-ground perception) were confounded by the testing procedure. Rubin (1969) later demonstrated that under different testing procedures there were no differences between brain-injured and non-brain-injured retarded persons in figure-background responses. The differences between the findings of Strauss and Rubin are attributable to *how* figure-background perception was measured. It seems likely that Strauss was measuring perceptual speed because of his method of measurement. To the extent that trait or skill scores include variance attributable to method of measurement, these scores may lack validity.

Enabling Behaviors

Several behaviors are assumed in any testing situation. We must assume that the subject is fluent in the language in which the test is prepared and administered if there are any verbal components to the test directions or test responses. Yet in many states with substantial Spanish-speaking populations, students whose primary language is not English are tested in English. Intelligence testing in English of non-English-speaking children was sufficiently commonplace that a group of parents brought suit against a school district (*Diana* v. *State Board of Education* 1970). Deaf children are routinely given the Performance subtests of the Wechsler intelligence scales (Levine, 1974) even though they cannot *hear* the directions. Children with extreme communication problems (speech impediments, for example) often are required to respond orally to test questions. Such obvious limitations or absences of enabling behaviors are frequently overlooked in testing situations even though they invalidate the test results.

Item Selection

Test items often presume that the subjects taking the test have had exposure to concepts and skills measured by the test. For example, standardized achievement tests presume that the students taking the tests have been exposed to similar curricula. If a teacher has not taught the content being tested, the results of the achievement test are invalid.

Administration Errors

Unless a test is administered according to the standardized procedures, the results are invalid. Suppose Ms. Williams wished to demonstrate how effective her teaching was by administering an intelligence test and an achievement test to her class. She allows the children five minutes less than the standardized time limits on the intelligence test and five minutes more on the standardized achievement test. The result is that the children earn scores lower than their true intelligence (since they did not have enough time) and scores higher than their true achievement (since they had too much time). The apparent results, that slow children had learned more than anticipated, would not be valid.

Norms

Scores based on the performance of unrepresentative norms lead to incorrect estimates of relative standing in the general population. To the extent that the normative sample is systematically unrepresentative, in either central tendency or variability, the inferences based on such scores are incorrect and invalid.

SUMMARY

Validity is the only technical characteristic of a test in which we are interested. All other technical considerations, such as reliability, are subsumed under the issue of validity and are analyzed separately to simplify the issue of validity. We must know if a test measures what it purports to measure and if scores derived from the test are accurate. Adequate norms, reliability, and lack of bias are all necessary conditions for validity. None—separately or in total—is sufficient to guarantee validity.

When the necessary conditions for validity are met, systematic validation can proceed. The content may be inspected to see if each item is valid and to insure that all aspects of the domain are represented. If a standard or criterion of known validity is available, the test should be compared to that standard. In the absence of a known standard, construct validation should proceed. In this case, directional predictions are made based on the constructed trait; these predictions are empirically tested.

STUDY QUESTIONS

1. Why must test authors demonstrate validity for their tests?
2. What is the relationship between reliability and validity?
3. Identify three factors that must be considered in the establishment of content validity.
4. Ms. Wilson uses a new math curriculum to teach her class of third graders. She uses a traditional math test to assess pupil progress. All pupils score in the bottom quartile according to the test norms. What can Ms. Wilson legitimately conclude?
5. There are many tests whose manuals include absolutely no evidence as to validity. These tests are used in schools to make important educational decisions about children. Under what circumstances could such tests be used?

6. Test author G presents interitem correlation coefficients as evidence for the validity of his scale. To what extent are these coefficients evidence of validity?
7. Kim Ngo, a recent arrival from a Vietnamese orphanage, speaks no English. When she enrolls in a U.S. school, her intelligence is assessed by means of a verbal test that has English directions and requires English responses. Kim performs poorly on the test, earning an IQ of 37. The tester concludes that Kim is a trainable mentally retarded child and recommends placement in a special class. Identify two major errors in the interpretation of the test results.
8. Professor Johnson develops a test that he claims can be used to identify children with learning disabilities who will profit from perceptual-motor training. What must he do to demonstrate that his test is valid?

ADDITIONAL READING

American Educational Research Association, American Psychological Association, & National Council on Measurement in Education. (1985). *Standards for educational and psychological testing*. Washington, DC: American Psychological Association.

Bagnato, S. (1982). Developmental scales and developmental curricula: Forging a linkage for early intervention. In J. T. Neisworth (Ed.), *Assessment in special education*. Rockville, MD: Aspen Systems.

Kazdin, A. (1982). *Single-case research designs*. New York: Oxford University Press. (Chapter 2: Behavioral assessment.)

PART 3

ASSESSMENT OF PROCESSES: DOMAINS SAMPLED AND REPRESENTATIVE TESTS

Part 3 is a description of the most common domains in which assessment of processes, or abilities, is conducted. In this part, we consider behaviors that represent one or more underlying hypothetical constructs, such as intelligence and oral language. The behaviors sampled by tests in the domains under consideration in this part allow educators to draw inferences about students' underlying abilities. Thus, for example, in assessment of processes reading may be assessed to analyze a person's intellectual ability or expressive competence rather than to evaluate his or her word-recognition skills.

Each chapter focuses on a different process, and each is developed in a similar way. The chapter opens with an explanation of why the domain is assessed. We then provide a general overview of the components of the domain

(that is, the behaviors that are usually assessed) and discuss the more commonly used tests within the domain. Each chapter concludes with some suggestions for coping with problems in assessing the domain, followed by a general summary of chapter content.

We examine five factors in our evaluations of tests. First, we describe the general format of the test and the specific behaviors that the test is designed to sample. The descriptions allow the reader to evaluate the extent to which specific tests sample the domain. Second, we describe the kinds of scores that the test provides for the practitioner. This gives information about the meaning and interpretation of those scores. Third, we examine the standardization sample for each test. This enables the reader to judge—recalling the discussion in Chapter 6—the adequacy of the norm group and to evaluate the appropriateness of each test for use with specific populations of students. Fourth, we evaluate the evidence of reliability for each test, using the standards set forth in Chapter 7. Fifth, for each device we examine evidence of its validity and evaluate the adequacy of the evidence in light of the standards set forth in Chapter 8. Finally, there is a summary for each test.

Two principles guided our development of Part 3. First, we did not include all the available measures for each domain. Rather, we selected representative and commonly used devices in each area. *The Mental Measurements Yearbooks* are an excellent source that provides reviews of standardized tests not reviewed here. These yearbooks are a compendium of critical test reviews by individuals who are authorities in assessment.

Second, in evaluating the technical adequacy of each test, we restricted our evaluation to in-

formation included in the test manuals. There were two major reasons for this decision. First, as stated in the *Standards for Educational and Psychological Tests* (APA, 1985), test authors are responsible for providing all necessary technical information in their test manuals. The test authors must have some basis for claiming that their tests are valid. Therefore, we searched the manuals for the technical information that provides the support for the test authors' contentions. Second, an attempt to include the vast body of research literature on commonly used tests would have resulted in a multivolume opus that would be impossible to publish as a current work. Entire books have been written on the subject of using and interpreting single tests. We urge our readers to peruse the literature and to examine the research that bears on tests in which they might be interested. We might add that test users also have a responsibility in this area.

C·H·A·P·T·E·R 9

ASSESSMENT OF INTELLIGENCE: AN OVERVIEW

No other area of assessment has generated as much attention, controversy, and debate as "intelligence" testing. For centuries philosophers, psychologists, educators, and laypeople have debated the meaning of intelligence. Numerous definitions of the term *intelligence* have been proposed, each definition serving as a stimulus for counterdefinitions and counterproposals. Several theories have been advanced to describe and explain intelligence and its development. The extent to which intelligence is genetically or environmentally determined has been of special concern. Genetic determinists, environmental determinists, and interactionists have all observed differences in the intelligence test performances of different populations of children. The interpretation of group differences in intelligence measurements and the practice of testing the intelligence of schoolchildren have been topics of recurrent controversy and debate, aired in professional journals, the popular press, and on television. In some instances the courts have acted to curtail or halt intelligence assessment in the public schools; in others the courts have defined what intelligence assessment must consist of. Debate and controversy have flourished about whether intelligence tests should be given, what intelligence tests measure, and how different levels of performance attained by different populations of children are to be explained.

No one, however, has seen a thing called intelligence. Rather, we observe differences in the ways people behave—either differences in everyday behavior in a variety of situations or differences in responses to standard stimuli or sets of stimuli; then we *infer* a construct called *intelligence*. In this sense, intelligence is an inferred entity, a term or construct we use to explain differences in present behavior and to predict differences in future behavior.

We have repeatedly stressed the fact that any test is a sample of behavior. So, too, intelligence tests are samples of behavior. Regardless of how an individual's performance is viewed and interpreted, intelligence tests and items on those tests simply sample behaviors. A variety of different kinds of behavior samplings are used to assess intelligence; in most cases, the kinds of behaviors sampled reflect a test author's conception of intelligence. In this chapter we review the kinds of behaviors sampled by intelligence tests with particular emphasis on the psychological demands of different test items as a function of pupil characteristics.

INTELLIGENCE TESTS AS SAMPLES OF BEHAVIOR

There is a hypothetical domain of items that could be used to assess intelligence. In practice, it is impossible to administer every item in the domain to a child whose intelligence we want to assess. The dots in Figure 9.1 represent different items in the domain of behaviors that could be used to assess intelligence. No two tests contain identical samples of behavior; some tests overlap in the kinds of behaviors they sample, and others do not. No test samples all possible behaviors in the domain. In Figure 9.1 we see that tests A and D sample different behaviors. Both tests assess some behaviors sampled by test E. None of the tests sample all the possible behaviors in the domain.

The characterization of behaviors sampled by intelligence tests is complex. Some persons have, for example, argued that intelligence tests assess a student's capacity to profit from instruction, while others argue that such tests assess merely what has been learned; some have characterized intelligence tests as either verbal or nonverbal; some characterize intelligence tests as either culturally biased or culture fair. In actuality, nearly any contention regarding what it is that intelligence tests measure can be supported. The relative merit of competing opinions, theories, and contentions is primarily a function of the interaction between the characteristics of an individual and the psycho-

FIGURE 9.1   Intelligence Tests as Samples of Behavior from a Larger Domain of Behaviors

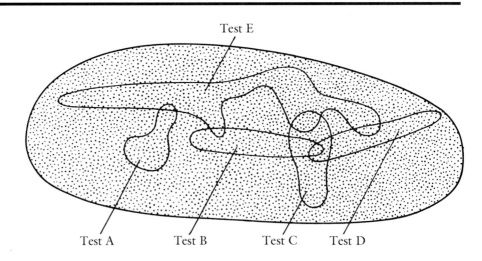

logical demands of items in an intelligence test. It is also a function of the stimulus and response requirements of the items.

There are many kinds of "nonverbal" behavior samples. A test might require children to point to objects in response to directions read by the examiner, to build block towers, to manipulate colored blocks in order to reproduce a design, or to copy symbols or designs on paper. Similarly, there are many kinds of "verbal" behavior samples. We could, for example, ask children factual questions, like "Who wrote *Huckleberry Finn?*" We could ask them to define words or to identify similarities and differences in words or objects. We could ask children to state actions they would take in specific social situations or ask them to repeat sequences of digits. Test items may be presented orally, or the test takers may have to read the items themselves.

Similar behaviors may be assessed in different ways. In assessing vocabulary, for example, the examiner may ask children to define words, to name pictures, to select a synonym of a stimulus word, or to point to pictures depicting words read by the examiner. All four kinds of assessments are called *vocabulary tests*, yet they sample different behaviors. The psychological demands of the items change with the ways the behavior is assessed.

In evaluating children's performances on intelligence tests, teachers, administrators, counselors, and diagnostic specialists must go beyond test names and scores to look at the kind or kinds of behaviors sampled on the test. They must be willing to question the ways test stimuli are presented to a child, to question the response requirements, and to evaluate the psychological demands placed on a child.

THE EFFECT OF PUPIL CHARACTERISTICS ON ASSESSMENT OF INTELLIGENCE

Acculturation is the most important characteristic in evaluating a child's performance on intelligence tests. *Acculturation,* as we have stated earlier, refers to a child's particular set of background experiences and opportunities to learn in both formal and informal educational settings. This, in turn, depends on the experiences available in the child's environment (that is, culture) and the length of time the child has had to assimilate those experiences. The culture in which a child lives and the length of time that child has lived in that culture effectively determine the psychological demands a test item presents. Simply knowing the kind of behavior sampled by a test is not enough, for the same test item may create different psychological demands for different children.

Suppose, for example, that we assess intelligence by asking children to tell how hail and sleet are alike. Children may fail the item for very different reasons. A child who does not know what hail and sleet are stands little chance of telling how hail and sleet are alike. He will fail the item simply because he does not know the meanings of the words. Another child may know what hail is and what sleet is but fail the item because she is unable to integrate these two words into a conceptual category (precipitation). The psychological demand of the item changes as a function of the children's acculturation. For the child who has not learned the meanings of the words, the item assesses vocabulary. For the child who knows the meanings of the words, the item is a generalization task.

In considering children's performance on intelligence tests, we need to know how acculturation affects test performance. Items on intelligence tests range along a continuum from items that sample fundamental psychological behaviors relatively unaffected by learning history to items that sample primarily learned behavior. To determine exactly what is being assessed, we need to know the essential background of the child. Consider for a moment the following item:

> *Jeff went walking in the forest. He saw a porcupine that he tried to take home for a pet. It got away from him, but when he got home his father took him to the doctor. Why?*

For a student who knows what a porcupine is, that a porcupine has quills, and that quills are sharp, the item can assess comprehension, abstract reasoning, and problem-solving skill. The student who does not know any of that information may very well fail the item. In this case, failure is due not to an inability to comprehend or solve the problem but to a deficiency in background experience.

Similarly, we could ask a child to identify the seasons of the year. The experiences available in children's environments are reflected in the way they respond to this item. Children from central Illinois, who experience four discernibly different climatic conditions, may well respond, "Summer, fall, winter, and spring." Children from central Pennsylvania, who also experience four discernibly different climatic conditions but who live in an environment where hunting is prevalent, often respond, "Buck season, doe season, rabbit season, and squirrel season." Response differences are a function of experiential differences. Within specific cultures, both responses are logical and appropriate; only one is *scored* as correct.

Items on intelligence tests also sample different behaviors as a function of the age of the child assessed. Age and acculturation are positively related; older children in general have had more opportunities to acquire the skills assessed by intelligence tests. The performances of 5-year-old children on an item requiring them to tell how a cardinal, a bluejay, and a swallow are alike are almost entirely a function of their knowledge of the word meanings. Most college students know the meanings of the three words; for them the item assesses primarily their ability to identify similarities and integrate words or objects into a conceptual category. As children get older, they have increasing opportunity to acquire "the more abstruse elements of the collective intelligence of a culture" (Horn, 1965, p. 4).

The interaction between acculturation and the behavior sampled determines the psychological demands of an intelligence test item. For this reason, it is impossible to define exactly what intelligence tests assess. *Identical test items actually place different psychological demands on different children.* Thirteen kinds of behaviors sampled by intelligence tests are described in the next section of this chapter. For the sake of illustration, let us assume that there are only three discrete sets of background experiences (this is a very conservative estimate; there are probably many times this number in the United States alone). To further simplify our example, let us consider only the thirteen kinds of behaviors sampled by intelligence tests rather than the millions of items that could be used to sample each of the thirteen kinds. With these very restrictive conditions, there are still $(mn)!/m!n!$ possible interactions between behavior samples and types of acculturation. This very restrictive estimate produces more than 1.35×10^{32} interactions! No wonder there is controversy about what intelligence tests measure. They measure more things than we can conceive of; they measure different things for different children.

Used appropriately, intelligence tests can provide information that can lead to enhancement of individual opportunity and protection of the rights of students. Used inappropriately, they can restrict opportunity and rights.

The next two chapters review commonly used group-administered and individually administered intelligence tests, with particular reference to the kinds of behaviors sampled by those tests and their technical adequacy.

BEHAVIORS SAMPLED BY INTELLIGENCE TESTS

Regardless of the interpretation of measured intelligence, it is a fact that intelligence tests simply sample behaviors. This section describes the kinds of behaviors sampled.

Discrimination

Intelligence test items that sample skill in discrimination usually present a variety of stimuli and ask the student to find the one that is different from all the others. Figural, symbolic, or semantic discrimination may be assessed.

Figure 9.2 illustrates items assessing discrimination: items a and b assess discrimination of figures; items c and d assess symbolic discrimination; items e and f assess semantic discrimination. In each case, the student must identify the item that is different from the others. The psychological demand of the items, however, differs depending on the student's age and particular set of background experiences.

Generalization

Items assessing generalization present a stimulus and ask the student to identify which of several response possibilities goes with the stimulus. Again,

FIGURE 9.2   Items That Assess Figural, Symbolic, and Semantic Discrimination

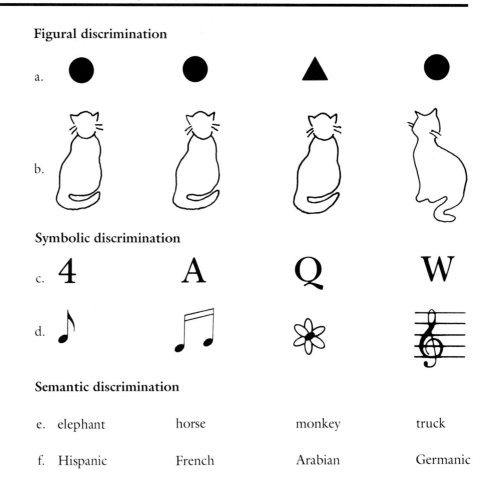

Figural discrimination

a.

b.

Symbolic discrimination

c.   4   A   Q   W

d.

Semantic discrimination

e.   elephant   horse   monkey   truck

f.   Hispanic   French   Arabian   Germanic the content of the items may be figural, symbolic, or semantic; the difficulty may range from simple matching to a more difficult type of classification. Figure 9.3 illustrates several items assessing generalization. In each case, the student is given a stimulus element and required to identify the one that is like it or that goes with it.

Motor Behavior

Many items on intelligence tests require a motor response. The intellectual level of very young children, for example, is often assessed by items requiring them to throw objects, walk, follow moving objects with their eyes, demonstrate a pincer grasp in picking up objects, build block towers, and place geometric forms in a recessed-form board. Most motor items at higher age levels are actually visual-motor items. The student may be required to copy geometric designs, trace paths through a maze, or reconstruct designs from memory. Obviously, since motor responses can be required for items assessing understanding and conceptualization, many items assess motor behavior at the same time that they assess other behaviors.

FIGURE 9.3   Items That Assess Figural, Symbolic, and Semantic Discrimination

Figural generalization

a.

b.

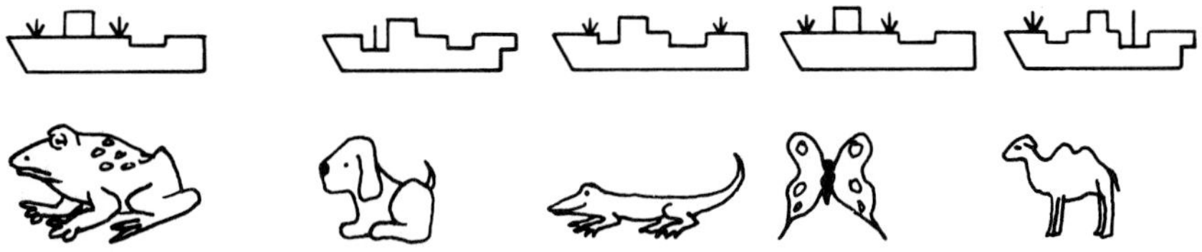

Symbolic generalization

| c. | J | H | 8 | 6 | 9 |
| d. | 81 | 21 | 23 | 26 | 25 |

Semantic generalization

| e. | tree | car | man | house | walk |
| f. | salvia | flashlight | frog | tulip | banana |

General Information

Items on intelligence tests sometimes require a student to answer specific factual questions, such as "In what direction would you travel if you were to go from Poland to Argentina?" and "What is the cube root of 8?" Essentially, such items are like the kinds of items in achievement tests; they assess primarily what has been learned.

Vocabulary

Many different kinds of test items are used to assess vocabulary. The student must name pictures in some cases and in others must point to objects in response to words read by the examiner. Some vocabulary items require the student to produce oral definitions of words, whereas others call for reading a definition and selecting one of several words to match the definition. Some tests score a student's definitions of words as simply pass or fail; others use a weighted scoring system to reflect the degree of abstraction used in defining words. The Wechsler Intelligence Scale for Children–Revised, for example, assigns zero points to incorrect definitions, one point to definitions that are descriptive (an orange is round) or functional (an orange is to eat), and two points to more abstract definitions (an orange is a citrus fruit).

Induction

Induction items present a series of examples and require the student to induce a governing principle. For example, the student is given a magnet and several different cloth, wooden, and metal objects and is asked to try to pick up the objects with the magnet. After several trials the student is asked to state a governing rule or principle about the kinds of objects magnets can pick up.

Comprehension

There are three kinds of items used to assess comprehension. The student gives evidence of comprehension of directions, printed material, or societal customs and mores. In some instances, the examiner presents a specific situation and asks what actions the student would take (for example, "What would you do if you saw a train approaching a washed-out bridge?"). In other cases, the examiner reads paragraphs to a student and then asks specific questions about the content of the paragraphs. In still other instances, the student is asked specific questions like "Why should we keep promises?"

Sequencing

Items assessing sequencing consist of a series of stimuli that have a progressive relationship among them, and the student must identify a response that continues the relationship. Four sequencing items are illustrated in Figure 9.4.

Detail Recognition

In general, not many tests or test items assess detail recognition. Those that do evaluate the completeness and detail with which a student solves problems. For example, certain drawing tests, such as the Goodenough-Harris, evaluate a student's drawing of a person on the basis of inclusion of detail. The more details in a student's drawing, the more credit the student earns. In other instances, items require a student to count the blocks in pictured piles of blocks in which some of the blocks are not directly visible, to copy geometric designs, or to identify missing parts in pictures. To do so correctly, the student must attend to detail in the stimulus drawings and reflect this attention to detail in making responses.

Analogies

"A is to B as C is to ___" is the usual form for analogies items. Element A is related to element B. The student must identify the response that has the

FIGURE 9.4   Items That Assess Sequencing Skill

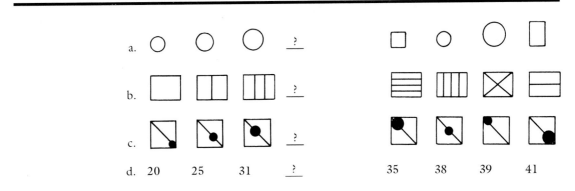

same relationship to C as B has to A. Figure 9.5 illustrates several different analogies items.

Abstract Reasoning

A variety of items on intelligence tests sample abstract reasoning ability. The Stanford-Binet Intelligence Scale, for example, presents absurd verbal statements and pictures and asks the student to identify the absurdity. It also includes a series of proverbs whose essential meanings the student must state. In the Stanford-Binet and other scales, arithmetic-reasoning problems are often thought to assess abstract reasoning.

Memory

Several different kinds of tasks assess memory: repetition of sequences of orally presented digits, reproduction of geometric designs from memory, verbatim repetition of sentences, and reconstruction of the essential meaning of paragraphs or stories. Simply saying that an item assesses memory is too simplistic. We need to ask, "Memory for what?" The psychological demand of a memory task changes in relation to both the method of assessment and the meaningfulness of the material to be recalled.

Pattern Completion

Some tests and test items require a student to select from several possibilities the one that supplies the missing part of a pattern or matrix. Figures 9.6 and

FIGURE 9.5   Analogies Items

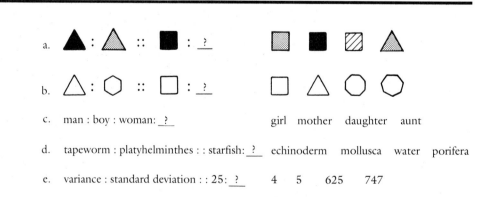

9.7 illustrate two different completion items. The item in Figure 9.6 requires identification of a missing part in a pattern. The item in Figure 9.7 calls for identification of the response that completes the matrix by continuing the horizontal, vertical, and diagonal sequences.

Summary

The practice of intellectual assessment of children is currently marked by controversy. However, much of that controversy could be set aside if intelligence tests were viewed appropriately. Intelligence tests are simply samples of behavior. And different intelligence tests sample different behaviors. For that reason, it is wrong to speak of a person's IQ. Instead, we can refer only to a

FIGURE 9.6   A Pattern-Completion Item

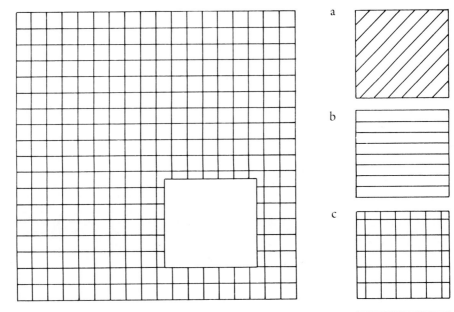

person's IQ on a specific test. An IQ on the Stanford-Binet Intelligence Scale is not derived from the same samples of behaviors as an IQ on any other intelligence test. Because the behavior samples are different for different tests, one must always ask, "IQ *on what test?*"

The same test may make different psychological demands on test takers, depending on their ages and acculturation. Test results mean different things for different students. It is imperative that we be especially aware of the relationship between a person's acculturation and the acculturation of the norm group to which that person is compared.

Intelligence tests are samples of behavior. While many different kinds of behaviors are sampled by these tests, we have described 13 kinds: discrimination, generalization, motor behavior, general information, vocabulary, induction, comprehension, sequencing, detail recognition, analogies, abstract reasoning, memory, pattern completion.

FIGURE 9.7   A Matrix-Completion Item

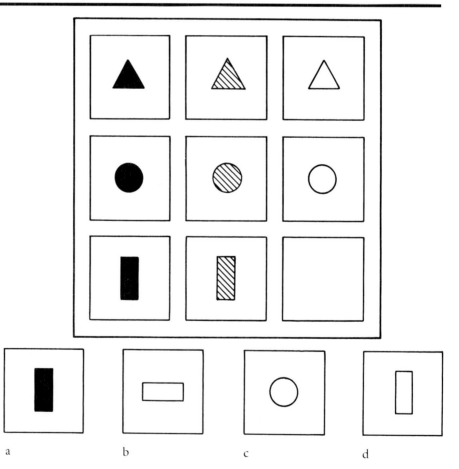

STUDY QUESTIONS

1. How would you demonstrate that a particular test item measured intelligence?
2. Describe at least three kinds of behaviors sampled by intelligence tests.
3. Bill Jones fails an item requiring him to state the difference between an optimist and a pessimist. Give two explanations for Bill's failure.
4. The school psychologist tells you that Emily Andrews has an IQ of 89. What additional information do you need before you are able to know the meaning of the score?
5. Using the categorization of behavior samplings described in this chapter, identify the kind or kinds of behaviors sampled by the following test items.
   a. How many legs does an octopus have?
   b. In what way are *first* and *last* alike?
   c. Find the one that is different: (1) table (2) bed (3) pillow (4) chair.
   d. Who wrote *Macbeth*?
   e. Window is to sill as door is to ___. (1) knob (2) entrance (3) threshold (4) pane
   f. Define *hieroglyphic*.
   g. Identify the one that comes next: 3, 6, 9, ___. (1) 12 (2) 11 (3) 18 (4) 15
6. Public Law 94-142 requires nondiscriminatory assessment of handicapped children. How can you demonstrate that a test is nondiscriminatory?

ADDITIONAL READING

Bersoff, D. N. (1973). Silk purses into sows' ears: The decline of psychological testing and a suggestion for its redemption. *American Psychologist, 10,* 892–899.

Cancro, R. (Ed.). (1980). *Intelligence: Genetic and environmental contributions.* New York: Grune & Stratton.

Cronbach, L. J. (1975). Five decades of public controversy over mental testing. *American Psychologist, 30,* 1–14.

McClelland, D. (1973). Testing for competence rather than for "intelligence." *American Psychologist, 1,* 1–14.

Siegel, L. S. (1989). IQ is irrelevant to the definition of learning disabilities. *Journal of Learning Disabilities, 22,* 469–479.

Torgeson, J. K. (1989). Why IQ is relevant to the definition of learning disabilities. *Journal of Learning Disabilities, 22,* 484–486.

C·H·A·P·T·E·R 10

ASSESSMENT OF INTELLIGENCE: INDIVIDUAL TESTS

In Chapter 9 we discussed the various kinds of behaviors sampled by intelligence tests, indicating that different tests sample different behaviors. In this chapter we will review the most commonly used individually administered intelligence tests with special reference to the kinds of behaviors they sample and to their technical adequacy.

Few individual intelligence tests can or should be administered by classroom teachers. Yet, over the last few years, test developers have developed intelligence tests with the specific intent that teachers or other nonpsychologists would be able to administer them. For example, the Test of Nonverbal Intelligence is specifically designed to be given by teachers. The Slosson Intelligence Test is described as equivalent to the Stanford-Binet Intelligence Scale, yet it can be given by people with no formal training in assessment. You will recall that one of the basic assumptions underlying psychoeducational assessment is that the person who uses tests is adequately trained to administer, score, and interpret them. The correct administration, scoring, and interpretation of individual intelligence tests is complex. Such tests should be used only by licensed or certified psychologists, who have specific training in their use.

Three kinds of individually administered intelligence tests are reviewed in this chapter. First, we review the most commonly used global measures of intelligence—the Stanford-Binet Intelligence Scale, the three Wechsler scales, the Slosson Intelligence Test, the Detroit Tests of Learning Aptitude, and the McCarthy Scales of Children's Abilities. In general, these tests sample the thirteen different kinds of behavior described in Chapter 9.

The second section of this chapter reviews the most commonly used picture vocabulary tests, instruments that assess receptive vocabulary but yield IQs.

Many children have handicaps (for example, blindness, deafness, and physical handicaps) that interfere with their capability to respond to traditional general intelligence tests. This fact has led several test authors to develop individually administered tests designed to assess the intelligence of blind, deaf, physically handicapped, and multiply handicapped persons. In a sense, the old adage "Necessity is the mother of invention" applies to these devices. The third section of this chapter is a review of individually administered tests designed for use with special populations of children.

Why Do We Give Individual Intelligence Tests?

Individually administered intelligence tests are most frequently used for making educational placement decisions. State special education standards typically specify that the collection of data about intellectual functioning must be included in the decision-making process for placement decisions and that these data must come from individual intellectual evaluation by a certified psychologist.

General Intelligence Tests
Stanford-Binet Intelligence Scale: Fourth Edition

The fourth edition of the Stanford-Binet (SB) (Thorndike, Hagen, & Sattler, 1985) is the latest version of the scale originally developed by Alfred Binet in 1905 and revised for American children by Terman and Merrill (1916, 1937). The 1960 version of the scale combined the best items from earlier forms into one form (L–M) and provided new norms with deviation IQs. Although the scale (Terman & Merrill, 1973) was renormed for the 1972 normative edition, this edition was not a revision because the 1960 items were used.

The fourth edition maintains some continuity with the past, but also brings the SB up to date. Additionally, it eliminates age scores because—even though the concept of mental age played an important role in earlier editions of the scale—age scales have several drawbacks. Like its predecessors, the new SB is an individually administered, norm-referenced measure of general intelligence that can be given to persons between the ages of 2 and 23.

Fifteen subtests are grouped into four areas: verbal reasoning, quantitative reasoning, abstract/visual reasoning, and short-term memory. The authors retained as many types of items from the 1960 version as could be fit into one of these four areas. Because of the extended range of ages, not all test takers are given all subtests; a complete battery requires from eight to thirteen subtests. Nevertheless, under certain circumstances (for screening, the identification of gifted students, or the assessment of students with school-learning difficulties), various abbreviated test batteries may also be used. The specific subtests are listed below according to the behavior sampled.

Verbal Reasoning

Vocabulary There are forty-six vocabulary items. The first fourteen use a picture vocabulary format. The remainder are presented orally and visually (on a printed form) and answered orally.

Comprehension The forty-two comprehension items require a test taker to explain why something is done or what should be done (for example, the sample items "Why do buildings have fire escapes?" and "Why should lawyers be licensed?").

Absurdities This thirty-two-item subtest requires a test taker to explain why the pictures presented are absurd (for example, one of a fish being walked).

Verbal Relations The subject is presented with four objects and must explain in what way three of them are alike and the fourth is different. (For example, in response to the sample item "Jim, Bob, Kate, not John," the test taker is expected to answer that the first three names are nicknames, or informal names, and the last is not.)

QUANTITATIVE REASONING

Quantitative This subtest assesses computation skills using forty-eight problems in two formats. The first twelve questions, designed for youngsters, require the test taker to use a counting tray and blocks to answer mathematical questions (for example, questions about counting). Questions geared to older individuals take the form of pictures or written questions.

Number Series The test taker is presented with a series of numbers and expected to induce the rule that governs the series. (For example, a student presented with the sample sequence 4, 9, 16, 25, 36, __ is expected to complete the series with 49, because $4 = 2^2$, $9 = $

3^2, $16 = 4^2$, $25 = 5^2$, $36 = 6^2$, and $49 = 7^2$.) There are twenty-six problems in this subtest.

Equation Building The test taker is presented with a sequence of numbers and mathematical symbols and instructed to arrange them in a way that forms a valid equation. (For example, a student given the sample series 2, 2, 8, 4, ×, +, = is expected to reformulate the sequence as $2 \times 2 + 4 = 8$.) There are eighteen equations.

ABSTRACT/VISUAL REASONING

Pattern Analysis Because the SB covers a wide range of ages, two sets of materials are used in this subtest. A three-hole form board is used with very young children, who must place the geometric forms in the correct holes or combine parts to make the geometric forms and then place them in the correct holes. Older individuals are given up to nine cubes with various geometric patterns; they are then shown a stimulus design and asked to reproduce it with the cubes. Credit is awarded on the basis of accuracy and completion within the time limits.

Copying The twenty-eight items on this subtest consist of designs of increasing complexity to be copied by the test taker. The type of copying required depends on the level of the test. At the lower levels, the designs are copied with blocks. At the higher levels, the designs are drawn with a pencil.

Matrices Two types of problems are given in this subtest. The first twenty-two problems, designed for younger children, are multiple-choice matrix-completion problems. The first twelve involve 2×2 matrices; the next ten involve 3×3 matrices. The last four problems, for older children, require the test taker to complete the matrices by writing the correct responses. The format of each of these problems is the same: a 3×3 matrix in which each of the nine stimuli is actually a smaller 3×3 matrix.

Paper Folding and Cutting   This eighteen-item, multiple-choice subtest consists of pictures. Each item has two parts: the item stem shows how a rectangular sheet of paper is folded and cut; the response options include one that correctly shows what the paper would look like after it had been cut and unfolded. The most difficult item has three folds and one area cut out.

SHORT-TERM MEMORY

Bead Memory   Beads of different colors (red, white, blue) and shapes (flat and round, spherical, conical, cylindrical) are used in this subtest. The type of items used depends on the level at which testing occurs. On lower-level items, the subject is required to look at one bead for 2 seconds (or two beads for 3 seconds) and then correctly identify the bead (beads) on a card containing assorted pictures of beads. At higher levels, the subject looks for 5 seconds at a picture of colored beads of different shapes strung on a stick and then must reproduce the design with his or her own beads and stick.

Memory for Sentences   The examiner reads a sentence and the test taker must repeat that sentence verbatim. The forty-two sentences range from simple (of this type: "Marv walked the cat") to complex (of this type: "Books and reading were now a very important part of Rosemary's everyday plans, opening new worlds and bringing new adventures her way").

Memory for Digits   After listening to a sequence of digits, the test taker must repeat it. Half of the sequences are to be repeated backward.

Memory for Objects   This subtest assesses visual sequential memory with fourteen items. After showing a picture of a common object for one second and then another picture of a different object for one second, the examiner shows a picture containing several objects, including the two that were shown previously. The test taker must select the previously shown pictures in the order in which they were shown. At the highest level, a subject may be shown eight objects and asked to recall them in order.

Scores   Raw scores for each subtest are converted to Standard Age Scores (SAS). These scores have a mean of 50 and a standard deviation of 8. Subtest scores are combined into area scores and an overall composite score, each with a mean of 100 and a standard deviation of 16. Extensive tables are provided for these conversions. The procedures for extrapolating scores at the extremes are carefully reported and appear appropriate.

NORMS

The normative sample was selected on the basis of five variables: age, sex, ethnicity (white, black, Hispanic, and Asian/Pacific Islander), geographic region, and community size. Extensive tables provided in the technical manual indicate reasonably good correspondence on each of these variables. Nevertheless, when an appropriate number of subjects with particular characteristics could not be located, those who were tested were weighted so as to count for more than one; similarly, when there were too many subjects with a particular characteristic, each was weighted so as to count for less than one.

RELIABILITY

Internal consistency (KR-20), SEMs, and stability coefficients are reported for each subtest, for each area, and for the composite at each age level. As would be expected, subtest reliabilities are lower than composite reliabilities. The test authors recommend that the composite score "be used as the primary source of information for making decisions" (Thorndike, Hagen, & Sattler, 1986, p. 38). All KR-20s for these SAS composites are excellent; they range from a low of .95 to a high of .99. Test-retest data were available for two groups of children, five-year-olds ($n = 57$) and eight-year-olds ($n = 55$). Stability coefficients for these two groups were .91 and .90.

KR-20s for the areas are based on different numbers of subtests. The more subtests, the higher the reliability. For abstract reasoning, all reliabilities exceed .90 except when two subtests are used at ages 2 and 3. For quantitative reasoning, internal consistencies based on one subtest are all lower than .90; those based on two or more subtests are all higher than .90 with the exception of those for seven-year-olds when a two-test composite is used. For short-term memory, all area scores have reliabilities exceeding .90 when three or four subtests are used. When only two subtests are used, nine of the seventeen age groups have short-term-memory-area reliabilities in the high .80s; whereas the rest are in the low .90s. Stabilities for areas ranged from a low of .51 (quantitative reasoning at age 5) to a high of .88 (verbal reasoning, also at age 5).

VALIDITY

The authors explain the SB within the context of current theoretical formulations about intelligence, justifying the development of a scale that assesses "g." The primary validity of interest for an intelligence scale is its construct validity. For the new SB, construct validity was established by conducting factor analyses to confirm a "g" factor and factors for each of the areas. Although "g" held up across ages, the factor structure varied for different age groups. For example, the quantitative factor did not emerge until after age 11.

Several concurrent validity studies were also conducted with the new SB. In one study, using a sample of children between about 2 and 10 years of age, the old SB (form L-M) correlated with the new composite IQ ($r = .81$). In another study, using a sample of children between about 6 and 13 years of age, the Wechsler Intelligence Scale for Children–Revised Full Scale IQ was highly correlated with the SB composite IQ ($r = .83$). The correlation of the new SB was .80 with the Wechsler Preschool and Primary Scale of Intelligence and .91 with the Wechsler Adult Intelligence Scale–Revised. For a sample of children (mean age = 70-0, standard deviation = 2-5), the correlation of the SB with the Mental Processing Composite of the Kaufman Assessment Battery for Children was .89.

Finally, eight studies were conducted that examined the performance of previously identified gifted, learning disabled, and mentally retarded students. These studies are difficult to interpret because criteria vary dramatically from state to state. No data are presented to indicate the degree of correspondence between decisions based on the new SB and the original decisions based on other devices. As would be expected, students classified as gifted received higher than average composite IQs (mean composite IQ = 123.3, $S = 11.2$); students classified as learning disabled received lower than average composite IQs (mean composite IQ = 85.1, $S = 14.6$); and students classified as mentally retarded received the lowest composite IQs (mean composite IQ = 54.9, $S = 16.2$).

SUMMARY

The new Stanford-Binet Intelligence Scale is a marked improvement over previous editions.

The behavior sample is psychologically interesting and the materials are appealing. Not only does the SB provide the technical data needed to evaluate the adequacy of its reliability and norms; the data indicate a well-normed and highly reliable device. There is also ample evidence of content and concurrent validity and some evidence of construct validity. It is unclear how effective the new SB will be in classifying exceptional students. It is becoming clear, however, that the SB requires significantly more time to administer than other individually administered tests of intelligence do.

THE WECHSLER SCALES

Three different measures of intelligence have been constructed by David Wechsler. Wechsler summarized his views on the concept of intelligence by stating that "intelligence is the overall capacity of an individual to understand and cope with the world around him" (Wechsler, 1974, p. 5). Wechsler states that his definition of intelligence differs from the conceptions of others in two important respects:

(1) *It conceives of intelligence as an overall or* global *entity; that is, a multidetermined and multifaceted entity rather than an independent, uniquely defined trait.*
(2) *It avoids singling out any ability (e.g., abstract reasoning), however esteemed as crucial or overwhelmingly important. In particular, it avoids equating general intelligence with intellectual ability.* (p. 5)

The original Wechsler scale, the Wechsler-Bellevue Intelligence Scale (1939), designed to assess the intelligence of adults, was revised in 1955 and called the Wechsler Adult Intelligence Scale (WAIS). Its present form is called the Wechsler Adult Intelligence Scale–Revised (WAIS-R). In 1949, Wechsler developed the Wechsler Intelligence Scale for Children (WISC). This scale was revised and restandardized in 1974; its present form is called the Wechsler Intelligence Scale for Children–Revised (WISC-R). In 1967, Wechsler developed a downward extension of the WISC, the Wechsler Preschool and Primary Scale of Intelligence (WPPSI). The WPPSI was revised and restandardized in 1989 and is now called the WPPSI-R. Although the three scales are similar in form and content, they are distinct scales designed for use with persons at different age levels. The WAIS-R is designed for use with individuals over 16 years of age; the WISC-R is designed to assess the intelligence of persons 6 through 16 years of age; the WPPSI-R is used with children ages 3 through 7. All three scales are point scales; all three include both verbal and performance subtests. A special edition of the WISC-R, standardized on deaf and hearing-impaired students, is published by Gallaudet University. Subtests of the three Wechsler scales are summarized in Table 10.1.

TABLE 10.1   Subtests of the Three Wechsler Scales

	WAIS-R	WISC-R	WPPSI-R
Verbal subtests			
Information	X	X	X
Comprehension	X	X	X
Similarities	X	X	X
Arithmetic	X	X	X
Vocabulary	X	X	X
Digit Span	X	S[b]	
Sentences			S
Performance subtests			
Picture Completion	S	X	X
Picture Arrangement	X	X	
Block Design	X	X	X
Object Assembly	X	X	X
Coding[a]	X	X	X
Mazes		S	X
Geometric Design			X

[a] Called Digit Symbol on the WAIS-R and Animal Pegs on the WPPSI-R.

[b] S's in the table indicate that although the subtest is included in the scale, it is considered a supplementary subtest and was not used in establishing IQ tables.

Although the Wechsler scales differ in terms of age-level appropriateness, they sample similar behaviors. Descriptions of the behaviors sampled by each of the verbal and performance subtests follows; differences in format among the three scales are noted where appropriate.

Information   The Information subtest assesses ability to answer specific factual questions. The content is learned; it consists of information that a person is expected to have acquired in both formal and informal educational settings. The examinee is asked questions such as "Which fast food franchise is represented by the symbol of a colonel?"

Comprehension   The Comprehension subtest assesses ability to comprehend verbal directions or to understand specific customs and mores.

The examinee is asked questions such as "Why is it important to wear boots after a large snowfall?"

Similarities   This subtest requires identification of similarities or commonalities in superficially unrelated verbal stimuli.

Arithmetic   This subtest assesses ability to solve problems requiring the application of arithmetic operations. Individual items range from relatively simple counting tasks on the WPPSI to conceptually and computationally more difficult problems on the WISC-R and the WAIS.

Vocabulary   Items on the Vocabulary subtest assess ability to define words. For the WPPSI-R, the Vocabulary subtest is a two-part test. At the lower age levels, children are required to name pictured objects. At higher age levels, the child defines words.

Digit Span   This subtest assesses immediate recall of orally presented digits. There is no Digit Span subtest for the WPPSI-R.

Sentences   This subtest is included only in the WPPSI-R. It assesses ability to repeat sentences verbatim.

Picture Completion   This subtest assesses the ability to identify missing parts in pictures.

Picture Arrangement   The Picture Arrangement subtest assesses comprehension, sequencing, and identification of relationships by requiring a person to place pictures in sequence to produce a logically correct story.

Block Design   This subtest assesses ability to manipulate blocks in order to reproduce a visually presented stimulus design.

Object Assembly   This subtest assesses ability to place disjointed puzzle pieces together to form complete objects. The WPPSI-R now includes an Object Assembly subtest; the subtest was not included in the WPPSI.

Coding (Animal Pegs for WPPSI-R)   This subtest assesses the ability to associate certain symbols with others and to copy them on paper. The WPPSI-R uses the Animal Pegs subtest in place of the Coding subtest. Instead of copying symbols on paper, the child must associate certain colored cubes with specific animals and match them.

Mazes   The Mazes subtest assesses ability to trace a path through progressively more difficult mazes.

Geometric Design   This subtest appears on only the WPPSI-R. Two distinct types of tasks are included. The first section is a visual recognition task. The child looks at a simple design and, with the stimulus in full view, picks one like it from a response array. The remaining items require the child to copy a geometric design by drawing.

SCORES

Raw scores obtained on the three Wechsler scales are transformed to scaled scores with a mean of 10 and a standard deviation of 3. The scaled scores for verbal subtests, performance subtests, and all subtests combined are added and then transformed to obtain verbal, performance, and full-scale IQs. IQs for the Wechsler scales are deviation IQs with a mean of 100 and a standard deviation of 15. For the WPPSI-R and the WISC-R, but not for the WAIS-R, raw scores may be transformed to test ages. Test ages represent the average performance on each of the subtests by individuals of specific ages.

The Wechsler intelligence scales employ a differential scoring system for some of the subtests. Responses for the Information, Digit Span, Sentences, Picture Completion, and Geometric Designs subtests are scored pass-fail. A weighted scoring system is used for the Comprehension, Similarities, and Vocabulary subtests. Incorrect responses receive a score of 0, lower-level or lower-quality responses are assigned a score of 1, and more abstract responses are assigned a score of 2. The remainder of the subtests are timed. Individuals who complete the tasks in relatively short periods of time receive more credit. These differential weightings of responses must be given special consideration, especially when the timed tests are used with children who demonstrate motoric impairments that interfere with the speed of response.

NORMS

All three Wechsler intelligence scales were standardized by selecting stratified samples and having individual examiners around the country administer the tests to specified kinds of individuals.

The WAIS-R was standardized "based on groups considered representative of the United States adult population" (Wechsler, 1981, p. 16). A stratified sampling plan based on age, sex, race, geographic region, occupation, education, and urban-rural residence was used. Proportions of specific kinds of individuals were included commensurate with their representation in the 1950 census. The WAIS-R was standardized on 1,880 adults, and extensive tables in the manual compare the percentage of the U.S. population to the percentage of specific kinds of individuals in the norms.

The WISC-R was standardized on 2,200 children ages 6½ to 16½. The standardization group was stratified on the basis of age, sex, race, geographic region, occupation of head of household, and urban-rural residence according to 1970 U.S. Census information.

The WPPSI-R was administered to over 2,100 children, including the 1,700 children used for norming and an oversample of 400 minority children used to investigate item bias. The sample was stratified by age, and within age on the basis of sex, geographic region, ethnicity, and parental education and occupation. The standardization sample is made up of a hundred boys and a hundred girls at each age in half-year age intervals. Tables in the manual show the match of proportions in the standardization sample to proportions in 1986 census data. The sample is representative of the U.S. population of children ages 3-7.

RELIABILITY

Internal-consistency reliability is reported for the WAIS-R, WISC-R, and WPPSI-R in the forms of split-half reliability coefficients. The reliabilities differ for the specific subtests and the age levels on which the coefficients are based. Ranges of reliability are reported for the three scales in Table 10.2. Reliabilities for the separate subtests are reliabilities of scaled scores, whereas reliabilities for verbal, performance, and full-scale IQs are reliabilities for the IQs. Reliabilities for the Coding (Digit Symbol) subtest on the WAIS-R, the Digit Span and Coding subtests of the WISC-R, and the Coding subtest (Animal Pegs) of the WPPSI-R are test-retest reliabilities. Test-retest reliabilities are reported for all subtests of the WISC-R in the test manual and range from .63 to .95.

Reliabilities for the WPPSI-R subtests are low. All reliabilities are below .90 with three exceptions: Information at ages 3 and 4-5, Picture Completion at age 4-5. Reliabilities of the WPPSI-R subtests are especially low at age 7. Reliabilities of composite scores are considerably higher than those for subtests. We recommend that interpretations of the WPPSI-R be at the composite score level rather than at the subtest level.

VALIDITY

No evidence for the validity of the WAIS-R is included in the manual. Instead, it is argued that (1) the WAIS-R and WAIS overlap considerably in content, (2) there are many studies of the validity of the WAIS, and (3) the WAIS-R will no doubt correlate with other measures of

TABLE 10.2   Split-Half Reliabilities for Subtests of the Three Wechsler Scales

	WAIS-R	WISC-R	WPPSI-R
Verbal subtests			
Information	.87–.91	.67–.90	.62–.90
Comprehension	.77–.90	.69–.87	.59–.88
Similarities	.78–.87	.74–.87	.54–.89
Arithmetic	.73–.87	.69–.81	.66–.81
Vocabulary	.94–.96	.70–.92	.74–.87
Digit Span	.70–.89[a]	.71–.84[a]	—
Sentences	—	—	.73–.88
Verbal IQ	.95–.97	.91–.96	.86–.96
Performance subtests			
Picture Completion	.71–.89	.68–.85	.72–.89
Picture Arrangement	.66–.82	.69–.78	—
Block Design	.83–.89	.80–.90	.79–.88
Object Assembly	.52–.73	.63–.76	.54–.70
Coding[a]	.73–.86[a]	.63–.80[a]	.58[a]
Mazes	—	.62–.82	.65–.85
Geometric Design	—	—	.68–.86
Performance IQ	.86–.94	.89–.91	.85–.93
Full-scale IQ	.96–.98	.95–.96	.90–.97

[a] Test-retest reliability

global intelligence as well as the WAIS did. In fact, 20 percent of the items on the WAIS-R are new items. It cannot be asserted that the WAIS-R is valid because the Wechsler-Bellevue and WAIS were valid.

Three concurrent validity studies were used to ascertain the relationship between performance on the WISC-R and on other measures of intelligence. In the first study, fifty 6-year-old children were administered both the WISC-R and the WPPSI. The WISC-R full-scale IQ and the WPPSI full-scale IQ had an .82 correlation. Individual verbal subtests correlated more highly with the WPPSI verbal IQ than with the WPPSI performance IQ. Similarly, individual performance subtests correlated more highly with the WPPSI performance IQ than with the WPPSI verbal IQ. In a second study, forty children aged 16 years, 11 months, were

given the WISC-R and the WAIS; the full-scale IQs on the two devices had a .95 correlation. Verbal IQs on the two devices were intercorrelated .96; performance IQs, .83. A third study was conducted to compare performance on the WISC-R with performance on the Stanford-Binet Intelligence Scale. Small samples of children (twenty-seven to thirty-three) at four ages were given both tests. Average correlations between 1972 Stanford-Binet IQs and WISC-R verbal, performance, and full-scale IQs were .71, .60, and .73, respectively. The WAIS, WPPSI, and Stanford-Binet have been revised and renormed since publication of the WISC-R.

Evidence for the validity of the WPPSI-R is presented in the manual. Much of the evidence is evidence for the validity of the WPPSI. Since the WPPSI-R includes 50 percent new items and has been restandardized, evidence for validity of the WPPSI is irrelevant to validity of the WPPSI-R.

The WPPSI-R is shown to correlate very highly with the WISC-R for fifty students ages 72–86 months living in Jacksonville, Florida. Correlations with the Stanford-Binet 4 were shown to be moderate. Performance on the WPPSI-R is more closely related to performance on the McCarthy Scales than to performance on the Stanford-Binet 4. Correlations between performance on the WPPSI-R and the Kaufman Assessment Battery for Children were low.

Scores earned by children on the WPPSI-R are generally lower than scores they earn on other measures. It is reported in the manual that student scores on the WPPSI-R Full Scale IQ are 8 points lower than their scores on the WPPSI, 7 points lower than their scores on the WISC-R, 2 points lower than their scores on the Stanford-Binet 4, and 6 points lower than their scores on the Kaufman Assessment Battery for Children.

SUMMARY

The three Wechsler intelligence scales (WAIS-R, WISC-R, WPPSI-R) are widely used individually administered intelligence tests. Although they are designed for different age levels, the three scales are similar in content and format. Evidence for the reliability of the three scales is good. Reliabilities are much lower for subtests, and subtest scores should not be used in making placement decisions. Evidence for validity, as presented in the manuals, is either nonexistent (WAIS-R) or very limited (WISC-R and WPPSI-R).

SLOSSON INTELLIGENCE TEST

The Slosson Intelligence Test (SIT) (Slosson, 1971) is a relatively short screening test used to estimate 1972 Stanford-Binet IQs. The test includes many items that appear in the 1972 Stanford-Binet, and the authors of the 1981 norms book for the SIT state that "the SIT and the SB are in most respects alternate forms of the same test instrument" (Armstrong & Jensen, 1981, p. 14). The test is merely designed to generate a number—an estimate of Stanford-Binet IQ. Whereas the Stanford-Binet is designed to give an examiner both a quantitative and a qualitative picture of intellectual functioning, the SIT is designed merely to yield a score—a quantitative index of intellectual functioning.

The SIT is designed to be administered by teachers, guidance counselors, principals, psychologists, school nurses, and "other responsible persons who, in their professional work, often need to evaluate an individual's mental ability" (Slosson, 1971, p. iii). The author does not report an age range of individuals who may be tested with the Slosson. Items range from the .5-month level to the 27-year level; the 1981 standardization was on people from 27 months to 17 years, 2 months. Apparently, the author (Slosson, 1971) believes the test is appropriate for nearly anyone, as there are directions in the manual for testing infants, those who have "reading handicaps" or "language handicaps," the blind, the hard of hearing, those with organic impairments, the emotionally disturbed, and the "deprived." There are, though, no data on the use of the test with these groups. Behaviors sampled by the SIT include most of the behaviors described and discussed in Chapter 9.

Scores

Raw scores for the SIT may be transformed to deviation IQs with a mean of 100 and a standard deviation of 16. To do so, the examiner does not use the procedures recommended in the manual, but uses the publication *Slosson Intelligence Test: 1981 Norms Tables* (Armstrong & Jensen, 1981). IQs may also be expressed as percentile ranks, normal curve equivalents, *T*-scores, or stanines.

Norms

The normative sample for the SIT consisted of a potpourri of individuals who are described by Slosson (1971) as follows:

> The children and adults used in obtaining comparative results came from both urban and rural populations in New York State. The referrals came from cooperative nursery schools, public, parochial and private schools, from junior and senior high school. They came from gifted as well as retarded classes—white, negro, and some American Indian. Some came from a city Youth Bureau, some from a Home for Boys. The very young children resided in an infant home. The adults came from the general population, from various professional groups, from a university graduate school, from a state school for the retarded and from a county jail.
>
> Many of these individuals were difficult to test as they were disturbed, negativistic, withdrawn, and many had reading difficulties. Some suffered from neurological disorders or other defects. The only cases which were excluded from this study were individuals who could not speak English. (p. iv)

Items were selected on the basis of the performance of this group. Between 1968 and 1977 a sample of individuals was given both the Stanford-Binet Intelligence Scale and the SIT in order to develop a new set of norms for the SIT. The sample comprised 1,109 people, ages 27 months to 17 years, 2 months. All were from New England states and are not further described. Thus, in using the 1981 norms we know only that the individuals we test are being compared to an unspecified sample of people who live in the New England states.

A new set of norms tables for the SIT was published in 1985 (Jensen & Armstrong, 1985). This is not a new set of norms, but a reprinting of the 1981 norms along with IQ scores for very low-functioning children ages 2–0 to 5–11. The new scores are estimates and are not based on actual performance of low-functioning young children.

Reliability

The only reliability data reported for the 1981 norms edition of the SIT are "parallel forms" reliability. The authors argue that since the Stanford-Binet and SIT are "parallel forms of the same instrument," they can use data on mean differences between scores on the two tests to estimate reliability. The reasoning is circular. The SIT norms were designed by equating scores on the two instruments. Then, the authors find they correlate highly. The two measures are not, in fact, parallel forms, and the arguments made for reliability are invalid.

Validity

Arguments for the validity of the scale are based on high correlations with the Stanford-Binet. The authors argue that since the Stanford-Binet and SIT correlate .975, the two can be used interchangeably.

SUMMARY

The Slosson Intelligence Test is a screening instrument designed to give estimates of IQs on the Stanford-Binet. It was standardized on an unspecified sample of people in New England. Evidence for reliability and validity are based on correlations with the Stanford-Binet, a test to which it was statistically equated during development. Those who use the SIT to assess children are advised to use the Stanford-Binet, as it provides a more in-depth and qualitative evaluation than the SIT.

DETROIT TESTS OF LEARNING APTITUDE–2

The Detroit Tests of Learning Aptitude–2 (DTLA-2) (Hammill, 1985) is a revision of the Detroit Tests of Learning Aptitude originally published in 1935 and most recently published in 1967 (Baker & Leland, 1967). The test is described as a measure of *aptitude*, a term the author defines using the *Random House Dictionary* definition: "*1.* Capability; ability; innate or acquired capacity for something; talent *2.* Readiness in learning; intelligence" (*The Random House Dictionary of the English Language*, 1967, p. 74). There are three principal uses for the test: "(a) to determine strengths and weaknesses among intellectual abilities, (b) to identify children and youths who are significantly below their peers in aptitude, and (c) to serve as a measurement device in research studies investigating aptitude, intelligence, and cognitive behavior" (Hammill, 1985, p. 8). The DTLA-2 is designed for use with students ages 6-0 through 17-11 and takes between 50 minutes and 2 hours to administer. See the next section for a description of an earlier version of the scale, the Detroit Tests of Learning Aptitude–Primary (DTLA-P), for use with children ages 3-0 through 9-11. The eleven subtests that make up the DTLA-2 are as follows.

Word Opposites A stimulus word is read aloud, and the student is asked to state orally a word that means the opposite of the stimulus word.

Sentence Imitation The examiner reads a sentence and the student must repeat the sentence precisely.

Oral Directions The examiner gives a series of relatively complex directions orally, and the student must carry out these directions, in pencil, on a sheet of paper.

Word Sequences The student is required to repeat a series of unrelated and isolated words read by the examiner.

Story Construction The student is shown pictures and asked to make up stories in response to the pictures.

Design Reproduction Geometric forms are presented for specified time intervals and then removed. The student must draw the forms from memory.

Object Sequences The student is shown a series of pictured objects for a short time interval. After the pictures have been removed, the student is given a response sheet with the pictures in scrambled order. The student must write a numeral below each picture to indicate its position in the original display.

Symbolic Relations The student is shown a design and then must select from among six

TABLE 10.3   Domains, Composite Scores, and Subtests for the Detroit Tests of Learning Aptitude–2

Domains and Composites	Subtests
Linguistic Domain	Word Opposites
Verbal Aptititude Composite	Sentence Imitation
Nonverbal Aptitude Composite	Oral Directions
Cognitive Domain	Word Sequences
Conceptual Aptitude Composite	Story Construction
Structural Aptitude Composite	Design Reproduction
Attention Domain	Object Sequences
Attention-Enhanced Aptitude Composite	Symbolic Relations
Attention-Reduced Aptitude Composite	Conceptual Matching
Motor Domain	Word Fragments
Motor-Enhanced Aptitude Composite	Letter Sequences
Motor-Reduced Aptitude Composite	

possible responses the pattern that completes the design. The items are from the Test of Nonverbal Intelligence (Brown, Sherbenou, & Dollar, 1982).

Conceptual Matching   The student is presented with a stimulus picture and ten response pictures. The task is to select the response picture that best matches the stimulus picture. Matching is in terms of concepts rather than perceptual attributes of the pictures.

Word Fragments   The student is asked to read aloud a series of words that have various parts missing. The test is a measure of closure.

Letter Sequences   The student is shown a series of lowercase letters. After the series has been removed, the student must write down the letters in order.

The DTLA-2 provides nine composite scores in addition to the eleven subtest scores. The composites are grouped into four domains. The domains and the composites that comprise each, as well as the subtests, are listed in Table 10.3. For some of the DTLA-2 subtests there are specific basal and ceiling rules. All items of the Oral Directions, Story Construction, Object Sequences, and Letter Sequences subtests are administered. On the remaining subtests, examiners start testing at a specified point and continue until a ceiling is reached. On all tests except Design Reproduction, the ceiling is that point at which the student has failed five consecutive items. On Design Reproduction the ceiling is reached when the student has received a score of zero on three consecutive drawings.

SCORES

A raw score, percentile, and standard score are obtained for each of the subtests. The standard scores have a mean of 10 and a standard deviation of 3. In addition, the examiner can obtain a quotient for each of the following composites: General Aptitude, Verbal Aptitude, Conceptual Aptitude, Attention-Reduced Aptitude, and Motor-Reduced Aptitude. These quotients are summed and converted to a General Intelligence, or Aptitude, Quotient. Each of the quotients has a mean of 100 and a standard deviation of 15.

NORMS

The DTLA-2 was standardized on 1,532 individuals living in thirty states. The sample was obtained by asking users of the 1935 DTLA to test approximately twenty children. In addition, teams of examiners went into each of the geographic regions to administer the test. The author argues that this process produced a representative norm sample, but he does not describe specifically how the sample was stratified. He presents data in the manual showing the percentages of the DTLA-2 sample representative of each sex, residential area, race, geographic area, ethnicity, parental educational level, and age. He also shows the national census data for these same characteristics. There is a close match between the national census data and the test sample, but without additional information the norm sample cannot be considered a stratified sample.

RELIABILITY

Data on internal-consistency and test-retest reliability are presented in the manual. Reliability coefficients for the subtests ranged from .76 to .97; 88 percent of the coefficients exceeded .80, and 38 percent exceeded .90. Reliability coefficients for the composites all exceeded .90. Test-retest reliability was established by giving the test twice to a group of thirty-three white, suburban, middle-class students who attended private school in Austin, Texas. The students ranged in age from 6 to 17, and the test was given at two-week intervals. The obtained reliabilities for both subtest and composite scores were below .80 except for the Word Opposites subtest and the Verbal

Quotient. Although there is good evidence for internal consistency, data on test-retest reliability are not convincing.

VALIDITY

In an effort to establish concurrent validity, data on how the standardization sample subjects performed on other tests were obtained from their records. Seventy-six students had been given the WISC-R, and twenty-five students had been given the Peabody Picture Vocabulary Test (*not* the PPVT-R). Times of test administration are not specified; all of the students were either enrolled in special education classes or being screened for special education placement. Correlations of the subtest scores ranged from .42 to .76 with the WISC-R and from .40 to .72 with the PPVT. Correlations of the DTLA-2 composites ranged from .54 to .84 with the WISC-R and from .61 to .79 with the PPVT. These data are not convincing: the sample is unrepresentative, the PPVT is obsolete, and variability between testing times is uncontrolled.

As further evidence for the validity of the DTLA-2, the author demonstrates that scores on the DTLA-2 increase with age. The subtests are highly correlated, and twelve students with scores below 80 on the WISC-R scored below 80 on the DTLA-2. There were also moderate correlations between the DTLA-2 and SRA Achievement Series scores of seventy-seven students in a public school in Texas.

SUMMARY

The Detroit Tests of Learning Aptitude–2 is a major revision of the Detroit Tests of Learning Aptitude first published in 1935. The test is used to provide a measure of learning aptitude in nine composite areas. There are questions regarding the extent to which the test was normed on a stratified sample of the U.S. population. Although there is good evidence for the internal consistency of the test, data on test-retest reliability are not convincing. There is limited information on the validity of the test.

Detroit Tests of Learning Aptitude–Primary

The Detroit Tests of Learning Aptitude–Primary (DTLA-P) (Hammill & Bryant, 1986) is a special level of the DTLA-2 designed for use with children ages 3-0 to 9-0. Although the test measures the same basic domains (linguistic, cognitive, attention, and motor) as the DTLA-2, it is much shorter and utilizes a different testing format. The DTLA-2 consists of 340 items grouped into eleven subtests; the DTLA-P consists of 130 items arranged in developmental order from the easiest to the most difficult. Users, however, are able to compute eight subtest scores. The names of the DTLA-P subtests are the same as the names of the DTLA-2 composites: Verbal Aptitude Subtest, Nonverbal Aptitude Subtest, Conceptual Aptitude Subtest, Structural Aptitude Subtest, Attention-Enhanced Aptitude Subtest, Attention-Reduced Aptitude Subtest, Motor-Enhanced Aptitude Subtest, and Motor-Reduced Aptitude Subtest. The DTLA-P can be given in 15 to 45 minutes, depending on the age and ability of the child. Basals and ceilings are used to shorten testing time; starting points are specified for each age level. Most of the names used by the authors to categorize the kinds of items in the DTLA-P are the same as those used for the DTLA-2 subtests: Articulation, Conceptual Matching, Design Reproduction, Digit Sequences, Draw-a-Person, Letter Sequences, Motor Directions, Object Sequences, Oral Directions, Picture Fragments, Picture Identification, Sentence Imitation, Symbolic Relations, Visual Discrimination, Word Opposites, and Word Sequences.

In selecting items for the DTLA-P, the authors conducted two preliminary studies. First the test was given to children attending two preschools in Texas. Item discrimination and item difficulty statistics were then computed. The best items were incorporated into a revised test, which was given to two other groups of students attending two preschools in Texas. The final 130 items were then selected.

Scores

A raw score, percentile, and standard score are obtained for each subtest. Standard scores for subtests have a mean of 100 and a standard deviation of 15.

Norms

The DTLA-P was standardized on 1,676 children from thirty-six states. The sample was selected by asking users of the DTLA-2 to test twenty to thirty students in their area by administering the DTLA-P. Individuals who had assisted in the development of other tests put out by the same publisher also gave the DTLA-P. Finally, teams of examiners trained by the authors went into the various geographic regions and administered the test. According to the authors, "the sites were selected particularly because their demographic characteristics were similar to those of the nation as a whole" (Hammill & Bryant, 1986, p. 33). The authors provide tables in the test manual showing the proportions of the sample representative of each sex, residential area, race, geographic area, and ethnic group.

RELIABILITY

Data on internal-consistency and test-retest reliability are provided. Internal-consistency reliability coefficients were computed on a subset of children from the standardization sample. All coefficients exceeded .90. The authors report the results of two investigations of test-retest reliability. In the first, sixty-seven students from a parochial school in Cedar Park, Texas, took the test twice at one-week intervals. In the second, children enrolled in a Head Start program in Austin, Texas, took the test twice at one-week intervals. All but two of the reliability coefficients exceeded .80.

VALIDITY

Validity data for the DTLA-P were obtained by asking those who gave the test as part of the standardization program to record other tests the students had taken, dates of testing, and scores obtained. Results were obtained for four aptitude measures (DTLA-2, WISC-R, Slosson Intelligence Scale, and PPVT-R) and for four achievement tests (SRA, CAT, Metropolitan Readiness Test, and WRAT). The authors report correlations of performance on the various measures with performance on the DTLA-P. Correlations are for an unspecified sample of students. We are told neither the ages nor characteristics of the sample. Correlations between the DTLA-P subtests and other measures of aptitude exceed those between the DTLA-P and other measures of achievement. Additional data on validity consist of demonstrations that students' scores on the test increase with age and that the subtests are highly intercorrelated. The authors conclude that the test results are highly related to measures of achievement on the basis of correlations between scores earned on the test and scores earned on other measures of achievement, collected from pupil records.

SUMMARY

The DTLA-P is a downward extension of the DTLA-2, intended to be used with children between 3 and 9 years of age. Users of the test obtain scores for each of eight different subtests. Information on how the norm sample for the test was stratified is incomplete. There is good evidence for the reliability of the scale, but data on validity are scarce.

McCarthy Scales of Children's Abilities

The McCarthy Scales of Children's Abilities (MSCA) (McCarthy, 1972) were designed to evaluate the general intellectual level of children (ages 2½ to 8½) as well as their strengths and weaknesses in a number of ability areas. The test consists of eighteen subtests that make up six scales: Verbal, Perceptual-Performance, Quantitative, Memory, Motor, and General Cognitive. The General Cognitive scale is a composite of the Verbal, Perceptual-Performance, and Quantitative scales. The interrelationships among the eighteen separate subtests and the six scales are shown in Figure 10.1.

The behaviors sampled by the subtests are described by the author as follows.

Block Building   Children copy four structures that the examiner has constructed. The author suggests that these items provide an opportunity to observe children's manipulative skills and perception of spatial relations.

Puzzle Solving   In this subtest children are required to assemble puzzle pieces to form six common animals and foods. The items meas-

FIGURE 10.1   Interrelationship of the Six Scales and Eighteen Subtests of the MSCA.

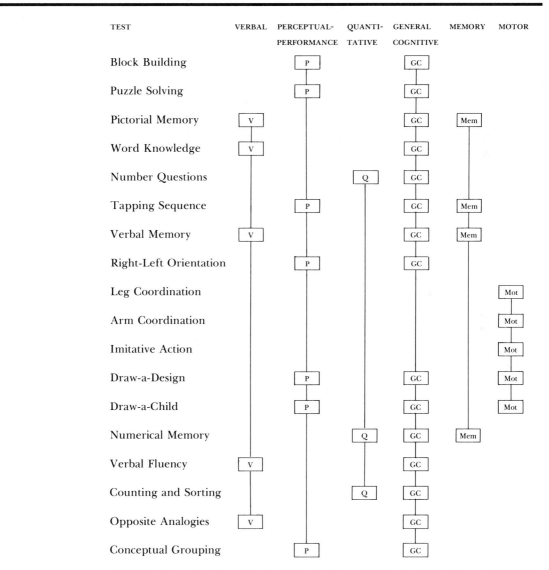

TEST	VERBAL	PERCEPTUAL-PERFORMANCE	QUANTI-TATIVE	GENERAL COGNITIVE	MEMORY	MOTOR
Block Building		P		GC		
Puzzle Solving		P		GC		
Pictorial Memory	V			GC	Mem	
Word Knowledge	V			GC		
Number Questions			Q	GC		
Tapping Sequence		P		GC	Mem	
Verbal Memory	V			GC	Mem	
Right-Left Orientation		P		GC		
Leg Coordination						Mot
Arm Coordination						Mot
Imitative Action						Mot
Draw-a-Design		P		GC		Mot
Draw-a-Child		P		GC		Mot
Numerical Memory			Q	GC	Mem	
Verbal Fluency	V			GC		
Counting and Sorting			Q	GC		
Opposite Analogies	V			GC		
Conceptual Grouping		P		GC		

ure perceptual and motor skills as well as general cognition.

Pictorial Memory   In this subtest children are shown a card with six pictured objects on it. The objects are named by the examiner, and children are then asked to recall what they saw. The test measures immediate memory, general cognition, and verbal ability.

Word Knowledge   This subtest consists of two parts. In Part 1 children are required to point to five common objects and name four additional objects shown to them on cards. Part 2 is an oral vocabulary test requiring children to define words.

Number Questions   Children are given twelve questions requiring quantitative thinking and involving solution of addition, subtraction, multiplication, and division problems.

Tapping Sequence   This subtest requires children to imitate the examiner's performance on a four-note xylophone. Memory, perceptual-motor coordination, and general cognition are said to be measured.

Verbal Memory   This is a two-part test. Part 1 requires children to repeat words and sentences. Part 2 requires them to recall the highlights of a paragraph read by the examiner.

Right-Left Orientation   Children are required to demonstrate knowledge of left and right with regard to their own bodies and then to demonstrate generalization of left and right to a picture of a boy. This subtest is not administered to children younger than 5.

Leg Coordination   Items requiring children to engage in a variety of exercises, such as walking backward and on tiptoe, are used to assess the maturity of leg coordination.

Arm Coordination   Development of the arms is assessed in a variety of gamelike activities.

Imitative Action   Eye preference is assessed by requiring children to sight through a plastic tube.

Draw-a-Design   Children are required to copy various geometric designs.

Draw-a-Child   This subtest requires males to draw a boy and females to draw a girl.

Numerical Memory   This subtest assesses immediate recall by requiring children to repeat sequences of digits both forward and backward.

Verbal Fluency   This subtest requires children to classify and think categorically. Children must name words that fall into each of four different categories within a time limit.

Counting and Sorting   Children are required to count blocks and to sort them into quantitative categories (for example, two piles with *the same* number).

Opposite Analogies   Children are required to provide opposites of key words in statements spoken by the examiner (for instance, "Milk is *cold*, but coffee is ____").

Conceptual Grouping   Children must manipulate from one to three variables to discover classification rules for problems.

All directions for administering the test are clear and specific. Procedures for scoring are clearly described; an eight-step procedure is outlined. Scores are described in language that teachers can easily understand.

SCORES

Four kinds of scores are obtained on the MSCA: a general cognitive index, scale indexes, percentile ranks, and MA. The author states that the general cognitive index "is a scaled score; it is not a quotient" (p. 24). The score has a mean of 100 and a standard deviation of 16. Separate indexes are obtained for each of the other five major scales; they have a mean of 50 and a standard deviation of 10. Tables in the manual are used to transform scaled scores into percentile ranks and to provide estimated MAs for performance on the general cognitive scale.

NORMS

One hundred children at each of ten age levels participated in the standardization of the MSCA; the sample was stratified on the basis of sex, age, "color," geographic region, father's occupation, and urban-rural residence. Proportions in the normative sample approximate very closely the 1970 U.S. Census data. The norms for this test are now out of date.

RELIABILITY

Reliability data consist of internal-consistency coefficients for all but three subtests of the MSCA. For these three, internal-consistency estimates were viewed as inappropriate, and test-retest coefficients were computed. Reliability coefficients and standard errors of

measurement for the six MSCA scales are reported in Table 10.4. Reliabilities for the Verbal and General Cognitive scales are excellent; coefficients for the other scales are lower.

VALIDITY

Studies of both predictive and concurrent validity are reported in the manual. Thirty-one children were tested using the MSCA and then tested four months later using the Metropolitan Achievement Test. Correlations among the six scales of the MSCA and the six scales of the MAT were high for the Perceptual-Performance and Quantitative scales, mediocre for the General Cognitive Scale, and poor for the Verbal, Memory, and Motor scales. The last three MSCA scales had correlations averaging .15, .26, and .03 with the MAT. The author rightfully states that the results should be interpreted with caution because of the small size of the sample.

To establish concurrent validity, MSCA scores were correlated with scores obtained on the Stanford-Binet and the Wechsler Preschool and Primary Scale of Intelligence (WPPSI). The sample consisted of thirty-five white children (aged 6 to $6\frac{1}{2}$) enrolled in a Catholic school in New York City. The obtained intercorrelations are reported in Table 10.5. The results lend some support to the concurrent validity of the MSCA.

SUMMARY

The tasks used in the MSCA are interesting and enjoyable; the directions are clear; the standardization is out of date, and reliability is excellent. Evidence about validity of the MSCA is very limited. Certain claims for the usefulness of the test with exceptional children ap-

TABLE 10.4   Reliability Coefficients and Standard Errors of Measurement of the Six MSCA Scales, by Age, for the Standardization Sample

Age in Years	N	Verbal		Perceptual-Performance		Quantitative		General Cognitive		Memory		Motor	
		r	SEM	r	SEM	r	SEM	r	SEM	r	SEM	r	SEM
2½	102	.90	3.2	.76	4.8	.77	4.9	.93	4.2	.78	4.6	.84	4.0
3	104	.89	3.2	.87	3.6	.82	4.2	.94	3.8	.73	5.0	.82	4.2
3½	100	.92	2.8	.90	3.2	.83	4.2	.96	3.4	.83	4.1	.84	4.1
4	102	.90	3.2	.86	3.6	.78	5.3	.91	4.7	.83	4.0	.78	4.6
4½	104	.88	3.5	.89	3.3	.79	4.6	.94	3.8	.74	5.0	.84	4.1
5	102	.87	3.6	.87	3.7	.86	3.7	.94	3.9	.78	4.9	.82	4.3
5½	104	.87	3.5	.84	3.9	.86	3.7	.93	4.2	.72	5.3	.80	4.5
6½	104	.84	3.9	.77	4.7	.80	4.3	.90	5.0	.84	4.0	.69	5.5
7½	104	.90	3.3	.84	4.1	.82	4.1	.94	3.9	.83	4.0	.75	5.1
8½	106	.86	3.7	.75	5.0	.83	4.2	.92	4.5	.82	4.3	.60	6.2
Average and SEM for the 10 Age Groups[a]		.88	3.4	.84	4.0	.81	4.3	.93	4.1	.79	4.5	.79	4.7

NOTE: The reliability coefficients presented here are based on split-half correlations corrected by the Spearman-Brown formula for the component tests, except for the Memory tests, Right-Left Orientation, and Draw-a-Child, for which that method was inappropriate. For these, test-retest correlations, based on smaller groups, and corrected for restriction of range, were used in the computation of Scale reliability coefficients (Guilford, 1954, pp 392–393).

The standard errors of measurement are in GCI units for the General Cognitive Scale, and in Scale Index units for the other five Scales. . . . Standard deviations . . . were used to compute the standard errors of measurement.

[a]The average coefficients were obtained by using Fisher's z transformation (Walker & Lev, 1953, p. 254).

SOURCE: From the *Manual for the McCarthy Scales of Children's Abilities*. Copyright © 1970, 1972 by The Psychological Corporation, San Antonio, Texas. Reproduced by permission. All rights reserved.

pear unsubstantiated for two reasons: no exceptional children were included in the standardization, and there is no evidence for the validity of the scale with specific groups. If school personnel wish to make normative comparisons, they will do better to use a measure with more up-to-date norms.

PICTURE VOCABULARY TESTS

A number of picture vocabulary tests are among the most widely used tests for assessment of children's intelligence. Before describing individual picture vocabulary tests, it is important to state what these devices measure. The tests are *not* measures of intelligence per se; rather, they measure only one aspect of intelligence, receptive vocabulary. Picture vocabulary tests present pictures to a child, who is asked to identify those pictures that correspond to words read by the examiner. Some authors of picture vocabulary measures state that the

TABLE 10.5 Coefficients of Correlation between MSCA Scale Indexes and IQs Obtained on the Wechsler Preschool and Primary Scale of Intelligence (WPPSI) and Stanford–Binet

MSCA Scales	WPPSI IQ			Stanford–Binet (Form L-M) IQ	MSCA Scale Index	
	Verbal	Performance	Full–Scale		Mean	SD
Verbal	.51	.43	.54	.66	52.5	8.2
Perceptual–Performance	.47	.59	.61	.70	53.4	10.3
Quantitative	.41	.27	.38	.41	50.0	8.4
General Cognitive	.63	.62	.71	.81	104.0	13.3
Memory	.42	.39	.46	.67	51.0	8.6
Motor	.02	.10	.07	.06	51.5	7.3
Mean	106.7	104.6	106.3	115.5		
Standard Deviation	10.9	12.4	11.1	14.2		

NOTE: Intervals between the administration of the MSCA and each of the other tests ranged from three to twenty days. Testing order was counterbalanced. $N = 35$ first-grade children aged 6 to 6½.
SOURCE: **Data** from the *Manual for the McCarthy Scales of Children's Abilities.* Copyright © 1970, 1972 by The Psychological Corporation, San Antonio, Texas. Reproduced by permission. All rights reserved.

tests measure receptive vocabulary; others equate receptive vocabulary with intelligence and claim that their tests assess intelligence. Because the tests measure only one aspect of intelligence, they should not be used to make placement decisions.

FULL-RANGE PICTURE VOCABULARY TEST

The Full-Range Picture Vocabulary Test (Ammons & Ammons, 1948) is designed to assess the "intelligence" of individuals from 2 years of age through adulthood. Materials for the test consist of thirteen plates with four pictures on each plate, a one-page manual, and an answer sheet with norms printed on the back. Directions for administering the test are complex. For each plate, there are words representing levels of performance. Point levels are assigned to each of the words on a given plate and "represent approximately the mental age at which fifty percent of a representative population would fail the word" (Ammons & Ammons, 1948, p. 1). Test takers are given words for in-

dividual cards until they pass three consecutive levels and fail three. However, three plates have only three words, while two plates have only two words. Administration is complicated; while there may be only three words for certain plates, the words may represent levels that are very disparate. The examiner must assume "hypothetical levels" for certain plates.

SCORES

Although administration is based on levels completed, scoring is based on number of *items* answered correctly. A table of norms is used to transform raw scores to MAs. Interpolation is often necessary because MAs are not specified for all possible raw scores. The authors state that a Wechsler-like scale of IQs accompanies each test kit. The scale was not included in our specimen kit.

NORMS

The authors of the FRPVT state that "the present norms are based on 589 representative cases from 2 years of age to adult level" (p. 1). There is no specification or description of the population on whom this test was standardized. The norms for this test are very badly out of date.

RELIABILITY

The one-page manual for the FRPVT does not include reliability data. In the manual for the Quick Test (Ammons & Ammons, 1962), the authors of the FRPVT state that

> critics of the FRPV not familiar with its widespread use and our extensive research program have implied or stated that the FRPV is "poorly standardized," etc. Actually, this is not at all the case. Rather, since shortly after the FRPV

was made available for use, there has been so much research with it that we have not been able to keep up with the findings. One of the consequences of this widespread use has been that we have been unable to prepare a comprehensive manual, although many separate articles reporting various aspects of work with the FRPV have been published. In order to make sure that a QT manual would be published, we deliberately refrained from releasing the QT until this manual was ready, reporting all experience and known research to date. If our experience with the FRPV is any indication, we may never get caught up again. (p. i)

VALIDITY

There is no evidence for the validity of the FRPVT.

SUMMARY

The FRPVT and its accompanying manual violate the majority of the standards for educational and psychological tests published by the joint committee of the American Psychological Association, the American Educational Research Association, and the National Council on Measurement in Education.

QUICK TEST

The Quick Test (Ammons & Ammons, 1962) is described by its authors as the "little brother of the Full Range Picture Vocabulary Test (FRPV), one of the most widely used brief tests of intelligence" (p. i). There are three forms of the Quick Test, each consisting of one plate of four drawings and a series of words that the examiner reads. The child or adult taking the test is required to point to the picture that

most nearly represents the meaning of the word read by the examiner. The authors state that the single forms of the Quick Test can be given in 2 minutes or less, that "it can be seen that the three forms of the QT are 'short forms' of the FRPV, which itself is a very brief, but highly reliable and valid, test of intelligence" (p. i). You will note that in our review of the Full Range Picture Vocabulary Test (above), we call attention to the fact that there is no evidence for the reliability and validity of the FRPVT.

SCORES

Raw scores for the Quick Test consist of the number of correct responses between the basal and the ceiling. Raw scores may be transformed to MAs and ratio IQs for children and to deviation IQs ($\overline{X} = 100$, $S = 15$) for adults. Actually, seven MAs and seven IQs are obtained (for form 1, form 2, form 3, forms 1 and 2 combined, forms 1 and 3 combined, forms 2 and 3 combined, and forms 1, 2, and 3 combined).

NORMS

The Quick Test was standardized on 458 white children and adults from geographically restricted areas (parts of Montana and Louisville, Kentucky). The authors state that they attempted to control for age, grade, occupation of parents, and sex. They state, "We did not attempt any geographical control for practical reasons and because previous work with the FRPV had indicated such control was very likely not important" (p. 121). The test is inadequately standardized, and the norms are out of date.

RELIABILITY

Ten studies are cited in the Quick Test manual to support the contention that the test is reliable. All ten studies are equivalent-form reliability studies. There are no reported investigations of either internal-consistency or test-retest reliability. Equivalent-form reliabilities

range from .60 to .96. Apparently, very disparate scores are often earned on the three forms of the Quick Test. The authors state,

> From time to time, FRPV or QT users have written to us, quite disturbed to find a testee who has shown a difference of two or three years in mental age on different forms of the test. Relatively inexperienced testers are inclined to say that the test is at fault, which of course it may be. However, in most instances, these discrepancies are well within the range which would be expected from the standard error of a test score. The tester only notices the few very large discrepancies, disregarding the far more numerous times when performances have been very similar. The tester should note that almost never has a large discrepancy been found for a good-sized group. Discrepancies are usually due to peculiar performance on a few (one to three) items and may very well have clinical significance. (p. 137)

Since reliability and standard error of measurement are inversely related, we wonder how the authors can claim that the test is highly reliable and still dismiss large discrepancies as "within the range which would be expected from the standard error of a test score."

VALIDITY

Validity data for the Quick Test consist of both concurrent and predictive data. Concurrent validity was studied by correlating performance on the Quick Test with performance on the FRPVT. Since the Quick Test is the "little brother" of the FRPVT, the reported correlations of .62 to .93 are not surprising.

Predictive validity was established by correlating performance on the Quick Test with school grades and scores on achievement tests. Intercorrelations with subtests of the Iowa

Tests of Basic Skills were found to range from .32 to .59.

SUMMARY

The Quick Test is a very brief measure of verbal intelligence that has many limitations for use in decision making. Standardization was carried out in a geographically circumscribed area, the norms are out of date, evidence regarding reliability is limited to equivalent-form reliability, and validity evidence is limited.

PEABODY PICTURE VOCABULARY TEST–REVISED

The Peabody Picture Vocabulary Test–Revised (PPVT-R) (Dunn & Dunn, 1981) is an individually administered, norm-referenced measure of receptive (hearing) vocabulary designed to provide an index of achievement and/or scholastic aptitude. The authors of the test state that

> The PPVT-R is designed primarily to measure a subject's receptive (hearing) vocabulary for Standard American English. In this sense, it is an achievement test, since it shows the extent of English vocabulary acquisition.
>
> Another function is to provide a quick estimate of one major aspect of verbal ability for subjects who have grown up in a standard English-speaking environment. In this sense, it is a scholastic aptitude test. It is not, however, a comprehensive test of general intelligence. Instead, it measures only one important facet of general intelligence: vocabulary. (Dunn & Dunn, 1981)

The PPVT-R, a revision of the Peabody Picture Vocabulary Test that originally appeared in 1959 and later in 1965, contains two-thirds new items. There are two parallel forms of the test (forms L and M), and the test may be administered to persons between 2½ and 40 years of age.

The PPVT-R is administered in easel format, with the examiner showing an individual a series of plates on which four pictures are drawn. The examiner reads a stimulus word for each plate, and the person being tested points to the picture that best represents the stimulus word. The PPVT-R is an untimed power test, and it usually takes from 10 to 15 minutes to administer. The test is accompanied by both a manual and a technical manual, the latter providing extensive data on the development and technical characteristics of the test.

SCORES

The student's raw score is the number of pictures correctly identified between basal and ceiling items. Because the test employs a multiple-choice format, the basal is the highest level at which a person makes eight consecutive correct responses; the ceiling is defined as that point at which a person makes six errors in eight consecutive items. Raw scores may be transformed to age equivalents, standard scores ($\overline{X} = 100$, $S = 15$), percentile ranks, and stanines. True score confidence bands are provided for obtained scores, and the authors use asymmetrical confidence intervals (see Chapter 7) for extreme scores.

Norms

The development of the PPVT-R began with a four-stage item tryout program between 1976 and 1978. A total of 9,099 persons were tested using 684 experimental items. This initial item tryout was followed by administration of 504 items (252 per form) to 5,717 persons as part of an item-calibration study. Subjects for this phase of test development were selected from a sample drawn on the basis of geographic region, rural-urban residence, socioeconomic status, and race (in preschool and grade 1 only). Both traditional item analysis and Rasch-Wright latent trait methods were used to select final items for the two forms of the test.

The PPVT-R was standardized on a representative national sample of 4,200 students, ages 2½ through 18, and on 828 adults. The 2½ to 18 sample was selected on the basis of geographic region, parental occupation, sex, race, and community size. Data in the technical manual illustrate close agreement between sample proportions and 1970 U.S. Census proportions. The adult sample was selected in proportion to the 1970 U.S. Census occupational data, and according to geographic region and sex. Again, the composition of the adult sample closely approximates census data.

Reliability

Extensive reliability data are provided in the technical manual for the PPVT-R. The section on reliability begins with a description of the relationship between performance on the 1965 and 1981 editions of the test. These data are of heuristic interest only, owing to extensive revision of the test.

Three kinds of reliability data are reported for the PPVT-R: split-half indices of internal consistency; immediate test-retest reliability us-

ing alternate forms; and delayed (9–31 days delay) test-retest reliability using alternate forms. Split-half reliability coefficients ranged from .67 to .88 with a median of .80 on form L, and from .61 to .88 with a median of .81 on form M for the younger (ages 2½ to 18) population, and from .80 to .85 with a median of .82 on form L for the adult population. Immediate test-retest data were collected on 642 children and adolescents. Reliabilities for raw scores for single-age groups ranged from .73 to .91 with a median reliability of .82. Reliabilities for standard scores for single-age groups ranged from .71 to .89 with a median of .79.

Delayed test-retest data were obtained by administering the test to 962 children and adolescents. Reliabilities for raw scores for single-age groups ranged from .52 to .90 (median = .78), and reliabilities for standard scores for single-age groups ranged from .54 to .90 (median = .77). The PPVT-R has satisfactory reliability for screening purposes, the intended use of the test.

Validity

There are no data in the PPVT-R manual on the validity of the test.

Summary

The PPVT-R is an individually administered, norm-referenced measure of hearing vocabulary. The test is well developed and adequately standardized. Data in the technical manual indicate adequate reliability for screening purposes, but there are no data on validity of the measure. Overall, the technical characteristics of this scale far surpass those of other picture vocabulary tests. Used properly and with awareness that it samples only receptive vocab- ulary, the PPVT-R can serve as an extremely useful screening device.

SCALES FOR SPECIAL POPULATIONS

As noted in the introduction to this chapter, a variety of devices have been developed to assess the intellectual capability of people who have difficulty responding to traditional devices. Assessment of special populations is usually carried out by one of the three following practices.

1. *Adapting Test Items* In some cases, examiners change the procedures for administering an item to compensate for the handicaps of the person they are testing. Items normally timed are presented without time limits; verbal items are presented in pantomime; and so on. In such efforts, examiners often "forget" to consider the fact that the test is standardized using standardized procedures. If, as is usually the case, examiners use the published norms for the test, they may make inappropriate comparisons. The children on whom the test was standardized will have been tested using procedures *different* from those adapted procedures an examiner chooses to use.

2. *Using Response-fair Tests* In other cases, examiners select tests to which the person can respond with minimal difficulty. Some tests, for example, employ no verbal instructions and require no verbalized responses. Deaf persons *can* respond and items *can* be given to deaf persons. However, many of the tests that *can* be given are standardized on nonhandicapped persons. The acculturation of the handicapped differs from that of the nonhandicapped. In this instance the normative comparisons are unfair because the acculturation of those tested differs from the acculturation of those on whom the test is standardized.

3. *Using Tests Designed for and Standardized on Handicapped Populations* In still other cases, when examiners are required to test persons who demonstrate specific handicaps, they choose to use tests developed for use with and standardized on specific groups of handicapped individuals. A limited number of such devices are available, but they have the distinct advantages of appropriateness in both response requirements and normative comparisons.

In assessing special populations, examiners must be concerned with two restrictions. They must be sure that response requirements are fair and reasonable—that is, that the person being tested can reasonably be expected to be able to respond. They must be cautious also in the use of norms—in being reasonably certain that those they test have had comparable acculturation to those in the normative sample. The remainder of this chapter describes devices most often used with special populations.

THE NEBRASKA TEST OF LEARNING APTITUDE

The Nebraska Test of Learning Aptitude (NTLA) (Hiskey, 1966) is an individually administered test designed to assess the learning aptitude of deaf and hearing individuals between 3 and 16 years of age. The NTLA has twelve subtests with instructions for pantomime administration of the test to deaf persons and verbal directions for use with hearing children. To use the NTLA, the examiner must have considerable experience in individual intellectual assessment. To assess deaf children, the examiner should have specialized preparation and considerable experience working with the deaf. The manual for the NTLA includes suggestions about specific procedures to use in establishing rapport with deaf children, including suggested ways of correcting mistakes and of giving the child nonverbal reinforcement.

The NTLA may be administered either by pantomime or by verbal directions. The test was standardized using pantomime directions with deaf children and verbal directions with hearing children. For that reason, if pantomime directions are used, the scoring must be based on the norms for deaf children. If verbal directions are used, scoring must be based on the norms for hearing children.

Each of the twelve subtests is a power test beginning with very simple items designed to give the child practice in the kind of behavior being sampled. Response requirements in all subtests are nonverbal, requiring a choice (by pointing) of several alternatives or a motor response such as stringing beads or drawing parts of pictures. Some subtests are administered only to three- to ten-year-olds; some are administered to all ages; others are given only to those 11 years old or older. A description of the twelve subtests follows.

Bead Patterns (ages 3 to 10)   This subtest assesses ability to string beads, copy bead pat-

terns, and reproduce bead patterns from memory.

Memory for Color (ages 3 to 10)   This subtest assesses ability to remember a visually presented series of colors after a short delay.

Picture Identification (ages 3 to 10)   This subtest assesses ability to match identical pictures of increasing complexity.

Picture Association (ages 3 to 10)   This subtest assesses the ability to match pictures to other picture pairs on the basis of perceptual and conceptual relationships.

Paper Folding (ages 3 to 10)   This subtest assesses ability to fold pieces of paper to reproduce a sequence of folds previously made by the examiner.

Visual Attention Span (all ages)   This subtest assesses ability to remember sequences of pictures after a short delay.

Block Patterns (all ages)   This subtest assesses ability to build block patterns from pictorial representations including three-dimensional arrays. The test taker is allowed 2 minutes to build each pattern and receives bonus points for faster solutions.

Completion of Drawings (all ages)   This subtest assesses ability to isolate missing parts in line drawings and to draw in missing parts with a pencil.

Memory for Digits (11 and above; omitted if mental retardation is suspected)   This subtest assesses ability to reproduce sequences of visually presented digits. A sequence on a card is shown, the card is removed, and the test taker must reproduce the sequence using plastic digits.

Puzzle Blocks (ages 11 and above) This subtest assesses ability to assemble disjointed cubes into a whole. It employs varying time limits, and bonus points are given for rapid solutions.

Picture Analogies (ages 11 and above) This subtest assesses ability to solve visually presented analogies. Three pictures are shown and there is a relationship between the first two. The third picture bears the same relationship to a fourth picture that must be chosen from a response bank.

Spatial Reasoning (ages 11 and above) This subtest presents a whole figure and several samples of disjointed parts. It requires identification of the samples that could be put together to form the whole objects.

The NTLA is a point scale; that is, the child earns points on the specific subtests that are administered. Different subtests employ different ceiling rules. Criteria for stopping each of the subtests are adequately described in the test manual.

SCORES

The kinds of scores obtained for the NTLA depend on how the test is administered. As noted earlier, the NTLA may be administered either in pantomime or verbally. When the test is administered in pantomime, the norms for deaf children are used to obtain a learning age (LA) and a learning quotient (LQ). When the test is administered verbally, the norms for hearing children are used to obtain a mental age (MA) and an intelligence quotient (IQ). Both scores and quotients are based on the median subtest learning ages and mental ages. Hiskey recom-

mends that in interpreting the test performance of hearing children, teachers and diagnostic specialists rely primarily on the MA. He advises that the learning age and learning quotient obtained for deaf children are not equivalent or comparable to MAs and IQs. He recommends that the learning age should be the only score used to interpret the performance of deaf children.

NORMS

The NTLA was originally developed in 1941. Norms for hearing children were first published in 1957, and the revised edition of the test with norms for both deaf and hearing children was published in 1966 (Hiskey, 1966). The standardization sample for the 1941 edition included 466 children enrolled in state schools for the deaf in seven midwestern states and in one day school for the deaf in Lincoln, Nebraska.

In the revision and restandardization of the NTLA, Hiskey added one subtest (Spatial Relations) and many more difficult items. The revised NTLA was administered to 1,107 deaf children and 1,101 hearing children between the ages of 2-6 and 17-5 in ten "widely separate states." The deaf children were primarily from state schools for the deaf with no other data reported on the nature of the normative sample. The hearing children were selected on the basis of their parents' occupational levels with reference to the percentages found in the 1960 census. Hiskey states that "the samples included representatives from minority groups, although no effort was made to obtain a specified percentage of such children" (p. 10).

For the purpose of establishing age norms, the children from both samples were divided into fifteen age groups (all children between 2-6 and 3-5 were placed in the 3-year-old group, and so on). The number of children at each year level varied more for the deaf (25 to 106) than for the hearing (47 to 85). The samples of 3- and 4-year-old deaf children and the samples of older hearing children were limited in size. The final item placement was based on the performance of *deaf* children, and there are no comparisons reported in the manual between the performances of deaf children and hearing children. Thus, while evidence is reported on the increasing difficulty of items within subtests for deaf children, comparable data for hearing children are not reported.

The published norms are based on the performances of 1,079 deaf children and 1,074 hearing children. As noted earlier, both samples are inadequately described. And, the norms for the NTLA are badly out of date.

RELIABILITY

The only reliability data presented in the manual for the NTLA are split-half reliabilities for the standardization groups. Hiskey reports split-half reliabilities of .95 for the 3- to 10-year-old deaf group, .92 for the 11- to 17-year-old deaf group, .93 for 3- to 10-year-old hearing children, and .90 for 11- to 17-year-old hearing children. No data about the standard errors of measurement are included in the manual.

Hiskey does report data on the internal consistency of the test but does so in an effort to demonstrate validity for the measure. In citing evidence of content validity, Hiskey reports subtest intercorrelations and correlations of each subtest learning age with the median learning age for the entire test. There are no data on the reliabilities of the individual subtests. Hiskey states that "studies in the near future will provide additional evidence of reliability based on re-test results after varying periods of time have elapsed" (p. 16). We have

searched the literature and have failed to find these studies.

VALIDITY

Hiskey states that "the best evidence of the validity of a test is to be found in its successful use over a period of years. Research reported during the past twenty years indicates that the original scale has been a valid instrument" (p. 12). He provides very little empirical evidence to support his contention. Data on validity consist of reported concurrent validity and evidence about correlation of subtest learning ages with median learning ages for the total test.

Hiskey reports correlations between subtest learning ages and the median learning age for the total test ranging from .55 to .89 for 3- to 10-year-old deaf children, from .59 to .67 for 11- to 17-year-old deaf children, from .51 to .77 for 3- to 10-year-old hearing children, and from .54 to .67 for 11- to 17-year-old hearing children.

Most data about the concurrent validity of the NTLA are based on the earlier edition of the test. Hiskey does, however, report the following concurrent validity coefficients for the 1966 revision of the NTLA: .86 for 99 hearing children (ages 3 to 10) between NTLA and Stanford-Binet IQs; .78 between the NTLA and Stanford-Binet IQs for fifty hearing children between 11 and 17 years of age; .82 between WISC and NTLA IQs for fifty-two hearing children between 5 and 11 years of age.

SUMMARY

The NTLA is an individually administered measure of learning aptitude standardized on both deaf and hearing children. The test is administered by pantomime procedures for deaf children and by verbal instructions for hearing children. When administering the test, the examiner must be especially careful to use the appropriate set of normative data. The test was standardized using pantomime procedures for deaf children and verbal instructions for hearing children. The standardization samples are not described fully enough, and the norms are out of date.

Reliability data for the NTLA are limited. No subtest reliabilities are reported; only split-half reliabilities for the entire scale are included in the manual. Validity data consist of reported correlations between subtest learning ages and the median learning age for the total test, data on the earlier edition of the test, and concurrent correlations of the NTLA scores with scores of hearing children on the Stanford-Binet and the WISC.

The Nebraska Test of Learning Aptitude is the best available device for the assessment of the learning aptitude of deaf children between 5 and 12 years of age. Because of limited technical data, and especially the datedness and inadequacy of the norm group, results on the test must be interpreted with considerable caution.

BLIND LEARNING APTITUDE TEST

The Blind Learning Aptitude Test (BLAT) (Newland, 1969)[1] was developed for assessing the learning aptitude of young blind children. Newland (1969) states that the BLAT was devised to give a clearer picture of the learning potential of young blind children than was possible using existent measures. He states,

> While a certain amount and kind of light could be thrown on their basic learning capacities by means of more widely used individual tests, the kinds of behaviors sampled by such tests did not yield as full, and early, psychological information as is needed, particularly at the time such children entered upon formal educational programs—whether in residential or day schools. In a psychological sense, young blind children come into such programs from a much more diversified background of acculturation than do non-impaired children. (p. 1)

In developing materials for the BLAT, Newland states, he used five guiding principles:

> (1) the test items were to be bas-relief form, consisting of dots and lines; (2) the spatial discriminations to be made by the child among these dots and lines were to be greater than those called for in the reading of Braille; (3) no stimulus materials, other than the directions, were to be verbal in nature, (4) verbalization of response was not to be required in solving the items or in specifying the solutions to items. Pointing behavior was to be accepted although accompanying verbalization could be accepted; (5) a variety of test-element patterns was to be developed, all of which would necessitate eduction of relationships and/or correlates by the child. (p. 1)

Newland designed the BLAT to sample "six discernibly different kinds of behavior." His description of the kinds of behaviors sampled is comparable to our descriptions of items assessing discrimination, generalization, sequencing, analogies, and pattern or matrix completion.

---

1. All quotations from the *Manual for the Blind Learning Aptitude Test* used in this discussion are copyrighted by T. Ernest Newland and reprinted by his permission.

The BLAT was standardized on individuals from 6 to 20 years of age, but it is intended primarily for children between 6 and 12 years of age. There is a unique feature in the administration of BLAT subtests: training items are presented before the actual administration of subtest items. This allows the examiner to be certain that a child understands the kind of behavior required before being asked to demonstrate the behavior for a scored test item.

Scores

Two scores, learning-aptitude test age and learning-aptitude test quotient, are obtained from the BLAT. Newland (1969) describes the test age by stating that

> a child who earns a given score on BLAT can be regarded as having earned a BLAT test age which is the midpoint of an age range. This is indicative of the level of his learning capability as a blind child, as reflected by his performance on the kinds of behavior being sampled by BLAT. (p. 19)

The learning quotient is a deviation score with a mean of 100 and a standard deviation of 15.

Norms

The BLAT was standardized on 961 blind students in both residential and day schools. The standardization sample was stratified on the basis of geographic region, age, sex, race, and socioeconomic status. Extensive tables comparing standardization data to U.S. Census data appear in the manual. In most instances BLAT sample proportions are closely comparable to the census proportions. The norms for this test are now out of date.

Reliability

Two kinds of reliability were ascertained for the BLAT. Internal consistency of the test for all 961 children in the standardization sample was .93. Test-retest reliability was reported as .87 for a sample of 93 children ranging in age from 10 through 16 who were retested seven months after the original testing. There was a median gain of 5.8 points between the original testing and subsequent retesting.

Validity

Validity for the BLAT was demonstrated in three ways. Newland states that estimates of concurrent validity would have limited value because "the 'intelligence' tests generally used with young blind children were regarded as having limited value in sampling learning potential—due to the nature of behavior samplings made and the very widely differing kinds and amounts of acculturation among blind children" (p. 10).

To establish validity for the BLAT it was demonstrated that performance on BLAT

> (1) progressively improves across random samples of increasing chronological age levels;
> (2) correlates well enough with performances on the Hayes-Binet and the WISC Verbal to suggest that the measurements are in a comparable domain, yet low enough to suggest differences in the behavior samplings; and
> (3) correlates promisingly with measured educational achievement as compared with correlations between performances on the Hayes-Binet and WISC Verbal and measured educational achievement. (Newland, 1969, p. 10)

SUMMARY

The Blind Learning Aptitude Test uses a bas-relief format and six different kinds of behavior samples to assess the intelligence of blind children between 6 and 12 years of age. The BLAT was standardized on blind children whose characteristics closely approximate census proportions, but the norms are now out of date. The test is sufficiently reliable to be used in making important decisions about children. Validity of the test is still based largely on theoretical postulates. The BLAT is currently the most adequate test for assessing the learning aptitude of young blind children.

ARTHUR ADAPTATION OF THE LEITER INTERNATIONAL PERFORMANCE SCALE

The Leiter International Performance Scale was first constructed by Russell Leiter in 1929 for the purpose of assessing the intelligence of children who might experience difficulty responding to a verbal test: the deaf, the hard of hearing, those who demonstrate speech difficulties, the bilingual, and those who do not speak English. The 1929 scale was an experimental edition; subsequent revisions were published in 1934, 1936, 1938, 1940, and 1948. In 1950, Grace Arthur published an adaptation (AALIPS) of the Leiter International Performance Scale.

The AALIPS is an untimed, nonverbal age scale containing sixty items ranging from the 2-year to the 12-year level. The 1948 edition of the LIPS contains additional items and can be used to assess the intelligence of persons 2 through 18 years of age. The test materials for the LIPS and the AALIPS are identical through the 12-year level.

Materials for the AALIPS consist of a response frame with an adjustable card holder and two trays of response blocks with corresponding stimulus cards (see Figure 10.2). All tests are administered by placing a stimulus card on the response frame and pantomiming the directions. The child responds by placing blocks in the response frame. The actual tasks range from matching colors and forms to completion of patterns, analogous designs, and classification of objects. Behaviors predominantly sampled, therefore, include discrimination, generalization, sequencing, analogies, and pattern completion. Most items require considerable perceptual organization and discrimination.

The directions for administering the scale that are included in the manual are confusing. They're illustrated by black-and-white pictures that, unfortunately, are of little assistance with items in which color is the discriminative feature in both administration and solution. Colored pictures would facilitate ease of administration; the use of black-and-white pictures necessitates reading an entire page of instructions in order to ascertain proper alignment of stimulus cards and pictures and to insure correct standardized administration.

SCORES

A major shortcoming of the AALIPS is the fact that the correct answers (arrangements of blocks) to test questions are not included in the manual. Examiners must judge the correctness of a child's response on the basis of what they believe the correct response should be. We suggest that examiners solve the problems themselves before giving the test to children, that they obtain the consensus of others (preferably, reasonably "bright" persons) about the correctness of their responses, and that they then mark the blocks using a coding system to avoid scoring errors.

Two scores, MA and a ratio IQ, are obtained by administering the AALIPS. There are four subtests at each age level of the test. The child earns a certain number of months' credit for each subtest passed and the number of months are summed to produce a mental age. Only items between the child's basal and ceiling are administered. A basal is located by identifying the level at which a child answers all items correctly. A double ceiling is attained; the child must fail all items at two consecutive year levels before testing is discontinued. Comparisons of the AALIPS with other intelligence tests (that is, the WISC and Stanford-Binet) have consistently shown that scores on the

AALIPS tend to be about five points lower than those earned on other scales. Arthur devised a bonus system that raises the basal and increases credit for subtests passed at the various year levels, thus bringing scores on the AALIPS into line with those on other tests.

NORMS

Normative data for the LIPS are not included in the AALIPS manual. The AALIPS, on the other hand, was standardized on only 289 children. All 289 came from a homogeneous middle-class, midwestern, metropolitan background. There were few children at either extreme of the socioeconomic scale and apparently few or none who were the kind of children for whom the scale was originally developed—that is, children who experience dif-

FIGURE 10.2   An Item from the Leiter International Performance Scale

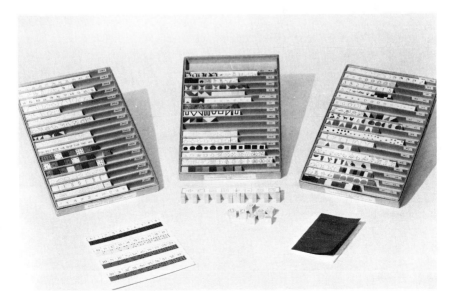

SOURCE: Photo courtesy Stoelting Company.

ficulty responding to a verbal scale. The norms for the AALIPS are badly out of date. They are forty years old.

RELIABILITY AND VALIDITY

No reliability data are published in the manual for the AALIPS. Arthur reports a number of studies as evidence for the concurrent validity of the AALIPS. Correlations between performance on the AALIPS and on the Stanford-Binet Intelligence Scale for 4-, 5-, 7-, and 8-year-old children ranged from .69 to .93; for a sample of mentally retarded and brain-injured children these correlations were between .56 and .86. The AALIPS correlates more highly with the performance scale (from .79 to .80) than with the verbal scale (.40 to .78) of the WISC.

SUMMARY

The AALIPS is, in theory and design, a test that holds considerable promise for the intellectual assessment of children who have difficulty responding verbally. It lacks the necessary technical characteristics to make it psychometrically adequate. The test is inadequately standardized, the norms are dated, and few data about its reliability and validity are given in the manual. Until this test is made technically adequate, its use should be restricted to procurement of qualitative information by only the most experienced examiners.

PICTORIAL TEST OF INTELLIGENCE

The Pictorial Test of Intelligence (PTI) (French, 1964) was designed "to provide an easily administered, objectively scored individual testing instrument to be used in assessing the general intellectual level of both normal and handicapped children between the ages of three and eight" (p. 1). The test employs an objective, multiple-choice format and requires no verbal response; children respond either by pointing or, in the case of those who cannot point, by focusing their eyes on specific response items.

The PTI includes six subtests designed to assess general mental ability. All items are administered by showing the child a large picture card containing four response possibilities. The child points to or focuses on one of the four drawings in response to orally presented directions. According to the author, the six subtests sample the following behaviors.

Picture Vocabulary This subtest assesses verbal comprehension. The child must identify the response that best fits the meaning of a stimulus word read by the examiner.

Form Discrimination This subtest assesses perceptual organization. The child is shown increasingly complex stimulus drawings on a second card and must match these to one of four response drawings.

Information and Comprehension The child must demonstrate a "range of knowledge, general understanding, and verbal comprehension" by pointing to pictures in response to verbal statements read by the examiner.

Similarities This subtest requires the child to identify which of four pictures does not belong in either a perceptual or conceptual category with the other three.

Size and Number This subtest assesses quantitative language (for example, *bigger*), enumeration, and word problems that require skills ranging from the addition of single-digit numbers to those needed to perform multiple arithmetic operations in the same problem.

Immediate Recall This subtest assesses "ability to retain momentary perceptions of size, space, and form relationships." The examiner presents a stimulus card for five seconds, removes it, and then asks the child to identify the identical stimulus on the four-choice response card.

SCORES

Raw scores for the PTI are obtained by objective scoring of the multiple-choice responses. Raw scores may be transformed to MAs, percentiles, and deviation IQs ($\overline{X} = 100$, $S = 16$). All children take every item of the test; there are no basal and ceiling rules. A short form of the test, which may be administered to 3- and 4-year-old children, provides the same kinds of scores as the long form.

NORMS

As we mentioned in Chapter 6, the PTI is a most adequately standardized device. The standardization sample consisted of 1,830 children selected as representative of the population of children ages 3 through 8 living in the United States. 1960 census data were used, and the sample was stratified on the basis of geographic region, community size, occupational level of head of household, and sex. Race was not employed as a specific stratification variable, since the author believed that "the most appropriate procedure would be to include all races with socioeconomic status as the prime

control variable" (p. 12). Extensive tables in the manual compare proportions of individuals in the normative sample with proportions in the population of the United States. All children who participated in the normative sample were individually tested by experienced psychologists. Unfortunately, the norms for this test have not been updated since 1960. Thus, the norms are out of date, and examiners should now make comparative judgments only with the utmost of caution.

RELIABILITY

Both internal-consistency and test-retest reliability data are reported in the PTI manual. Internal-consistency coefficients were computed separately for each age level and ranged from .87 to .93. Separate internal-consistency estimates for the short form were .86 at age 3 and .88 at age 4.

Five studies investigated the test-retest reliability of the PTI. The results of these studies, time intervals between testings, and the age levels of the children are reported in Table 10.6. The PTI has the necessary reliability to be used in making important educational decisions.

VALIDITY

Content validity for the PTI was inferred on the basis of item selection and test development. Predictive validity for the test is based on studies of its predecessor, the North Central Individual Test of Mental Ability (NCITMA). Concurrent validity of the PTI was established by correlating performance on the scale with performance on the Stanford-Binet, WISC, and Columbia Mental Maturity Scale. Correlations obtained for a sample of thirty-two first graders are reported in Table 10.7. However,

TABLE 10.6 Summary of Studies on Test-Retest Reliability for the PTI

Age	Time Lapse	r	N
3, 4; 8, 9	54–56 mos.	.69[a]	49
3, 4, 5	3–6 wks.	.96	27
5	2–6 wks	.91	31
6	2–4 wks.	.90	30
7	2–4 wks.	.94	25

[a]NCITMA (ages 3 and 4) vs. PTI (ages 8 and 9).

SOURCE: *Manual for the Pictorial Test of Intelligence* (p. 19) by J. L. French, 1964, Chicago: The Riverside Publishing Co. Copyright 1964. Reproduced by permission of the Publisher, The Riverside Publishing Company, 8420 Bryn Mawr Ave., Chicago, IL 60631.

for this same sample the means and standard deviations differed considerably (PTI: $\overline{X}$ = 114.5, S = 8.2; Stanford-Binet: $\overline{X}$ = 113.6, S = 17.6; and WISC: $\overline{X}$ = 101.5, S = 10.1).

The performance of thirty-two first graders on the PTI correlated .61 with their performance on the Lorge-Thorndike Intelligence Scale (now the Cognitive Abilities Test), while the PTI performance of thirty first graders correlated .62 with their earlier scores on the California Test of Mental Maturity.

Construct validity was established by demonstrating increasing scores with chronological ages and occupational level of children's parents.

SUMMARY

The Pictorial Test of Intelligence is an individually administered device composed of six separate subtests designed to assess general mental ability. The test does not require the child to respond verbally and is thus suitable for administration to children who experience difficulty making verbal responses (young children with speech and language difficulties, with cerebral palsy, and so on). The test is adequately standardized, but the norms are now out of date. The PTI has the necessary reliability to be used in making important educational decisions.

TABLE 10.7 Correlations of PTI Total Test and Subtests with Other Intelligence Tests (32 first graders)

Subtests	Stanford-Binet MA	WISC Scores			CMMS IQ	PTI Total
		Full-Scale	Verbal	Performance		
Picture Vocabulary	.45	.38	.38	.33	.42	.55
Form Discrimination	.53	.56	.52	.49	.45	.68
Information and Comprehension	.41	.56	.23	.16	.22	.48
Similarities	.55	.25	.41	.23	.40	.63
Size and Number	.52	.50	.53	.42	.38	.74
Immediate Recall	.22	.14	.10	.14	.26	.38
Total raw scores	.77	.67	.71	.55	.61	—

SOURCE: *Manual for the Pictorial Test of Intelligence* (p. 21) by J. L. French, 1964, Chicago: The Riverside Publishing Co. Copyright 1964. Reproduced by permission of the Publisher, The Riverside Publishing Company, 8420 Bryn Mawr Ave., Chicago, IL 60631.

COLUMBIA MENTAL MATURITY SCALE

The Columbia Mental Maturity Scale (CMMS) (Burgemeister, Blum, & Lorge, 1972) is an individually administered device that assesses general reasoning ability by requiring a child to make visual-perceptual discriminations in order to classify and relate series of pictures, colors, forms, and symbols. The ninety-two figural and pictorial classification items that make up the scale are arranged in eight overlapping levels and may be used with children between 3 years, 6 months, and 9 years, 11 months, of age. Children take the level of the test appropriate for their chronological age. The authors describe administration of the scale as follows.

Each item consists of a series of from three to five drawings printed on a 6-by-19-inch card. . . . The objects depicted are, in general, within the range of experience of most American children, even those whose environmental backgrounds have been limited. . . . For each item the child is asked to look at all the pictures on the card, select the one which is different from, or unrelated to, the others, and indicate his choice by pointing to it. In order to do this, he must formulate a rule for organizing the pictures so as to exclude just one. The bases for discrimination range from the perception of rather gross differences in color, size, or form, to recognition of very subtle relations in pairs of pictures so as to exclude one from the series of drawings. (p. 7)

Administration of the CMMS takes from 15 to 20 minutes. The child is taught the task by three training items and then takes the appropriate age level of the test.

SCORES

The raw score for the CMMS is simply the number of items answered correctly. Raw scores may be converted to age-deviation scores, percentile ranks, stanines, and a maturity index. The age-deviation score is a standard score with a mean of 100 and a standard deviation of 16. Maturity indexes are essentially comparable to MAs, although they are more global, encompassing ranges rather than being specific MAs. A maturity index of 4U, for example, indicates that the child earned the same score on the test as did those in the standardization group who were in the range from 4 years, 6 months, to 4 years, 11 months. The symbols U and L are used to depict upper and lower ranges of a given year level.

NORMS

The CMMS was standardized on 2,600 children stratified on the basis of geographic region, race, parental occupation, age, and sex. Proportions of children in each of the demographic groups closely approximate 1960 U.S. Census data, with one exception. Figures reported for community size indicate that a greater proportion of children in the normative sample were from large cities (43.74 percent) than is true of the general population (28.5 percent). The selection of the normative sample was in all other ways exemplary.

RELIABILITY

Both internal-consistency (split-half) and test-retest reliability are reported in the CMMS manual. The internal-consistency coefficients ranged from .85 to .91. Test-retest reliability for three different age groups ranged from .84 to .86. Children gained an average of 4.6 age-deviation score points between administrations.

VALIDITY

Validity for the CMMS is based on two kinds of data: data indicating that scores on the test correlate substantially with scores on the Stanford Achievement Test (.31 to .61) and with scores on other intelligence tests. The CMMS scores of 353 children in grades 1 through 3 in a single school system correlated .62 to .69 with their scores on the Otis-Lennon Mental Ability Test and .67 with their scores on the Stanford-Binet.

SUMMARY

The CMMS is an easily administered individual intelligence test designed to assess children's "reasoning ability." The test is adequately standardized and appears technically adequate. The instrument may be used to assess children who have difficulty responding verbally. It does, however, sample only two kinds of intellectual behavior, discrimination and classification; users must be careful not to overgeneralize the test results.

TEST OF NONVERBAL INTELLIGENCE

The Test of Nonverbal Intelligence (TONI) (Brown, Sherbenou, & Dollar, 1982) is a language-free intelligence test designed to be used in both screening and diagnosis with individuals between 5-0 and 85-11 years of age. The test is administered in pantomime, and those tested point to one of several responses presented in multiple-response array. Because no listening, speaking, reading, or writing is required in either the administration or scoring of this test, the test is especially useful with those who are unable to read or write or who may have impaired language abilities (for example, aphasic, non-English-speaking, culturally disadvantaged, mentally retarded, learning disabled, or deaf students). The test is designed to be administered individually, though the authors claim it can be group administered. They state, "Although the TONI should be administered individually, it is possible for a trained and experienced examiner to administer the test to a small group of two to five subjects with no loss of accuracy or stability" (p. 20). The authors provide no evidence to support this latter contention, so the test is best restricted to individual administration. The test is untimed and takes about 15 minutes.

There are two forms of the TONI; each has fifty items arranged in order of difficulty. The test is designed to assess one aspect of intelligence—problem solving. This aspect was selected because it was thought to be a general component of intelligence as well as a basic prerequisite of functional independence. All TONI items require test takers to solve problems by identifying relationships among abstract figures. The subject must point to the one response among several alternatives that best fits a missing part in a pattern or matrix. The test item shown in Figure 9.7 is an example of the kind of item used in the TONI.

In developing the TONI, the authors wanted to put together a set of items that could be administered in pantomime and responded to by pointing. They also wanted items that were both abstract (nonmeaningful) and figural. An initial pool of 307 test items was developed by reviewing the content and format of other nonverbal and performance tests of intelligence. These items were reviewed by an unspecified number of professors, graduate students, school psychologists, psychometrists, and special education teachers. Items that these experts thought were too ambiguous, that were symbolic, or that involved language were eliminated from the item pool. This left 183 items. These items were further reduced by giving the test to an unspecified sample of 322 students in grades K, 1, 3, 5, 7 and 9, and to young adults ages 18–35 and older adults ages 65–86. The number of items was reduced on the basis of indices of item difficulty and item discriminating power, and 50 items were assigned to each of the two forms of the test.

SCORES

Two kinds of scores, percentile ranks and TONI quotients, may be obtained. TONI quotients are standard scores with a mean of 100 and a standard deviation of 15. Thus, they are like the IQs earned on other intelligence tests. In fact, in some tables in the manual they are called "TONI quotient deviation IQs."

NORMS

The authors report that the TONI was standardized on 1,929 subjects from twenty-eight states, ages 5-0 to 85-11, stratified on the basis of sex, race, ethnicity, domicile (urban, rural), geographic location, parental occupation and education (for children), and occupation and education (for adults). Close inspection of tables provided in the manual shows, however, that 45 percent of the norm sample lived in two states (25 percent from Texas, 20 percent from Kansas). No other state was represented by more than 9 percent of the sample; only 13 percent of the sample was from the Northeast. In fact, 89 percent of the sample came from seven states. Data on race, ethnicity, sex, and domicile indicate close approximation to 1980 census figures.

RELIABILITY

Data on internal-consistency and alternate-form reliability are reported in the test manual. No data are presented on test-retest reliability. Internal consistency was evaluated in two ways. First, the authors used coefficient alpha to ascertain internal consistency on 400 cases drawn randomly across the age range from the standardization sample. All correlation coefficients exceeded .90. The authors also used a KR-21 procedure to examine internal consistency, and all coefficients except those for 5- and 6-year-old children exceeded .80. Most exceeded .90. The authors shade scores for five- and six-year-olds in their norm tables to remind users that reliabilities are lower at this age level.

The authors also report alternate-form reliabilities for 1,888 subjects. These are in the .80 to .90 range, with only one coefficient (at age range 8-6 to 10-11) below .80. This coefficient is .78. In addition, data on the reliability of the test are presented for four groups of handicapped students: 10 educable mentally retarded students, 30 deaf students, and two groups ($N = 11$ and 16) of learning disabled students. Internal consistency was at least .80. The authors present sufficient data to demonstrate that the TONI is a reliable measure.

VALIDITY

Data from eight concurrent validity studies are presented. Three studies were conducted with normal students, the other five used groups of handicapped students. All validity coefficients exceeded .35; 41 percent exceeded .80. The number of students in groups on whom validity data was collected was small. One troublesome feature is that correlations of the TONI with other measures of intelligence were nearly the same as correlations with measures of achievement.

To establish the construct validity of this measure—that is, to show that the test measures intelligence—the authors demonstrated that the test discriminates well between normal and mentally retarded students.

Summary

The TONI is an individually administered nonverbal measure of problem-solving ability. The test is adequately standardized and there is good evidence that this is a reliable measure. Evidence on validity is presented in the test manual, but that evidence is limited. The TONI should be especially useful in screening the intellectual functioning of students in instances when it is unwise or not feasible to use a verbal measure.

Coping with Dilemmas in Current Practice

The biggest difficulty encountered in trying to use individual intelligence tests is a problem of definition. What is intelligence? We noted in Chapter 9 that intelligence is an inferred construct. No one has seen a thing called *intelligence*. Yet there are many tests of this thing that no one has seen, and assessors are regularly required to assess it. Most of the definitions of conditions requiring or eligible for special education include reference to cognitive functioning, intelligence, or capability. Mentally retarded students are said to have too little of it, gifted students have more than most. Learning disabled students are said to have average intelligence but fail to demonstrate school performance commensurate with the amount of it they have.

Those who assess intelligence, and most diagnostic personnel are required to do so, must recognize that they can only infer intelligence from a sample of behavior derived through testing. Assessors must pay special attention to the kinds of behaviors sampled by intelligence tests. Two considerations are especially important. First, intelligence tests are usually administered for the purpose of making a prediction about future academic performance. In selecting an intelligence test, one must always ask, "What is the relationship between the kind(s) of behavior sampled by the test and the kind(s) of behavior I am trying to predict?" The closer the relationship, the better the prediction. It is wise to try to select tests that sample behaviors related as closely as possible to the behaviors one is trying to predict.

Second, one must always consider the psychological demand of intelligence test items. In particular, when different kinds of intelligence tests are used to assess handicapped students, it is very important to be aware of the stimulus and response demands of the items. The descriptions of kinds of behaviors sampled by intelligence tests provided in the last chapter should be helpful. When we assess students' intelligence we want the test results to reflect intelligence, not sensory dysfunction.

It is important to remember that intelligence is not a fixed thing that we measure. Rather, it is an inferred entity, one that is understood best by evaluating the ways in which individuals who have different kinds of acculturation perform several different kinds of tasks. Intelligence tests differ markedly; individuals differ markedly. Evaluations of the intelligence of an individual must be understood as a function of the interaction between the skills and characteristics the individual brings to a test setting and the behaviors sampled by the test.

SUMMARY

Many different individually administered tests are currently used to assess intelligence. The tests differ considerably in their basic design, the kinds of behaviors they sample, and their technical adequacy. In evaluating performance on intelligence tests, it is especially important that teachers and examiners go beyond obtained scores to consider the specific tests on which the scores were obtained and the kinds of behaviors sampled by those tests. Detailed information facilitates that evaluation.

There are many individually administered tests designed to assess the intelligence of special populations. Individual intellectual assessment of children with specific handicaps should be carried out using tests designed to minimize the effects of the handicaps on their performances.

STUDY QUESTIONS

1. The Stanford-Binet Intelligence Scale and the Wechsler Intelligence Scale for Children–Revised are the two intelligence tests most frequently used with schoolage children. Identify similarities and differences in the domains of behavior sampled by these two tests.
2. Why is it inappropriate to use the same intelligence tests with sensorily or physically handicapped children as with children who do not have such handicaps?
3. Identify the major advantages of using the Stanford-Binet Intelligence Scale instead of the Slosson Intelligence Test.
4. In Chapter 9, we stated that IQs earned on different intelligence tests are not comparable. Using the Peabody Picture Vocabulary Test–Revised, the Quick Test, and the Wechsler Intelligence Scale for Children–Revised, support the statement.
5. The Performance sections of the Wechsler scales are the tests most commonly used today to assess the intelligence of deaf children. What are the major shortcomings of this practice? What alternatives exist?

6. Using the manual for any of the individual tests described in this chapter, characterize the domain or domains of behaviors sampled by any ten items. Use the domains described in Chapter 9.
7. For what reasons would school personnel give individual intelligence tests?

ADDITIONAL READING

Gerweck, S., & Ysseldyke, J. E. (1974). Limitations of current psychological practices for the intellectual assessment of the hearing impaired. A response to the Levine survey. *Volta Review, 77,* 243–248.

Sattler, J. (1988). *Assessment of children's intelligence and other special abilities* (3rd ed.). San Diego: Jerome M. Sattler. (Chapter 4: Issues related to the measurement and change of intelligence; Chapter 5: testing children; Chapter 8: Stanford-Binet Intelligence Scale: Fourth Edition; Chapter 11: Interpreting the WISC-R.)

Sattler, J., & Tozier, L. (1971). A review of intelligence test modifications used with the cerebral palsied and other handicapped groups. *Journal of Special Education, 4,* 391–398.

C•H•A•P•T•E•R 11

ASSESSMENT OF INTELLIGENCE: GROUP TESTS

Group intelligence tests differ from one another in three ways. First, they differ in format. Whereas some group tests consist of a single battery to be administered in one sitting, others contain a number of subscales or subtests and are administered in two or more sittings. Second, they differ in the kinds of scores they provide. Some provide IQs and/or mental ages based on a global performance; others provide the same kinds of scores, but they are differentiated into subscale scores (for example, verbal, performance, and total; language, nonlanguage, and total). Third, some group intelligence tests are speed tests (timed), and others are power tests (untimed).

WHY DO WE ADMINISTER GROUP INTELLIGENCE TESTS?

Group intelligence tests are used for one of two purposes. Most often, they are routinely administered as screening devices to identify those who are different enough from average to warrant further assessment. Their merit, in this case, is that they can be administered relatively quickly by teachers to large numbers of students. Their drawback is that they suffer from the same limitations as any group test: they can be made to yield qualitative information only with difficulty, and they require that students can sit still for about twenty minutes, that they can mark with a pencil, and, often, that they can read.

Group intelligence tests are also used to provide descriptive information about the level of capability of students in a classroom, district, or even state. They are, on occasion, used in place of or in addition to achievement tests to track students. When used in this way, they set expectations; they are thought to indicate the level of achievement to be expected in individual classrooms or districts.

Specific Group Tests of Intelligence
Culture Fair Intelligence Tests

Three different scales comprise the Culture Fair Intelligence Tests. Scale 1 (Cattell, 1950) is used with students between 4 and 8 years of age. Scale 2 (Cattell & Cattell, 1960a) is used with those who are between 8 and 14 years of age; scale 3 (Cattell & Cattell, 1963) is used with those who are over 14 years of age. The Culture Fair Intelligence Tests are unique among group intelligence tests, and it is helpful to note the rationale for the tests and the theoretical orientation of their author.

According to Cattell (1962), the motivation for construction of the Culture Fair Intelligence Tests "was originally the need for a test which would fairly measure the intelligence of persons having different languages and cultures, or influenced by very different social status and education" (p. 5). Cattell (1973a) states that "the Culture Fair Intelligence Tests measure individual intelligence in a manner designed to reduce, as much as possible, the influence of verbal fluency, culture climate, and educational level" (p. 5).

Cattell believes culture-fair intelligence tests are more adequate measures of learning potential than are traditional intelligence tests. The latter, he argues, are contaminated by the effects of prior learning. Many have argued that scores on the Culture Fair Intelligence Tests do not effectively predict academic achievement. Cattell (1973b) states that the tests have been criticized because "within the same year and among students all in the same kind of school, the Culture Fair does not correlate with ('predict') achievement quite so highly as the traditional test" (p. 8). Cattell (1973b) states that

this is not only admitted, but treasured by the exponent of the newer tests. The reason that the traditional test gives a better immediate "pre-

diction" is that it already contains an appreciable admixture of the school achievement it is supposed to predict. If all we want to do is predict, in March, children's school achievement in, say, July, we can do better than any intelligence test by predicting from their school achievement scores in March. The very object of an intelligence test, however, is to be analytical. As we study any individual child we are interested in the discrepancy *between his native intelligence and his school achievement, and the more clearly and reliably this is brought out, the better the test. The claim of the Culture Fair Tests is that it will make a more fair selection for future performance when the passage of some years has given a chance for the present accidental inequalities of achievement opportunity to be ironed out. (p. 8)*

The Culture Fair Intelligence Tests are designed to measure general mental ability and, with the exception of some parts of scale 1, consist entirely of figural analogies and figural reasoning items. Time limits are 22 minutes for scale 1 and 12½ minutes each for scales 2 and 3. Only parts of scale 1 can be group administered; the scale consists of eight different subtests; some are individually administered, while others are group administered. Only four of the subtests make up the group test, and only four are judged by Cattell to be culture fair. Subtests of scales 1, 2, and 3 are listed in Table 11.1. As we noted earlier, scale 1 contains eight subtests. Four of these make up the group-administered version of the scale; the behaviors they sample are as follows.

Substitution   This subtest is a coding task that requires the student to associate symbols with pictures and to copy them on paper.

TABLE 11.1 Subtests of the Three Scales of the Culture Fair Intelligence Tests

Scale 1	Scales 2 and 3
Substitution[a,b]	Series
Classification[b]	Classification
Mazes[a,b]	Matrices
Selecting Named	Conditions
Objects[a]	(Typology)
Following Directions	
Wrong Pictures	
Riddles	
Similarities[a,b]	

[a] Group-administered form
[b] Fully culture-fair form

Mazes The student is required to trace paths out of increasingly complex mazes.

Selecting Named Objects This subtest is essentially a picture vocabulary task requiring the student to identify pictures of words read aloud by the examiner. This is one of the subtests that, according to the author, is not culture fair.

Similarities The student is required to identify which of several response pictures is just like a stimulus picture.

Scales 2 and 3 are made up of the same four subtests. Behaviors sampled by these subtests are as follows.

Series The student is given a sequence of figures having some progressive relationship to one another and is required to choose from four possible responses the figure that continues the progressive relationship. The first item in Figure 11.1 is a Series item.

Classification The student is given five figures and is required to identify which picture is

different from the other four. The second item in Figure 11.1 is a Classification item.

Matrices The student is given a matrix and is required to identify the response that is the missing element in the matrix. The third item in Figure 11.1 is a Matrices item.

Conditions (Typology) The student is given a stimulus figure in which a dot is placed in a certain relationship (that is, inside the circle, but outside the square). The student must identify that response element in which the dot is in the same relationship to the other elements as in the stimulus figure (that is, *inside* the circle, but *outside* the square). The fourth item in Figure 11.1 is a Conditions item.

SCORES

In taking scale 1, students mark their responses in consumable test booklets, and the booklets are hand scored. Raw scores may be transformed to mental ages or to ratio IQs. The ratio IQs have a mean of 100, but a standard deviation of approximately 20. Cattell believes the higher standard deviations obtained from culture-fair tests are more nearly correct values than those obtained from traditional intelligence tests because "the reduced scatter in traditional intelligence tests is probably due to a contamination of intelligence with achievement" (1962, p. 14). One must remember, therefore, that an IQ of 120 on scale 1 is the standard-score equivalent of an IQ of 116 on the Stanford-Binet Intelligence Scale. Similarly, an IQ of 60 on scale 1 is the standard score equivalent of an IQ of 68 on the Stanford-Binet. Ratio IQs obtained for scale 1 may be transformed to percentiles on an IQ distribution with a standard deviation of 20.

On scales 2 and 3 of the Culture Fair Intelligence Tests, students respond on answer sheets that may be machine scored or scored by hand using a stencil. Raw scores on these scales may be transformed to mental ages and to three different IQs, each having a mean of 100 but standard deviations of 24.4, 24, or 16. The first two distributions are recommended for use when doing research on practical application of the tests and when one wishes to obtain the full spread of IQs typically obtained in administration of the device. The third distribution is a distribution of normalized standard scores with the standard deviation set at the standard deviation of "attainment-contaminated" tests. The distribution is used when one wishes to compare the results obtained on the Culture Fair Intelligence Tests with those obtained on more traditional intelligence tests.

NORMS

The populations on whom the Culture Fair Intelligence Tests were standardized are inadequately described in the manuals. And the norms for all three scales are out of date. Cattell states that scale 1 was standardized on "more than 400 cases combining American

FIGURE 11.1 Items Representative of Subtests of the Culture Fair Intelligence Tests

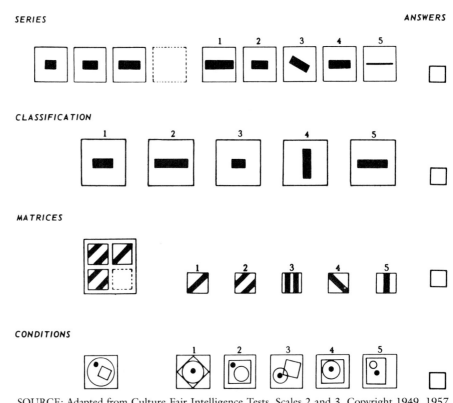

SOURCE: Adapted from Culture Fair Intelligence Tests, Scales 2 and 3. Copyright 1949, 1957 by the Institute for Personality and Ability Testing, Inc. Reproduced by permission.

and British samples" (1962, p. 12). He states that scale 2 was standardized on 4,328 boys and girls from varied regions of the United States and Great Britain. The sample was apparently not stratified on the basis of any population characteristics. Norms for scale 3 were based on "3,140 cases, consisting of American high school students equally divided among freshmen, sophomores, juniors, and seniors, and young adults in a stratified job sample" (Cattell, 1973a, p. 21). There are no data in the manuals regarding the specific characteristics of the standardization samples.

for the use of scale 2 with those under 11 years of age.

Reliability for scale 3 is reported in terms of internal-consistency and equivalent-form reliability for 202 high school students. Internal-consistency coefficients ranged from .51 to .68 for form A and from .53 to .64 for form B. Equivalent-form reliability ranged from .32 to .68.

Reliability for the Culture Fair Intelligence Tests sometimes approaches the necessary values for use of the test in screening. However, reliability data are incomplete.

RELIABILITY

Data about reliability and validity of the three scales are reported in a separate Technical Supplement for scales 2 and 3 (Cattell, 1973b). Both internal-consistency and test-retest data are reported for scale 1 on the basis of the test performance of 113 elementary school children of unspecified ages. Test-retest reliability based on the performances of 57 Head Start children over an unspecified time interval was reported to be .80 for the total test and to range from .57 to .71 for the subtests.

Three kinds of reliability data—internal-consistency, equivalent-form, and test-retest—are reported for scale 2. Based on the performances of 102 female Job Corps applicants, internal consistency for scale 2 was reported to range from .77 to .81 for form A and from .71 to .76 for form B. Split-half reliability, ranging from .95 to .97, was computed from a sample of 200 Mexican and U.S. subjects. Equivalent-form reliability for scale 2 ranged from .58 to .72 with individuals of various ages. Test-retest reliability over an unspecified time interval was .82 for 200 U.S. high school students and .85 for 450 eleven-year-old British secondary school students. There are no reliability data

VALIDITY

The majority of evidence for the validity of the scales rests on a series of factor-analytic studies conducted by Cattell. Essentially, Cattell extracted a general ability factor ("g") and then correlated performance on each of the subtests with that factor. According to Cattell and Cattell, "The real basis of validity of an intelligence test is its correlation with the 'construct' or concept of intelligence in the general ability factor" (1960b, p. 5). Cattell reports that correlations of the subtests with "g" range from .53 to .99.

Additional evidence for the validity of scale 1 consists of reported correlations with the Stanford-Binet (r = .62 for 25 "underprivileged children") and the Goodenough-Harris (r = .46 for 72 unspecified children). Scale 2 has been correlated with a number of other tests, and the correlations are reported in Table 11.2. Samples ranged in size from 186 to 1,000 and came from both the United States and Hong Kong. Validity for scale 3 is based on studies conducted with individuals in Taiwan and mainland China. Cattell reports that the scale correlated .29 with a critical-thinking test, .22 with teacher ratings of intelligence,

TABLE 11.2 Correlations of Scores on Scale 2 of the Culture Fair Intelligence Tests with Scores Earned on Other Intelligence Tests

Test	Correlation with Scale 2
Otis Beta	.49
Pintner General Ability	.69
WISC Verbal	.62
WISC Performance	.63
WISC Full Scale	.72

.23 with total grade average, .32 with math test scores, and .31 with math grades.

In addition, a number of studies are cited in the manual for scale 2 of the Culture Fair Intelligence Tests that provide evidence, according to the author, of immunity of the tests from specific cultural influences.

SUMMARY

The Culture Fair Intelligence Tests provide the examiner with a nontraditional approach to the assessment of intelligence. The tests assess intelligence with relatively little contamination by formal instruction. In evaluating how much meaningful information for one's own setting the tests provide, one must examine both the kind of information sought and one's own theoretical approach to intelligence testing. In interpreting the scores students earn on the scales, one must be especially aware of the large standard deviations of obtained scores. Two major shortcomings of the Culture Fair Intelligence Tests are the inadequate description of the standardization group and the fact that the norms are very out of date.

COGNITIVE ABILITIES TEST

The Cognitive Abilities Test (CogAT) (Thorndike & Hagen, 1986) is a further development of the Lorge-Thorndike Intelligence Tests, which first appeared in 1954. The Iowa Tests of Basic Skills, the Tests of Achievement and Proficiency, and the CogAT comprise the Riverside Basic Skills Assessment Program. There are ten levels of the CogAT. Levels 1 and 2 make up the primary battery. Level 1 is appropriate for use in kindergarten and grade 1, and level 2 is to be used in grades 2 and 3. The other eight levels of the test (levels A through H) are published in a multilevel edition in a single test booklet. Items in the multilevel edition range from easy third-grade items to very difficult items at the twelfth-grade level. Examinees start and stop at different points, depending on the level being administered. The inclusion of eight levels of the test in a single multilevel edition allows teachers to administer levels of difficulty appropriate to the ability of their students. The scales increase in difficulty in very small steps. For students who attain little more than chance-level performance, the next easier level of the scale may be administered; whereas for those who get nearly every item correct, the next more difficult level may be administered. Practice tests are available for all subtests in the scale.

The primary battery is designed to assess the extent to which the child has developed the ability to comprehend oral English; the ability to follow directions; the ability to hold material in short-term memory; effective strategies for scanning pictorial and figural stimuli to obtain either specific or general information; a store of general information and concepts; the ability to compare stimuli and detect similarities and differences in relative size; the ability to classify or order familiar objects; and the ability to use quantitative and special relationships and concepts.

The multilevel edition of the CogAT was constructed to provide a variety of tasks that require the student to discover and use relationships to solve problems. The tasks use verbal, numerical, and nonverbal symbols.

Although both the primary battery and the multilevel edition include three separate batteries—verbal, quantitative, and nonverbal—the subtests included in the two editions differ. The various subtests are described below.

VERBAL BATTERY—LEVELS 1 AND 2

Oral Vocabulary The examiner reads a word aloud, and the student must mark the picture that illustrates it.

Verbal Classification The examiner reads aloud three things that are members of a conceptual category, and the child must mark the one of four possible response pictures that belongs to the same category.

QUANTITATIVE BATTERY—LEVELS 1 AND 2

Quantitative Concepts The examiner asks the child to mark the picture illustrating a particular quantitative concept (for example, "Mark the one that shows a whole apple").

Relational Concepts The examiner asks the child to mark the picture illustrating a particular relational concept (for example, biggest, tallest, beside) read aloud by the examiner.

NONVERBAL BATTERY—LEVELS 1 AND 2

Figure Matrices The student must select from among four response choices the one that best completes a stimulus figure.

Figure Classifications The child is shown three figures that are alike in some way and must select from among four response possibi-

lities the one figure that is like the three stimulus figures.

VERBAL BATTERY—MULTILEVEL EDITION

Sentence Completion The student reads a sentence with a missing word and must select the response word that most appropriately fills the blank.

Verbal Classification The student is given three or four words that are members of a conceptual category and must identify which response word best fits into the same category as the stimulus words.

Verbal Analogies The student must complete verbal analogies of the nature A : B : C : __.

QUANTITATIVE BATTERY—MULTILEVEL EDITION

Quantitative Relations The student must make judgments about relative sizes or amounts of material. Given two quantities (one might be 2 + 4 and the other 2 × 4), the student must identify which one is greater.

Number Series Given a series of numbers that have a progressive relationship to one another, the student must select the number that best completes the relationship.

Equation Building The student must construct correct equations, using numbers and symbols for mathematical operations.

NONVERBAL BATTERY—MULTILEVEL EDITION

Figure Classification Given three figures that are alike in some way, the student must identify the response figure that best fits into the same conceptual category.

Figure Analogies   The student must complete figural analogies of the nature $\triangle : \triangle :: \bigcirc : \underline{}$.

Figure Analysis   The student is given parts of figures and must identify the whole figure that could be formed by putting the parts together.

The entire primary battery requires no reading. The primary battery is administered in three sessions ranging from 35 to 40 minutes each. The multilevel edition is also administered in three sessions. Though administration time necessarily is longer, actual working time is 60 minutes for each of the three batteries of the multilevel edition.

Scores

Transformed scores obtained from the CogAT include standard scores by ages (IQs with a mean of 100 and a standard deviation of 16), percentiles and stanines by age, and percentile ranks and stanines by grade. Separate scores may be obtained for the Verbal, Quantitative, and Nonverbal batteries. No total score for the combination of the three batteries is provided, and the authors rightly recommend that no total score be used.

Norms

The CogAT was standardized concurrently with the Iowa Tests of Basic Skills (Hieronymus, Hoover, & Lindquist, 1986) and the Tests of Achievement and Proficiency (Scannell, 1986). The three measures were standardized on a national sample of about 332,000 students, 14,000 at each grade level. A carefully selected stratified national sample was used. All public school districts in the United States were stratified first on the basis of size

of enrollment, and then on the basis of geographic region. Districts were then stratified on the basis of socioeconomic status within the district, taking into account the median years of education of the population over 18 years of age as well as median family income. After school districts were stratified on the basis of size, geographic region, and socioeconomic status, districts were invited to participate. Once districts agreed to participate, further sample selection occurred. On the basis of previous achievement data, buildings within school districts were selected to be representative of achievement within the districts. Data provided in the test manual show the relationship of the sample to census figures on district size, region of the country, district socioeconomic status, and ethnic characteristics.

In addition to the public school norm, norms are provided for Catholic schools and for private non-Catholic schools. Catholic schools were selected on the basis of geographic region and size of the diocesan school system of which they were members. Private non-Catholic schools were selected on the basis of region and type of school—Baptist, Lutheran, Seventh Day Adventist, other church, and nonchurch.

There are seven separate sets of norms so that student performance can be compared to different groups. There are national, interpolated, local, large city, Catholic, high socioeconomic, and low socioeconomic norms.

Reliability

Data on internal-consistency reliability are reported for the Verbal, Quantitative, and Nonverbal batteries based on the performance of students in the fall 1984 standardization sample. This sample was very large, including about 14,000 students per grade. All reliability coefficients exceeded .83. There is good evidence for the internal consistency of the CogAT.

No other reliability data are reported in the preliminary technical manual. The authors do describe test-retest reliability and alternate-form reliability for earlier editions of the test. These editions differed from the current one, however, so the data are not helpful.

VALIDITY

All validity data in the preliminary technical manual for the CogAT are on earlier editions of the test. There are no data on the validity of the 1986 CogAT. Perhaps these will appear in a final version of the manual.

SUMMARY

The Cognitive Abilities Test consists of three batteries (Verbal, Quantitative, and Nonverbal) designed to measure the intelligence of students in kindergarten through grade 12. The procedures used in standardizing this test are exemplary. Evidence for internal-consistency reliability is good, but there are no data on other forms of reliability. There are no data on the validity of the CogAT.

EDUCATIONAL ABILITY SERIES

The Educational Ability Series (EAS) (Thurstone, 1978) is a group-administered ability test available only as an option with the SRA Achievement Series. The test cannot be separately purchased and administered. There are eight levels (A through H) of the test, matched to the eight levels of the SRA Achievement Series. The test comprises both a verbal and a nonverbal battery. Behaviors sampled by the subtests are as follows.

Picture and Word Vocabulary   This subtest measures a student's knowledge of word meanings by requiring the student to match a stimulus word with a response word or picture.

Number   This subtest measures a student's skill in understanding quantitative concepts.

Picture Grouping   This subtest assesses a student's ability to classify pictured objects. The student is required to identify which of four pictured objects differs from the other three.

Spatial   This subtest assesses development of skill in identifying spatial relationships. Early levels of the test require students to visualize relationships among shapes; at later levels, students are required to identify which of four given forms could be constructed by putting four shapes together.

Number and Series   This subtest assesses pupils' skills in computation and sequencing.

Word Groupings   This subtest assesses skill in identifying the one of four words that does not fit a conceptual category.

SCORES

Several different derived scores are obtained for the EAS. The first is a quotient score with a standard deviation of 16 and a "sliding mean" that begins at 100 at kindergarten and increases by 0.5 each grade year until grade 10, where it is 105. Users may obtain Growth Scale Values (GSVs), standard scores ranging from 20 to 780, that make it easier to contrast change (growth or loss) over time with that of the standardization sample. Users may also obtain percentile and stanine scores.

NORMS

The EAS was standardized concurrently with the SRA Achievement Series (Naslund, Thorpe, & Lefever, 1978) on 83,681 students in 383 schools in eighty-one districts in spring 1978. An additional standardization was completed on 129,900 students in 457 schools in ninety-two districts in fall 1978. A three-stage sampling design was used; stratification of school districts on the basis of geographic region was followed by random sampling of schools within districts and a random sampling of classes within schools. Sample weighting procedures were used to improve the representativeness of the standardization sample. Specific demographic data on the standardization sample are included in Technical Report No. 1.

RELIABILITY

The authors report internal-consistency reliabilities based on scores earned by those who participated in both fall and spring standardizations of the scale. Reliabilities are reported separately by grade level and range from .77 to .93. Most exceed .80. There are no data on test-retest reliability.

VALIDITY

Data on validity of the EAS are limited to correlations of scores on the measure with scores earned on subtests of the SRA Achievement Series. These are reported separately by grade level and range from .28 to .80.

SUMMARY

The Educational Ability Series is a norm-referenced ability measure developed for use with the SRA Achievement Series. The test includes both a verbal and a nonverbal battery. The test is adequately standardized, though data on reliability and validity are limited.

HENMON-NELSON TESTS OF MENTAL ABILITY

The Henmon-Nelson Tests of Mental Ability (Lamke, Nelson, & French, 1973; Nelson & French, 1974) are "designed to measure those aspects of mental ability which are important for success in school work" (p. 3). There are four levels of the test, designed for assessment of children in grades kindergarten through 2, 3 through 6, 6 through 9, and 9 through 12. The Primary form, for kindergarten through grade 2, contains eighty-six items and is published as a consumable test booklet in which pupils record their responses directly. The other three levels each contain ninety items and have an accompanying self-scoring answer sheet so that the test booklets may be reused. Each level takes approximately 30 minutes to administer. The Primary form (kindergarten through grade 2) includes three subtests: Listening, Vocabulary, and Size and Number. These are designed to measure the following behaviors.

Listening   This subtest assesses knowledge of factual information, reasoning ability, and understanding of logical relationships. In each case, information is read to the student, who is then required to identify pictures.

Vocabulary   This subtest assesses understanding of words by requiring the student to identify which of four pictures best matches a word read by the examiner.

Size and Number   This subtest assesses understanding of basic spatial and numerical concepts by measuring "perception and recognition of size, number comprehension, ability to count, and ability to solve simple arithmetic problems" (Nelson & French, 1974, p. 4).

The remainder of the Henmon-Nelson levels do not include subtests but sample several different behaviors that are combined in a global score. A description of how these behaviors are sampled follows.

Vocabulary   The student is required to identify synonyms for stimulus words.

Sentence Completion   The student is required to select which of five response choices best completes a sentence.

Opposites   The student is required to identify antonyms for stimulus words.

General Information   The student is required to answer specific factual questions.

Verbal Analogies   The student is required to complete verbal relationships of the nature A : B : : C : ?.

Verbal Classification   The student is required to identify which of five response possibilities does not belong with the other four.

Verbal Inference   The student is given verbal information and must solve problems by inference.

Number Series   The student is given a sequence of numbers having some relationship to one another and must identify the number or numbers that continue the relationship.

Arithmetic Reasoning   The student is required to solve arithmetic problems employing one or more computational operations.

Figure Analogies   The student is required to solve analogies that employ symbols as stimuli.

SCORES

Raw scores that students earn on the Henmon-Nelson may be transformed to deviation IQs (mean = 100, standard deviation = 16), percentile ranks, and stanines.

NORMS

The levels of the Henmon-Nelson for grades 3 through 12 were standardized on 48,000 pupils (4,000 from each grade plus an additional 4,000 per grade in grades 6 and 9). The Primary form was standardized on 5,000 children from the same schools as those used in the standardization of the other levels. The standardization was completed in regular classes, and the sample was stratified only on the basis of community size and geographic region. The authors provide descriptive tables for community size and geographic region, comparing sample proportions to U.S. population proportions. They do not provide descriptive data about individual students in the standardization sample. The norms for this test are now seriously out of date.

RELIABILITY

Reliability data for the Henmon-Nelson consist of internal-consistency coefficients (split-half reliability estimates corrected by the Spearman-Brown formula) for each of the levels by grade. These coefficients are reported in

Table 11.3. The reported reliabilities are satisfactory for the use of the test as a screening instrument. No test-retest reliabilities are reported.

VALIDITY

Validity data are reported separately in the Primary manual and the manual for grades 3 through 12. The authors of the Henmon-Nelson report concurrent validity for the Primary form based on correlations of scores earned on the Henmon-Nelson and scores earned on the Metropolitan Achievement Test (MAT) by thirty disadvantaged children (the author's definition of *disadvantaged* is not given) and thirty nondisadvantaged children. For the combined groups, the total score on the Henmon-Nelson correlated .72 with the total score on the MAT, while subtest correlations ranged from .41 to .73.

Two sets of validity data are reported for the levels of the test for grades 3 through 12, but they cover specifically grades 3, 6, and 9 only. The Lorge-Thorndike Intelligence Test (grades 3 and 6), the Otis-Lennon Mental Ability Test (grade 9), and the Iowa Tests of Basic Skills were administered to three hundred pupils "representative of those enrolled in grades 3, 6, and 9 in Clearfield, Pennsylvania," during the spring of the year. The following fall the Henmon-Nelson was given. Correlations between the Henmon-Nelson and the Lorge-Thorndike ranged from .78 to .83; those between the Henmon-Nelson and the Otis-Lennon, from .75 to .82. Correlations between scores earned on the Henmon-Nelson and scores earned on subtests of the ITBS ranged from .60 to .86. Predictive validity requires that the predictor test be given first. What the authors have done, in fact, is to establish predictive validity for the other tests using the Henmon-Nelson as a criterion. There are no validity data on other grades or samples

TABLE 11.3   Odd-Even Reliability Coefficients for the Henmon-Nelson Tests of Mental Ability

Level	Grade	r (Corrected)
Primary	K	.84
Primary	1	.89
Primary	2	.88
3–6	3	.95
3–6	4	.96
3–6	5	.96
3–6	6	.97
6–9	6	.95
6–9	7	.94
6–9	8	.95
6–9	9	.95
9–12	9	.93
9–12	10	.95
9–12	11	.95
9–12	12	.96

SOURCE: From *Examiner's Manual for the Henmon-Nelson Tests of Mental Ability, 1973 Revision* (p. 38) by T. Lamke, M. Nelson, and J. French, 1973, Chicago: The Riverside Publishing Co. Copyright 1973. *Examiner's Manual for the Henmon-Nelson Tests of Mental Ability, Primary Form 1* (p. 31) by M. Nelson and J. French, 1974, Chicago: The Riverside Publishing Co. Copyright 1974. Reproduced by permission of the Publisher, The Riverside Publishing Company, 8420 Bryn Mawr Ave., Chicago, IL 60631.

of pupils. The authors state that "since the 1973 Revision retains the essential characteristics of the earlier Henmon-Nelson forms, it is reasonable to expect that Form I [for grades 3–6] will show similar patterns of relationships with achievement tests" (p. 41).

SUMMARY

The Henmon-Nelson Tests of Mental Ability are quickly administered group tests of mental ability. Levels of the scale for grades 3 through 12 are revisions of the earlier forms of the test. The level appropriate for use in kindergarten through grade 2 is a new downward extension of the test. While data about the reliability of the scale indicate adequate reliability for use of the test in screening, there are some serious questions about the adequacy of standardization of the scale. Data regarding validity are inadequate, and the norms are out of date.

OTIS-LENNON SCHOOL ABILITY TEST

The Otis-Lennon School Ability Test (OLSAT) (Otis & Lennon, 1989) is the latest in a series of intelligence tests that date back to 1918. The OLSAT requires a student to perform tasks such as detecting similarities and differences, solving analogies and matrices, classifying, and sequencing as a measure of those verbal, quantitative, and figural reasoning skills most closely related to scholastic achievement. The test is designed to assess "the examinee's ability to cope with school learning tasks, to suggest their possible placement for school learning functions, and to evaluate their achievement in relation to the talents they bring to school learning situations" (Otis & Lennon, 1989, p. 9).

There are seven levels (designated A through G) of the OLSAT used to assess abilities of students in K through grade 12. This most recent edition of the test includes two subtests more than previous editions. There is a separate test for each grade, K–3; thereafter, there is a multilevel edition of the test. At levels A and B (kindergarten and first grade) the entire test is dictated. Level C (grade 3) contains two self-administered subtests, with the remainder of the test dictated. All other levels (D – G) are self-administered. The twenty-one different types of items that comprise the OLSAT fall into five clusters.

SCORES

Raw scores earned on the OLSAT may be converted to one or more derived score: scaled scores, school ability indices (with a mean of 100 and a standard deviation of 16), percentile ranks, stanines, or normal curve equivalents (NCE).

NORMS

The OLSAT was standardized in both fall and spring, 1988. The spring standardization sample consisted of 175,000 students from 1,000 school districts, while the fall standardization was on 135,000 students. The sampling of students was carried out taking into account socioeconomic status (SES), urbanicity, region of the country, and ethnicity. There was no specific stratification on the basis of age, grade, or gender. The sampling distribution is reported, but cross tabulations are not. The sample is not a stratified sample; for example, we do not know how many students from the northeast were from urban environments.

RELIABILITY

At each level, KR-20s are reported for each age and grade. All reliability coefficients exceed .76, with most ranging from .80 to .89. Reliability coefficients for the 1989 edition of the OLSAT are lower than those for previous editions. There are no data on test stability.

VALIDITY

The authors of the OLSAT argue that construct validity of the measure is shown by demonstrating the high consistency of scores across all levels of the test. This is more a validity than a reliability argument. Evidence for validity is presented in the form of high correlations with the most recent edition of the test, and high correlations between the OLSAT and the Stanford Achievement Test. The authors show that scores on the verbal subtests of the OLSAT are better predictors of performance on verbal (language and reading) subtests of the SAT, while performance on the nonverbal section is more predictive of scores on the SAT mathematics subtests.

SUMMARY

The OLSAT is a quickly administered group test of intelligence for which there exists reasonable evidence of internal consistency. There is no support for stability. Evidence for validity is limited. The authors do not report the stratification of the standardization sample.

COPING WITH DILEMMAS IN CURRENT PRACTICE

A number of specific limitations are inherent in the construction and use of group intelligence tests. The first limitation is that most tests have a number of levels designed for use in specific grades (for example, level A for kindergarten through third grade, level B for third through sixth grade). Tests are typically standardized by grade. Students of different ages are enrolled in the same grade; students of the same age are enrolled in different grades. Test authors use interpolation to compute mental ages for students based on grade sampling. In earlier discussions, an age score was defined as the average score earned by individuals of a given age. Let us now consider a problem.

Suppose that an intelligence test has a level Q, which is designed to measure the intelligence of students in grades 6 through 9. As is typical of group intelligence tests, the test is standardized on students in grades 6 through 9, students who range in age from approximately 10 to 15 or 16 years. Norms are based on this age range. The test is later administered to Stanley, age 10-8, who earns a mental age of 7-3. How can this be? Stanley, who is 10 years, 8 months old, could not possibly earn the same score as is typically earned on the test by students who are 7 years, 3 months old, since no 7-year, 3-month-old students were included in the normative sample. The score is based on an extrapolation.

The second limitation is that most group intelligence tests, while standardized on large numbers of students, often are not standardized on representative populations. Most are standardized on school districts, not on individual students. An effort is made to select representative districts, but not necessarily a representative population of individuals. Yet, the normative tables for group intelligence tests typically provide scores for individuals, not for groups.

The third limitation is that most group intelligence tests are standardized on volunteer samples. In the process of standardizing the test, representative districts are selected and are asked to participate. Those districts refusing, for any number of reasons, are replaced by "comparable" districts. This process of replacement may introduce bias into the standardization.

Finally, it must be remembered that when tests are standardized in public schools, those students who are excluded from school are also excluded from the standardization population. Severely retarded students, severely disturbed students, and dropouts are excluded from the norms. Similarly, most authors of group intelligence tests do not describe the extent to which they included students enrolled in special education classes in their standardization samples. Exclusion of students with low IQs biases the norms; the range of performance of the standardization group is reduced, and the standard deviation is decreased. It is extremely important for the authors of group tests to provide tables in test manuals illustrating the composition of the standardization sample. In doing so, it is preferable to include descriptions of the kinds of individuals on whom a test was standardized rather than descriptions of districts.

Many school districts have done away with the use of group intelligence tests for several reasons: the tests have been alleged to discriminate against members of racial and cultural minorities; they provide teachers with limited information for instructional planning; the administration of group intelligence tests produces scores, and teachers may form unrealistic or inaccurate expectancies or stereotypes based on the scores.

In spite of limitations and problems, however, group intelligence tests are still used. Those who use the tests must recognize that they are sampling behaviors and must be aware of the behaviors sampled by the test. School personnel give group intelligence tests to predict future performance, usually future achievement. It is, therefore, wise to use group intelligence tests and group achievement tests that have been standardized on the same population. We recommend that school personnel first select the group achievement test to be used and then choose the group intelligence test that has been standardized on the same population. The following pairs of tests have been standardized on identical groups of students: Otis-Lennon School Ability Test and Stanford Achievement Test, Cognitive Abilities Test and Iowa Tests of Basic Skills, Otis-Lennon School Ability Test and Metropolitan Achievement Tests, and Educational Ability Series and SRA Achievement Series.

SUMMARY

Group intelligence tests are used primarily as screening devices; they are designed to identify those whose intellectual development deviates significantly enough from "normal" to warrant individual intellectual assessment. Many different group intelligence tests are currently used in the schools. A review of the most commonly used group tests illustrates the many kinds of behaviors sampled in the assessment of intelligence. When teachers evaluate students' performances on group intelligence tests, they must go beyond obtained scores to look at the kinds of behaviors sampled by the tests. When selecting group intelligence tests, teachers must evaluate the extent to which specific tests are standardized on samples of students to whom they want to compare their pupils and the extent to which the tests are technically adequate for their own purposes.

STUDY QUESTIONS

1. Obtain a copy of any group intelligence test and identify the domains of behaviors sampled by at least ten *items*. Use the domains described in Chapter 9.
2. Identify at least four major factors a teacher must consider when administering a group intelligence test to students.
3. Why would school personnel give group intelligence tests to students?
4. Suppose you had to decide which group intelligence test to give in your school. What factors would you consider in selecting a test? Which test might you select? Justify your answer.
5. Of what value to classroom teachers are scores from group-administered intelligence tests?

ADDITIONAL READING

Conoley, J. C., & Kramer, J. J. (1989). *Buros tenth mental measurements yearbook*. Lincoln, NE: University of Nebraska Press.

C•H•A•P•T•E•R 12

ASSESSMENT OF SENSORY ACUITY

The *first* thing to check when a child is having academic or social difficulties is whether that child is receiving environmental information adequately and properly. In efforts to identify why children experience difficulties, we too often overlook the obvious in search of the subtle. Vision and hearing difficulties do interfere with the educational progress of a significant number of schoolchildren. The teacher's role in assessment of sensory acuity is twofold. First, the teacher must be aware of behaviors that may indicate sensory difficulties and thus must have at least an embryonic knowledge of the kinds of sensory difficulties children experience. Second, the teacher must know the instructional implications of sensory difficulties. Informed communication with vision and hearing specialists is the most effective way to gain such information. The teacher must have basic knowledge about procedures used to assess sensory acuity in order to comprehend and use data from specialists. This chapter, therefore, differs from previous chapters. It provides basic knowledge about the kinds of vision and hearing difficulties pupils experience as well as an overview of procedures and devices used to assess sensory acuity.

WHY DO WE ASSESS SENSORY ACUITY?

Difficulties in seeing or hearing are among the most obvious reasons that students experience academic and behavioral difficulties in school. They also generally are the kinds of difficulties most easily corrected or compensated for. The link between sensory difficulties and academic problems is easy to appreciate. The fact that sensory difficulties may cause behavioral problems, while not so obvious, has also been established.

VISUAL DIFFICULTIES

There are three ways in which vision may be limited: visual acuity may be limited; the field of vision may be restricted; or color vision may be imperfect.

233

Visual acuity refers to the clarity or sharpness with which a person sees. You probably have heard it said that a keen-sighted person has "perfect" vision—20/20 in both eyes.[1] The person might more accurately be described as demonstrating "normal" vision; the numbers 20/20 simply indicate that the person is able to see a standard-sized object from a standard number of feet away. This method of measuring visual acuity is derived from the use of the Snellen Wall Chart. A person is described as having 20/20 vision who at 20 feet is able to distinguish letters an average person can distinguish at 20 feet. A rating of 20/200 means that the person can distinguish letters at 20 feet that the average person can distinguish at 200 feet. Conversely, 20/10 vision means the person is able to distinguish letters at 20 feet that the average person can only distinguish at 10 feet. The former demonstrates limited vision, while the latter demonstrates better than average distant visual acuity.

The field of vision may be restricted in two ways. A person may demonstrate normal central visual acuity with a restricted peripheral field; this is usually referred to as *tunnel vision*. Or a person may have a *scotoma*, a spot without vision. If the spot occurs in the middle of the eye, it may result in central vision impairment.

Color vision is determined by the discrimination of three qualities of color: hue, saturation, and brightness. The essential difference between colorblind and normal persons is that hues that appear different to normal persons look the same to a colorblind person. Colorblind persons frequently do not know they are colorblind unless they have been tested and told so. They see the same things that other individuals see, and they usually have learned to call them by the same color names. Colorblindness is not an all-or-nothing thing. Most colorblindness is partial; the person has difficulty distinguishing certain colors, usually red and green. Total colorblindness is extremely rare. Colorblindness is an inherited trait found in about one out of twelve males and one out of two hundred females. There is no cure for colorblindness, but the condition is not usually regarded as a handicap.

Few people are totally blind; many have at least light perception and some light projection, either of which helps for mobility. Blindness, for legal purposes, is defined as

> *central visual acuity of 20/200 or less in the better eye, with correcting glasses, or central visual acuity of more than 20/200 if there is a field defect in which the peripheral field has contracted to such an extent that the widest diameter of visual field subtends an angular distance no greater than 20 degrees. (Hurlin, 1962, p. 8)*

Blindness may be either congenital or acquired. Congenital blindness or blindness acquired prior to age 5 has the most serious educational implications.

1. It is also said that hindsight is always 20/20.

It has been said that more people are blinded by definition (the legal definition cited above) than by any other cause (Greenwood, 1963, cited in Barraga, 1976). According to Barraga (1976, p. 13),[2]

> *the term* visually handicapped *is being used widely at present to denote the total group of children who have impairments in the structure or functioning of the visual sense organ—the eye—irrespective of the nature and extent of the impairment. This term has gained acceptance because the impairment causes a limitation that, even with the best possible correction, interferes with incidental or normal learning through the sense of vision. (Taylor, 1973, p. 156)*

When we deal with children, we are concerned primarily with visual handicaps that require special educational provisions. Barraga differentiates among three categories of visual handicaps; these are as follows.

> Blind. *This term [is] used to refer to children who have only light perception without projection, or those who are totally without the sense of vision (Faye, 1970). . . . Educationally, the blind child is one who learns through braille and related media without the use of vision (Halliday, 1970), although perception of light may be present and useful in orientation and movement.*
>
> Low Vision. *Children who have limitations in distance vision but are able to see objects and materials when they are within a few inches or at a maximum of a few feet away are another subgroup. Most low-vision children will be able to use their vision for many school learning activities, a few for visual reading perhaps, whereas others may need to use tactual materials and possibly even braille to supplement printed and other visual materials. . . . Under no circumstances should low-vision children be referred to as "blind."*
>
> Visually Limited. *This term refers to children who in some way are limited in their use of vision under average circumstances. They may have difficulty seeing learning materials without special lighting, or they may be unable to see distant objects unless the objects are moving, or they may need to wear prescriptive lenses or use optical aids and special materials to function visually. Visually limited children will be considered for all educational purposes and under all circumstances as seeing children. (1976, p. 14)*

Estimates of the number of schoolage children who experience visual difficulties range from 5 to 33 percent. Obviously, estimates differ as a function of the definition used and the screening devices employed.

Teachers must be consistently on the lookout for signs of visual difficulty. When children complain of frequent headaches, dizziness, sensitivity to light, or blurred vision, efforts must be made to evaluate the extent to which they

---

2. Quotations from Barraga's *Visual Handicaps and Learning: A Developmental Approach* used in this discussion are copyright 1976 by Wadsworth Publishing Company, Inc.

are seeing properly. Obvious signs of possible visual difficulty include crossed eyes; turned-out eyes; red, swollen, or encrusted eyelids; constant rapid movement of the eyes; watery eyes or discharges; and haziness in the pupils. These, too, should receive special attention in the form of referral for vision screening (U.S. Public Health Service, 1971).

Certain behaviors indicate possible visual difficulties. According to the U.S. Public Health Service (1971), behaviors indicative of potential visual difficulties include holding books unusually close to or far from the eyes while reading; frequent blinking, squinting, or rubbing of the eyes; abnormal head tilting or turning; inattention in blackboard lessons; poor alignment in written work; unusual choice of colors in artwork; confusion of certain letters of the alphabet in reading (*o*'s and *a*'s, *e*'s and *c*'s, *b*'s and *h*'s, *n*'s and *r*'s); inability or reluctance to participate in games requiring distance vision or visual accuracy; and irritability when doing close work.

VISION TESTING IN THE SCHOOLS

Most schools now have vision-screening programs, but the effectiveness of these programs is varied. Two fundamentally different kinds of tests are used: those that screen only central visual acuity at a distance and those that assess both central visual acuity and a number of other visual capabilities.

The Basic Test

The standard Snellen Wall Chart is the most commonly used screening test to assess visual acuity. The test consists simply of a wall chart of standard-sized letters that a child is asked to read at a distance of 20 feet. The test provides limited information about vision, assessing only central visual acuity at a distance of 20 feet. Specific difficulties may be encountered in using the test with some schoolage children. First, children may be unable to read the letters or to discriminate between letters like *F* and *P*. Second, children can often memorize the letters ahead of time. Third, the letters of the alphabet differ in legibility and lend themselves to guessing. The practical criterion for referral using this test is acuity of 20/40 or less in either eye for children in kindergarten through third grade, and 20/30 or less in either eye for those who are older (National Society for the Prevention of Blindness, 1961).

An adaptation of the Snellen Wall Chart, the Snellen E Test, is the most commonly used test with preschool children and those who are unable to read. The letter *E* is presented with its arms facing in one of four directions and the person being tested is asked either to name the direction, to point, or to hold up a letter *E* to match the stimulus. Again, this test assesses only central visual acuity.

More Comprehensive Tests

Several tests assess more aspects of vision than central visual acuity. The Massachusetts Vision Test, introduced in 1940, assesses (1) visual acuity using the Snellen E, (2) *accommodative ability* (the automatic adjustment of the eyes for seeing at different distances) using a plus lens, and (3) muscle imbalance.

Whereas the basic screening tests measure only visual acuity from a distance, the Keystone Telebinocular assesses fourteen different visual skills. The instrument measures the visual functioning of each eye separately and the functioning of both eyes together. In taking this test, students sit in front of a telebinocular instrument, view three-dimensional test slides, and tell the examiner what they see. Visual functioning is assessed at both near point (16 inches) and far point (20 inches); the distances are produced optically, and children remain seated in front of the instrument throughout testing.

Several alternative tests may be administered using the Keystone Telebinocular: a screening test, a comprehensive test battery, the Keystone Plus-Lens Test, the Keystone Primary Skills Test, and the Keystone Periometer Test. Skills tested in the screening test are as follows:

Far Point	*Near Point*
Simultaneous perception	Fusion
Fusion	Vertical eye posture
Color and depth perception	Usable vision
Usable vision	

Skills tested in the comprehensive test battery are as follows:

Far Point	*Near Point*
Simultaneous perception	Fusion
Fusion	Vertical eye posture
Vertical and lateral eye posture	Usable vision of each eye and both eyes together
Depth perception	
Color discrimination	
Usable vision of each eye and both eyes together	

The Bausch and Lomb Orthorater is another instrument used for a more comprehensive assessment of visual functioning. The device assesses farsightedness, muscle balance at both near and far points, and visual acuity using the Snellen E. Like the Keystone Telebinocular, it is a relatively expensive instrument.

The Titmus Vision Tester, illustrated in Figure 12.1, is increasingly used for screening in public school settings. The device is used to assess both acuity and *phoria* (the tendency of the visual axis to turn in or out, up or down) at far and near points. In addition, slides are available to assess preschool children.

In selecting devices to screen visual functioning, it is imperative that the practitioner select devices that are diagnostically accurate; that is, devices that identify individuals who do indeed have visual difficulties. Error in the direction of overreferral to ophthalmologists and optometrists is better than missing anyone who has vision difficulties. Comparative studies of screening devices are difficult to locate. Studies summarized in bulletins published by the National Society for Prevention of Blindness (1961) and by the U.S. Public Health Service (1971) indicate that the Snellen Wall Chart continues to be a relatively effective screening test.

FUNCTIONAL VISION ASSESSMENT

More and more, educators are recognizing the limitations of assessing visual acuity with traditional measures. They note that students with similar ratings on measures of acuity vary considerably in their actual classroom functioning.

FIGURE 12.1   A Titmus Vision Tester

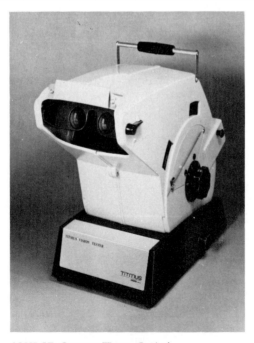

SOURCE: Courtesy Titmus Optical.

A significant effort is under way to develop in-school measures of residual vision and of functional vision. Researchers at the University of Minnesota have been working on the Minnesota Functional Vision Assessment (MFVA) (Knowlton, 1988). They have produced eight subtests, each designed to assess an aspect of functional vision: acuity, binocular coordination, contrast, color, motion, functional fields, accommodation, and illusion. This assessment instrument is for use in the regular school environment.

Assessment of Color Vision

As we have indicated earlier, colorblindness is not usually an educationally handicapping condition. Nevertheless, it is important that color vision be assessed, primarily so that colorblind children and their parents can know that the children have this condition.

Colorblindness is a stable trait, and one we ought to be able to assess with considerable reliability and validity. However, current devices used to assess color vision are not as reliable and valid as would be expected. Adam, Doran, and Modan (1967) state that "it has repeatedly been stressed by experts in the field of color vision (e.g., Franceschetti, 1928; Wright, 1947; Waardenburg et al., 1963) that an accurate diagnosis of color vision can be attained only by the use of an anomaloscope" (p. 297). An *anomaloscope* is a scientific instrument that requires that a person indicate if two simultaneously presented light spots are of approximately equal brightness and if they are the same color. Salvia and Ysseldyke (1972) investigated the validity of measures of colorblindness as compared to the anomaloscope with mentally retarded boys. Validities were low; the tests misdiagnosed from 7 to 30 percent of the boys.

If measures of colorblindness are used with students, we recommend that at least two different tests be given. If a student is identified as colorblind on both tests, there is a strong likelihood that the student is colorblind.

A description of the tests most commonly used to assess color vision follows.

Farnsworth Dichotomous Test for Color Blindness

The Farnsworth Dichotomous Test for Color Blindness (Farnsworth, 1947) consists of fifteen colored bottle caps that the student is asked to order with respect to a reference cap so that each cap is more like the preceding cap than any other. Diagnosis is made by plotting the order of the caps selected on a response sheet.

AO H-R-R Pseudoisochromatic Plates

The AO H-R-R Pseudoisochromatic Plates (Hardy, Rand, & Rittler, 1957) consists of twenty plates. Each plate is divided into four quadrants with background patterns and color (gray) identical for each quadrant and for each plate. In one or two of the quadrants, a symbol may appear, with no more than two symbols per plate. Subjects are asked to state what they see and where they see it.

Dvorine Pseudo-isochromatic Plates

The Dvorine Pseudo-isochromatic Plates (Dvorine, 1953) consists of fourteen number plates and seven trail plates with multicolor dots and a number (or trail) embedded in a contrasting color. Subjects are asked to read the number or trace the trail with a fine brush.

Ishihara Color Blind Test

The Ishihara Color Blind Test (Ishihara, 1970) consists of fourteen plates similar in composition to those in the Dvorine Test. There are seven number plates and seven trail plates. Subjects are asked to name the number or trace the trail with a fine brush.

ASSESSMENT OF HEARING DIFFICULTIES[3]
Signs of Hearing Loss

Early detection of hearing problems is imperative in preschool and schoolage children so that appropriate remedial or compensatory procedures can be instituted. Children with hearing problems characteristically fail to pay attention, provide wrong answers to simple questions, frequently ask to have words or sentences repeated, and hear better in quiet conditions and when watching the teacher's face. Such children often function below their educational potential, are withdrawn, or exhibit behavior problems. Children who are repeatedly sick, have frequent earaches, colds or other upper respiratory infections, allergies, or fluid draining from their ears may also have a concomitant hearing problem. And children who don't speak clearly or who show other types of speech or language problems, as well as children who fail to discrim-

---

3. This section was specially written for this book by Dr. Tom Frank, Professor of Audiology, Department of Communication Disorders, College of Health and Human Development, The Pennsylvania State University.

inate between sounds or words with similar vowels but different consonants, may also have a hearing problem. Finally, some preschool and schoolage children are more at risk for hearing problems, including those having cranio-facial anomalies such as children with cleft palate or Down syndrome, children from a lower socioeconomic class, American Indians and Eskimos, and children classified as learning disabled or retarded.

Any child, regardless of age, having one or more of the hearing-loss symptoms listed above or being at risk for hearing loss should be referred for a hearing test. For schoolage children and depending on the school system, the hearing test may be given by the school nurse, speech-language pathologist, hearing therapist, audiologist, or a trained technician. These professionals have been trained to test hearing efficiently and accurately.

If a hearing problem is detected or the child is difficult to test, making the results questionable, the child should be referred to a doctor specializing in disorders of the ear, called an *otologist* or *otolaryngologist*, or to a specialist in hearing evaluation and rehabilitation, called an *audiologist*. The otologist and audiologist often work together as a team. For children in a preschool setting, additional support personnel for assessing hearing problems may not be available. Such children should be referred to their family physician or directly to an otologist or an audiologist.

Anatomy and Physiology

The assessment of hearing loss and hearing problems in preschool or school-age children is an exacting procedure that requires an understanding of the anatomy and physiology of the auditory system.

The auditory system can be divided into two parts, the *peripheral* and the *central*. The peripheral auditory system can be further divided into three parts. Going from the outside in, these peripheral parts are known as the *outer*, *middle*, and *inner ear*. Each part makes a significant contribution to hearing. The outer ear contains the part we can see, known as the *pinna* or *auricle*, and the ear canal. The outer ear functions as a resonator so that some sounds, especially in the higher frequencies, are presented to the eardrum at a more intense level than their actual intensity level in the environment. The middle ear is an air-filled cavity in the *temporal bone* of the skull and contains the *eardrum* or *tympanic membrane*; three connected bones known as the *malleus, incus,* and *stapes* (collectively called the *ossicles*); and the *Eustachian tube.* The function of the Eustachian tube is to allow air into the middle ear so that the air pressure in the middle ear is the same as in the environment. When a sound strikes the eardrum, it moves back and forth and conveys that movement first to the malleus, then to the incus, and finally to the stapes, which connects to the inner ear. The hearing function of the middle ear is to act as a mechanical transformer so that air-borne sounds striking the eardrum are conveyed to the fluid-filled inner ear with only a minimal loss in energy. The inner ear contains two parts and the origin of the nerve of hearing called the *VIII cranial* or *acoustic nerve*. One part of the inner ear, the *vestibular system*, is responsible for balance, and the other part, the *cochlea*, is responsible for hearing. The cochlea is shaped like a snail and contains three fluid-filled portions; the middle portion, known as the *scala media* contains the *organ of Corti* and is the most important, because it also contains a series of outer and inner hair cells. The hearing function of the inner ear is to convert cochlear fluid movement to a neural output. This is initiated by the mechanical-type movement of the stapes, which creates a movement of the cochlear fluid that acts to stimulate the hair cells. In turn, the output of the hair cells initiates a neural discharge directed to the acoustic nerve, which conveys the neural signal to the central auditory system.

The central auditory system can be divided into two parts, the *brainstem* and the auditory portion of the *temporal lobe* or *cortex*. The neural output of the acoustic nerve is directed to the lower brainstem. Neural tracks within the brainstem convey the neural activity up the brainstem to primary and secondary auditory area of the temporal cortex on each side of the brain. The hearing function of the primary and secondary auditory portion of the temporal cortex is to sample, analyze, and associate the neural input with learned experiences to derive the sense of auditory perception and to appropriately change our listening behaviors. This process is very complex and is not completely understood.

Modes of Hearing

The sensation of hearing can be initiated in either (or both) of two modes: air conduction and bone conduction. Both hearing screening and threshold testing use the air-conduction mode. Hearing thresholds, obtained by testing both air- and bone-conduction modes, help define the type of hearing loss. The severity of hearing loss is defined by testing the air-conduction mode.

Air-conduction hearing occurs when the sense of hearing is initiated by an air-borne sound that enters the outer ear and passes the middle and inner ear and the central auditory system. The vast majority of our everyday hearing experiences occur by air conduction; for example, listening to a teacher's voice or to television. To test hearing, air-conduction signals can be transmitted to the ear via a loudspeaker but are more commonly transmitted through an earphone placed on the outer ear, especially to screen hearing and test threshold. *Bone-conduction* hearing occurs when the head is mechanically vibrated, so that the sense of hearing is initiated in the inner ear with little or no participation of the outer or middle ear. Hearing by bone conduction occurs when we listen to ourselves speak. To test hearing, bone-conduction signals are transmitted to the ear via a small vibrator commonly placed behind the outer ear on the mastoid bone. Normal hearing by air conduction depends on the normal function of the outer, middle, and inner ear and neural pathways beyond, while normal hearing by bone conduction depends on the normal function of the inner ear and beyond.

Audiometer

Hearing screening, hearing-threshold testing, and other types of hearing tests are conducted with an electronic instrument called an *audiometer*. There are many types of audiometers, differentiated by their functions. Some audiometers are meant only for hearing screening, while others are meant for very complex diagnostic hearing testing. Hearing screening audiometers typically present discrete-frequency air-conducted pure tones at a set output level. However, the type of audiometer most commonly used in school settings is known as a *pure-tone audiometer*, which can be used for both hearing screening and threshold testing. A pure-tone audiometer equipped with earphones is shown in Figure 12.2.

A pure-tone audiometer consists of an electronic oscillator that generates pure tones that can be directed to an earphone (one for each ear) for air conduction testing. Some pure-tone audiometers used for screening also can direct a pure-tone to a bone vibrator. However, only air conduction or earphone testing is done for hearing screening. All pure-tone audiometers produce signals at discrete frequencies called pure tones, hence the name, at octave and half-octave intervals over the frequency range that contains all of the sounds used for understanding speech. The term Hertz (Hz), after a German physicist, Heinrich Rudolph Hertz, defines frequency as the number of events or cycles per second. Frequency can be described by the subjective impression it creates, known as *pitch*. A 125 Hz tone has a very low pitch, while an 8000 Hz tone has a very high pitch. The highest pitch on a piano is about 4000 Hz.

The pure-tone audiometer also contains an amplifier and an attenuator that can be adjusted in discrete steps to increase or decrease the sound pressure level output of the earphones. Sound pressure level output can be quantified by a measurement unit known as a *decibel* (dB). A decibel does not have a fixed absolute value. Rather, it is simply a ratio relating one value to another. Since a normal hearing ear does not have the same sound pressure level hearing thresholds at each frequency, audiometers are internally calibrated to a decibel scale called hearing level (HL). As a result, 0 dB HL represents average normal hearing for a pure-tone at each frequency. The hearing level can be varied from −10 for all frequencies to at least 110 dB for most of the frequencies. The physical intensity of a sound creates a subjective impression known as loudness. The relation between intensity and loudness is that as intensity increases loudness increases. For example, a 1000 Hz pure tone at 60 dB HL would be perceived louder than the same frequency tone presented at 40 dB HL. As mentioned previously, 0 dB HL is the threshold of normal hearing, while 40 to 50 dB HL may be thought of as the range of normal everyday speech, and 80 to 90 dB HL would correspond to a very loud shout.

Pure-tone audiometers are also equipped with a silent switch used to turn the pure tone on and off and a switch that activates the right or left earphone or bone vibrator. Further, a pure-tone audiometer has switches, buttons, or dials to control the frequency and hearing level. The American National Standards Institute (ANSI) has issued detailed specifications for audiometers and all pure-tone audiometers sold in the United States conform to these specifications.

Hearing Screening

The primary purpose of hearing assessment in a school situation is to identify children with educationally significant hearing problems. Experience has indi-

FIGURE 12.2   A Portable Pure-Tone Audiometer and Earphones

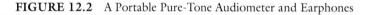

The power switch is located at the bottom right of the audiometer. The intensity (hearing level) of the pure tone is shown in the top right window and the frequency is shown in the top left window. The intensity and frequency can be changed by dials on the right and left side of the audiometer respectively. When one of the stimulus switches, on the top right and left of the audiometer, is depressed, a pure tone will be presented. The ear selector switch is located at the middle, bottom. The pulse, stimulation on, and FM switches can be used to control the presentation mode of a pure tone.
SOURCE: Courtesy of Maico Hearing Instruments, 7375 Bush Lake Road, Minneapolis, MN 55439

cated that teachers or parents may not be able to identify a child with an educationally significant hearing loss. Sometimes teachers and parents identify a normal child as having hearing loss. Thus subjective estimates of a child's hearing ability are not always reliable and more objective testing must be conducted. This is the purpose of hearing screening.

The identification of preschool and schoolage children with hearing problems usually falls within the realm of a hearing-screening program that may also be called a "hearing conservation" or a "hearing-loss identification" program or "identification audiometry." The vast majority of school systems have hearing-screening programs. In fact, almost all states have laws requiring hearing screening of schoolage children. Unfortunately, hearing screening for many children in preschool programs is not mandated by state or federal laws. Therefore many preschool children who have educationally significant hearing losses are not being identified and may become educationally delayed. Hearing-screening programs generally have three components: the actual hearing screening, follow-up hearing-threshold tests for those who fail the screening, and referral.

At one time, group hearing-screening programs were very popular. However, research shows that group hearing tests have lower validity and reliability compared with individual testing. Therefore, hearing should be screened for one child at a time. The additional time required to screen a large number of children on an individual basis is probably more effective in identifying children with hearing problems and is probably more cost-efficient than screening groups of children.

The American Speech-Language-Hearing Association (ASHA) has developed guidelines for hearing screening (ASHA, 1985). These guidelines recommend that hearing be screened annually for children functioning at a developmental level of 3 years through grade 3 and high-risk children regardless of grade. High-risk children are those who have repeated a grade; require special education; are new to the school; are absent during the hearing screening (a technical category—an untested child is "at risk" per se); failed previous hearing screenings; have speech, language, or communication problems; are suspected of having a hearing impairment or have a medical problem associated with hearing impairment (for example, chronic earaches or allergies), and those involved in course work around loud noise (such as band, woodworking, and auto repair). Some state laws mandate that children receive routine hearing screening. For example, Pennsylvania regulations require screening for all children in kindergarten, grades 1, 2, 3, 7, and 11, and those in special ungraded classes.

When hearing screening is conducted, the child is instructed to respond, even if the tone is very soft, by raising his or her hand. For older children, a response button may be used. Some preschool and younger schoolage children must be taught or be conditioned to respond. The tester then places earphones directly on the child's ears, making sure that there is no hair in between the earphone and the opening to the ear canal, that glasses have been removed, and earrings removed if they cause a problem. The child should be seated so that he or she cannot see the examiner. Because earphones are employed for hearing screening, the child's entire auditory system is being stimulated. That is, the child's hearing is being tested by air conduction.

ASHA (1985) has recommended using the frequencies 500, 1,000, 2,000, and 4,000 Hertz (Hz) at a hearing level (HL) of 20 dB (decibels). However, if acoustic-immittance screening (discussed later) is also conducted, screening at 500 Hz can be excluded. ASHA's choice of frequencies relates to the fact that hearing speech sounds in the range of 500 to 4,000 Hz is crucial for understanding speech. ASHA regards 20 dB HL as the upper range of normal hearing for children. It should be noted that many states having regulations pertaining to hearing screening specifying hearing-screening frequencies and hearing levels. For example, in Pennsylvania schoolage children are screened at 250, 500, 1,000, 2,000, and 4,000 Hz at 25 dB HL.

The ASHA (1985) recommendations can be used to provide an example of the procedures for a hearing screening. At this point the child has received the instructions and has been fitted with the earphones. Next, the audiometer hearing-level dial is set to 20 dB HL and a 500-Hz tone is directed to the right earphone, presented, and the child's response is noted. Then the pure tone is changed to 1,000 Hz, presented, and the child's response is noted. This continues at 2,000 and 4,000 Hz. Then the other ear is tested the same way. Needless to say, all hearing testing should always be done in a very quiet room, separated not only acoustically but also by distance from noisy parts of the school. Excessive external noise will have the influence of covering up or masking a pure tone, causing many children to fail the hearing screening when they really have normal hearing.

The ASHA (1985) criterion for failing is the failure to respond at the hearing-screening level at any frequency in either ear. However, states having hearing-screening regulations also have criteria for failure. In Pennsylvania, the criterion for failing is not responding to two or more tones at 25 dB HL in one or both ears. Regardless of the failure criteria, all failures should be retested immediately. This is done by removing the earphones, providing a more careful set of instructions, and repeating the screening test using the same procedures. However, some preschool children may need to have the initial screening tone presented at 40 to 50 dB so that they know what to listen for and can be conditioned to respond. Then the tone should be adjusted to the screening level and the screening test should be repeated.

Hearing-Threshold Testing

Children who fail the hearing screening and repeated screening, should receive a more detailed hearing test in school or be referred to an audiologist or an otologist. The more detailed test is known as a *pure-tone threshold test* or *pure-tone audiometry*. The purpose of this test is to determine the child's hearing thresholds for different pure-frequency tones. For this testing, hearing is measured using earphones (air conduction) and a bone vibrator (bone conduction). However, bone conduction should never be assessed in a school setting because many variables may influence the results, especially external noise. Bone-conduction testing should only be done in a very sound-proofed environment (audiometric test booth) by an audiologist or otologist.

For the pure-tone air-conduction threshold testing, the frequencies tested (listed in sequence) are usually 1,000, 2,000, 4,000, 8,000, 1,000 (recheck), 500, and 250 Hz. One ear is tested before the other ear. Initially, a pure tone is presented loudly enough so the child responds. The examiner then decreases the hearing level in 10-dB steps, presenting a tone at each decreasing 10-dB step, until the child stops responding. Then the level of the tone is increased in 5-dB steps until a response is noted. The tone is then decreased and increased in a bracketing fashion (10-dB down, 5-dB up) several times until a hearing level corresponding to the child's threshold is determined. *Threshold* is usually defined as the lowest hearing level at which a minimum of two out of three ascending (going from inaudibility to audibility) responses occurred. This procedure is continued for each frequency tested by air and by bone conduction for each ear. However, bone-conduction testing is limited to the frequency range of 250 to 4,000 Hz due to the output limitations of a bone vibrator.

In some situations, hearing thresholds must be obtained for one ear when a noise-type signal is directed to the other ear. This is called *masking*, and the resultant hearing threshold for the ear being tested is called a *masked threshold*. Masking is necessary so that the ear not being tested (nontest ear) is eliminated from responding to a pure tone directed to the ear being tested (test ear). Masking is meant to produce an artificial temporary hearing loss in the nontest ear so that the true hearing threshold of the test ear can be obtained. Masked thresholds should only be obtained by an audiologist or otologist.

The hearing-threshold levels obtained as a result of the pure-tone threshold test can be expressed numerically. However, it is more common to plot the hearing thresholds on a graph called an *audiogram*, as shown in Figure 12.3. On the audiogram, frequency in Hertz (Hz) is shown along the top of the audiogram in octave intervals from 125 to 8,000 Hz, and audiometric half-octave intervals at 750, 1,500, 3,000, and 6,000 Hz are also shown. Hearing level in decibels (dB) is shown along the side of the audiogram from −10 to 120 dB in 10-dB steps. The symbols plotted on the audiogram correspond to the hearing threshold for each ear at each frequency tested, using earphones (air conduction) or a bone vibrator (bone conduction) when the thresholds were unmasked or masked. Each audiogram contains an adjacent legend that defines the meaning of the symbols. An audiogram legend is shown in Figure 12.4. For example, an "O" indicates an unmasked air-conduction threshold for the right ear, and an "X" indicates an unmasked air-conduction threshold for the left ear. It is common practice to mark thresholds for the right ear in red and for the left ear in blue.

The criteria for failing a pure-tone threshold test are generally the same as for the hearing screening. Children who fail the air-conduction hearing-threshold test in school should be referred to an audiologist or an otologist for further testing and diagnosis of their suspected hearing loss.

Acoustic-Immittance Screening

Even though the pure-tone air-conduction screening and the threshold test are commonly used to identify children with educationally significant hearing

FIGURE 12.3   Audiogram Showing Frequency in Hertz (Hz) (top) and Hearing Level in Decibels (dB) (side)

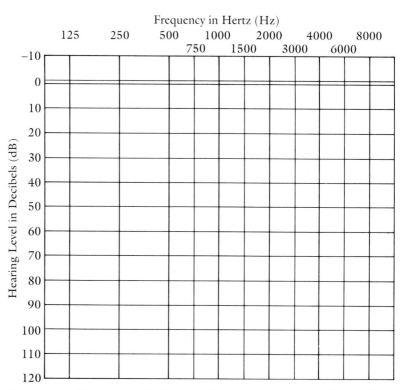

Average normal hearing is 0 dB HL at each frequency and the range of normal is from −10 to 20 dB regardless of frequency.

SOURCE: American Speech-Language-Hearing Association. (1990). Guidelines for Audiometric Symbols, *ASHA, 32* (Suppl. 2), 25–30. Reprinted with permission of the publisher.

loss, they have a number of drawbacks. Both the amount of external noise in the test environment and the rapport between the child and the examiner influence the results. Also, some normal-hearing children might fail these tests because they are immature or inattentive, or because they don't understand the instructions. Moreover, some children may pass these tests although they have a minor hearing problem or a fluctuating hearing loss, usually due to abnormal conditions of the middle ear. Consequently, several school systems and states have initiated another type of screening test, used alone or in conjunction with pure-tone screening. This test is known as *acoustic-immittance screening*; however, it has also been called "impedance audiometry," "admittance audiometry," "oto-admittance," "middle-ear screening," "tympanometry," or "tympanometric screening." Acoustic-immittance screening is designed to detect abnormal conditions of the outer or middle ear, not to detect educationally significant hearing losses. Disorders of the middle ear are the largest cause of educationally significant hearing loss in children, especially for preschool and young schoolage children.

The acoustic-immittance screening consists of inspecting each ear canal for signs of wax blockage and abnormal conditions. If such problems are not

FIGURE 12.4   Audiogram Legend Showing the Meaning of Symbols Plotted on an Audiogram

Audiogram Legend

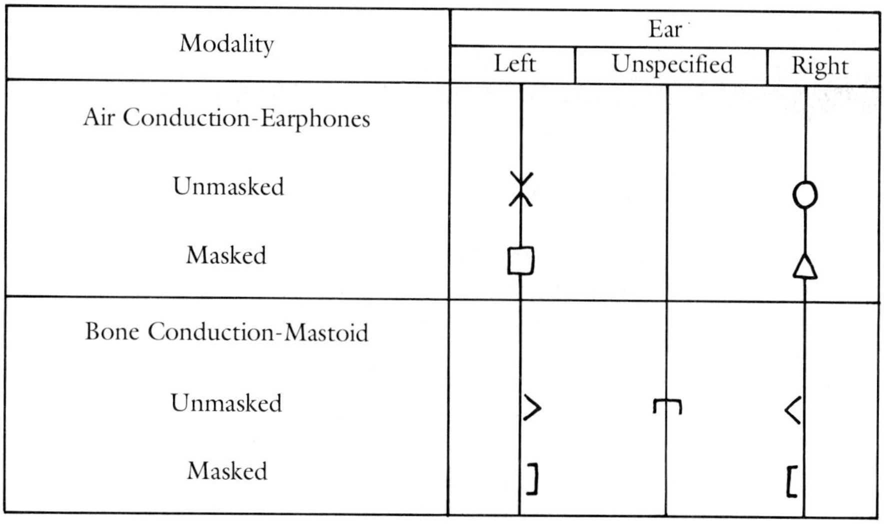

Modality	Ear		
	Left	Unspecified	Right
Air Conduction-Earphones			
Unmasked	X		O
Masked	⊡		△
Bone Conduction-Mastoid			
Unmasked	>	⊓	<
Masked	]		[

This legend shows the symbols for air conduction unmasked and masked thresholds and for bone conduction unmasked and masked thresholds when a bone vibrator is placed on the mastoid bone behind the ear. It should be noted that there are many other symbols that can be used to plot hearing thresholds. The symbols shown in this figure are the most commonly used.
SOURCE: American Speech-Language-Hearing Association. (1990). Guidelines for Audiometric Symbols, *ASHA, 32* (Suppl. 2), 25–30. Reprinted with permission of the publisher.

found, the mobility of the middle ear is then measured. This is done using a specially designed instrument generically known as a "middle-ear screener," "tympanogram screener," "middle-ear analyzer," or an "impedance or admittance meter." Figure 12.5 shows a photograph of a middle-ear screening instrument. Middle-ear screening is done by inserting a probe tip, which may be hand held or held in place with a headband, into the ear canal to obtain an air-tight seal. Once the ear canal is sealed, air pressure in the canal is varied over a range from about +200 to −400 deca Pascal (daPA) while the immittance or compliance of the middle ear is being sampled. The procedure takes less than 10 seconds. Many middle-ear screening instruments are automatic so that measurements begin when the ear canal is sealed.

The result of the testing is usually plotted on a graph known as a *tympanogram*. A tympanogram shows the acoustic immittance or compliance of the middle ear on the *y* axis as a function of air pressure on the *x* axis. Figure 12.6 shows a tympanogram observed for a normal middle ear and for middle ears that have a pathologic condition. Since almost all middle-ear pathologies affect the movement of the middle ear, acoustic-immittance testing is a sensitive screening for middle-ear disorders. Children who fail the middle-ear screening (abnormal tympanogram) may be immediately referred for further testing and diagnosis or (most often) are retested in four to six weeks. If they fail the re-screening, they should be referred for additional testing and diagnosis.

It is important to recognize that screening for middle-ear disorders is not the same as screening for hearing loss. It is very possible that a child could have a middle-ear disorder but yet pass a pure-tone screening. Likewise, a child could have an educationally significant hearing loss and pass the middle-ear screening. To differentiate, note that the primary goal of pure-tone screening is to identify children with educationally significant hearing loss, while the primary goal of acoustic-immittance screening is to identify children with middle-ear disorders. It is in the best health interests of preschool and schoolage children to have both a pure-tone and an acoustic-immittance screening conducted in the same session.

Types of Hearing Loss

As noted, the sense of hearing can be initiated by air and by bone conduction. When hearing thresholds are obtained for both air- and bone-conducted pure tones, the type of hearing loss can be defined.

Normal hearing for preschool and schoolage children is usually defined within a range around 0 dB HL from −10 to 20 dB HL. The audiogram in Figure 12.7 shows the air-conduction thresholds for a 6-year-old girl having normal hearing in each ear from 250 to 8,000 Hz. Note that the right- and left-ear air-conduction symbols show about-average normal hearing (0 dB HL) and lie within the normal range of −10 to 20 dB HL. In this case, bone-conduction thresholds were not measured, because the child had normal air-conduction hearing.

If a child has a hearing loss caused by an abnormal condition (pathology) in the outer ear, such as wax (*cerumen*) buildup in the ear canal, or an abnormal condition of the middle ear, such as fluid in the middle ear (*otitis media*) or a perforation in the eardrum, bone-conduction hearing will be normal be-

FIGURE 12.5 Middle-Ear Screening Instrument

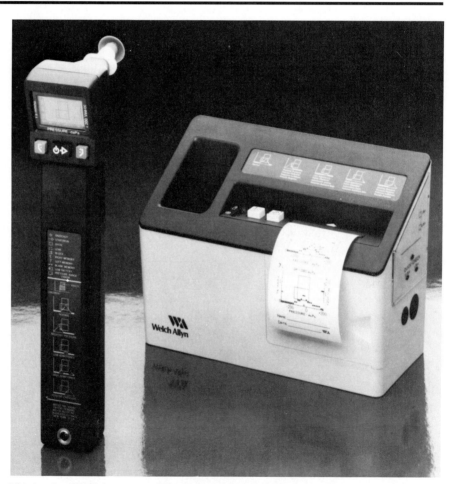

This is a hand-held instrument. When inserted into a child's ear canal and an air-tight seal is obtained, the instrument will automatically sample the immittance of the middle ear. When the instrument is inserted into its power charging stand, a tympanogram will automatically be printed.

SOURCE: Courtesy of Welch Allyn, Inc., 4341 State Street Road, Skaneateles Falls, NY 13153-0220

cause the inner ear is not affected. However, the child's hearing by air conduction will be abnormal, because the hearing problem (dysfunction) is due
to a pathology in the outer or middle ear or both. This type of hearing loss
(normal bone but abnormal air-conduction hearing) is known as a *conductive
hearing loss* because the pathology has affected the sound-conducting mechanisms of the outer or middle ear or both. The audiogram in Figure 12.8
shows the air- and bone-conduction thresholds of a 5-year-old girl having a
mild, bilateral (both ears), conductive hearing loss due to middle-ear fluid.
Note that the bone-conduction masked thresholds are normal but the air-
conduction thresholds are abnormal (>20 dB HL). This child failed the
pure-tone screening and threshold test and was classified as having an educa-

FIGURE 12.6   Tympanogram Configurations for a Normal Middle Ear (a) and for Middle Ears
Having a Pathologic Condition (b to e)

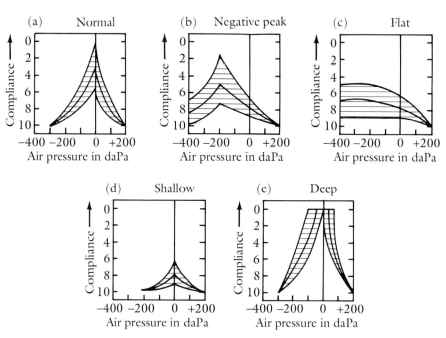

Each tympanogram shows compliance on the y axis, air pressure on the x axis, and a shaded area
used for interpreting the tympanogram. Tympanogram a is normal. Tympanogram b is called
negative peak and is observed in children having negative pressure in their middle ear. Tympanogram c is called flat and is commonly observed in children having middle ear fluid. Tympanogram d is called shallow and is observed when the middle ear is stiffer than normal but does not
contain fluid. Tympanogram e is called deep and is observed in children who have a flaccid eardrum or dysarticulation of the middle ear bones.
SOURCE: Bess, F. H., and Humes, L. E., *Audiology: The Fundamentals* (Baltimore: Williams &
Wilkins, 1990), Figure 4.15. Used with permission of the publisher and author.

tionally significant hearing loss in each ear. The child was referred to an audiologist and otologist for further testing. After the middle-ear fluid problem
was resolved by medication, her air-conduction hearing returned to normal.

If a child has a hearing loss due to a dysfunction of the inner ear, bone- as
well as air-conduction hearing will be equally abnormal (except in cases of
severe, severe to profound, or profound hearing loss, because the bone vibrator has a more limited output than an earphone). This type of loss (abnormal
bone and equally abnormal air-conduction hearing) is known as a *sensorineural, cochlear,* or *neurosensory* hearing loss. There are many causes of a sensorineural hearing loss, such as noise exposure, inheritance, ototoxic drugs,
mumps, measles, and head trauma. The audiogram in Figure 12.9 is for a
7-year-old boy having a mild to moderate, bilateral, high-frequency, sensorineural hearing loss, probably due to a very high fever in infancy. Note that
for the higher frequencies the bone- and air-conduction thresholds are
equally abnormal (>20 dB HL). This child also failed the pure-tone screening
and threshold test and was classified as having an educationally significant

FIGURE 12.7   Audiogram for a 6-Year-Old Girl Having Normal Air-Conduction Hearing in Each
Ear from 250 to 8,000 Hz

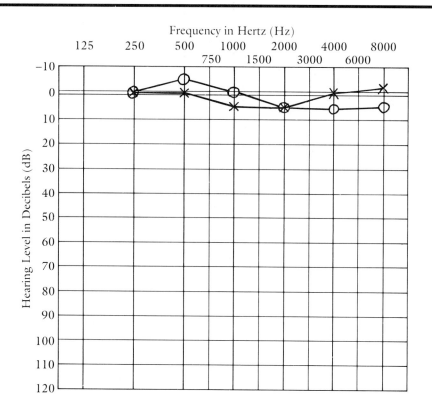

hearing loss in each ear. The child was referred to an audiologist and otologist and consequently fitted with a hearing aid for each ear.

A hearing loss can also be a combination of a conductive and sensorineural hearing loss. This type is known as a *mixed hearing loss* (abnormal bone- and even more abnormal air-conduction hearing). For example, a mixed loss could arise if a child had middle-ear fluid and inner-ear hair-cell dysfunction.

Recently, another type of hearing problem has been identified. This type of hearing problem is related to the function and processing capabilities of the central auditory system and is called a *central auditory processing dysfunction* or *central auditory hearing loss.* Children who have a central auditory processing dysfunction generally pass hearing screenings and threshold tests because they have normal air-conduction hearing and respond well to speech spoken at a normal level. However, these children may have difficulty under-

FIGURE 12.8   Audiogram for a 5-Year-Old Girl Having a Mild, Bilateral (each ear), Conductive Hearing Loss Due to Middle-Ear Fluid

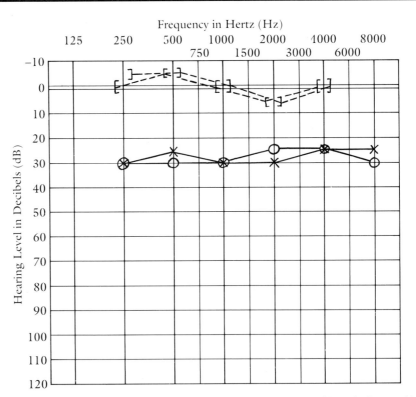

Note that her bone conductions thresholds were normal and were obtained when masking was directed to the non-test ear. However, her air conduction thresholds were abnormal and demonstrated an educationally significant hearing loss.

standing speech in a noisy background, as would occur in a classroom, problems with auditory memory or auditory sequential memory, sounding out words (phonetics), or in reading comprehension. These types of problems can be very educationally significant and frustrating to the child, teacher, and parents. Any child who passes a hearing screening but is still suspected of having a hearing problem should be considered a candidate for central auditory processing testing.

Testing for central auditory processing is very complex, and often the results are difficult to interpret. Children suspected of having a central auditory processing problem should be evaluated by a team of professionals representing many disciplines. If a central auditory problem is diagnosed, new teaching and learning strategies may need to be developed to reduce the educational significance of the problem. These strategies can be provided by special education teachers, speech-language pathologists, and school psychologists.

FIGURE 12.9   Audiogram for a 7-Year-Old Boy Having a Mild to Moderate, Bilateral, High-Frequency, Sensorineural Hearing Loss

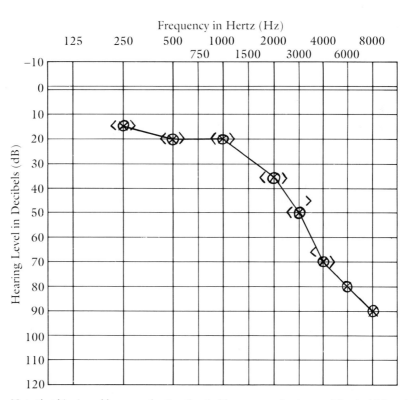

Note that his air and bone conduction thresholds were equally abnormal for the higher pitches.

Severity of Hearing Loss

Besides providing a way to judge type of hearing loss, a pure-tone threshold test also provides valuable information regarding the severity of hearing loss for individual frequencies and frequency regions. This information is very important for understanding speech and fitting hearing aids. There are many ways to calculate hearing loss severity, and many classification schemes. The most common method to determine severity is based on the average better-ear air-conduction hearing threshold. This is done by determining the lowest air-conduction hearing threshold, regardless of ear, at 500, 1,000, and 2,000 Hz, and then determining the average hearing level. This measure is usually referred to as the "better-ear three-frequency average." The frequencies 500, 1,000, and 2,000 Hz, called the *speech frequencies*, were chosen because the majority of sounds needed for understanding speech are contained between 500 to 2,000 Hz. The average hearing loss can then be described or classified in reference to a severity category and in relation to hearing and understanding speech. Figure 12.10 shows an audiogram providing a classification of hearing impairment by severity and handicap for hearing speech. For example, a child with an average hearing loss of 35 dB would be classified as having a mild hearing loss and would have difficulty hearing whispered or faint speech. As another example, a child with a hearing loss of 80 dB would be classified as having a severe hearing impairment and could only understand shouted or amplified speech.

Other Types of Hearing Testing

In addition to pure-tone audiometry, audiologists conduct several other hearing- and middle-ear-function tests. These tests aid in diagnosis and hearing-aid fitting and are beyond the scope of this section. However, I will discuss two important and routine tests that employ speech as the test signal. One test is used to determine a hearing threshold for speech, known as a *speech-recognition threshold* (SRT). The other test is used to determine word-recognition ability, known as a word-recognition score (WRS). (This test was earlier known as a *speech-discrimination* or *speech-intelligibility test*.) Generally, both the SRT and WRS are obtained via earphones for each ear separately and via a loudspeaker located in an audiometric test booth. When testing is done via the loudspeaker, only the better-hearing ear responds. In cases where each ear hears at the same level, the advantage of binaural (both ears) compared with monaural (one ear) hearing can usually be demonstrated.

The SRT is determined by having the child repeat back or point to pictures of bisyllabic words spoken (hotdog) with a spondaic stress pattern while the hearing level is varied. The SRT is defined as the lowest hearing level at which the child responds to 50 percent of the words. The SRT is used to check the validity of the air-conducted pure-tone hearing threshold, to provide an estimate of the child's threshold for speech, and to guide the fit of hearing aids.

A WRS is usually determined by having the child repeat back or point to pictures of words when the words are presented at a hearing level loud enough to produce maximum recognition. A WRS is simply the percentage of words correctly heard. A WRS can also be determined when the words are presented through a loudspeaker when the words are presented at a hearing level corresponding to the level of normal conversational speech. This testing is very important for estimating the child's hearing handicap for speech. For example, if a child had a WRS of 90 percent in his or her better-hearing ear

FIGURE 12.10   Classification of the Severity of Hearing Impairment in Relation to Hearing Handicap for Speech Recognition Shown on an Audiogram

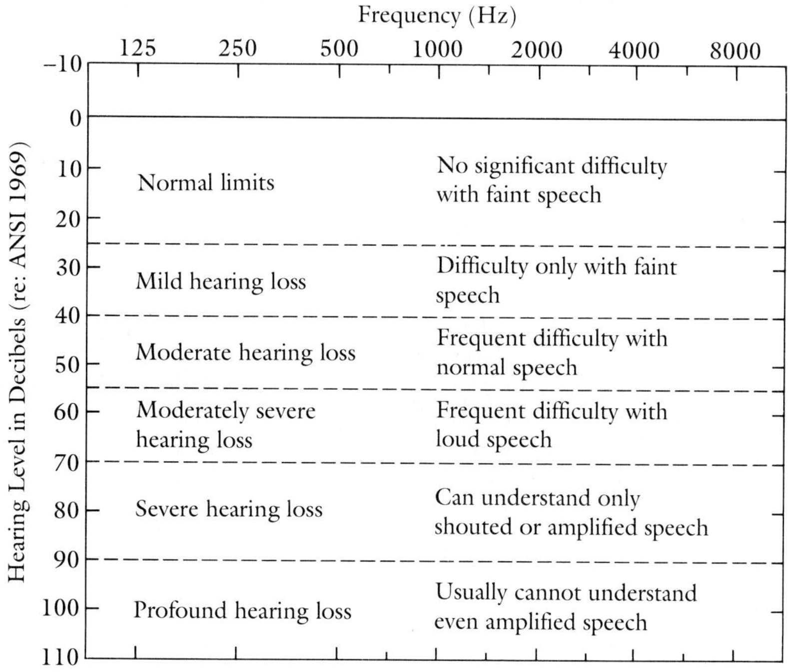

SOURCE: Bess, F. H., and Humes, L. E., *Audiology: The Fundamentals* (Baltimore: Williams & Wilkins, 1990), Figure 4.3. Used with permission of the publisher and author.

when speech was presented loud enough to be heard but only had a WRS of 20 percent when speech was presented at a normal level, the child would be very educationally handicapped for hearing speech. This result would also indicate that if speech were made louder through the use of a hearing aid or hearing loss was medically corrected to normal, the child's WRS would increase from 20 percent to about 90 percent, drastically decreasing the educational significance of the child's hearing loss.

Speech Understanding and Hearing Loss

Recall that children with a conductive hearing loss have a normal inner ear. Such children can perceive speech normally if it is loud enough to overcome the hearing loss. The effect of a 30- to 40-dB conductive hearing loss can be simulated by wearing a foam-type earplug in each ear. If you had such a loss, you would be able to hear normal conversation speech but at a very reduced level. You would have to strain to understand what had been said, and would not be able to hear people talking at a distance. In addition, you might not be able to hear yourself walk, hear whispers, or turn to correct pages in a text. Imagine what it is like for a child to sit in a classroom for five hours, unable to hear and understand everything that is being said!

Children with a sensorineural hearing loss have abnormal function of the inner ear, and the severity of the hearing loss usually increases as frequency increases. These children often report that they can hear someone talking but they cannot always understand what has been said sometimes even with the use of a hearing aid. This occurs because the child is hearing the lower-frequency vowel sounds, which carry the power of speech, but cannot hear the high-pitched consonants, which carry the intelligibility of speech. It is difficult to simulate the effects of a sensorineural hearing loss. However, try listening to a radio station when your radio is slightly mistuned, then turn down the level and increase the base. You will notice that you can hear speech but not understand what has been said.

Children who have sensorineural hearing loss have extreme difficulties hearing in a noisy environment. In most classrooms, the teacher's voice is only about 6 to 10 dB louder than the background noise. Research has clearly demonstrated that if the signal (teacher's voice) to noise (classroom noise) is improved, children with sensorineural loss—and, for that matter, normal-hearing children—will have better speech understanding. This improvement can be achieved by simply talking louder or the better way is to acoustically treat the classroom to reduce the level of the noise. An audiologist can recommend ways to improve the signal-to-noise ratio for increasing speech understanding. Research has also demonstrated that a child with sensorineural hearing loss will have improved understanding for speech when speech is better articulated, spoken directly at the child, and at a slightly slower rate.

Diagnosing a Hearing Loss

An audiologist or otologist can diagnose the extent of a hearing problem in reference to the type of hearing loss (conductive, sensorineural, or mixed), ears involved, and severity. An otologist can diagnose the cause of the hearing loss. Often the audiologist and otologist work together as a team, because each has a particular area of expertise. For example, the otologist is trained from a medical standpoint and has expertise in physical examining of the ears and in treating ear disorders. If the child has a conductive or mixed hearing loss, the otologist can usually provide the appropriate treatment (drug therapy or surgery). The audiologist is trained from an academic and paramedical standpoint and has expertise in hearing assessment and rehabilitation. If a child has an educationally significant hearing loss due to a noncorrectable conductive or mixed hearing loss or a sensorineural hearing loss, the audiologist can prescribe, fit, and monitor the use of hearing aids. The audiologist can make recommendations to teachers, hearing therapists, speech-language pathologists, and parents concerning the child's hearing ability in different listening environments. And the audiologist has expertise in testing the hearing of nonverbal children and those who are difficult to test.

The Most Common Problem—Otitis Media

The most common type of hearing problem in preschool and schoolage children is a conductive hearing loss due to middle-ear fluid. This condition is commonly called *otitis media with effusion* (fluid) and can have several causes. However, almost all the causes are related to dysfunction of the Eustachian tube. Some children have many episodes of otitis media and earaches, especially in early childhood. These children might be categorized as "otitis-media prone." Hearing loss due to otitis media is usually mild, fluctuates (some days more hearing loss than others), and is usually temporary until the fluid dissipates and the eardrum and middle ear return to normal. Generally, otitis media is treated by drug therapy. If this is not successful, the fluid can be removed surgically and a small tube is placed in the eardrum. This surgical procedure is called a *myringotomy with tubal insertion*. The small tube, called a *pressure-equalization (PE) tube*, temporarily takes over the function of the Eustachian tube by allowing air to enter the middle-ear space. A PE tube usually works its way out of the eardrum over time, and can be removed if necessary.

The association between (1) otitis media and (2) speech and language development and learning is not well known. However, some research has suggested that children who have chronic otitis media have more speech and language delays and learning problems than do children free of middle-ear disease.

After appropriate treatment for conductive hearing loss, hearing ability can almost always be restored to normal. In some cases where this is not possible and if the hearing loss is educationally significant, the use of hearing aids should be seriously considered.

The causes of sensorineural hearing loss are far too numerous to describe in this section. However, an educationally significant moderate or more severe sensorineural hearing loss will almost always be detected before a child enters a preschool. On the other hand, educationally significant, sensorineural hearing losses in just one ear (unilateral) or bilateral in the very high frequencies, or bilateral and very mild in all frequencies, are usually detected in kindergarten or first grade. A sensorineural hearing loss will not respond to medical or surgical treatment. For the vast majority of children with sensorineural hearing loss, hearing aids are very helpful.

Recall that children with a mixed hearing loss have a conductive plus a sensorineural hearing loss. Generally, mixed hearing losses in children are caused by a pathology that creates a conductive loss on top of an existing sensorineural hearing loss. The otologist can usually alleviate the conductive part of the hearing loss by medical or surgical treatment. However, in some cases the conductive part of the mixed loss cannot be corrected. If a mixed hearing loss is educationally significant following medical or surgical treatment, the use of hearing aids is warranted.

School Help for the Child

A preschool or schoolage child with a hearing problem should receive assistance from the teacher. The teacher should discuss classroom management of a hearing-impaired child with special support personnel such as a hearing therapist or speech-language pathologist. Preferential seating close to the teacher and talking just a little louder and slower improves the signal-to-noise ratio, thus maximizing a child's ability to hear and to read lips. Of course, if the teacher moves around the room and talks at a distance to the hearing-impaired child, the benefits of preferential seating are lost, especially for a child with a unilateral hearing loss. The teacher must be able to cope with children who have fluctuating hearing loss or permanent hearing loss and wear hearing aids. Sometimes children with fluctuating hearing loss pass a pure-tone hearing and acoustic-immittance screening. The teacher should help arrange to have hearing tested on a day when such children show poor hearing. For children who wear hearing aids, the teacher should ask the hearing therapist, speech-language pathologist, or audiologist for instruction on classroom maintenance of a hearing aid, especially for preschool and young schoolage children. This may require knowing how to put a hearing aid in an ear, adjusting the volume control, and changing the battery. Children with central auditory processing problems are hard to identify, and many require special instruction. Different teaching modes may be needed to maximize the hearing abilities of such children.

Coping with Dilemmas in Current Practice

There are fewer difficulties in accurately assessing sensory acuity than there are in other kinds of assessment. Those who assess vision or hearing acuity are assessing relatively stable human characteristics. There are well-accepted objective standards of performance for making decisions about the nature and extent of vision or hearing difficulties. With the exception of color vision, the relationship between sensory difficulties and performance in the curriculum is well understood and established. And there are known treatments (corrective lenses or hearing aids) for most mild vision or hearing problems. There are also known methods for coping with severe vision or hearing problems.

The major dilemma confronted in assessment of sensory acuity is that, with the exception of routine screening, assessment is done by people outside the school. Students who have serious vision problems are assessed by optometrists or ophthalmologists. Those who have serious hearing problems are assessed by audiologists or ear, nose, and throat specialists. Communication between specialists outside the school and school personnel may be difficult— because specialists are not familiar with the curriculum, do not understand the educational relevance of their diagnoses, or do not take the necessary time to speak with school personnel about their findings for individual children. Difficulty may also come about when school personnel do not understand the vocabulary used by those who assess vision and hearing problems. Problems are most effectively overcome in situations in which there is very good communication and ongoing interaction among school personnel and out-of-school specialists.

Summary

Vision and hearing difficulties can have a significant effect on the performance of children in educational environments. A basic overview of the kinds of vision and hearing difficulties children experience and of the procedures used to assess sensory acuity, can help school personnel decide how to intervene.

Screening tests of both visual and auditory acuity must be individually administered. Individually administered screening tests that are appropriate and reasonably effective have been reviewed. The actual diagnosis of sensory difficulties must be completed by specialists: ophthalmologists, optometrists, audiologists, and otologists.

STUDY QUESTIONS

1. Identify several characteristics (behaviors) that a student might demonstrate that would make you question whether that individual is seeing adequately.
2. Identify several characteristics (behaviors) that might make you question whether a student is hearing adequately.

ADDITIONAL READINGS

American-Speech-Language-Hearing Association. (1985). Guidelines for identification audiometry. *ASHA 27*, 49–53.

Bauman, M. K., & Kropf, C. A. (1979). Psychological tests used with blind and visually handicapped persons. *School Psychology Review, 8*, 257–270.

Bradley-Johnson, S. (1986). *Psychoeducational assessment of visually impaired and blind students.* Austin, TX: Pro-Ed.

Sullivan, P. M., & Vernon, M. (1979). Psychological assessment of hearing impaired children. *School Psychology Review, 8*, 271–290.

Vernon, M., Bair, R., & Lotz, S. (1979). Psychological evaluation and testing of children who are deaf-blind. *School Psychology Review, 8*, 291–295.

C·H·A·P·T·E·R 13

ASSESSMENT OF ORAL LANGUAGE

Coauthored by
Stephen Camarata[1]
Vanderbilt University

There are many ways of defining language. Educators, psychologists, linguists, and speech-language pathologists often have different perspectives on which skills comprise language. Not surprisingly, these differing perspectives on language have resulted in the current plethora of language-assessment instruments on the market, each with an apparently unique and/or oblique method of assessing language. Because of this, the nature of oral language can be rather elusive. Indeed, one could argue that certain kinds of tasks touted as oral language actually fall outside of the construct. As we examine the currently available instruments used to assess oral language, bear in mind that theoretical perspectives on the nature of language have been changing dramatically over the past three decades. Similarly, the technology used to assess language has shadowed the theoretical shifts. Yet new instruments do not displace established tests in the way that new theories replace older models. Rather, the new instruments typically are squeezed into an already crowded field. In order to meaningfully compare instruments arising from quite different theoretical models, the reader must have some understanding of the theoretical underpinnings of each particular instrument. A detailed presentation of a wide variety of theoretical perspectives is beyond the scope of this chapter; instead we present (1) a current description of language and (2) a brief description of several of the major theories of language that have been adapted to assess oral language.

DEFINITION OF ORAL LANGUAGE
Linguistic Aspects

In a way, the definition of language has come full circle. Language theorists have long been interested in describing the various structural aspects of language (see Bloomfield, 1933). This emphasis was followed by a shift to explanatory mechanisms (for example, Osgood, 1962) and a fragmentation of

1. Parts of this chapter are based upon a previous version prepared by Ed Klein.

language with an emphasis on specific dominant components (for example, sentence structure—see Chomsky, 1957). More recently, theorists have returned to descriptive kinds of structural analyses (for example, Lahey, 1988). In the current literature, there is a consensus on the basic definition of language: from a broad, cross-disciplinary perspective, *language can be defined as a code for conveying ideas* (Bloom & Lahey, 1978; Fromkin & Rodman, 1978; Reich, 1986). Although there is some variation, language theorists also propose five basic components to describe the code: phonology, semantics, morphology, syntax, and pragmatics. Figure 13.1 presents a graphic representation of these aspects of language.

In order to examine the basic parts of oral language, consider a typical sentence such as "The girl is running away." At the most basic level, such a sentence includes speech sounds. For example, the word *is* includes a consonant sound and a vowel sound. This aspect of oral language is defined as *phonology* (Fromkin & Rodman, 1978). It should be noted that many speech-language pathologists also use the term *articulation* to describe speech sound production. Although there are some subtle differences in how these terms are used (Ingram, 1976), the term *articulation* is considered to be synonymous with the term *phonology* in this chapter. In addition to speech sounds, the preceding sentence also contains words (such as *the* and *girl*). The study of word meanings is defined as *semantics*. Although the scope of the term *semantics* can extend beyond individual words to include sentence meaning (for example, Filmore, 1968), the term generally applies to word-level meaning.

Closer examination of the sentence indicates that some of the words can contain affixes (suffixes and/or prefixes). For example, the word *running* includes the root word *run* and the progressive suffix *ing*. The description of such affixes falls within the domain of the term *morphology*. Morphology also includes auxiliary and copula forms of the verb *be* (such as the auxiliary verb *is*) and function words (such as *the* in the preceding sentence). In addition to

FIGURE 13.1   Linguistic Aspects of Language

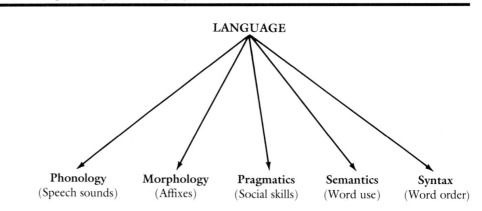

LANGUAGE

Phonology	Morphology	Pragmatics	Semantics	Syntax
(Speech sounds)	(Affixes)	(Social skills)	(Word use)	(Word order)

sounds and words, the example sentence includes a specific word order. This aspect of oral language is known as *syntax*, and includes the rules for arranging the words into a sentence. Another name for the combination of syntax and morphology that may be more familiar to educators is the term *grammar*. The term *grammar* is synonymous with a combination of *syntax* and *morphology* in this chapter.

Finally, the example sentence occurred within a certain linguistic context (for example, providing an example within this chapter). The social context that a sentence appears in is defined as *pragmatics*. In order to illustrate how pragmatics applies to oral language, consider the sentence "Can you close the door?" spoken in two different contexts. In the first case, imagine that a professor has spoken this sentence to a student sitting next to an open door. In this example, the sentence clearly is a request (to close the door). In the second case, imagine that a patient is receiving physical therapy, and the therapist is trying to determine the extent of the patient's residual physical capabilities. In this example, the question should be interpreted literally ("Are you able to close the door?"). In each of these cases, the phonology, semantics, morphology, and syntax are precisely the same, yet the sentence means different things based on the context. Pragmatics has only recently appeared in oral-language theory (see Prutting & Kirshner, 1987), and few standardized assessments are available to evaluate this aspect of language. However, it will become increasingly important within assessment, because the ultimate communicative success of oral-language users depends on using language correctly within a shifting social context.

Thus, language is defined as a code for conveying ideas, a code that includes phonology, semantics, morphology, syntax, and pragmatics. One advantage of adopting this descriptive framework is that it encompasses widely divergent theoretical models for assessment. For example, the Bloom and Lahey (1978) term *content* is included in semantics, whereas *form* can be captured within phonology, morphology, and syntax. Similarly, *sound blending* within an information-processing model (Osgood, 1962) is a part of the phonological domain. The descriptive model is therefore well suited to evaluating assessment instruments constructed with different theoretical underpinnings. Therefore, the following review of standardized assessment instruments is organized within this basic framework for defining oral language.

Finally, one might ask whether this particular definition has any advantages over explanatory (for example, Osgood, 1962) or component-specific (for example, Chomsky, 1957) definitions of language. The construct validity of any of the competing models of language is directly related to the degree to which the model captures actual language behavior. The parts of the linguistic definition represent well-established areas of language inquiry; each basic level of analysis can be observed in any oral-language conversation. Although many tests reviewed here assess only one aspect of language, some include tasks designed to assess several aspects of oral language.

Metalinguistic Aspects

A final term that requires explanation within the definition of oral language, *metalinguistic*, refers to direct examination of the structural aspects of language. For example, a metalinguistic analysis of the *phonological* structure of the example sentence "The girl is running away" reveals that it includes fifteen phonemes. Similarly, a metalinguistic analysis of the *syntactic* structure of the example sentence indicates that the basic structure of the sentence is simple, active, and declarative. The phonics approach to reading could be considered metalinguistic: the child is taught that each letter represents a sound and these sounds can be compiled into words that are then compiled into sentences and so on. Many assessment instruments used with older children involve metalinguistic tasks.

Expressive and Receptive Language

Oral language includes both speaking and listening. That is, speaking can be considered an output mode, while listening involves receiving and analyzing input. Therefore, each of the preceding components of language has both a receptive and an expressive aspect. A synonym for *receptive language* is *comprehension*; a synonym for *expressive language* is *production*. Many tests assess only speaking or only listening. Although a child can have difficulties with both the expressive and receptive aspects of oral language, it is not unusual for a child to have problems in only one of these modalities (for example, expressive skills deficits with normal abilities within the receptive domain). Performance in one modality does not always predict performance in the other. For example, normal speech comprehension does not necessarily mean that the child will have normal speech-production abilities. Although less common, a child with relatively normal expressive skills may have problems with receptive language. Therefore, a complete oral-language assessment includes examination of both modalities. A schematic of these modalities across the basic language domains is shown in Figure 13.2.

WHY ASSESS ORAL LANGUAGE?

There are two primary reasons for assessing oral-language abilities. First, well-developed language abilities are desirable in and of themselves. The ability to converse and express oneself is a goal held by or for most individuals. Those who have difficulties with various aspects of language are often eligible for special services from speech and language specialists or from special educators (usually specialists in learning disabilities). The second reason for assessing oral-language function is that various language processes and skills are believed to underlie subsequent development. For example, recent research indicates that difficulties in oral language are related to the incidence of behavior disorders (see Camarata, Hughes & Ruhl, 1988). Consequently, identifying and remediating oral-language disorders is believed to have a broad, general, and positive effect on personal and academic development.

A HISTORICAL PERSPECTIVE ON ORAL LANGUAGE

As noted earlier, the instruments designed to assess oral language have mirrored the shifting theoretical positions on describing the nature of oral language. At the risk of oversimplification, we can say that the evolution of test development has included instruments designed to test specific aspects of language to the exclusion of others (such as syntax); information-processing capabilities; cognitive capabilities; and a combination of two or more of the basic language areas (phonology, semantics, morphology, syntax, and pragmatics). Note that although the models that were used to construct these instruments have been discarded or modified extensively, the actual instruments may have remained relatively intact. Moreover, the instrument may possess some utility that was not evident within the theoretical model (for example, digit span may no longer be thought to be a precursor to language development, but it may serve to validly identify language-impaired children). However, it is important to determine what aspect of language a particular

FIGURE 13.2   A Model of Language Subskills

Channels of Communication		Phonology	Morphology and Syntax	Semantics	Pragmatics	Ultimate Language Skill
	Reception	Hearing and discrimination of speech sounds	Understanding grammatical structure of language	Understanding vocabulary meaning concepts	Understanding speaker intentions	Understanding spoken language
	Expression	Articulation of speech sounds	Using the grammatical structure of language	Using vocabulary meaning concepts	Using awareness of social aspects of language	Talking

instrument actually assesses. Therefore, let us examine this evolution in a bit more detail.

Specific-Components Models

Until recently, the assessment of oral language simply meant the assessment of expressive phonology, or, more precisely, it meant articulation (Berry & Eisenson, 1956; Van Riper, 1939). Consequently, the assessment instruments developed during this time included no other information about language (for example, the Templin-Darley Test of Articulation). This period was followed by a shift to syntax. Chomsky (1957) spearheaded the movement to new models of grammar, and assessment instruments of syntax soon appeared (such as the Northwestern Syntax Screening Test). This work had a profound effect on language assessment in that it now extended beyond speech sounds. However, although phonology and syntax remain an important part of oral-language assessment, a comprehensive evaluation extends beyond these specific abilities.

Information-Processing Models

The work of Lashly (1953), Miller (1951) and Osgood (1963) lead to models of language that paralleled the development of the computer. Within these models, a series of processing levels needed to complete language comprehension and production are outlined. For example, language comprehension requires that a listener detect the sounds as they travel across the air, filter the relevant signals, and assign meaning to the message. Such models do not focus on the structural aspects of language; rather, the mechanisms for processing the linguistic signal are described. Assessment instruments designed using this model of oral language include a series of tasks designed to assess each of the processing levels thought to contribute to normal language use (such as the Illinois Test of Psycholinguistic Abilities).

Cognitive Models

Piaget (1955) and Vygotsky (1962) have stressed the cognitive bases of language; arguing that oral language arises from the development of more general cognitive structures. For example, Brown (1973) argued that early word use arises from the Piagetian cognitive structure of object permanence. Assessment instruments generated from this theoretical perspective include cognitive tasks thought to relate to language performance (such as the Early Language Inventory). Most intelligence-assessment instruments include items and/or subtests that assess oral language (such as the Weschler Intelligence Scale for Children). Several are exclusively language oriented (such as the Peabody Picture Vocabulary Test).

OTHER CONSIDERATIONS IN THE ASSESSMENT OF ORAL LANGUAGE

Cultural Diversity

Certain factors outside of test content or construction must be considered when undertaking a valid assessment of a child's language competence. First, a child's *cultural background must be considered*. Although most U.S. children learn English, the form of English that they learn depends on where they were born, who their parents are, and so on. For example, in central Pennsylvania a child might say, "My hands need washed," rather than the more standard "My hands need to be washed." In New York City, a child learning Black English might say "birfday" instead of "birthday" or "he be running" instead of "he is running." These and other culturally determined alternative constructions and pronunciations are not incorrect or inferior; they are just different. Indeed, they are appropriate within the child's surrounding community. For example, a number of studies of Black English have shown that it has its own rules of pronunciation, structure, and meaning—and that those rules are at least as complex as those of Standard American English (Wolfram, 1971).

For many years, all nonstandard U.S. dialects were viewed as inferior. Children who did not speak or write in Standard American English were diagnosed as having language disorders. This error has been recognized. Children should be viewed as having a language disorder only if they exhibit disordered production of their own primary language or dialect. If the latter is not the case, then they are simply producing an acceptable language variation. This is not meant to imply that children with language variations should not be taught Standard American English. Knowledge of Standard American English is vital if a person is to progress academically, socially, and economically. Thus, a child should be taught Standard American English, not because other dialects are inherently inferior, but because it allows that child greater access to the general U.S. cultural community (Salvia & Ysseldyke, 1978). However, children who do not speak it should not be viewed as language disordered.

TABLE 13.1   Tests Discussed Elsewhere in This Book That Provide Information about Auditory Discrimination, Letter-Sound Associations, Sound Blending, and Other Receptive Skills

California Achievement Tests
Diagnostic Reading Scales
Durrell Analysis of Reading Difficulty
Gates-McKillop-Horowitz Reading Diagnostic Tests
Iowa Tests of Basic Skills
Kaufman Assessment Battery for Children
Metropolitan Achievement Tests
SRA Achievement Tests
Stanford Achievement Test
Stanford Diagnostic Reading Test
Woodcock-Johnson Psychoeducational Battery

The factor of cultural background becomes particularly important when considering the language assessment devices that are currently available, including those listed in Tables 13.1 through 13.4. Ideally, a child should be compared with others in the same language community in order to determine the existence or nonexistence of a language disorder. Again, ideally, there should be separate norms for each language community, including Standard American English. Unfortunately, the normative samples of most language tests are heterogenous. Thus, scores on these tests may not be valid indicators of a child's language ability. As a final example, consider plate 25 of the Peabody Picture Vocabulary Test (PPVT). This plate contains four pictures, and the examiner is supposed to say, "Show me the wiener." There are many places in this country where the only word for that item is *hot dog* or *frankfurter*. Relatedly, there are many places in this country (for example, northern California) where *wiener* has an anatomical referent. Yet, because the test was standardized using *wiener*, the examiner is required to use that term. If the child has never heard the word *wiener*, or if the word has been learned with a different meaning, he or she is penalized and receives a lower score, although the error is cultural and not a semantic or intellectual deficiency. If there are a number of such items on a test, a child's score can hardly be considered a valid indicator of language ability.

Developmental Considerations

A second major consideration in the assessment of language is the child's *age*, especially if the test being used is criterion-referenced rather than norm-referenced. It is important for a teacher to be aware that language is develop-

TABLE 13.2   Listing of the Most Frequently Used Articulation-Assessment Tests

Name of Test	Author	Publisher	Date of Publication
Arizona Articulation Proficiency Scale	J. Fudala	Western Psychological Services, Los Angeles, CA	1970
A Deep Test of Articulation	E. McDonald	Stanwix House, Pittsburgh, PA	1964
Fisher-Logemann Test of Articulation Competence	H. Fisher & J. Logemann	The Riverside Publishing Company, Chicago, IL	1971
Goldman-Fristoe Test of Articulation[a]	R. Goldman & M. Fristoe	American Guidance Service, Inc., Circle Pines, MN	1986
Phonological Process Analysis[a]	F. Weiner	University Park Press Baltimore, MD	1979
Photo Articulation Test	K. Pendergast, S. Dickey, J. Selmar & A. Soder	Interstate Printers & Publishers, Danville, IL	1969
Predictive Screening Test of Articulation, 3rd ed.	C. Van Riper & R. Erickson	Continuing Education Office, Western Michigan University, Kalamazoo, MI	1973
Templin-Darley Tests of Articulation, 2nd ed.	M. Templin & F. Darley	Bureau of Educational Research, University of Iowa, Iowa City, IA	1969

[a] Reviewed in this chapter.

mental; some sounds, linguistic structures, and even semantic elements are correctly produced at an earlier age than others. Thus, it is not unusual or an indication of language disorder for a two-year-old child to say, "Kitty house," for "The cat is in the house," although the same phrase *would* be an indication of disorder in a three-year-old. It is important to be aware of the developmental norms for language acquisition and to use those norms when making judgments about a child's language competence.

Similarly, it is important to note that some tasks designed to assess oral language are developmental in nature. For example, most 2-year-old children can repeat only one or two digits, whereas older children can repeat much longer number strings. However, a task such as repeating digits should not be viewed

TABLE 13.3 Tests Discussed Elsewhere in This Book That Provide Information About Grammatical Usage

California Achievement Tests	Iowa Tests of Basic Skills
Diagnostic Reading Scales	Metropolitan Achievement Tests
Durrell Analysis of Reading Difficulty	Peabody Individual Achievement Test
Gates-MacGinitie Reading Tests	Stanford Achievement Test
Gilmore Oral Reading Test	Stanford Diagnostic Reading Test
Gray Oral Reading Test–Revised	Woodcock Reading Mastery Tests–Revised

as a precursor to language acquisition. Such skills develop in conjunction *with* language. Therefore, many of the tasks used for the purpose of assessing oral language may not be useful for planning treatment.

GOALS OF A LANGUAGE ASSESSMENT SESSION

The chapter thus far has been serving to lay the groundwork for evaluating instruments used to assess oral language. However, a description of the goals of a language-assessment session must be provided in order to put the use of standard assessment instruments into proper perspective. According to Lahey (1988), the basic objectives of a session to assess oral language include: (1) determining whether the child has a language disorder, (2) determining the goals of intervention, (3) planning procedures for intervention, and (4) determining prognosis (adapted from Table 6-1 in Lahey, 1988, p. 125). As noted, standardized oral-language assessments may not be directly useful for determining the goals of treatment or planning intervention, because the instruments may not directly reflect the child's everyday language use. Rather, such instruments are particularly useful in meeting the first objective: identifying the child as having a language disorder. That is, a psychometrically valid instrument used to assess oral language, that meets a majority of the standardization criteria, is particularly well suited for comparing a child's performance to the normal population. Standardized instruments are perhaps the only reliable and valid method for doing so.

Conversely, standardized instruments used to assess oral language are not constructed to assess a child's conversational abilities. Yet such information is needed for determining treatment goals and for planning intervention (the second and third objectives). Conversational-language assessment uses non-standard procedures such as those outlined by Lee (1976), Miller (1981), or Tyack and Gottsleben (1972). Therefore, to meet all the goals of oral-language assessment, a session should include both a nonstandard assessment

TABLE 13.4   Tests Discussed Elsewhere in This Book That Provide Information About a Child's Vocabulary

Boehm Test of Basic Concepts–Revised	Metropolitan Achievement Tests
California Achievement Tests	Metropolitan Readiness Tests
Cognitive Abilities Test	Otis-Lennon School Ability Test
Culture Fair Intelligence Tests	Peabody Individual Achievement Test
Diagnostic Reading Scales	Peabody Picture Vocabulary Test
Durrell Analysis of Reading Difficulty	Pictorial Test of Intelligence
Educational Ability Series	SRA Achievement Series
Full-Range Picture Vocabulary Test	Stanford Achievement Test
Gates-MacGinitie Reading Tests	Stanford-Binet Intelligence Scale:
Gates-McKillop-Horowitz Reading	4th ed.
Diagnostic Tests	Stanford Diagnostic Reading Test
Gilmore Oral Reading Test	Test of Adolescent Language
Gray Oral Reading Test–Revised	Tests of Basic Experiences 2
Henmon-Nelson Tests of Mental Ability	Test of Nonverbal Intelligence
Iowa Tests of Basic Skills	Wechsler Intelligence Scale for
Kaufman Assessment Battery for	Children–Revised
Children	Woodcock-Johnson Psychoeducational
Lee-Clark Reading Readiness Test	Battery
McCarthy Scales of Children's Abilities	

of conversational-language abilities and administration of a psychometrically sound standardized instrument. A discussion of these methods of language assessment is presented later.

OBSERVING LANGUAGE BEHAVIOR

There has been some disagreement among language professionals concerning the most valid method of evaluating a child's language performance, especially in the expressive channel of communication. In all, there are three procedures used to gather a sample of a child's language behavior: spontaneous, imitative, and elicited.

Spontaneous Language

One school of thought holds that the only valid measure of a child's language abilities is one that studies the language that the child produces spontaneously (for example, see Miller, 1981). Using this procedure, fifty to one hundred consecutive utterances produced as the child is talking to an adult or playing with toys are recorded. With an older child, conversations or storytelling tasks are often used. The child's utterances are then analyzed in terms of phonology, semantics, morphology, syntax, and pragmatics in order to provide information on the child's conversational abilities. Because the construct of pragmatics has been developed only recently, few standard assessment instruments are available to sample this domain. Therefore, spontaneous language-sampling procedures are widely used to evaluate pragmatic abilities (see Prutting & Kirshner, 1987). Although the analysis of a child's spontaneous language production is not found on any standard instruments that assess oral language, some interest has been shown in standard assessment of handwriting and spelling skills in an uncontrived, spontaneous situation (for example, the Test of Written Language by Hammill and Larsen).

Imitation

Imitation tasks require a child to repeat directly the word, phrase, or sentence produced by the examiner. One might assume that such tasks bear little relation to spontaneous performance, but some evidence suggests that such tasks are valid predictors of spontaneous production. In fact, several investigators have demonstrated that children's imitative language is essentially the same in content and structure as their spontaneous language (Brown & Bellugi, 1964; Ervin, 1964; Slobin & Welsh, 1973; Connell & Myles-Zitzer, 1982; Lahey, Launer & Schiff-Myers, 1983). Evidently, the children translate the adult sentences into their own language system and then repeat the sentences using their own language rules. Thus, a young child might imitate "The boy is running and jumping" as "boy run and jump." Because of this, imitation seems to be a valuable tool for providing information about a child's language abilities. One caution should be noted, however. Features of a child's language systems can be obtained using imitation only if the stimulus sentences are long enough to tax the child's memory, as a child will imitate perfectly any sentence *if the length of that sentence is within memory capacity* (Slobin & Welsh, 1973).

In addition, imitation does not preclude the need for spontaneous sampling, because the examiner needs the information derived from direct observation of conversational skills. Rather, the imitation tasks should be used to augment the information obtained within the spontaneous sample, as such tasks can be used to elicit forms that the child did not attempt in the conversations. Standardized imitation tasks are widely used in instruments that assess oral language (such as the Test of Language Development and the Illinois Test of Psycholinguistic Abilities). Assessment devices that use imitation usually contain a number of grammatically loaded words, phrases, or sentences that children are asked to imitate. The examiner records and transcribes the children's responses and then analyzes their phonology, morphology, and syntax. (Semantics and pragmatics are rarely assessed using an imitative mode.) Finally, imitation generally is used only in assessing expressive oral language.

Elicited Language[1]

Using a picture stimulus to elicit language involves no imitation on the part of the child but cannot be classified as a totally spontaneous procedure. In this task, the child is presented with a picture or pictures of objects or action scenes and asked to do one of the following: (1) point to the correct object (a task eliciting receptive vocabulary), (2) point to the action picture that best describes a sentence (receptive language, including vocabulary), (3) name the picture (expressive vocabulary), or (4) describe the picture (expressive language, including vocabulary).

A Comparison of Spontaneous, Imitation, and Picture Formats

There are advantages and disadvantages to all three modes of language elicitation. The use of spontaneous language samples has two major advantages. First, a child's spontaneous language is undoubtedly the best and most natural indicator of everyday language performance. Second, the informality of the procedure often allows the examiner to assess all children quite easily, without the difficulties sometimes associated with formal testing ambience. The disadvantages associated with this procedure relate to the nonstandard nature of the data collection. Although some aspects of language sampling are stable across a variety of parameters, there is much wider variability than is seen with standardized assessments. In addition, language sampling requires detailed analyses across language domains, a procedure that is relatively more time consuming than administering a standardized instrument. Finally, because the examiner does not directly control the selection of target words and phrases, young children may be difficult to understand, or there may be several different interpretations of what the child intended to say. Moreover, the child may have avoided, or not had an opportunity to attempt a particular structure that is of interest to the examiner.

The use of imitation overcomes many of the disadvantages inherent in the spontaneous approach. An imitation task will often assess many different language elements and provide a representative view of a child's language system. Also, because of the structure of the test, the examiner knows at all times what elements of language are being assessed. Thus, even the language abilities of a child with a severe language disorder (especially a severe phonological disorder) can be quantified. Finally, imitation devices can be administered much more quickly than spontaneous language samples. Unfortunately, the

1. Although only stimulus pictures are described in this section, some tests use concrete objects rather than pictures.

advantages of the spontaneous approach become the disadvantages of the imitative method. First, a child's auditory memory may have some effect on the results. For example, an echolalic child may score highly on an imitative test, without demonstrating productive knowledge of the language structures being imitated. Second, part of a sentence may be repeated exactly because the utterance is too simple or short to place a load on the child's memory. Therefore, accurate production is not necessarily evidence that the child uses the structure spontaneously. However, inaccurate productions often reflect a child's lack of mastery of the structure. Thus, one should draw conclusions only about a child's errors from an imitative test. A third disadvantage to imitative tests is that they are often quite boring to the child. Not all children will sit still for the time required to repeat fifty to one hundred sentences without any other stimulation such as pictures or toys.

The use of pictures to elicit language production is an attempt to overcome the disadvantages of both imitation and spontaneous language. Pictures are easy to administer, are interesting to children, and require minimal administration time. They can be structured to test desired language elements and yet retain some of the spontaneity of spontaneous language samples, because children have to formulate the language on their own. As there is no limitation, results are not dependent on the children's word retention skills. Despite these advantages, a major disadvantage limits the usefulness of picture stimuli in language assessment. It is difficult to create pictures guaranteed to elicit specific language elements. Even though it is probably easiest to create pictures for object identification, difficulties arise even in this area. Thus, the disadvantage seen in spontaneous sampling is evident with picture stimuli as well; the child may not produce or attempt to produce the desired language structure.

To summarize, all three methods of elicitation have advantages and disadvantages. The examiner must decide which elements of language should be tested, which method(s) of elicitation is (are) most appropriate for assessing those elements, and which assessment devices satisfy these needs. It should not be surprising that more than one test is often necessary to assess all aspects of language (phonology, semantics, morphology, syntax, and pragmatics), both receptively and expressively. As noted, standardized instruments should be supplemented with measures of conversational abilities within any assessment of oral language. Also, the different language domains are often best suited for assessment within different elicitation procedures. For example, picture stimuli are particularly well suited for assessing phonological abilities, because the examiner should know the intended production. Similarly, imitation tasks are often employed to assess morphological abilities, as the child having difficulty with this domain often deletes suffixes and prefixes during imitation. Finally, because assessment of pragmatics involves determining the child's conversational use of language, this domain should be assessed within spontaneous production.

Summary

Language is defined as a code for conveying ideas with the code consisting of phonology, semantics, morphology, syntax, and pragmatics. In addition, language includes both input and output modalities. A comprehensive assessment of oral language will include information for all these domains across both modalities. Finally, standardized instruments to assess oral language are typically used to identify a child as language-disordered and to indicate areas of weakness. Moreover, the structure of the standardized assessment instrument is predicated on the model of language that was used to construct the test. Therefore, the following review of specific oral-language tests will include references to these factors.

SPECIFIC TESTS—EXPRESSIVE AND RECEPTIVE

GOLDMAN-FRISTOE TEST OF ARTICULATION

Language Component Assessed   Phonology

Communication Channel   Expressive

The Goldman-Fristoe Test of Articulation (GFTA) (Goldman & Fristoe, 1986) is one of the more popular tools developed to assess phonology. It is an individually administered, criterion-referenced device in which most consonant sounds and eleven common consonant blends (*st*, for example) are elicited in differing levels of complexity (word, sentence) and in a variety of word positions (beginning, middle, and end of word). Although the device does not specifically measure vowels, the examiner can still get a fairly good idea of a child's vowel production, since all vowels and diphthongs are used at least once within the stimulus words. The GFTA is divided into three sections.

Sounds-in-Words   In this subtest, thirty-five pictures of familiar objects are presented to the child, who must either name the picture or answer questions pertaining to it. In all, forty-four responses are elicited, including eleven common consonant blends and all single consonant sounds except *zh*; medial position *h, w, wh,* and *y*; and final position voiced *th* (as in *bathe*).

Sounds-in-Sentences   This subtest is designed to elicit a sample of a child's speech in a more complex, spontaneous context. The examiner reads two stories aloud to the child while presenting four or five pictures illustrating each story. After the story is read, the examiner again presents the pictures to the child, who recounts the story. The story is loaded with sounds most commonly misarticulated by children, and the examiner appraises the child's speech-sound production in this more complex context (sentences).

Stimulability   After the first two subtests are completed, the examiner returns to the sounds the child has misarticulated and tries to stimulate correct production by means of a three-step procedure explained in the instructions. The purpose of this subtest is to predict the child's performance within intervention. This clinical information then leads to a decision regarding prognosis for and length of that intervention.

The GFTA differs from some other articulation tests by assessing more than one speech sound at a time. This places a greater load on the listening abilities of the examiner, although many individuals using this test seem to have no problem listening for more than one sound in a given word. The stimulus pictures are large and colorful, making the test very motivating for young children. However, older children might find the device too juvenile, especially compared with the black-and-white pictures of a test such as the Arizona Articulation Proficiency Scale (Fudala, 1970).

Although classroom teachers may administer the GFTA, they should score only the *number* of errors the child makes. A more detailed analysis of these errors requires familiarity with the International Phonetic Alphabet.

Scores

Percentile ranks (based on the National Speech and Hearing Survey conducted by Hill in 1971) are available for schoolage students for the Sounds-in-Words and Stimulability subtests. In addition, percentile ranks are also available for children between 2 and 5 years of age. These norms are from the 1983 sample used to standardize the Khan-Lewis Phonolog-

ical Analysis. Pertinent characteristics of the children making up these norms are not described.

Reliability

Percent agreement data are presented in the manual for three types of generalization. The stability of a child's correctness of production of each sound on two subtests (Sounds-in-Words and Sounds-in-Sentences) was assessed with a one-week interval between assessments. Data were collected on thirty-seven children between the ages of 4 and 8 who were assessed by eight certified (Certificate of Clinical Competence) clinicians. Only median stabilities for each subtest are presented; neither data for each sound nor ranges of values are reported. For Sounds-in-Words, the median reliability was 95 percent; for Sounds-in-Sentences, it was 94 percent; and for the specific type of error made (e.g., omission, distortion, etc.) on Sounds-in-Words, it was 89 percent.

Intrarater agreement (stability of the rater over time) was assessed by having six judges, described only as having had "at least one semester of experience" using the test, evaluate the tape-recorded responses of four individuals who had articulation problems judged to range from mild to severe. Only medians are presented. For presence or absence of error and for the type of error, the median stability was 91 percent.

Interrater agreement was also assessed for Sounds-in-Words. Six judges, described only as having had "at least one semester of experience" using the test, evaluated the tape-recorded responses of four individuals who had articulation problems judged to range from mild to severe. Again, only medians are presented. For presence or absence of error for the sounds, the median was 92 percent; for type of error, the median was 88 percent.

VALIDITY

Because the GFTA is often used as a criterion-referenced device, content validity is most important. The test does seem to have adequately sampled speech sounds. However, no measures of validity are reported.

SUMMARY

The GFTA is an individually administered criterion-referenced device that has supplemental norms. The norms are more than fifteen years old for all but the two- to five-year-olds. Reliability data are inadequately reported, but do appear adequate for at least half of the sample. Validity is a matter of whether the content is appropriate for the user's purposes.

PHONOLOGICAL PROCESS ANALYSIS

Language Component Assessed   Phonology

Communication Channel   Expressive

The Phonological Process Analysis (PPA) (Weiner, 1979) is one of the first attempts to assess a child's articulation abilities in a manner other than examining the child's isolated speech-sound production. Instead, the PPA assumes that there are speech-production rules or patterns that cut across single sounds. These rules, or processes, "are based on such factors as sound environment, syllable structure" and differences in the distinctive features of sounds (Weiner, 1979, p. 1). The PPA is an individually administered, criterion-referenced device that assesses sixteen such phonological rules that might explain a child's speech-production problems.

For each rule tested, there are four to eight stimulus words. Each word is elicited twice from the child. The first mode of elicitation used is delayed imitation, where the child is shown an action picture and read an incomplete sentence. For example, "Uncle George is running fast. Uncle George, be careful; you are running too _____." The child must complete the sentence. Then, the examiner elicits the same stimulus word a second time by asking, "What is Uncle George doing?" The de-

sired response is "running too fast." If the child does not respond correctly to these modes of elicitation, immediate imitation might be required. The examiner transcribes both responses for each stimulus word tested onto a process profile and analyzes the data to determine whether a child is having particular problems with any specific phonological rules. In addition, all responses should be tape-recorded for verification and better analysis of the live transcription.

Although the PPA takes 45 minutes to complete with a cooperative child, it is not necessary to administer the entire analysis in one session. In fact, the examiner might not want to assess all phonological rules with every child.

SCORES

Because the PPA is an unnormed, criterion-referenced device, there is no attempt to attribute scores to a child's responses. The examiner does, however, indicate the percentage of times the child has correctly used the given rule. If the percentage is less than 100 percent, the examiner must determine the extent to which the misuse of that rule is contributing to the child's speech problems. If the examiner decides that the child's misuse of the rule is a significant factor, a program of intervention should be developed to teach the given rule to the child.

RELIABILITY

No reliability data accompany the PPA.

VALIDITY

The content validity of the PPA appears satisfactory. Weiner states that the 136 test items included in the PPA were those that most often assessed the desired phonological rules in a group of 100 children with phonological disorders. It should be noted that neither the sever-

ity nor the type of these children's phonological problems was described. Also, there is no information concerning whether some of the instructions and presentations might be too difficult for younger children.

The types of items included seem an appropriate measure of the test domain. The sample of items seems extensive enough to measure satisfactorily the sixteen phonological rules. Finally, the items assess the rules using two elicitation modes, delayed imitation and recall.

SUMMARY

The PPA is an individually administered, criterion-referenced test intended to assess the child's use of the phonological rules inherent in the production of speech. The lack of reliability and validity data is a weakness in the construction of the instrument.

AUDITORY DISCRIMINATION TEST

Language Component Assessed   Phonology

Communication Channel   Receptive

The Auditory Discrimination Test (ADT) (Wepman, revised 1973) is an individually administered, norm-referenced device intended to measure the auditory discrimination abilities of 5- to 8-year-old children. The procedure used to equate the two forms of the ADT is not specified in the technical information. Each form contains forty pairs of words, ten of which are identical and thirty of which differ from each other in only one phoneme. In the different-word pairs, the location of the differing phoneme is the medial position for vowels and the initial and/or final position for consonants. To administer the device, the ex-

aminer reads each word pair. The child must indicate whether the two words are the same or different.

SCORES

The child receives one point for each correct recognition of different-word pairs, for a possible raw score of 30. The technical manual provides tables with which the examiner can convert raw scores to a five-point rating scale. The scale appears to be based on percentile ranks for those for whom the test is valid. The test is deemed invalid if the child scores below 10 on the different-word pairs, or below 7 on the same-word pairs.

Norms

No data are given concerning either the children in the normative sample or any of their characteristics.

Reliability

Two types of reliability data are presented in the ADT. Test-retest reliability was undertaken twice, with good stability coefficients of 0.91 and 0.95. In addition, alternate-form reliability was estimated as 0.92. Neither the sample used to estimate the reliability coefficients nor the time interval between test administrations is discussed in the manual.

Validity

Of eight studies presented in the manual that purport to establish the validity of the ADT, only seven are truly studies of validity. These seven studies provide information regarding construct validity.

Three of the seven validity studies indicate that there is a significant relationship between age and auditory discrimination score. As children get older, their auditory discrimination scores increase.

Two studies attempt to establish a relationship between auditory discrimination (as measured by the ADT) and reading. In fact, these studies report significant differences in reading scores between those students with adequate auditory discrimination and those with inadequate auditory discrimination. However, when the data are studied closely, some curious facts emerge. The first graders showing adequate auditory discrimination had a mean reading score of 2.2, while the other group (inadequate) had a 1.9 reading grade level. Both of these groups are well above normal reading ability.

Another validity study compared the scores of students in grade 1 on the ADT and the Metropolitan Achievement Tests (MAT). Wepman reports significant correlations between subtests of the MAT and the ADT and implies a causative connection between school achievement and auditory discrimination. However, the correlations found were only between .235 and .348, statistically significant but trivial.

In a final study, Wepman reports a significant difference between the auditory discrimination abilities of children with articulation problems and those without. However, there have been many studies in this same area, and Rees (1973), in a thorough examination of research on this relationship, has not proven the connection between auditory discrimination and speech ability. More recent reviews (see Grunewell, 1981) and experiments (see Locke, 1980a, b) have substantiated this conclusion.

No evidence of content or criterion-related validity is presented in the manual. After assessing the content of the ADT, it is questionable whether the items appropriately and completely measure the domain. For example, the two words in the different-word pairs differ only in placement of the articulators. There is no pair that tests discrimination of (1) acoustic characteristics [such as a stop-burst sound *(t)* versus an affricate *(ch)*], or (2) voicing of the sound versus nonvoicing (*s* versus *z*, for example). Also, some of the more frequently misarticulated sounds (*r, l, w, y*) are not even included in the test. In fact, Winitz (1975) concludes that the Auditory Discrimination Test does not provide the information needed to validly assess a child's auditory discrimination abilities.

SUMMARY

The purpose of the ADT is to assess the auditory discrimination skills of children 5 to 8 years of age. It is individually administered and norm-referenced, although the sample on which the norms are based is not described in the manual. Reliability is high, although the sample used is not described and there is no information concerning the time interval between test administration. The validity of the ADT seems very questionable. Construct validity is open to question, and content validity seems quite poor. No mention is made of criterion validity. The ADT should be used only with caution and with a thorough knowledge of its shortcomings.

TEST OF ADOLESCENT LANGUAGE—2

Language Components Assessed   Semantics, morphology, and syntax

Communication Channels   Receptive and expressive

The revised edition of the Test of Adolescent Language: A Multidimensional Approach to Assessment (TOAL-2) (Hammill, Brown, Larsen, & Wiederholt, 1987) is a norm-referenced device designed for adolescents between the ages of 12 and 18. It is intended to identify areas of relative strength and weakness, document academic progress, and identify those who might profit from programs of language intervention. Six of the subtests may be administered in groups; two (Speaking/Vocabulary and Speaking/Grammar) must be administered individually. The TOAL-2 was designed to assess receptive and expressive, spoken and written vocabulary (semantics) and grammar (morphology and syntax). These abilities are assessed through the eight subtests described below.

Listening/Vocabulary In this thirty-five-item picture vocabulary subtest, the adolescent must select two pictures that relate to the stimulus word read by the examiner.

Listening/Grammar Each of the thirty-five items in this subtest contains three sentences that are read aloud to the adolescent, who must select the two sentences that have the same meaning.

Speaking/Vocabulary In this subtest, the examiner reads a stimulus word and the adolescent must use it in a meaningful sentence. The subtest contains twenty-five stimulus words.

Writing/Vocabulary The adolescent is required to read a stimulus word and write a meaningful sentence using that word within this subtest. The subtest contains thirty items.

Speaking/Grammar In this subtest, the examiner reads a sentence to the adolescent, who must then repeat it. There are 30 stimulus items.

Reading/Vocabulary The adolescent is presented with up to thirty items in this subtest. Each item consists of three stimulus words and a multiple-choice array containing four additional words. The adolescent must select from the array two words that go with the stimulus words.

Reading/Grammar The adolescent is presented with up to twenty-five items, each of which contains five sentences. The adolescent must find the two sentences that mean "almost the same thing."

Writing/Grammar Each of the seventeen items in this subtest contains two or three sentences of varying complexity. The adolescent is instructed to combine the sentences into one. The simple sentences prompt grammatically more complex constructions.

SCORES

Several types of scores are available. The eight subtest scores can be transformed into standard scores (mean = 10, standard deviation = 3). Standard scores (mean = 100, standard deviation = 15) are also available for the TOAL-2 total score and each of the ten composite scores: Listening, Speaking, Reading, Writing, Spoken Language, Written Language, Vocabulary, Grammar, Receptive Language, and Expressive Language.

NORMS

The TOAL-2 was normed on a total of 2,628 adolescents between 12 and 18 years of age. These adolescents make up six normative groups (17- and 18-year–olds are combined) of unknown size. A table on page 7 of the TOAL-2 manual shows that the normative sample corresponds closely to the overall population of adolescents at the time of the 1985 census. There is no more than a 5 percent difference between the TOAL-2 sample and the population with respect to sex, residence (urban/rural), race, ethnicity, and geographic region (four U.S. regions and Canada).

RELIABILITY

Three types of reliability data are presented. First, coefficient alpha was computed for each subtest, each composite, and the total score for each age group. Of the forty-eight age-by-subtest coefficients, sixteen are less than .90, but none is lower than .80. All sixty of the composite-by-age coefficients exceed .90, as do the six total composites. Second, one stability coefficient was computed for fifty-two adolescents attending different grades in a parochial school in Kansas City, Missouri. These adolescents took TOAL, however—not the revised version (TOAL-2). Only two coefficients for composite scores are less than .90, but no reliability data are presented for subtests. Third, data are presented on interscorer agreement of six raters on the three subtests that utilize subjective scoring. For Writing/Vocabulary, the correlations between raters ranged from .70 to .95; for Speaking/Vocabulary, correlations ranged from .86 to .99; and for Writing/Grammar, they ranged from .91 to .99. Calculations of the percentage of interscorer agreement, based on the same data, yielded different results. Only the Speaking/Vocabulary subtest attained a minimum of 90 percent agreement among all raters. Because several items presented difficulties in scoring, the authors revised the criteria for scoring these items. Unfortunately, the revised scoring criteria were not empirically tested, and the revised items were not identified.

VALIDITY

The authors provide a discussion of the selection of formats for subtests. Evidence of criterion-related validity for the first edition of the test is presented. Moderate correlations are reported between TOAL and the Peabody Picture Vocabulary Test, a subtest of the Detroit Tests of Learning Aptitude, the reading and language totals from the Comprehensive Test of Basic Skills, the total score from the Test of Written Language, and the Test of Language Competence. Because TOAL and TOAL-2 are very highly correlated, these correlations can be assumed for TOAL-2 as well as TOAL. In addition, the authors note that the TOAL correlated with intelligence and that students previously identified as mentally retarded or learning disabled attained lower scores. No data are provided to indicate that the TOAL-2 is sufficiently sensitive to monitor a child's progress, and no data are provided to demonstrate that the TOAL-2 identifies students who might profit from programs of language intervention.

SUMMARY

TOAL-2 is a norm-referenced device that assesses three aspects of language—semantics, morphology, and syntax—via both the receptive and expressive channels. Expressive and receptive skills are sampled using both oral and written modes of communication. The composite scores have good internal consistency, and the reported stability and interscorer reliability are adequate, although this information is based on limited samples. In addition, evidence of criterion-related validity is presented. Moreover, the TOAL-2 is a useful instrument that was constructed with higher psychometric rigor than most instruments reviewed in this chapter.

TEST OF AUDITORY COMPREHENSION OF LANGUAGE–REVISED

Language Components Assessed   Morphology, syntax, and some semantics

Communication Channel   Receptive

The Test of Auditory Comprehension of Language–Revised (TACL-R) (Carrow-Woolfolk, 1985) is an individually administered, norm-referenced test designed to assess the language comprehension of children between the ages of 3 years, 0 months and 9 years, 11 months. TACL-R consists of 120 test items in which a child selects, from a set of three pictures, the one picture that best represents a word or sentence read to the child by the examiner. An oral response is not required. Basal and ceiling criteria speed the administration of the test.

Test items are arranged in three categories. Category I assesses the literal meaning of various words and basic word relations (for example, "riding a little bicycle"). Category II as-

sesses grammatical morphemes (for example, past tense, noun and verb agreement). Category III assesses the ability to derive meaning from elaborated sentences (for example, active and passive voices, direct and indirect objects).

The author states that TACL-R scores are useful for identifying children with language problems, for measuring school readiness, for program planning, and for program monitoring.

SCORES

Various tables are provided in the examiner's manual (Carrow-Woolfolk, 1985) for converting raw scores to percentile ranks and age equivalents. A student's performances are compared to those of one of ten age groups: six 6-month norm groups (from 3 years, 0 months to 5 years, 11 months) and four 1-year norm groups (from 6 years, 0 months to 9 years, 11 months). In addition, a table is presented for converting percentile ranks to z-scores, T-scores, deviation quotients (mean = 100, standard deviation = 15), and normal curve equivalents. This table is based on the assumption that the raw scores are normally distributed. However, no data are presented to indicate whether this assumption is valid.

NORMS

A stratified sample of 1,003 children was selected to correspond to the population at the time of the 1980 U.S. census. Stratification variables within each age group included family occupation, ethnic/racial background, sex, and geographical factors (such as region of the United States and community size). The obtained sample was differentially weighted (some children were counted as more than one child) to adjust the norm characteristics so that they would correspond exactly to the census data.

RELIABILITY

Forty split-half estimates of internal consistency (corrected by the Spearman-Brown formula) were computed (ten age groups on three category scores and a total score). For Category I, coefficients ranged from .73 to .95, with half of the coefficients equaling or exceeding .90. Category II coefficients ranged from .82 to .95; four of the ten coefficients were less than .90. For Category III, the coefficients ranged from .86 to .96, with only two coefficients less than .90. As expected, the reli-

ability of the total score was higher; except for one group—8 years, 0 months to 8 years, 11 months—all coefficients exceeded .91. However, the reliability for this age group was consistently low. Stability coefficients for the four scores equaled or exceeded .90, except for Category III (rxx = .89).

VALIDITY

Evidence is presented for the content validity of TACL-R. A wide variety of language elements are assessed. The author also presents evidence for construct validity by demonstrating that TACL-R is correlated with age and hence is developmental. Also, performances of the children in the normative sample corresponded to the expected progression of subtest difficulty (Category I was easier than Category II, which in turn was easier than Category III). Additionally, the performances of the children in the norm sample were better than the performances of children with language disorders. The results of several studies are presented to establish the criterion validity of the TACL-R. However, the data in these studies are difficult to interpret.

Finally, no data are presented to demonstrate that TACL-R scores are useful for identifying children with language problems, for determining school readiness, for planning educational or therapeutic programs, or for monitoring the therapeutic program of an individual student.

SUMMARY

TACL-R is an individually administered device intended to assess receptive morphological, syntactic, and semantic abilities of children between 3 and 12 years of age. Reliability data for total scores is high, but category-score reliability is variable. Some evidence of validity is presented. The total score appears to be the most reliable and valid indicator of comprehension ability.

TEST OF LANGUAGE DEVELOPMENT 2, PRIMARY

Language Components Assessed Semantics, morphology, syntax, and phonology

Communication Channels Expressive and receptive

The Test of Language Development, Primary (TOLD-P) (Hammill & Newcomer, 1982b) is a norm-referenced, individually administered device intended to identify children with language problems, to ascertain a child's language strengths and weaknesses, to evaluate pupil progress in language programs, and to facilitate research. TOLD-P can be administered to children between the ages of 4-0 and 8-11. Various aspects of language are assessed by the following seven subtests.

Picture Vocabulary This twenty-five-item subtest requires a child to point to the one picture in a group of four that best represents the stimulus word read by the tester.

Oral Vocabulary This twenty-item subtest requires a child to define words orally.

Grammatic Understanding This twenty-five-item subtest requires a child to select from a group of three pictures the one that best represents a sentence read by the tester.

Sentence Imitation This thirty-item subtest requires a child to repeat, verbatim, sentences that vary in length from five words to twelve words and that vary considerably in grammatical form.

Grammatic Completion This thirty-item subtest requires a child to complete sentences by supplying appropriate plurals, possessives, tenses, adjectival comparisons, and so forth.

Word Discrimination This twenty-five-item subtest requires a child to say whether two words read by the examiner are the same or different. The words differ from each other in only the beginning, middle, or ending phoneme.

Word Articulation This twenty-item subtest uses pictures of familiar things to prompt speech.

SCORES

Subtest raw scores can be transformed into Language Ages (based on mean performances), percentiles, and standard scores (mean = 10, standard deviation = 3). Subtests can be combined into five composites: Syntax (Grammatic Understanding, Sentence Imitation, and Grammatic Completion); Semantics (Picture Vocabulary and Oral Vocabulary); Speaking (Oral Vocabulary, Sentence Imitation, and Grammatic Completion); Listening (Picture Vocabulary and Grammatic Understanding); and Spoken Language (all subtests). Composites are appropriately obtained by adding the subtest scaled scores and converting this sum to a scaled score with a mean of 100 and a standard deviation of 15. The composites are based on only fifty children at each age (250 children), however, rather than the entire sample (1,836 children).

NORMS

TOLD-P was normed on 1,836 children between 4 and 8 years of age. The distribution of children at each age is not reported. Children came from nineteen states and British Columbia, Canada. A table on page 32 of the TOLD-P manual shows that the normative sample approximates the population at the time of the 1980 census. The difference between TOLD-P and the population with respect to sex is 1 percent; residence (urban/rural), 6 percent; race, less than 1 percent; geographic region (four U.S. regions), 11 percent; and occupation of parents, 11 percent. Nonetheless, these data are insufficient for interpreting the adequacy of the normative sample. Norms are important because they are used to derive standard scores for each age group. Therefore, correspondence between the sample and the population *at each age* is important. Moreover, no sampling plan is discussed; readers are told neither the criteria for inclusion in the sample nor the method of subject selection.

RELIABILITY

Split-half reliability estimates are presented that are based on the performance of part of the standardization sample (only fifty children at each age). For the seven subtests at the five age groups, eleven of the thirty-five corrected coefficients equal or exceed .90. For the composites, eleven of the thirty-five corrected coefficients also equal or exceed .90. Similar coef-

ficients are reported from other studies that assessed special samples.

Stability (with a 5-day interval) was estimated from the performances of twenty-one children who ranged in age from 4 to 8. All but two subtests had stabilities in excess of .90. However, because raw scores were used to estimate stability and raw scores on TOLD-P are correlated with age (see section on Validity), the obtained coefficients were systematically inflated and cannot be used.

VALIDITY

Several types of validity data are presented for TOLD-P. The authors try to establish content validity by arguing that their subtests measure the same things as subtests of other devices used to assess language and by showing that a group of experts felt that the items included in the test were measuring the appropriate domains. However, no evidence is presented to show that the subtests sample the intended domains systematically or completely. To establish criterion-related validity, the authors discuss several studies showing that various TOLD-P subtests correlate with other appropriate language measures at each age. Evidence offered for construct validity is in the form of correlations of TOLD-P scores with age, intelligence, academic achievement, and school readiness. Further evidence offered is in the form of intercorrelations of subtests and factor analyses. Finally, TOLD-P differentiates handicapped students from nonhandicapped students.

SUMMARY

TOLD-P is an individually administered, norm-referenced test designed to assess expressive and receptive semantics, syntax, and phonology. The quality of the norms is unclear. The reliability is adequate for screening and occasionally for classification decisions. The item sample seems too sparse for the test to be used for either program planning or program evaluation. Validity appears adequate for general purposes.

TEST OF LANGUAGE DEVELOPMENT, INTERMEDIATE

Language Components Assessed   Semantics, morphology, syntax, and phonology

Communication Channels   Expressive and receptive

The Test of Language Development, Intermediate (TOLD-I) (Hammill & Newcomer, 1982a) is a norm-referenced, individually administered device designed for use with children between the ages of 8-6 and 12-11. In addition to facilitating research, TOLD-I is intended to identify children with language problems, to ascertain a child's language strengths and weaknesses, and to evaluate pupil progress in language programs. Various aspects of language are assessed by the following five subtests.

Sentence Combining   In this twenty-five-item subtest, a child must combine two or more simple sentences into a compound, complex, or compound-complex sentence incorporating all the essential information in the original simple sentences.

Characteristics   This fifty-item true-false subtest requires a child to tell whether a statement is correct. All statements take the form "All [noun] is/are [noun/adjective]."

Word Ordering   In this twenty-item subtest of syntactic ability, a child is presented with a sentence in which the words have been scrambled. The child must reorder the words to make a correct English sentence.

Generals   This twenty-five-item subtest requires a child to find a superordinate for three words that are read by the examiner.

Grammatic Comprehension   In this forty-item subtest, a child must state whether a given sentence is grammatically correct. Ten sentences are correct, and thirty are incorrect.

SCORES

Subtest raw scores can be transformed int percentiles and standard scores (mean = 10, standard deviation = 3). Subtests can be combined into five composites: Syntax (Grammatic Comprehension, Sentence Combining, and Word Ordering); Semantics (Characteristics and Generals); Speaking (Sentence Combining, Word Ordering, and Generals); Listening (Characteristics and Grammatic Comprehension); and Spoken Language (all subtests).

Composites are appropriately obtained by adding the subtest scaled scores and converting this sum to a scaled score with a mean of 100 and a standard deviation of 15. The Composites are based on fifty children at each age, however, rather than the entire sample.

NORMS

The TOLD-I was normed on 871 children between the ages of 8-6 and 12-11. The distribution of children at each age is unreported. Children came from thirteen states. A table on page 18 of the TOLD-I manual shows that the normative sample approximates the population at the time of the 1980 census. There is no difference between TOLD-I and the population with respect to sex; the difference with respect to residence (urban/rural) is 1 percent; race, 6 percent; geographic region (four U.S. regions), 8 percent; and occupation of parents, 6 percent. However, no sampling plan is discussed; readers are told neither the criteria for inclusion in the sample nor the method of actual subject selection.

RELIABILITY

Coefficient alpha was computed from the performances of fifty children from the standardization sample at each age. For the five subtests at the four age groups, twelve of the twenty coefficients equal or exceed .90. For the composites, all twenty coefficients equal or exceed .90.

Stability (with a one-week interval) was estimated from the performances of 30 fifth- and sixth-grade students. Two subtests had stabilities of less than .90; all composites exceeded

.90. No stability data are provided for other grades or ages.

VALIDITY

Three types of validity are discussed in the TOLD-I manual. First, expert opinion about what the items might be measuring is offered to support content validity. The expert opinion does not attest to the completeness of the domain, however. Second, criterion validity was investigated by correlating TOLD-I scores and scores from the Test of Adolescent Language for a group of thirty students. The obtained correlations were corrected to determine the maximum possible correlation between the scores if they were all completely reliable. The median correlation was .56. Finally, several types of evidence of construct validity are presented. Language scores are associated with chronological age, TOLD-I scores are associated with achievement, and TOLD-I differentiates groups of handicapped students (who might be expected to have poorer language skills) from nonhandicapped students.

SUMMARY

TOLD-I is an individually administered, norm-referenced test designed to assess expressive and receptive semantics, morphology, syntax, and phonology. The internal consistency of the composites is high, as is the stability for the sampled grade levels. Some evidence of construct validity is presented, as is evidence for criterion-related and content validity. As with the other tests in this series (the TOAL-2 and TOLD-2, P), the TOLD-I meets a higher number of psychometric criteria than many tests designed to evaluate oral language

CARROW ELICITED LANGUAGE INVENTORY

Language Components Assessed   Morphology and syntax

Communication Channel   Expressive

The Carrow Elicited Language Inventory (CELI) (Carrow, 1974) is one of the few formal tests designed to give the examiner information about a child's expressive grammatical competence. Although quantification of a child's abilities is possible and normative data are provided, the CELI is best used as a criterion-referenced device that allows the examiner to determine which specific elements of language the child is producing incorrectly.

The CELI is an individually administered device consisting of fifty-one grammatically loaded sentences and one phrase. The lengths of the stimuli range from two to ten words, with an average length of six words. Within these sentences, the following grammatical forms are tested: 41 pronouns (including six different types), 14 prepositions (in four contexts), 7 conjunctions, 41 articles (in two contexts), 9 adverbs, 5 Wh questions, 13 negatives (in three contexts), 59 nouns (including singular and plural), 7 adjectives, 103 verbs (twenty types), 8 infinitives, and 1 gerund.

To administer the test, the examiner presents a stimulus sentence and requests the child to imitate that sentence. Ideally, the child's responses should be taped so that there can be two levels of analysis: one immediate and one after listening to the tape. The scoring sheet is in the form of a matrix, with the grammatical categories listed horizontally and the sentences listed vertically in the order that they are presented to the child. The examiner identifies and analyzes the elements in the sentence that the child has produced incorrectly. In addition a second score sheet, called the verb protocol, allows for a detailed analysis of the verb errors

a child is making. This is helpful because a large percentage of grammatical errors made by children involve verbs. The verb protocol is suggested if the child's verb score falls below the tenth percentile. However, it can be profitably used with children above that cutoff point.

The test itself takes about 20 to 30 minutes to administer, depending on the child's attention span (which can be a problem as the only stimuli are the verbal sentences). The analysis, however, can take up to 45 minutes. Detailed training of prospective examiners, including a training tape and "practice children" included within the kit, is recommended. Although the CELI was developed for use by speech-language pathologists, the manual states that any examiner with a language background will be able to administer and use the test.

Finally, the manual warns that the test should not be used with the following groups of children: (1) those with such severe misarticulation that the examiner cannot understand what is being said, and (2) those with echolalia.

SCORES

The number of grammatical errors the child makes is summed to provide the total error score, from which other kinds of scores may be obtained. An error score in each of the grammatical subcategories can also be obtained. Percentile ranks are given that correspond to the child's total and subcategory error scores. Stanines have been provided for each age level and subcategory.

As has been stated, the CELI is best used as a criterion-referenced device. In fact, the normative scores provided have some problems that are not explained within the technical manual. For example, from age 36 months to 79 months, the expected error score decreases. This is unsurprising. However, from 79 months to 95 months, the error score begins to rise again. Although the author claims that perhaps a test ceiling has been reached at 79 months and that the increased error score is due to random factors, this hypothesis has not been tested. A second problem with the scores provided is the instability of both the subcategory error scores. The author states, "With the exception of the verb subscore in the grammar categories . . . the performance of the five, six, and seven year old children in the subcategories was relatively homogeneous within each age group. Consequently, the percentile scores must be interpreted with caution" (Carrow, 1974). As a result, a 7-year-old child who makes no contraction errors will be at the one-hundredth percentile, while one who makes just one error will be at the fifteenth percentile. Also, because the scores of each of the groups are so homogeneous, a child can achieve a score of 31 at age 3-11 and be placed in the seventy-sixth percentile, and yet one month later, if the child achieves the same score at 4-0, the child is placed in the twenty-eighth percentile. It seems, then, that the range of the age groups used in computing the scores (1 year) is too large to trace the development of language accurately with this task.

Norms

The CELI was standardized on a restricted group of 475 white middle-class children aged 3-0 to 7-11 coming from homes where only Standard American English was spoken. The author acknowledges that this is a narrowly defined group and indicates the intent to gather additional data on language-disordered children and children speaking the major dialects of English. All children within the original norming group were selected from day-care centers and church schools in middle-income neighborhoods in Houston, Texas. Children who had any speech or language disorders were eliminated from the sample.

Reliability

Three measures of reliability are provided for the CELI. Test-retest reliability was determined for twenty-five children (five each across five age levels), selected at random and retested after two weeks. The same examiner performed both tests. The stability coefficient obtained was 0.98.

Two measures of interrater reliability were obtained. First, two examiners listened to and scored ten randomly selected tapes of children's responses, with a resulting reliability coefficient of 0.98. Second, two examiners administered the test to twenty children, ten of whom were diagnosed as having language disorders. Responses were transcribed live and scored, with a resultant correlation coefficient of 0.99.

Validity

Because the CELI is best used as a criterion-referenced test, much of its validity rests on its content validity. Although the author makes little reference to content validity in the test manual, the wide variety of language structures sampled appears to indicate a content-valid test. However, it also appears that certain structures are inadequately sampled; for these structures, more caution is desirable when making conclusions about a child's language abilities.

Evidence of concurrent validity is presented in the technical manual. First, the CELI was compared with the Developmental Sentence Scoring (DSS) procedure by Lee and Canter (1971), a widely used procedure for analyzing children's language abilities. The correlation between the two measures was –0.79. Because the CELI uses error scores and the DSS uses "correct" scores, a negative correlation is observed. Content validity was tested by obtaining scores on the CELI for twenty children. These scores were ranked according to severity and then compared with a ranking of these children according to the external clinical judgment of expert observers. The number of judges conducting this evaluation was not reported in the manual. The rank order correlation (rho) between the CELI and the rank of the children by the judges was 0.77.

Finally, Carrow presents some evidence of construct validity. The correlation coefficient between total error score and age was –0.62. Also, the manual presents some evidence that the CELI successfully separates children with language disorders from those with normal language.

Summary

The CELI is an individually administered device designed to measure the expressive morphological and syntactic abilities of children between 3 and 8 years of age. Reliability and validity data appear adequate, and more than adequate if the CELI is used as a criterion-referenced device.

NORTHWESTERN SYNTAX SCREENING TEST

Language Components Assessed   Syntax, morphology

Communication Channels   Receptive and expressive

For many years, the only formal device commonly used to evaluate a child's language structure was the Northwestern Syntax Screening Test (NSST) (Lee, 1969). Although other tests are now on the market, the NSST is still very popular in many areas. The NSST is an individually administered device, essentially a screening instrument to distinguish children who may have problems in the area of receptive or expressive morphology or syntax. It consists of two parts, the first of which screens a child's comprehension abilities. In part one, the child is shown a page with four black-and-white drawings and then told, "I'm going to tell you about these pictures. When I'm done, you show me the right pictures." The examiner then reads a pair of sentences to the child in the order given on the test form. After reading the sentence pair, the examiner repeats the sentence that has an asterisk after it, and the child must point to the correct picture. Then the examiner repeats the other sentence, and the child must point to the picture that illustrates *that* sentence. This continues for twenty pages and sentence pairs, with the child pointing to the picture that illustrates the sentence.

Part two has a slightly different format and screens expressive language. In part two, the child is shown a page with two pictures on it. The examiner says, "I will tell you about these pictures. When I am done, you say just what I say." The examiner presents the pair of sentences in the order that they appear on the test form, then points to the asterisked picture and asks, "What is this picture?" The child has to repeat the correct sentence from the sentence pair. The examiner then points to the other picture and asks the same question. This procedure is repeated with twenty sentence pairs. In the receptive section, the response is judged correct if the child points to the correct picture. In the expressive section, the response is considered correct if either verbatim responses or responses using equivalent grammatical structures are spoken.

The NSST contains twenty sentence pairs for each communication channel and assesses the following grammatical elements: plurals, verb tenses, pronouns, prepositions, negatives, possessives, passives, subject-verb agreement, Wh questions, and question-statement differences.

SCORES

The child receives a score of 1 for each correct response. Thus, a child can receives a score 0, 1, or 2 for each of the sentence pairs, for a total possible score of 40 for each part.

The total raw score on each section can be converted to percentile ranges (second, tenth, twenty-fifth, fiftieth, seventy-fifth, and ninetieth). If a child scores below the 2nd percentile (more than 2 standard deviations below the mean), the manual states that "the children are almost certain to be in need of interventional language teaching." If a child's score is between the 2nd and 10th percentile, further investigation is recommended before the child is enrolled in an intervention program.

NORMS

The NSST was standardized on 344 children between the ages of 3 years and 7 years, 11 months. The number of children in each age group varied from 34 (at 7-0 to 7-11) to 160 (at 5-0 to 5-11). Normal nursery school or public school classes were used to provide the normative group, and the children's teachers reported on handicapping conditions that would contribute to inadequate language development. The children in the sample generally came from middle- and upper-middle-class midwestern homes in which Standard American English was spoken.

RELIABILITY

No reliability information is provided in the manual.

VALIDITY

The validity of the NSST rests on its content validity when used as instructed. Although the sample of test items measuring the various grammatical constructions is limited, the author appropriately warns against using the NSST as anything but as a screening device. No data are reported in the manual that correlate performance on the NSST with any other language measure.

SUMMARY

The NSST is a screening test of language comprehension and expression, with a sample of morphological and syntactic elements included. No reliability data are presented. In the manual, the author states best the uses of the

NSST: "The NSST is intended to be used as a screening instrument only; it is, in no sense, to be considered a measurement of a child's general language skill nor even as an 'in depth' study of syntax." No direct measures of reliability or validity are reported.

ILLINOIS TEST OF PSYCHOLINGUISTIC ABILITIES

Language Components Assessed   Some morphology, some semantics; other "psycholinguistic" activities that theoretically underlie communication

Communication Channels   Receptive and expressive

The revised edition of the Illinois Test of Psycholinguistic Abilities (ITPA) (Kirk, McCarthy, & Kirk, 1968) is an individually administered, norm-referenced test that has norms for children between the ages of 2 years, 4 months and 10 years, 3 months. The ITPA was designed to measure a child's relative ability to understand, process, and produce both verbal and nonverbal language and was theoretically based on an adaptation of the information-processing model of oral language (see Osgood, 1962). The test contains ten regularly administered and two optional subtests, each designed to minimize the demands of any factor other than that being measured. For example, the auditory reception and visual reception subtests attempt to minimize response demands for the child by requiring only yes-no or pointing responses.

The format of the ITPA includes three hypothetical components of communication: (1) the channels of communication, including sensory input and verbal or motor response; (2) psycholinguistic processes, including reception, association, and expression; and (3) levels of organization, which encompass representational and automatic activities. At the representational level, some form of mediation is required, in contrast to the automatic level, where "the individual's habits of functioning are less voluntary but highly organized and integrated" (Paraskevopoulos & Kirk, 1969, p.

14). The twelve subtests of the ITPA and the behaviors sampled by each follow.

Auditory Reception (AR)   This subtest presents a series of yes-no questions such as, "Do dogs eat?" The syntactic form of the question remains constant until the upper level of the scale, where adjectives are inserted before the noun ("Do wingless birds soar?"). The child responds by nodding or saying *yes* or *no*. This subtest measures receptive vocabulary, a part of semantics.

Visual Reception (VR)   In this subtest, the child is shown a stimulus picture (a German Shepherd dog, for example). After this picture is removed, the child is shown a card having four pictures and instructed to point to one similar to the original picture. Among those four pictures might be another dog (for example, a Chihuahua). This subtest is meant to parallel the auditory reception subtest, while using a different sensory modality.

Auditory Association (AA)   This subtest measures another aspect of semantic comprehension, verbal analogies. The child is presented with, for example, the following incomplete statement: "Brother is a boy. Sister is a _____." The child has to complete the unfinished phrase orally.

Visual Association (VA)   In this subtest, the child is presented with a picture surrounded by four other pictures, one of which goes with the picture in the center. For example, the center picture might be a hammer, surrounded by four pictures, one of which is a nail. The child is then asked to point to the surrounding picture that goes with the picture in the center. At the upper level of the subtest, the task changes so that the child is presented with three pictures (tennis ball, tennis racket, baseball bat) and a blank. The child is instructed to find a picture out of an array of four pictures that goes with the third (baseball bat) as the first goes with the second.

Verbal Expression (VE)   In this subtest, the child is shown an object (such as a block), and is instructed to tell the examiner everything about it. Scoring is based on the number of correct, discrete statements the child makes about the object.

Manual Expression (ME)   This subtest measures a child's understanding of the use of some common objects. After being shown a picture object (for example, a telephone), the child must gesturally show how to use it (that is, the child must dial and talk into a receiver).

Grammatic Closure (GC)   In this subtest, the child is presented with a picture such as that depicted in Figure 13.3 and an incomplete statement such as "Here is one die; here are two ____." The child must complete the statement by supplying the correct word (in this case, "dice"). This subtest is essentially a test of morphology.

Auditory Closure (AC)   This is an optional subtest requiring that a child complete a word that has been presented orally with one or more missing phonemes. For example, the examiner says "olli-op" and asks the child, "What am I talking about?" The child must repeat the entire word (*lollipop*). The authors claim that this function "occurs in everyday life situations such as understanding foreign accents, speech defects, or poor telephone connections" (Paraskevopoulos & Kirk, 1969, p. 21).

FIGURE 13.3   An Example of the Format Used in the Grammatic Closure Subtest of the Illinois Test of Psycholinguistic Abilities

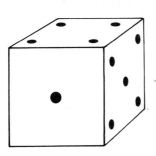

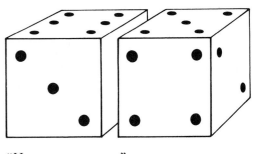

"Here is one die."   "Here are two ____."

Sound Blending (SB) Also optional, this subtest requires the examiner to say a word, but pause for one-half second between syllables ["type-(pause)-wri-(pause)-ter"]. The child must put the syllables together and say the word as a whole.

Visual Closure (VC) In this subtest, the child must recognize familiar objects when only part of the object is pictured. For example, the child is shown a pictured object like a dog and then a complex scene with many objects in it. Within that scene are many partially depicted dogs (for example, just a tail). The child is given 30 seconds to find as many incomplete target objects as possible.

Auditory Sequential Memory (ASM) This subtest requires the examiner to present a sequence of digits orally to the child at half-second intervals. The child is expected to say the oral digit pattern correctly.

Visual Sequential Memory (VSM) In this subtest, the child is presented a card containing a sequence of two or more meaningless designs and given a number of chips, each containing one design. The child looks at the design sequence on the card for 5 seconds and then is requested to reproduce the sequence in correct order from memory, using the chips.

Scores

Various types of scores can be computed from the number of correct responses a child makes for each subtest and the total number of correct responses on the entire test.

Scaled Scores (SS) Raw scores can be converted to scaled scores (SS) having a mean of 36 and a standard deviation of 6. A composite SS is computed based on the total of raw-score points. Because the raw-score variances differ, the different subtests are not equally weighted. This means that in the total score, some subtests are weighted more heavily than others.

Psycholinguistic Ages (PLAs) PLAs are available for the total score, as well as for each subtest. The authors obtained the PLAs by plotting a graph of mean CAs and mean raw scores for the eight age groups tested in the normative sample. After this, means were conducted and intermediate values were calculated. These values are the PLAs. Since Paraskevopoulos and Kirk (1969) present data showing that the "standard deviations of PLA vary from test to test and from age to age" (p. 91), PLAs for different subtests and ages are not comparable.

Psycholinguistic Quotients (PLQs) PLQs are ratio scores (100 PLA/CA). Because of this, PLQs for different subtests, like PLAs, cannot be compared due to the unequal standard deviations. In addition, the technical manual states that "since the standardization sample was comprised of average children, *deviation* PLQs could not be computed without questionable extrapolations" (Paraskevopoulos & Kirk, 1969, p. 80). However, only fourteen pages later, the manual claims that the composite scaled score, "in contrast to the PLQ, is essentially comparable in nature to a *deviation* intelligence quotient" (p. 94). This seems strange in that the composite scaled score is based on the same sample as the PLQ. And the manual has already stated that the sample of average children was too restricted to be able to compute deviation scores without making questionable assumptions.

Percentage Score A percentage score that can be interpreted as a percentile rank for average deviations is also presented in the technical manual. The average deviation (AD) can be obtained by performing the following computations: (1) Subtract the *mean* of a given child's scaled scores from the child's scaled scores on each of the subtests. (2) Sum these differences (there will be twelve of them if twelve subtests are administered). Ignore the + and − signs. (3) Divide this sum by the number of scores. The percentage of children in the normative group whose AD was greater than or equal to the computed AD is shown in a table.

Norms

The ITPA was standardized on a restricted group of children. It is interesting that although the test was designed "for use with children encountering learning difficulties" (Paraskevopoulos & Kirk, 1969, p. 51), children who were having problems in school were systematically excluded from the normative sample. In fact, the children included in the norm groups were "only those children demonstrating average intellectual functioning, average school achievement, average characteristics of personal social adjustment, sensory motor integrity, and coming from predominantly English speaking families" (pp. 51–52). The norm sample included 962 children between the ages of 2-7 and 10-1. These children lived in Bloomington, Illinois; Danville, Illinois; Decatur, Illinois; Madison, Wisconsin; and Urbana, Illinois. These communities were selected because of "practical requirements of being middle-class communities" (Paraskevopoulos & Kirk, 1969, p. 57). Schoolage children were selected by sampling only schools that school administrators judged to be predominantly middle-class. In addition, only classes of normal children were sampled. In or-

der to obtain the preschool sample, younger siblings of the school sample were tested, as were children referred "mostly by mothers of preschool siblings" (pp. 55–56).

The norm sample contains approximately 4 percent black children; substantially less than the national average. This can be explained by the fact that schools in the communities selected were excluded from the sample if they had more than a 10 percent black enrollment. The authors indicate that the five communities making up the sample are representative of the entire U.S. population (1960 census), at least in terms of education, median family income, and occupation of residents. However, these comparisons are misleading in that the group of children selected was not a random sample of residents within the five communities. The occupations of the sample children's fathers are presented and correspond to countrywide data on occupations given in the 1960 census. It should be noted that sampling based upon the 1960 census may not be current.

Finally, information is presented about the intelligence of the children in the normative sample, as measured by the Stanford-Binet (1960). Although the mean of the sample IQs was approximately 100, the standard deviation of the IQs in the sample was approximately 8, indicating a restricted sample.

Reliability

A thorough description of reliability data is provided in the technical manual accompanying the ITPA. For each of the eight age groups, and for each of the twelve subtests, internal-consistency estimates (generally KR-20) have been computed, yielding ninety-six reliability coefficients. Of these coefficients, nine equal or exceed .90. Also, only four of the twelve subtests have *any* reliability coef-

TABLE 13.5 Ranges of Reliability Estimates for Subtests of the ITPA

Subtests	Internal Consistency[a]	Test-Retest[a]
AR	.84–.91	.36–.56
VR	.73–.87	.21–.36
AA	.74–.85	.62–.71
VA	.75–.82	.32–.57
VE	.51–.79	.45–.49
ME	.77–.83	.40–.51
GC	.60–.74	.49–.72
AC	.45–.84	.36–.52
SB	.78–.91	.30–.63
VC	.49–.70	.57–.68
ASM	.74–.90	.61–.86
VSM	.51–.96	.12–.50
Composite	.87–.93	.70–.83

[a] Not corrected for restriction in intelligence range.

ficients at or above .90. The composite reliability coefficients for each age level are higher, with only two of the eight age levels having coefficients below .90. However, most of the discussion on the uses and interpretation of the ITPA refers to the subtest scores and not to the composite score, the part of the test that has higher internal consistency. Column one of Table 13.5 lists the ranges of internal-consistency estimates for each ITPA subtest.

Test-retest reliabilities are also reported in the technical manual and are lower than the internal-consistency estimates. The test-retest coefficients were computed for the following three age levels, using a 5- to 6-month interval: four-year-olds (n = 71), six-year-olds (n = 55), and eight-year-olds (n = 72). Of the thirty-six subtest coefficients reported (twelve subtests at three age levels), twenty-seven, or 75 percent, had reported reliability coefficients below .60, and eighteen coefficients, or fully half, were below .50. Only two of the thirty-six coefficients were above .72. The estimate for

composite test-retest reliability is higher than the subtest estimates. The four-year-olds achieved an estimate of .83, but the reliability coefficients for the six- and eight-year-olds were .70. Column two of Table 13.5 illustrates the range of test-retest reliabilities for the twelve subtests of the ITPA.

Finally, the technical manual provides other data, including SEMs for raw scores, scaled scores, and PLAs (in months). Median reliability estimates for difference scores among subtests, based on the internal-consistency reliability estimates and median SEMs of scaled score differences are also calculated. Coefficients indicating excellent interscorer reliability for the Verbal Expression subtest are presented.

VALIDITY

No validity data are reported within the technical manual.

SUMMARY

The ITPA is a widely used instrument based on the information-processing model of language. Extensive reliability information is presented, but no measures of validity. In addition, several of the reliability coefficients are below optimal levels. The ITPA was an innovative instrument that contributed tasks that appear on more recently developed instruments to assess oral language (such as the grammatic-closure format is found on the TOLD series). However, the primary bases for this test are metalinguistic or nonlinguistic. Therefore the reader should not use this instrument as the sole language-assessment instrument nor should intervention be constructed using the ITPA tasks as a model.

COPING WITH DILEMMAS IN CURRENT PRACTICE

Three issues are particularly troublesome in the assessment of oral language: (1) ensuring that the elicited language assessment is a true reflection of the child's general spontaneous language capacity, (2) using the results of standardized tests to generate effective therapy, (3) adapting assessment to individuals who do not match the characteristics of the standardization sample. All of these dilemmas stem from the limited nature of the standardized tests and must be addressed in practice.

From a practical standpoint, the clinician must use standardized tests to identify a language impaired child. Yet, as noted earlier in this chapter, such instruments may not directly measure a child's true language abilities. Thus, the clinician must supplement the standard tests with nonstandard spontaneous language sampling. Additionally, if possible, the child should be observed in a number of settings outside the formal testing situation. After the spontaneous samples have been gathered, the results of these analyses should be compared to the performance or the standardized tests.

Selection of targets for intervention is one of the more difficult tasks facing the clinician. Many standardized tests that are useful for identifying language disorders in children may not lend themselves to efficient treatment. The clinician must evaluate the results of both the standard and nonstandard assessment procedures and decide which language skills are most important to the child. Although it is tempting to simply train the child to perform better on a particular test (hence boosting performance on that instrument), the clinician must bear in mind that such tasks are often metalinguistic in nature and will not ultimately result in generalized language skills. Rather, the focus of treatment should be on those language behaviors and structures that are needed for improved language competence in the home and in the classroom.

Finally, in today's oral language assessment environment, with a plethora of multicultural and socioeconomic variation in the caseloads, a clinician is bound to encounter many children who differ in one or more respects from the standardization sample of a particular test. Indeed, clinicians are likely to see children who do not match the standardization sample of *any* standardized test. When this occurs, the clinician must interpret conservatively the scores derived from these tests. Information from nonstandard assessments becomes even more important and the clinician should obtain reports from parents, teachers, and peers regarding their impressions of the child's language competence. Additionally, the clinician should determine whether local norms have been developed for the standard and nonstandard assessment procedures. As noted earlier, it is inappropriate to treat multicultural language differences as if they were language disorders. However, the clinician performing an assessment must judge whether the child's language is disordered within his or her language community and what impact such disorders may have on classroom performance and communication skills generally.

SUMMARY

The primary function of standard oral-language tests is to identify language disorders. Assessment sessions should include nonstandard measures such as language sampling to augment the results observed on standard instruments. The assessment session should also include measures of all aspects of oral language, including phonology, semantics, morphology, syntax, and pragmatics across both receptive and expressive channels.

A review of standardized tests indicates that psychometric principles used in constructing these instruments have generally not been applied. Such a conclusion has been verified in the literature (for example, see McCauley & Swisher, 1984). Although more recent tests have generally included more detailed psychometric data, the basic challenge of upgrading the standards remains. Moreover, the mismatch between the standard instruments and the content of the field remains large. Standard measures of language sampling are needed, as are reliable and valid instruments designed to measure pragmatics. The commercial success of the TOLD series suggests that the field would welcome new instruments that meet a majority of the psychometric criteria outlined elsewhere in this book.

Finally, a review of the first edition of this book indicates that the theoretical basis of language has been changing dramatically over the past decade. The first edition included only three components of language. The "new" areas of language represent new constructs that fill gaps in the earlier models of language. As noted elsewhere in this book, the testing technology lags behind the theoretical frontiers. The readers should thus be aware that new instruments will be designed to assess these domains and that such tests may change the way oral language is assessed.

STUDY QUESTIONS

1. Define *oral language,* and identify the five components of language.
2. Define *metalinguistic,* and describe a task that is metalinguistic in nature.
3. Why should a standard assessment instrument be used to identify language disorders?
4. Why should language-sampling procedures be included in the assessment session?
5. What are the three techniques for obtaining language from the child?

6. Design an assessment session that includes information on all aspects of language across both comprehension and production. Be sure to include a list of specific tests required to complete the session. Don't forget to include language sampling.

ADDITIONAL READINGS

Lahey, M. (1988). *Language disorders and language development.* New York: Macmillan.

Miller, J. (1981). *Assessing language production in children.* Austin, TX: Pro-Ed, Inc.

Reed, V. (1986). *An introduction to children with language disorders.* New York: Macmillan.

C·H·A·P·T·E·R 14

ASSESSMENT OF
PERCEPTUAL-MOTOR SKILLS

Educators and psychologists have operated for quite some time under the assumption that adequate perceptual-motor development is important both in and of itself and as a prerequisite to the development of academic skills. A wide variety of devices designed to assess children's perceptual-motor functioning are in use in the public schools today. While many measures of learning aptitude include items designed to assess perceptual or motor skills and while many readiness tests assess aspects of perceptual-motor development, this chapter focuses on those devices designed specifically and exclusively to assess perceptual-motor skills.

WHY DO WE ASSESS
PERCEPTUAL-MOTOR SKILLS?

Perceptual-motor assessment typically takes place for one of several purposes. In some cases, the perceptual-motor skills of entire classes of students are assessed in an effort to identify those with perceptual-motor difficulties so that training programs can be instituted to prevent incipient learning difficulties. Students who perform poorly on perceptual-motor devices are said to demonstrate perceptual-motor problems thought to contribute to or cause learning problems. In other cases, students having academic difficulties are assessed by means of perceptual-motor tests in an effort to identify the extent to which perceptual-motor difficulties may be causing the academic difficulties. In both instances, efforts are made to identify perceptual-motor problems so that training programs can be prescribed. Finally, perceptual-motor tests are widely used to diagnose brain injury.

The Interesting Past and Problematical Present of Perceptual-Motor Assessment

The practice of perceptual-motor assessment, while relatively new, has an interesting history. In the early 1900s gestalt psychology was born with a paper by Max Wertheimer that reported the work of Wertheimer, Kurt Koffka, and Wolfgang Kohler on perceptual phenomena such as apparent movement and afterimages. In 1923 Wertheimer put together a set of empirical statements known as the *principles of perceptual organization*. Gestalt psychologists, while certainly concerned with other aspects of psychology, made perception their major study. The early work of Wertheimer and his associates is apparent even today in the assessment of perceptual-motor development.

More recently, Hallahan and Cruickshank (1973) traced the history of the study of perceptual-motor problems in mentally retarded, brain-injured, and learning disabled children. According to Hallahan and Cruickshank, the historical roots of current practices in perceptual-motor assessment can be traced to the early work of Goldstein and of Werner and Strauss. Goldstein (1927, 1936, 1939) was engaged in the study of soldiers who had suffered traumatic head injuries during World War I. According to Hallahan and Cruickshank (1973), "Goldstein . . . found in his patients . . . the psychological characteristics of concrete behavior, meticulosity, perseveration, figure-background confusion, forced responsiveness to stimuli, and catastrophic reaction" (p. 59).

In the mid-1940s the two German psychologists Heinz Werner and Alfred Strauss began to study the behavioral pathology evidenced by brain-injured persons. In a series of studies at the Wayne County Training School in Detroit, Michigan, Werner and Strauss studied two kinds of brain-injured subjects: brain-injured retardates, and nonretardates who had experienced traumatic head injury from an automobile accident, a fall, a gunshot wound, or other similar incident. Their early research resulted in a list of behavioral characteristics said to differentiate brain-injured and non-brain-injured persons. The tests that were constructed to assess these behavioral characteristics are used today for that purpose.

Hallahan and Cruickshank state that "for Werner and Strauss it became a major concern to learn whether the psychological manifestations of brain injury found in adults by Goldstein would also be observable in children" (p. 60). Despite this interest in children, it must be remembered that the subjects studied in early investigations and on whom early tests were developed differ significantly from the children we currently assess using perceptual-motor tests. Subjects in early investigations were primarily adults who exhibited focal brain injury in the form of tissue damage, lesions, or tumors. To generalize characteristics of such persons to children with "diffuse brain injury" ignores neurological differences as well as developmental differences between children and adults. Many current perceptual-motor tests were developed using a criterion-group approach; they were developed to differentiate between *groups* of persons known to have sustained brain injury and non-brain-injured persons. They are currently used to differentiate between *individuals* whose problems may be due to brain injury and those who have no proven injury to the central nervous system.

While perceptual-motor tests have been used for some time to diagnose brain injury, recently there has been a dramatic and significant increase in the use of various perceptual-motor devices to diagnose learning disabilities. According to Hallahan and Cruickshank (1973), the contemporary leaders in the field of learning disabilities, who were responsible for its origin and development and for the development of the major perceptual-motor tests, were at one time associates or students of Werner and Strauss or were at least significantly influenced by their work. William Cruickshank, Samuel Kirk, and Newell Kephart were all associated with the Wayne County Training School at the time Werner and Strauss were engaged in their early investigations. Gerald Getman, an optometrist, later worked with Kephart at Purdue University, while Ray Barsch worked with both Getman and Strauss. Marianne Frostig, while not a direct associate of Werner and Strauss, has stated that she was significantly influenced by their early investigations (Hallahan & Cruickshank, 1973).

The associates of Werner and Strauss went on to apply their early work to the study of behavioral pathology in nonretarded children who were experiencing learning difficulty. While Kirk emphasized psycholinguistic disabilities and with his students constructed the Illinois Test of Psycholinguistic Abilities, the others stressed perceptual problems. Cruickshank focused on brain-injured children and children with cerebral palsy, and Kephart, Getman, Barsch, and Frostig focused on the academic correlates of perceptual-motor problems.

Out of the long history of interest in perception and perceptual problems among adults and brain-injured retardates has grown today a particular concern for the perceptual and motor problems of nonretarded children who fail academically. The thinking underlying this concern is illustrated by statements made by Frostig, Lefever, and Whittlesey (1966).

It is most important that a child's perceptual disabilities, if any exist, be discovered as early as possible. All research to date which has explored the child's general classroom behavior has confirmed the authors' original finding that kindergarten and first-grade children with visual perceptual disabilities are likely to be rated by their teachers as maladjusted in the classroom; not only do they frequently find academic learning difficult, but their ability to adjust to the social and emotional demands of classroom procedures is often impaired.

Identification and training of children with visual perceptual disabilities during the preschool years or at the time of school entrance would help prevent many instances of school failure and maladjustment caused [emphasis added] by visual perceptual difficulties. Although some children may overcome these difficulties at a later age, there is as yet no method to predict whether a child will be able to do so without help. . . . The authors' research has shown that visual perceptual difficulties, regardless of etiology, can be ameliorated by specific training. Pinpointing the areas of a child's visual perceptual difficulties and measuring their severity is helpful and is often necessary in designing the most efficient training program to aid in overcoming the disabilities. (p. 6)

The writers of the preceding paragraphs (they are also the authors of the Developmental Test of Visual Perception) do not cite empirical support for their contentions. We would argue that the claims made are unwarranted. The majority of the research does not support the contention that children with visual-perceptual disabilities are likely to be rated as maladjusted. At most, it can demonstrate simply that children who are rated as maladjusted also perform poorly on perceptual-motor tests. Furthermore, the authors recommend assessment of perceptual-motor difficulties under the assumption that remediation of identified disabilities will lead to greater academic success, and yet reviews of the efficacy of perceptual-motor training demonstrate that it is grossly ineffective in improving academic performance (Mann, 1971; Hammill & Wiederholt, 1973; Ysseldyke, 1973).

What the majority of the research *has* shown is that most perceptual-motor tests are unreliable. We do not know what they measure, because they do not measure anything consistently. Unlike the majority of intelligence and achievement tests, the tests used to assess perceptual-motor skills in children are technically inadequate. And for the most part they are neither theoretically nor psychometrically sound. For example, they are designed to assess perceptual-motor abilities under the assumption that such abilities cause academic success or academic failure (see Ysseldyke & Salvia, 1974). Or they are designed to assess hypothetical constructs like figure-ground perception and body image and differentiation but do not do so with consistency (see Ysseldyke, 1973; Ysseldyke & Salvia, 1974). Or they may be based on criterion keying, an approach that can lead to logical fallacies of undistributed middle terms (all canaries eat birdseed; Esmeralda eats birdseed; therefore, Esmeralda is a canary).

In short, the devices currently used to assess children's perceptual-motor skills are extremely inadequate. The real danger is that reliance on such tests in planning interventions for children may actually lead to assigning children to activities that do them absolutely no good. While we believe that few currently available perceptual-motor devices approach either theoretical or psychometrical adequacy, we review those that are most often used.

SPECIFIC TESTS OF PERCEPTUAL-MOTOR SKILLS

BENDER VISUAL MOTOR GESTALT TEST

The Bender Visual Motor Gestalt Test (BVMGT), consisting of nine geometric designs to be copied on paper, was originally developed by Loretta Bender in 1938. The designs in the test were first used by Wertheimer in 1923 to illustrate the perceptual principles of gestalt psychology. Bender used the designs in a test to differentiate brain-injured from non-brain-injured adults and to detect signs of emotional disturbance. The test has gained widespread popularity among clinical psychologists and has become one of the most frequently administered psychometric devices.

Administration of the BVMGT consists simply of presenting nine geometric designs, one at a time, to a subject who is asked to copy each of them on a plain sheet of paper. Although Bender provided criteria for scoring the test, a variety of other scoring systems have been developed, the most common of which is the system developed by Elizabeth Koppitz in 1963. The impetus for Koppitz's work arose from her experience in a child guidance clinic, where she was reportedly impressed with the frequency of perceptual problems among children with learning or emotional difficulties.

The Koppitz scoring system, restricted to use with children between 5 and 11 years of age, is the system most often used by psychologists in school settings. In 1963, Koppitz published a text describing the scoring system, the various uses of the BVMGT with children, normative data for the scoring system, and limited information about reliability and validity. In 1975, Koppitz published volume 2 of *The Bender Gestalt Test for Young Children*, a compilation and synthesis of research on the BVMGT between 1963 and 1973. This latter text is a commendable effort that eliminates the need to search the literature for research on the test.

Our discussion of the BVMGT is based entirely on use of the Koppitz scoring system with the test.

SCORES

When scoring according to the Koppitz system, the examiner records the number of errors on each of the nine separate geometric forms. Four kinds of errors are recorded.

Distortion of Shape   Errors are scored as distortion of shape when a child's reproduction of the stimulus design is so misshapen that the general configuration is lost. If a child converts dots to circles, alters the relative size of components of the stimulus drawing, or in other ways distorts the design, errors are recorded.

Perseveration   Perseveration errors are recorded when a child fails to stop after completing the required drawing—for example, a child is asked to copy eleven dots in a row and then copies significantly more than eleven.

Integration   Integration errors consist of a failure to juxtapose correctly parts of a design, as illustrated in Figure 14.1. In drawing a, the components of the design fail to meet. In drawing b, they overlap.

Rotation   Rotation errors are recorded when a child rotates a design by more than 45 degrees or rotates the stimulus card, even though the drawing is correctly copied. Reversals are

180-degree rotations and are scored as rotation errors.

More than one error can be scored on each drawing. The total number of possible errors is twenty-five. The examiner adds the number of errors to obtain a total raw score for the test. The higher the total raw score, the poorer the performance.

The Koppitz manual (1963) contains a normative table reporting means and standard deviations of error scores for specific age levels in half-year intervals. This normative table, based on the 1963 standardization of the test, is used to transform error scores to developmental ages. The 1975 publication reporting research on the BVMGT from 1963 to 1973 includes two features. A new set of examples for scoring individual items has been included to eliminate the scoring difficulties that examiners reported to the author. It also includes a new set of normative tables based on a 1974 renorming of the test. This set of tables can be used to convert error scores to age equivalents and to percentile ranks.

NORMS

Two sets of norms are now available for the Koppitz scoring system. The test was originally standardized on 1,104 children from forty-six classes in twelve public schools. The schools were reportedly selected from rural, urban, and suburban areas in unspecified proportions. The original normative sample included 637 boys and 467 girls. There are no data in the 1963 manual on the geographic areas the sample was drawn from or their demographic characteristics. In volume 2 (1975), Koppitz reports that 98 percent of the original sample was white.

Koppitz renormed the test in 1974 in an effort to achieve a more representative sample of American schoolchildren. The 1974 normative sample included 975 children between the ages of 5 and 11. A geographic cross section was not attained: 15 percent of the children were from the West, 2 percent were from the South, and 83 percent were from the Northeast. Racial balance is more nearly representative; 86 percent of the sample was white, 8.5 percent black, 4.5 percent were either Mexican-American or Puerto Rican, and 1 percent was Asian. There is no indication of the socioeconomic level of the sample; Koppitz states that research has demonstrated that socioeconomic status is not an important variable in children's performance on the BVMGT. Community size is adequately described; 7 percent were from rural communities, 31 percent were from small towns, 36 percent from suburbs, and 26 percent were from large metropolitan areas.

The sample sizes for half-year-interval age groups in both the 1963 and 1974 norms are unevenly distributed. For the 1963 norms, the norm group ranged in size from 27 children at ages 10-0 to 10-5 to 180 children at ages 6-6 to 6-11. For the 1974 norms, the norm group ranges in size from 47 children (at ages 5-0 to 5-5, 7-6 to 7-11, and 9-6 to 9-11) to 175 chil-

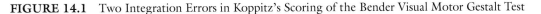

FIGURE 14.1   Two Integration Errors in Koppitz's Scoring of the Bender Visual Motor Gestalt Test

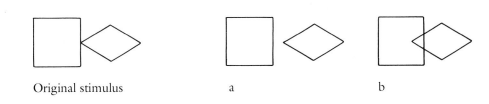

Original stimulus   a   b

dren at ages 6-0 to 6-5. Another major difficulty was present in the 1963 standardization: after age 8-6 the standard deviations for raw scores exceeded the means. For the 1974 norms, the standard deviations after age 8-6 are about equal to the means.

RELIABILITY

Two kinds of reliability data are reported for the BVMGT. Koppitz (1975) summarizes twenty-three studies of the interscorer reliability for her scoring system. Interscorer reliabilities ranged from .79 to .99, with 81 percent exceeding .89. The revised set of scoring examples that Koppitz published in 1975 after test users reported scoring difficulties will probably facilitate interscorer agreement in scoring a child's performance.

In her 1975 addition to the 1963 manual, Koppitz reports research on factors she believes may affect performance on the scale. Her review of research on the effects of motivation, task familiarization, verbal labeling, tracing and copying, and specific perceptual-motor training led to the conclusion that the BVMGT does indeed serve mainly as a measure of children's level of maturation in integration of perceptual and motor functions. Only secondarily does it reflect their various learning experiences with specific perceptual-motor tasks.

The 1975 manual also summarizes the results of nine test-retest reliability studies with normal elementary schoolchildren. Reliability coefficients ranged from .50 to .90 (mean = 71.48; mode = .76). On the basis of her review, Koppitz made a claim for the essential reliability of the BVMGT scores for normal children. Yet five of the nine reliability studies she reports are on kindergarten children only; and only one of twenty-five reported coefficients exceeds the standard of .90 recommended for

tests used to make important decisions. As Koppitz valuably cautions, "Certainly no diagnosis or major decision should ever be made on the basis of a single scoring point, nor for that matter on the basis of a youngster's total Developmental Bender Test score" (p. 29).

VALIDITY

The construct of *visual-motor perception* is never adequately defined in either Koppitz manual. There is no evidence about the extent to which the test assesses visual-motor perception; the copying of nine designs is believed to be a measure of visual perception because some experts say it is one.

Koppitz (1975) cites several uses for the BVMGT and reports research on each of the suggested uses. She reports correlations of performance on the BVMGT and performance on measures of intelligence, academic achievement, and visual perception. She also cites evidence for use of the test in diagnosing minimal brain dysfunction and emotional disturbance. The paragraphs that follow describe some of her findings and recommendations.

In her 1963 manual, Koppitz reported results of tests of the relationship between scores earned on the BVMGT and scores earned on intelligence tests. She concluded that the BVMGT may be substituted "with some confidence" for a screening test of intelligence. She stated,

> In clinical and school settings psychologists are constantly faced with the problem of how to use their limited time most economically. A full scale intelligence test usually requires so much time that only a brief period is left for other tests or an interview. The author has used the Bender test frequently with young children of normal intelligence who primarily seemed to show emotional problems and revealed no

learning difficulties. The Bender test not only gives the examiner a rough measure of the youngster's intellectual ability, but also serves as a nonthreatening introduction to the interview. Children tend to enjoy copying the Bender designs, and in some cases the Bender figures evoke associations and spontaneous comments which can lead to further discussions. In most cases the Bender Test will suffice to rule out mental retardation or serious perceptual problems associated with neurological impairment and the examiner can use most of his/her time for projective tests and an interview rather than spending it on a lengthy intelligence test which offers little insight into the dynamics of the child's emotional problems. (p. 51)

In the 1975 addition to the 1963 manual, Koppitz continues to support the use of the BVMGT as a rough test of intelligence:

The statement "The Bender Gestalt Test can be used with some degree of confidence as a short nonverbal intelligence test for young children, particularly for screening purposes" (Koppitz, 1963, p. 50) has been supported by a number of recent studies. But as I previously suggested, the Bender Test should if possible be combined with a brief verbal test. (p. 47)

The BVMGT is *not* an intelligence test but a measure of a child's skill in copying geometric designs. It provides a very limited sample of behavior; in fact, of the thirteen kinds of behaviors described in Chapter 9 as being regularly sampled in intelligence tests, the Bender samples only one. In our opinion, the BVMGT should never be used as, or substituted for, a measure of intellectual functioning.

Koppitz (1975) reviews numerous investigations of the relationship between children's performance on the BVMGT and their academic achievement. Good students and poor students, she concludes, tend as groups to make significantly different total scores on the test. Furthermore, the scores normal children earn show a positive correlation with their academic achievement. Koppitz uses observed differences to conclude that scores earned on the BVMGT

appear to be most successful in predicting overall school functioning and rate of progress in total achievement. A child with a marked discrepancy between IQ and Bender Test scores usually has specific learning difficulties. LD pupils and slow learners mature at a significantly slower rate in visual-motor integration, as measured on the Bender Test, than do well-functioning children. Scores from repeated administrations of the Bender Test are good indicators of progress a child is making, and they are helpful in planning an individualized educational program. (p. 70)

Children who perform well in school may well do better on the BVMGT than children who experience academic difficulty. But as Koppitz herself states, the test cannot be used to predict the academic performance of *individual* children (1975, p. 70). Moreover, Koppitz has not provided evidence to support the contention that the test facilitates individualization of instruction. To do so would require demonstration of an interaction between test performance and success under different forms (methods, techniques) of instruction—demonstration, in other words, of evidence for aptitude-treatment interactions.

Koppitz (1975) reviewed many studies of the use of the BVMGT to diagnose minimal brain dysfunction in schoolchildren. She concluded that the test is a valuable aid for this purpose but should never be used in isolation. Rather, she believes test results are valuable when combined with other medical and behavioral data.

Koppitz (1975) also claims that recent research gives additional validity to the ten indicators of emotional problems that she delineated in her 1963 text. Although she again provides notes of caution indicating that not all children with poor Bender protocols have emotional problems, she does state that "the presence of three or more emotional indicators on a Bender Test protocol tends to reflect emotional difficulties that warrant further investigation" (p. 92).

Koppitz (1975) provides evidence to support the contention that performance on the BVMGT is significantly related to performance on other visual-perceptual measures. She does not report the extent to which pupils who achieve low scores on the BVMGT perform well on these other tests or vice versa.

The BVMGT is, quite simply, a measure of skill development in copying geometric designs. It is *not* designed as a measure of intelligence, predictor of achievement, or measure of emotional disturbance or minimal brain dysfunction. Using it for any of these purposes is risky.

Summary

The BVMGT requires the child to copy nine geometric designs. The test was originally developed by Bender, who used designs developed earlier by Wertheimer. Koppitz has developed a scoring system for the test, and her system is designed for ages 5 to 11. The BVMGT is today one of the most widely used psychometric devices. The most recent standardization of the test was 1974, so the norms are nearly 20 years old.

Reliability for the BVMGT is relatively low, at least too low for use in making placement decisions. Yet, performance on the test is used as a criterion in the differential identification of children as brain injured, perceptually handicapped, or emotionally disturbed. Validity for the BVMGT is currently not clearly established. The authors have not empirically demonstrated that the test measures visual-motor perception or that it discriminates individual cases of brain injury, perceptual handicap, or emotional disturbance. The test certainly provides a very limited sample of perceptual-motor behavior, and, for this reason if for no other, one would have to be extremely cautious in interpreting and using its results.

A statement by Koppitz is a fitting conclusion to our discussion of her test. "The very fact," she writes, "that the Bender Test is so appealing and is easy to administer presents a certain danger. Because it is so deceptively simple, it is probably one of the most overrated, most misunderstood, and most maligned tests currently in use" (1975, p. 2).

DEVELOPMENTAL TEST OF VISUAL PERCEPTION

The Developmental Test of Visual Perception (DTVP) (Frostig, Maslow, Lefever, & Whittlesey, 1964; Frostig, Lefever, & Whittlesey, 1966) is designed to measure "five operationally-defined perceptual skills" (Frostig et al., 1966, p. 5): eye-hand coordination, figure-ground perception, form constancy, position in space, and spatial relations. The areas were selected for assessment, according to the authors, because (1) they are critical for the acquisition of academic skills; (2) they affect the total organism to a greater extent than other functions such as color vision or tone discrimination; (3) they develop relatively early in life; (4) they are frequently disturbed in children diagnosed as neurologically handicapped; and (5) they are suitable for group testing.

The DTVP consists of a thirty-five-page consumable pupil response booklet. There are two manuals for the test, a standardization manual (Frostig et al., 1966), and an administration and scoring manual (Frostig et al., 1964). The test can be individually or group administered; it takes about 40 minutes. Behaviors sampled by each of the five subtests are described by the authors.

Eye-Hand Coordination This subtest assesses skill in drawing various kinds of continuous lines within boundaries and from point to point.

Figure-Ground Perception This subtest assesses skill in identifying figures as distinct from increasingly complex backgrounds and in discriminating intersecting and hidden geometric figures.

Form Constancy This subtest assesses skill in recognizing various geometric shapes regardless of size or orientation.

Position in Space This subtest assesses skill in discriminating reversals and rotations of figures in a series.

Spatial Relations This subtest assesses skill in copying patterns using dots as guide points. The child is shown a sample pattern and required to copy it by following the dots.

SCORES

Scoring of the DTVP is objective. Ample scoring examples and in some cases scoring stencils are provided. Points earned depend on the quality of a child's responses to test items, and

a raw score is earned for each of the subtests. Three kinds of derived scores are obtained for the DTVP: perceptual ages, scale scores, and perceptual quotients. Perceptual ages are age-equivalent scores and are derived separately for each subtest. The scale score is a ratio score obtained by dividing the perceptual age by the chronological age and multiplying by 10.[1]

Thus, a child who is 6 years, 6 months old who has a perceptual age on the DTVP of 5 years, 3 months is given a scale score of 8.3. In the scoring procedures for the DTVP, the scale score is rounded to the nearest whole number. The perceptual quotient is a deviation score obtained by adding the subtest scale scores and using a table in the manual. The perceptual quotients are constructed so that a perceptual quotient of 100 is always at the fiftieth percentile; one of 90 is always at the twenty-fifth percentile; one of 110 is always at the seventy-fifth percentile; and so on.

Procedures recommended in the manual for the DTVP for transforming raw scores to scale scores and perceptual quotients are unnecessarily complex. Without really giving a rationale for doing so, the authors employ four different scoring procedures depending on the age of the child assessed. For children between the ages of 3 and 4, a table is used to convert raw scores to perceptual ages. These perceptual ages are then divided by chronological age to obtain scale scores. However, in all cases, regardless of the raw score, a constant score of 10 is assigned to a child's performance on the Spatial Relations subtest. For children between 4 and 8 years of age, different tables for different chronological ages are used to convert raw

---

1. The scale score obtained for the DTVP is *not* a scaled score. Scaled scores are standard scores and have a predetermined mean and standard deviation (see also the scaled scores for the Wechsler Intelligence Scale for Children–Revised). The scale scores for the DTVP are ratios. These ratios have different means and different standard deviations for children of different ages.

scores to scale scores and to obtain perceptual quotients.

A child between 8 and 10 years of age who receives the maximum perceptual age for any subtest is credited with a scale score of 10. It is, however, possible for a child who does *not* earn the maximum perceptual age to earn a higher scale score, and thus a higher perceptual quotient, than a child who earns the maximum score. Let us assume that two children, Amy and Christopher, who are both 8 years, 1 month old, take the DTVP. On subtest 1, Eye-Hand Coordination, Amy earns a raw score of 19, while Christopher earns a raw score of 20. Using Table 1 in the DTVP manual, Amy earns a perceptual age of 9-6, while Christopher earns a perceptual age of 10+. To obtain scale scores, the perceptual age is divided by the chronological age; the quotient is multiplied by 10; and the product is rounded to the nearest whole number. Amy earns a scale score of 12 ($114/97 \times 10 = 11.7$). Christopher, however, because he obtained the maximum perceptual age, is assigned a scale score of 10. A child who earns a maximum perceptual age on every subtest *cannot* earn a perceptual quotient greater than 100. Think for a moment what this must do to the reliability of the test. Raw scores and scale scores can actually be inversely related, and there is a ceiling effect.

Finally, the authors of the DTVP state that "any child of 10 years or more who does not receive the maximum Perceptual Age Equivalent for any subtest is presumed to have difficulty in the area measured" (1966, p. 31). *The transformed scores for the DTVP are not only confusing; they are questionably derived and therefore absolutely must not be used in making diagnostic decisions.*

The authors of the DTVP state that scale scores of less than 8 indicate perceptual-motor weaknesses in need of remediation. They further state that "it has been found very helpful to use a perceptual quotient of 90 as the cutoff point in the scores of kindergarten children, below which a child should receive special training" (1964, p. 479). Such interpretations simply cannot be made when the scores obtained on the DTVP do not have consistent meaning.

NORMS

The 1963 edition of the DTVP was standardized on 2,116 children, between 107 and 240 children at each half-year level between the ages of 3 and 9. The authors (1964) do state, though, that the test was designed primarily for use with young children. The entire sample was drawn from nursery schools and public elementary schools in southern California. The sample was selected on the basis of the following considerations: (1) an attempt to get a stratified sample of children from different socioeconomic levels, (2) the willingness of schools to cooperate, and (3) the proximity to Frostig's research center. By Frostig's own admission the sample has some serious shortcomings. The sample was drawn from a geographically and socioeconomically restricted area. It was overwhelmingly middle class (93 percent), despite the reported attempt to obtain a stratified sample of children from different socioeconomic backgrounds, and it had little minority representation (a few Chicanos, fewer Orientals, and no blacks). Nowhere in the manual is there a report of the sex, grade level, or occupation and education of the parents of those in the normative group.

In Chapter 2, on the administration of tests, we discussed optimal group size for testing. The standardization of the DTVP was completed by testing *no fewer* than fifteen kindergarten and first-grade children at one time. Nursery schoolchildren were tested in groups of two to eight. The norms for this test are out of date.

RELIABILITY

Frostig et al. (1964) report the results of three test-retest reliability studies carried out in 1960 with a small sample of fifty children who were experiencing learning difficulties. The test-retest reliability for the perceptual quotient was reported as .98 using the full range of ages. In a second study of two groups of thirty-five first graders and two groups of thirty-seven second graders a reliability of .80 was obtained. Test-retest reliability for subtest scale scores, however, ranged from .42 (Figure-Ground) to .80 (Form Constancy).

A third study was conducted in 1962 to ascertain test-retest reliability when the device was administered by trained personnel who were not psychologists or psychometricians. The test was given to three kindergarten and three first-grade classes with a fourteen-day interval between test and retest. Obtained reliability coefficients for subtest scale scores ranged from .29 (Eye-Hand Coordination) to .74 (Form Constancy) for kindergarten children and from .39 (Eye-Hand Coordination and Figure-Ground) to .68 (Form Constancy) for first graders. The reliability coefficient for the total scale score was .69.

Split-half reliabilities obtained for the total scale score for the various age levels were .89 (5 to 6 years) to .68 (6 to 7 years) to .82 (7 to 8 years) to .78 (8 to 9 years). Reliabilities decreased with increasing age.

The low reliabilities for individual subtests certainly raise serious questions about their use in differential diagnosis, the very procedure Frostig recommends. You will recall that tests should have reliabilities in excess of .90 to be used in differential diagnosis and in making instructional decisions. Reliabilities for subtests

of the DTVP come nowhere near this figure. The test is suitable only for screening.

VALIDITY

Frostig et al. (1964) report two validity studies in the manual for the DTVP. Correlations between total scale scores on the DTVP and teacher ratings of classroom adjustment, motor coordination, and intellectual functioning were .44, .50, and .50 respectively. The authors state that "the correlation found between teacher ratings of classroom adjustment and scores on the Frostig Test (1961 standardization) suggests the correctness of the hypothesis that disturbances in visual perception during the early school years are likely to be reflected in disturbances in classroom behavior" (p. 492).

In showing a moderate correlation between scores on the DTVP and teacher ratings the authors have demonstrated only a relationship, not necessarily a cause-effect relationship. The study does not provide validity evidence for the scale. It does not prove that the test measures what it is designed to measure. Such proof constitutes evidence of a test's validity. The DTVP was designed to assess visual-motor skills, not classroom adjustment or intellectual functioning.

The second validity study—based on the contention that the Goodenough-Harris Test is a measure of intellectual functioning, perceptual development, and personality—was designed to ascertain to what extent the DTVP and the Goodenough-Harris measured factors in common. Correlations between scores on the DTVP and the Goodenough-Harris were .46 for kindergarten, .32 for first-grade, and .36 for second-grade children.

As mentioned above, the test authors believe that for kindergarten children a perceptual quotient of 90 on the DTVP should be used as a cutoff point below which a child should receive visual-perceptual remediation. They also maintain that "a child's ability to learn to read is affected by his visual perceptual development" (1964, p. 493). To support these contentions, the authors conducted a study in a laboratory school classroom at UCLA. They report,

> A group of 25 children between the ages of 4½ and 6½ were to be exposed to reading material but not forced to use it. All who used it were to be given training in word attack skills, phonics, observation of configuration, and use of contextual clues. The Frostig test was administered in July, 1962, and eight of the children were found to have visual perceptual quotients of 90 or below. It was predicted that these eight children would not attempt to learn to read because of their difficulties. This prediction proved to be highly accurate. In October, 1962, the children were rated for reading achievement. None of the children with a visual perceptual quotient below 90 had begun to read; of the two children with a perceptual quotient of 90, one had learned to read very well, while the other had not. Only one of the children with a PQ above 90 showed reading difficulties.
> (p. 495)

The authors simply cannot use the obtained data to support their contention. Such support would require a carefully controlled study accounting for the fact that the observed differences were not a function of intellectual level, some other variable, or teacher expectancy. The validity data reported in the manual for the DTVP do not support the authors' contention that the test measures five operationally defined perceptual skills.

SUMMARY

The DTVP is a group-administered test designed to assess what the author has defined as five relatively independent components of visual perception. Data about the reliability of the scale obviously indicate that the five areas are not consistently assessed, and factor-analytic studies have pretty well dismissed the notion that the five areas are independently assessed.

Individual subtests of the DTVP lack the necessary reliability and validity to be used in diagnostic prescriptive teaching. We simply cannot put a great deal of faith in the accuracy (freedom from error) of the scores a child earns on the DTVP subtests.

In its composite form, as reflected by the perceptual quotient, the DTVP is a relatively reliable measure for theoretical and research purposes. The total test provides a global score indicative of overall visual-perceptual skill development. Performance on the DTVP must be interpreted with considerable caution. Normative comparisons should not be made; the norms are now out of date.

MEMORY FOR DESIGNS TEST

The Memory for Designs Test (Graham & Kendall, 1960) assesses the ability of persons over 8 years old to copy geometric designs from memory. The express purpose of the test is to provide an instrument to use in research on organic impairment and to use as an adjunct test in a battery of tests administered to persons suspected of being brain-injured. The Memory for Designs Test is administered by asking a person to copy fifteen geometric designs, each of which is individually exposed for a period of 5 seconds and then withdrawn. Administration time usually requires about 10 minutes.

Scores

Individual designs are scored in terms of the number and kinds of errors in the subject's drawing. The total score, the sum of scores for individual drawings, is used to judge the person's performance. Scores for each of the fifteen drawings are assigned on a four-point scale, described by the authors as follows.

0 A score of 0 is assigned to a satisfactory reproduction or to an omitted design.
1 A score of 1 is assigned when more than two easily identifiable errors are made but the general configuration of the design is retained.
2 A score of 2 is given when the general configuration of the design has been lost.
3 A score of 3 is given when the design is reversed or rotated.

According to the authors, the weight given to different types of errors was assigned on an empirical basis. Because rotation errors were observed to be more prevalent in brain-injured subjects, such errors are penalized more heavily. The assignment of a score of 0 for omitted designs is based on the observation that about as many brain-injured as non-brain-injured persons omit designs.

In addition to the raw score, a difference score is obtained for performance on the Memory for Designs Test. The difference score statistically controls for the effects of chronological age and vocabulary level. Older individuals and those of higher intellectual level are expected to make fewer errors on the Memory for Designs Test.

Raw scores are interpreted in such a way that for adults a score of 12 or greater is seen as indicative of "brain damage," a score of 5 to 11 is interpreted as "borderline" performance, and a raw score of 0 to 4 is interpreted as "normal" performance.

To obtain difference scores, values are assigned to both chronological age and vocabulary level (as assessed by the Vocabulary section of the Stanford-Binet or the Wechsler scales), and the score for Vocabulary level is subtracted from the score for chronological age. The difference score is used to ascertain the presence or absence of brain injury.

Norms

The norms for the Memory for Designs Test are based on eight groups of persons who participated in research on the test. The subjects were obtained from various clinics and hospitals in the St. Louis area. Some subjects took the test as part of a psychological examination or under the guise that it was a part of a routine medical examination. Others were informed that they were participating in research. To be included in the normative sample, subjects had to have had formal schooling to at least a third-grade level and a vocabulary equivalent to a Stanford-Binet IQ of at least 70; they had to complete at least eleven of the fifteen designs; and they had to demonstrate that they had no marked motor incoordination or uncorrected defect in near vision. For child subjects, the educational restriction was dropped, but the child had to have an IQ of at least 70 on the Stanford-Binet or Wechsler-Bellevue scale.[2]

It is quite difficult to get a handle on the actual normative sample for the Memory for Designs Test. Those who participated in the standardization included persons with a variety of brain disorders including more than fifteen different classifications of both acute and chronic conditions, persons with idiopathic epilepsy and various forms of psychosis, and a

---

2. The Wechsler-Bellevue is an adult test.

TABLE 14.1   Index of Reliability on the Memory for Designs Test, and Difference in Mean Raw Scores on Test and Immediate Retest for Various Samples

Sample	N	Reliability	Mean Difference
Control children	(32)	.81	.41
Test score 8	22		−.41
Test score 8	10		1.60
Control adults	(45)	.85	2.22
Test score 8	17		1.82
Test score 8	28		2.46
Brain-disordered	(27)	.88	3.30
Special adult	(98)		
Mental deficiency diagnosis or low vocabulary	34	.72	2.32
Questionable diagnosis	41	.90	1.66
Over 60 years, mixed diagnosis	23	.86	1.44
Total	202	.89	1.89

SOURCE: Reprinted with permission of authors and publisher from F. K. Graham and B. S. Kendall, Memory for Designs Test: Revised general manual. *Perceptual and Motor Skills,* 1960, *11,* 147–188, Monograph Supplement 2-VII. Table 10.

"normal" group of persons. The test was normed on a total of 535 normal persons, 47 subjects who had idiopathic epilepsy, and 243 who suffered some form of brain injury. Subjects ranged in age from 8 to 70 years. Normative comparisons should not be made using this test. There simply is too much confusion about the nature of the norm group, and the norms are out of date.

RELIABILITY

Three kinds of reliability are reported in the Memory for Designs manual. Interscorer reliability, obtained by the two authors independently scoring 140 protocols, is reported as .99. Split-half reliabilities for the performance of the same 140 subjects is reported to be .92.

Test-retest reliabilities on readministrations within 24 hours to select groups of subjects are reported in Table 14.1. Reliability indexes are in the .80s with the exception of the group with low vocabulary scores. The average Memory for Designs score for all groups was 1.89 lower on the retest than on the original test. The authors attribute this improvement in performance to a practice effect.

VALIDITY

Validity data consist primarily of criterion validity scores showing that brain-injured individuals earn lower scores on the test than do non-brain-injured persons. The test does differentiate between the groups, and the scores on the test do demonstrate little correlation with either age or intelligence. Just because the test differentiates between groups does not mean that it measures what it says it measures.

SUMMARY

The Memory for Designs Test was originally constructed for the purpose of identifying brain-injured persons. Scores obtained on the device are reasonably reliable compared to those obtained on other perceptual-motor devices, and the test does discriminate between groups of brain-injured and non-brain-injured persons. The user of the test must, however, be cautious because it is very easy to make errors in logic. The test uses a criterion-group approach. A person who performs *like* a brain-injured person is not necessarily brain-injured. The Memory for Designs Test assesses skill in copying designs from memory; it does *not* assess brain injury. The diagnosis of an individual as brain-injured on the basis of relative difficulty in copying designs is quite clearly and simply an inference. As long as test results are viewed in this manner, there is little problem. To view the results as factual indicators of the extent of brain injury is simply inappropriate. The norms for the Memory for Designs Test are out of date.

DEVELOPMENTAL TEST OF VISUAL-MOTOR INTEGRATION

The Developmental Test of Visual-Motor Integration (Beery, 1989) is designed to assess visual perception and motor coordination in students ages 2 to 19. It is intended for use primarily with prekindergarten children and those enrolled in the early grades. The test may be administered individually or to groups. The test consists of twenty-four geometric designs of increasing difficulty to be copied with a pencil on paper. The test can be administered and scored by a classroom teacher and usually takes about 15 minutes. Scoring is relatively easy as the designs are scored pass-fail, and individual protocols can be scored in a few minutes.

SCORES

The manual for the VMI includes two pages of scoring information for each of the twenty-four designs. The child's reproduction of each design is scored pass-fail, and criteria for successful performance are clearly articulated. A raw score for the total test is obtained by adding the number of correct reproductions up to three consecutive failures. Normative tables provided in the manual allow the examiner to convert the total raw score to a developmental age equivalent. Scoring procedures for the VMI were changed in 1989. The twenty-four forms were weighted according to their developmental difficulties. The range of possible scores was expanded from 1–24 to 1–50. The author argues that new scores correlate highly with scores earned using the previous scoring procedures, and that the technical data for earlier versions of the test still apply to the most recent (1989) edition.

NORMS

The VMI was originally standardized on 1,030 children in rural, urban, and suburban Illinois. In 1981 the test was cross-validated with samples of children "from various ethnic and income groups in California" (p. 10). In 1988 the test was again cross-validated with an unspecified group of students "from several eastern, northern and southern states" (p. 10). The norm sample is not representative with respect to ethnicity and residence of the students. The norms are based on the performance of an unspecified group of 5,824 individuals. Norm-referenced use of the test should be discouraged, as the tester does not know the nature of the group to whom tested individuals are being compared.

RELIABILITY

The author summarizes the results of many different reliability studies conducted by others since initial publication of the VMI. Ten studies of interscorer reliability are listed, and it is reported that reliability coefficients ranged from .58 to .99 with a median of .93. Five studies of test-retest reliability are mentioned, and a range of .63 to .92 is reported. Four studies of split-half reliability are reported, with coefficients ranging from .66 to .93 and a median of .79. The samples for these studies are not described.

VALIDITY

The author summarizes studies by many different investigators but does not describe these studies specifically. He reports that scores on the VMI correlate .42 with a measure of handwriting, about .50 with readiness tests, .89 with chronological age, .41 to .82 with performance on the Bender Visual Motor Gestalt Test, and .37 to .59 with mental age. Studies of the relationship between performance on the VMI and later achievement show mixed results. Some investigators have found moderately strong relationships; others report little relationship.

SUMMARY

The VMI is designed to assess the integration of visual and motor skills by asking the child to copy geometric designs. As is the case with other such tests, the behavior sampling is limited, although the twenty-four items on the VMI certainly provide a larger sample of behavior than is provided by the nine items on the Bender Visual Motor Gestalt Test or the fifteen items on the Memory for Designs Test. The VMI has relatively high reliability and validity in comparison to other measures of perceptual-motor skills.

PURDUE PERCEPTUAL-MOTOR SURVEY

The Purdue Perceptual-Motor Survey (PPMS) (Roach & Kephart, 1966) was developed "to assess qualitatively the perceptual-motor abilities of children in the early grades" (p. 2). The survey, which consists of eleven subtests designed to measure some aspect of perceptual-motor development, includes twenty-two scorable items. The authors of the survey state that "the survey was not designed for diagnosis, per se, but to allow the clinician to observe perceptual-motor behavior in a series of behavioral performances" (p. 11).

Criteria used to include items in the PPMS are described by the authors in the test manual. Each item had to

(1) tap some perceptual-motor area; (2) be easy to administer and require a minimum of special equipment; (3) be representative of behavior familiar to all children; (4) have scoring

criteria simple enough and clear enough that a minimum amount of training would be necessary for administration; and (5) not be over-structured so that it elicits a learned response. (p. 11)

Most items in the survey were chosen to be used with second, third, and fourth graders. The normative data are on children between 6 and 10 years of age. Items on the PPMS are grouped into five areas: Balance and Posture, Body Image and Differentiation, Perceptual-Motor Match, Ocular Control, and Form Perception. Each area samples certain behaviors.

Balance and Posture Two activities, walking a balance beam and jumping, are used to assess balance and postural flexibility. The items are not precisely scored; rather, the examiner makes an effort to identify the extent to which children have "a general balance problem." The tasks assess the extent to which children use both sides of their bodies in a bilateral activity, shift from one side to the other in a smooth, well-coordinated fashion, and demonstrate rhythmic and coordinated control.

Body Image and Differentiation Five tasks are used to assess body image and differentiation. These include (1) Identification of Body Parts, (2) Imitation of Movement, (3) Obstacle Course, (4) Kraus-Weber, and (5) Angels in the Snow. In general, the tasks assess the extent to which children have knowledge of their body parts, can imitate movement, can avoid obstacles, have good physical strength, and can move their bodies as directed.

Perceptual-Motor Match The match between perceptual information and motor response is assessed by two activities in which children are asked to draw several geometric forms on a chalkboard and to engage in rhythmic writing. Chalkboard activities include (1) drawing a circle, (2) drawing two circles simultaneously, one with each hand, (3) drawing a lateral line, and (4) drawing two straight vertical lines simultaneously. In the rhythmic writing task, children reproduce on paper eight patterns drawn on the chalkboard by the examiner. They must reproduce the patterns accurately, with a free rhythmic flow, and must make certain "perceptual-motor adjustments" in doing so.

Ocular Control The ability of children to establish and maintain contact with a visual target is assessed by means of four tasks requiring them to maintain eye contact with a penlight. The examiner evaluates the extent to which children are able to move their eyes (as opposed to the entire head) smoothly in following the movements of a flashlight. Ocular control for both eyes and for each eye individually is assessed. In addition, convergence of the eyes in focusing on objects is evaluated.

Form Perception The extent to which children demonstrate adequate form perception and can reproduce geometric designs is assessed by asking them to copy seven simple geometric forms: circle, cross, square, triangle, horizontal diamond, vertical diamond, and divided rectangle.

SCORES

Scoring for the PPMS is subjective and largely qualitative. While numbers are assigned as scores, they are used to designate the quality of a child's perceptual-motor behaviors. The record form for the PPMS includes a series of check lists for each task. The check lists enable the examiner to take note of the specific difficulties a child experiences on each of the tasks.

The authors of the PPMS stress the fact that the survey is not a test but a device for designating problem areas. They state that "the probable level of measurement is ordinal" (p. 13).[3]

NORMS

The PPMS was standardized on fifty children at each of the first four grades. Only children known to be free of motor defect who had not been referred to an agency for evaluation of their academic achievement were included in the normative sample. By administering the Wide Range Achievement Test (WRAT), the authors established the fact that all children studied were achieving at or above grade level. They report that

> every child that participated in the study from the normative group was achieving at least within his assigned grade level. . . . Since the data were collected in midyear, this meant that children were achieving at various levels at or above grade placement. For example, some third graders were achieving at grade three, zero month, in spelling, while others were achieving at a much higher level. In all, the range of achievement was known to be varied. (p. 14)

The reader of the manual is led to believe that all children earned scores on the WRAT no lower than the lower limit of their grade level (for example, no lower than 3.0). In the next sentence of the manual, however, the authors report that "it was assumed that intelligence, like achievement, was randomly distributed in the normative sample" (p. 14). The authors do not report data about the actual range of achievement and intelligence of children in the normative sample.

3. *Ordinal* refers to rank order as discussed in Chapter 4.

The authors do report the sex and socioeconomic status of children in the normative sample, but these data are reported only in the validity section of the manual. One needs to refer to validity tables to identify the numbers of children representing each specific socioeconomic group. The norms for the PPMS are out of date.

RELIABILITY

The authors report a test-retest reliability of the PPMS of .95. They state that this coefficient was based on the performance of thirty children selected randomly from the normative sample and that the test-retest interval was one week.

VALIDITY

To establish validity for the PPMS, the authors compared the performance of students in the normative sample to that of a clinic sample of ninety-seven nonachievers matched for grade level and age with the normative group. The items of the scale were validated by demonstrating that the nonclinic children performed at a significantly higher level than the clinic children on all but two items of the scale.

Additional validity studies were performed to illustrate that performance on items on the survey increases with higher grade level and with higher socioeconomic status. Performances on only two items increased significantly with grade level, while means for the six socioeconomic groups were in the order 5, 4, 1, 2, 3, 6. Thus, the authors' own research failed to support their contentions about grade and socioeconomic status. The authors do not demonstrate that the survey measures what it says it measures.

Summary

The Purdue Perceptual-Motor Survey is designed to provide qualitative information regarding the extent to which children demonstrate adequately developed perceptual-motor skills. Because standardization was limited, and the norms are out of date, the survey cannot be used for the purpose of making normative comparisons. Although good test-retest reliability has been demonstrated, validity of the scale is questionable. Individual teachers must judge whether they are willing to accept the authors' contention that the development of adequate perceptual-motor skills is a necessary prerequisite to the acquisition of academic skills. Such a claim is, to date, without support.

Coping with Dilemmas in Current Practice

The assessment of perceptual-motor skills is incredibly problematic. There are many obvious problems. First, it is very difficult to define perception, and therefore difficult to come up with measures of it. Yet school personnel assume, and in fact insist, that adequate perceptual-motor development is a necessary prerequisite to acquiring reading skills. Often, assessors are asked to find out whether students have perceptual-motor problems. Without adequate definition, with no technically adequate tests, and with no evidence that there are specific, effective interventions for students with perceptual-motor problems, the assessor is in a difficult bind.

We are of the opinion that if assessments cannot be done properly, they should not be done at all. This is one domain in which we believe that formal assessment using standardized tests is of little value. Rather, we encourage those who are concerned about development of perceptual-motor skills to engage in direct systematic observation in the natural environment in which these skills actually occur.

Summary

Educational personnel typically assess perceptual-motor skills for one of three reasons: prevention, remediation, and differential diagnosis. The use of perceptual-motor tests to identify children who demonstrate perceptual-motor difficulties is based on the assumption that without special perceptual-motor training, these children will experience academic difficulties. They are used to try to ascertain whether perceptual-motor difficulties are causing academic difficulties and must therefore be remediated. Third, perceptual-motor tests are used diagnostically to identify brain injury and emotional difficulties.

This chapter reviewed the most commonly used perceptual-motor tests. Most are out of date. Most lack the necessary reliability to be used in making important instructional decisions. Likewise, they lack demonstrated validity; we simply cannot say with much certainty that the tests measure what they purport to measure.

The practice of perceptual-motor assessment is linked directly to perceptual-motor training or remediation. There is a tremendous lack of empirical evidence to support the claim that specific perceptual-motor training facilitates the acquisition of academic skills or improves the chances of academic success. Perceptual-motor training will improve *perceptual-motor* functioning. When the purpose of perceptual-motor assessment is to identify specific important perceptual and motor behaviors that children have not yet mastered, some of the devices reviewed in this chapter may provide useful information; performance on individual items will indicate the extent to which specific skills (for example, walking along a straight line) have been mastered. There is no support for the use of perceptual-motor tests in planning programs designed to facilitate academic learning or to remediate academic difficulties.

STUDY QUESTIONS

1. Homer, age 6-3, takes two visual-perceptual tests, the Developmental Test of Visual Perception (DTVP) and the Developmental Test of Visual-Motor Integration (VMI). On the DTVP he earns a developmental age of 5-6, and on the VMI he earns a developmental age of 7-4. Give two different explanations for the discrepancy between the scores.
2. Original measures of perceptual-motor characteristics were shown to discriminate between brain-injured and non-brain-injured adults. Identify at least two major problems in the current use of these tests to diagnose brain injury in schoolage children.
3. Brairdale School decides to implement a preschool screening program to identify children with perceptual-motor problems. The decision is made to evaluate all four-year-olds in the community with the Memory for Designs Test, the Developmental Test of Visual Perception, and the Purdue Perceptual-Motor Survey. You are on the team charged with implementation of this screening project. Would you object to the proposed screening, and if so, why?
4. Identify at least three major problems in current perceptual-motor assessment practices.
5. A local school district in Boston, Massachusetts, uses the DTVP to screen kindergarten youngsters for potential perceptual-motor problems. To whom are these children being compared?

6. Performance on the Bender Visual Motor Gestalt Test is used as a criterion in the differential identification of children as brain-injured, perceptually handicapped, or emotionally disturbed. Why must the examiner use caution in interpreting and using BVMGT test results for this purpose?

ADDITIONAL READING

Arter, J., & Jenkins, J. R. (1979). Differential diagnosis—prescriptive teaching: A critical appraisal. *Review of Educational Research, 49,* 517–556.

Conoley, J. C., & Kramer, J. J. (1989). *Buros tenth mental measurements yearbook.* Lincoln, NE: University of Nebraska Press.

Mann, L. (1971). Perceptual training revisited: The training of nothing at all. *Rehabilitation Literature, 32,* 322–335.

Yates, A. J. (1954). The validity of some psychological tests of brain damage. *Psychological Bulletin, 51,* 359–379.

Ysseldyke, J. E., & Algozzine, B. (1979). Perspectives on assessment of learning disabled students. *Learning Disability Quarterly, 2,* 3–15.

C·H·A·P·T·E·R 15

ASSESSMENT OF PERSONALITY

Personality development is a nebulous concept, ill-defined and subjectively measured. No one has seen a thing called personality. In fact, you could probably debate long and hard about the meaning of adequate personality development. Personality is never assessed. Rather, we observe and/or measure behaviors and infer a thing called personality. Inadequate or inappropriate personality functioning is inferred when a person does not behave according to social expectations. Behavior is evaluated in terms of the degree to which it is disturbing—either to the individual exhibiting the behavior or to people who come into contact with that individual.

Tests of personality and social-emotional behavior use items from several other domains of measurement (reading and writing, motor development, perceptual-motor integration, and so on). However, in the assessment of personality or social-emotional behavior, relative levels of skill development are *not* assessed. What is assessed is how skills are typically used and how that use is interpreted. In social-emotional assessment, we do not look at the level of oral vocabulary; we look at how a person uses words. For instance, a person might use words in an "aggressive" manner—swearing, threatening, and so on. We do not look at drawings to assess the completeness of a human figure or the integration of circles and squares; we interpret drawings as indicative of underlying feelings and emotions.

WHY DO WE ASSESS PERSONALITY?

In any social system there are individuals who exhibit behaviors that are disturbing to other people. Schools are social systems, and in schools the behavior of some students is bothersome to teachers or to other students. If such disturbing behaviors are exhibited often enough or strongly enough, the student can have significant difficulty profiting from instruction or can seriously disrupt the "orderly affairs" of the school. In its simplest sense, personality tests are used to decide what is wrong with the student so decisions can be made about him or her.

In the 1950s and 1960s, the use of personality tests was narrowly directed at making classification decisions about students. Students were classified as emotionally disturbed, behavior disordered, or socially maladjusted based on test-demonstrated evidence of pathology (Batsche & Peterson, 1983). Tests were used to identify "deep," "hidden," and "private" aspects of personality. Children were identified as normal or abnormal, as members of normal or clinical populations, based on their test performance. Elaborate systems of classifying students were developed, and elaborate classification manuals were designed to help assessors.

In recent years the use in schools of personality measures, especially projective measures, has diminished greatly. In part, this is due to changes in the theoretical beliefs of those who assess students—and to the ways in which assessors are educated. More importantly, it is due to a change in thinking about the purposes of assessment. When Public Law 94-142 was passed, the bottom line in assessment became establishment of instructional interventions for students. Personality measures provide very little information about what to teach or how to teach.

An Overview of Personality Assessment

Personality tests have been developed within the framework of "dynamic" psychology, including psychoanalysis and phenomenology. Various theorists hold that there are internal causes of behavior and that the identification of these causes will facilitate both an understanding of behavior and behavior change. In some cases, test authors design instruments to assess specific personality types, traits, or characteristics, such as aggression, withdrawal, dominance, paranoia, cyclothymia, and hysteria. Other test authors set out to identify needs, such as the need for affiliation and the need for nurturance, that allegedly motivate behavior.

Personality measures are usually constructed in one of two ways: a criterion-group approach or a factor-analytic approach.

The criterion-group approach is characterized by efforts to differentiate among certain groups of persons in the same way that tests of brain injury attempt to differentiate between brain-injured and non-brain-injured individuals. Thus, a test author might wish to develop a test to differentiate among hypochondriacs, hysterics, manic-depressives, and paranoid schizophrenics. Items are chosen that the author believes may distinguish personality types. They are then administered to individuals who have been previously diagnosed as hypochondriacs, and so on. Items that adequately discriminate among known groups are included in the scale. The scale is then applied to individuals who have not yet been classified, under the presumption that if the test can distinguish previously identified *groups* of individuals it can distinguish among unclassified *individuals*. An individual who responds like members of a criterion group is said to exhibit a "personality" characteristic of the criterion group.

The factor-analytic approach to personality-test construction is a statistical procedure for developing tests. Items believed to assess personality are administered to many persons, and scores are then factor-analyzed to identify clusters of intercorrelated items. These clusters of items are examined for common features and then named. Items that do not fit into clusters are disregarded.

Methods of Measuring Personality

Walker (1973) provided a comprehensive guide to personality measures available for use with children. In it she identified five categories of measurement: attitude scales, measures of general personality and emotional development, measures of interests or preferences, measures of behavioral traits, and measures of self-concept. We have categorized the most commonly used personality tests according to Walker's system. These tests are listed in Table 15.1.

Walker also identified several different kinds of measurement techniques, originally described by Lindzey (1959), that are used to assess personality. A description of these techniques follows.

Projective Techniques

Projective personality assessment is accomplished by showing ambiguous stimuli such as pictures of inkblots, and then asking children to describe what they see. Projective techniques also include interpretations of drawings, word associations, sentence completion, choosing pictures that fit moods, and creative expression (puppetry, doll-play tasks, and so on). Theoretically, projective techniques allow children to assign their own thoughts, feelings, needs, and motives to ambiguous, essentially neutral stimuli. Children theoretically project aspects of their personalities in their responses.

Rating Scales

There are several types of rating scales; generally a parent, teacher, peer, or "significant other" in a child's environment must rate the extent to which that child demonstrates certain undesirable behaviors. Most rating scales are check lists designed to identify whether the child demonstrates certain behaviors believed to indicate some underlying pathology. Other rating scales require, in addition, that the rater estimate the frequency with which these behaviors are exhibited.

Self-report Measures

The self-report is a very common technique in personality assessment. It is used more frequently with adults than with children, however. Individuals being assessed are asked to reveal common behaviors in which they engage or to identify inner feelings. The devices used with children routinely ask them to identify feelings by checking happy or sad faces on a response form.

Situational Measures

According to Walker, "situational measures refer to a wide range of situations, ranging from highly structured to almost totally unstructured, that are designed to reveal to the tester something about an individual's personality" (1973, p. 31). Peer-acceptance scales and sociometric techniques are situational measures.

Observational Procedures

Most observational procedures used to assess personality or emotional characteristics are systematic. "Direct observation is the only procedure that allows one to observe the behavior as it occurs in the natural situation, thus reducing the chance of making incorrect assumptions" (Walker, 1973, p. 26).

Whatever technique is employed, it is only a vehicle for eliciting responses that are believed to represent a person's "true" inner state—feelings, drives, and so on. Responses are seldom interpreted at face value but are more often believed to be symbolic or representative. Consequently, the skill of the examiner is far more important than the device or vehicle for eliciting a person's responses.

Technical Characteristics

Scores

The particular kinds of scores obtained for personality measures vary with the kind of measure used. Scoring systems range from elaborate multifactor systems with profiles to nonquantifiable interpretive information. Entire books and manuals have been written to describe scoring and interpretation proce-

TABLE 15.1   Commonly Used Measures of Personality and Socioemotional Development

Projective Measures of Personality

Blacky Pictures Test (Blum, 1967)
Children's Apperception Test (Bellak & Bellak, 1974)
Children's Apperceptive Story Telling Test (Schneider, 1989)
Draw-a-Person (Urban, 1963)
Holtzman Ink Blot Technique (Holtzman, 1972)
House-Tree-Person (Buck & Jolles, 1966)
Human Figures Drawing Test (Koppitz, 1968)
Rorschach Ink Blot Technique (Rorschach, 1966)
School Apperception Method (Solomon & Starr, 1968)
Thematic Apperception Test (Murray & Bellak, 1973)

Paper-Pencil Measures of Personality

Children's Personality Questionnaire (Porter & Cattell, 1982)
Early School Personality Questionnaire (Coan & Cattell, 1970)
Edwards Personal Preference Schedule (Edwards, 1966)
Family Relations Test (Bene & Anthony, 1957)
High School Personality Questionnaire (Cattell, Cattell, & Johns, 1984)
Index of Personality Characteristics (1988)
Minnesota Multiphasic Personality Inventory (Butcher, 1989)
Personality Inventory for Children (Wirt, Lachar, Klinedinst, Seat, & Broen, 1984)
Revised Children's Manifest Anxiety Scale (Reynolds & Richmond, 1985)
Reynolds Adolescent Depression Scale (Reynolds, 1987)
Sixteen Personality Factor Questionnaire (Cattell & IPAT Staff, 1986)
Test of Early Socioemotional Development (Hresko & Brown, 1984)

dures (for example, Exner, 1966; Hutt & Briskin, 1960; Piotrowski, 1957). Some devices include very little information about scoring and interpretation.

Norms

Most personality assessment devices have inadequate norms. Walker states that "very few instruments have adequate standardization norms that are representative for a wide range of children of varying ethnic groups, intelligence levels, and socioeconomic backgrounds" (1973, p. 37).

Reliability

Many authors of personality measures do not report evidence of the reliability of their tests. When reliability data are reported, the reliabilities are generally too low to warrant use of the tests in making important educational decisions about individual children.

TABLE 15.1   Commonly Used Measures of Personality and Socioemotional Development (cont.)

Problem Behavior Check lists

Behavior Evaluation Scale (McCarney, Leigh & Cornbleet, 1983)
Behavior Rating Profile (Brown & Hammill, 1983)
Child Behavior Check list for Ages 2–3 (Achenbach, 1986)
Child Behavior Check list for Ages 4–16 (Achenbach & Edelbrock, 1986)
Comprehensive Behavior Rating Scale for Children (Neeper, Lahey, & Frick, 1990)
Conners Parent Rating Scale (Conners, 1985)
Conners Teacher Rating Scale (Conners, 1985)
Devereaux Adolescent Behavior Rating Scale (Spivack, Spotts, & Haimes, 1967)
Devereux Child Behavior Rating Scale (Spivack & Spotts, 1966)
Devereux Elementary School Behavior Rating Scale (Spivack & Swift, 1967)
Revised Behavior Problem Checklist (Quay & Peterson, 1987)
Portland Problem Behavior Checklist–Revised (Waksman, 1984)
Walker Problem Identification Checklist (Walker, 1983)

Measures of Self-Concept and Self-Esteem

Coopersmith Self Esteem Inventories (Coopersmith, 1982)
Piers-Harris Children's Self Concept Scale (Piers & Harris, 1984)
Self Description Questionnaire (Marsh, 1988)
Tennessee Self Concept Inventory (Fitts, 1965)

Measures of Social Competence

Kohn Social Competence Scale (Kohn, 1986)
Social Skills Rating System (Gresham & Elliott, 1990)
Waksman Social Skills Rating Scale (Waksman, 1983)
Walker-McConnell Scale of Social Competence and School Adjustment (Walker & McConnell, 1988)

Validity

Definition of traits, characteristics, needs, and behaviors assessed by personality measures is not a common practice among test authors. Moreover, any effort to describe the specific behaviors sampled by the myriad of personality devices would be pointless, since the interpretation of the behaviors is of primary interest. Yet the absence of operational definitions creates a situation in which it is difficult to determine just what a test is designed to measure. Given this fact, it is impossible to assess how well the test measures what it purports to measure. According to Walker,

> *Underlying these inadequate socioemotional measures for young children is an inadequate and immature socioemotional developmental theory. No one theory to date satisfactorily describes the socioemotional aspects of man's development. More specifically, no theory is advanced enough to guide the development of a socioemotional measurement technology for young children. (1973, p. 40)*

Coping with Dilemmas in Current Practice

School personnel are required to make decisions about eligibility of students for placement in classes for the "emotionally disturbed," or "behavior disordered." Students often are said to be disturbed or disordered based on their performance on personality measures. Despite this fact, there are no reliable and valid measures of specific personality traits or disorders and no reliable or valid measures of social or emotional maturity or development. We suggest that school personnel refrain from using personality measures, especially projective tests.

During the last fifteen to twenty years, there has been a shift in emphasis in psychology from "dynamic" psychology to a more objective study of behavior. There is an increased emphasis on the study of observable, operationally defined behaviors and deemphasis of unobservable thoughts, motives, drives, and traits that supposedly cause behavior. Most personality tests were originally designed to enable psychologists to get at those hidden aspects that supposedly cause persons to act in certain ways.

Along with a shift in theoretical orientation, there has developed an increased concern for accountability. Psychologists have been called on repeatedly to defend their activities and have had considerable difficulty defending the practice of personality assessment, in terms of both the psychometric adequacy of the devices and the educational relevance of the information provided by those devices. Psychologists today operate at nearly polar extremes. There are those who routinely administer personality tests as parts of larger assessment batteries, believing that by using the tests they will be able to pinpoint pathology. Others openly reject the use of personality tests, believing that the devices are psychometrically inadequate and educationally irrelevant. They rely instead on interviewing and on formal and informal observation to gather information about interpersonal functioning.

Along with a shift in orientation and an increased skepticism about the adequacy of personality devices and the relevance of information obtained, concern for the privacy of the individual has increased. Not long ago, congressional hearings debated the extent to which personality assessment constituted an invasion of privacy. Schools are now required by law to gain informed consent from parents before assessing children and may only maintain and disseminate *verified* information about a child. It has been increasingly difficult to convince parents that personality assessment *should* take place, and there is no way to verify the information gathered by personality tests.

Decisions about services to students who demonstrate behaviors that bother teachers are better made by collecting data through direct observation in classrooms. If school personnel document the frequency and duration of occurrence of behaviors that bother people, and if they also have data on extent of occurrence of those behaviors in students' agemates or grademates, then decisions about who should be served can be based on normative peer comparisons.

SUMMARY

In the assessment of personality, the *interpretation* of a person's behavior is of primary concern. Behaviors sampled by the tests and procedures discussed in this chapter may be the same as those discussed in earlier chapters; the interpretations of these behaviors are couched in different terms, however, since the purpose of assessment is no longer the mastery of skills and facts.

The assessment of personality takes different forms depending on the theoretical context in which the particular test or method was developed. Most often, the aim of personality assessment is to discover the underlying causes of behavior. The hypothetical causes vary with the theoretical orientation of the test authors. Five methods of assessing personality were discussed: projective techniques, rating scales, self-report measures, situational measures, and observational procedures. All of these techniques are best thought of as ways of eliciting responses, which the examiner then interprets.

STUDY QUESTIONS

1. Select any personality test and review the following:
   a. kinds of behaviors sampled
   b. adequacy of the norms
   c. evidence of reliability
   d. evidence of validity
2. For what reasons might personality tests be used in public school settings?
3. How might one validate a test of aggression?
4. Identify three major techniques for personality assessment.

ADDITIONAL READING

Anastasi, A. (1976). *Psychological testing.* New York: Macmillan. (Part 5: Personality tests, pp. 493–616.)

Barnett, D. W. (1986). Personality assessment and children: A critical appraisal and emerging trends. *Special Services in the Schools, 2,* 121–140.

Buros, O. K. (Ed.). (1970). *Personality tests and reviews.* Highland Park, NJ: Gryphon Press.

Conoley, J. C., & Kramer, J. J. (1989). *Buros tenth mental measurements yearbook*. Lincoln, NE: University of Nebraska Press.

Edelbrook, C. (1983). Problems and issues in using rating scales to assess child personality and psychopathology. *School Psychology Review, 12,* 293–299.

Fuller, G. B., & Goh, D. S. (1983). Current practices in the assessment of personality and behavior by school psychologists. *School Psychology Review, 12,* 240–243.

Knoff, H. M. (1983). Projective/personality assessment in the schools [Special issue]. *School Psychology Review, 12,* 375–451.

Walker, D. K. (1973). *Socioemotional measures for preschool and kindergarten children*. San Francisco: Jossey-Bass.

PART 4

Assessment of Skills: Domains Sampled and Representative Tests

Part 4 is an analysis of the most common domains in which assessment of skill attainment is conducted. Unlike Part 3, where the emphasis was on hypothetical constructs, such as intelligence, that are presumed to influence the learning of behavior, skills, and concepts, this part focuses primarily on evaluation of the learned behavior itself. For example, we are interested in a person's skill in reading words, not because the ability to read words suggests intellectual ability or school aptitude, but because the reading of words is important in and of itself.

Chapters 16 through 22 are organized in the same way as the chapters in Part 3, but each chapter in this section focuses on a different domain of achievement. The two principles that guided our development of both Part 3 and Part 4 bear repeating here. First, we did not attempt to cover all available measures for each domain. Instead, we have selected representative and commonly used tests in each area. *Buros Mental Measurements Yearbooks* provide an important resource for critical reviews of all currently available tests for readers who want information about devices that we have not evaluated in the text.

Second, our evaluation of the technical adequacy of each test is restricted to information contained in the test manual. We did not try to present a comprehensive review of the research literature for two reasons. In the first place, as stated in the Standards for Educational and Psychological Testing, test authors are responsible for providing all necessary technical information in their test manuals; they must have

C·H·A·P·T·E·R 16

ASSESSMENT OF ACADEMIC ACHIEVEMENT WITH MULTIPLE-SKILL DEVICES

Achievement tests are the most frequently used tests in educational settings. Multiple-skill achievement tests evaluate knowledge and understanding in several curricular areas; for example, in reading and math. They are intended to assess the extent to which students have profited from schooling and other life experiences compared to others of the same age or grade. Consequently, most achievement tests are norm-referenced, although some are criterion-referenced. Both norm-referenced and criterion-referenced tests are designed in consultation with subject-matter experts and are believed to reflect national curricular trends in general.

Various kinds of tests were described in Chapter 2. Achievement tests can be classified along several dimensions; perhaps the most important one describes their specificity and density of content. Diagnostic achievement tests have dense content; they have many more items to assess specific skills and concepts and allow finer analyses to pinpoint specific strengths and weaknesses in academic development. Tests with fewer items per skill allow comparisons among test takers but lack a sufficient number of items to pinpoint strengths and weaknesses. These tests may be useful for screening to estimate a student's current general level of functioning in comparison to other students; they estimate the extent to which an individual has acquired the skills and concepts that other students of the same age have acquired. Another important dimension is the number of students who can be tested at once. Tests are designed to be given to groups of students or to individual students. Generally, group tests require students to read and write or mark answers; individually administered tests may require an examiner to read questions to a student and may allow students to respond orally. The primary advantage of individually administered tests is that they afford examiners the opportunity to observe students working and solving problems. Therefore, examiners can glean valuable qualitative information in addition to the quantitative information that scores provide. Finally, it should be noted that a group test may be appropriately given to one student at a time, but individual tests should not be given to a group of students.

Figure 16.1 shows the different categories of achievement tests. The Stanford Achievement Test is, for example, both a norm- and a criterion-referenced (objective-referenced), group-administered screening test that samples skill development in many content areas. The Stanford Diagnostic Reading Test is both a norm-referenced, group-administered and a criterion-referenced, individually administered diagnostic test that samples skill-development strengths and weaknesses in the single skill of reading. The SDRT is intended to provide a classroom teacher with a more detailed analysis of students' strengths and weaknesses in reading, which may be of assistance in program planning and evaluation.

The most obvious advantage of multiple-skill achievement tests is that they can provide teachers with data showing the extent to which their pupils have acquired information and skills. By using group-administered, multiple-skill

FIGURE 16.1   Categories of Achievement Tests

Screening Devices

		Norm-referenced		Criterion-referenced	
		Single Skill	Multiple Skill	Single Skill	Multiple Skill
Group Administered		Gates-MacGinitie	California Achievement Test Iowa Tests of Basic Skills Metropolitan Achievement Tests (Survey Battery) SRA Achievement Series Stanford Achievement Test Series	None	California Achievement Test Iowa Tests of Basic Skills Metropolitan Achievement Tests (Instructional Batteries) SRA Achievement Series Stanford Achievement Test Series
Individually Administered		Test of Mathematical Abilities	Kaufman Test of Educational Achievement Peabody Individual Achievement Test–Revised Wide Range Achievement Test–Revised Woodcock-Johnson Psychoeducational Battery Kaufman Assessment Battery for Children Basic Academic Skills Individual Screener	None	Basic Academic Skills Individual Screener

batteries, teachers can obtain a considerable amount of information in a relatively short time.

In selecting a multiple-skill achievement test, teachers must consider three factors. First, teachers must evaluate evidence for content validity, the most important kind of validity for achievement tests. Many multiple-skill tests have a general content validity—the test measures important concepts and skills that are generally part of most curricula. As such, their content is suitable for assessing general attainment. However, if a test is to be used to assess the extent to which students have profited from school instruction (that is, student achievement), more than general content validity is required: The test must match the instruction provided. Tests that do not match instruction lack content validity, and decisions based on such tests should be tempered. Second, teachers must evaluate the adequacy of each test's norms by asking

Diagnostic Devices

	Norm-referenced		Criterion-referenced	
	Single Skill	Multiple Skill	Single Skill	Multiple Skill
Group Administered	Stanford Diagnostic Reading Test Stanford Diagnostic Mathematics Test	None	Prescriptive Reading Inventory Diagnostic Mathematics Inventory Stanford Diagnostic Mathematics Test	None
Individually Administered	Gray Oral Reading Test–Revised Durrell Analysis of Reading Difficulty Diagnostic Reading Scales Gates-McKillop-Horowitz Reading Diagnostic Tests Gilmore Oral Reading Test Woodcock Reading Mastery Tests–Revised Test of Written Language Test of Written Spelling 2 Test of Reading Comprehension Formal Reading Inventory Test of Language Development Test of Adolescent Language	None	KeyMath–Revised Stanford Diagnostic Reading Test Standardized Reading Inventory	BRIGANCE® Diagnostic Inventories

whether the normative group is composed of the kinds of individuals to whom they wish to compare their students. If a test is used to estimate general attainment, a representative sample of students from across the nation is preferred. However, if a test is used to estimate achievement in a school system, local norms are probably better. Third, teachers should examine the extent to which a total test and its components have the reliability necessary for making decisions about what students have learned.

WHY DO WE ASSESS ACHIEVEMENT?

The very term *screening device* reflects the major purpose of these tests. Achievement tests are used most often to screen students in an effort to identify those who demonstrate relatively low-level, average, or high-level attainment in comparison to their peers. Achievement tests provide a global estimate of academic skill development and may be used to identify individual students for whom educational intervention is necessary—either in the form of remediation (for those who demonstrate relatively low-level skill development) or in the form of academic enrichment (for those who exhibit exceptionally high-level skill development). However, screening tests have limited behavior samples and lower requirements for reliability. Therefore, students who are identified with screening tests should be further assessed with diagnostic tests to verify their need for educational intervention.

Although multiple-skill, group-administered achievement tests are usually considered to be screening devices, they are occasionally used in classification or placement decisions. In principle, such a use is generally inappropriate, although it may be justifiable—or even desirable—when the group tests (for example, the Stanford Achievement Test Series or the Metropolitan Achievement Tests) contain behavior samples that are more complete than those contained in some individually administered tests of achievement used for placement (such as the Wide Range Achievement Test–Revised). Use of an achievement test with a better behavior sample is desirable if the tester goes beyond the scores earned to examine performance on specific test items.

Multiple-skill achievement tests may also be used for progress evaluation. Most school districts have routine testing programs at various grade levels to evaluate the extent to which pupils in their schools are progressing in comparison with some national standard. Scores on achievement tests provide communities, school boards, and parents with an index of the quality of schooling. Schools and, indeed, the teachers within those schools are often subject to question when pupils fail to demonstrate expected progress.

Finally, achievement tests are used to evaluate the relative effectiveness of alternative curricula. Brown School may choose to use the Scott, Foresman Reading Series in third grade, while Green School decides to use the Lippincott Reading Program. If school personnel can assume that children were at relatively comparable reading levels when they entered the third grade, then achievement tests may be administered at the end of the year to ascertain the relative effectiveness of the Scott, Foresman and Lippincott programs. There are, of course, many assumptions in such evaluations (for example, that the quality of individual teachers and the instructional environment are comparable in the two schools) and many research pitfalls that must be avoided if comparative evaluation is to have meaning.

Specific Tests of Academic Achievement

The remainder of this chapter is addressed specifically to multiple-skill devices and examines five popular group-administered multiple-skill batteries (the California Achievement Tests, the Iowa Tests of Basic Skills, the Metropolitan Achievement Tests, the SRA Achievement Series, and the Stanford Achievement Test Series), four individually administered multiple-skill batteries (the Basic Achievement Skills Individual Screener, the Kaufman Test of Educational Achievement, the Peabody Individual Achievement Test, and the Wide Range Achievement Test–Revised), and one individually administered, criterion-referenced, multiple-skill battery (the BRIGANCE® Diagnostic Inventories). Later chapters provide discussions of both screening and diagnostic tests that are devoted to specific content areas such as reading.

California Achievement Tests

The California Achievement Tests (CAT) (CTB/McGraw-Hill, 1985a) is a set of norm-referenced tests from which mastery scores for specific instructional objectives can also be obtained. The tests are used to assess skill development in seven content areas in grades K through 12. The tests include measures of skill development in reading, spelling, language, mathematics, study skills, science, and social studies. There are two forms of the test (CAT E and F). Form E is available at eleven overlapping levels; form F is available at eight levels (levels 13 to 20). A "locator test" is available; it may be used as a pretest to determine the appropriate level of the test to be administered. Use of the locator test facilitates functional-level testing—that is, assessment of students

at their functional level rather than their grade-placement level. There are four practice tests, which may be used to give students experience in taking standardized tests—one for level 10, one for levels 11 and 12, one for level 13, and one for levels 14 to 20. Testing time ranges from about 2 1/2 hours at kindergarten to 6 hours, 48 minutes at grades 3 through 12. Recommended grade ranges and time limits for the various levels of the CAT are listed in Table 16.1.

Several materials accompany the CAT. There are examiner's manuals for levels 10, 11, 12, and 13 and a combined manual for levels 14 to 20. A test coordinator's handbook describes the development and content of the tests and provides a set of guidelines for test interpreta-

TABLE 16.1   Recommended Grade Ranges and Time Limits for Subtests of the California Achievement Tests

Complete Battery		
Grades K.0–K.9	Level 10	2 hours, 34 minutes
Grades K.6–2.2	Level 11	2 hours, 55 minutes
Grades 1.6–3.2	Level 12	2 hours, 35 minutes
Grades 2.6–4.2	Level 13	4 hours, 54 minutes
Grades 3.6–5.2	Level 14	6 hours, 48 minutes
Grades 4.6–6.2	Level 15	6 hours, 48 minutes
Grades 5.6–7.2	Level 16	6 hours, 48 minutes
Grades 6.6–8.2	Level 17	6 hours, 48 minutes
Grades 7.6–9.2	Level 18	6 hours, 48 minutes
Grades 8.6–11.2	Level 19	6 hours, 48 minutes
Grades 10.6–12.9	Level 20	6 hours, 48 minutes

tion. A class management guide provides instructions for norm-referenced and criterion-referenced use and interpretation of the test results, as well as selected instructional activities matched to the objectives assessed by the test. Technical information is included in two separate technical bulletins. Technical Bulletin 1 (CTB/McGraw-Hill, 1985b) includes a description of the norming procedures and the standardization sample. It also includes a description of reliability and validity studies that are to be done. Technical Bulletin 2 (CTB/McGraw-Hill, 1986) includes a description of some reliability and validity information and a description of item difficulty levels.

Subtests included in specific levels of the CAT are shown in Table 16.2. Specific behaviors sampled by these subtests are described below.

Reading   This content area includes four subtests at level 10, and three subtests at each of the other levels.

1. *Visual Recognition*   The student is required to distinguish letters by recognizing single letters that are orally presented, recognizing uppercase and lowercase forms of the same letter, and matching letter groups.

2. *Sound Recognition*   This subtest assesses the student's skill in recognizing sounds in spoken words. The student is required to identify pictures of objects that have the same initial or final consonant sounds as words read by the examiner, and to identify pictures of objects whose names rhyme with words read by the examiner.

3. *Word Analysis*   This subtest measures the student's skill in decoding and in using structural clues to identify the proper pronunciation and meaning of unfamiliar words.

4. *Vocabulary*   This subtest measures the student's understanding of word meaning. The student is required to identify words that fit categories, that have the same meaning, or that have opposite meanings. Students are also required to use context clues to identify the intended meaning of words that have multiple meanings.

5. *Comprehension*   This subtest assesses literal, inferential, and evaluative comprehension by requiring the student to derive meaning from written sentences and passages.

Spelling   The single subtest in this content area, which is not given at level 10, assesses

TABLE 16.2 Subtests at Each of the Ten Levels of the California Achievement Test

Content Area	Subtest	10	11	12	13	14	15	16	17	18	19	20
Reading	Visual Recognition	*										
	Sound Recognition	*										
	Word Analysis		*	*	*	*	*	*				
	Vocabulary	*	*	*	*	*	*	*	*	*	*	*
	Comprehension	*	*	*	*	*	*	*	*	*	*	*
Spelling	Spelling			*	*	*	*	*	*	*	*	*
Language	Language Mechanics			*	*	*	*	*	*	*	*	*
	Language Expression	*	*	*	*	*	*	*	*	*	*	*
Mathematics	Mathematics Computation		*	*	*	*	*	*	*	*	*	*
	Mathematics Concepts and Applications	*	*	*	*	*	*	*	*	*	*	*
Study Skills	Study Skills					*	*	*	*	*	*	*
Science	Science			*	*	*	*	*	*	*	*	*
Social Studies	Social Studies			*	*	*	*	*	*	*	*	*

the student's skill in identifying incorrectly spelled words used in sentences.

Language There are two subtests in this content area, although only one—Language Expression—is given at level 10.

1. *Language Mechanics* This subtest measures capitalization and punctuation skills. Students are required to edit passages presented in differing formats.
2. *Language Expression* This subtest assesses the student's skill in effective written expression, including the use of various parts of speech and the formation and organization of sentences and paragraphs.

Mathematics Two subtests are included in this content area, although only one—Mathematics Concepts and Applications—is given at level 10.

1. *Mathematics Computation* This subtest assesses the student's skill in solving addition, subtraction, multiplication, and division problems involving whole numbers, fractions, mixed numbers, decimals, and algebraic expressions.
2. *Mathematics Concepts and Applications* This subtest assesses the student's skill in understanding and applying a wide range of mathematical concepts involving numeration, number sentences, number theory, problem solving, measurement, and geometry.

Study Skills Items in the single subtest in this content area relate to parts of books, dictionary conventions, library skills, graphic information, and study techniques. The subtest measures the student's skill in finding and using information.

Science   The single subtest in this content area measures the student's understanding of scientific language, concepts, and methods of inquiry. Item content is drawn from each of the major areas of science.

Social Studies   Items in the single subtest in this content area measure understanding of the social sciences, including geography, economics, history, political science, and sociology.

SCORES

Five kinds of scores may be obtained for the CAT: percentile ranks, stanines, grade equivalents, normal curve equivalents, and scale scores (ranging from 000 to 999). The tests may be either hand-scored or submitted to the publisher for machine scoring. A variety of information systems are available, including individual test records, graphic frequency distributions, summary reports, error analyses, and class test records. Schools may obtain criterion-referenced data on objectives mastered by individuals or by classes, norm-referenced data comparing pupil performance to national norms, or demographic norm reports comparing class or school performance to the performances of schools of comparable demographic makeup.

NORMS

There are both fall and spring norms for the CAT. In the fall of 1984, the test was given to 300,000 students in grades K through 12 at public, private, and Catholic schools. The test was administered jointly with the Prescriptive Reading Inventory Reading System and the Diagnostic Mathematics Inventory Mathematics System. In the spring of 1985, the test was administered to 230,000 students. Three separate samples were used in norming the CAT: public, private, and Catholic. The samples were stratified on the basis of geographic region, community type (urban, rural, suburban), and district size. Once actual districts had been selected and had agreed to participate, schools within districts were stratified on the basis of the percent of students below the poverty level.

RELIABILITY

Data on reliability are not included in the examiner's manuals, but they do appear in the technical manuals, which must be obtained separately. In Technical Manual 1, the authors outline the kinds of reliability and validity studies that are to be completed. In Technical Manual 2, they provide the results of a few of the studies.

Data on reliability are restricted to internal consistency. The authors provide internal-consistency coefficients for each of the subtests at each level of the CAT. At level 12 and above, internal-consistency coefficients are satisfactory. All exceed .80 except for the Science and Social Studies subtests at level 12. The reliabilities for these two subtests are .68 and .66, respectively. At level 10 only 28 percent of the subtests have reliabilities that exceed .80, and at level 11 only half the subtests have reliabilities that exceed .80. There are no data on test-retest reliability or on alternate-forms reliability for the CAT.

VALIDITY

Data on validity of the CAT are limited to an illustration that the percentage of students mastering objectives increases with age and a report of correlation of the CAT with the Test of Cognitive Skills, a measure of learning aptitude.

Summary

The California Achievement Tests is a group-administered, norm-referenced measure of pupils' skill development in reading, spelling, language, mathematics, science, and social studies. The tests are adequately standardized. Data on reliability are limited to evidence of internal consistency and suggest that the CAT may not be suitable for screening at all grades. Data on validity are limited.

Iowa Tests of Basic Skills and the Tests of Achievement and Proficiency

The Iowa Tests of Basic Skills (ITBS) (Hieronymus, Hoover & Lindquist, 1986) and the Tests of Achievement and Proficiency (TAP) (Scannell, 1986) are norm-referenced and criterion-referenced tests designed to assess broad general functioning rather than specific facts and content. Both tests serve as continuous measures of growth in fundamental skills necessary to academic and later life success. The tests were designed to be used for multiple purposes, among which are (1) determination of students' developmental levels to assist in adapting instruction, (2) identification of specific qualitative strengths and weaknesses, (3) identification of readiness both to begin instruction and to proceed to the next step in instruction, (4) provision of data to assist in grouping students, (5) evaluation of strengths or weaknesses in entire group performance, (6) provision of information on pupil progress toward meeting instructional goals, and (7) provision to parents of objective, meaningful reports of their children's progress in learning basic skills.

The ITBS measures skills in vocabulary, reading, writing, methods of studying, listening, and mathematics. Two supplementary subtests measure skills in science and social studies. The ITBS is used in grades K through 9. The TAP measures advanced skills of the high school curriculum, assessing achievement in reading comprehension, written expression, listening, mathematics, use of information sources, science, and social studies. Subtests of the ITBS and TAP are listed in Table 16.3. There are ten levels of the ITBS and four levels of the TAP. Levels 5 and 6 are the early primary battery used in kindergarten and first grade; levels 7 and 8 are the primary battery used in grades 1.7 to 3.5. Levels 9 to 14 make up the multilevel battery of the ITBS used in grades 3 through 9; levels 15 to 18 comprise the TAP. Levels are essentially equivalent to chronological age, and there are two forms at each level. There is a basic battery (nine of the fifteen subtests), which is a shorter version of the complete battery.

Following is a list of the subtests of the ITBS and the skills they assess.

Listening   The Listening subtest, which is available in a separate test booklet, is included at all levels of the ITBS. Skills assessed include comprehending literal meaning and inferential meaning, following directions, concept development, attention span, understanding sequence, comprehending numerical and spatial relationships, predicting outcomes, understanding a speaker's purpose, and understanding the relevance of details.

Writing   The Writing subtest, published in a separate booklet, is available for all levels of the ITBS. It assesses the student's skill in writing

TABLE 16.3   Content of the Basic Skills Assessment Program Achievement Tests

	Iowa Tests of Basic Skills (Grades K–9)			Tests of Achievement and Proficiency (Grades 9–12)	
	Levels Available				
Subtest	Early Primary Battery	Primary Battery	Multilevel Battery	Subtest	Levels Available
Listening	5–6	7–8	9–14	Listening	15–18
Writing	5–6	7–8	9–14	Writing	15–18
Vocabulary	5–6	7–8	9–14[a]		
Word Analysis	5–6	7–8[a]			
Reading Comprehension	5–6	7–8	9–14	Reading Comprehension	15–18
				Written Expression	15–18
				Using Sources of Information	15–18
Language Skills	5–6			Language Skills	
Spelling	—	7–8[a]	9–14[a]	Spelling	15–18
Capitalization	—	7–8	9–14	Capitalization	15–18
Punctuation	—	7–8	9–14	Punctuation	15–18
Usage	—	7–8	9–14	Usage	15–18
Work Study Skills	—	7–8	9–14	Language Organization	15–18
Visual Materials	—	7–8	9–14	Letters and Themes	15–18
Reference Materials	—	7–8	9–14		
Mathematics Skills	5–6			Mathematics	15–18
Mathematics Concepts	—	7–8[a]	9–14[a]		
Mathematics Problems	—	7–8[a]	9–14[a]		
Mathematics Computation	—	7–8[a]	9–14[a]		
Science	—	—	9–14	Science	15–18
Social Studies	—	—	9–14	Social Studies	15–18

[a]Subtests in Basic Battery.

reports, persuasive arguments, explanations, descriptions, and narration.

Word Analysis   This subtest is available only at the levels of the test intended for use in kindergarten through third grade. At the lower levels (levels 5 and 6), the subtest provides information on skill development in letter recognition, letter-sound correspondence, identifying initial sounds, identifying final sounds, rhyming sounds, and word building. At levels 7 and 8, this subtest assesses the student's skill in identifying initial, medial, and final sounds and silent letters; initial and final substitution;

identifying vowel sounds, affixes, and inflections; and forming compound words.

Vocabulary   This subtest assesses the student's skill in determining the meanings of words in context.

Reading Comprehension   At levels 5 and 6, this subtest assesses word recognition, word attack, and literal and inferential comprehension. At the remaining levels, the subtest assesses skill development in literal comprehension, inferential comprehension, and generalization.

Language Skills This subtest assesses skills in four subareas: spelling, capitalization, punctuation, and usage. The spelling section is a measure of recognition, in which students identify one of four words as being the correct spelling of a word read by the teacher. The capitalization section requires students to identify words that should be capitalized in sentences or paragraphs. The punctuation section requires children to identify those places in sentences that need specific punctuation marks. The usage section assesses knowledge of grammatical rules by requiring students to identify which of three alternative sentences employs correct usage.

Work Study Skills This subtest, included at only levels 7 to 14 of the ITBS, assesses generalized skill development in three areas: map reading, reading graphs and tables, and knowledge and uses of references. The map-reading section requires students to answer specific questions by reading maps. The second section assesses similar skills by requiring students to answer specific questions by reading graphs and tables. The section on use of references requires students to demonstrate knowledge of how to alphabetize, read tables of contents, use a dictionary, classify information, and indicate reference sources for specific material.

Mathematics Skills Two kinds of math tests are included in the ITBS. The first assesses knowledge of mathematical concepts, and the second requires students to solve computational problems and written problems. At lower levels of the test, the directions are read to the students; at upper levels, students must read the directions themselves.

Science This subtest is available for levels 7 through 14 of the ITBS. It assesses the student's knowledge, understanding, and ability to evaluate facts and concepts on the nature of

science and in the content areas of life science, earth and space science, physics, chemistry, health, and safety.

Social Studies This subtest is available for levels 7 through 14 of the ITBS. It includes an assessment of the student's knowledge, understanding, and ability to evaluate facts and concepts in economics, geography, political science, anthropology, and related social sciences.

The subtests of the TAP and the skills they assess are as follows.

Listening This subtest measures the extent to which students can remember exactly what they hear, identify word meanings in context, remember main points and details, distinguish between fact and opinion, listen to a lecture, and detect bias and prejudice. The TAP is the only achievement test that includes a measure of listening appropriate for use with high school students.

Writing This subtest assesses student skill development in writing passages or reports that involve narration, explanation, analysis, and argumentation.

Reading Comprehension This subtest assesses the student's skill in factual and inferential comprehension, as well as skill in generalizing from what has been read.

Language Skills There are six sections in the Language Skills subtest for the TAP. Four of these are identical in kind and format to parts of the ITBS Language Skills subtest: spelling, punctuation, capitalization, and usage. In addition, the TAP includes measures of the student's skill in language organization and knowledge of appropriate forms for letters and themes.

Using Sources of Information This subtest assesses the extent to which the student can act independently to locate and interpret information.

Mathematics   This subtest measures both the understanding of mathematical principles and the use of basic mathematics in managing the quantitative aspects of everyday living.

Social Studies   This subtest is similar in form and content to its counterpart on the ITBS.

Science   This subtest measures knowledge and skill in applying scientific concepts. In addition, it assesses the student's knowledge of the scientific method, including matters of instrumentation, hypothesis formation, and experimental methodology. Content is drawn from biology, chemistry, physics, earth and space science, and general science.

NORMS

The ITBS and TAP were standardized concurrently with the Cognitive Abilities Test (Thorndike & Hagen, 1986). These measures were standardized on a national sample of about 332,000 students, 14,000 at each grade level. A carefully selected stratified national sample was used. All public school districts in the United States were stratified first on the basis of size of enrollment, and then on the basis of geographic region. Districts were then stratified on the basis of socioeconomic status within the district, taking into account median years of education of the population over age 18 as well as median family income. Once districts had been selected and had agreed to participate, further sample selection was accomplished by selecting buildings that would be representative of the distribution of achievement within the selected districts. Data provided in the test manuals show the relationship

of the sample to census figures on district size, region of the country, district socioeconomic status, and ethnic characteristics.

In addition to the public school norm sample, norms are provided for Catholic schools and for private non-Catholic schools. Catholic schools were selected on the basis of geographic region and size of the diocesan school system of which they were members. Private non-Catholic schools were selected on the basis of region and type of school—Baptist, Lutheran, Seventh Day Adventist, other church, and nonchurch. There are seven separate sets of norms—national, interpolated, local, large city, Catholic, high socioeconomic, and low socioeconomic—so that student performance can be compared to different groups.

RELIABILITY

Internal-consistency reliability data are based on the performance of the fall 1984 standardization sample. Because major areas of the tests (for example, language total and mathematics total) are most often used in norm-referenced interpretation, these are the reliabilities of greatest concern. Reliabilities for the ITBS range from .71 to .91 at the kindergarten and first-grade levels, and from .67 to .95 for the multilevel edition of the test. At the kindergarten level, the Word Analysis and Mathematics subtests are the only subtests whose reliabilities are sufficient for the tests to be used in making screening decisions about individuals (that is, the reliabilities for these subtests exceed .80). At the first-grade level, only the Word Analysis and Reading subtests have reliabilities high enough for the tests to be used in making screening decisions about individuals. At the second- and third-grade levels, the reliability for the Listening subtest is too low for the test to be used in making screening decisions about individuals.

Data on internal-consistency reliability of the TAP are based on the performance of the fall 1984 standardization sample. The reliability coefficients for the TAP all exceed .85.

There are no data on the stability of the 1986 ITBS or TAP. Data are presented in the manuals, but these data are based on previous editions of the tests.

VALIDITY

The authors of the ITBS and TAP attempted to ensure content validity by following a number of steps in the development of the tests. Curriculum guides, textbooks, and research were searched in order to write the items. Potential items were tried out on a large sample of students in Iowa schools. Item selection was based on the performance of this sample group, and selected items were reviewed for bias.

There are no data on the construct validity or criterion validity of the ITBS or the TAP. Data are presented in the manuals, but they are based on previous editions of the tests.

SUMMARY

The Iowa Tests of Basic Skills and the Tests of Achievement and Proficiency are a comprehensive battery designed to assess broad functional skills in grades K through 12. Development and standardization of the tests appear exemplary. From the internal-consistency data presented in the manual, reliability is variable. Test users should check the manual to ascertain the reliability for the relevant grades and subtests. There are no data on the long-term stability (test-retest reliability) of either the ITBS or the TAP. Users must judge the content validity of these tests for their particular use. There are no data on either the construct validity or the criterion-related validity of the 1986 editions of the ITBS and the TAP.

METROPOLITAN ACHIEVEMENT TESTS

The Metropolitan Achievement Tests (MAT6) is the sixth edition in a series that began in 1930. This most recent edition differs from traditional achievement tests in that it is a two-component system made up of two "sets" of tests: Survey and Diagnostic. This two-component system was developed in recognition of the multiple needs of test users. The MAT6 Survey Battery (Prescott, Balow, Hogan, & Farr, 1984) is a group-administered test designed to provide a global evaluation of pupil skill development in five curricular areas: reading, mathematics, language, social studies, and science. The MAT6 Survey Battery provides both norm-referenced and criterion-referenced interpretation, is published in eight

overlapping levels for grades K through 12.9, and requires from 1 hour, 35 minutes to 4 hours, 14 minutes to administer. Primary uses of the MAT6 Survey Battery are screening, monitoring group performance, and evaluating the overall instructional program. The subtests at each of the specific levels of the battery are shown in Table 16.4.

There are three Diagnostic Batteries in the MAT6 series: the Reading Diagnostic Tests (Farr, Prescott, Balow, & Hogan, 1986), the Mathematics Diagnostic Tests (Hogan, Farr, Prescott, & Balow, 1986), and the Language Diagnostic Tests (Balow, Hogan, Farr, & Prescott, 1986). These are designed primarily for use by classroom teachers and curriculum spe-

TABLE 16.4   Subtests at Each Level of the MAT6 Survey Battery

Subtests	Preprimer Grade K.0–K.9	Primer Grades K.5–1.9	Primary 1 Grades 1.5–2.9	Primary 2 Grades 2.5–3.9	Elementary Grades 3.5–4.9	Intermediate Grades 5.0–6.9	Advanced Grades 7.0–9.9	Advanced 2 Grades 10.0–12.9
Reading	*							
Vocabulary		*	*	*	*	*	*	*
Word-Recognition Skills		*	*	*	*			
Reading Comprehension		*	*	*	*	*	*	*
Mathematics	*	*						
Mathematics: Concepts			*	*	*	*	*	
Mathematics: Problem Solving			*	*	*	*	*	
Mathematics: Computation			*	*	*	*	*	
Spelling			*	*	*	*	*	*
Language	*	*	*	*	*	*	*	*
Science			*	*	*	*	*	*
Social Studies			*	*	*	*	*	*
Research Skills					*	*	*	*

cialists for the purposes of instructional planning and evaluation of specific parts of the curriculum. The tests are designed to provide information on the educational performance of individual pupils in terms of specific instructional objectives. Each Diagnostic Battery is a group-administered test that can be interpreted in either a norm-referenced or a criterion-referenced manner; each is published in six nonoverlapping levels from grades K.5 to 12.9. Administration times range from 1 hour, 19 minutes to 3 hours, 43 minutes.

The MAT6 Reading Diagnostic Battery samples behaviors in eleven content areas: visual discrimination, letter recognition, auditory discrimination, sight vocabulary, consonant sounds, vowel sounds, vocabulary in context, word part clues, rate of comprehension, skimming and scanning, and reading comprehension. The MAT6 Mathematics Diagnostic Battery includes samples of behavior in six areas: numeration, geometry and measurement, problem solving, computation with whole numbers, computation with decimals and fractions, and graphs and statistics. The MAT6 Language Diagnostic Battery includes subtests in the following six areas: listening comprehension, punctuation and capitalization, usage, written expression, spelling, and study skills.

The survey test and the three diagnostic batteries include practice tests for teachers to use in preparing students to take the test. Teacher's manuals for both the survey test and the diagnostic batteries include detailed content outlines as well as lists of instructional objectives measured by each MAT6 item. The manuals also include extensive guidelines for interpretation of the test results.

There is an MAT6 Writing Test, which is optional. The test assesses a student's writing ability in a free-response, work-sample format. The student is given a prompt and must prepare a written essay.

The MAT6 Survey Test is composed of items selected from the diagnostic batteries. Behaviors sampled by each of the subtests in the survey battery are as follows.

Reading This subtest appears only at the Pre-primer level. All directions are read to the student. The test is a measure of auditory discrimination, visual discrimination, and letter recognition.

Vocabulary This subtest, which must be read by the pupil, assesses skill in deriving meaning from words in context.

Word-Recognition Skills Skill in identifying consonant sounds, vowel sounds, and word parts is measured by this subtest.

Reading Comprehension This subtest assesses the student's skill in recognizing detail and sequence; inferring meaning, cause and effect, main idea, and character analysis; and drawing conclusions.

Mathematics This subtest, which appears at the Preprimer and Primer levels only, assesses basic concepts of number and units, shapes, and money.

Mathematics: Concepts Concepts of number (through one hundred), shapes, figures, money, and time are assessed in this subtest.

Mathematics: Problem Solving At lower levels of this subtest, the teacher dictates word problems; at higher levels, the student reads word problems. The student must either solve the problem or identify the number sentence needed to solve the problem.

Mathematics: Computation This subtest measures skill development in addition, subtraction, multiplication, and division.

Spelling In this subtest, the student must select the correct spelling of a word dictated in a sentence.

Language This subtest measures skill development in listening comprehension at the lower levels of the test and in punctuation, capitalization, and grammar at all levels.

Science This subtest assesses the student's knowledge of basic science facts and concepts derived from physical, earth and space, and life sciences. Also assessed are inquiry skills and skill in critical analysis.

Social Studies This subtest assesses knowledge and comprehension of facts and concepts from the subject matter areas of geography, economics, history, political science, sociology, anthropology, and psychology.

Research Skills This subtest, which is included in levels of the test intended for use beyond third grade, measures skill development in using library resources and other methods of collecting data.

SCORES

Raw scores and nine kinds of derived scores can be obtained for subtests and components of the MAT6. Derived scores include scaled scores, percentile ranks, grade equivalents, normal curve equivalents, performance indicators, instructional reading levels, independent reading levels, frustration reading levels, and instructional mathematics levels. Normal curve equivalents are *z*-scores used primarily for research purposes. Performance indicators are used to describe the student's performance on each content cluster of MAT6, relative to the performance of a nationwide sample of students at the same grade level. Instructional reading levels are indices of the highest level at which pupils can read without experiencing frustration. Independent reading levels are criterion-referenced scores indicating the level of material a student can read with ease and efficiency. Frustration reading levels are criterion-referenced scores showing the level at which the student will find materials too difficult to comprehend even with instruction. Instructional mathematics levels are criterion-referenced scores suggesting the level of basal mathematics textbook that would be most appropriate for the student.

Manuals for the MAT6 include, in addition to the derived scores, tables reporting the percentage of students in the national standardization sample who passed each item in the tests.

The MAT6 may be hand-scored or submitted to the publisher for computerized scoring. The scoring service may be used to obtain class summary reports, norm-referenced analyses for classes and for individual pupils, and criterion-referenced analyses for classes and for individuals.

NORMS

The MAT6 was standardized during the 1984–1985 school year; both fall and spring norms were developed. More than 200,000 students participated in each of the standardizations. Variables considered in selection of the standardization sample included geographic region, school system enrollment, and socioeconomic status. Although there are tables in the manual indicating a correspondence between sample characteristics and characteristics of the U.S. school enrollment, there is no indication that the authors employed a stratified sampling procedure.

RELIABILITY

Data on internal-consistency reliability and alternate-form reliability (except at the Primer level) are provided in the MAT6 manual. Internal-consistency and alternate-form reliability coefficients exceed .80 at the Intermediate and Advanced levels of the test. At the Primary 1 level, half of the internal-consistency coefficients are below .80, and 60 percent of the alternate-form reliability coefficients are below .80. At the Primary 2 level, 40 percent of the subtests have internal-consistency reliabilities below .80. At the Elementary level, 30 percent of the alternate-form reliability coefficients are below .80. There are no data on test-retest reliability of the MAT6.

VALIDITY

The authors of the MAT6 quite accurately explain that judgments about content validity will have to be made by those who use the test. They indicate, however, that validity of the test is supported by expert opinion (that of the professionals who made judgments about inclusion of items and teachers who thought the test measured the content of their curriculum). And, although they cannot be considered validity data, data are presented showing the correlation of performance on the MAT6 with performance on the Otis-Lennon School Ability Test.

Summary

The Metropolitan Achievement Tests (sixth edition) is a norm-referenced and criterion-referenced achievement test designed for use in grades K through 12. The test was standardized on a national sample of students, although the procedures used for stratification of the standardization sample are unclear. Data are provided indicating that from grade 3 upward the test is reliable. Judgments about validity must be made by users, who must consider the extent to which the test samples what they teach.

SRA ACHIEVEMENT SERIES

TABLE 16.5 Levels of the SRA Achievement Series, Grades for Which They Are Appropriate, and Administration Time

Level	Grades	Administration Time
A	K.2–1.1	2:00[a]
B	1.2–2.1	2:45
C	2.2–3.1	3:10
D	3.2–4.1	2:47
E	4.2–6.1	4:35
F	6.2–8.1	4:35
G	8.2–10.1	4:35
H	9.1–12.2	4:45

[a] Administration time is in hours and minutes.

The SRA Achievement Series (Naslund, Thorpe, & Lefever, 1978) is a group-administered, norm- and criterion-referenced battery of tests designed to assess skill development in basic curriculum areas in grades K through 12. The SRA series assesses skill development in reading, mathematics, language arts, social studies, sciences, and use of reference materials.

There are eight nonoverlapping levels of the series. Levels of the test, grade levels for which they are appropriate, and administration time in hours and minutes are summarized in Table 16.5. Specific subtests and levels at which they appear are listed in Table 16.6.

Subtests of the SRA Achievement Series and the behaviors they sample are as follows.

Reading: Visual Discrimination Pupils are required to match shapes and letters.

Reading: Auditory Discrimination Pupils are required to determine whether two words or letter sounds are alike.

Reading: Letters and Sounds This subtest assesses skill in matching uppercase and lowercase letters, recognizing letters, identifying beginning or ending consonant sounds, identifying vowel sounds, and identifying letters or pictures that stand for ending consonant or vowel sounds.

Reading: Listening Comprehension Assessed in this subtest is skill in understanding directions, grasping details, summarizing, perceiving relationships, drawing conclusions, and understanding the vocabulary of material read to the student.

Reading: Vocabulary This subtest assesses skill in identification of antonyms and synonyms, literal meanings of words, meanings of idioms, and meanings of figurative expressions.

Reading: Comprehension This subtest measures skill in understanding sentences, grasping details, summarizing, drawing conclusions, perceiving relationships, and understanding the author.

TABLE 16.6   Subtests at the Eight Levels of the SRA Achievement Series

	Levels							
Subtests	A	B	C	D	E	F	G	H
Reading: Visual Discrimination	X	X						
Reading: Auditory Discrimination	X	X						
Reading: Letters and Sounds	X	X	X					
Reading: Listening Comprehension	X	X	X					
Reading: Vocabulary		X	X	X	X	X	X	X
Reading: Comprehension		X	X	X	X	X	X	X
Mathematics: Concepts	X	X	X	X	X	X	X	X
Mathematics: Computation		X	X	X	X	X	X	X
Mathematics: Problem Solving					X	X	X	X
Language Arts: Mechanics			X	X	X	X	X	
Language Arts: Usage			X	X	X	X	X	X
Language Arts: Spelling			X	X	X	X	X	X
Reference Materials					X	X	X	X
Social Studies					X	X	X	X
Science					X	X	X	X

Mathematics: Concepts   At the early levels (A to D), this subtest assesses skill in identifying numerals, sets, the meanings of operations and fractions, counting, place value, odd and even numbers, recognition of shapes, spatial relationships, patterns, relative size, time on a clock, money, and problem solving. At the later levels (E to H), this subtest measures conceptual understanding of whole numbers (including place values, factors, and multiples), fractions and decimals, geometry and measurement, and prealgebraic relationships.

Mathematics: Computation   This subtest measures skill in addition, subtraction, multiplication, and division facts and algorithms; whole numbers, mixed numbers, and fractions; decimals; money; percents; and signed numbers.

Mathematics: Problem Solving   Word problems are used to assess skill in solving whole-number problems; problems including fractions and decimals; multiple-step problems;

rate, proportion, and percent problems; and problems involving the use of geometry, statistics, and probability.

Language Arts: Mechanics   Skill in capitalization, alphabetization, and punctuation is assessed.

Language Arts: Usage   This subtest assesses knowledge of correct usage of verbs, pronouns, adjectives, and adverbs; sentence structure; sentence transformation; and clarity.

Language Arts: Spelling   Different formats are used at different levels to assess the development of spelling skills. At level C, the student must identify which of four alternative spellings of a word is correct. At level D, words are given in context so that context cues may be used to figure out the correct spelling. In levels E to H, spelling words are given in phrases only.

Reference Materials   This subtest assesses skill in using such reference materials as dictionaries, books, encyclopedias, card catalogs, maps, tables, and graphs.

Social Studies   Major social studies concepts and skills are assessed rather than specific content.

Science   This subtest assesses science knowledge, comprehension of science concepts, and scientific inquiry.

The SRA Achievement Series is accompanied by a User's Guide that describes the series, includes overgeneralized teaching suggestions for improving skills in each subtest area, and lists skill areas matched to items assessing those skill areas. Three technical manuals are available for use with the SRA series. Manual 1 reports general data on development and standardization of Form 1; Manual 2 reports similar data on Form 2 and includes demographic data on the standardization sample; Manual 3 reports data on reliability and validity studies of the series.

SCORES

A variety of transformed scores are reported for the SRA series. Grade equivalents, stanines, national and local percentiles, and national percentile bands are among the more traditional scores. In addition, users may obtain normal curve equivalents; special percentiles for Title I, large cities, and nonpublic schools; growth-scale values; and scores indicating percentage and ratio correct.

Normal curve equivalents are standard scores with a mean of 50 and a standard deviation of 20. Growth-scale values are standard scores ranging from 20 to 780, computed separately for each subtest. They enable the user to contrast change (growth or loss) over time in stu-

dent performance with that of the norming sample. The percentage correct and ratio correct scores are simply indicative of the student's proportion of correct responses to total possible correct responses.

NORMS

The SRA Achievement Series was standardized concurrently with the Educational Ability Series (EAS) (Thurstone, 1978). At level H the series was standardized concurrently with the EAS, the Iowa Tests of Educational Development (Lindquist & Feldt, 1980) and the Short Tests of Educational Ability (Chicago: Science Research Associates, n.d.).

A number of developmental steps preceded standardization of the series. Initial content planning was completed by searching textbooks, supplementary curricular materials, and other achievement tests. Item writing was carried out by teachers, educational writers, and curriculum specialists who were given content specifications, objectives, and format. Item editing for content and for sex and minority bias was completed before pretesting. Item pretesting consisted of administration of the preliminary test to 49,524 students from 979 classes in 226 schools for 154 cities in 38 states. Although the authors provide no data on procedures or criteria used to select the pretest sample, they do provide data on the grade level, minority representation, and community type and size from which the pretest sample was drawn. Following item analysis, the final test was selected.

Standardization was completed on 83,681 students in 383 schools in 81 districts in spring 1978 and on 129,900 students in 457 schools in 92 districts in fall 1978. A three-stage sampling design was used; stratification of school districts on the basis of geographic region was followed by random sampling of schools within selected districts and random sampling of classes within schools. Sample weighting procedures were used to improve the representativeness of the standardization sample. Specific demographic data on the standardization sample appear in Technical Manual 3.

RELIABILITY

Three kinds of reliability data are reported in the technical reports that accompany the SRA Achievement Series. Internal-consistency coefficients were reported for both fall and spring standardization samples. Reliability coefficients range from .54 to .94. Median reliabilities for subtests at each level of the test are listed in Table 16.7.

Alternate-form reliabilities are reported based on the performance of 1,300 students. They range from .87 to .94 for the composite score, with the majority of subtest reliabilities between .70 and .88. One-year test-retest reliabilities for the composite score ranged from .88 to .94, while test-retest reliabilities for the majority of subtests were between .66 and .91.

TABLE 16.7 Median Internal-Consistency Reliabilities for the SRA Achievement Series (Spring and Fall Standardization Samples)

Level	Grade	Spring	Fall
A	K	.85	.82
A	1	.79	.83
A	2	—	.71
B	1	.87	—
B	2	.87	.85
B	3	—	.78
C	2	.86	—
C	3	.85	.85
C	4	—	.84
D	3	.89	—
D	4	.89	.89
D	5	—	.90
E	4	.89	—
E	5	.91	.89
E	6	—	.91
F	5	.86	—
F	6	.89	.88
F	7	.90	.90
F	8	—	.91
G	7	.86	—
G	8	.88	.87
G	9	.88	.87
G	10	—	.88
H	9	.88	.87
H	10	.89	.89
H	11	.90	.90
H	12	.92	.91

VALIDITY

Validity data consist of correlations between performance on the SRA Achievement Series and course grades, and between the test and other achievement tests. Correlations with course grades ranged from .43 to .79. The following correlations were reported with scores on other achievement tests: Iowa Tests of Basic Skills (.60 to .93), Metropolitan Achievement Tests (.71 to .82), California Test of Basic Skills (.45 to .90).

SUMMARY

The SRA Achievement Series is a group-administered test assessing skill development in reading, mathematics, language arts, social studies, science, and the use of reference materials. Although its developers claim the test is both norm-referenced and criterion-referenced, the only criterion-referenced feature is a listing of items that sample objectives; it is not a criterion-referenced test.

Data in technical reports that accompany this test indicate appropriate standardization.

STANFORD ACHIEVEMENT TEST SERIES

The Stanford Achievement Test Series is made up of three separate measures. The Stanford Early School Achievement Test (SESAT) (Madden, Gardner, & Collins, 1983) is in its second edition and is intended for use in kindergarten and first grade. The Stanford Achievement Test (SAT) (Gardner, Rudman, Karlsen, & Merwin, 1982) is in its seventh edition and is used in first grade through ninth grade. The Test of Academic Skills (TASK) (Gardner, Callis, Merwin, & Rudman, 1982) is in its second edition and is used in eighth grade through community college. All forms and levels of the test are group administered. The test is both norm-referenced and criterion-referenced.

There are ten levels of the Stanford Achievement Test Series and five to eleven subtests at each level. Subtests at each level of the series as well as number of items per subtest and the administration time are listed in Table 16.8. No subtest occurs at all levels.

Assessors must decide whether to use a Basic Battery or a Complete Battery. The Basic Battery at all levels includes all subtests except the Science and Social Science subtests. Assessors may also decide to assess students in only reading, mathematics, or listening comprehension. The publishers have provided separate booklets including all reading tests, all mathematics tests, and the listening tests. Total administration time ranges from 2 hours, 15 minutes to 4 hours, 15 minutes for the Basic Battery. Administration time for the Complete Battery ranges from 2 hours, 10 minutes to 5 hours, 15 minutes. An optional Writing Test that assesses four types of writing—describing, narrating, explaining, and reasoning—is available with the Stanford Achievement Test.

The test has variable reliability suitable for screening purposes and adequate validity.

Five reports called "Stanford Bulletins" are also available. These bulletins describe (1) reading assessment, (2) the Writing Test, (3) diagnosing comprehension, (4) testing in the secondary schools, and (5) assessment of effective listening. The bulletins include descriptions of ways in which the tests may be used to improve instruction.

Following is a description of subtests of the Stanford series and behaviors they sample.

Sounds and Letters This subtest is included only in SESAT 1 and 2. It is an assessment of the abilities to match beginning or ending sounds in words, to recognize letters, and to match sounds to letters.

Word Study Skills This is a measure of the student's skills in decoding words and identifying relationships between sounds and letters.

Word Reading This is a measure of the ability to recognize words by (1) matching spoken words to pictures, (2) identifying printed words that name particular illustrations, and (3) identifying printed words that describe or are associated with a picture.

Sentence Reading This subtest is at the SESAT 2 level only. It is an assessment of students' skill in identifying pictures that illustrate sentences they read.

Reading Comprehension Students are required to read passages that assess textual, functional, and recreational reading skills. Questions are asked at the end of each passage

TABLE 16.8   Subtests and Levels for the Stanford Achievement Test Series

Subtest	Test Levels and Recommended Grade Ranges							
	SESAT 1 K.0–K.9		SESAT 2 K.5–1.9		Primary 1 1.5–2.9		Primary 2 2.5–3.9	
	Items	Time*	Items	Time*	Items	Time*	Items	Time*
Sounds and Letters	44	30	45	25				
Word Study Skills					36	20	48	25
Word Reading	30	15	38	20	33	20	33	20
Reading Comprehension			30	20**	40	25	40	25
Vocabulary					35	20	38	20
Listening to Words and Stories	45	30	45	30				
Listening Comprehension					28	20	30	20
Spelling					30	20	30	20
Language/English†								
Concepts of Number					34	25	34	20
Mathematics Computation					45	45	38	30
Mathematics Applications							36	25
Mathematics	40	30	50	30				
Environment	38	25	40	20	27	20	27	20
Science								
Social Science								
TOTAL BASIC BATTERY								
TOTAL COMPLETE BATTERY	197	2 hrs. 10 min.	248	2 hrs. 25 min.	311	3 hrs. 35 min.	351	3 hrs. 45 min.

*Time for each subtest is in minutes.
**Sentence Reading at SESAT 2 level.
†An optional Writing Test is also available at levels Primary 3 through TASK 2.
SOURCE: From Stanford Achievement Test: 7th Edition. Copyright © 1982, 1983, 1984, 1986 by Harcourt Brace, Jovanovich, Inc. Reproduced by permission. All rights reserved.

as an assessment of literal and inferential comprehension.

Vocabulary   Students are asked to select words that best fit definitions read by the examiner. The measure thus provides an assessment of word knowledge independent of ability to read definitions.

Listening to Words and Stories   This subtest is an assessment of ability to remember details, follow directions, identify cause and effect, identify main ideas, and understand aspects of language structure. Students must demonstrate knowledge of word meanings and skill in comprehending what is read to them.

Listening Comprehension   This is an assessment of students' ability to process information that is read to them.

Spelling   Students are given four words and must identify the one that is misspelled.

TABLE 16.8   Subtests and Levels for the Stanford Achievement Test Series (cont.)

Test Levels and Recommended Grade Ranges											
Primary 3 3.5–4.9		Intermediate 1 4.5–5.9		Intermediate 2 5.5–7.9		Advanced 7.0–9.9		TASK 1 8.0–12.9		TASK 2 9.0–13	
Items	Time*	Items	Time*	Items	Time*	Items	Time*	Items	Time*	Items	Time*
54	30	60	35	60	35						
60	30	60	30	60	30	60	30	50	30	50	30
38	20	36	20	36	20	40	20	37	20	37	20
40	30	40	30	40	30	40	30				
36	15	40	15	50	15	50	15	40	15	40	15
46	30	53	30	53	30	59	30	54	30	54	30
34	20	34	20	34	20	34	20				
42	35	44	40	44	40	44	40				
38	35	40	35	40	35	40	35				
								48	40	48	40
44	25	60	30	60	30	60	30	50	25	50	25
44	25	60	30	60	30	60	30	50	25	50	25
388	4 hrs. 5 min.	407	4hrs. 15 min.	417	4 hrs. 15 min.	367	3 hrs. 40 min.	229	2 hrs. 15 min.	229	2 hrs. 15 min.
476	4 hrs. 55 min.	527	5 hrs. 15 min.	537	5 hrs. 15 min.	487	4 hrs. 40 min.	329	3 hrs. 5 min.	329	3 hrs. 5 min.

Language/English   This subtest is organized into three parts: (1) language conventions including punctuation, capitalization, and so on, (2) language sensitivity including tasks such as recognition of complete sentences, and (3) reference skills.

Mathematics   At the SESAT 1 and 2 levels there is a single mathematics measure. The test assesses skill in counting, knowledge of basic number concepts, knowledge of geometric shapes and forms, understanding of comparative language of mathematics, and knowledge of basic addition and subtraction facts.

Concepts of Number   This subtest measures understanding of basic number concepts.

Mathematics Computation   Students are required to solve computation problems in this subtest.

Mathematics Applications   This subtest assesses students' ability to apply mathematics skills to the solution of problems.

Science   Students' understanding of the facts and concepts of the biological and physical sciences is measured. The subtest also assesses inquiry skills in science.

Social Science This subtest measures skill development in geography, history, anthropology, sociology, political science, and economics.

Environment The Science and Social Science subtests are combined at the early levels of the test in an assessment of concepts about the social and natural environment.

In addition to the subtests listed, scores may be obtained for assessing skills in using information and writing. The using information score is obtained by separately scoring selected items from the Mathematics, Language, Science, and Social Science subtests. The score provides an index of a student's ability to use reference materials and to read graphs and charts. The writing score is obtained by administering the optional Writing Test.

There are two special editions of the Stanford Achievement Test: one for assessing blind or partially sighted students and one for assessing deaf students. The edition for use with blind or partially sighted students can be obtained in either braille or large print from the American Printing House for the Blind, and the edition for hearing-impaired students may be obtained from Gallaudet University. Both special editions were standardized on the respective handicapped populations.

We noted earlier that the Stanford series is both norm-referenced and criterion-referenced. To facilitate criterion-referenced use of the tests, the authors have prepared a set of indexes of instructional objectives. These include a detailed listing of the behavior(s) sampled by each test item. Also indicated is the difficulty level of the item for students in particular grades at different times of the year.

SCORES

A variety of transformed scores are obtained for the Stanford series: stanines, grade-equivalent scores, percentiles, age scores, and various standard scores. The tests may be scored by hand or submitted to the publisher for machine scoring. By submitting the protocols to the publisher's scoring service, it is possible to obtain record sheets for individual students, forms for reporting test results to parents, item analyses, class profiles, profiles comparing individual achievement with individual capability, analyses of each student's performance in attainment of specific objectives, local norms, and so forth.

NORMS

Several factors were taken into account in the design of the national standardization for the Stanford series. Except for the SESAT 1 and 2 and the Primary 1 levels, the test was standardized in both the fall and the spring. So, separate norms are provided for schools whose students must be tested at specific times of the year. For the SESAT 1 and 2 and the Primary 1 levels, the test was standardized at midyear.

The Stanford series was standardized simultaneously with the Otis-Lennon School Ability Test. This enabled the authors to account for the ability levels of the students in the standardization population and also to develop a set of tables for comparison of ability level to achievement.

Sample selection was based on several variables including school district size, geographic region, socioeconomic status, and public/nonpublic status. About 450,000 students participated in the standardization of the series. Tables are included in the norms booklets showing the percentage of different types of students who participated and comparing those percentages to national census data. There is close correspondence between standardization sample makeup and the makeup of the 1970 census.

RELIABILITY

Reliability data for the SESAT, SAT, and TASK consist of KR-20 internal-consistency coefficients and alternate-form reliability coefficients for each level of the test. Reliability coefficients range from .76 to .96. Most coefficients are between .85 and .90. Nearly all of the lower coefficients are for the listening comprehension subtest. Extensive tables listing reliability coefficients and standard errors of measurement are included in the norms booklets and technical manual for the test.

VALIDITY

As for any achievement test, the validity of the Stanford series rests primarily on its content validity. Items for the series were originally written by the test authors and submitted to a group of subject-matter experts to establish the content accuracy. Several measurement experts edited the items, and the items were then reviewed by general editors for writing clarity. The test items were submitted to a group of minority-group persons who screened the items in terms of the appropriateness of content for various cultural groups. Finally, a group of teachers were asked to evaluate the clarity of both the instructions and the items.

Empirical validity was established on the basis of two factors: an increasing difficulty of items with higher grade levels, and a moderate to high relationship with previous Stanford Achievement Tests and with the previous Metropolitan Achievement Tests. The authors state that three other factors were used to establish validity: (1) internal consistency, (2) correlation of obtained scores with scores expected on the basis of performance on the Otis-Lennon, and (3) "continuing reviews by representatives of minority and other groups." The first two are of very limited utility in establishing validity; internal consistency is an issue that pertains to reliability, and correlations with measures of intelligence were convenient for the publisher to obtain but offer more validity information for the intelligence test. The third we have previously discussed under content validity.

SUMMARY

The Stanford Achievement Test Series is comprised of the SESAT, SAT, and TASK. The tests provide a comprehensive continuous assessment of skill development in a variety of content areas. Standardization, reliability, and validity are adequate for screening purposes.

BASIC ACHIEVEMENT SKILLS INDIVIDUAL SCREENER

Basic Achievement Skills Individual Screener (BASIS) (Sonnenschein, 1983) is an individually administered achievement test that assesses pupil skills in reading, mathematics, spelling, and writing. The test takes less than one hour and provides both norm- and criterion-referenced interpretation. Normative scores are available for pupils in grades 1 to 12. Criterion-referenced use involves assessment of

pupil performance on clusters of test items. Each cluster reflects the curriculum of a specific grade, and grade-referenced placement scores are obtained that describe achievement in basic skills. These scores are used to derive classroom and textbook placement suggestions.

BASIS may be administered by teachers, resource teachers, or school psychologists. Examiners do not give all items of the test, but instead administer clusters of items appropriate to the student's developmental level. Clusters of items range from readiness to grade 8 in reading and mathematics, and from grade 1 to grade 8 in spelling. Testing starts with administration of relatively easy clusters and proceeds until the student fails to reach criterion on one of the more difficult graded clusters. Behaviors sampled by subtests of BASIS are as follows.

Reading This subtest measures comprehension of graded passages. The student supplies missing words in paragraphs. At early levels, students read words and sentences; at the readiness level, they must identify letters.

Mathematics This subtest measures computational skill by requiring the student to complete paper-and-pencil computation problems and word problems that are read to the student.

Spelling The student must write words dictated by the person giving the test.

Writing The student must write for 10 minutes on a subject that will elicit descriptive writing.

SCORES

Both norm-referenced and criterion-referenced scores are obtained for BASIS. Both grade and age scores are expressed as standard scores, percentile ranks, stanines, grade equivalents, age equivalents, and normal curve equivalents. Criterion-referenced scores, called grade-referenced placements, may also be obtained. These scores are used to recommend the grade or textbook level at which a student should be instructed in each subject.

NORMS

In developing items for the test, the authors reviewed the most commonly used textbooks in each subject-matter area, selected those objectives that formed the essence of the curriculum, and developed items to measure those objectives. The authors focused on computation and problem solving in mathematics, on comprehension in reading, and on production from dictation in spelling. An item analysis was conducted in spring 1981 by administering the test to between 1,900 and 2,000 students. BASIS was standardized in the fall of 1972 on more than 3,200 students who were representative of students in grades 1-12. The sample was stratified on the basis of grade, sex, geographic region, socioeconomic status, and ethnic representation. The authors report characteristics of the sample in comparison to 1970 national census figures. Sample distribution was very close to population distribution on all characteristics.

RELIABILITY

Several different indices of reliability were derived using the standardization group as a sample. Internal-consistency coefficients for the math, reading, and spelling subtest at each grade level all exceed .85. All but four coefficients exceed .90. Test-retest reliabilities were computed for a subsample (about 20 percent) of the standardization group. All test-retest reliabilities exceed .80.

VALIDITY

Content validity was established by initial selection of items and later demonstration that items difficulty increased with grade level. Validity was also investigated by correlating performance on the BASIS with performance on unspecified achievement tests. Correlations ranged from .30 to .72. All correlations except one were greater than .43. Correlations between BASIS scores and report card grades consistently exceeded .40.

The authors of BASIS also conducted a number of studies on the validity of the test for use with special populations of children. First, the authors established correlations between performance on the BASIS reading subtest and scores on two reading achievement tests (Metropolitan Achievement Test and Degrees of Reading Power) using 49 mainstreamed students. Correlations were .61 and .64. Instructional reading levels (from MAT) were in consistent agreement with the grade-referenced placements on BASIS. For 35 third-grade learning-disabled students, correlations between BASIS subtests and comparable content subtests of the MAT and WRAT ranged from .40 to .74. For 29 severely learning-disabled seventh and eighth graders, BASIS reading correlated .60 with Woodcock Reading Mastery

Test scores. BASIS correlated .44 to .57 with Metropolitan Achievement Test scores for 34 gifted fourth- and fifth-grade students. BASIS subtests correlated with WRAT subtests .44 (Math), .19 (Reading), and .90 (Spelling) for 26 educable mentally retarded junior high school students. Correlations between BASIS, WRAT, and California Achievement Test scores for 25 emotionally handicapped sixth, seventh, and eighth graders ranged from .51 to .81. For 22 hearing-impaired students in grades 4, 5, and 6, correlations between BASIS scores and comparable content CAT scores ranged from .71 to .83.

SUMMARY

BASIS is an individually administered achievement test that samples behaviors in reading, mathematics, spelling, and writing. The test is norm-referenced and offers limited criterion-referenced interpretation. The test norms may now be outdated. Reliability is suitable for screening purposes, and validity is adequate.

KAUFMAN TEST OF EDUCATIONAL ACHIEVEMENT

The Kaufman Test of Educational Achievement (KTEA) is an individually administered norm-referenced multiple-skill achievement test that can be used with students in the first through twelfth grades. The KTEA comes in two quite different forms: the Comprehensive Form (CF) (Kaufman & Kaufman, 1985a, c) and the Brief Form (BF) (Kaufman & Kaufman, 1985a, b). The BF requires from 10 to 35 minutes to administer and the CF from 20 to 75 minutes, depending on a child's grade. Both forms use the easel-kit format.

Both forms of the KTEA are intended for use in program planning, program evaluation, making placement decisions, self-appraisal, and personnel selection. They are also recommended by the Kaufmans for use in estimating "social adaptive" functioning and assisting governmental social agencies in "their decision making process regarding adoption, welfare, court cases, vocational rehabilitation, and the like" (1985b, p. 11). In addition, the BF is recommended for screening, and the CF can be used to assess a pupil's strengths and weaknesses.

Although the tests bear the same name and have some similarities in content, they are quite different. Consequently, we will for the most part treat the forms separately.

The Comprehensive Form (CF) contains five subtests.

Reading Decoding   This sixty-item subtest requires a student to identify letters and then to read phonetic and nonphonetic words of increasing difficulty.

Reading Comprehension   This subtest contains two types of items. Twelve questions require a student to respond gesturally or orally to commands given in printed sentences. The remaining thirty-eight questions require a student to read material and then answer literal and inferential questions about it. The complexity and variety of language structures increase over the course of the subtest.

Mathematics Applications   This subtest assesses a student's "ability to solve real-world problems by the application of mathematics knowledge" (1985c, p. 196). The sixty items are of two types: math concepts and applications in practical situations. All problems are read to the student, who has available various visual materials (illustrations, graphs, and so forth).

Mathematics Computation   This sixty-item subtest assesses a student's skill in solving problems involving basic operations, exponents, symbols, abbreviations, and algebraic equations.

Spelling   This subtest assesses a student's ability to spell fifty words. The tester says each word and uses it in a sentence. (Students who are unable to write are allowed to spell orally.)

The Brief Form (BF) provides global assessment of skill in reading, mathematics, and spelling.

Reading   This subtest contains fifty-two items. The first twenty-three items require letter identification and word decoding; the remaining items are similar to those on the CF Reading Comprehension subtest.

Mathematics   This subtest contains fifty-two items that assess arithmetic concepts, applications, reasoning, and computational skill. The first twenty-five problems require written computation. The remaining problems are read to the student, who has available various visual materials (such as illustrations, graphs, and so forth).

Spelling   This forty-word subtest is similar in form to the CF Spelling subtest.

Scores

For individual subtest scores and composite scores (reading, mathematics, and battery), normalized standard scores (for the CF, mean = 100 and standard deviation = 15, and the values are approximately the same for the BF) are available by grade or age for either the spring or the fall. Composites are based on raw score totals; thus subtests are not equally weighted within composites. Percentile ranks, stanines, and normal curve equivalents are also available, as are age and grade equivalents.

Finally, a teacher can conduct an error analysis of each subtest of the CF. Errors made consistently by a student are noted, and the number of errors is compared to the number made by students in the norm sample.

Norms

For the Comprehensive Form, separate norms are provided for spring and fall. The spring sample consisted of 1,409 students and the fall sample contained 1,067, with no fewer than 100 students per grade. The authors have done an exemplary job of describing and documenting the characteristics of the normative samples. The samples were stratified within each grade level by sex, geographic region, socioeconomic status, and racial/ethnic group to represent the proportions in the 1983 or 1984 census report.[1]

Comprehensive tables document the correspondence of the standardization samples to the population on each of the stratification variables. Overall, geographic representation is good, although the Northeast is overrepresented (and the North Central and South underrepresented) in the eleventh and twelfth grades. The socioeconomic composition of the sample (represented by parental education) varies somewhat across grades from the national average, but never by more than 8 percent and usually by much less. The racial/ethnic composition of the sample closely approximates that of the U.S. population at all grades.

The norms for the Brief Form were equated to the norms for the Comprehensive Form by testing 589 students (from 49 to 61 per grade) with both forms and equating their scores. The BF sample "was carefully selected to match the demographic characteristics of the nationally representative Comprehensive Form norm group" (Kaufman & Kaufman, 1985b, p. 96);

1. Sampling was based on the most recent report containing the desired data.

it was also stratified within each grade level with respect to sex, geographic region, socioeconomic status, and racial/ethnic background.

Reliability

For the Comprehensive Form, the average of the spring and fall split-half estimates of reliability for each subtest and composite at each grade level are presented. Reliabilities for the five subtests, corrected by the Spearman-Brown formula, range from .87 to .96; eleven of the sixty grade-by-subtest coefficients are in the .80s, and the remainder are in the .90s. The reliabilities for the reading, math, and battery composites all exceed .92. Stability data are based on the performances of 172 students who were retested between one and thirty-five days after their first testing. Data were combined for grades 1 to 6 and grades 7 to 12. All correlations for subtests and composites exceed .90, although these coefficients should be considered inflated estimates. The correlations of achievement with grade are confounded with stability.

For the Brief Form, split-half estimates of reliability, corrected with the Spearman-Brown formula, were computed for each subtest and composite at each grade level and at each age level from 6 to 18. For the subtests by grades, these estimates range from .72 to .97; of the thirty-six coefficients, only seven equal or exceed .90. For the composites by ages, only one coefficient ($r_{xx} = .89$) falls below .90. Stability data are based on the performances of 153 students who were retested between one and twenty-five days after their first testing. As with the Comprehensive Form, data were combined for grades 1 to 6 and grades 7 to 12. For subtests, stability coefficients ranged from .84 to .90; one of the six coefficients equaled .90.

For the composites, both coefficients exceeded .90, although these coefficients should also be considered inflated estimates.

VALIDITY

The validity of both forms was established in essentially the same ways. First, the content of the KTEA was carefully selected to assess the general domains covered by the tests. Because content varies considerably from curriculum to curriculum, however, the test user must verify that the content of the KTEA subtests and composites is appropriate for the particular curriculum being used with the students who are being tested.

To demonstrate construct validity, increases of subtest and composite scores across grades and ages are shown. Some evidence of criterion-related validity is presented in the form of correlations between the KTEA forms and the Wide Range Achievement Test or the Peabody Individual Achievement Test. Correlations with the Kaufman Assessment Battery for Children and the Peabody Picture Vocabulary Test are presented, but it is unclear why these correlations would help establish validity.

Finally, for the CF, data from previously administered group achievement tests are reviewed. Although there are some methodological problems with these data, they do demonstrate the expected relationships with the KTEA.

No data are offered to establish that either form is effective for program planning, program evaluation, placement decisions, self-appraisal, personnel selection, or estimating "social adaptive" functioning.

SUMMARY

The Kaufman Test of Educational Achievement forms are individually administered, norm-referenced tests. The content of subtests on the CF appears well selected. The content of the BF is less well defined; the reading and mathematics subtests seemed to have been formed by combining the two reading subtests and the two mathematics subtests on the CF. Thus their content demands vary considerably across grades and are not conceptually homogeneous.

The technical characteristics of the KTEA vary in adequacy. The normative samples are adequate. Internal consistencies for subtests vary from adequate for screening to adequate for more important decisions. The composites have good internal consistency. Stability cannot be accurately assessed from the data presented. Sufficient evidence for the test's validity is offered to make the case for general adequacy. As with any achievement test, however, the most critical concern is content validity. Users must be sensitive to the correspondence of the KTEA's content with a student's curriculum.

PEABODY INDIVIDUAL ACHIEVEMENT TEST–REVISED

The Peabody Individual Achievement Test–Revised (PIAT-R) (Markwardt, 1989) is a norm-referenced, individually administered test designed to provide a wide-range screening measure of academic achievement in six content areas. The test can be used with students in kindergarten through twelfth grade. PIAT-R test materials are contained in four easel kits—one for each volume of the test. Easel-kit volumes present stimulus materials to the student at eye level; the examiner's instructions are placed on the reverse side (see Figure

16.2). The student can see one side of the response plate, while the examiner can see both sides. The test includes a test record and a separate response booklet for written expression. The author lists the following as recommended uses for the PIAT-R: individual evaluation, guidance and counseling, admissions and transfers, grouping students, progress evaluation, and personnel selection.

The original PIAT (Dunn & Markwardt, 1970) included five subtests. The Written Expression subtest is new to the revised edition of the test. Other changes made in revising the test included development of updated norms, addition of test items, and inclusion of more contemporary content. About 65 percent of the items are new to the PIAT-R. Behaviors sampled by the six subtests of the PIAT-R follow.

Mathematics This subtest contains 100 multiple-choice items ranging from items that assess such early skills as matching, discriminating, and recognizing numerals to items that as-

FIGURE 16.2   Easel Kit for the Peabody Individual Achievement Test–Revised

SOURCE: *Peabody Individual Achievement Test–Revised (PIAT-R)* by Frederick C. Markwardt, Jr. Circle Pines, MN: American Guidance Service. Copyright 1989. All rights reserved. Photo courtesy American Guidance Service, Inc.

sess advanced concepts in geometry and trigonometry. The test is a measure of the student's knowledge and application of math concepts and facts.

Reading Recognition This subtest also contains 100 items ranging in difficulty from preschool level through high school level. Items assess skill development in matching letters, naming capital and lower-case letters, and recognizing words in isolation.

Reading Comprehension This subtest contains 81 multiple-choice items assessing skill development in understanding what is read. After reading a sentence the student must indicate comprehension by choosing the correct picture out of a group of four.

Spelling This subtest consists of 100 items sampling behaviors from kindergarten level through high school level. Initial items assess the student's ability to distinguish a printed letter of the alphabet from pictured objects and to associate letter symbols with speech sounds. More difficult items assess the student's ability to identify, from a response bank of four words, the correct spelling of a word read aloud by the examiner.

General Information This subtest consists of 100 orally presented questions that the student must answer verbally. Items assess the extent to which the student has learned facts in social studies, science, sports, and the fine arts.

Written Expression This subtest assesses written-language skills at two levels. Level I, appropriate for students in kindergarten and first grade, is a measure of prewriting skills such as skill in copying and writing letters, words, and sentences from dictation. At Level II, students write a story in response to a picture prompt.

SCORES

Five subtests of the PIAT-R are scored in the same way. The student's response to each item is scored pass-fail for all subtests except Written Expression. On these five subtests raw scores are converted to grade and age equivalents, grade and age-based standard scores, percentile ranks, normal curve equivalents, and stanines. Written Expression is scored differently from the other subtests. The examiner uses a set of scoring criteria included in an appendix in the test manual. At Level I the examiner scores the student's writing of his or her name, and then scores eighteen items pass-fail. For these more difficult items at Level I, the student must earn a specified number of subcredits to pass the item. Methods for assigning subcredits are specified clearly in the manual. At Level II the student generates a free response, and the assessor examines the response for certain specified characteristics. For example, the student is given credit for each letter correctly capitalized, each correct punctuation, and absence of inappropriate words. Scores earned on the Written Expression subtest include grade-based stanines and developmental scaled scores (with a mean of 8 and a standard deviation of about 3).

Three composite scores are used to summarize student performance on the PIAT-R: Total Reading, Total Test, and Written Language. Total Reading is described as an overall measure of "reading ability," and is obtained by combining scores on Reading Recognition and Reading Comprehension. The Total Test score is obtained by combining performance of the student on the General Information, Reading Recognition, Reading Comprehension, Mathematics and Spelling subtests. A third composite score is optional. This is the Written Language composite score and is obtained by combining performance on the Spelling and Written Expression subtests.

NORMS

The PIAT-R was standardized on 1,563 students in grades K–12 in 33 communities nationwide. An additional 175 kindergarten students took the test to establish fall norms. The standardization plan called for assessing 159 students at each grade K–2, 125 at each grade 3–8, and 100 students at each grade 9–12. The minor deviations from this plan were a result of attrition. The standardization sample was stratified within geographic region on the basis of sex, socioeconomic status, and race or ethnic group. Percentages in each of these stratification cells are reported in the manual. For the most part, the sample proportions approximated census proportions. The norms are not representative of geographic region at grade 12, where there is overrepresentation of students from the Northeast. The norms are not representative of sex at grade 1 and of race at grade 11.

RELIABILITY

Several kinds of reliability data are presented in the manual for the PIAT-R and are based on the performance of students in the standardization sample. Reliability data are reported separately for the Written Expression subtest and the other five subtests.

Excluding the Written Language subtest, split-half reliabilities for the PIAT-R are high. All exceed .90 with the exception of the Math and Spelling subtests at kindergarten and the Spelling subtest at grade 11. All internal-consistency coefficients exceeded .90, with the exception of Math and Spelling at kindergarten level. Test-retest reliabilities are generally high; 66 percent exceed .90, while 90 percent exceed .80.

Internal-consistency and interrater reliability are reported for the Written Expression subtest. At Level I the internal consistencies range from .61 to .69. For Level II they range from .69 to .91. All except two internal-consistency coefficients for Written Expression are below .90. Interrater reliability for Level I was .56 and for Level II, .58.

Except for Written Language, the subtests of the PIAT-R are reliable enough to be used in making screening decisions. The reliability of the Written Expression subtest is such that it should be used only for experimental purposes.

VALIDITY

Two kinds of validity information, content validity and construct validity, are reported in the manual. Content validity is largely a matter of expert opinion.

Concurrent validity was said to be established by correlating scores on the PIAT-R, an achievement test, with scores on the Peabody Picture Vocabulary Test–Revised, a measure of receptive vocabulary. These data cannot be considered particularly relevant to the test's validity.

SUMMARY

The Peabody Individual Achievement Test–Revised is designed to provide screening information on development of skills in six academic areas. Its standardization appears good. Internal consistencies are generally adequate for use in making important educational decisions about individuals. Validity of the PIAT rests on its content validity. Teachers need to assess its appropriateness for the curricula they use.

WIDE RANGE ACHIEVEMENT TEST–REVISED

The Wide Range Achievement Test–Revised (WRAT-R) (Jastak & Wilkinson, 1984) is an individually administered, norm-referenced, paper-and-pencil test.

The authors state that the WRAT-R is intended to be used in measuring the "codes which are needed to learn the basic skills of reading, spelling, and arithmetic" (p. 1). The 1984 edition is the sixth in a series that was originally developed in 1936. There are two levels of this test: Level I is for students ages 5-0 to 11-11, and Level II is for those ages 12-0 to 74. The two levels are available in separate forms. There are three subtests at each level:

Reading This subtest assesses skill in letter recognition, letter naming, and pronunciation of words in isolation.

Spelling This subtest assesses skills in copying marks onto paper, writing one's name, and writing single words from dictation.

Arithmetic This subtest assesses skills in counting, reading numerals, solving orally presented problems, and performing written computation of arithmetic problems.

SCORES

Three types of scores are obtained for each of the subtests of the WRAT-R: grade equivalents, percentiles, and standard scores. The standard scores have a mean of 100 and a standard deviation of 15. Grade equivalents are not reported with decimals but rather with letters indicating the ordinal nature of the scores. A student who earns the same score as was earned by the average beginning sixth grader in the standardization sample receives a score of 6B. A score of 6E is used to designate performance comparable to that of students at the end of sixth grade. The authors appropriately caution users against adding or subtracting grade equivalents from one administration to another. As we noted earlier in this text, grade equivalents should not be used at all.

NORMS

The WRAT-R was standardized on 5,600 individuals, 200 in each age group. The authors state that they used a stratified sampling approach in establishing the norms for this test, but data included in the manual indicate clearly that the standardization sample is not representative of the U.S. population. The authors say they stratified the norm sample on the basis of age, sex, race, geographic region, and metropolitan residence. They include in their manual a set of tables showing the proportion of people living in each region of the United States, the proportion of each race, and so forth. The data are from the 1982 *Rand McNally Commercial Atlas and Marketing Guide*. The authors, however, do *not* report either the numbers or the proportions of students drawn from each stratification category for purposes of standardization. The test was standardized in seventeen states, only one of which is from the north central region.

RELIABILITY

The section in the manual on reliability of the WRAT-R is incomprehensible, so it is impossible to say whether the data presented are correct. The reliabilities reported as indicative of internal consistencies are unlikely to be the reliabilities of anything. Reliability is usually defined as the ratio of true *variance* to true plus error *variance*. The authors report the ratio of true *standard deviation* to true plus error *standard deviation*. Test-retest reliability coefficients are reported for a number of students drawn from the standardization sample. The group is not described; the reliability coefficients ranged from .79 to .96 over an unspecified time interval.

VALIDITY

The most important kind of validity for an achievement test is content validity. If the test does not assess the content of the curriculum, then interpretations based on obtained results may be very misleading. Although subtests of the WRAT-R sample only very limited aspects of reading, spelling, and arithmetic curricula, the authors do not question its content validity. They state, in fact, that "the content validity of the WRAT-R is apparent" (p. 62). A teacher who adjusted a student's reading curriculum on the basis of scores obtained on the Reading subtest of the WRAT-R would be on shaky ground indeed. The subtest assesses only skill in decoding isolated words and is not designed to measure the derivation of meaning from those words. Similarly, the Arithmetic subtest is simply a measure of the student's computational skills. Data on other aspects of validity are restricted to data on earlier editions of the test.

SUMMARY

The Wide Range Achievement Test–Revised is an individually administered achievement test designed to assess academic content in three areas. The test is not standardized on a representative national group. Evidence for reliability is questionable, and there is no evidence for the validity of the test. A very limited set of behaviors is sampled in each of the three subtests.

BRIGANCE® DIAGNOSTIC INVENTORIES[2]

The BRIGANCE® Diagnostic Inventories consist of three batteries:

The Diagnostic Inventory of Early Development (Brigance, 1978), which is intended for use with individuals with developmental ages less than 7 years, the Diagnostic Inventory of Basic Skills (Brigance, 1977), which is intended for use with children functioning from kindergarten through sixth grade, and the Diagnostic Inventory of Essential Skills (Brigance, 1980), which is intended for use in secondary programs. Each inventory is a criterion-referenced multiple-skill battery.

The three inventories are highly similar in purpose and format. Figure 16.3 illustrates an assessment from the early-development inventory. The child's page contains the test stimuli. The examiner's page contains the suggested directions for administering the items, the rule

2. BRIGANCE® is a trademark of Curriculum Associates, Inc., North Billerica, Mass.

FIGURE 16.3   Sample from BRIGANCE® Diagnostic Inventory of Early Development

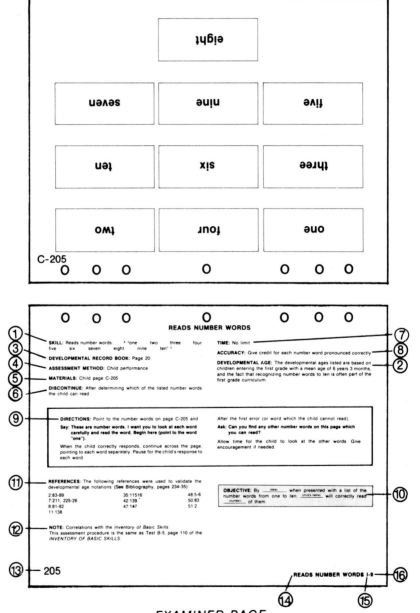

CHILD PAGE
(Oriented for the child
facing the examiner.)

EXAMINER PAGE

FIGURE 16.3.   Sample from BRIGANCE® Diagnostic Inventory of Early Development (cont.)

MODEL OF FORMAT

FOR AN ASSESSMENT PROCEDURE

WITH A CHILD PAGE

1. **SKILL:** A general statement of the skill being assessed. When appropriate, the skill sequence in the *Developmental Record Book* is also listed.

2. **DEVELOPMENTAL AGE NOTATION:** The numbers preceding a sequence indicate the year and month the child usually begins to learn or master that skill. Those following indicate when mastery is usually accomplished. Example: for ⁴⁻⁷, read 4 years and 7 months developmental age.

   In addition, the developmental ages are explained or discussed in a separate note where necessary.

3. **DEVELOPMENTAL RECORD BOOK:** The page on which this skill is listed in the *Developmental Record Book.*

4. **ASSESSMENT METHODS:** The means recommended for assessing.

5. **MATERIALS:** Materials which are needed for the assessment.

6. **DISCONTINUE:** Indicates the number of items the child may fail before you discontinue the assessment of skills in this sequence.

7. **TIME:** Time limits suggested for the child's response.

8. **ACCURACY:** Explanation of scoring criteria.

9. **DIRECTIONS:** The recommended directions for assessing the skills sequence. Recommended phrasing of instructions or questions is clearly labeled, indented and printed in bold face type.

10. **OBJECTIVE:** The objective for the skills being assessed is stated, and is a valuable resource for developing individualized education programs (IEP's).

11. **REFERENCES:** the numbers listed correspond to the sources used to establish and validate the skill sequences and developmental ages. References are found in the *Bibliography* on page 246-7.

12. **NOTES:** Helpful notes on observations, resources or diagnosing are listed here.

13. Examiner's page number.

14. Skill assessed.

15. The first letter, "I," indicates the section, where all basic reading skills are located.

16. This number indicates the ninth of the skills sequenced in the basic reading section of the *Inventory.*

SOURCE: BRIGANCE® Diagnostic Inventory of Early Development. Copyright © 1978, Curriculum Associates, Inc. Reprinted by permission.

for discontinuing the test, the criteria for scoring, the instructional objective for the item being assessed, and several other useful bits of information. Each inventory is intended to assess mastery of the skill or concept; consequently, testers are urged to adapt the testing procedures as necessary to insure valid assessment. Administering the inventories thus requires some professional judgment, although no special training is required. Each inventory assesses observable behavior or products and is scored objectively except for some rating forms in the essential skills inventory. Each inventory is comprehensive: the early development inventory assesses 98 skill sequences; the basic-skills inventory, 140 skill sequences; and the essential-skills inventory, 165 skill sequences. As is true of most criterion-referenced systems, the inventories provide the educator with lists of mastered and unmastered skills from which strengths and weaknesses as well as potential instructional objectives can be inferred.

In addition to being criterion-referenced, the Diagnostic Inventory of Early Development is also "normative-referenced." Developmental skills are assigned developmental ages not by norming the items, but by consulting several texts in which age norms for the skills are published. Moreover, the texts are referenced to each skill so that the user can check the sources for any skill of particular interest. Eleven subscales make up the early-development inventories.

1. Four preambulatory motor sequences (for example, supine, prone, sitting, and standing positions)
2. Thirteen gross motor sequences (for example, walking, catching, rhythm)
3. Nine fine motor sequences (for example, eye/finger/hand manipulations, painting)
4. Eleven self-help sequences (for example, eating, unfastening, toileting, household chores)
5. Three prespeech sequences (receptive language, gestures, and vocalization)
6. Ten speech and language sequences (syntax, social speech, singing)
7. Thirteen general knowledge and comprehension sequences (for example, body parts, colors, weather, community helpers)
8. Five readiness sequences (for example, response to and experience with books, lowercase letters)
9. Eleven basic reading sequences (for example, auditory discrimination, vowels, reading common signs)
10. Seven manuscript-writing sequences (for example, printing capital letters sequentially, printing simple sentences)

11. Twelve math sequences (for example, rote counting, writing dictated numerals, recognition of money)

In addition to being criterion-referenced, the Diagnostic Inventory of Basic Skills is "text-referenced." Grade levels are determined by the level at which the material is first taught, not by the level at which half of the students have learned the material. This inventory is composed of four subscales. The Readiness subscale contains twenty-four sequences ranging from developmental skills (such as color recognition, identification of body parts, articulation of sounds) to more academic enabling skills (among them, recognition of upper- and lowercase letters, number recognition, writing letters).

Reading   This subscale contains four subparts.

1. Six word-recognition sequences (for example, basic sight vocabulary)
2. Three reading sequences (oral reading comprehension, literal comprehension [recall], oral reading rate)
3. Nineteen word-analysis sequences (such as auditory discrimination, initial sounds auditorily and visually, prefixes and suffixes, syllabication)
4. Five vocabulary sequences (context clues, classification, analogies, antonyms, and homonyms)

Language Arts   This subscale contains four subparts.

1. Three handwriting sequences (cursive lowercase, cursive capitals, personal data)
2. Three grammar sequences (capitalization, punctuation, and parts of speech)

3. Four spelling sequences (initial consonants, initial clusters, suffixes, and prefixes)
4. Nine reference skills (such as dictionary use, maps)

Mathematics   This subscale has four parts.

1. Thirteen number sequences (for example, rote counting, writing numbers from dictation, decimals)
2. Seventeen operations sequences (such as addition combinations, division by decimals)
3. Twenty-five measurement sequences (four dealing with money, nine with time, four with the calendar, three with linear measurement, three with weight [including thermometer], and two with liquids)
4. Eight geometry sequences (for example, two-dimensional squares, three-dimensional cylinder)

The Diagnostic Inventory of Essential Skills focuses on "skills which have been identified as essential for mastery if the student is to be able to function successfully and with the greatest degree of independence as a citizen, consumer, worker, and family member" (Brigance, 1980, p. v). Unlike the other two inventories, this one has two forms (A and B) for several parts; it also contains nine rating scales to assess health practices and attitudes, self-concept, general attitude, personality, responsibility and self-discipline, job interview preparation, job interview, auto safety, and communication skills. The 165 skill sequences are divided into two parts: academic skills and applied skills. The academic skills include

1. Oral reading (graded from second to eleventh grade)

2. Reading comprehension (graded from third to eleventh grade)
3. Functional word recognition (basic sight vocabulary, directions, abbreviations, signs, numbers)
4. Word analysis (such as vowel sounds, digraphs, and diphthongs, prefixes and suffixes)
5. Reference skills (for example, alphabetizing, using library card catalogue)
6. Graphic representations (TV schedule, graphs, and so forth)
7. Writing (including cursive letter formation, punctuation, letter writing)
8. Filling out forms
9. Spelling (for example, calendar words, initial consonants)
10. Numbers (such as recognition, writing from dictation)
11. Arithmetic functions (basic operations)
12. Computation of whole numbers
13. Fractions
14. Decimals
15. Percent
16. Measurement (money, time, metric and English linear, temperature, reading meters and gauges)
17. Metrics
18. Math vocabulary

The applied skills include

1. Health and safety
2. Vocational
3. Food and clothing (for example, reading directions or labels, selection by best price for quantity)
4. Communication and telephone

Too comprehensive to be administered in its entirety, the essential-skill inventory should be administered selectively. Grade-placement tests are intended to provide a way to identify starting places for detailed assessments in word recognition, writing, spelling, and math.

Scores

The scores from the diagnostic inventories are mastered/unmastered on each skill sequence. These scores can be displayed on pupil record forms and class record forms. No summary scores are obtained. The normative-referenced and test-referenced features should not be thought of as scores.

Norms

The inventories are criterion-referenced, so norms are not required.

Reliability

No reliability data are provided. At a minimum, alternate-form reliability estimates should be provided on tests with two forms,

and interrater agreement should be provided on the rating scales.

Validity

The content validity of the inventories is the overriding concern. Although there are subtle differences in the content validity of the three devices, they are highly similar. All were developed by review of appropriate literature, and all were submitted to field testing. A detailed description of these procedures is absent. Nonetheless, inspection of the content of the inventories indicates comprehensive coverage, careful preparation, and meticulous selection of items.

Summary

The BRIGANCE® Diagnostic Inventories offer comprehensive criterion-referenced assessment of important skills, concepts, and behavior. They are appropriately used with individuals ranging from infants through adolescents. The content validity of the devices is most acceptable. However, in the absence of information about reliability, the usefulness of the scales in planning and evaluating instruction for handicapped pupils is undetermined.

Getting the Most Mileage Out of an Achievement Test

The achievement tests described in this chapter provide the teacher with global scores in areas such as word meaning and work-study skills. While global scores can help us in screening children, they generally lack the specificity to help us in planning individualized instructional programs. Merely knowing that Emily earned a standard score of 85 on the Mathematics Computation subtest of the Metropolitan Achievement Tests does not tell us what math skills Emily has. In addition, a teacher cannot rely on test names as an indication of what is measured by a specific test. For example, a reading score of 115 on the Wide Range Achievement Test tells a teacher nothing about reading comprehension or rate of oral reading.

A teacher must look at any screening test—at *any* test, for that matter—in terms of the *behaviors* sampled by that test. Let's take a case in point. Suppose Richard earned a standard score of 70 on a spelling subtest. What do we know about Richard?

We know Richard earned enough raw score points to place him two standard deviations below the mean of students in his grade. That is *all* we know without going beyond the score and looking at the kinds of behaviors sampled by the test. The test title tells us only that the test measures skill development in spelling. But we still do not know *what* Richard did to earn a score of 70.

First, we need to ask, "What is the nature of the behaviors sampled by the test?" Spelling tests can be of several kinds. Richard may have been asked to write a word read by his teacher, as is the case in the Spelling subtest of the Wide Range Achievement Test. Such a behavior sampling demands that he recall the correct spelling of a word and actually produce that correct spelling in writing. On the other hand, Richard's score of 70 may have been earned on a spelling test that asked him to recognize the correct spelling of a word. For example, the Spelling subtest of the Peabody Individual Achievement Test presents the student with four alternative spellings of a word (like *empti*, *empty*, *impty*, *emity*), and the teacher asks a child to point to the word *empty*. Such an item demands recognition and pointing rather than recall and production. We need to look first at the nature of the behaviors sampled by the test.

Second, a teacher must look at the specific items a student passes or fails. This requires actually going back to the original test protocol to analyze the specific nature of skill development in a given area. We need to ask, "What kinds of items did the child fail?" and to look for consistent patterns among the failures. In trying to identify the nature of spelling errors, the teacher needs to ask such questions as "Does the student consistently demonstrate errors in spelling words with long vowels? with silent *e*'s? with specific consonant blends?" and so on. The search is for specific patterns of errors, and the teacher tries to ascertain the relative degree of consistency in making certain errors. Of course, finding error patterns requires that the test content be sufficiently dense to allow a student to make the same error at least two times.

Similar procedures are followed with any screening device. Quite obviously, the information achieved is not nearly as specific as the information we get from diagnostic tests. Administration of an achievement test that is a screening test gives the classroom teacher a general idea of where to start with any additional diagnostic assessment.

Coping with Dilemmas in Current Practice

Two limitations affect the use of achievement tests as screening devices. As was noted earlier, unless the content of an achievement test reflects the content of the curriculum, the obtained results are meaningless. If students are instructed in new math but tested with traditional math achievement tests, they may well perform poorly. Yet the obtained results cannot be said to reflect accurately and validly a student's level of skill development in math. Jenkins and Pany (1978) compared the contents of four separate reading achievement tests with the contents of five commercial reading series at grades 1 and 2. Their major concern was the extent to which students might earn different scores on different tests of reading achievement simply as a function of the degree of overlap in content between tests and curricula. Jenkins and Pany calculated the grade scores that would be earned by students who had mastered the words taught in the respective curricula and who had correctly read those words on the four tests. Grade scores are reported in Table 16.9. It is apparent that different curricula result in different performance on different tests. Those charged with the selection of achievement tests must go beyond a casual inspection of test items. They should construct a table of specifications for each area of the curriculum to be tested and compare prospective tests on that table. Only then will they be able to make valid judgments about the relative correspondence of test content and curriculum.

A second limitation is inherent in the way most achievement tests are administered. Most achievement tests are group administered, and teachers giving a group-administered test are unable to observe individual pupil performance. They may lose valuable information about how a student goes about solving problems, analyzing words, and spelling because they cannot observe individual behavior directly. Then, because most screening devices provide global scores by content areas, teachers must actually return to a student's test blank or answer sheet to investigate the kinds of errors made. Otherwise, teachers are left with a score but little information about how the score was obtained and no systematic analysis of skill-development strengths and weaknesses.

Summary

Screening devices used to assess academic achievement provide a global picture of a student's skill development in academic content areas. Screening tests must be selected on the basis of the kinds of behavior each test samples, the adequacy of its norms, its reliability, and its validity. When selecting an

TABLE 16.9 Grade-Equivalent Scores Obtained by Matching Specific Reading Text Words to Standardized Reading Test Words

Curriculum	PIAT	MAT Word Knowledge	MAT Word Analysis	SDRT	WRAT
Bank Street Reading Series					
Grade 1	1.5	1.0	1.1	1.8	2.0
Grade 2	2.8	2.5	1.2	2.9	2.7
Keys to Reading					
Grade 1	2.0	1.4	1.2	2.2	2.2
Grade 2	3.3	1.9	1.0	3.0	3.0
Reading 360					
Grade 1	1.5	1.0	1.0	1.4	1.7
Grade 2	2.2	2.1	1.0	2.7	2.3
SRA Reading Program					
Grade 1	1.5	1.2	1.3	1.0	2.1
Grade 2	3.1	2.5	1.4	2.9	3.5
Sullivan Associates Programmed Reading					
Grade 1	1.8	1.4	1.2	1.1	2.0
Grade 2	2.2	2.4	1.1	2.5	2.5

SOURCE: From "Standardized Achievement Tests: How Useful for Special Education?" by J. Jenkins & D. Pany, 1978, *Exceptional Children, 44,* p. 450. Copyright 1978 by The Council for Exceptional Children, 1920 Association Drive, Reston, VA 22091. Reprinted by permission.

achievement test or when evaluating the results of a student's performance on an achievement test, the classroom teacher needs to take into careful consideration not only the technical characteristics of the test but also the extent to which the behaviors sampled represent the goals and objectives of the student's curriculum. The teacher can adapt certain techniques for administering group tests and for getting the most mileage out of the results of group tests.

STUDY QUESTIONS

1. State at least three different reasons for administering the screening tests described in this chapter.
2. Differentiate between screening tests and diagnostic tests.
3. Identify at least four important considerations in selecting a specific achievement test for use with the third graders in your local school system.
4. Identify similarities and differences in the domains of behavior sampled by the California Achievement Tests, the Iowa Tests of Basic Skills, and the Peabody Individual Achievement Test–Revised.

5. Ms. Epstein decides to assess the achievement of her fifth-grade pupils. She believes her pupils are unusually "slow" and estimates that, in general, they are functioning on about a third-grade level. She decides to use Primary Level III of the SAT. What difficulties will she face in doing so?

6. Mr. Spencer, a fourth-grade teacher in Bemidji, Minnesota, wants to group students in his class for reading instruction. He administers the reading recognition subtest of the Wide Range Achievement Test and assigns students to groups on the basis of the grade scores they earn on the test. Which of the basic assumptions underlying assessment has Mr. Spencer violated? How might he make this grouping decision?

ADDITIONAL READING

Conoley, J. C., & Kramer, J. J. (1989). *Buros tenth mental measurements yearbook*. Lincoln, NE: University of Nebraska Press.

Gronlund, N. E. (1973). *Preparing criterion-referenced tests for classroom instruction*. New York: Macmillan.

Gronlund, N. E. (1982). *Constructing achievement tests*. Englewood Cliffs, NJ: Prentice-Hall.

Jenkins, J., & Pany, D. (1978). Standardized achievement tests: How useful for special education? *Exceptional Children, 44*, 448–453.

C·H·A·P·T·E·R 17

ASSESSMENT OF READING

In Chapter 16 we described multiple-skill achievement tests. These tests provide relatively global information about a student's achievement. Often, school personnel need more specific information. In this chapter we provide a detailed description of the kinds of behaviors sampled by reading tests; we then describe commonly used reading tests, both norm-referenced and criterion-referenced.

WHY DO WE ASSESS READING SKILLS?

Reading is thought to be the most fundamental skill students acquire through the process of schooling. Students who experience difficulty reading can be expected to have difficulty with nearly all academic curriculum content. It should not surprise you to learn that "difficulty reading" is the most frequently stated reason why students are referred for psychoeducational evaluation.

Diagnostic tests are designed to help school personnel pinpoint students' strengths and weaknesses in reading and to help plan appropriate educational interventions for them. They are used to give teachers a systematic, relatively specific picture of where pupils stand in development of specific reading skills.

Another reason to use reading tests is to spot common problems within groups of children. One of the authors recently consulted at a school in which pupils consistently performed above grade level in all areas of the curriculum but one: reading. Students in that school nearly all earned below-average scores on the reading subtests of the Metropolitan Achievement Test. A diagnostic reading test was used to pinpoint skill deficiencies that students consistently demonstrated. Once specific deficiencies were identified, teachers were able to explore alternative explanations for the deficiencies. Teachers learned that the skills were not systematically taught in the math curriculum used by the school. They then identified skills they thought were very important to teach and added those skills to the curriculum.

Norm-referenced diagnostic reading tests provide information about relative standing in development of reading skills. This information might be used for making classification or placement decisions and for making program evaluation decisions. Norm-referenced diagnostic reading tests may be used in instructional planning, but when that is the case users must go beyond the derived scores to analyze pupil performance of the specific behaviors sampled by the test. Knowledge of grade scores, age scores, percentile ranks, and stanines is of limited value in instructional planning. For example, knowing where Heather stands relative to other students does not help a teacher decide how to teach Heather to read.

Skills Assessed by Diagnostic Reading Tests

Reading is a complex behavior composed of many skills. No diagnostic reading test assesses all aspects of reading completely. Rather, the test samples specific reading or reading-related behaviors. The particular behaviors assessed by any one test are simply those behaviors that the test authors believe are most important to assess. In a broad sense, several different categories of behaviors are sampled by diagnostic reading tests. Specific tests or subtests assess oral reading skills, comprehension skills, word-attack skills, and rate of reading. A variety of supplementary subtests are included in a number of diagnostic reading tests.

Assessment of Oral Reading Skills

A number of tests or parts of tests are designed to assess the accuracy and fluency of a student's oral reading. Oral reading tests consist of series of paragraphs arranged sequentially from very easy paragraphs to relatively difficult ones. The student reads aloud while the examiner notes both the kinds of errors made and the behaviors that characterize the student's oral reading. Two commonly used tests, the Gray Oral Reading Test–Revised and the Gilmore Oral Reading Test, are designed specifically to assess skill development in oral reading. Four other commonly used tests, the Formal Reading Inventory, the Gates-McKillop-Horowitz Reading Diagnostic Tests, the Durrell Analysis of Reading Difficulty, and the Standardized Reading Inventory, include oral reading subtests.

Different oral reading tests record different behaviors as errors or miscues in oral reading. A description follows of the behaviors demonstrated as each specific kind of error takes place.

Aid If a student either hesitates for a time without making an audible effort to pronounce a word or appears to be attempting for 10 seconds to pronounce the word, the examiner pronounces the word and records an error. The error is recorded by an underlined bracket.

Gross Mispronunciation of a Word "A gross mispronunciation is one in which the pupil's pronunciation of a word bears so little resemblance to the proper pronunciation that the examiner must be looking at the word to recognize it" (Gray & Robinson, 1967, p. 5). An example of a gross mispronunciation is one in which the pupil reads the word *encounters* as "actors." The examiner records the error phonetically above the mispronounced word.

Omission of a Word or Group of Words Omissions consist of skipping individual words or groups of words. The examiner simply circles the word or group of words omitted.

Insertion of a Word or Group of Words Insertions consist of the student's putting one or more words into the sentence being read. The student may, for example, read the dog as "the mean dog." Insertions are recorded by placing a caret (^) in the sentence and writing in the word or words inserted.

Substitution of One Meaningful Word for Another Substitutions consist of the actual replacement of one or more words in the passage by one or more meaningful words. The student might read *is* as "it" or *dense* as "depress." Children often replace entire sequences of words with others as illustrated in the reading of *He is his own mechanic* as "He sat on his own machine." The examiner records substitutions by underlining the word or words substituted and writing in the substitutions. Some oral reading tests require that examiners record the specific kind of substitution error. Substitutions are classified as those of meaning similarity (the words have similar meanings), function similarity (the two words have syntactically similar functions), graphic/phoneme similarity (the words sound alike), or comprising a combination of the above.

Repetition Repetition consists of repeating words or groups of words while attempting to read sentences or paragraphs. In some cases if a student repeats a group of words to correct an error, the original error is struck but a repetition error is recorded. In other cases such behaviors are recorded simply as spontaneous corrections. Repetitions are recorded by underlining the repeated word or words with a wavy line. Errors due to stuttering are not recorded as repetition errors.

Inversion, or Changing of Word Order Errors of inversion are recorded when the child changes the order of words appearing in a sentence. Inversions are indicated as follows: *house the.*

Partial Mispronunciation   A partial mispronunciation can be one of several different kinds of errors. The examiner may have to pronounce *part* of a word for a student (an aid); the student may phonetically mispronounce specific letters by reading words like *red* as "reed"; the student may omit part of a word, insert elements of words, make errors in syllabication, accent, or inversion. Such errors are recorded phonetically and scored as partial mispronunciations.

Disregard of Punctuation   The student may fail to observe punctuation—that is, may not pause for a comma, stop for a period, or indicate by vocal inflection a question mark or exclamation point. These errors of disregard of punctuation are recorded by circling the punctuation mark.

Hesitation   The student hesitates for two or more seconds before pronouncing a word. The error is recorded as a check (✓) over the word. If the examiner then pronounces the word, it is recorded ✓p.

In addition to making a systematic analysis of oral reading errors, the examiner can note the behaviors that characterize a student's oral reading. Although, certainly, any characteristics may be observed, the indicators of difficulty more frequently looked for include head movement, finger pointing, loss of place, word-by-word reading, poor phrasing, lack of expression, reading in a monotonous tone, and reading in a strained voice.

Assessment of Comprehension Skills

Diagnostic reading tests assess six kinds of comprehension skills: literal comprehension, inferential comprehension, listening comprehension, critical comprehension, affective comprehension, and lexical comprehension. Assessment of *literal comprehension* is usually accomplished by asking a number of factual questions based directly on the content of a paragraph or story the student has read. The answers to such questions appear directly in the story or paragraph. Such comprehension tests require specific recall of material read and for that reason are sometimes characterized as memory tests—appropriately, unless, of course, the passage is available for the student to refer to when responding to the questions.

Inferential comprehension tests require interpretation and extension of what has been read. The student must demonstrate an ability to derive meaning from printed paragraphs or stories. Assessment of *listening comprehension* is accomplished by reading a story or paragraph to a student and then asking questions based on recall or understanding of the material read. Listening comprehension tests can measure both literal and inferential comprehension.

Critical comprehension tests assess the student's skill in analyzing, evaluating, or making judgments about what is read. *Affective comprehension* tests involve personal and emotional responses to the text. *Lexical comprehension* tests pertain to knowledge of key vocabulary words. Though students can answer the questions correctly without reading the text, these tests do give examiners information on the extent to which poor performance is a function of lack of knowledge of the meanings of specific words.

In the process of assessing the development of comprehension skills, it is absolutely necessary for the teacher or diagnostic specialist to examine critically how those skills are assessed. The method by which comprehension skills are assessed may muddy the waters, in that pupil performance may depend more on other traits or skills than on comprehension of what is read. When literal comprehension is assessed by asking the student to read a passage and recall, without observing the passage, what has been read, performance may depend more on memory than on reading comprehension. Similarly, asking students to infer meaning on the basis of what they have read probably requires as much cognition as comprehension. In our opinion, the best way to assess comprehension is to ask students to state or paraphrase what they have read.

Assessment of Word-Attack Skills

Word-attack or word-analysis skills are those used "to derive the meaning and/or pronunciation of a word through phonics, structural analysis, or context clues" (Ekwall, 1970, p. 4). Children must decode words before they can gain meaning from the printed page. Since word-analysis difficulties are among the principal reasons why children have trouble reading, a variety of subtests of commonly used diagnostic reading tests specifically assess word-analysis skills.

Subtests assessing skill in word analysis range from such basic assessments as analysis of a student's skill in associating letters with sounds to tests of blending and syllabication. Subtests that assess skill in associating letters with sounds are generally of a format in which the examiner reads a word aloud and the child must identify the consonant, vowel, consonant cluster, or digraph that has the same sound as the beginning, middle, or ending letter in the words. Syllabication subtests present polysyllabic words, and the child must either divide the word into syllables or circle specific syllables. Blending subtests, on the other hand, are of three types. First, the examiner may read syllables out loud ("wa - ter - mel - on," for example) and ask the child to pronounce the word. Second, the child may be asked to read word parts and pronounce whole words. Third, the child may be presented with alternative beginning, middle, and ending sounds and asked to produce a word. Figure

17.1 illustrates the third method used with the Stanford Diagnostic Reading Test.

Assessment of Word-Recognition Skills

Subtests of diagnostic reading tests that assess a pupil's word-recognition skills are designed to ascertain what many call *sight vocabulary*. A person learns the correct pronunciation of letters and words through a variety of experiences. The more exposure a person has to specific words and the more familiar those words become, the more readily the person recognizes those words and pronounces them. Well-known words require very little reliance on word-attack skills. Most readers of this book immediately recognize the word *hemorrhage* and do not have to employ phonetic skills to pronounce it. On the other hand, words like *nephrocystanastomosis* are not a part of the sight vocabulary of most of us. The word slows us down; we use phonetics to analyze it.

Word-recognition subtests form a major part of most diagnostic reading tests. Some tests use paper tachistoscopes to expose words for brief periods of time (usually one-half second). Students who recognize many words are said to have good sight vocabularies or good word-recognition skills. Other subtests assess letter recognition, recognition of words in isolation, and recognition of words in context.

Assessment of Rate of Reading

Reading rate is generally played down in the diagnostic assessment of reading difficulties. There are, however, some exceptions. Two levels of the Stanford Diagnostic Reading Test have subtests to assess rate of reading. On the other hand, tests such as the Gray Oral Reading Test–Revised are timed, with time affecting the score a pupil receives. A pupil who reads a passage on the GORT-R slowly but makes no errors in reading can earn a lower score than a rapid reader who makes one or two errors in reading.

FIGURE 17.1   An Item That Assesses Blending Skill

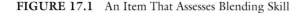
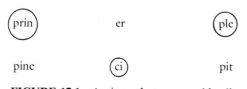

FIGURE 17.1   An item that assesses blending skill
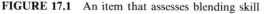

Assessment of Other Reading and Reading-Related Behaviors

A variety of subtests that fit none of the above categories are included in diagnostic reading tests as either major or supplementary subtests. Examples of such tests include oral vocabulary, spelling, handwriting, and auditory discrimination. In most cases such subtests are included simply to provide the examiner with additional diagnostic information.

ORAL READING TESTS

GATES-MACGINITIE READING TESTS

The 1978 edition of the Gates-MacGinitie Reading Tests (MacGinitie, 1978) is the most recent in a series that began with publication of the Gates Silent Reading Test and the Gates Primary Reading Tests in 1926. The series consists of norm-referenced screening tests designed to assess skill development in reading from kindergarten through twelfth grade. There are seven levels of the tests, with at least two forms at each level; there are three forms for use in grades 4 through 9. Testing time is about 55 minutes for each level.

The specific subtests and the behaviors they sample follow.

Vocabulary   This subtest assesses reading vocabulary. The actual demand of the task varies with grade level. The Vocabulary subtest at grades 1, 2, and 3, for example, presents the child with four printed words and a picture illustrating one of the words. The child must circle the word that best corresponds to the picture. From grade level 4 through grade level 12, the student is presented with a stimulus word and five additional words. The student must identify the response word that has the same meaning as the stimulus word.

Comprehension   This subtest assesses ability to read and understand whole sentences and paragraphs. In grades 1 and 2 the child must read a selection and choose the picture that best describes its content. In grade 3, the child reads a paragraph and then selects, from among four response choices, the best answer to specific questions about the paragraph. In grades 4 through 12 the student is presented with paragraphs in which there are a number of blank spaces. The student must select from five response alternatives the word or phrase that best fits in the blank.

SCORES

Raw scores for the Vocabulary and Comprehension subtests are simply the number of items correct. Raw scores are not obtained for the level of the test used in grades 1-0 to 1-9 (level R), because the subtests are very short. For level R, normative information is given descriptively (low, average, high). Raw scores for the other levels of the test may be transformed to normal curve equivalents, percentile ranks, stanines, grade equivalents, and extended scale scores.

TABLE 17.1 Alternate-Form Reliabilities for the Gates-MacGinitie Reading Tests

Level	Vocabulary	Comprehension	Total
A	.88–.90	.89	.92–.94
B	.88–.90	.86	.92
C	.89–.90	.85–.86	.93
D	.86–.89	.83–.84	.91–.92
E	.86–.90	.82–.87	.89–.93
F	.86–.87	.77–.83	.89–.91

NORMS

The Gates-MacGinitie Reading Tests were standardized in October 1976, February 1977 (level A only), and May 1977. The sample was selected to correspond to 1970 census data: geographic region, district enrollment size, and the school district's socioeconomic status (median family income and median years of education completed by adults). A total of 65,000 students (approximately 5,000 per grade) were assessed. The author states that districts were selected to produce within each region a representative proportion of black and Hispanic students. There are no demographic data in the manuals that accompany this test describing the specific characteristics of the sample or contrasting sample proportions with population proportions.

RELIABILITY

Three kinds of reliability data—internal-consistency, alternate-form, and test-retest—are reported in the technical manual for the Gates-MacGinitie Reading Tests. Internal-consistency coefficients based on the performance of pupils in the standardization sample are all greater than .85, with most being greater than .90. Alternate-form reliabilities are reported for all levels. These are sum-marized for levels A to F in Table 17.1. Alternate-form reliability for the total test at level R was .91, but for subtests reliability ranged only from .57 to .78. Test-retest reliability, based on correlations between pupils' performances in October and May, ranged from .77 to .89.

VALIDITY

Two indexes of validity are reported for the Gates-MacGinitie Reading Tests. The author reports correlations ranging from .74 to .94 with the first edition of the test. He also reports correlations with corresponding subtests of the Metropolitan Achievement Test at grades 5-8 and 8-8. Correlations at grade 5-8 were .88 (Vocabulary), .83 (Comprehension), and .91 (Total); at grade 8-8 correlations were .86 (Vocabulary), .80 (Comprehension), and .88 (Total).

SUMMARY

The second edition of the Gates-MacGinitie Reading Tests provides a comprehensive assessment of reading skills in two domains: vocabulary and comprehension. Data on the specific makeup of the standardization group are not provided. Evidence for reliability and validity of the tests is adequate.

FORMAL READING INVENTORY

The Formal Reading Inventory (FRI) (Wieder-holt, 1986) is an individually administered, norm-referenced measure of a student's skill development in oral and silent reading. The test is appropriate for use with students in grades 1 through 12 (ages 6-6 through 17-11). There are four forms of the test. Forms A and C are read silently; Forms B and D are read orally. Forms B and D are identical in every respect to the two forms of the Gray Oral Reading Test–Revised. Materials for the FRI consist of a reusable student book of reading passages, an examiner's manual, and examiner's worksheets. Each form of the test contains thirteen reading passages, each of which is followed by five multiple-choice comprehension questions. It takes about 15 minutes to administer each form of the test.

In developing the stories for the FRI, specific effort was made to control for density of words, length of words and sentences, complexity of sentence structure, structure of sentences, logical connections between sentences and clauses, and coherence of topics. The readability levels of the paragraphs were assessed by five different readability formulas: Flesch, Fry, Dale-Chall, Farr-Jenkins-Patterson, and Danielson-Bryan. Three separate word lists were used to control the vocabulary level of words in the FRI passages. In developing the comprehension questions, special care was taken to ensure that the level of vocabulary used in the questions did not exceed that used in the stories. Four kinds of reading comprehension are assessed: literal, inferential, critical, and affective. The questions were written so as to be passage dependent—an effort was made to eliminate the possibility that the correct response would be chosen primarily on the basis of similarities in text features.

By administering the FRI, the examiner obtains two kinds of information: (a) an analysis and classification of the kinds of oral reading miscues the student makes and (b) a silent reading comprehension quotient. Miscues are further examined and categorized as to type only if they are substitutions. The following categories of substitution miscues are recorded:

Meaning Similarity Miscues are scored in this category when the examiner judges that the miscue consisted of the student's substituting one word for another one having essentially the same meaning (for example, the student read menace as "threat").

Function Similarity These are miscues in which one word is substituted for another one having a "syntactically similar function." The number of such miscues is a measure of the student's use of correct grammatical forms in reading. The examiner must judge whether a substituted word has the same grammatical function as the original printed word.

Graphic/Phonemic Similarity Miscues are scored in this category when the examiner decides that the word substituted looks like and/or sounds like the original word (for example, the student read *thought* as "through").

Multiple Sources Miscues are scored in this category when they fit more than one of the types of miscues listed above.

Self-Correction Miscues are scored in this category when the student corrects an error in oral reading. These miscues are recorded to differentiate readers who correct their errors from those who do not.

In addition to recording formally the five kinds of oral reading miscues described above, examiners make note of other kinds of miscues. These include errors of dialect, reversals, omissions, and additions. The examiner also makes note of such oral reading behaviors as slow reading rate, word-by-word reading, poor phrasing, lack of expression, pitch too high or low, voice too soft or strained, poor enunciation, disregard of punctuation, head movement, finger pointing, loss of place, holding the book far away or very close, nervousness, and poor attitude.

The kinds of miscues students make are recorded directly on the FRI worksheet. An illustration of the recording procedure is reproduced in Figure 17.2. The student's responses to the five multiple-choice comprehension questions are simply scored pass-fail.

SCORES

Scores obtained from administering the FRI include a silent reading comprehension quotient, a percentile score for silent reading comprehension, and a classification of oral reading miscues. Because the two forms of the test read orally (Forms B and D) are identical to the Gray Oral Reading Test–Revised (Wiederholt & Bryant, 1986), the GORT-R manual can be used to obtain an oral reading comprehension score and an oral reading quotient.

The silent reading comprehension quotient has a mean of 100 and a standard deviation of 15. For the categorical analysis of oral reading miscues, the examiner notes the total number of miscues made and the number of each type.

NORMS

The FRI was standardized on 1,737 children from twelve states (Florida, Iowa, Illinois, Kan-

sas, Louisiana, Missouri, Mississippi, New York, Ohio, South Carolina, Texas, and Washington). The author reports a breakdown of the normative sample in terms of sex, area of residence (urban, rural), race, geographic area, and ethnicity, though no indication is given of how the sample was stratified. The percentages for students in the sample are reasonably close to the percentages for the population as revealed by census data, but these figures may be misleading. For example, although the percentage of the sample coming from the West (20 percent) was identical to the percentage of the U.S. population in the West according to census data, the only western state from which standardization data were collected was Washington. The author does not provide data on the socioeconomic status of those who make up the standardization group.

RELIABILITY

Two kinds of reliability data are provided in the FRI manual. Data on the internal consistency of the test are reported based on twenty-five protocols selected at random for each age level in the standardization population. All internal-consistency coefficients exceeded .92. Alternate-form reliability was computed by correlating scores of the standardization sample for Forms A and C of the test. The correlation was .75.

VALIDITY

Two studies were conducted to ascertain the concurrent validity of the FRI. In the first study, 190 children in grades 1 through 6 in Tacoma, Washington, took the FRI and the Comprehensive Tests of Basic Skills. In a second study, 114 children in grades 4, 5, 6, 8, and 10 from a school district in Westlake,

Texas, took the FRI and the California Achievement Test. Correlations between the FRI and the total reading score on the CTBS ranged from .21 for Form A to .46 for Form D.

FIGURE 17.2 An Illustration of the Recording Procedure for the Formal Reading Inventory

---

Story 10

1. For days the zoologist had scoured the protected area for a coyote den.
   [annotations: scored, project, idea]

2. Unless she could stake one out for field study, it would be impossible to docu-
   [annotations: strake, the]

3. ment her theory that a coyote is a social creature staunchly devoted to its family
   [annotations: a, and]

4. and clan, not the loner of popular imagination. The wildlife sanctuary had
   [annotations: immigration, security]

5. seemed the ideal setting for tracking coyotes, for there the detested adversary
   [annotations: the, the]

6. of sheep ranchers was afforded refuge from the wholesale onslaughts of trap-
   [annotations: refuse, loss]

7. ping, shooting, and poisoning. But years of this guerilla warfare had conditioned
   [annotations: position, gorilla, continued]

8. in the species a wariness that made coyote sightings a rarity. Seasoned by com-
   [annotations: to speeches, had]

9. bat, the species had evolved a highly suspicious nature that honed its survival
   [annotations: specious, regarded, honed]

10. instincts and thwarted efforts aimed at its extermination. Yet this same trait, as
    [annotations: alert, and as and, and]

11. the zoologist was forced to acknowledge with frustration, had endowed it with
    [annotations: in the knowledge and, that]

12. the uncanny ability to elude scientific scrutiny.
    [annotations: unscanny, vidulg, certainty]

1. ✓   2. _____   3. _____   4. _____   5. _____

SOURCE: From *Formal Reading Inventory, Examiner's Manual* (p. 51) by J. L. Wiederholt, 1986, Austin, TX: Pro-Ed. Copyright 1986 by J. L. Wiederholt. Reprinted by permission of Pro-Ed.

Correlations between the FRI and the total reading score for the CAT ranged from .37 for Form A to .69 for Form B. In an effort to establish construct validity, the author shows that FRI scores increase with age, that the stories become progressively more difficult throughout the test, that children with subnormal reading comprehension performance on the Comprehensive Test of Basic Skills earn low scores on the FRI, and that correlations between the FRI and a measure of intelligence are high. This latter finding is based on a very small sample (seventeen adolescent females) and on correlations with only one test (the Detroit Tests of Learning Aptitude–2). Yet the correlations with intelligence are as high as or higher than the correlations with other measures of reading.

SUMMARY

The Formal Reading Inventory (FRI) is an individually administered, norm-referenced measure that provides users with an assessment of silent reading comprehension and an analysis of the kinds of oral reading miscues students make. Forms B and D of this scale, which are used to assess oral reading, are identical to the Gray Oral Reading Test–Revised. The FRI requires students to read paragraphs orally or silently and then answer comprehension questions. The extent to which the norms for this test are based on a representative sample of students is questionable. Evidence for reliability is restricted to internal consistency, which is very good.

GRAY ORAL READING TEST–REVISED

The Gray Oral Reading Test–Revised (GORT-R) (Wiederholt & Bryant, 1986) is an individually administered, norm-referenced measure of skill development in oral reading. Students are required to read paragraphs orally and to respond to a set of comprehension questions for each paragraph. The GORT-R, a revision of the Gray Oral Reading Test most recently published by Gray and Robinson in 1967, is intended for students between the ages of 7-0 and 7-11. Specific basal and ceiling rules are used to limit testing time, which ranges from 15 to 30 minutes.

The authors of the GORT-R state four purposes for the test: "(a) to help identify those students who are significantly below their peers in oral reading proficiency and who may profit from additional help; (b) to aid in determining the particular kinds of reading strengths and weaknesses that individual students possess; (c) to document students' progress in reading as a consequence of special intervention programs; and (d) to serve as a measurement device in investigations where researchers are studying the reading abilities of school age students" (p. 7).

In the manual the authors go into elaborate detail describing the extensive care with which the oral reading passages for the GORT-R were developed. They describe how specific care was taken to ensure that the comprehension questions that followed each passage were written to assess literal, inferential, critical, and affective comprehension. In fact, the two forms of the Gray Oral Reading Test–Revised are identical in every way to Forms B and D of the Formal Reading Inventory (Wiederholt, 1986). The distinction between the two tests is simply that with the GORT-R the examiner can obtain an oral reading coefficient, separate indices of rate and comprehension, and a percentage score for each of the specific kinds of miscues, whereas with the FRI the examiner obtains only a classification of oral reading miscues.

SCORES

Scores on the GORT-R are based on measures of rate (time in seconds) and oral reading miscues (called deviations from print). The two measures are combined to generate an overall passage score. Passage scores range from 0 to 9. Passage scores are combined to form an oral reading quotient, a score with a mean of 100 and a standard deviation of 15.

On the GORT-R, any deviation from print is scored as an oral reading miscue unless the deviation is the result of normal speech variations. The examiner records both the number and kinds of miscues (the kinds are identical to those scored on the FRI). On the FRI, the examiner simply records the number of errors of a given type. For the GORT-R, that number is also converted into a percentage.

NORMS

The GORT-R was standardized on 1,401 children from fifteen states. The authors show the relationship between their sample distribution and the U.S. population distribution with respect to sex, place of residence (urban, rural), race, ethnicity, and geographic region. The proportions are reasonably comparable; however, the actual number of states participating is limited, there are no data on the socioeconomic status of the standardization sample, and we are not told how the sample was stratified.

RELIABILITY

Data are reported on internal-consistency and alternate-form reliability. To establish internal consistency, twenty-five protocols were randomly selected from each age level of the standardization sample. Reliability coefficients in all instances exceeded .83. To examine alternate-form reliability, the protocols of one hundred students were randomly selected from across the age range in the standardization sample. Alternate-form reliabilities for the comprehension score, the passage score, and the oral reading quotient were .80, .81, and .83, respectively. The GORT-R demonstrates satisfactory reliability.

VALIDITY

Early in the manual for the GORT-R the authors list several purposes of the test. They do not provide evidence of the validity of the scale for those purposes. Rather, data are provided on content, criterion-related, and construct validity. The authors argue that the test has good content validity because of the procedures followed in test construction. Specifically, they argue that the reading passages were written to control for "density of words, length of words and sentences, complexity of sentence structure, structure of sentences, logical connections between sentences and clauses, and coherence of topics" (p. 4).

Concurrent validity was examined by taking scores earned on other tests from the files of students who participated in the standardization population. Thus the other test scores are for students from a variety of school districts who took the tests at a variety of points in time. Data are reported on the correlation of the scores of 108 students in grades 9 through 12 on the GORT-R and the Iowa Tests of Educational Development. Correlations ranged from .28 to .47. The GORT-R scores of an unspecified number of students were correlated with their scores on Form C of the Formal Reading Inventory; correlations ranged from .44 to .66. The GORT-R scores of seventy-four students in grades 3 and 4 were correlated with their scores on the Comprehensive Test of

Basic Skills: Reading, Total Score. Correlations ranged from .40 to .49. Finally, three elementary teachers rated the overall reading of thirty-seven students on a 5-point scale. The correlations between their judgments and GORT-R scores ranged from .47 to .78.

The authors examined the construct validity of the GORT-R by showing that GORT-R scores increase with age and that GORT-R scores are highly correlated with measures of other language abilities and total achievement. Yet in another study the authors illustrate that scores on the GORT-R are more highly correlated with performance on measures of intelligence than with performance on other measures of reading skill development.

SUMMARY

The Gray Oral Reading Test–Revised is a 1986 revision of the 1967 Gray Oral Reading Test. The GORT-R was developed by establishing a set of norms and technical characteristics for two of the four subtests of the Formal Reading Inventory. Forms B and D of the FRI are identical in every respect to the GORT-R. The two measures have separate norms, but it is difficult to judge the representativeness of the norms for either test. There is more evidence for the technical adequacy of the GORT-R than for that of the FRI. Those who wish to use this test might simply purchase the FRI and a manual for the GORT-R.

GILMORE ORAL READING TEST

The Gilmore Oral Reading Test (Gilmore & Gilmore, 1968) is an individually administered test designed to assess skill development in oral reading from grades 1 through 8. The test consists of two forms, C and D, that assess the accuracy of oral reading, reading comprehension, and rate of reading. Each form of the test contains ten paragraphs of increasing difficulty. These ten paragraphs form a continuous story. Administration of the test generally takes 15 to 20 minutes.

The Gilmore is very much like the Gray Oral Reading Test–Revised with one major exception. A score earned on the Gray is a function of both the number of errors in oral reading and the rate of reading. The grade scores on the Gilmore are a function only of the errors made. Although the test is timed, rate is not used in arriving at the grade score.

The Gilmore provides a systematic analysis of the kinds of errors the student makes in oral reading. The kinds of errors recorded for the Gilmore include (1) substitutions, (2) mispro-

nunciations, (3) words pronounced by the examiner (aids), (4) disregard of punctuation, (5) insertions, (6) hesitations, (7) repetitions, and (8) omissions. Substitution errors, aids, insertions, repetitions, and omissions are errors we discussed earlier and are scored identically to the errors of the same name on the Gray Oral Reading Test–Revised. Errors counted as gross mispronunciations and partial mispronunciations in the Gray are grouped into the category of "mispronunciations" on the Gilmore.

Errors scored as disregard of punctuation on the Gilmore consist of failures to observe punctuation, while a hesitation error is scored each time the pupil hesitates for at least two seconds before pronouncing a word. Whereas repetitions of words or phrases to correct other kinds of errors were counted as repetition errors in the Gray Oral, they do not count as repetition errors in the Gilmore. According to the Gilmore manual, a pupil who immediately corrects an error does not erase the error. The error is still counted.

TABLE 17.2 Performance Ratings for Accuracy and Comprehension on the Gilmore Oral Reading Test

Rating	Stanine	Percentile Band	Percentage of Pupils
Superior	9	Above 95	4
Above average	7, 8	77–95	19
Average	4, 5, 6	23–76	54
Below average	2, 3	4–22	19
Poor	1	Below 4	4

There are quite obvious differences in the kinds of errors scored on the Gray and the Gilmore. It is imperative, therefore, that in using and interpreting the two tests the teacher look beyond the grade scores earned to note the kinds of errors the pupil has made.

SCORES

Two kinds of scores, grade scores and performance ratings, are provided by the Gilmore. The student earns both grade scores and performance ratings (poor, below average, average, above average, and superior) for accuracy and comprehension. Performance ratings for accuracy and comprehension are based on stanines as shown in Table 17.2. Rate of reading is scored as slow, average, or fast. Within each grade, those whose rate of reading is within the top quartile are designated as fast readers, those in the bottom quartile as slow readers, and those in the two middle quartiles as average.

As in the Gray Oral Reading Test–Revised, grade scores—and in this case performance ratings, too—are global scores. The information of most use in designing programs of instruction is provided by the systematic analysis of errors in oral reading.

NORMS

Standardization of the Gilmore was completed in 1967 in eighteen schools in six school systems selected to include students from a variety of socioeconomic backgrounds. The total normative sample included 4,455 pupils in grades 1 through 8. Form C was administered to 2,246 students, while form D was given to 2,209 students. There are no data in the test manual on the sex, ethnic background, or reading curriculum of the students in the normative sample.

RELIABILITY

The only reliability data reported in the test manual are alternate-form reliabilities for fifty-one students in grade 3 and fifty-five students in grade 6. Reliabilities are reported in Table 17.3. There are no data on test-retest reliability for the Gilmore Oral Reading Test.

TABLE 17.3 Alternate-Form Reliability Data for the Gilmore Oral Reading Test

Grade	N	Accuracy	Comprehension	Rate
3	51	.94	.60	.70
6	55	.84	.53	.54

VALIDITY

No validity was established for the current Gilmore. There are validity data in the manual, but these data are for an earlier edition (Form A) of the test.

SUMMARY

The Gilmore Oral Reading Test is an individually administered test designed to assess oral reading skills, reading comprehension, and rate of reading. The student earns grade scores for accuracy and comprehension as well as performance ratings on all three scales.

The test was standardized on 4,455 children, who are inadequately described in the manual. Reliability data consist of alternate-form coefficients, all but one of which are considerably lower than the .90 standard. There are no data reported in the manual regarding the validity of forms C and D. The Gilmore Oral Reading Test may provide the experienced examiner with diagnostic information with which to construct instructional hypotheses. Its technical characteristics are such that one must use the test with caution.

DIAGNOSTIC READING TESTS

GATES-MCKILLOP-HOROWITZ READING DIAGNOSTIC TESTS

The Gates-McKillop-Horowitz Reading Diagnostic Tests (Gates, McKillop, & Horowitz, 1981) are a revision of the Gates-McKillop Reading Diagnostic Tests (Gates & McKillop, 1962). The tests consist of a battery of fourteen individually administered subtests and parts of subtests designed to assess skill development in reading. The tests are used with students in grades 1 through 6. No set battery of subtests must be given to each child; rather, the examiner is to select those measures thought necessary.

The manual for the Gates-McKillop-Horowitz states no specific qualifications as necessary for administering the tests. Most subtests are easy enough for a classroom teacher with little testing experience to administer. Scoring and interpretation, are, however, complex and difficult for even the most experienced examiner.

Behaviors sampled by the tests follow.

Oral Reading The Oral Reading subtest of the Gates-McKillop-Horowitz is like the Gray and Gilmore oral reading tests. The errors recorded for this subtest include hesitations, omissions, additions, repetitions, and mispronunciations. Mispronunciations are scored in terms of the kind of error made, including directional errors (inversions); words with wrong beginnings, wrong middles, or wrong endings; words wrong in several parts; and accent errors.

Words: Flash This subtest purports to assess sight vocabulary. A cardboard tachistoscope is provided to the examiner to use to expose single words for one-half second. The student reads the words aloud.

Words: Untimed This subtest is said to be a measure of word-attack skills. The student is required to read words without time restriction.

Knowledge of Word Parts: Word Attack This subtest has six parts, all assessing skill development in word attack:

1. *Syllabication* The pupil is shown nonsense words divided into syllables and is asked to read the words aloud. The examiner records errors phonetically.
2. *Recognizing and Blending Common Word Parts* This part of the subtest is complex, both in administration and in scoring. The examiner asks the student to read nonsense words like *drack* and *glebe*. When the child reads a nonsense word incorrectly, the word is presented in two parts ("dr-ack") and the pupil is requested to pronounce the parts and to blend them to pronounce the nonsense word.
3. *Reading Words* The student is shown nonsense words and required to read them. The examiner records errors phonetically.
4. *Giving Letter Sounds* The pupil is shown letters and asked to give their sounds.
5. *Naming Capital Letters* The student is shown capital letters and asked to name them.
6. *Naming Lowercase Letters* The student is shown lowercase letters and asked to name them.

Recognizing the Visual Form of Sounds This subtest contains one part called Vowels. The examiner reads nonsense words and the student is asked to identify the vowel that produces the vowel sound in each word.

Auditory Blending The examiner pronounces words part by part: "z-ip." The child must blend the parts to say the word.

Auditory Discrimination This subtest assesses skill in discriminating among common English phonemes.

Written Expression Two measures compose the Written Expression subtest:

1. *Spelling* The student writes words dictated by the examiner.
2. *Informal Writing Sample* The child writes on any topic. There are no formal criteria for scoring performance; rather, the examiner evaluates the pupil's performance on the basis of two criteria: expression of ideas and handwriting.

SCORES AND NORMS

A number of normative tables appear in the Gates-McKillop-Horowitz manual, but there is no information on the nature of the group on whom the test was standardized. Pupil performance is evaluated in two ways. For four subtests, grade scores are provided. These are, in turn, assigned a rating of high, medium, low, or very low relative to the student's grade. For the rest of the tests, there are no scoring standards. The authors simply provide guidelines for interpretation. Ratings for grade scores are based on the authors' opinion.

We commented earlier on the relative educational meaninglessness of scores that compare children to one another; transformed scores earned on the Gates-McKillop-Horowitz have little meaning. Normative comparisons provide very limited help in teachers' attempts to differentiate instruction. That process is further complicated by the use of grade scores—the kinds of scores that are most frequently misinterpreted. The value of the Gates-McKillop-Horowitz is limited to its clinical use. It may provide a skilled examiner with a sample of items that can be used to identify specific skill-development strengths and weaknesses in reading; however, to accomplish this, the examiner will have to go beyond scores and look at performance on individual items.

RELIABILITY

The authors report the results of two reliability studies. The first was completed on an unspecified group of twenty-seven students who took the Oral Reading subtest twice. Scores on the first administration correlated .94 with scores on the second administration. The other study was one of interscorer reliability. In our opinion, the reliability of this measure has not been established.

VALIDITY

The authors report an investigation of the validity of the measure by correlating pupil performance on this test with performance on the Gates-MacGinitie and the Metropolitan Achievement Tests. Only a range of coefficients is given (.68-.96) and the user is not told the number of coefficients for specific levels. The sample is not satisfactorily described. There is no evidence for the validity of the scale.

SUMMARY

The Gates-McKillop-Horowitz Reading Diagnostic Tests are a widely used diagnostic instrument in spite of significant limitations. The manual provides normative tables without including a description of the population on whom the test was standardized. The many scores obtained on the tests are subject to misinterpretation. Evidence for reliability and validity is unsatisfactory.

DURRELL ANALYSIS OF READING DIFFICULTY

The Durrell Analysis of Reading Difficulty (DARD) (Durrell & Catterson, 1980) is designed to assist diagnostic personnel in estimating general level of reading achievement and identifying specific strengths and weaknesses in reading. The test covers a range of reading ability from the nonreader or prereading level to the sixth-grade level. The 1980 edition of the test is the third edition in a series originally published in 1937.

The DARD is administered individually and is designed to be used by experienced teachers. The authors state that the administration of the test is best learned under the direction of a person who has had experience in analyzing and correcting reading difficulties. Test materials include a booklet of reading paragraphs to be used in the major subtests, a manual of directions, an individual record book, and a cardboard tachistoscope with accompanying test cards and word lists. Test administration takes about 30 to 90 minutes. The DARD samples several different reading and reading-related behaviors. The subtests and behaviors they sample follow.

Oral Reading This subtest consists of eight paragraphs of increasing difficulty that the child is required to read aloud. The subtest is scored in much the same manner as the Gray, the Gilmore, and the Oral Reading subtest of the Gates-McKillop-Horowitz. The child responds to literal comprehension questions following the reading of each paragraph.

Silent Reading The Silent Reading subtest contains eight paragraphs of comparable difficulty to those in the Oral Reading subtest. The examiner tests and records voluntary memory (simple recall), prompted memory (responses to specific questions), and eye movement.

Listening Comprehension The examiner reads the six paragraphs of this subtest aloud and asks specific comprehension questions. The most difficult paragraph in which the child misses no more than one comprehension question is identified, by grade and score, as the child's listening comprehension level.

Word Recognition and Word Analysis This subtest contains several parts. The examiner uses a cardboard tachistoscope, exposing words for one-half second, to assess word-recognition skills. When the child reads a word unsuccessfully, the same word is presented in an untimed format. The student is then asked to name the letters seen and is given an opportunity to sound out the word.

Listening Vocabulary This subtest contains the same words as those listed in the Word Recognition and Word Analysis subtest. The child must point to pictures to indicate an understanding of words read by the examiner. The examiner can compare performance on this subtest (a measure of words understood in speech) with performance on the Word Recognition and Word Analysis subtest (a measure of words understood in print).

Pronunciation of Word Elements This subtest measures the child's skill in pronouncing sounds (letters, blends, digraphs, phonograms, and affixes) in isolation.

Spelling This subtest measures the pupil's skill in writing and spelling correctly words read by the examiner.

Visual Memory of Words The student is required to remember the visual pattern of words long enough to circle them (for students whose oral reading level is grade 3 or below) or to write them down.

Auditory Analysis of Words and Elements The student is required to identify sounds in words (children whose oral reading is at or below third-grade level) or to spell words phonetically.

Prereading Phonics Abilities Inventories Two new measures (syntax matching and identifying letter names in spoken words) have been added to three subtests—identifying phonemes, naming letters, and writing letters—from previous editions of the DARD. Together they form a measure of prereading abilities. These measures are designed to help evaluate prereading phonics skills necessary for success in learning to read.

SCORES

Most subtests of the DARD provide raw scores that can be converted to grade scores. However, in interpreting pupil performance, the greatest emphasis is placed on the check list of instructional needs that follows each subtest. The comprehensive check lists are completed by the examiner following administration of each subtest.

NORMS

The DARD was standardized on "carefully selected populations in six school systems in different geographic regions" (Durrell & Catterson, 1980, p. 8). The names of the school districts are listed in the test manual, but we know little more than that about the normative population. A total of 1,224 students participated in standardization of the test. Students were selected because they were enrolled in districts chosen by university personnel in graduate reading programs. The authors state that "factors such as language backgrounds, socioeconomic status, ethnic characteristics, and curriculum emphasis were taken into consideration in choosing the particular schools and classrooms from which the children were selected for testing" (p. 56).

Students in the six school districts were given the Metropolitan Achievement Tests. Forty children in each grade who earned average scores (4th, 5th, or 6th stanine) on the MAT were given the Durrell. The authors do not provide data on the sex, ages, socioeconomic status, or nature of reading curriculum for the standardization group.

RELIABILITY

Reliability was assessed in several ways. For the Oral Reading and Silent Reading subtests, the authors correlated reading time for adjacent paragraphs. Correlations were .85 for oral reading and .80 for silent reading. These are not reliability data. What is needed is information on consistency over time on the same, similar, or parallel levels of passages. For each of the additional subtests, the authors computed internal consistency using the Kuder-Richardson 21 formula. Reliabilities ranged from .63 to .97. Reliabilities exceeded .80 for eight of the thirteen subtests. No data are reported on test-retest reliability.

VALIDITY

The section on validity in the DARD manual consists primarily of a discussion of the concept of validity, with little actual validity data presented. Initially, the authors make the case for expert opinion, stating that the device has been used and modified since 1937 and that the "stability of the content of the test from revision to revision attests to current professional confidence in its general validity." Stability of test content, of course, reflects only the fact that the authors have not made major changes in the test.

The authors do report one validity study. They correlated September measures of first-grade pupils' scores on the prereading inventory with their reading achievement at the end of first grade. Correlations ranged from "about .55" to "about .65." The authors do not say how many students participated in the study, they do not describe those who participated, and they do not say what test was used to measure reading achievement.

SUMMARY

The DARD is designed to assist classroom teachers to delineate specific skill-development strengths and weaknesses in reading. As long as the examiner and user of the test data place little emphasis on scores obtained and look instead at the qualitative information afforded by the test, the results may be useful in making tentative hypotheses about the nature of a child's reading difficulties. The norm-referenced use of the test is hindered by inadequate standardization, absence of a description of the norm group, limited data on reliability, and limited validity.

STANFORD DIAGNOSTIC READING TEST

The 1984 Stanford Diagnostic Reading Test (SDRT) (Karlsen & Gardner, 1985) is the third edition of a test originally published in 1966. The SDRT is a group-administered diagnostic test designed to identify specific strengths and weaknesses in reading. It provides detailed coverage of skills in decoding, vocabulary, comprehension, and reading rate. Because the test is intended for use with low achievers, it contains more easy questions than do most achievement tests.

There are four overlapping levels of the SDRT, with two parallel forms (G and H) at each level. The Red Level is designed to be used at the end of grade 1, in grade 2, and with low achievers in grade 3. The Green Level is intended for use in grades 3 and 4 and with very low achievers in grade 5. The Brown Level is to be used in grades 5 through 8 and with very low achieving high school students. The Blue Level is intended for use from the end of eighth grade through the community college level.

The SDRT can be group administered by a classroom teacher. Four skill domains are sampled by the test, though not all domains are sampled at all levels. Subtests and skill domains sampled by the SDRT are reported in Figure 17.3. Behaviors sampled are as follows.

Auditory Vocabulary This subtest assesses the language competence of students without requiring them to read. Words were selected from three general content areas: reading and literature, mathematics and science, and social studies and the arts. At the Red Level, students must identify pictures of words read by the ex-

aminer. At the Green and Brown levels, pupils select the word or words that best fit the meaning of a sentence read by the examiner.

Vocabulary This subtest appears only at the Blue Level. Words included in the test were selected from lists of the words that are encountered most commonly in the high school curriculum. Students must recognize the meanings of words in the context of passages from the areas of reading and literature, mathematics and science, and social studies and the arts.

Auditory Discrimination This subtest appears at the Red and Green levels only. The subtest assesses skill in hearing similar and different sounds in words. Students are asked to determine whether two dictated words have the same beginning, middle, and ending sounds.

Phonetic Analysis This subtest appears at all levels of the SDRT. At the Red Level, students must identify letters that represent beginning and ending sounds of words. At the Green and Brown levels, the task is to identify sounds in words and match these to common or variant spellings of the sound. At the Blue Level, focus is on rather unusual letter-sound combinations.

Structural Analysis This subtest appears at all but the Red Level of the test. At the Green Level, the test includes two parts. Students must identify the first syllable of two-syllable words, and they must identify common word parts and blend them into words. At the Brown and Blue levels, the subtest requires stu-

FIGURE 17.3   Subtests and Skill Domains of the Stanford Diagnostic Reading Test

Decoding			
RED LEVEL	**GREEN LEVEL**	**BROWN LEVEL**	**BLUE LEVEL**
TEST 2: Auditory Discrimination Consonants (15 Items) Vowels (15 Items)	TEST 2: Auditory Discrimination Consonants (15 Items) Vowels (15 Items)		
TEST 3: Phonetic Analysis Consonants (24 Items) Vowels (16 Items)	TEST 3: Phonetic Analysis Consonants (15 Items) Vowels (15 Items)	TEST 3: Phonetic Analysis Consonants (15 Items) Vowels (15 Items)	TEST 4: Phonetic Analysis Consonants (15 Items) Vowels (15 Items)
	TEST 4: Structural Analysis Word Division (24 Items) Blending (24 Items)	TEST 4: Structural Analysis Word Division (48 Items) Blending (30 Items)	TEST 5: Structural Analysis Affixes (15 Items) Syllables (15 Items)

Vocabulary			
RED LEVEL	**GREEN LEVEL**	**BROWN LEVEL**	**BLUE LEVEL**
TEST 1: Auditory Vocabulary (36 Items)	TEST 1: Auditory Vocabulary (40 Items)	TEST 1: Auditory Vocabulary (40 Items)	TEST 2: Vocabulary (30 Items) TEST 3: Word Parts (30 Items)

Comprehension			
RED LEVEL	**GREEN LEVEL**	**BROWN LEVEL**	**BLUE LEVEL**
TEST 4: Word Reading (30 Items) TEST 5: Reading Comprehension Sentence Reading (28 Items) Paragraph Comprehension (20 Items)	TEST 5: Reading Comprehension Literal Comprehension (24 Items) Inferential Comprehension (24 Items)	TEST 2: Reading Comprehension (Items measure two skills) Literal Comprehension (30 Items) Inferential Comprehension (30 Items) and Textual Reading (20 Items) Functional Reading (20 Items) Recreational Reading (20 Items)	TEST 1: Reading Comprehension (Items measure two skills) Literal Comprehension (30 Items) Inferential Comprehension (30 Items) and Textual Reading (20 Items) Functional Reading (20 Items) Recreational Reading (20 Items)

Rate			
RED LEVEL	**GREEN LEVEL**	**BROWN LEVEL**	**BLUE LEVEL**
		TEST 5: Reading Rate (33 Items)	TEST 6: Scanning and Skimming (32 Items) TEST 7: Fast Reading (30 Items)

dents to divide three-syllable words into syllables.

Word Parts   This vocabulary subtest is at the Blue Level only. It assesses students' knowledge of word parts such as prefixes, suffixes, root words, and word roots.

Word Reading   This subtest, which is at the Red Level only, measures skill in recognizing and attaching meaning to words.

Reading Comprehension   There is a reading comprehension subtest at each level of the SDRT, but the methods of sampling the behaviors differ at the various levels. At the Red Level, students must identify the pictures that best represent sentences they read, and they must read and understand sentences and paragraphs presented in a multiple-choice cloze[1] format. At the Green Level, literal and inferential comprehension are assessed by requiring students to respond to multiple-choice questions in cloze format. At the Brown and Blue levels, literal and inferential comprehension are assessed by means of textual, functional, and recreational reading passages followed by questions.

---

1.   The "cloze" procedure is a technique in which words are omitted from a sentence. To close the sentence correctly, the student must comprehend the story. Many programmed texts use a cloze format. The modified cloze format used in the SDRT gives the student a choice of several words. The following is an illustration:

Elephants are well known as animals that never forget. But Henry was a strange elephant who, unlike other elephants, always ___ things.

(a) wanted (b) forgot (c) remembered (d) liked

Reading Rate   This subtest, which is at the Brown Level only, assesses skill in reading easy material quickly.

Scanning and Skimming   This subtest is at the Blue Level only. There are two parts to the subtest. The first measures skill in scanning an article or chapter for specific information. In the second, students must extract both general and specific information from an article in a short period of time.

Fast Reading   At the Blue Level only, this subtest measures skill in reading easy material quickly with comprehension.

SCORES

The SDRT is both norm-referenced and criterion-referenced. It can be used to assess a pupil's performance relative to the performance of others, and it can be used to pinpoint individual pupils' strengths and weaknesses in specific reading skills.

Students respond either in the test booklets or on machine-readable answer sheets. The test can, therefore, be either hand scored or machine scored. Six kinds of scores can be obtained; which scores are useful depends on the purpose for which the test has been administered.

Raw scores are obtained for each subtest and can be transformed to "Progress Indicators," percentile ranks, stanines, grade equivalents, and scaled scores. Progress Indicators are criterion-referenced scores, whereas the other four scores are norm-referenced. Progress Indicators are "+" or "−" indications as to whether a pupil achieved a predetermined cutoff score in a specific skill domain; they show whether a pupil demonstrates mastery of specific skills important to the various stages in the process of learning to read effectively. It is reported that

> *in setting the Progress Indicator cutoff scores, the SDRT authors were guided by the relative importance of each skill to the reading process, by the location of these skills in the developmental sequence, and by the performance of students at different achievement levels on the items measuring these skills. (Karlsen & Gardner, 1985, p. 13)*

The manual for each level of the SDRT includes an appendix that lists specific instructional objectives assessed by each level of the test.

The norm-referenced scores obtained by administering the SDRT can be used for a variety of purposes. The authors suggest that comparisons to national norms be made using percentile ranks, stanines, or normal curve equivalents. Detailed procedures for the use of stanines to group students for instructional purposes are included in the manuals. Scaled scores, because they are comparable across both grades and levels, are most useful in evaluating pupil growth and in interpreting the performance of pupils who are tested out of level (for example, the scores of a fifth grader who has taken the Red Level).

A number of reports can be generated from the SDRT by making use of the publisher's computer scoring service. Examiners can obtain an Individual Diagnostic Report, which contains a detailed analysis of the performance of a single pupil. They can also obtain a Class Summary Report. This report shows the average scores earned by the pupils on each of the subtests. It also provides an analysis of skill development for the class by indicating the number of students in the class who obtained a Progress Indicator of "+" and the number who obtained a Progress Indicator of "−." Examiners can obtain a Master List Report, consisting of a listing of scores for all students in a class. They can obtain a Parent Report designed specifically for sending test results home to parents. Or they can obtain a Pupil Item Analysis showing the raw scores earned by a particular student on each subtest and cluster, as well as the student's response to each item.

NORMS

In selecting the standardization sample for the SDRT, the authors used a stratified random-sampling technique. Socioeconomic status, school-system enrollment, and geographic region were the stratification variables. School-system data were obtained from the United States Office of Education's 1970 census tapes. The tapes were used to generate a random sample of 3,000 school districts. A composite socioeconomic-status index for each system was determined by weighting family income twice and averaging it with the median years of parental schooling. Age and sex were not controlled in standardizing the SDRT.

School districts within each of the stratified cells were invited to participate in standardization of the test. A random sample of consenting districts within each cell was selected. The SDRT was standardized during the fall of 1983 and spring of 1984. Thirty-three school systems participated in the fall standardization, forty-eight in the spring standardization. The test was standardized on about 30,000 students in grades 2 through 12 in the fall; it was standardized on about 34,000 students in grades 1 through 12 in the spring.

RELIABILITY

Two kinds of reliability data are provided for the SDRT. Data on internal consistency are provided for all but the speeded subtests. Data on alternate-form reliability are reported for the speeded subtests. All but two of the internal-consistency coefficients exceed .80. The reliability of the Auditory Vocabulary subtest is .79 at grade 2 and .76 at grade 3. Alternate-form reliabilities for the rate measures are generally lower. These range from .66 to .78.

VALIDITY

Data are provided on content validity and criterion-related validity. The authors state that the test's content validity, like the content validity of any other measure of academic achievement, must be based on an evaluation of the extent to which the test content reflects local curricular content. Criterion-related validity was established by correlating performance on the SDRT subtests with performance on their counterparts on the Stanford Achievement Test. The correlations range from .67 to .88 at the Red Level, .68 to .87 at the Green Level, .69 to .87 at the Brown Level, and .64 to .74 at the Blue Level.

SUMMARY

The Stanford Diagnostic Reading Test is a group-administered device that is both norm and criterion referenced. The device was exceptionally well standardized and is reliable enough to be used in pinpointing specific domains of reading in which pupils demonstrate skill-development strengths and weaknesses. Validity for the SDRT, as for any achievement measure, must be judged relative to the content of local curricula.

DIAGNOSTIC READING SCALES

The Diagnostic Reading Scales (Spache, 1981) are a series of individually administered tests designed to provide standardized evaluations of oral and silent reading skills and of auditory comprehension. The tests consist of three lists of words to be recognized, twenty-two reading passages of graduated difficulty, and twelve supplementary word analysis and phonics tests. The scales can be used with students in grades 1 through 7 and, according to the author, with junior and senior high school students who are functioning below normal in reading.

The word lists are administered as an assessment of a child's skill in pronouncing words in isolation. According to the author, the word lists serve three purposes: to estimate the instructional level of reading, to reveal the child's methods of word attack and word analysis, and to evaluate sight vocabulary. The reading passages are used to assess literal and inferential comprehension of material read orally or silently by the child and of material read to the child. The author states that the passages are useful in identifying suitable reading material for the student and in determining the nature and extent of a student's reading errors and the student's reading speed and reading potential.

The twelve word analysis and phonics tests are initial consonants, final consonants, consonant digraphs, consonant blends, initial-consonant substitution, initial-consonant sounds recognized auditorily, auditory discrimination, short and long vowel sounds, vowels with *r*, vowel diphthongs and digraphs, common syllables, and blending. The subtests are designed to give the examiner a detailed analysis of phonic knowledge and word-analysis skills. Total administration time for the Diagnostic Reading Scales is about 60 minutes, and all student responses are oral.

SCORES

The word lists are administered to determine which of the several reading passages should be used as a starting point for the assessment of oral, silent, and auditory comprehension skills. The author states that on the basis of a child's score in oral reading the teacher can ascertain the child's instructional level, that is, the level at which instruction in reading should be given. Performance in comprehension of passages read silently is used to ascertain the child's independent level, the grade level at which the child can read recreational and supplementary reading materials. Performance in auditory comprehension is used as an assessment of the child's "potential reading level."

As in the case with most diagnostic reading tests, the most valuable information is obtained by careful analysis of the kinds of errors the child makes in oral reading and on the six supplementary subtests.

NORMS

The Diagnostic Reading Scales were originally standardized in 1963 on an unspecified population of students. The test was revised in 1972 and again in 1981. As part of each revision, the author conducted a study and used results of pupil performance to rearrange the items on the test. The 1981 version of the Diagnostic Reading Scales is not identical to the 1963 edition. As part of revising the scale, in 1981 the test was given to a sample of 534 students. The norm group is not described sufficiently in the manual.

In a section of the manual entitled "Validity," the author describes 534 students. He says that the students attended grades 1 through 8 in sixty-six school districts in thirty-two states, and that there were approximately equal numbers of males and females and a rep-

resentative number of black and Hispanic students. The norms are not described in such a way as to enable a user to know the nature of those to whom an examinee is being compared.

RELIABILITY

Data on reliability of the Diagnostic Reading Scales are reported in a separate technical manual. With minor exceptions, reliability data are on earlier versions of the test. The author does say that alternate-form reliabilities were computed on an unspecified number of students in grades 1 through 8. He does not report correlation coefficients by grade level, but says they averaged .89.

Data on test-retest reliability are reported only for grades 1 and 2, and only for the word-analysis and phonics subtests. Data are on an unspecified number of students. Correlation coefficients ranged from .09 (initial consonant sounds recognized auditorily) to .93. Only half of the twenty-four coefficients exceed .80.

Data on internal consistency are reported only for an unspecified number of students in grades 1 and 2. All but three of the twenty-four coefficients reported exceed .80. No data on reliability are reported for students in upper grades. The author argues that these students earn a ceiling too easily.

VALIDITY

Much space in the technical manual is devoted to a discussion of validity. Again, though, nearly all data reported are on the 1963 and 1972 editions of the test. One validity study is reported on the 1981 scale. The author reports that test scores are higher with increases in grade level, teacher estimates of reading level, level of classroom reader, and scores on reading tests. The latter information is derived from a number of different reading tests. Data on validity are not convincing. The author reports that the sample on whom validity and reliability data were based included far more older than younger students and an excessive number of cases scoring at the high end of the scale.

SUMMARY

The Diagnostic Reading Scales are an individually administered series of scales designed to as-

sess oral and silent reading skills and auditory comprehension. The manual includes normative tables, but it does not provide an adequate description of the nature of the group on whom the test was standardized. A separate technical manual includes data on reliability and validity, though most of this information is on earlier versions of the test. Evidence for the technical adequacy of the 1981 scales is very limited. At best, the scales are useful for screening purposes.

WOODCOCK READING MASTERY TESTS–REVISED

The Woodcock Reading Mastery Tests–Revised (Woodcock, 1987) is a battery of six individually administered tests used to assess development of readiness skills, basic reading skills, and reading comprehension skills in students from kindergartners to college seniors and in adults up to 75 years of age. The complete materials for the test are contained in an easel kit similar to the easel kit illustrated earlier for the Peabody Individual Achievement Test (Figure 16.2). There are two alternative forms of the test, G and H. Form G includes all six tests; Form H includes only the four reading-achievement tests (it does not include the readiness measures). The six tests that make up the WRMT-R battery are as follows.

Visual-Auditory Learning In a miniature learning-to-read task, the student is required to associate unfamiliar visual stimuli (rebuses) with familiar oral words and to translate sequences of rebuses into sentences. The test is the same as the Visual-Auditory Learning subtest of the Woodcock-Johnson Psychoeducational Battery.

Letter Identification This test assesses skill in naming or pronouncing (the student is permitted to do either) letters of the alphabet. Both upper- and lowercase letters are used, and the letters are presented in a variety of type styles.

Word Identification This test measures skill in pronouncing words in isolation.

Word Attack This test assesses skill in using phonic and structural analysis to read nonsense words.

Word Comprehension Three subtests make up this test: Antonyms, Synonyms, and Analogies. In the Antonyms subtest, the student must read a word and then provide a word that means the opposite; in the Synonyms subtest, words with similar meanings must be provided. In the Analogies subtest, the student must read a pair of words, ascertain the relationship between the two words, read a third word, and then supply a word that has the same relationship to the third word as exists between the initial pair of words read. Separate scores can be obtained for comprehension of words in different content areas: General Reading Vocabulary, Science-Mathematics Vocabulary, Social Studies Vocabulary, and Humanities Vocabulary.

Passage Comprehension This test uses a modified cloze procedure. The student's task is to read silently a passage that has a word missing and then tell the examiner a word that could appropriately fill the blank space. The passages are actual passages drawn from newspaper articles and textbooks.

The six tests of the WRMT-R are organized into three clusters. The Readiness Cluster is composed of the Visual-Auditory Learning and Letter Identification tests. The Word Identification and Word Attack tests make up the Basic Skills Cluster. The Word Comprehension and Passage Comprehension tests make up the Reading Comprehension Cluster.

There are several differences between the WRMT-R and the 1973 edition of the tests. A readiness section has been added to the battery, and the Word Comprehension test has been expanded to include three different samples of behavior—finding analogies, antonyms, and synonyms. Reading vocabulary is assessed in four content areas, listed above. More sample items have been incorporated into the WRMT-R. A Short Scale has been developed that involves only the administration and scoring of the Word Identification and Passage Comprehension tests. Several diagnostic aids have been added that, in addition to facilitating error analysis, enable the examiner to compare performance on the WRMT-R with performance on either the Goldman-Fristoe-Woodcock or the Woodcock-Johnson. Scoring, procedures for recording scores, and procedures for creating visual displays of scores have been simplified.

A special microcomputer scoring program, ASSIST, can be used to compute and report all derived scores for the WRMT-R. Also available is a report to parents, which conveys test results, explains student performance, and describes each of the WRMT-R tests.

SCORES

Woodcock (1987) describes three options for interpreting the WRMT-R, four levels of interpretive information for the WRMT-R (or any other test), and nine kinds of derived scores.

The three options for interpreting the WRMT-R are designed to provide differing degrees of precision. At the lowest level, examiners can simply plot raw scores from the WRMT-R, the Goldman-Fristoe-Woodcock Auditory Skills Test Battery, and the Woodcock-Johnson Psychoeducational Battery on an Instructional Level Profile and/or on three diagnostic profiles. When the Instructional Level Profile has been completed, approximate grade equivalents and instructional ranges can be observed, and strengths and weaknesses across WRMT-R tests and subtests of the other two tests can be seen. An Instructional Level Profile from the WRMT-R Test Record is shown in Figure 17.4. At a middle level of interpretation, the examiner goes to the norm tables and gets the total reading score as well as percentile ranks and relative performance indices (RPIs) for each of the subtests. At the highest level, the examiner uses the norm tables to get exact grade equivalents, age equivalents, a variety of standard scores, confidence bands for RPIs, and percentile ranks.

Woodcock describes four levels of interpretive information for the WRMT-R. The examiner can engage in analysis of errors in the responses that students make to individual items; the examiner can describe the student's level of development by reporting such derived scores as grade equivalents and age equivalents; the examiner can describe the quality of the student's performance by reporting Relative Performance Indicators, difference scores, or instructional ranges; or the examiner can report the student's standing in a group by reporting percentile rank or standard scores.

Many derived scores can be obtained for the WRMT-R. Some (for example, *W*-scores) are complex, and a reasonably sophisticated knowledge of measurement is required to understand them. We have chosen not to describe those scores here. The kinds of scores obtained from the WRMT-R include grade equivalents, age equivalents, relative performance indices, in-

FIGURE 17.4   Instructional-Level Profile from the WRMT-R Test Record

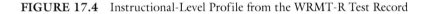

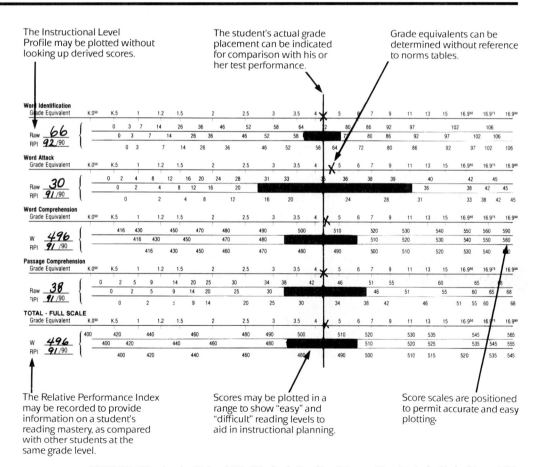

SOURCE: Woodcock, Richard W. *Woodcock Reading Mastery Test–Revised.* Circle Pines, MN: American Guidance Service, copyright 1987. Reprinted by permission of American Guidance Service, Inc.

structional ranges, percentile ranks, and standard scores. The RPI provides an index of a student's expected quality of performance on tasks of a given level of difficulty. Woodcock (1987) states,

> *An RPI is like the index used with the Snellen Chart to describe visual acuity. On the Snellen Index, 20/20 vision indicates a person can distinguish at a distance of 20 feet what people with normal vision can see at 20 feet. A person with 20/100 vision has to be at 20 feet to see what people with normal vision can see at 100 feet. (p. 40).*

RPIs are used to indicate percentage mastery and therefore are indicative of quality of performance rather than standing within a group.

Instructional range is designed to provide a guide to the level of instruction that would be appropriate for a student. The range includes that interval between instructional activities or materials that are too easy and those that are too difficult and therefore frustrating. Instructional levels are indicated by the shaded areas in Figure 17.4

In addition to obtaining scores, examiners can complete a number of visual profiles of scores: the Instructional Level Profile noted above, a Percentile Rank Profile, and three diagnostic profiles (a Diagnostic Readiness Profile, a Diagnostic Basic Skills Profile, and a Diagnostic Comprehension Profile). Completion of these profiles enables examiners, teachers, and parents to visualize the strengths and weaknesses of the student's performance on the six tests and to compare the student's performance on the WRMT-R with that on the Goldman-Fristoe-Woodcock and the Woodcock-Johnson Psychoeducational Battery.

NORMS

The WRMT-T was standardized on 6,089 students in sixty geographically diverse communities. Subjects were randomly selected using a sampling design stratified on the basis of geographic region, community size, sex, race, and ethnic origin. The college sample was stratified on the basis of type of college (public, private, university, two-year college, four-year college), in addition to the above factors. The adult sample was stratified on the basis of number of years of education, occupational status, and occupational type, in addition to the "core factors" noted above. A table in the manual compares the proportion of the sample in each of the stratification categories with the proportion of the U.S. population in that category. Standardization data were gathered throughout the school year, and continuous-year norms are provided.

RELIABILITY

Data are provided on the internal-consistency reliability of the WRMT-R. These data are for all tests and clusters and are provided separately for grades 1, 3, 5, 8, and 11 and for college and adult groups. Reliabilities for clusters exceed .80; in all but three cases they exceed .90. With one exception, reliabilities for the six tests exceed .80; most exceed .90. There are no data on the test-retest reliability of the WRMT-R.

VALIDITY

Several kinds of validity are discussed in the manual for the WRMT-R. The case for content validity is made on the basis of expert judgment and the Rasch scaling procedures used in constructing the test. Users of the test will have to make judgements about the extent to which the test measures mastery of the content of their curriculum.

Evidence for concurrent validity is good. Data are presented showing correlations of the WRMT-R with the reading subtests of the Woodcock-Johnson Psychoeducational Battery. Correlations among subtests measuring similar behaviors are high. There is good evidence for the convergent validity of the scale. That is, performance on specific tests correlates more highly with performance on other measures of similar reading behaviors than with performance on measures of different reading behaviors.

SUMMARY

The Woodcock Reading Mastery Tests–Revised, a revision of a scale that was originally published in 1973, includes six separate measures of pupil skill development in reading and reading comprehension. The WRMT-R has expanded and updated norms and now includes a readiness component. The test is also normed on college students and adults. The several new diagnostic aids that have been developed look as if they will be useful. The test is appropriately and adequately normed, and evidence for internal-consistency reliability is good. There are no data on test-retest reliability. Evidence for validity of the tests is good.

MEASURES OF
READING COMPREHENSION

TEST OF READING COMPREHENSION

The Test of Reading Comprehension: Revised Edition (TORC) (Brown, Hammill & Wiederholt, 1986) is an individually administered, norm-referenced measure of students' understanding of written language. The test may, on occasion, be given to groups of three to five students; it is appropriate for use with students ages 7-0 to 17-11. In developing the TORC, the authors set out to construct a measure of comprehension of written language that was independent of any instructional program; used multiple formats or styles to assess reading comprehension; minimized the likelihood of obtaining correct responses solely as a result of general information, memorization, or guessing; used a silent rather than an oral reading format; and was not loaded with vocabulary from any specific content area. For the most part, they were successful. The authors clearly

state that any results obtained from this measure are to be treated as instructional hypotheses to be confirmed through more individualized, direct behaviorally focused strategies.

The TORC is made up of eight subtests. Four of the subtests are combined to form a "General Reading Comprehension Core," three subtests are measures of content-specific vocabularies, and one subtest is a measure of the student's skill in reading the directions of schoolwork. The names of the subtests and a brief description of each follow.

General Vocabulary The student is required to read three stimulus words that are related in some way and then select from four response words the two that are related to the three stimulus words.

Syntactic Similarities The student is given five sentences and must select the two that are most nearly the same in meaning.

Paragraph Reading The student is required to read paragraphs and then answer five multiple-choice questions for each paragraph. The questions differ in their demands. One question requires the selection of a "best title" for the paragraph, two questions require the literal recall of story details, one question requires the inference of meaning, and one question requires the making of a negative inference.

Sentence Sequencing Each item consists of five randomly ordered sentences, which the student must order in such a way that they make a meaningful story.

Mathematics Vocabulary The format of this subtest is identical to that of the General Vocabulary subtest. The words are taken from recent mathematics textbooks.

Social-Studies Vocabulary The format of this subtest is identical to that of the General Vocabulary subtest. The words are taken from recent social-studies textbooks.

Science Vocabulary The format of this subtest is identical to that of the General Vocabulary subtest. The words are taken from recent science textbooks.

Reading the Directions of Schoolwork This subtest is designed for younger and remedial readers. The student must read a set of directions and then carry them out on an answer sheet.

The TORC contains a relatively limited number of items for a measure spanning a 10-year age range. Six of the subtests contain

twenty-five items; Sentence Sequencing contains ten items; and the Paragraph Reading subtest contains six reading passages, each of which is followed by five questions. Item selection was based on the performance of 120 elementary school students in grades 2 through 6 in one school district in Austin, Texas. The authors used the performance of these students to reduce the test from an initial 358 items to the 185 items that make up the test.

The authors of the TORC identify five purposes for using the test:

(1) to determine a student's relative reading comprehension status in relation to a normative group; (2) to determine how well a student or group of students can comprehend written language when a program-independent measure is needed; (3) to examine strengths and weaknesses from one subtest to another for diagnostic purposes; (4) to compare relative performance in reading comprehension tasks with other conceptual abilities when appropriate measures are available; (5) to compare TORC performances with other language behaviors to determine relative strengths and weaknesses; and (6) to investigate behaviors related to reading comprehension and to study the construct itself. (p. 15)

SCORES

Raw scores, percentiles, and standard scores may be obtained for each subtest. In addition, an overall Reading Comprehension Quotient may be calculated. Standard scores have a mean of 10 and a standard deviation of 3. The Reading Comprehension Quotient is obtained by adding the standard scores for the General Vocabulary, Syntactic Similarities, Paragraph Reading, and Sentence Sequencing subtests. These four subtests comprise the General Reading Comprehension Core. The Reading

Comprehension Quotient has a mean of 100 and a standard deviation of 15.

NORMS

The TORC was standardized on a sample of 2,492 children from thirteen states. The Revised Edition of this test is basically an expanded-norm edition. That is, the authors added to the original 1978 normative sample by obtaining data on an unspecified number of additional students. These data were obtained by getting users of the scale to submit twenty protocols each and by sending a team of personnel into selected areas to administer the TORC. The authors do not indicate the extent to which this approach resulted in a representative sample. They do provide data on sex, residence (urban, rural), and geographic area for students in the normative sample, and they demonstrate that on two of these three factors (sex and residence) the sample distribution closely matches the population as characterized by census data. No data are provided on the race or socioeconomic status of those who participated in the standardization of this test. Also, no data are provided on the crosstabs of sample characteristics. For example, data are not provided on the number of females who were from urban environments in the West. These data are necessary to make judgments about the representativeness of the norm group.

RELIABILITY

The authors of the TORC provide data on two kinds of reliability: internal consistency and test-retest. Internal-consistency coefficients were computed for each of the individual subtests at each age. Eighty percent of those coefficients exceed .90, and all but one of the ninety-six coefficients exceed the desirable standard .80.

VALIDITY

The authors have not done a convincing job of illustrating that the TORC is, indeed, a measure of reading comprehension. First, the rationale for inclusion of the eight subtests as measures of reading comprehension is not convincing. This is especially true for the subtests that measure content-specific vocabulary in mathematics, social studies, and science. Also, criterion-related validity studies raise some major questions. The authors report the results of five such studies. The investigations were conducted with very specific samples (for example, fifty-four boys and girls attending second and third grade in Norman, Oklahoma; twenty-eight adolescent girls attending a residential treatment center in Austin, Texas). Sample size ranged from twenty-eight to ninety-four, and performance on the TORC was correlated with performance on other measures of reading, intelligence, mathematics, and language arts. Correlations of TORC subtests with measures of intelligence and measures of mathematics achievement are as high as correlations with other measures of reading, language arts, and reading comprehension.

SUMMARY

The Test of Reading Comprehension is a norm-referenced measure designed to provide an evaluation of students' comprehension of written language. In addition to a Reading Comprehension Quotient, based on pupil performance on four subtests, the test provides users with an assessment of pupil performance in content-specific vocabulary and in following the directions of schoolwork. There is some question about the adequacy of the norms. In general, TORC appears sufficiently reliable for making important individual decisions about students, but the extent to which the test measures reading comprehension is uncertain.

CRITERION-REFERENCED TESTING IN READING

The tests we have discussed to this point are norm-referenced tests, which are designed to compare individuals to their peers. Criterion-referenced diagnostic testing in reading is a practice that dates from the late 1960s. Criterion-referenced diagnostic reading tests are designed to analyze systematically an individual's strengths and weaknesses without comparing that individual to others. The principle objective of criterion-referenced tests is to assess the specific skills a pupil does and does not have and to relate the assessment to curricular content. Criterion-referenced assessment is tied to instructional objectives, and individual items are designed to assess mastery of specific objectives.

While all criterion-referenced reading tests are based on task analyses of reading, the particular skills assessed and their sequences differ from test to test. This is because different authors view reading in different ways and see the sequence of development of reading skills differently. For this reason, it is especially important with criterion-referenced tests, as with norm-referenced tests, that teachers pay special attention to the behaviors and sequences of behaviors sampled by the tests.

Because normative comparisons are not made in criterion-referenced assessment, no derived scores are calculated. For that reason, many authors of criterion-referenced tests downplay the importance of reliability for their scales. But reliable assessment *is* important in criterion-referenced assessment. For criterion-referenced tests we are not concerned with the consistency of derived scores. We are concerned with the consistency of responses to items when all items in the domain are assessed. If a different pattern of item scores is obtained each time an individual takes the test, we begin to question the reliability of the device. Because criterion-referenced devices generally contain relatively limited samples of behavior, it is important that test authors report the consistency with which their tests assess each specific behavior. Test authors *can* and should report test-retest reliabilities for each item. We are concerned with the consistency with which the test samples the domain of possible test items when the domain is not exhausted. When alternate forms of a criterion-referenced test are available, the authors should report correlations between performances on the two forms.

STANDARDIZED READING INVENTORY

The Standardized Reading Inventory (SRI) (Newcomer, 1986) is an individually administered measure of skill development in oral and silent reading, appropriate for use with students whose reading competence does not exceed the eighth-grade level. The test provides information on both word recognition and reading comprehension and is designed to be used to diagnose the nature of reading difficulties of students who are experiencing reading problems. The author indicates that the test can be administered in 15 to 45 minutes but recommends that users allot 1 hour for testing. Materials for this scale consist of a test manual; a student booklet containing word lists, reading passages, and comprehension questions; and summary/record sheets. After reading the word lists, the student reads passages first orally and then silently. There are two forms of the test: Form A and Form B.

In administering the SRI, the examiner first asks the student to read the words from the graded word list that is two grades below the student's estimated reading level. If the student misreads three or more words, the examiner drops down to an easier list. The student continues reading words in isolation until three or more words on a list are misread. The student then is required to read passages, beginning with the passage that corresponds to the highest grade level at which the student attained an independent level in reading the word lists. The student reads each passage aloud, while the examiner records errors in oral reading. The student then reads the same passages silently and responds to a set of comprehension questions for each passage.

SCORES

The SRI is scored in such a way that examiners obtain an indication of whether word recogni-

tion skills and reading comprehension are at an independent, instructional, or frustration level. An instructional level is defined as a score that is plus or minus one standard deviation from the mean; an independent level, a score that is more than one standard deviation above the mean; and a frustration level, a score that is more than one standard deviation below the mean. In practice, for Word Recognition, an independent level is that level at which the student misreads fewer than two words; the instructional level is that level at which two words are misread; the frustration level is that level at which the student misreads three or more words. For the oral reading passages, there are specified criteria for independent, instructional, and frustration levels for both word recognition and comprehension.

In developing the SRI, the author first compiled lists of new words that are included as typical words in five popular basal reading series: Scott Foresman Basics in Reading, Houghton Mifflin Reading Series, HBJ Bookmark Reading Program, Macmillan Reading Series, and Ginn Reading Series. Words presented at the same grade level in two or more reading series were designated as key words, and these words were then used in writing the reading passages. The author states, "In composing the passages, the total number of words, total number of sentences, and the number of words per sentence were held relatively constant for the forms of the passages at each grade level; but the number of key words and novel words varied" (p. 6).

NORMS

There are no norms for the SRI. The author argues that the SRI is a criterion-referenced test that is standardized. She uses Hammill's definition of standardized assessment instruments as instruments that possess "(a) set administration procedures, (b) objective scoring criteria, and (c) specified guidelines for interpreting results" (Newcomer, 1986 p. 1).

RELIABILITY

Three types of reliability are presented for the SRI: test-retest, alternate form, and interscorer. Test-retest reliability data are based on the performance of thirty third-grade children in a single school district on levels 2, 3 and 4 of the SRI. The test was given twice at an interval of one week. Test-retest reliabilities ranged from .83 for level 2 of form A to .92 for level 4 of Form B.

Alternate-form reliability was established by correlating performance on forms A and B for the 288 children who took the test as part of the standardization process. This sample included twenty-four students reading at the pre-primer level, twenty-four at the primer level, and thirty each at levels 1 through 8. The students took the test so that the difficulty of the passages could be calibrated. Alternate-form coefficients ranged from .70 to .97 for Word Recognition and from .71 to .96 for Reading Comprehension. For Word Recognition, acceptable levels of reliability were obtained only after the grade-one level.

To establish interscorer reliability, the author and a colleague scored thirty completed protocols. There was 97 percent agreement for both Word Recognition and Reading Comprehension. The author and a colleague also scored tape-recorded performances of twenty students. Interscorer agreement on the instructional level exceeded 90 percent.

The reliability coefficients for the SRI indicate satisfactory reliability, though coefficients are based on limited samples of students.

VALIDITY

The author goes to considerable trouble to demonstrate the content validity of the SRI. This is as it should be for criterion-referenced measures. Yet passages were selected for the test and placed at specified grade levels based on the performances of 288 children from a single school district in suburban Philadelphia. Designated reading levels were established by getting data on the performance of students on end-of-book tests at specified levels and, in some instances, performance on the Stanford Achievement Test.

Criterion-related validity was established by correlating results of performance on the SRI with the results of performance on the reading section of the Standford Achievement Test. Subjects were thirty fifth graders from a suburban Philadelphia school district. Correlation of the SAT reading score was .74 with the SRI Word Recognition score and .74 with the SRI Reading Comprehension score.

Further evidence for validity of the test is provided: scores on the SRI increase with age, performance on the test is highly correlated with intelligence, and good readers perform significantly better than poor readers.

SUMMARY

The Standardized Reading Inventory is a criterion-referenced measure of pupil skill development in both oral and silent reading. The test provides users with an assessment of the nature of oral reading errors and of comprehension of material read silently. There are no norms for this test; the author argues that the test is a standardized criterion-referenced measure. Reliability coefficients are variable so test users must consult the manual at specific ages to determine the test's suitability for various educational decisions. There is good evidence for the validity of the test.

PRESCRIPTIVE READING INVENTORY

The Prescriptive Reading Inventory Reading System (PRI/RS) (CTB/McGraw-Hill, 1980) is a criterion-referenced assessment and instruction program incorporated into a reading system for use in planning and managing instruction in reading and language arts in grades K through 9. The system is designed to be used by teachers in placing students at appropriate instructional levels, diagnosing specific instructional strengths and weaknesses, prescribing appropriate materials and activities, and monitoring pupil progress toward mastery of instructional objectives.

The PRI/RS assesses skills in four discrete skill areas of reading and language arts: Oral Language and Oral Comprehension, Word Attack and Usage (including Word Analysis, Vocabulary, and Word Usage), Comprehension (literal, interpretive, and critical), and Reading Applications (Study Skills and Content Area Reading). There are five overlapping levels of the test, intended for use at specific grade levels: Level A (grades K through 1), B (grades 1 through 2), C (grades 2 through 3), D (grades 4 through 6), and E (grades 7 through 9).

Three kinds of criterion-referenced assessment can be carried out with the PRI/RS. The examiner can conduct a skill area assessment, a category objectives assessment, or an instructional objectives assessment. Skill area assessments are broad diagnoses of skill mastery in areas such as Vocabulary or Word Analysis. Assessment of category objectives consists of assessment of terminal reading objectives such as sound and symbol correspondence. Examiners also can use the PRI/RS to assess mastery of very specific instructional objectives such as mastery of sounds of single consonants. The entire PRI Reading System assesses mastery of 171 objectives across the five levels. Objectives may be assessed at more than one level.

Examiners chose from two systems in using the PRI/RS: System 1 and System 2. Each of these systems represents a unique approach to reading instruction. "System 1, the graded approach to reading assessment, deals with students' reading abilities in *all* skill clusters at a *particular* level. System 2, the multigraded approach to reading assessment, deals with proficiency in a *particular* skill cluster across *several* levels" (CTB/McGraw-Hill, 1980, p. 3). System 1 of the PRI Reading System includes three assessment instruments ranging from very broad to very specific. The broadest measure is the Skill Areas Survey, and the most precise is the Instructional Objectives Inventory. Midway between these is the Category Objectives Test. When System 2 is used, the examiner goes through two activities in assessing the student. First a PRI Reading System Placement Test is given to identify the student's instructional level in each of the skill areas. Then a Skill Diagnostic Test is administered to ascertain whether the student has mastered specific instructional objectives within the specific skill area.

The PRI/RS is indexed to kits of instructional materials. There are five kits for System 1 and four kits for System 2. Among other things, the kits include a teacher's guide, teacher resource files, tutor activities, student worksheets, mastery tests, and continuous progress logs.

SCORES

Traditional derived scores such as grade equivalents and age scores are not provided for the PRI. Because the device is criterion-referenced, scores consist of relatively detailed analyses of objectives mastered. Five kinds of reports are used for the purpose of interpreting pupil and class performance on the PRI.

1. *Individual Diagnostic Maps* Show the extent to which a student has mastered specific reading objectives at age and grade level
2. *Class Diagnostic Maps* Summarize the performance of each pupil in a class on items assessing each of the specific objectives
3. *Class Grouping Reports* Identify groups of students who share common reading difficulties and who may be grouped together for instructional purposes
4. *Individual Study Guides* Cross-reference reading objectives assessed in the PRI/RS with page numbers in basal reading series where the objectives are taught
5. *Program Reference Guides* Cross-reference each basal reading series in its entirety to each of the objectives assessed by the PRI/RS

While this battery is cross-referenced to basal readers, an *Interpretive Handbook* is also provided, identifying numerous specific instructional exercises that can be used to teach to areas of deficiency.

NORMS

Normative scores can be obtained for the PRI/RS, but the process for doing so is relatively risky. Scores earned by an unspecified number and kind of students on the PRI/RS were correlated with scores they earned on Form C of the California Achievement Test (CAT). These correlations are used to estimate the scores the students would have earned had they taken the CAT. In addition, the information is for a previous edition of the CAT. We recommend that users restrict themselves to criterion-referenced use of the PRI/RS.

RELIABILITY AND VALIDITY

No data on consistency of student performance are provided for the PRI. The developers do report a study of the validity of the device. The PRI and the Reading section of the California Achievement Test were administered to the students who participated in the field testing. This procedure was used in an effort to check the extent to which the performance of the sample of students was comparable to that of a representative national sample. Although no specific data are reported on the relationship of pupil performance on the two tests, the developers stated that no adjustments to the PRI/RS were seen to be necessary. Validity rests largely on expert opinion. There are no data in the manual on the validity of the recommended grouping of students for instructional purposes.

SUMMARY

The Prescriptive Reading Inventory Reading System is a criterion-referenced assessment and instruction program designed to address mastery of prereading behaviors and desired reading behaviors in grades K through 9. Five kinds of reports are available that may be of considerable assistance in pinpointing individual pupil strengths and weaknesses, evaluating individual pupil progress, grouping students for instructional purposes, and evaluating program effectiveness.

The cross-referencing of this system to the most widely used basal readers has two specific advantages: those who use the test do not have to purchase an entire curriculum, and teachers can readily shift materials for individual students who experience difficulty learning in specific curricula.

COPING WITH DILEMMAS IN CURRENT PRACTICE

There are three major problems in the diagnostic assessment of reading strengths and weaknesses. The first is the problem of curriculum match. Students enrolled in different reading curricula have different opportunities to learn specific skills. Reading series differ in the skills that are taught, in the emphasis placed on different skills, in the sequence in which skills are taught, and the time at which skills are taught. Tests differ in the skills that are assessed. Thus, it can be expected that pupils studying different curricula will perform differently on the same reading test. It can also be expected that pupils studying the same curriculum will perform differently on different reading tests. Diagnostic personnel must be very careful to examine the match between skills taught in the student's curriculum and skills tested on the test. Most teacher's manuals for reading series include a listing of the skills taught at each level in the series. Many authors of diagnostic reading tests now include in test manuals a list of the objectives measured by the test. At the very least, assessors should carefully examine the extent to which the test measures what has been taught. Ideally, assessors would select specific parts of tests to measure exactly what has been taught. To the extent that there is a difference between what has been taught and what is tested, the test is not a valid measure.

A second problem is the selection of tests that are appropriate for making different kinds of educational decisions. We noted that there are different types of diagnostic reading tests. In making classification decisions, tests must be individually administered. One may either use an individually administered test or give a group test to one individual. In making instructional planning decisions, the most precise and helpful information will be obtained by giving individually administered criterion-referenced measures. One can, of course, systematically analyze pupil performance on a norm-referenced test, but the approach is difficult and time-consuming. It may also be futile since norm-referenced tests usually do not contain a sufficient number of items on which to base a diagnosis.

When evaluating individual pupil progress, the assessor must consider carefully the kinds of comparisons he or she wants to make. If one wants to compare pupils to others their age, norm-referenced measures are useful. If, on the other hand, one wants to know the extent to which individual pupils are mastering curriculum objectives, criterion-referenced measures are the tests of choice.

The third problem in reading is that there are few technically adequate tests. We have noted that for very many "norm-referenced" reading tests there is no description, or an inadequate description, of the groups on which the tests were standardized. Others were inadequately standardized. There is no evidence on the reliability and/or validity of many diagnostic reading tests. For others, reliability is not sufficient for use in making decisions about individuals. Diagnostic personnel should refrain from using technically inadequate measures. At the very least, they must operate with full awareness of the technical limitations of the devices they use.

The fourth problem is one of generalization. Assessors are faced with the very difficult task of describing or predicting pupil performance in reading. Yet, reading itself is difficult to describe. Reading is a complex behavior composed of subskills. Those who engage in reading diagnosis will do well to describe pupil performance in terms of specific skills or subskills (like recognition of words in isolation, listening comprehension, specific word-attack skills, and so on). They will do well also to limit predictions to making statements about probable performance of specific reading behaviors, not probable performance in reading.

SUMMARY

In this chapter we have reviewed the kinds of behaviors sampled by diagnostic reading tests. Several specific norm-referenced and criterion-referenced tests have been evaluated in terms of the kinds of behaviors they sample and their technical adequacy. Most of the norm-referenced devices clearly lack the technical characteristics necessary for use in making specific instructional decisions. Many do not present evidence of reliability and validity. In fact, some tests (Gates-McKillop-Horowitz, Durrell, and Diagnostic Reading Scales) present the consumer with numerous normative tables for interpreting test data without even describing the nature of the normative population.

The criterion-referenced tests described in this chapter are designed to pinpoint skill-development strengths and weaknesses, provide teachers with instructional objectives, and direct teachers to materials that help teach to those objectives. We do not yet have sufficient empirical evidence to judge the extent to which criterion-referenced tests meet their stated objectives. Teachers need to judge for their own purposes the adequacy of the behavior samplings and the sequences of behaviors sampled. The systems still contain many rough spots that must be smoothed out.

How, then, do teachers and diagnostic specialists assess skill development in reading and prescribe developmental, corrective, or remedial programs? Reliance on scores provided by diagnostic reading tests is indeed precarious. Teachers and diagnostic specialists must rely on the qualitative information obtained in testing. Some tests provide checklists of observed difficulties, and these may be of considerable help in identifying individual pupil's reading characteristics.

In assessing reading strengths and weaknesses, teachers must first ask themselves what kinds of behaviors they want to assess. Specific subtests of larger batteries may then be used to assess those behaviors. Teachers should choose the subtests that are technically most accurate. Interpretation must be in terms of behaviors sampled rather than in terms of subtest names.

STUDY QUESTIONS

1. For what purpose are diagnostic reading tests given?
2. What are the relative merits and limitations in using criterion-referenced diagnostic reading tests? In using norm-referenced tests?
3. Several shortcomings have been noted for each of the specific norm-referenced diagnostic reading tests described in this chapter. What shortcomings do most of the tests have in common?
4. Deirdre, a student in Mr. Albert's fifth-grade class, has considerable difficulty reading. Mr. Albert wants to know at what level to begin reading instruction. Given the state of the art in diagnostic testing in reading, describe some alternative ways for Mr. Albert to identify a starting point.
5. You are teaching reading to a third-grade class. The school psychologist assesses one of the children in your class and reports that the child earned a grade score of 1.6 in reading. What additional information would you ask the psychologist to give you?
6. When teachers use criterion-referenced reading tests, they often find that the sequence in which specific individuals learn reading skills differs from the sequence of skills assessed by the test. How might this be explained?
7. It has been argued that norms are more important for screening tests than for diagnostic tests. Why?

ADDITIONAL READING

Buros, O. K. (Ed.). (1968). *Reading tests and reviews.* Highland Park, NJ: Gryphon Press.

Conoley, J. C., & Kramer, J. J. (1989). *Buros tenth mental measurements yearbook.* Lincoln, NE: University of Nebraska Press.

Guthrie, J. T. (1973). Models of reading and reading disability. *Journal of Educational Psychology, 65,* 9–18.

Salvia, J. & Hughes, C. (1990). *Curriculum-based assessment: Testing what is taught.* New York: Macmillan. (Chapter 6: CBA in reading.)

C·H·A·P·T·E·R 18

ASSESSMENT OF MATHEMATICS

Diagnostic testing in mathematics is designed to identify specific strengths and weaknesses in skill development. We have seen that all major achievement tests designed to assess multiple skills include subtests that measure mathematics skills. These tests are necessarily global and attempt to assess a wide range of skills. In most cases, the number of items assessing specific math skills is insufficient for diagnostic purposes. Diagnostic testing in mathematics is more specific, providing a detailed assessment of skill development within specific areas.

There are fewer diagnostic math tests than diagnostic reading tests, but math assessment is more clear-cut. Because the successful performance of some mathematical operations clearly depends on the successful performance of other operations (for instance, multiplication depends on addition), it is relatively easier to sequence skill development and assessment in math than in reading. Diagnostic math tests generally sample similar behaviors. They sample various contents or mathematical concepts, various operations, and various applications of mathematical facts and principles.

WHY DO WE ASSESS MATHEMATICS?

There are several reasons to assess mathematics skills. First, we are often interested in evaluating a person's attainments in math. We may use diagnostic tests in mathematics to assess a person's readiness for instruction (in mathematics and other subjects) or to determine eligibility for employment. Second, all public school programs, with the exception of programs for the profoundly retarded, teach mathematical facts and concepts. Thus, teachers need to know if pupils have mastered particular facts and concepts. Diagnostic math tests are intended to provide sufficiently detailed information so that teachers can plan and evaluate instructional programs. Finally, diagnostic math tests are occasionally used to make classification decisions. Individually administered tests are usually required for classification and placement decisions. Therefore, we often see diagnostic math tests used to establish eligibility for programs for children with learning disabilities in mathematics.

Behaviors Sampled by Diagnostic Mathematics Tests

Behaviors sampled by diagnostic math tests have been classified by Connolly, Nachtman, and Pritchett (1976). A description of those behavior samples follows.

Content

A number of content areas are assessed by diagnostic math tests. Facts, knowledge, and concepts necessary for the successful performance of mathematical operations and for meaningful applications of math are assessed in each of the following content areas.

Numeration   Diagnostic math subtests assess knowledge of the number system. Items include those that assess identification of quantities and set value, rounding, identification of missing numbers in sequences, and counting.

Fractions   In nearly all cases and especially in tests designed to be used with students who are beyond fourth grade, understanding of basic concepts about fractions, decimals, and percentages is assessed.

Algebra   Some diagnostic math tests include subtests or items designed to assess knowledge and understanding of principles involved in the solution of linear and quadratic equations.

Geometry   Items that assess knowledge of geometry typically measure skill in recognizing specific shapes and, in some cases, understanding of theorems.

Operations

Subtests and items designed to assess children's skill in carrying out fundamental arithmetic operations include measures of counting, computation, and arithmetic reasoning.

Counting   Items designed to assess skill in counting usually require the student to count dots or objects and to select or write numerals to represent the number of objects counted.

Computation   Items and subtests designed to assess computational skills range from those that sample the traditional arithmetic operations of addition, subtraction, multiplication, and division to those that require the student to complete as many as four computational operations in problem-solving tasks. Items designed to assess specific operations generally range from those that require performance of the operation in the form of word problems to those that require the written solution of relatively complex computational problems.

Arithmetic Reasoning   Arithmetic-reasoning subtests require the solution of problems with missing number facts.

Applications

Diagnostic math tests assess students' skills in applying mathematical facts and concepts to the solution of problems. Tasks generally include the following kinds of behavior samplings.

Measurement   Items assessing measurement require the recognition and application of common measurement units and the practical application of length, weight, and temperature measures.

Problem Solving   Problem-solving tasks require students to solve "story problems" that are read to them or that they read themselves. Four kinds of problems are generally included: (1) those requiring only a one-step mathematical operation, (2) those requiring more than one computational operation, (3) those requiring the student to differentiate between essential and nonessential information in solving problems, and (4) those requiring the student to demonstrate logical thinking by solving problems with missing elements.

Reading Graphs and Tables   The application of mathematical skills and concepts may be assessed by requiring the student to read graphs and tables in the solution of problems.

Money and Budgeting   The application of mathematical skills and concepts may be assessed by requiring the student to solve money problems. Items include those that assess the extent to which the student can make value judgments about purchasing articles, can interpret budgets, and can comprehend checks and checking accounts.

Time The application of mathematical facts and concepts to the solution of problems involving time includes test items requiring the student to read clocks and to identify time intervals, holidays, and seasons.

SPECIFIC DIAGNOSTIC MATHEMATICS TESTS

This chapter reviews four diagnostic mathematics tests: the KeyMath–Revised, the Stanford Diagnostic Mathematics Test, the Test of Mathematical Abilities, and the Diagnostic Mathematics Inventory/Mathematics Systems.

KEYMATH–REVISED

KeyMath–Revised: A Diagnostic Inventory of Essential Mathematics (KeyMath-R) (Connolly, 1988) is an individually administered, norm-referenced device. The basic testing materials consist of two easels that contain testing items and directions for presenting and scoring items. Four uses are offered for the test: instructional planning, comparison of students, evaluation of educational progress, and curriculum evaluation.

There are two forms of KeyMath-R (Forms A and B), and each contains 258 items. Total math performance is divided into three areas. The area of Basic Concepts is composed of three subtests: numeration, rational numbers, and geometry. The Operations area consists of addition, subtraction, multiplication, division, and mental computation. The area of Applications contains items assessing measurement, time and money, estimation, interpretation of data, and problem solving. Each subtest is composed of domains or subsubtests. There are three or four domains per subtest for a total of 43 domains. For example, the subtest of rational numbers consists of three domains (frac-

tions, decimals, and percents). Only on the subtests in Operations is written computation permitted.

SCORES

Both percentiles and standard scores with a mean of 10 and a standard deviation of 3 are available for each subtest. For area and total test performance, six derived scores are provided: standard scores (with a mean of 100 and standard deviation of 15), normal curve equivalents, stanines, percentiles, and age and grade equivalents. Finally, KeyMath-R provides a rather unusual score for domains. (A domain is a subdivision of a subtest; for example, in the measurement subtest, there are four domains: comparisons, using nonstandard units, using standard units of length and area, and using standard units of weight and capacity.) Domain Performance scores divide student performances into strong (top quartile), average (middle quartiles) or weak (bottom quartile);

the usefulness of domain scores for instructional planning is unclear. A microcomputer program is available to convert raw scores and construct profiles.

NORMS

A total of 1,798 students (873 in the fall and 925 in the spring) from kindergarten through eighth grade were tested for the national standardization. The sample was stratified on the basis of geographic region, grade, sex, socioeconomic status (inferred from the educational attainment of the parents), and racial/ethnic status. For each grade, the demographic characteristics of KeyMath-R's sample is compared to the U.S. population. Regional representation is quite close to the census figures although the standardization sample was drawn from only 22 locations in sixteen states; Pennsylvania and Texas had the most testing sites (4 and 3, respectively). Representation by educational attainment is quite close to the national proportions; representation by racial or ethnic group slightly overrepresents minorities, but this overrepresentation should have little, if any, practical effect. Finally, minor differences in the norms of forms A and B were removed statistically.

RELIABILITY

Alternate-form reliability was estimated by retesting about 70 percent of the students in grades K, 2, 4, 6, and 8 at two- and four-week intervals. However, Connolly does not report estimated reliability by grade; rather, he reports pooled (across-grade) coefficients. Only the total score may be sufficiently reliable for making important educational decisions for students; all subtest and area estimates of reliability are less than .85.

Split-half reliabilities (using an odd-even split and Spearman-Brown correction) were also estimated by grade and age.[1]

For students in kindergarten through the second grade, total scores are consistently reliable enough to make decisions for individuals; area subtests fluctuate so the test user must determine if a particular age-area combination is sufficiently reliable for interpretation. After second grade, area scores have acceptable reliability, and total scores have excellent reliability; however, because basal and ceiling rules were applied to the test scores, the obtained split-half estimates are likely to be inflated.

A third method of estimating reliability based on item-response theory was used. The results of this analysis are essentially the same as those obtained using split-half estimates.

No reliability data are provided for domain scores. No stability coefficients are reported although stability can be inferred from the alternate-form reliability coefficients.

VALIDITY

Little evidence of construct validity is presented. What is offered is a demonstration of mean score progressions from grade to grade. No evidence of concurrent validity is presented. However, for most achievement tests, these indices of validity are less important than evidence of content validity. Limited evidence for KeyMath-R's content validity comes from the careful development of a table of specifications to guide item development. As always is the case, however, test users should inspect the test's content to make sure that it conforms to the curriculum followed by the students who are assessed.

1. We believe that the reliability estimates based on age are somewhat misleading because several age groups are contained within any grade. Consequently, the range of ability would likely be extended.

Summary

From its title and claims made in its manual, KeyMath-R is intended as a diagnostic test. The standardization of the test appears to be generally adequate. Before third grade, only the total score is sufficiently reliable for diagnostic purposes; after second grade, area and total scores are sufficiently reliable. Because of the low reliabilities of subtests and the absence of reliability information for domains, users should avoid making inferences about a student's instructional strengths and weaknesses based on subtest and domain scores. For the four uses that are proffered for the test, no evidence of KeyMath-R's validity for instructional planning, evaluation of educational progress, or curriculum evaluation is presented. Some evidence for the validity of comparing students' global performances is presented.

STANFORD DIAGNOSTIC MATHEMATICS TEST

The Stanford Diagnostic Mathematics Test (SDMT) (Beatty, Gardner, Madden, & Karlsen, 1985) is the third edition of this group-administered, norm-referenced device, intended for use with pupils in the second through twelfth grades. The test comes in four booklets for overlapping levels—red, green, brown, and blue (see the first column of Table 18.1).

The SDMT has two purposes; it serves as a diagnostic test for classroom teachers and as a test for program evaluation for school administrators. The content is arranged in three subtests.

Number System and Numeration The tasks included in this subtest range from identifying numerals and comparing sets to working with fractions and more complex arithmetic operations. The items are noncomputational; they are designed to assess pupils' understanding of numbers and their properties.

Computation This subtest assesses knowledge of the primary facts and algorithms of addition, subtraction, multiplication, and division, as well as methods for solving simple and compound number sentences.

Applications This subtest assesses skill in applying basic mathematical facts and principles. Items range in difficulty from those that require students to solve simple story problems and to select correct models for solving one-step problems to those that require students to solve multiple-step and measurement problems and to read tables and graphs.

Scores

Content-referenced and norm-referenced scores are available for each subtest, and norm-referenced scores are available for the total score. Content-referenced scores are raw scores (the number correct) and Progress Indicators. Progress Indicators, expressed as "+" and "–," are intended "to identify those pupils who have demonstrated sufficient competence in specific mathematics skills to make satisfactory progress in the regular mathematics program" (p. 10). The basis of these scores is not made explicit.

Norm-referenced scores consist of percentiles, stanines, normal curve equivalents, grade equivalents, and scaled scores that are standardized across grades. The scaled scores create

TABLE 18.1 KR-20 Estimates of Internal Consistency of the Subtests of the Stanford Diagnostic Math Test

Level/Grade/Form	Subtest 1	Subtest 2	Subtest 3	Total
Red Level				
Grade 2				
Form G	.86	.88	.82	.94
Form H	.87	.87	.83	.94
Grade 3				
Form G	.84	.84	.82	.92
Form H	.86	.82	.83	.93
Grade 4				
Form G	.74	.82	.78	.89
Form H	.78	.80	.71	.88
Green Level				
Grade 4				
Form G	.85	.91	.88	.95
Form H	.86	.92	.87	.95
Grade 5				
Form G	.86	.91	.88	.95
Form H	.85	.91	.88	.95
Grade 6				
Form G	.84	.86	.88	.93
Form H	.85	.91	.88	.94
Brown Level				
Grade 6				
Form G	.86	.92	.90	.96
Form H	.86	.91	.88	.96
Grade 7				
Form G	.87	.90	.90	.95
Form H	.86	.91	.88	.95
Grade 8				
Form G	.88	.91	.89	.95
Form H	.87	.89	.87	.95
Blue Level				
Grade 8				
Form G	.89	.92	.85	.96
Form H	.89	.92	.86	.96
Grade 9				
Form G	.90	.93	.89	.96
Form H	.90	.92	.87	.96
Grade 10				
Form G	.90	.91	.87	.96
Form H	.90	.91	.87	.96
Grade 11				
Form G	.90	.92	.88	.96
Form H	.90	.91	.88	.96
Grade 12				
Form G	.91	.92	.87	.96
Form H	.91	.92	.89	.96

some problems because "each subtest and total score has its own system" (p. 12); scaled scores are not equivalent across subtests and totals.

NORMS

Norms are provided for spring and fall testing. However, the characteristics of the sample and several specifics of the sampling plan used to select the normative sample are not discussed in the technical manuals.

Data from the school census conducted in 1970 by the U.S. Office of Education were used to stratify schools on the basis of the districts' socioeconomic levels (family income and educational attainment of adults in the community) and pupil enrollments. An unspecified number of SES-by-enrollment cells were created for each grade level, and from four to six school districts per cell were chosen at random to participate. The final sample contains an unspecified number of students from an unspecified number of school districts. The sample does approximate the population (as reflected in the 1983 school census) closely with respect to district size (within 5 percent) and ethnic group (6 percent); however, with respect to geographic area the fall sample overrepresents the southeastern part of the United States by 24 percent.

RELIABILITY

KR-20 estimates of internal consistency are presented for all combinations of subtests and totals, forms and grades. These values are shown in Table 18.1. For the total score, only the reliability coefficients for grade 4 fail to exceed .90. For the individual combinations of form, grade, and subtest, the eighty-four KR-20s are lower: four coefficients are less

than .80; fifty coefficients are less than .90; the remaining thirty equal or exceed .90. Thus most of the subtests are not sufficiently reliable for use in making important educational decisions.

No stability data are presented, and no data are presented on the reliability of Progress Indicators.

VALIDITY

The absence of a description of how items were selected or developed makes evaluation of the SDMT's content validity difficult. The content validity, as with any achievement test, depends on the match between curriculum and test; test users themselves must evaluate the content validity.

Limited evidence of concurrent validity is presented. The subtests and total of the SDMT are highly correlated with the corresponding subtests and total of the Stanford Achievement Test in grades 2 through 8; r's range from .64 to .89. For the upper grades, the authors report only the correlation of the total scores ($r = .84$).

Finally, no evidence is presented to show that Progress Indicators are valid. Evidence is presented to show that the SMDT correlates with the Otis-Lennon School Ability Test, but it is not clear why these correlations would establish the validity of the SDMT as a diagnostic achievement test.

SUMMARY

The Stanford Diagnostic Mathematics Test is a group-administered achievement test intended for use as a diagnostic test by classroom teachers and as a test for program evaluation by school administrators. The norms are inadequately described. The subtests lack sufficient reliability for the SDMT to be used as a diagnostic tool. Its validity for use in program eval-uation will depend on its relevance to the particular program being evaluated.

TEST OF MATHEMATICAL ABILITIES

The Test of Mathematical Abilities (TOMA) (Brown & McEntire, 1984) is a norm-referenced device intended for use with students in grades 3 through 12 or between the ages of 8-6 and 18-11. The TOMA provides information about a student's skills in computation and in solving word problems as well as about attitudes toward mathematics, mathematical vocabulary, and general cultural application of information. It is intended to identify students who are significantly ahead of or behind their agemates in mathematical ability, to determine strengths and weaknesses of the students, to document progress, and to serve as a useful research tool. Four of the subtests may be group administered; general information must be individually administered. The 107 test items are grouped into five subtests.

Attitude Toward Math   The 15 items in this subtest are based on the Estes Attitude Scales. Students use a three-point scale to rate their feelings about mathematics.

Vocabulary   The student must define 20 terms in writing.

Computation   Students solve 25 problems in their answer booklets.

General Information   Each of the 30 questions in this subtest requires an oral response to "cultural-social-practical applications of mathematics."

Story Problems   Students solve 17 word problems in their answer booklets.

SCORES

Derived scores are reported by ages (half years from 8-0 to 10-0, then one-year intervals from 10 to 18-11), not by grades. Standard scores have a mean of 10 and a standard deviation of 3. A *math quotient* is obtained by adding the standard scores from each subtest. Math quotients have a mean of 100 and a standard deviation of 15. Percentile ranks as well as age and grade equivalents are also available.

NORMS

The TOMA was standardized on 1,560 students living in five states. Although the five states seems rather few, the final sample is within 7 percent of the 1980 census proportions for urban-rural residence, race, and region of residence. However, no data are presented for socioeconomic status (education or income) of the parents of the students in the sample.

RELIABILITY

The subtest scores are of considerably greater interest than total scores (which do not seem to us to be readily interpretable). Coefficient alpha for each of the 50 combinations of age group (10) and subtest (5) ranged from .57 for computation at age 11 to .97 for computation at age 8-6 to 8-11. Only twelve of the fifty coefficients equaled or exceeded .90. Two studies examined the stability of TOMA. One used twenty-three normal 11-year-old students; reliabilities ranged from .71 (Attitude Toward Math) to .81 (General Information). In the second study, learning-disabled students between ages 9 and 17 were tested. However, crossing so many age levels tends to inflate seriously estimates of reliability. (Indeed, for the norming sample, age correlated with test scores about .60.) SEMs based on internal-consistency estimates are also reported.

VALIDITY

No evidence of content validity is presented.

Criterion-related validity was established by correlating the TOMA scores with the math subtests of the PIAT and the WRAT as well as with the KeyMath Diagnostic Arithmetic Test. Using these three tests as the criterion, the TOMA subtests of computation and story problems are of particular interest since their behavior samples are similar. The TOMA computation correlates .45 with the PIAT, but is nonsignificant with the WRAT. Story problems correlate .36 with the PIAT, but .37 with the WRAT despite the fact that there are no word problems on the WRAT. None of the criterion measures seems appropriate for attitude toward math. (Indeed, correlations between math attitudes and achievement might better be construed as construct validity.) All of the TOMA subtests correlate modestly with KeyMath total score.

Construct validity was established by showing that the TOMA scores increased with age, that the four subtests requiring cognitive skills were correlated with the WISC-R and the Slosson IQs, and that learning-disabled students earned significantly lower scores than normal students on the TOMA.

SUMMARY

The TOMA is a group-administered and an individually administered norm-referenced test that assesses several aspects of mathematical ability. The quality of the norms is difficult to assess. They appear representative on the dimensions of urban-rural residence, geographic region, and race. No data are presented on social status of the parents of the children in the normative sample or on the curricula in which the students were enrolled. The internal-consistency reliability is adequate for screening decisions and occasionally adequate for important educational decisions. Stability is unknown for all but one subtest. No evidence of content validity is presented, and only limited evidence of criterion-related and construct validity is provided.

DIAGNOSTIC MATHEMATICS INVENTORY/ MATHEMATICS SYSTEMS

Diagnostic Mathematics Inventory/Mathematics Systems (DMI/MS) (Gessell, 1983) is a criterion-referenced assessment and instruction program incorporated into a set of systems for use in mathematics instruction. There are two systems: System 1 is a graded system, and System 2 is an ungraded, objectives-based system. The two systems include identical material packaged in different ways. The systems are used to place students at their instructional level, diagnose specific strengths and weaknesses in mathematics, prescribe appropriate instructional materials and activities, and monitor pupil progress. The test is designed for use with students in grades K.6 through 8.9. The test component is accompanied by an instructional program, but the test is also cross-referenced to a wide range of basal mathematics series.

The DMI/MS is used to provide teachers with an assessment of skill development in four major content areas of mathematics: Whole Numbers, Fractions and Decimals, Measurement and Geometry, and Problem Solving and Special Topics. Materials included with the test provide teachers with a very detailed list of the specific skills assessed in each of these content areas. The areas are divided into twenty-nine categories of objectives, which are subdivided into eighty-two instructional objectives. The Whole Numbers domain includes an assessment of students' concepts of whole numbers as well as their skill in performing operations using whole numbers. The Fractions and Decimals domain includes an assessment of students' concepts of fractions as well as their skill in performing arithmetic operations using fractions and decimals. The Mathematics and Geometry domain includes items assessing knowledge of metric and customary units of measurement as well as those assessing geometric concepts and operations. The Problem Solving and Special Topics domain is a set of items assessing the ability to apply mathematics skills to the solution of word problems and problems involving graphs, basic statistics and probability, and prealgebra. The DMI/MS has seven levels: Level A (grades K.6 through 1.5), Level B (grades 1.6 through 2.5), Level C (grades 2.6 through 3.5), Level D (grades 3.6 through 4.5), Level E (grades 4.6 through 5.5), Level F (grades 5.6 through 6.5) and Level G (grades 6.6 through 8.9 and up). Content of the DMI/MS was selected based on a review of the content of fourteen basal mathematics series. The DMI/MS is available on microcomputer disks.

SCORES

Scores on the DMI/MS are available in the following five report formats.

Objectives Mastery Report   This report, provided for the class, identifies for each student those objectives mastered and not mastered.

Common Error Report   This report, available for individual students and for a class of students, provides information on errors made often. It is used by the teacher to identify aspects of instruction that many students are not mastering.

Individual Diagnostic Report   This report, available for individual students, provides a listing of objectives mastered and not mastered as well as an analysis of the common errors made.

Class Grouping Report   This report is a specific list of the students who demonstrated mastery of each of the objectives in the system.

Estimated Norms Report   This report consists of a set of estimated normative scores for students who took the DMI/MS.

NORMS

Normative scores can be obtained for the DMI/MS, but the process for doing so is relatively risky. Scores earned by an unspecified number and kind of students on the DMI/MS were correlated with the scores they earned on Form C of the California Achievement Test and Form U of the Comprehensive Tests of Basic Skills. The correlations are used to estimate the scores students would have earned had they taken the CAT or the CTBS. Previous editions of the CAT and CTBS were used in the process of developing estimated norms. We recommend that users restrict themselves to criterion-referenced use of the DMI/MS.

RELIABILITY AND VALIDITY

The DMI/MS is a criterion-referenced mathematics test. Traditional reliability and validity data are not included in the manuals for the DMI/MS.

SUMMARY

The DMI/MS is one of the most complete diagnostic-prescriptive inventories we have seen. The system can be used to assess pupil mastery of objectives in twenty-nine instructional categories. Objectives are cross-referenced to mathematics textbooks and supplementary materials. The DMI/MS should be extremely useful to teachers and other educational personnel in planning specific individualized educational programs in mathematics.

COPING WITH DILEMMAS IN CURRENT PRACTICE

There are three major problems in the diagnostic assessment of mathematical skills. The first problem is the recurring issue of curriculum match. There is considerable variation in math curricula. This variation means that the diagnostic math tests will not be equally representative for all curricula—or even appropriate for some commonly used ones. As a result, great care must be exercised in using diagnostic math tests to make various educational decisions. Diagnosticians must be extremely careful to note the match between test content and curriculum. This usually involves far more than a quick inspection of test items by someone unfamiliar with the specific classroom curriculum. For example, a diagnostician could inspect the teacher's manual to ensure that the test assesses only material that has been taught and that there is reasonable correspondence between the relative emphasis placed on teaching the material and testing the material. To do this, the diagnostician may have to develop a table of specifications for the math curriculum and compare test items to that table. However, once a table of specifications has been developed for the curriculum, a better procedure would be to select items from a criterion-referenced system to fit the cells in the table exactly.

The next problem is selecting an appropriate test for the type of decision that needs to be made. School personnel are usually required to use individually administered norm-referenced devices in classification decisions. Decisions about a pupil's eligibility for special services, however, need not be based on detailed information about a pupil's strengths and weaknesses, as provided by diagnostic tests; diagnosticians are interested in a pupil's relative standing. In our opinion the best achievement survey tests are subtests of group-administered tests. A practical solution is not to use a diagnostic math test for classification decisions but to administer individually a subtest from one of the better group achievement tests.

The third problem is that most of the diagnostic tests in mathematics do not test a sufficiently detailed sample of facts and concepts (although the DMI/MS may be an exception). Consequently, one must generalize from a student's performance on the items tested to performance on the items that are not tested. The reliabilities of the subtests on diagnostic math tests are often not high enough for educators to make such a generalization with any great degree of confidence. As a result, these tests are not too useful in assessing readiness or in assessing strengths and weaknesses in order to plan instructional programs. We believe that the preferred practice in diagnostic testing in mathematics is for teachers to develop criterion-referenced achievement tests that exactly parallel the curriculum being taught.

Summary

In this chapter we have reviewed the kinds of behaviors sampled by diagnostic mathematics tests and have evaluated the most commonly used tests in terms of the kinds of behaviors they sample and their technical adequacy. The four tests reviewed in this chapter are designed essentially to provide teachers and diagnostic specialists with specified information on those math skills that pupils have and have not mastered. Compared to diagnostic testing in reading, diagnostic testing in math puts less emphasis on the provision of scores.

The tests described in this chapter differ in their technical adequacy for use in making instructional decisions for students. Knowledge of pupil mastery of specific math skills as gained from administration of one or more of the tests, along with knowledge of the general sequence of development of math skills, can help teachers design curricular content for individuals.

Study Questions

1. Identify four ways a teacher can interpret the performance of a pupil on KeyMath-R.
2. The Stanford Diagnostic Mathematics Test is both norm-referenced and criterion-referenced. Under what circumstances would a teacher want to use the norms for the SDMT?
3. Given the state of the art in diagnostic assessment in math, identify at least two ways a classroom teacher can pinpoint a starting place for teaching math to an individual pupil.
4. You are teaching arithmetic to a third-grade class. The local school psychologist assesses one of the children in your class and reports that the

child earned a grade equivalent of 5.6 in arithmetic. What additional information would you ask the psychologist to give you?

ADDITIONAL READING

Ashlock, R. (1976). *Error patterns in computation* (2nd ed.). Columbus, OH: Merrill.

Conoley, J. C., & Kramer, J. J. (1989). *Buros tenth mental measurements yearbook*. Lincoln, NE: University of Nebraska Press.

Reisman, F. (1982). Strategies for mathematics disorders. In C. Reynolds and T. Gutkin (Eds.), *Handbook of school psychology*. New York: Wiley.

CHAPTER 19

ASSESSMENT OF WRITTEN LANGUAGE

Written expression is the end product of a considerable amount of intellectual activity: the formation of ideas, their elaboration, their sequencing, and so forth. Much of what we consider to be writing is a creative endeavor. One's ability to use words to excite, to depict vividly, to imply is far more than a mechanical set of skills that can be taught, although they can be polished and honed. However, several aspects of written language can be thought of as skills that can be taught and mastered. These skills have been separated from those in Chapter 13 on oral language because they are routinely taught in school. The written encoding of language requires that we observe certain conventions—rules. These conventions are taught in school and learned by students. Several components of written language are assessed: spelling, punctuation and capitalization, grammar, word usage, penmanship, and, occasionally, outlining and organizing.

Spelling is often assessed as part of several standardized tests: the California Achievement Tests, the Iowa Tests of Basic Skills and Tests of Achievement and Proficiency, the Metropolitan Achievement Tests, the SRA Achievement Series, the Stanford Achievement Test, the Wide Range Achievement Test–Revised, the Peabody Individual Achievement Test–Revised, the BRIGANCE® Diagnostic Inventory of Basic Skills, the Durrell Analysis of Reading Difficulty, and the Woodcock-Johnson Psychoeducational Battery. However, the spelling words that students are to learn vary considerably from curriculum to curriculum. For example, Ames (1965) examined seven spelling series and found that they introduce an average of 3,200 words between the second and eighth grades. However, only about 1,300 words were common to all the series; about 1,700 words were taught in only one series. Moreover, the words taught in several series varied considerably in their grade placement, sometimes by as many as *five* grades.

Mechanics (capitalization and punctuation) are also assessed on several achievement batteries: the California Achievement Tests, the Iowa Tests of Basic Skills and Tests of Achievement and Proficiency, the Metropolitan Achievement Tests, the SRA Achievement Series, the Stanford Achievement Test, the BRIGANCE® Diagnostic Inventory of Basic Skills, and the Woodcock-Johnson Psychoeducational Battery. Again, standardized tests are not well suited to measuring achievement in these areas since the grade level at which these skills are taught varies so much from one curriculum to another. To be valid, the measurement of achievement in these areas must be closely tied to the curriculum being taught. In capitalization and punctuation, for example, pupils may learn that a sentence always begins with a capital letter in kindergarten, first grade, second grade, or later. They may learn that commercial brand names are capitalized in the sixth grade or several grades earlier. Students may be taught that the apostrophe in "it's" makes the word a contraction of "it is" in the second or third grade but may still be studying "it's" in high school. Finally, in assessing word usage, organization, and penmanship we must take into account the emphasis that individual teachers place on these components of written language and when and how students are taught.

The more usual way to assess written language is to conduct an informal evaluation of a student's written work and to develop vocabulary and spelling tests that parallel the curriculum. In this way teachers can be sure that they are measuring precisely what has been taught. Most teachers' editions of language arts series contain scope and sequence charts that specify fairly clearly the objectives that are taught in each unit. From these charts teachers can develop appropriate criterion-referenced tests.

WHY DO WE ASSESS WRITTEN LANGUAGE?

Written language and spelling are regularly taught in school, and these areas are singled out for assessment in PL 94-142. Consequently, we assess written language and spelling for the same reasons we assess any achievement area. We may use tests to screen for pupils who exhibit difficulties in various aspects of written language. We may use tests to ascertain eligibility for special educational services for the language-impaired or learning-disabled. We may use language tests as an aid in planning instructional programs. Finally, we may use language tests to evaluate the progress of individual pupils.

TESTS OF WRITTEN EXPRESSION AND SPELLING

TEST OF WRITTEN LANGUAGE-2

The Test of Written Language–2 (TOWL-2) (Hammill & Larsen, 1988) is a norm-referenced device designed to assess written-language competence of students between the ages of 7 years, 6 months and 17 years, 11 months. Although designed to be administered to individual students, the authors claim that it can be given to groups; the only proviso given for group administration is to "stop testing when the vast majority of the individuals in the group have attained a ceiling" (p. 13). Because the test scores are based on individual administration, great care should be exercised in interpreting the results of group administration. The recommended uses of TOWL-2 include identifying students with writing difficulties, determining strengths and weaknesses of individual students, evaluating student progress, and doing research.

TOWL-2 is published with two alternate forms, A and B. On each form, ten subtests are combined into three composite scores: Overall Written Language (a composite of all subtests), Contrived Writing (a composite based on five subtests), and Spontaneous Writing (a composite based on the other five subtests). Contrived Writing is defined by the test authors as "the ability to write when measured by tests having contrived formats" (Hammill & Larsen, 1988, p. 6). Later in the test manual these formats are elaborated as "traditional, standardized test formats" (p. 46). Following are brief descriptions of the five contrived-writing subtests and their formats.

Vocabulary   This area is assessed by having a student write correct sentences using stimulus words.

Spelling   The TOWL-2 assesses spelling by having a student write sentences from dictation.

Style   This aspect is assessed by evaluating the punctuation and capitalization of words in dictated sentences.

Logical Sentences   This area is assessed by having students rewrite illogical sentences so that they make sense.

Sentence Combining   TOWL-2 requires students to write one grammatically correct sentence based on the information in several, short, visually presented sentences.

Spontaneous Writing is assessed from a "free, spontaneously produced essay" (p. 46). On the TOWL-2, a student is asked to write a story using one of two pictures as a story starter. After the story has been written (and the other five subtests administered), the story is scored on five dimensions. Each dimension is treated as a subtest. Following are brief descriptions of how these subtests are scored.

Thematic Maturity   This aspect is assessed by evaluating a student's story on the presence of 30 different elements (for example, paragraph usage, naming objects depicted in the stimulus, definite story ending, presence of a moral or philosophic theme, and so forth).

Contextual Vocabulary   This area is evaluated by counting the number of different seven-letter words contained in the story.

Syntactic Maturity   TOWL-2 evaluates this factor by counting the number of grammatically correct words in the story. Spelling and punctuation errors are not counted as grammatical errors.

Contextual Spelling   This subtest is evaluated by counting the number of different words that have been spelled correctly.

Contextual Style   This subtest is evaluated on the basis of the number of different punctuation and capitalization rules used in the story. Rules are given different point values. For example, a period at the end of sentence and capitalizing the first word of a sentence each are awarded one point; a comma after an introductory clause and capitalizing proper adjectives (for example, *American*) are awarded three points.

Scores

Raw scores for each subtest can be converted to percentiles or standard scores. The standard scores have a mean of 10 and a standard deviation of 3; the percentiles appear to be those associated with standard scores in a normal distribution rather than those obtained, although no discussion to confirm or disconfirm this impression was found in the test manual. Composite quotients are standard scores with a mean of 100 and a standard deviation of 15.

Raw-score conversions are based on age rather than grade. However, written expression is not a trait that develops independently of schooling; much of TOWL-2's content (for example, spelling, punctuation, and paragraph usage among others) is systematically taught in school. Therefore, grade conversions are more appropriate. Furthermore, students of the same age may receive instruction in two or three different grades. Because skill levels should be more closely related to grade than age, age norms will likely be more variable than grade norms, and estimates of reliability may be somewhat inflated.

Norms

TOWL-2 was standardized on 2,216 students from 19 states. Overall, the sample approximates the characteristics of people living in the United States on selected demographic variables. Urbanites and Hispanics are slightly overrepresented; Westerners are substantially overrepresented (25 percent of people in the norm group versus 20 percent of U.S. population), while Southerners are substantially un-

derrepresented (29 versus 34 percent). Because the test authors have provided demographic data only for the entire sample, the representativeness of the normative sample at each age is unknown. However, because the data from the total sample are averages, the samples at specific age groups are probably less representative than the total sample.

Reliability

Three types of reliability are discussed in the TOWL-2 manual: interscorer reliability, internal consistency, and stability with alternate forms. Interscorer reliability was estimated by having two scorers each evaluate 20 protocols selected to represent short, medium, and long stories written by third, seventh, and tenth graders. With the exception of an anomalous value for sentence combining on Form A, all interscorer correlations exceed .90.

Internal-consistency (that is, split-half and coefficient-alpha) estimates of reliability are incompletely reported. Coefficient alpha was computed for the five Contrived subtests while split-half estimates, corrected by the Spearman-Brown formula, were computed for the five Spontaneous subtests. The data reported in the test manual are based on the performances of 25 students randomly selected from each age group. Adjacent age groups between the ages of 7 and 14 were then combined to create groups of 50 students (for example, seven- and eight-year-olds); the fifteen-, sixteen-, and seventeen-year-olds were combined into one group of 75 students. Combining age groups is undesirable for two reasons. First, because raw scores must be used to estimate both alpha and split-half coefficients, the combined ranges of ability underlying the correlations are needlessly extended. Therefore, these estimates of reliability are likely inflated. Second, reliability estimates should be reported for each score at each age. Because TOWL-2 subtest reliability coefficients seem to increase with age, test users should be cautious when interpreting subtests with students younger than 10 years old. Conclusions about the internal consistency of TOWL-2 must be tempered; reliability estimates appearing in the test manual are probably maximum values. In general, TOWL-2 subtests probably have adequate internal consistency for screening purposes; composite scores probably have adequate reliability for decisions about individual students.

Alternate-form reliability (with an average testing interval of two days) are based on 77 students who lived in Austin, Texas. Because standard scores were used in the analysis, the range of ability underlying the correlation should not be affected. All the obtained coefficients are less than .90. Moreover, the internal-consistency estimates that are presented often contradict the notion that A and B are truly alternate forms. The data from the 7- to 8-year-old age group readily illustrate the problem: the Form A vocabulary subtest has a reliability of .83 while the Form B vocabulary subtest has a reliability coefficient of .95; Form A contextual spelling has an estimated reliability of .97 while Form B contextual spelling has an estimated reliability of .70.

Stability was estimated by statistically removing the average error associated with internal consistency from the alternate-form estimate of reliability. However, because there is considerable variation in the internal-consistency estimates between the two forms of the test, the average internal consistency for any subtest or composite will overestimate the stability on one form while underestimating the stability on the other form. Given this problem, TOWL-2 scores should not be considered sufficiently stable for purposes other than screening.

VALIDITY

Some claim for content validity can be made from the way the test was developed, the completeness of the dimensions of written language, and the methods by which competence in written language is assessed. Those major aspects of written language that lend themselves to objective appraisal are assessed. However, more subjective aspects (for example, content generation, cohesion, audience considerations) are not. The subtest and total scores are intuitively interpretable. The interpretation of the Contrived Writing and Spontaneous Writing composites is more problematic because they represent testing format rather than test content. Moreover, the results of factor-analytic studies (discussed later) suggest that TOWL-2 subtests assess only one general factor—general written language.

Evidence for TOWL-2's criterion-related validity comes from two studies. The first study relates the TOWL-2 performance of 68 students of unknown demographic characteristics to their performance on the Language Arts subtest of the SRA Achievement Test. The obtained correlations support a claim for the criterion-related validity of the contrived subtests but offer less support for the validity of the spontaneous subtests. In the second study, TOWL-2 essays of 51 private school students from Austin, Texas, who were enrolled in grades 2 through 7 were evaluated. The essays were graded holistically and with the TOWL-2 criteria. The correlation of holistic ratings with the total TOWL-2 score was .61; all other correlations were less than .50. However, because it is unclear if raw or standard scores were used in the statistical analyses, the correlations may be inflated.

Several types of evidence for TOWL-2's construct validity are offered in the test manual. In our opinion, three studies bear on a claim for TOWL-2's construct validity. First, the test correlates modestly with grade. Second, a subsample of learning-disabled students who participated in the standardization of the test earned substantially lower scores on TOWL-2. Third, different procedures were used to factor-analyze the test. The different procedures resulted in different factoral structures; this finding suggests that the factor structure of TOWL-2 is not robust. However, neither solution found more than two factors, and in both factor analyses the factors identified were consistent with the test's structure.

SUMMARY

The content and structure of TOWL-2 appear appropriate. The representativeness of the test's norms at each age cannot be evaluated with the data presented in the test manual, and age norms are used rather than grade norms. Interscorer reliability is excellent. The internal consistencies of composite and total scores are probably high enough to use in making individual decisions. Although the means and standard deviations of forms A and B appear equivalent, the internal consistencies of subtests within forms do not support the hypothesis that the forms are equivalent. Because of the lack of equivalence of the two test forms, stability data are not readily interpretable. Because of the difficulties with the presentation of norms and reliability data, the validity of TOWL-2 scores is unclear. Although the validity of the test's content appears acceptable, the validity of the quantification of student performance should not be assumed. Consequently, the validity of TOWL-2's ability to identification is not established. The data presented in the test manual do not support the contention that TOWL-2 can be used to determine strengths and weaknesses of individual students or to evaluate the progress of individual students.

TEST OF WRITTEN SPELLING, 2

Test of Written Spelling, 2 (TWS-2) (Larsen & Hammill, 1986) is the most recent edition of this individually administered, norm-referenced test, intended to assess the spelling ability of students ranging in age from 6-6 to 18-5. TWS-2 is based on the realization that some words are spelled phonetically and need not be taught or learned by memorization, whereas other words are irregular and must be memorized individually. Consequently, there are two subtests on TWS-2.

Predictable Words This subtest contains fifty words whose spellings are consistently governed by the rules of Standard American English.

Unpredictable Words This subtest contains fifty words that could not be spelled by computer even after more than two thousand rules of English spelling were applied.

A three-step process is used to administer TWS-2—the examiner reads the word, uses the word in a sentence, and reads the word a second time in isolation. The student then writes the word. Basal and ceiling levels (five consecutive correct responses and five consecutive incorrect responses, respectively) speed administration, which can usually be accomplished in less than 25 minutes. Guidelines for group administration are also given (p. 6).[1]

SCORES

For each subtest and for the total score, raw scores are converted into percentiles and standard scores (called quotients) that have a mean of 100 and a standard deviation of 15.

NORMS

The TWS-2 was normed on over 3,800 students from fifteen states. The plan used to obtain the normative sample is not discussed. However, the sample is quite close (within 5 percent) to the population as revealed by the 1985 census with respect to sex, residence, race, and ethnicity. The north central region of the United States is underrepresented in the norms (18 percent of the sample, 25 percent of the national population), primarily to the benefit of the West.

RELIABILITY

Internal consistency was estimated with coefficient alpha by examining the responses of fifty students from the standardization sample. A total of thirty-nine coefficients were obtained (two subtests and a total score for thirteen age groups). Only two subtests had coefficients less than .90: Predictable Words and Unpredictable Words for the 6-year-old group. Stability (two-week interval) was estimated from the

performances of 160 students in the first through eighth grades at one school in Michigan. Again the coefficients were extremely high. Only one coefficient was less than .90 (Predictable Words for second graders).

VALIDITY

Content validity is of the greatest importance. The TWS-2 is one of only a few tests that precisely relate test content to the content taught in various curricula. Each of the words included in the original TWS appeared in ten basal spelling series. Additional words were added to the TWS-2 to test students between the ages of 13 and 18 and to strengthen the test for younger students. New words for the TWS-2 were selected from the reading core vocabulary in the EDL Core Vocabularies in Reading, Mathematics, Science, and Social Studies. Evidence of criterion-related validity is offered in the form of correlations between the TWS and the spelling subtests of the Durrell Analysis of Reading Difficulty, the Wide Range Achievement Test, the California Achievement Tests, and the SRA Achievement Series. (Because the TWS and the TWS-2 are highly correlated—$r > .90$—correlations between the TWS-2 and those tests can safely be assumed.) These studies are poorly described, however, and the large correlations between measures must be interpreted cautiously. The correlation of TWS-2 scores with age and the poor performance of learning-disabled students are cited as evidence of construct validity.

SUMMARY

The Test of Written Spelling, 2 is a norm-referenced, individually administered device de-

---

1. The number of words is fixed for the group; thus basals and ceilings may not be obtained for all students.

signed to assess spelling ability in students between the ages of 6-6 and 18-5. The test has adequate norms, good reliability, and content validity.

SLINGERLAND SCREENING TESTS FOR IDENTIFYING CHILDREN WITH SPECIFIC LANGUAGE DISABILITY

The Slingerland Screening Tests for Identifying Children with Specific Language Disability (Slingerland, 1970) are intended to identify those children "with potential language difficulties and those with already present specific language disabilities who are in need of special attention . . ." (Slingerland, 1970, p. xx). Although the title of the test and the promotional materials claim that the test identifies children with language disabilities, the test actually assesses visual, auditory, and kinesthetic abilities believed to form the foundation upon which later language learning is built. Neither theoretical nor empirical evidence is presented by Slingerland in the technical manuals to support the link between the test content and language disability.

The test is available at four levels: form A (end of first grade or beginning of second grade), form B (end of second grade or beginning of third grade), form C (end of third grade or beginning of fourth grade), and form D (beginning or end of grades 5 and 6). Separate manuals are available for forms A, B, and C (Slingerland, 1970) and form D (Slingerland, 1974). Eight subtests are regularly administered at all levels; a ninth subtest is administered on form D. The subtests can be given to groups of students. In addition, optional, individually administered subtests to assess auditory ability are available.

Descriptions of the nine regularly administered subtests follow.

Copying from a Wall Chart The student has the choice of copying a story in either manuscript or cursive writing.

Copying Words in Isolation The student copies ten words presented in manuscript style.

Recalling Words, Numbers, and Letters Students turn their answer booklets over and place their pencils on the floor. The teacher shows a stimulus (for example, "our") to the class for "approximately 10 seconds," withdraws the stimulus, pauses for "a few seconds," and instructs the students to find what they saw in a horizontal multiple-choice array. Students pick up their pencils, turn their answer sheets over, and mark their selection. The motor task is intended to interfere with recall.

Matching Words to Sample Students select from a vertical array of options the word that matches the word at the top of the column.

Drawing from Memory Students draw twelve stimuli (letters, words, numbers, and designs) from memory. Again, turning over their answer booklets and picking up their pencils from the floor are intended to interfere with recall.

Writing Letters, Numbers, and Words from Memory The teacher says the stimulus (for example, the letters "Ess," "Eye," "Wye"), pauses for "several seconds," and tells the students to pick up their pencils, turn over their booklets, and write what they heard. There are twelve stimuli. Students may use cursive or manuscript, but they can only use lower-case letters.

Writing the Initial and Ending Letter in Words   The teacher says one word at a time, and students write the initial letter of each of the ten words. Then the students are told to write the last letter of each of the next six words.

Recalling Words, Letters, and Numbers   The teacher reads the stimulus, pauses "for a few seconds," and asks the students to circle the one word, letter, or number read, choosing from a horizontal array of four options. There are twelve items.

Writing Answers to Questions (form D)   The students write down information requested by the teacher (for example, first and last name, name of the student's school).

Scores

Poor formations and self-corrections are summed, and, for unexplained reasons, both are treated as errors. Uncorrected errors, of course, are also treated as errors. Uncorrected errors include omissions, substitutions, insertions, reversals, inversions, transpositions, substitutions of capital letter for lowercase letter (or vice versa), poor integration of symbol parts (for example, failure to join the parts of a letter is an error), poor proportion (for drawings), misspellings, and poor spatial organization.

Scores on the first two subtests are summed and contrasted with the performance on the third through eighth subtests. Slingerland

(1970) advocates the use of "break-off points" —twelve to fifteen consistent errors on the third through eighth subtests are considered significant.

Reliability

A report by Fulmer (1980) accompanies the test materials. She studied 804 children in six school districts and provided data on the reliability of the Slingerland. For forms A through D, coefficient alpha was computed for visual and auditory composites and for the total score. For the visual composite, alpha ranged from .88 to .92; for the auditory composite, alpha ranged from .88 to .94. Coefficient alpha for total correct ranged from .93 to .96. Interscorer reliability was also computed for total errors for each form. Reliability ranged from .69 (form A) to .91 (form C); only form C had adequate interscorer reliability. Test-retest reliabilities for subtests and totals are also presented. The stabilities for subtests are generally dismal; of the thirty-three coefficients, only one exceeds .70, and only five exceed .59. Stabilities for the total scores range from .71 to .85. Fulmer also reported a study by Burns and Burns, who found generally higher stabilities for total scores (.86 to .96). Also of interest is stability of the categorization of students as "regular," "SLD," or "unready." Fulmer (1980) reports that from 71 to 87 percent of the time (depending on the grade level of the students) students were reclassified consistently upon retesting thirty days later. However, the classifications were based on more than the scores from the Slingerland.

Validity

Close examination of the Slingerland tests indicates that the content assesses perpetual-motor and memory functions in students. It is not a direct measure of language nor is it a direct measure of language disability, although it is conceivable that it predicts language function.

The empirical validity information does little to demonstrate that the device is a measure of language disability. Fulmer (1980) presents correlations between Slingerland total scores and scores from the Comprehensive Tests of Basic Skills. The numbers of students on whom the correlations are based range from nine to seventy-one; obtained correlations vary from $-.53$ to $-.86$. (The correlations are negative because errors are correlated with correct responses.) She also reports similar results from a study by Oliphant. Whatever the test measures, it correlates with achievement. Fulmer also conducted factor analysis of the Slingerland and found that the factor structure varied from age to age. This means that whatever the test is measuring differs at different ages. Finally, Fulmer reports a study that compared the performances of students recommended for placement in a SLD class with children who were not experiencing learning difficulties. "Generally, t-tests for the difference between mean errors on subtests for each group proved significant at the .05 level (except for some subtests on form C)" (Fulmer, 1980, p. 18).

The validity of the recommended interpretation of scores is not established in the manuals. No data are presented to demonstrate that a number of errors greater than the "break-off" might signal the possibility of specific language disability. Nor are data provided to show that difference between errors and errors plus self-corrections and poor formations is "an indication in itself of possible specific language disability," as Slingerland asserts (1970, p. 78).

SUMMARY

The Slingerland is an unnormed, group-administered screening device intended to identify children with specific language disabilities. The test has adequate consistency for screening, but it lacks adequate interscorer and test-retest reliability. The validity of the device has not been demonstrated. Indeed, the content of the test would lead one to assume that it is a test of perpetual abilities, not of language.

COPING WITH DILEMMAS IN CURRENT PRACTICE

The most serious problem in the assessment of written language is inserting a match between what is taught in the school curriculum and what is tested. The great variation in the time at which various skills and facts are taught renders a general test of achievement inappropriate. This dilemma also attends diagnostic assessment of written language. Commercially prepared tests have doubtful validity for planning individual programs and evaluating the progress of individual pupils. We recommend that teachers and diagnosticians construct criterion-referenced achievement tests that closely parallel the curricula that the students follow.

In those cases where normative data are required, there are three choices. Diagnosticians can select the devices that most closely parallel the curriculum, develop local norms, or select individual students for comparative purposes.

Care should be exercised in selecting *methods* of assessing language skills. For example, it is probably better to test pupils in ways that are familiar to them. Thus, if the teacher's weekly spelling test is from dictation, then spelling tests using dictation are probably superior to tests requiring the student to identify incorrectly spelled words.

SUMMARY

Written language and spelling are regularly assessed in the schools. Teachers routinely assess these skills with informal and criterion-referenced tests. Most standardized test batteries include subtests that assess language and spelling. Very few individually administered tests have been published that deal with these content areas. Three are reviewed in this chapter.

STUDY QUESTIONS

1. Why is it important to teach Standard American English in the public schools?
2. List and explain five components of written language.
3. Why is it important for spelling tests to correspond closely to the spelling words that teachers assign to their students?
4. List and explain three limitations on analyzing a pupil's English composition to assess skill in spelling, grammar, and punctuation.

ADDITIONAL READING

Cooper, C., & Odell, L. (1977). *Evaluating writing: Describing, measuring, judging.* Urbana, IL: National Council of Teachers of English. (Chapter 1: Holistic evaluation of writing; Chapter 2: Primary trait scoring.)

Graves, D. (1981). A new look at research on writing. In S. Haley-James (Ed.), *Perspectives on writing in grades 1–8.* Urbana, IL: National Council of Teachers of English.

Moss, P., Cole, N., & Khampalikit, C. (1982). A comparison of procedures to assess written language skills at grades 4, 7, and 10. *Journal of Educational Measurement, 19,* 37–47.

C·H·A·P·T·E·R 20

ASSESSMENT OF ADAPTIVE BEHAVIOR

Adaptive behavior is an elusive, deceptively simple concept. It refers to the extent to which individuals adapt themselves to the expectations of nature and society. Infants and preschool children are expected to conform to the normal course of maturation and development in language and cognitive functioning. The assessment of schoolage children and adolescents relies on the development of behaviors that enable them to perform adult roles. Adaptive behavior in adults is the conformity to and fulfillment of the roles that particular societies set for their adults. Adaptive behavior may also include avoidance of maladaptive behavior. What constitutes maladaptive behavior is determined by several factors: the social tolerance for particular behaviors, the context in which those behaviors are demonstrated, the status of the individual exhibiting the behavior, and the theoretical orientation of the person making the assessment.

The assessment of adaptive behavior differs from the assessment of other domains. Usually we just test the person. For adaptive behavior, we do not test the subject directly. Instead, we rely on the observation of a third person who is very familiar with the subject of the assessment. The diagnostician interviews this third person, who describes the typical behavior patterns of the subject. The subject's behavior is evaluated on this basis.

WHY DO WE ASSESS ADAPTIVE BEHAVIOR?

There are two major reasons for assessing adaptive behavior. The first is that mental retardation is generally defined, in part, as a failure in adaptive behavior. In theory, in order to classify a pupil as mentally retarded, one needs to assess adaptive behavior. More important, however, there are federal regulations and state school codes requiring that adaptive behavior be assessed before a pupil can be considered mentally retarded.

The second reason for assessing adaptive behavior is for program planning. Educational objectives in the domain of adaptive behavior are frequently developed for moderately and severely retarded individuals. Scales of adaptive behavior are often the source of educational goals.

TESTS OF ADAPTIVE BEHAVIOR

The five devices reviewed in the pages that follow are used most often with handicapped individuals. In addition, the Adaptive Behavior Inventory for Children (ABIC), which is a component of the System of Multicultural Pluralistic Assessment (SOMPA), is reviewed in Chapter 22.

VINELAND ADAPTIVE BEHAVIOR SCALE

The Vineland Adaptive Behavior Scale (VABS) is an individually administered scale given to an individual (such as a parent, caregiver, or teacher) familiar with the person who is the subject of the assessment. The VABS has been termed the 1984 revision of the Vineland Social Maturity Scale (VSMS). As would be expected, the revision entailed conversion of the old VSMS from an age scale to a much more modern point scale and complete restandardization. The revision is far more sweeping, however; thus the new VABS might better be considered a new device.

The VABS is available in three forms that have three separate technical manuals. Two forms are termed interview editions: the Expanded Form (Sparrow, Balla, & Cicchetti, 1984a) and the Survey Form (Sparrow, Balla, & Cicchetti, 1984b). The third form is the Classroom Edition (Harrison, 1985). The three forms vary in the number and types of items included as well as in the person who completes the form. The Survey Form contains 297 items and is intended to provide a general appraisal of the individual; it requires about 20 to 60 minutes to administer to a parent or caregiver. The Expanded Form contains 577 items and is intended to provide a comprehensive appraisal suitable for planning educational programs; it requires 60 to 90 minutes to administer to a parent or caregiver. The Classroom Edition contains 244 items and requires about 20 minutes for a teacher to complete.

Individual items form subdomains, and subdomains form domains. All three editions assess Communication, Daily Living Skills, Socialization, and Motor domains. The two interview editions also assess maladaptive behavior.

Communication This domain consists of three subdomains: receptive (for example, listens to a story for at least 20 minutes), expressive (for example, uses "around" as a preposition in a phrase), and written (for example, addresses letters correctly).

Daily Living This domain consists of three subdomains: personal (for example, dresses self completely, except for tying shoelaces), domestic (for example, puts clean clothes away without assistance), and community (for example, states current date when asked).

Socialization This domain consists of three subdomains: interpersonal (for example, shows desire to please caregiver), play and leisure time (for example, shares toys or possessions without being told to do so), and coping skills (for example, does not talk with food in mouth).

Motor Skills This domain consists of two subdomains: gross (for example, can jump over small objects) and fine (for example, can unlock key locks).

Maladaptive Behavior This domain consists of thirty-six behaviors. Part 1 contains twenty-seven maladaptive behaviors that are termed minor (for example, sucks thumb or finger, bites fingernails, is stubborn or sullen, and so forth); the nine behaviors included in Part 2 are considered more serious (for example, displays inappropriate sexual behavior, uses bizarre speech, rocks back and forth when sitting or standing).

The subdomains are not evenly distributed throughout the domain. For example, in Communication, the receptive subdomain is assessed, with one exception, totally in the first half of the domain, and the written subdomain is assessed exclusively in the second half of the domain.

SCORES

Within the Communication, Daily Living Skills, Socialization, and Motor domains, items between basal and ceiling are scored 2 (yes or usually), 1 (sometimes or partially), or 0 (no or never). Items may also be scored "DK" (respondent does not know) or "N" (no opportunity). In Part 1 of the Maladaptive Domain (minor maladaptive behaviors), items are scored 2 for usually, 1 for sometimes, or 0 for never or very seldom. In Part 2, items are scored for their intensity (severe, moderate, or absent). Subdomain scores are combined into domain scores, and the Communication, Daily Living Skills, Socialization, and Motor domains can be combined into an "Adaptive Behavior Composite."

Domain and composite scores can be transformed to standard scores (mean = 100, standard deviation = 15), percentile ranks, age equivalents, and adaptive levels—high (more than two standard deviations above the mean), moderately high (between one and two standard deviations above the mean), adequate (between one standard deviation above and one below the mean), moderately low (between one and two standard deviations below the mean), and low (more than two standard deviations below the mean).

NORMS

Several sets of norm groups are available. For the interview editions, a national sample of 3,000 individuals who ranged in age from newborn to 18 years, 11 months was tested. The sample is quite similar to the population at the time of the 1980 census in terms of geographic region, racial/ethnic group membership, parental education, and community size. For the Classroom Edition, 1,984 children between the ages of 3 and 12 years, 11 months were tested. The sample resembles the population at the time of the 1980 census with respect to racial/ethnic group membership. It appears unrepresentative with respect to geographic region (overrepresenting the north central region and underrepresenting the others), parental education (overrepresenting college educated and underrepresenting those with only a high school education or less), and community size (overrepresenting central city and underrepresenting rural areas). Supplementary samples are also available: institutionalized and noninstitutionalized mentally retarded adults and institutionalized children who were either emotionally disturbed, visually handicapped, or hearing impaired. The supplementary norms are not carefully described, but must be used for Part 2 of the Maladaptive Domain.

RELIABILITY

Interview Editions Internal consistency of the Survey Form was estimated by odd-even correlations corrected by the Spearman-Brown formula. For Communication, coefficients for the different age groups range from .73 to .94; only six of the fifteen coefficients equal or exceed .90. For Daily Living Skills, coefficients for the fifteen age groups range from .83 to .92; eight of the fifteen coefficients equal or exceed .90. For Socialization, the fifteen coefficients range from .78 to .94; only two of the fifteen coefficients equal or exceed .90. For Motor Skills, the six coefficients range from .70 to .95; only for the 0 to 0-11 age group is the reliability greater than .89. The estimated reliabilities for the Adaptive Behavior Composite are generally larger; the lowest coefficient is .89 for the 14-0 to 15-11 age group. Finally, the ten coefficients for Maladaptive Behavior (Part 1) ranged from .77 to .88. As could be anticipated, the estimated reliabilities for the subdomains are considerably lower.

The split-half correlations from the Survey Form were used "to estimate split-half reliability coefficients for the Expanded Form" (Sparrow, Balla, & Cicchetti, 1984a, p. 30).[1] For Communication, the reported coefficients for the fifteen age groups range from .84 to .97; only five of the fifteen coefficients are less than .90. For Daily Living Skills, coefficients for the fifteen age groups all exceed .90. For Socialization, the fifteen coefficients range from .88 to .97; only two of the fifteen coefficients are less than .90. For Motor Skills, the six coefficients range from .83 to .97; half of the coefficients are .90 or larger. The estimated reliabilities for the Adaptive Behavior Composite all exceed .93. The ten coefficients for Maladaptive Behavior (Part 1) range from .77 to .88. As could again be anticipated, the estimated reliabilities for the subdomains are considerably lower.

Stability is estimated by correlating raw scores for age groups. The fifteen age groups were combined into just six, however. Consequently, stability coefficients are inflated by the degree to which chronological age correlates with the raw scores. For Communication, the estimated stabilities for the six age groups ranged from .80 to .98; two coefficients were less than .90. For Daily Living Skills, the estimated stabilities ranged from .87 to .96; half of the coefficients were less than .90. For Socialization, they ranged from .77 to .92; only one exceeded .89. For the three combined age groups on the Motor Domain, two stability coefficients were below .90. Stability for the domain of maladaptive behavior ranged from .84 to .89 for the four age groups for which this domain is appropriate. The stability of composite scores is not reported.

Interrater agreement was assessed for 160 individuals who varied in age from 0-6 to 18-11. In these computations, the effect of chronological age on the correlations between rates was removed statistically.[2] For Communication and Daily Living Skills, interrater agreement exceeded .90; for Socialization and Motor Skills, it was less than .87.

Classroom Edition Coefficient alpha was used to estimate internal consistency for sub-

---

1. The procedure used rests on several assumptions; one requires that the "items in the Expanded Form constituted the complete universe from which a representative sample of about 48 percent was used to develop the Survey Form" (Sparrow, Balla, & Cicchetti, 1984a, p. 30). Of course if this assumption were met, then there would be no need to *estimate* reliability. Because the entire domain is supposedly tested by the Expanded Form, by most definitions the obtained scores must equal true scores. The amount of bias introduced by violating the assumptions is unknown.

2. First-order partial correlations were computed. Because this procedure was used for interrater agreement, it seems inconsistent not to have used it with stability estimates.

domains and domains for Forms A and E for ten age groups (a combined 3-0 to 4-11 group and nine one-year groups between 5-0 and 12-11). For Communication, alphas ranged from .88 to .95, with only one coefficient less than .89. For Daily Living Skills and Socialization, alphas ranged from .91 to .96. For Motor Skills, the two coefficients were .84 and .77. The Adaptive Behavior Composite exceeded .95 at each age.

VALIDITY

Evidence of the validity for the Classroom Edition and Survey Form comes from several sources. Content validity is difficult to assess because a precise definition of the domain to be assessed is never offered. The authors state that they conducted an intensive review of the child development literature and drew on their own clinical and research experiences to determine the four behavioral domains—Communication, Daily Living Skills, Socialization, and Motor Skills. How daily activities are related to adaptive behavior is unclear.

Evidence of construct validity comes from the correlation of VABS scores and chronological age. Results of factor analyses only partially confirm the subdomains, however. The differential performances of supplementary norm groups are also used to support the construct validity of the scale. In addition, correlations between VABS and intelligence-test scores are reported. Evidence for criterion-related validity comes from the correlation of the VABS with the original Vineland Social Maturity Scale, the Adaptive Behavior Inventory for Children, and the AAMD Adaptive Behavior Scale.

No independent evidence of criterion-related validity is offered for the Expanded Form. Rather, validity is estimated from correlations between the VABS Survey Form and the criterion measures discussed in the preceding paragraph.

SUMMARY

The Vineland Adaptive Behavior Scale is an individually administered, norm-referenced device intended to assess the adaptive and maladaptive behaviors of individuals under 19 years of age. Norming appears quite good. Reliability of the scale varies considerably, however, and only sometimes are the domains and subdomains suitable for use in making important individual decisions. Validity data are adequate.

AAMD ADAPTIVE BEHAVIOR SCALE FOR CHILDREN AND ADULTS

The American Association on Mental Deficiency Adaptive Behavior Scale for Children and Adults (AAMD ABS) (Nihira, Foster, Shellhaas, & Leland, 1975) is intended to provide information about "the way an individual maintains his or her personal independence in daily living or of how he or she meets the social expectations of his or her environment" (Nihira et al., 1975, p. 5). The authors state that scores from the AAMD ABS are useful for program planning and design, resource allocation, and program evaluation (pp. 44-45).

Like other measures of social competence, the scale may be administered to a third person, who is asked about the subject's performance. The scale may also be completed directly by diagnosticians if they are sufficiently familiar with the subjects. The scale consists of two parts. Part 1 contains sixty-six items that rate skill use in ten domains. There are several statements for each item. Some items require that the respondent check the one statement that best describes the subject; other items require that all statements applying to the subject be checked. Items are grouped into areas, and areas are grouped into domains. The ten domains that make up Part 1 are described below.

Independent Functioning   In this domain, skills are measured in eight areas: (1) four items relate to eating, from use of utensils to table manners; (2) two items deal with toilet use; (3) five items deal with cleanliness, from bathing to menstruation; (4) two items dealing with posture and clothing are clustered under the more general area of appearance; (5) one item assesses care of clothing; (6) three items measure dressing and undressing; (7) two items (sense of direction and use of public transportation) deal with travel; and (8) two items (telephone use and a miscellaneous item) assess other independent functioning.

Physical Development   In this domain, skills are measured by six items in two areas: (1) sensory function (vision and hearing) and (2) motor development (body balance, walking and running, control of hands, and limb function).

Economic Activity   In this domain, skills are assessed by four items in two areas: (1) money handling and budgeting, and (2) shopping skills.

Language Development   In this domain, skills are measured by nine items in three areas: (1) expression is assessed by five items (writing, preverbal expression, articulation, sentences, and word usage), (2) comprehension is assessed by two items (reading and complex instruc-

tions), and (3) social language development is assessed by two items (conversation and miscellaneous language development).

Numbers and Time   In this domain, skills are assessed by three items dealing with the understanding of numbers, time, and time concepts.

Domestic Activity   In this domain, skills are measured by six items in three areas: (1) cleaning (room cleaning and laundry), (2) kitchen (table setting, food preparation, and table clearing), and (3) other domestic activities.

Vocational Activity   In this domain, skills are assessed by three items in three areas: job complexity, job performance, and work habits.

Self-Direction   This domain consists of five items in three areas: (1) initiative (initiative and passivity), (2) perseverance (attention and persistence), and (3) leisure time.

Responsibility   In this domain, skills are measured by two items: personal belongings and general responsibility.

Socialization   In this domain, seven items sample both appropriate and inappropriate behaviors. Points are subtracted for inappropriate behavior.

Part 2 consists of forty-four items grouped into fourteen domains. All items in part 2 are scored in the same way. The respondent rates all statements in each item that apply to the subject with a 1 (occasionally) or a 2 (frequently). A description of the domains assessed in Part 2 follows.

Violent and Destructive Behavior   Five items assess personal violence, temper tantrums, and property damage.

Antisocial Behavior Six items assess teasing, bossiness, disruption, inconsiderate behavior, disrespect of others' property, and "angry" language (swearing, threatening, and so forth).

Rebellious Behavior Six items assess disobedience, noncompliance, or insubordination in matters related to regulations and routines; following instructions and requests; attitudes toward authority; absenteeism; running away; and misbehavior in group settings.

Untrustworthy Behavior This domain contains two items: lying and stealing.

Withdrawal This domain contains three items: inactivity, withdrawal, and shyness.

Stereotyped Behavior and Odd Mannerisms This domain contains two items described by the domain title.

Inappropriate Interpersonal Manners This domain contains one item.

Unacceptable Vocal Habits This domain also has one item.

Unacceptable or Eccentric Habits This domain contains four items: strange habits (for example, smelling everything), unacceptable oral habits (for example, biting fingernails), removing or tearing off clothing, and other eccentric habits (for example, sitting by things that vibrate).

Self-Abusive Behavior This domain contains one item.

Hyperactive Tendencies This domain also has one item.

Sexually Aberrant Behavior This domain contains four items dealing with masturbation, homosexuality, and socially unacceptable behavior such as rape.

Psychological Disturbance This domain contains seven items that explore possible emotional disturbances: overestimating own ability, reacting poorly to criticism, reacting poorly to frustration, demanding too much attention, feeling persecuted, having hypochondriacal tendencies, and having other signs of emotional disturbance (for example, vomiting when upset).

Use of Medication Use of medication for the control of hyperactivity, seizures, and so forth is considered by the authors of the scale to be maladaptive.

Three observations, applicable to statements on both parts of the scale, are especially noteworthy. First, many of the behaviors, when exhibited by normal individuals, are not considered maladaptive or aberrant (for example, "using prescribed medications," "sits with knees under chin," "pulls threads out of own clothing," and so on). Second, many statements are not only overly value-laden but also unnecessarily subjective. For example, hugging "too intensely" in public is viewed as unacceptable sexual behavior. One wonders to whom the hugging is too intense—the huggee or the observer? Third, there is a lack of proportion in the scale. For example, being overly seductive in appearance carries as much weight as raping someone. Similarly, one is given as many points for acting sick after an illness as for attempting suicide.

SCORES

Raw scores for domains are summed and may be converted into deciles (although the tables are labeled "percentile ranks"). (Deciles are not available for several domains for younger subjects.) In Part 1, the higher the decile rank, the better the development of the person. In Part 2, the higher the decile rank, the more maladaptive the person's behavior.

NORMS

Norms are based on the ratings of approximately four thousand persons residing in sixty-eight institutions. Eleven age groups were used, ranging from a 3-year-old group to a 50- to 69-year-old group. The number of persons in the age group ranges from 528 at 10 to 12 years of age to ninety-seven at 3 years of age. Mean IQs (tests unspecified) for each age group range from 28 at age 3 to 45.8 at ages 16 to 18.

There are several significant problems with the norms. First, the reference population for the scale is an institutionalized population. Thus any person being tested is being compared to individuals who have poor levels of adaptation, not to the overall population. Second, the ability levels of the comparison groups increase each year. Thus a person who maintains exactly the same relative position in the general population will receive lower scores on the AAMD ABS each year because of the increased ability levels in the comparison group. Third, although changes were made in several items and although there are directions "for conversion of scores on the 1969 form of ABS to equivalent scores on the 1974 Revision" (Nihira et al., 1975, p. 51), the norms of the two editions appear to be identical.

RELIABILITY

Only interrater reliability is considered in the manual. Pearson product-moment correlation coefficients were used to estimate agreement by attendants for 133 institutionalized persons who ranged in age from 4 to 69 and resided in one of three institutions. These coefficients, probably inflated because of range extension, ranged from .71 (Self-Direction) to .93 (Physical Development) for the first part and from .37 (Unacceptable Vocal Habits) to .77 (Use of Medications) for the second part. Only two domains have adequate reliability for use in making important educational decisions.

No evidence of stability or internal consistency is presented in the manual.

VALIDITY

The content validity of the scale is questionable for several reasons. First, the overriding concern is that the authors present no conceptualization of the domain used to guide inclusion and exclusion of items. Second, many items do not assess behavior; they assess physical and emotional states. Third, many items that are termed maladaptive on the scale probably should not be considered to be maladaptive.

Very limited evidence of the validity of the scale is presented in the technical manual. Factor analysis supports, in part, the division of the scale into two parts. Because the scale was developed from a series of factor-analytic studies, however, this finding is hardly surprising.

The summarized results of three unreferenced studies are offered as evidence of "practical validity." One study was summarized as showing that Part 1 scores agreed with clinical judgments about the level of adaptive behavior exhibited by institutionalized retarded adults. The second study was summarized as showing that the scores from Part 2 were different for people who had been placed into different administrative units, such as "medical, educational, vocational, preplacement, and release units" (Nihira et al., 1975, p. 48). The third study showed that three domain scores changed after a two-year intervention.

Summary

The AAMD ABS is poorly standardized, and its norms should now be considered old; pre- sented estimates of reliability are inadequate (no estimates of stability or internal consis- tency are provided); and evidence of validity is very limited. Although the scale is *not* labeled as an experimental device, it is best suited for that purpose. Moreover, it should probably not be used as a norm-referenced device.

AAMD Adaptive Behavior Scale, School Edition

Separate manuals and norms for the AAMD Adaptive Behavior Scale were prepared for use in the schools by Lambert, Windmiller, and colleagues. Three domains (Domestic Activity, Self-Abusive Behavior, and Sexually Aberrant Behavior) not readily observed in or pertinent to school were deleted. The AAMD Adaptive Behavior Scale, School Edition (ABS-SE) (Lambert & Windmiller, 1981) is the latest edition of the scale. The items remain essen- tially the same as those in the 1974 edition although some renaming has occurred. Teach- ers are the preferred respondents. The speci- men kit includes an Administration and In- structional Planning Manual, a Diagnostic and Technical Manual, an Instructional Planning Profile, a Diagnostic Profile, and a Parent's Guide: Using the Adaptive Behavior Scale to Identify Children's Special Needs.

The scale is intended to provide information about students' "personal independence and social skills and to reveal areas of functioning where special program planning" is needed (Lambert, Windmiller, Tharinger, & Cole, 1981, p. 3). Part 1 of the scale consists of nine domains intended to assess adaptive behavior; part 2 consists of twelve domains assessing per- sonality and behavior disorders. If the scale is given as an adjunct in instructional planning or program evaluation, the authors recommend combining the domains from part 1 into clus-

ters: physical development, cognitive develop- ment, personal independence, volitional skills, and socialization (Lambert et al., 1981). If a more general overview of adaptive behavior is desired, one can construct a "diagnostic" pro- file that consists of five clusters of domains (derived from factor analytic studies of adaptive behavior of adults and children):[3] personal self-sufficiency, community self-sufficiency, personal-social responsibility, social adjust- ment, and personal adjustment.

Scores

Raw scores are converted to scaled scores that have a mean of 10 and a standard deviation of 3. Raw scores are also converted to "converted

---

3. In the Diagnostic and Technical Manual, Lambert cites four studies to support her contention that there are five factors on the ABS-SE. Two studies were conducted with adults (Guarmaccia, 1976; Nihira, 1969a). Two studies were done with children and adolescents. Lambert and Nicoll (1976) found two factors in part 1 that they named functional autonomy and interpersonal adjustment; they also found two factors, named social responsibility and intrapersonal adjustment, in part 2. The second study by Nihira (1969b), using an earlier version of the AAMD Adaptive Behavior Scale with institutionalized retarded persons, found three factors: personal independence, social maladaption, and personal maladaption. It is unclear how these studies support the existence of five factors.

factor scores," which are in turn converted to "comparison scores." Comparison scores can be converted to cumulative percentages (the percentage of the sample earning lower scores).

The guidelines for interpreting the scores offered in the manual are misleading. We are told that "Domain score percentiles provide information about the relative standing of a student" (Lambert, 1981, p. 10) although there are no tables for converting to percentiles. (Cumulative frequencies are not percentiles; cumulative frequencies will differ substantially from percentiles when the samples are small or when several individuals earn the same raw score.) We are also told that serious deficits in adaptive behavior are indicated by percentile ranks below the 10th percentile (except for four domains where the critical number is the 15th percentile) and factor scores more than one standard deviation below the mean (that is, less than 7).

NORMS

The standardization sample consists of five samples and is inadequately described in the manuals. Sample 1 consists of 2,135 children from the 1974 standardization sample of 2,600 California children between the ages of 7 and 13 who were attending regular classes or classes for the educable or trainable mentally retarded in 1972-1973. Sample 2 consists of 3,220 children between the ages of 3 and 16 attending regular classes or classes for the educable or trainable mentally retarded in Florida. Sample 3 consists of 363 regular and trainable mentally retarded preschoolers (between the ages of 3 and 6) living in California and Florida. Sample 4 consists of 656 California educable and trainable mentally retarded persons between the ages of 6 and 16 "whose reevaluations indicated continued special education placement" (Lambert, 1981, p. 22). Sample 5

consists of 149 California adolescents between the ages of 13 and 16. Frequencies of individuals in the normative samples are provided by ethnic status, urbanization (urban, suburban, rural), classification (regular class, educable mentally retarded, trainable mentally retarded), and socioeconomic status (high, middle, and low). No data are presented to demonstrate that the sample is representative of any population. Only about 34 percent of the sample is considered "regular."

Separate norm tables are provided for students attending regular programs, programs for the educable mentally retarded (EMR), and programs for the trainable mentally retarded (TMR). For children between the ages of 3 to 4 and 6 to 7, conversion tables for regular and TMR pupils are available. From 7 to 8 to 15 to 16 conversion tables are available for regular, EMR, and TMR students. Tables for EMR students and TMR students are available for ages 16 to 17. The number of pupils in each age for each classification group varies considerably. Eighteen of the thirty-seven norm tables are based on fewer than 100 individuals. For TMR students, the size of the norm group varies from 29 to 110; for EMR students, size varies from 88 to 608; for students in regular classes, size varies from 39 to 320.

RELIABILITY

Coefficient alpha was used to compute the internal consistency of each factor score at each age for pupils in regular classes as well as for EMR students and TMR students. For regular-class pupils, reliabilities ranged from .96 to .38; forty-two of the sixty-five age x factor coefficients are less than .90. For EMR students, coefficients ranged from .95 to .34; thirty-five of the fifty age x factor coefficients are less than .90. For TMR students, coefficients ranged from .94 to .27; of the seventy age x factor coefficients, forty-eight are less than .90.

No reliability data for domain scores or for total or composite scores are reported. No data on stability are reported.

VALIDITY

Construct validity was established by correlating IQs and domain scores. The obtained correlations ranged from .18 to .63 for part 1 and from .28 to -.23 for part 2. Domain scores are associated with regular or EMR placement. Factor scores were also correlated with achievement test scores for both regular and EMR students in the Florida sample. Although there is considerable mention of factors in the ABS-SE, no data are presented demonstrating that five factors are obtained when one analyzes the ABS-SE.

Of special interest is the comparison score. The statistical procedures used were designed to optimize discriminations among regular students and EMR students and TMR students. The difficulty, of course, is that adaptive behavior is only one of several criteria used to

place pupils in special programs for the retarded.

No data are provided to demonstrate that critical scores (below the 10th or 15th percentile on domains or more than one standard deviation below the mean on factor scores) are indeed suggestive of unusual problems.

SUMMARY

The school edition of the AAMD Adaptive Behavior Scale contains essentially the same items that are found on the institutional instrument from which it was derived. However, it contains three fewer domains and some minor changes in wording. The norms are fast becoming dated, do not appear representative, and, in some of the norm groups, have a too limited number of children to provide stable interindividual comparisons. Although the avowed purpose of the instrument is to aid in placement and program-planning decisions, the reliability of the scale is not adequate for these purposes. Validity for the interpretation of the various scores is also suspect.

ADAPTIVE BEHAVIOR INVENTORY

The Adaptive Behavior Inventory (ABI) (Brown & Leigh, 1986a) is a norm-referenced scale appropriate for use with students who range in age from 6-0 to 18-11. The ABI is intended to be used to provide information about adaptive behavior during the diagnosis of mental retardation, to make intraindividual comparisons among various components of adaptive behavior, and to evaluate instructional programs designed to affect a student's adaptation. Like other adaptive behavior measures, it

is administered by having a respondent answer questions about the subject being assessed. The preferred respondent for the ABI is "the classroom teacher or other professional who has relevant contact with the student being assessed" (Brown & Leigh, 1986b, p. 4). It is particularly praiseworthy that ABI users are urged to postpone administration of the device if a rater cannot be found who has had sufficient contact with the student to provide complete and reliable information.

The ABI consists of five subtests that can be given independently in about five minutes each.

Self-Care Skills   This subtest contains thirty items that range from going from one school area to another to grooming to being aware of social-service agencies.

Communication Skills   This subtest contains thirty items that range from communicating one's needs orally to describing abstract ideas in writing.

Social Skills   This subtest contains thirty-two items that range from referring to others by name to sharing to organizing and leading groups.

Academic Skills   This subtest contains thirty items that range from identifying alphabet letters and one's own name to taking adequate notes to performing advanced mathematical tasks.

Occupational Skills   This subtest contains twenty-eight items that range from being punctual to supervising the work of others.

A short form of the ABI is also available. It contains a sample of items from each subtest.

SCORES

Individual items are scored using a four-point scale, through which the respondent indicates that a person does not perform the behavior (0 points), a person is beginning to perform the behavior (1 point), a person performs the behavior most of the time (3 points), and a person has mastered the behavior (4).

Raw scores on each subtest can be converted into percentiles and standard scores (mean = 100, standard deviation = 15). If four or five subtests are administered, a weighted composite deviation score can also be obtained.

NORMS

Two sets of norms are available. One set, the normal intelligence sample, is intended to be representative of students in the general U.S. population; the other set is intended to be representative of mentally retarded pupils in special educational programs and residential facilities. Sampling plans are not provided for either normative sample, and the samples are poorly described.

The normal intelligence sample is composed of about 1,300 individuals who ranged in age from 5-0 to 18-11 and resided in twenty-four states. This sample, as a whole, corresponds to the population at the time of the 1980 census in terms of sex, race, ethnicity, geographic area, and socioeconomic status. However, the correspondense of each age group on these characteristics is not described.

The mentally retarded sample is composed of about 1,100 individuals from the same age range drawn from the same twenty-four states. This sample, as a whole, corresponds to the population at the time of the 1980 census in terms of sex and measured IQ. The sample underrepresents students in special day schools.

RELIABILITY

Internal consistency was estimated by coefficient alpha. Adjacent age groups were combined (five- and six-year-olds, seven- and eight-year-olds, and so forth), and the responses for fifty individuals from each age group of the standardization groups were randomly selected. For the normal intelligence groups, forty-two coefficients were computed (five subtests and total score at the seven ages). The thirty-five subtest-by-age coefficients ranged from .86 (for the 5- and 6-year-old group) to .97; twenty-five of the thirty-five coefficients equaled or exceeded .90. All of the coefficients for the total ABI score exceeded .90. The internal consistency of the ABI short form also exceeded .90 for each of the age groups.

Stability was estimated by test-retest reliability using thirty-nine students of normal intelligence who ranged in age from 5 to 18 and fifty-six mentally retarded students who ranged in age from 6 to 18. The effects of age were held constant statistically.[4] Estimated stabilities for the subtests, the composite, and the short-form composite all exceeded .90.

VALIDITY

Validity data are reported superficially. Thus most of the evidence provided is difficult to evaluate. Inspection of the items included in the ABI may provide some evidence of content validity. Some items are too subjective, however, and criteria for scoring/marking each item may not be clear to the person completing the form. For example, teachers are asked to rate a student's performance on *intermediate* reading tasks, understanding of *basic* measurement concepts, knowledge of the *approximate* cost of common items, and so forth.

As evidence of criterion-related validity, the authors provide correlations with teacher judgments of adaptive behavior and modest to high correlations with the AAMD Adaptive Behavior Scale and the Vineland Adaptive Behavior Scale. These studies are incompletely described, however, so it is difficult to evaluate the ABI's criterion-related validity.

As evidence of construct validity, the authors offer the correlations of the ABI with achievement tests, intelligence tests, and age, as well as the intercorrelations of the ABI's subtests. Finally, to show construct validity, the performances of retarded and normal students in the standardization samples were compared. "In every instance, there were significant differences between each of the pairwise comparisons of the groups, with higher ABI means attributed to students in less restrictive classroom environments" (Brown & Leigh, 1986b, p. 40).

SUMMARY

The ABI is a norm-referenced scale that assesses five aspects of adaptive behavior through the ratings of the student's teacher. The norms appear adequate, and the device appears to have adequate reliability and validity.

SCALES OF INDEPENDENT BEHAVIOR

The Scales of Independent Behavior (SIB) (Bruininks, Woodcock, Weatherman, & Hill, 1984) is an individually administered,

norm-referenced device suitable for use with individuals ranging in age from infancy through adulthood. The SIB's primary use is "to identify individuals who lack adaptive functional independence in particular settings" (Bruininks, Woodcock, Weatherman, & Hill,

---

4. Partial correlation was used. In essence, this procedure gives the average test-retest correlation at each age.

1985, p. 3). Additional uses include aiding in the development of individualized education plans (IEPs) and individually prescribed programs (IPPs), in the selection and placement of individuals within programs of education and training, in guidance, in the assessment of individual gains following intervention, in program management and evaluation, and in research. Like other measures of adaptive behavior, the SIB is administered to a respondent who is thoroughly familiar with the subject who is being assessed.

Adaptive behavior items are arranged into fourteen subscales; subscales are grouped into four clusters. The Motor Skills cluster consists of two subscales: gross motor skills and fine motor skills. The Social Interaction and Communication Skills cluster consists of three subscales: social interaction, language comprehension, and language expression. The Personal Living Skills cluster consists of five subscales: eating and meal preparation, dressing, toileting, personal self-care, and domestic skills. The Community Living Skills cluster consists of four subscales: time and punctuality, money and value, work skills, and home and community orientation. The clusters can be combined into a total score called "Broad Independence." Also included in the SIB are four maladaptive behavior indices: General Maladaptive Behavior, Internalized Maladaptive Behavior, Asocial Maladaptive Behavior, and Externalized Maladaptive Behavior (Bruininks et al., 1985, pp. 11–12). Finally, two short-form options are available, the Short Form Scale and the Early Primary Scale.

Scores

A variety of norm-referenced scores are available for adaptive behavior: age equivalents, percentile ranks, standard scores (mean = 100, standard deviation = 15), and normal curve equivalents. Also available are instructional ranges, relative performance indices,[5] functioning levels ("very superior" to "severe deficit"), and adjusted adaptive behavior scores (comparisons with Woodcock-Johnson IQs). Three different scores are available for the maladaptive indices: stanines, maladaptive behavior indices, and levels of seriousness.

Norms

Norms, developed using Rasch scaling techniques, were based on interviews for over 1,700 subjects who ranged in age from 3 months to 44 years. A detailed sampling plan is provided. The normative sample was intended to approximate the U.S. population in terms of sex, race, community size (urban and urban fringe, outside urban area, rural), geographic region (eleven states in nine regions), and socioeconomic status. In the construction of the norms, individual subjects were weighted so that the figures would correspond exactly with those of the national census.

Reliability

Corrected split-half estimates of reliability are provided for each subscale and scale for thirteen age groups ranging from 0-3/0-11 to 29 years and older. The 182 reliability coefficients range from .00 to .95, with fourteen equaling or exceeding .90. Many of the poor reliabilities are the result of floor and ceiling effects. For example, the coefficients that equaled 0 were located at the 0-3/0-11 age group for behaviors such as domestic skills and time and punc-

5. The RPI is a fractional index (for example, 75/90) indicating "the percent of independence predicted for a given subject on a set of tasks that a reference group can perform with 90% accuracy" (Bruininks et al., 1985, p. 14).

tuality. When reliabilities are estimated across all age levels, however, no subscale has a reliability equal to or greater than .90. Cluster reliabilities are substantially higher: reliabilities for Motor Skills range from .64 to .93; Social and Communication Skills, from .85 to .93; Personal Living Skills, from .85 to .95; and Community Living Skills, from .67 to .94. The total score "Broad Independence" is very reliable, equaling or exceeding .95 for all age groups. Internal-consistency estimates are not provided for the maladaptive indices.

Stability estimates are provided for two age groups (6-8 and 10-11) for the adaptive subscales, clusters, Broad Independence, and maladaptive indices. For the 6-8 age group, subscale stabilities ranged from .67 to .94; only two subscales had coefficients equal to or greater than .90. For the 10-11 age group, stabilities ranged from .51 to .88. The clusters, as expected, had higher coefficients. Only for Motor Skills was the coefficient less than .90 for the younger group; for the older group, coefficients ranged from .71 to .88. Stabilities for Broad Independence for the older and younger groups were .96 and .87, respectively. The maladaptive indices for the two age groups ranged from .75 to .90.

Finally, data are provided on rater agreement and interinterviewer agreement. Correlations were very high—.90 or higher.

VALIDITY

Content validity was established through delineation of the domain and careful item selection. Criterion-related validity was investigated by correlating SIB scores with scores on the AAMD Adaptive Behavior Scale (Public School edition). Correlations between SIB cluster scores and ABS factor scores ranged from .59 to .91. Also, the SIB scores correlate moderately with Woodcock-Johnson Psychoeduca-

tional Battery Broad Cognitive scores. Maladaptive indices were correlated with results of the Revised Problem Behavior Checklist (RPBC) (Quay & Peterson, 1983); the pattern of correlations supports the validity of the SIB (for example, the Asocial Maladaptive Behavior Index of the SIB correlates better with scores on the Socialized Aggression, Attention Problems, and Motor Excess scales of the RPBC than with scores on the other subscales of the RPBC).

Construct validity was established in several ways. Adaptive behavior was demonstrated to increase with age (although maladaptive behavior was, essentially, unrelated to age). Several studies were conducted in which the scores of special populations (for example, trainable mentally retarded individuals) in several age ranges were compared to those of nonhandicapped persons drawn at random from the normative sample. The comparisons showed that the SIB consistently assigned lower adaptivity to handicapped persons. Moreover, differences in adaptive behavior were on expected dimensions. For example, hearing-impaired individuals earned significantly lower scores on the Social Interaction and Language Comprehension subscales and on the Social Interaction and Communication Skills cluster.

SUMMARY

The Scales of Independent Behavior is an individually administered, norm-referenced adaptive behavior scale that is useful with individuals ranging in age from infancy through adulthood. The SIB includes four clusters of adaptive behavior (Motor Skills, Social Interaction and Communication Skills, Personal Living Skills, and Community Living Skills) and four maladaptive behavior indices (General Maladaptive Behavior, Internalized Maladaptive Behavior, Asocial Maladaptive Behavior, and Externalized Maladaptive Behavior). Norms appear to be representative of the general U.S. population. Evidence for the SIB's reliability is mixed. Subscales and scales often have relatively poor reliability, although Broad Independence is highly reliable at all ages. Evidence for the validity of the scale is excellent.

COPING WITH DILEMMAS IN CURRENT PRACTICE

There are three severe problems in the use of currently available instruments to assess adaptive behavior. The first problem is professional consensus about what constitutes adaptive behavior. Reading the definitions offered in the scientific literature and inspecting the behaviors sampled by the various devices indicate a lack of agreement about adaptive behavior. Indeed, there is a broad range of behaviors sampled and orientations toward measurement. Without better agreement on the concept of adaptive behavior, one must exercise great care in making definitive statements about a person's adaptive behavior based on any one scale. In our opinion, diagnosticians should specify clearly the various aspects of adaptive behavior they wish to assess with one or more scales. In the absence of appropriate scales, the only option may be to develop one's own scale with local norms.

The second problem is more technical. Scales of adaptive behavior require that pupils be rated by people who are very familiar with them. There are numerous possibilities for bias; they range from ignorance to inaccurate statements about the student. There are at least three ways to deal with this potential problem. It is important for diagnosticians to encourage respondents to admit freely that they do not know particular facts about the pupil. Another strategy that a diagnostician can use is actual observation of the pupil. Many of the skills and behaviors assessed on the various adaptive behavior scales are observable and are of sufficiently high frequency that an observer would be able to note them in a relatively short time. A final strategy would be to interview two respondents about one pupil. Although it is possible that both respondents would be mistaken in their evaluations of a pupil, the risk should be substantially reduced.

The third problem is that scales of adaptive behavior are typically inadequate from a technical point of view. They are poorly normed (sometimes only on handicapped populations) and have limited reliability—two very serious shortcomings. If the norm samples are unrepresentative, they should not be used. An alternative to unrepresentative norms is simply to isolate one or two students to use for comparison. Teachers or parents can be asked to nominate individuals of the same age and sex who they believe have "adapted" successfully. The behavior of these adaptive peers can then be used to make rather simple comparisons. Although one or two children certainly are no substitute for a normative sample, they may prove adequate for some comparisons. Inadequate reliability poses a more serious problem. If interobserver agreement and internal consistency are inadequate, the definition of the domain and the particular behavior that is being observed will have to be reworked. For commercially prepared devices, this boils down to making up a new instrument. Until this is done, diagnosticians may be forced to rely on observations and more general appraisals of individuals within the peer group.

SUMMARY

In the assessment of adaptive behavior we are interested in what an individual regularly does, not what the individual is capable of doing. Ultimately, the behaviors of interest in adults are those that allow individuals to manage their affairs sufficiently well that they do not require societal intervention to protect them or others. The behaviors that are believed to be important vary from time to time and from theory to theory. In general, in the United States, adults are expected to exercise reasonable care of themselves (health, dressing, eating, and so on), to work, and to engage in socially acceptable recreational or leisure activities. In children and adolescents, the behaviors of interest are those that are believed to enable the desired adult behaviors and skills.

The assessment of adaptive behavior usually takes the form of a structured interview with a person (for example, a parent or teacher) who is very familiar with the person being assessed (the subject of the interview). The assessment of adaptive behavior has been plagued by inadequate instruments—scales that lack reliability and are poorly normed. One must select scales (or parts of scales) with great care.

STUDY QUESTIONS

1. How does the assessment of adaptive behavior differ from the assessment of academic achievement?
2. What criteria would be appropriate to classify a behavior as maladaptive?
3. With the introduction of computers and robots to American industry, what do you think will happen to current definitions of adaptive behavior?
4. Do you think adaptive behavior ranges from absent to highly developed, or does it range from absent to adequate? Why?

ADDITIONAL READING

Reschly, D. (1982). Assessing mild mental retardation: The influence of adaptive behavior, sociocultural status, and prospects for nonbiased assessment. In C. Reynolds and T. Gutkin (Eds.), *Handbook of school psychology* (pp. 220–236). New York: Wiley.

Schmidt, M., & Salvia, J. (1984). Adaptive behavior: A conceptual analysis. *Diagnostique, 9* (2), 117–125.

C·H·A·P·T·E·R 21

ASSESSMENT OF INFANTS, TODDLERS, AND PRESCHOOL CHILDREN

The format of this chapter differs from that of previous chapters for two reasons. First, in each of the preceding chapters tests of a particular domain were reviewed, but no particular domain of items or tests is uniquely used with infants, toddlers, and preschool children. Tests and techniques from many domains are used. Although downward extensions of other measures are often used with these children, the practice of assessing infants, toddlers, and preschool children is unique, because infants and preschool children are qualitatively different from children of elementary school age. Second, the uses to which assessment information is put at this level are different from the uses of the tests previously discussed.

To engage in accurate assessment at this level requires a good working knowledge of normal development for infants and preschoolers. And it requires a good understanding of the environments in which infants, toddlers, and preschool children spend their time. Thus, those who assess infants and preschool children must understand family systems and functioning and be able to work with families and caregivers in gathering assessment information. They must also know about the organization and meaning of infant behavior.

THE IMPETUS FOR ASSESSMENT OF INFANTS, TODDLERS, AND PRESCHOOL CHILDREN

School systems are playing an increasingly important role in assessment and intervention with infants, toddlers, and preschool children. Much of this activity is in direct response to recent legislation mandating that schools serve very young students who are handicapped. In the recent past, very young children who were handicapped received services from physicians, hospitals, developmental-achievement centers in communities, or from community mental-health centers. Public schools are now viewed as having responsibility for delivery of services to these children, and are now seen as legitimate providers of service.

Two factors have contributed to the push for early intervention and the assessment activities associated with it. First, developmental psychologists increasingly have shown the importance of early experience in the development of individuals. More importantly, they have shown that early experience is malleable, and have illustrated the developmental plasticity of intelligence. Earlier, psychologists thought that intelligence was fixed, so there was little reason to intervene in children's development to try to influence their later accomplishments. Second, the federal government now sponsors early-intervention programs, especially those designed for poor children, and federal legislation has been passed mandating early intervention for students who are handicapped.

The Handicapped Children's Early Education Assistance Act, passed by Congress in 1968 established the Handicapped Children's Early Education Model Program, which led to establishment of Child Service Demonstration Centers designed to show the effectiveness of early-intervention programs. In 1975, as part of Public Law 94-142, schools were required to serve children down to age 5. Major advances occurred with passage of Public Law 99-457 in 1986.

PL 99-457 has two major provisions, Part B and Part H, that pertain to assessment of infants, toddlers, and preschool children who are handicapped. Part B of the law says that by 1990–91 states must have in place services for children ages 3 to 5 who are handicapped. This part of the law extends PL 94-142 downward to age 3. States can serve any child who meets the criteria for one or more conditions specified in PL 94-142, but they do not have to assign the child a category. That is, they do not have to label preschool children in order to serve them.

Part H extends services to children birth to 3 years of age who have a physical or mental condition (such as cerebral palsy or Down syndrome) that has a high probability of resulting in developmental delay, or are at risk medically or environmentally for developmental delay, or have delays in one or more of the following areas: cognitive, physical, language and speech, psychosocial, or self-help. States must have services in place by the fifth year of their participation in these activities. Part H requires the development of an Individual Family Service Plan (IFSP) developed by a multidisciplinary team who meets with the parents. Components of the IFSP are as follows: (1) a statement of the child's present levels of development (cognitive, speech and language, psychosocial, motor, and self-help); (2) a statement of the family's strengths and needs relating to enhancing the child's development; (3) a statement of major outcomes expected to be achieved for the child and family, (4) the criteria, procedures, and timelines for determining progress; (5) the specific early-intervention services necessary to meet the unique needs of the child and family, including the method, frequency, and intensity of service; (6) the projected dates for initiation of services and expected duration; (7) the name of the case manager, and (8) the procedures for transition to early intervention in the preschool program.

PURPOSES OF ASSESSMENT OF INFANTS, TODDLERS, AND PRESCHOOL CHILDREN
Eligibility for Preschool Programs and Preschool Screening

We use readiness and developmental tests with young children much as we use achievement tests with students who are enrolled in schools—as measures of attainment before formal schooling. Since special education services are frequently available for preschoolers, some form of attainment testing is needed to ascertain whether a child needs or is eligible for some form of special service. When used with children about to enter school, tests give school personnel some idea of what to expect from incoming students. Such information may actually be used to exclude unready students or to track pupils into various programs. For children who have been in school for some time, tests may be used to assess beginning skills for particular curricula (music or math, for example).

Early screening is based on the notions of prevention and developmental plasticity. It is believed that the behavior and cognition of young children is malleable and that early intervention will facilitate appropriate development. The Early and Periodic Screening, Diagnosis and Treatment (EPSDT) program is a nationwide screening and referral-to-service program established in 1972. The goals of the program and (1) early identification of young children with special needs, and (2) connection of children from low-income families with medical services. Those who engage in screening of young children are often part of Child Find activities. Child Find is defined as "A systematic process of identifying infants and children who are eligible or potentially eligible for enrollment in intervention programs" (Wolery, 1989, p. 120).

Neurobiological Appraisal

Early-childhood special educators now are required to assess and develop interventions for newborn infants. Such assessment typically involves neurobiological appraisal, which has its origins in medicine (specifically in pediatrics and neurology) rather than in education.

TABLE 21.1   Tests Used in Assessment of Newborns

Assessment of Preterm Infant Behavior (Als, Lester, Tronick, & Brazelton, 1982)

Graham-Rosenblith Behavior Test for Neonates (Rosenblith, 1961)

Neurological Assessment of the Preterm and Full Term Newborn Infant
(Dubowitz & Dubowitz, 1981)

Neonatal Behavioral Assessment Scale (Brazelton, 1984)

Naturalistic Observation of the Preterm Infant (Als, 1984)

Neurobiological appraisal involves assessment in four areas: neurological integrity, behavioral organization and needs, temperament, and state of consciousness. When assessors examine neurological integrity, they look for signs of brain injury by looking at reflexes, postural responses, and developmental level. They assess behavioral organization by looking at the infant's competence in attending and responding to social stimuli. They examine temperament by looking at how infants relate to their caregivers (mothers or others). In doing so, they look at sensitivity, involvement, and responsiveness. Tests used in assessing newborns are listed in Table 21.1.

Assessors use these measures with neonates to assess such things as heart rate, color, respiratory regularity, visceral signs, posture, muscle tone, movements, states, attention, and quality of responsiveness.

A fourth major factor assessed in conducting infant appraisals is state of consciousness. Prechtl (1974) describes six states: quiet sleep, active sleep, drowsy, quiet awake, active awake, and distress. Infants are not assessed when they are asleep; the other states are defined in Table 21.2.

People who assess infants must take into account the infant's state. They should contact nursery attendants or parents and find out when the infant is alert and then arrange to test the infant at that time. Those who assess infants must be careful not to disturb them unduly. Infants show distress when approached by strangers. Bailey and Rouse (1989) report that "beginning at developmental age 6-8 months and continuing through approximately 18 months, infants show varying degrees of distress when approached by unfamiliar adults" (p. 49). Distance matters; so keep your distance. Infants show a better response to strangers when held by their caregiver. It is generally recommended that parents be present when infants are assessed. It is also strongly recommended that preschoolers be assessed in the *absence* of their parent(s). The exception, of course, is when toddlers or preschoolers are extremely fearful or shy. Many other factors must also be considered in assessing infants and preschoolers. Bailey and Rouse (1989, p. 50) state that "infants and preschoolers may have high activity levels, be easily distracted, display variable states and attention spans, be wary of strangers, and display inconsistent performance in strange situations."

TABLE 21.2   Infant States of Consciousness

Drowsy: eyes open and close; eyes are "heavy-lidded" and have dull, glazed appearance. Infant may respond to sensory stimuli although responses are usually delayed.

Quiet Awake: eyes wide open; limited motor activity, child is quite alert to environment, primarily through visual modality.

Active Awake: eyes wide open with accompanying motor activity; occasional periods of fussiness; increased sensitivity to disturbing contextual stimuli.

Distress: characterized by crying, grimacing, and increased motor activity

SOURCE: From Bailey, D. B., & Rouse, T. L. (1989), Procedural considerations in assessing infants and preschoolers with handicaps. In D. B. Bailey & M. Wolery (Eds.), *Assessing infants and preschoolers with handicaps.* Columbus, OH: Merrill. Pp. 48–49. Copyright © 1989 by Merrill Publishing. Reprinted with permission of Merrill, an imprint of Macmillan Publishing Company.

Instructional Planning

Early-childhood special educators now find themselves involved in the planning of instructional programs, treatments, or interventions with two new populations of children: medically high-risk infants (low-birth-weight infants) and special-needs infants and toddlers. When they assess newborn infants, they find themselves doing so for the purpose of providing information to physicians, parents, and community early-intervention programs. They do so for the express purpose of developing interventions for these very young children.

An expressed requirement of PL 99-457 is the development of an Individualized Family Service Plan. The components of this plan were specified earlier in this chapter. The plan is used to guide intervention with the infant, toddler, or preschool child.

Program Evaluation

Many measures currently available for use with very young children were developed exclusively for measuring attainment of goals in Head Start programs. Kelly and Surbeck (1985) report that well over two hundred assessment instruments were constructed and published during 1960–1980. In the 1960s Congress authorized the establishment of a set of programs known collectively as the Handicapped Children's Early Education Program. Each of these programs was required to have an evaluation plan. The limited availability of instruments that could be used to assess student gains led to the development of many new measures.

Assessment of Readiness

Readiness is usually considered essential for initial entry into school, although the concept of readiness can be appropriately applied at all levels of instruction. For example, to be ready for algebra instruction, the student must have mastered more basic mathematical concepts and operations. Readiness for higher-level academic instruction is usually conceptualized as mastery of prerequisite material. Readiness for school entry is a more complex topic. Readiness for the first grade or even kindergarten is a generalized readiness and refers to both academic and social readiness. Academic readiness is most often thought of in terms of reading readiness but properly includes readiness for all academic instruction. We must also consider, however, a child's readiness for the social milieu of school. In school, children must follow the directions of an adult other than their parent or guardian, must enter into cooperative ventures with their peers, must not present a physical threat to themselves or others, must have mastered many self-help skills such as toileting, and so on.

Readiness for school entry is further complicated because there are two different orientations toward the topic. The first, a *skill orientation*, was implicit in the foregoing discussion. It holds that readiness involves the skill development and knowledge prerequisite to *beginning* instruction. Academic and social instruction is viewed as a program of sequential skills and knowledge that is built on previously mastered skills and knowledge. From this perspective, skills learned in school build on skills learned at home. The second orientation, a *process orientation*, is further removed from direct instruction. Here readiness is viewed in terms of underlying processes (intelligence, discrimination, and so on) that are believed to be necessary for the acquisition of skills and knowledge. If the processes are mature or developed, the child is ready to learn, to acquire skills.

Traditionally, formal readiness assessment has dealt with academic-process testing. For the most part, the tests have been norm-referenced, and the abilities that are thought to underlie all, or at least most, academic skills are the most typically tested. Thus, intelligence or learning aptitude, which is believed to underlie all school subjects, is often a component of a readiness assessment. Indeed, intelligence tests were developed to predict school success and are often validated against achievement tests or teacher ratings. Entry into formal school programs is often predicated upon a mental age of 6 or more years. Intellectual readiness can be assessed by any of the better tests discussed in Chapters 10 and 11. Perceptual-motor development is also thought to underlie school achievement, particularly reading (see Chapter 14). Readiness tests often contain many items or subtests that are appropriately termed perceptual-motor. Although these items and tests are usually less predictive of school achievement than are intelligence tests, many people feel they are an important component of readiness. Language development (see Chapter 13) is obviously important for school success. Children must be fluent in the idiomatic English of their peers; they must also understand and use standard (formal) English.

The assessment of school readiness is *not* a unique kind of measurement. What makes a test a readiness test is not what the test measures or how the measuring is done; three distinctive features make a test a readiness test. First, readiness tests are typically administered before school entry or during kindergarten. Second, the tests are used to predict initial school success and to select those children who perform poorly—and thus are thought not to be ready for regular school experiences—for participation in remedial or compensatory educational programs or delayed school entry. Third, these tests often contain the word readiness in the test name.

TECHNICAL CONSIDERATIONS

School readiness is a deceptively simple concept. Knowledge of a child's readiness can provide the teacher with invaluable information that may ensure that the child enters an instructional sequence at an appropriate level or it can provide the teacher with a destructive self-fulfilling prophecy that may actually hamper a child's development. Since decisions made on the basis of readiness tests are so important, the validity of the tests is crucial.

The purposes of readiness tests are

1. To predict who is not ready for formal entry into academic instruction
2. To predict who will profit from either remedial or compensatory educational programs in which readiness skills or processes are developed

It is apparent from these two purposes that the academic development of many children must be followed and documented. When the same children are followed and their progress recorded, the data are called *longitudinal*. Readiness data *must* be longitudinal in both standardization and validation. Specifically, to validate a readiness test, a large number of children must be tested before they enter school and then be retested after a specific period of time in school—generally one year. Only in this way can we determine if children with poor scores on the readiness test perform poorly during actual schooling.

If readiness tests do indeed accurately identify which children will do poorly in school, the educator is faced with a choice of whether to admit a child to the regular school program or take another action. If the child is admitted to the regular school program, the only justification for the test having been administered is that it gives the teacher sufficient information to take steps to overcome the deficits in the child's readiness. Such a use for readiness tests is not justified when one views readiness as physiological maturation. However, if readiness is viewed as depending on skills or processes susceptible to environmental manipulation, there is some justification.

If the child is not admitted to the regular school program, the educator can choose either to delay entry into the regular program or to provide remedial or compensatory preschool or kindergarten programs. Either of these alternatives should be considered only in light of research data indicating that readiness tests are effective predictors of differential programming. In essence, aptitude-treatment interaction research is required to validate these uses. As an illustration of how this research might be accomplished, let us assume that a school district chooses to delay school entry for children who score poorly on a readiness test. To validate this action, it would be necessary to administer the test to a large number of children before admission to school and then divide the children randomly into two groups, admitting one group to school and delaying the entry of the other for, say, one year. After *both* groups had completed their first year of regular schooling (kindergarten or first grade), the groups would be compared on some measure of school success. Two of several possible outcomes are presented in Figure 21.1. In part a, no matter what their readiness score, children perform better if their school entry is delayed. A child scoring fairly low on readiness would earn a performance score at point A if entered immediately into school but at point A' if allowed to wait before entering; similarly, a child with high readiness would earn a higher performance score (B' as compared to B) with delayed entry. In short, there is no differential advantage afforded by delaying children who score poorly on the readiness test. In part b, by contrast, there is a significant aptitude-by-treatment interaction: children who score poorly on the readiness test perform better in school (at A' rather than A) when their entry is delayed; but children who score well on the readiness test perform better in school (at B rather than B') when they are immediately enrolled. The same type of research could be used to evaluate compensatory or remedial programs when placement decisions are based on readiness tests.

From the foregoing discussion, it is apparent that the validation of readiness tests is not a simple or convenient task. Validation takes a minimum of one or two years. It must take place in a variety of schools where distinctive features of the curriculum are carefully noted. It is possible that a particular readiness test may predict well who would profit from one type of remedial or compensatory program but not who would profit from another program. Similarly, the predictive validity may vary according to curriculum; one test may predict well a student's progress in one reading program but not predict that student's progress in another program.

Standardization sample norms are generally gathered for four groups; beginning kindergarten (September), middle kindergarten (January), end of kindergarten (June), and beginning first grade. Children tested for the norm group should also be retested at the end of first grade to determine predictive validity. In the area of readiness, perhaps more than any other, local longitudinal norms are very important.

FIGURE 21.1   Possible Interactions Between Readiness and Delayed School Entry

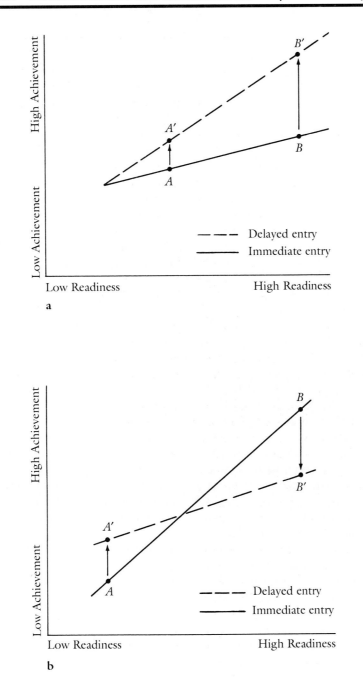

Although the foregoing discussion has stressed norms and predictive validity, reliability should not be overlooked. As can be recalled from Chapter 7, reliability has a definite effect on validity. An unreliable test must have poor predictive validity. Finally, readiness is an area where tests *are* routinely used to make important educational decisions about individual children. Consequently, readiness tests must meet the highest technical standards.

There is little correlation between measures of infant abilities and measures of preschool abilities in children of normal intelligence (Lewis & Sullivan, 1985). This finding has lead to much debate—debate about the extent to which the lack of a relationship reflects a defect in the instruments at this level, or the nature of infant development and the difference between behavioral repertoires of infants and preschoolers.

SPECIFIC TESTS OF SCHOOL READINESS

BATTELLE DEVELOPMENTAL INVENTORY

The Battelle Developmental Inventory (BDI) is a norm-referenced, individually administered assessment battery to test key developmental skills in children from birth to 8 years of age. It is intended to be administered by and used by those who teach infants, toddlers, and preschool children. The Battelle was initially developed by a team of investigators who were charged by the federal government with the task of evaluating the impact of the Handicapped Children's Early Education Program. The test was developed by selecting items from already existing tests and organizing them into five domains: personal-social, adaptive, motor, communication, and cognitive. Items selected were those thought to measure developmental milestones, and apparent gaps in development were filled by creating a few additional items. The test was piloted in 1980 on about five hundred children ages birth to 8 who were living in Ohio. In 1982–83 the test was standardized on a national sample, and the norms were recalibrated in 1987.

The Battelle is used to gather data on functioning in five domains, described as follows.

Personal-Social   In this domain are assessed abilities and characteristics that enable the child to engage in meaningful social interaction. Included are measures of the frequency and quality of interactions with adults, the child's ability to express feelings and emotions, development of self-awareness and self-worth, coping, and social development.

Adaptive Domain   This domain involves assessment of extent of independent functioning and attention. Included in this domain are measures of visual and auditory attention, eating-related behaviors, dressing skills, ability to assume responsibility, and toileting.

Motor Domain   In this domain are assessed muscle control, body coordination, locomotion, fine-muscle coordination, and perceptual-motor functioning.

Communication Domain   This domain involves assessing the development of reception and expression of information, thoughts, and ideas.

TABLE 21.3   Subdomains of the Battelle Developmental Inventory

Domains and Subdomains	BDI Number of Items	Screening Test Number of Items
Personal-social domain	85	20
Adult interaction	18	
Expression of feelings/affect	12	
Self-concept	14	
Peer interaction	17	
Coping	10	
Social role	14	
Adaptive domain	59	20
Attention	10	
Eating	14	
Dressing	10	
Personal responsibility	19	
Toileting	6	
Motor domain	62	20
Muscle control	6	
Body coordination	25	
Locomotion	13	
Fine muscle	18	
Perceptual motor	20	
Communication domain	39	18
Receptive	27	
Expressive	32	
Cognitive domain	56	18
Perceptual discrimination	10	
Memory	10	
Reasoning and academic skills	16	
Conceptual development	20	
Total	341	96

Cognitive Domain   In the cognitive domain are assessed ability to discriminate objects, memory, reasoning and judgment, and concept development.

For each domain there are a number of subdomains. These are shown in Table 21.3. There are 341 items on this scale. Each domain is published in a separate test booklet. This separation facilitates examination by more than one person at the same time. Data to be used in completing the response protocols are collected by (1) giving standardized test items, (2) holding interviews with the parents, and (3) making observations of the child in natural settings. There is a screeening version of the BDI, and this consists of 96 of the 341 items. Details on how to modify specific items for children who show specific kinds of handicaps are described in the manual.

It takes approximately 10 to 30 minutes to administer the Screening version of the BDI; it takes 10–15 minutes to give the scale to children who are younger than age 3 or older than age 5, and about 20–30 minutes to administer the screening version to those who are between 3 and 5. It takes approximately an hour to give the total scale to children under age 3 or older than 5. It takes 1.5 to 2 hours to give it to children between ages 3 and 5. The authors recommend that the scale be used for the following purposes: identification of developmental strengths and weaknesses, assessment of children considered "at risk," general preschool and kindergarten screening, IEP development and instructional planning, and monitoring of pupil progress.

SCORES

Individual items on the Battelle are scored using a three-point scoring system. Children receive two points when they respond according to a specified criterion. They earn one point when they attempt a response but do not meet the criterion. The child earns zero points when he or she cannot or will not attempt an item, or when the response is an extremely poor approximation of the desired response.

The BDI is arranged into domains, and for each domain there are components or subdomains. Those who use this scale can derive domain scores, component scores, or cluster scores. Scores may be obtained for the following ten major components: Personal-Social, Adaptive, Gross Motor, Fine Motor, Motor, Receptive, Expressive, Communication, Cognitive, Total Score.

The BDI is scored by examining the scores earned on the inventory in relation to cutoff scores. Cutoff scores and age equivalent scores may be computed for each of the ten major scores. Percentile ranks are provided for each of thirty component scores that may be derived for the BDI.

Performance on the BDI is evaluated on the basis of the individual's score relative to specified cutoffs. Three levels of cutoff are provided in the manual: performance 1.00, 1.50, and 2.00 below the mean. The authors provide three levels because decisions about program eligibility differ among states.

NORMS

The BDI was standardized during 1982–83 on a national sample stratified on the basis of geographic region, race, and sex within each age level. The test was given by 42 examiners at twenty-eight sites in 24 states. A total of 800 children participated in standardization of the BDI. The norms for this test were recalibrated in 1987 when it was learned that there were some inconsistencies in the norms tables.

RELIABILITY

Test-retest reliability is provided for an unspecified sample of 183 children drawn from the standardization group and given the test twice four weeks apart. Nearly all reliabilities exceed .90.

VALIDITY

The authors of the BDI address three forms of validity: content, construct, and criterion. Content validity is based on expert opinion.

Items for this scale were selected from other measures, and experts placed the items at specified levels and in specified domains. Construct validity was examined by looking at subtest intercorrelations. Evidence for concurrent validity is based on correlations with other measures. The BDI component scores were highly correlated with scores on the Vineland Adaptive Behavior Scale, and moderately correlated with performance on other scales. The test was developed by selecting items from other scales; the authors do not indicate overlap of the BDI with the other scales to which they relate it.

SUMMARY

The BDI is an individually administered norm-referenced measure of the development of the young child in five major domains. Standardization procedures look reasonable, but evidence for validity is limited.

BOEHM TEST OF BASIC CONCEPTS–REVISED

The Boehm Test of Basic Concepts–Revised (BTBC-R) (Boehm, 1986) differs somewhat in content from the original version: there are seven new items, one item was divided into two items, two items were deleted, and four items were moved to a downward extension of the test. Like the earlier edition, the BTBC-R is a group-administered, norm-referenced device that assesses knowledge of fifty abstract, relational concepts that occur frequently in preschool and primary curricula. The concepts are "both fundamental to understanding verbal instruction and essential for early school achievement" (Boehm, 1986, p. 1). The BTBC-R is intended primarily for use in identifying children who have not mastered the concepts and in identifying those concepts that a teacher should systematically teach. In addition, Boehm states that the test may be used as part of a battery to identify children who are "at risk" of learning problems and to evaluate the effectiveness of instruction in the concepts assessed. The test is available in two forms, C and D.

The fifty concepts are arranged in order of increasing difficulty in two booklets. Each booklet takes about 15 to 20 minutes to administer and includes three practice items. The testing format requires children to mark the picture that best answers the question read by the teacher (for example, "Mark the one where the boy is *next to* the horse"). The items can be categorized as spatial (for example, "next to"), quantitative (for example, "few"), temporal (for example, "after"), and miscellaneous (for example, "other").

SCORES

Two types of scores are provided: "pass" or "fail" on each item and a percentile rank for the total score. In addition, tables give the percentage of children passing each item. The interpretive data for the two types of scores are similar in several respects: both provide normative data for kindergarten, grade 1, and grade 2; both provide separate norms for the beginning of the year and the end of the year; and both provide a means of comparing a student's performance with that of the total sample and that of other students at the same socioeconomic level.

Forms C and D have separate sets of norms for the percentage of students passing each item. The percentile norms, however, are for Forms C and D combined. This is troublesome, because Forms C and D were standardized separately and were not equated for variations in the samples. Although Boehm claims that the two samples were selected to be comparable in ability, no specifics are given.

Norms

The standardization sample was intended to be broadly representative of the U.S. population, although it appears that only children from public school who attended regular classes were included. School district size and geographic area were the bases of stratification. The obtained data were statistically weighted to make the sample conform to the population with respect to the stratification variables.

Boehm claims that her sample is also representative of the socioeconomic levels of schools in the United States. "Participating districts were asked to select groups of school buildings that, together, would provide a sample representative of the range of schools within the districts" (p. 45). Her data are not convincing, however. [1]

Reliability

Although not presented as reliability data in the test manual, information on alternate-form reliability, based on the performances of 625 children, indicates poor reliability: .82 at kindergarten, .77 at first grade, and .65 at second grade. Twenty-four split-half reliability estimates (one for each form, grade/socioeconomic class, and total sample) are also pre-

sented. These range from .55 to .87; only ten coefficients exceed .80. Stability estimates (with an interval of one school year) are also given for each form at each grade. The six coefficients range from .55 to .88, with only two of the six exceeding .80.

Validity

Because the BTBC-R is essentially a specialized achievement test, its content validity is of primary concern. Substantial evidence is presented that the words are common, and some evidence is presented that they are important. Some evidence of predictive validity is also presented. The BTBC-R correlates modestly with achievement, assessed after one year. Boehm presents seventeen coefficients of correlation with achievement tests that range from .38 to .64 (median .4). No evidence is presented, however, to show that the BTBC-R can identify children who are "at risk" of learning problems.

Seven pages of the BTBC-R manual are devoted to a review of validity studies conducted with the BTBC. Because the contents of the two devices are so similar—about 80 percent overlap between the two devices—many of these studies are applicable to the BTBC-R. Studies reported indicate that the BTBC (1) had some criterion-related validity for achievement, readiness, and language; (2) was sensitive to instruction in the concepts tested; and (3) found no sex differences but did find differences among socioeconomic classes and among ethnic groups.

Summary

The Boehm Test of Basic Concepts–Revised is a group-administered test that assesses knowl-

---

1. To estimate the SES of her sample, Boehm used the percentage of children in each school who received subsidized lunches. Schools were classified as high SES if no more than 10 percent of the students were eligible for subsidized lunches and middle class if 11 to 50 percent of the students were eligible.

edge of fifty relational words. Although there is some evidence for the importance of the words (and hence for use of the test as a criterion-referenced device), the device has inadequate reliability and norms for purposes other than screening.

COMPREHENSIVE DEVELOPMENTAL SCALE

The Comprehensive Developmental Scale (Quick, Little, & Campbell, 1974), developed as part of project MEMPHIS, is an individually administered, multiple-skill "age scale" intended for use with children who are handicapped or have developmental deficiencies. It can be used with children between 3 months and 6 years of age. Intended to assess skills "important to later school learning" (p. 13), it can be "administered by teachers in a classroom setting through information gained by personal observation of the child or information given to the teacher by others knowledgeable about the child" (p. 16).

The scale consists of five subscales. Personal-Social Skills contains sixty items that deal with eating, dressing, interpersonal relationships, following directions, self-concept, safety, and general self-help. Gross Motor Skills contains forty items mainly dealing with developmental mobility (for example, rolling over, standing, walking), balance, and stair walking. Fine Motor Skills contains forty items dealing mainly with drawing, grasping, depositing objects in containers, using scissors, manipulating paper (for example, unwrapping, folding, page turning), and tower building. Language skills contains sixty items that assess vocabulary, grammar, morphology, and phonology. Perceptual-Cognitive Skills contains sixty items that in general resemble items found on tests of intelligence: drawing, early language (for example, naming), quantitative concepts, memory, and so on.

SCORES

Items on each scale are assigned to an age range. Raw scores are summed, and the age range to which the subtest total corresponds is the age score.

NORMS

There is no mention of the procedures used to assign ages to scale items, nor is there any mention of norms in the technical materials.

RELIABILITY

No evidence of any type of reliability is reported.

VALIDITY

No evidence of validity is presented.

SUMMARY

Project MEMPHIS's Comprehensive Developmental Scale is a device without technical data. It should be considered as an informal check list.

DENVER DEVELOPMENTAL SCREENING TEST

The Denver Developmental Screening Test (DDST) (Frankenburg, Dodds, Fandal, Kazuk, & Cohrs, 1975) is an individually administered, norm-referenced, multiple-skill device designed for the early identification of children with developmental and behavioral problems. It is intended for use with children from birth to 6 years of age. No special training is needed to administer the screening test, which requires approximately 20 minutes to give, score, and interpret. Test forms and the test manual are available in Spanish.

One hundred five skills are clustered into four general developmental areas that must be administered in the order in which they are discussed here. The first area is personal-social development. It contains twenty-three items. These can be clustered into three subareas: responding to another person (for example, smiling), playing (playing pat-a-cake, joining in interactive games), and self-care (dressing, washing, feeding). The second area, fine motor development, contains thirty items. These assess grasping and manipulation, building towers of various heights with blocks, drawing (for example, scribbling, drawing a person), and copying increasingly difficult geometric designs. The third area is language development. The twenty-one items in this area assess the ability of younger children to produce and imitate sounds and require older children to demonstrate factual knowledge (for example, parts of the body and composition of familiar objects) as well as command of more traditional measures of language development such as vocabulary and syntax. The thirty-one items in the fourth area, gross motor development, can be classified as requiring body control (for example, lifting the head, rolling over), mobility (walking, jumping in place), coordination (kicking a ball, riding a tricycle), and balance (balancing on one foot).

SCORES

All items are presented on the scoring sheet in the format shown in Figure 21.2. Across the top and bottom of the scoring sheet are age lines. The child's chronological age (CA) is computed, and a line at the appropriate age connects the top and bottom age lines. As shown in Figure 21.2, a child who is 3-6 has the age line drawn through skills 2 and 5. Each skill is enclosed in a rectangle with four discernible points along one of the horizontal sides. Vertical extensions of the four points intercept the age lines. For skill 1 in Figure 21.2, the vertical that goes from point A to the top age line intercepts the age line at about 2-1. This indicates that 25 percent of the children in the norm sample could perform skill 1 by the time they were about 2 years, 1 month old. Point B is the point at which 50 percent of the norm group could perform a skill. As shown in Figure 21.2, 50 percent of the children could perform skill 2 by age 3-4. Point C is the age at which 75 percent succeeded; 75 percent of the children could perform skill 4 by age 2-8. Point D is the age at which 90 percent successfully performed the skill. In Figure 21.2, 90 percent of the children in the norm group could perform skill 5 by age 4-1.

There is no formal basal rule for the scoring of the DDST.[2] Ceilings are not important since the purpose of the test is to determine developmental lags, not level of functioning. The examiner should administer all test items through which the child's age line passes, and testing in each area should not be terminated until the child passes three items and fails three items.

---

2. A basal age is the age at which a child performs all tasks correctly and below which the tester can assume that all items will be passed. A basal rule states the number of items a child must pass before a basal age can be assumed.

Each item may be scored "pass," "fail," "passed by report," "refusal," or "no opportunity." Passed and failed items are observed directly by the examiner. Items passed by report (skills such as washing and drying the hands) are items that are difficult or time-consuming to administer but that can be observed reliably by the child's parents. If a parent reports that the child performs the particular task, the item is scored as a pass. Refusals are items to which the child *will not* respond whether the items are administered by the examiner or by the parents. If the examiner feels that the child *cannot* perform the task, the item is scored as failed. No-opportunity scores indicate that the child has not had the chance to learn the skill; such items are not included in the interpretation of the results.

Two types of scores are used. The first score is called a *delay*. A delay is scored if the child fails an item that is passed by 90 percent of the children who are younger; thus, a delay is an item that is failed and lies to the left of the age-line vertical. The second score is the interpretation of the results as abnormal, questionable, untestable, and normal. An *abnormal* is scored when the child has (1) two delays in each of two sections or (2) one section with two delays and one section with one delay and in that same section "no passes intersecting the age line" (Frankenburg et al., 1975, p. 12). A *questionable* is scored (1) if the child has two or more delays in one section or (2) if the child has one delay and has not passed any items in that section through which the age line passes. An *untestable* is scored "when refusals occur in numbers large enough to cause the test result to be *questionable* or *abnormal* if they were scored as failures" (Frankenburg et al., 1975, p. 12). All other outcomes are scored as normal. If children earn scores other than *normal*, it is recommended that they be retested in two to three weeks. If the retest indicates other than normal and if the parents say the behavior

FIGURE 21.2   Sample Scoring Sheet for the DDST

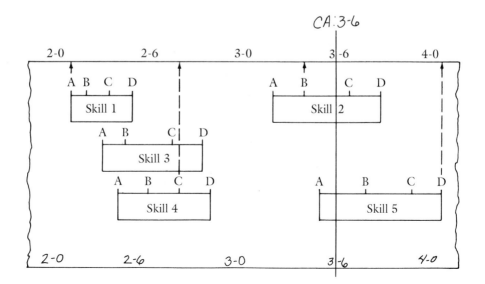

is typical, the children should be referred for further assessment.

Norms

The DDST was standardized on 543 boys and 493 girls from 2 weeks through 6-4 years of age who (we presume, although the test is not clear on this point) lived in Denver, Colorado. Children with serious, known handicaps or difficult births were excluded. The standardization sample approximated the 1960 census in terms of racial-ethnic composition and occupations of the children's fathers.

The number of children in the sample at various ages is limited and is not evenly distributed. The number of children (in one-month intervals) from 1 month to 14 months ranges from thirty-six to forty-three, while the total number of children between 5 and 6 years of age is forty-seven.

Reliability

The authors report stability data (one-week interval) for the performance of twenty children who ranged in age from 2 months to 5 years, 6 months and who were tested by the same examiner. For each of the twenty children, there was at least 90 percent agreement[3] on the pass-fail decisions on the items administered. The specimen kit also contains a reprint of an article by Frankenburg, Goldstein, and Camp (1971). There the test-retest reliability (percentage-agreement method) of abnormal, questionable, and normal classifications for 186 children was reported to be .97.

3. Number of agreements divided by number of agreements plus disagreements.

Interrater agreement was also evaluated during the standardization of DDST, since it was important to know if two different examiners would elicit the same performances and score them in the same way. Calculated by the percentage-agreement method, interrater reliability ranged from 80 to 95 percent agreement.

Validity

The authors can claim content validity by their method of item selection. They surveyed several intelligence and developmental tests and selected items from them. The authors also present data from the paper by Frankenburg, Goldstein, and Camp to demonstrate a strong relationship between classifications on the DDST (that is, abnormal, questionable, and normal) and scores on the Stanford Binet Intelligence Scale or the Revised Bayley Infant Scales. This study also indicates low proportions of false positives and false negatives.[4]

Summary

The Denver Developmental Screening Test is a quickly administered and scored device that assesses a child's development in four general areas: personal-social, fine-motor, language, and gross-motor. The device is intended to provide a gross estimate of delayed development and must be followed by a more intensive evaluation. The test's reliability and validity are adequate for a screening device, although the norms are questionable.

4. A *false positive* is a child who is diagnosed as abnormal but on subsequent evaluation is determined to be normal. A *false negative* is a child who is diagnosed as normal but on subsequent evaluation is determined to be abnormal.

DEVELOPMENTAL INDICATORS FOR THE ASSESSMENT OF LEARNING–REVISED

The Developmental Indicators for the Assessment of Learning–Revised (DIAL-R) (Mardell-Czudnowski & Goldenberg, 1990) is an individually administered screening test intended to assess motor, conceptual, and language skills of children from 2 to 6 years of age. Although individual children are screened, the testing procedures are designed to handle large numbers of children; different examiners administer different portions of the test to children who go from one testing area to another. DIAL-R is administered by a four-person screening team that includes one coordinator and three operators, one to administer each of the three DIAL-R screening areas. There are no special qualifications for the operators other than familiarity with the testing materials and procedures and limited special training.

The three subtests of the DIAL-R each consist of eight items. In some places in the test manual, it is suggested that individual items may be plotted as a profile.

Motor   In this subtest, the eight items are (1) catching a beanbag; (2) jumping, hopping, and skipping; (3) building with blocks; (4) touching the fingers of each hand with that hand's thumb; (5) cutting with scissors; (6) matching to sample; (7) copying letters and shapes; and (8) writing first name.

Concepts   In this subtest, the eight items are (1) naming nine colors; (2) pointing to various body parts; (3) rote counting; (4) one-to-one correspondence; (5) comprehending positions (for example, "put the block on the box"); (6) identifying fourteen concepts (for example, biggest, night, cold, least); (7) letter naming; and (8) sorting after observing the tester's sorting.

Language   In this subtest, the eight items are (1) articulating fifteen words; (2) giving personal data (for example, identifying one's own photograph, giving one's telephone number); (3) remembering a sequence of hand claps, repeating digits, and repeating sentences; (4) naming nine pictured nouns (for example, TV, phone, ambulance); (5) naming pictured verbs (for example, sleep, talk, comb); (6) naming foods eaten; (7) problem solving (that is, social comprehension questions); and (8) sentence length of the child's longest response.

SCORES

Scaled scores are computed for each item. However, these scores are not really scaled scores in the sense that they have the same means and standard deviations. Rather, they are age scores, given in one-year age ranges. These scores are summed for each area and converted to another scale: "potential problem," "OK," "potential advanced." Children earning scores of potential problem or potential advanced are to be followed up.

NORMS

DIAL-R was standardized in 1981–83 on 2,447 children living in six states. The primary goal was to produce norms that would be representative of the U.S. population of children two years through six years of age and that the sample was stratified on the basis of "age, sex, geographic region, size of community, and race" (p. 49). Noticeably missing is stratification on the basis of socioeconomic class, a variable that has been repeatedly shown to affect significantly the development of children. There are serious shortcomings in the variables that were actually used in stratification. For example, geographic region is sampled by two cities in each of four regions, and the cities are located in only six states. The cities were classified as large (over 50,000) and small (less than 50,000); the large cities are Freeport, New York; Joliet, Illinois; Jacksonville, Florida; and Honolulu, Hawaii. No 6-year-old children were included in the sample. Separate norms for whites and nonwhites are available.

The DIAL-R standardized data were reanalyzed in 1990 to provide norms for what is called the AGS version of the test. These are the norms to be used in interpreting pupil performance.

RELIABILITY

Test-retest reliabilities are not readily interpretable since they are computed across age groups. These coefficients range from .76 (Motor) to .90 (Concepts); the reliability of the total score is .87. No stability data are presented on the categorization of scores as "potential problem," "OK," and "potential gifted."

Coefficient alpha was also computed for each subtest at each three-month age group. Thus, there were forty-eight coefficients that ranged from .45 (Language at age 5-6) to .87 (Language at age 2-3); thirty-eight of the coefficients fall below .80, including Motor at all ages. For the total score, reliabilities range from .80 (5-3) to .92 (total at 2-2); none of the sixteen coefficients fall below .80. Thus, low reliability makes about three-fourths of the subtest scores unsuitable for screening purposes, but the total scores are suitable.

VALIDITY

Twenty-one of the twenty-four items on the DIAL-R were taken from the first edition of the DIAL. In selecting these twenty-one items, the test authors interviewed early childhood and kindergarten teachers to identify behaviors believed necessary for school success. The resulting list of behaviors was reviewed by a group of consultants. The bases for deleting DIAL items and adding DIAL-R items are not specified in the manual. Inspection of the individual items raises some questions. For example, many of the items on the Motor subtest make heavy intellectual demands. Indeed, one factor analytic study reported by Mardell-Czudnowski and Goldenberg indicates that the items on the DIAL-R actually cluster into only two factors: (1) Motor and Concepts and (2) Language.

Construct validity of the DIAL-R was established by showing that parts of the scale correlated with like-named parts of other scales and did not correlate highly with other-named scales. Evidence for criterion-related validity is mixed. The authors reanalyzed the standardization data in 1990, developing new norms. Many of the validity studies were completed using the norms for prior editions of the scale. Data in the manual support the criterion-related validity of the scale.

SUMMARY

DIAL-R is an individually administered screening device assessing development in domains of motor, conceptual, and language behavior. The norms are adequate, reliability is reasonable for the total scale but limited for subtests, and validity is clearly established. The DIAL-R is a useful and technically adequate screening device. Users are advised to use the total score rather than subtest scores in decision making.

DEVELOPMENTAL PROFILE II

The Developmental Profile II (DP-II) (Alpern, Boll, & Shearer, 1986) is an age scale designed to assess children's development from birth to age 9-6. The first and second editions of the scales differ slightly. Thirty-one of the items from the DP were not included in the DP-II—items above the 9-year, 6-month level and sexist items. The manual was also rewritten, but no new norms or items were developed. The DP-II can be administered as a parent interview in about 20 to 40 minutes by anyone who has been trained to use it, or it can be used as a "self-interview" that is completed by a teacher.

The DP-II contains 186 items arranged in five subscales, with usually three items per age level per subscale. The subscales are as follows:

The Physical Scale contains thirty-nine items that assess both gross and fine motor skills.

The Self-Help Scale consists of thirty-nine items that assess both survival and self-care.

The Social Scale contains thirty-six items that assess "expression of needs and feelings, interactions with others, sense of identity, and adherence to rules and regulations."

The Academic Scale consists of thirty-four items that assess cognitive functioning (for example, perception, memory, and categorization).

The Communication Scale contains thirty-eight items that assess verbal and nonverbal expression and language comprehension.

The DP-II is intended for several uses: screening, determining eligibility for special education and related services, planning individual educational programs, evaluating pupil progress, and evaluating educational programs for groups of children. However, its authors recommend that, when not used in conjunction with other assessment procedures, the DP-II be used only for screening.

SCORES

The DP-II is one of the few tests that rely on age scores. Age scores have been widely rejected as inadequate for the reasons discussed in Chapter 5.

Individual items are scored as "pass," "fail," or "no opportunity" (which is counted as "fail"). Individual items are combined to form an age score for each subscale. These subscale age scores are interpreted as "advanced" or "delayed." If the developmental age is greater than the chronological age, performance on the subscale is interpreted as advanced; if the developmental age is less than the chronological age, performance on the subscale is interpreted as delayed. Tables are also provided to interpret the magnitude of delays. One table shows the age at which 95 percent of the children in the standardization sample passed the items on each scale. Another table interprets the importance of delays as "delayed," "borderline," and "normal." These classifications are not, however, empirical; they are based on the clinical judgments of unspecified individuals.

NORMS

A total of 2,354 normal children ranging in age from 0 to 9-6 make up the normative sample for the DP-II. No sampling plan is discussed, but the few statistics that are presented indicate that the sample is not representative of the U.S. population. It is overwhelmingly middle class (80 percent), with only 9 percent lower-class and 11 percent upper-class children. The sample is also restricted geographically: 91 percent from the state of Indiana and 9 percent from the state of Washington.

RELIABILITY

The discussion of reliability offered in the technical manual of the DP-II does not conform to either psychometric or behavioral models of reliability. The authors present unorthodox estimates of reliability to demonstrate interscorer reliability, stability, and internal consistency. We are unable to evaluate these data in the form presented and must conclude that usable evidence of reliability is absent from the manual.

VALIDITY

Little evidence for content validity may be claimed because of the way in which the items

were selected for inclusion. There are (1) items from existing scales of intelligence, language, social abilities, and physical abilities; (2) items derived from normative data from the research literature in child development; (3) newly developed items. The factors considered in selecting items included age and sex bias and the performance of children of different ages on an item. No detailed descriptions are given of the domains sampled (and their parameters), however. Thus at other than the most general level, it is unclear what domains the content of the DP-II is intended to represent.

Evidence for other types of validity is also not convincing. Mothers and teachers have a high rate of agreement on children's performances, and there are modest correlations with the Stanford Binet (Form L-M). The studies cited tend to be flawed methodically, however.

SUMMARY

The Developmental Profile II is an individually administered screening device intended for use with children ranging in age from newborn to 9-6. The norms are unrepresentative, the degree of reliability is unknown, and evidence for validity is scant.

METROPOLITAN READINESS TESTS

The Metropolitan Readiness Tests (MRT) (Nurss & McGauvran, 1986) is the fifth edition of this group-administered test designed to assess a "diverse range of prereading skills" (p. 7) for children in preschool through the middle of kindergarten (Level 1) and "more advanced skills that are important in beginning reading and mathematics" (p. 7) for children

in the middle of kindergarten through the fall of first grade (Level 2). As might be expected, because the two levels have different behaviors, Level 1 subtests are described in general terms below.

Auditory Memory assesses immediate recall of words read by the tester.

Beginning Consonants assesses the discrimination of initial sounds.

Letter Recognition assesses both upper- and lowercase letters.

Visual Matching assesses a child's ability to match a series of letters, words, numbers, or other symbols.

School Language and Listening assesses "basic cognitive concepts, as well as complex grammatical structures"; "the questions require children to integrate and reorganize information, to draw inferences, and to analyze and evaluate" oral material (p. 8).

Following are brief descriptions of the Level 2 subtests.

Quantitative Language assesses various mathematical concepts (for example, one-to-one correspondence).

Beginning Consonants assesses discrimination of beginning consonants.

Sound-Letter Correspondence requires a child "to identify letters that correspond to specific sounds in words" (p. 8).

Visual Matching requires the matching of various arithmetic, English, and nonsense symbols.

Finding Patterns requires the child to find various arithmetic, English, and nonsense symbols embedded in larger groupings of symbols.

School Language is essentially the same as the School Language subtest in Level 1.

Listening is about the same as the Listening subtest in Level 1.

Quantitative Concepts assesses various mathematical concepts (for example, conservation and part-whole relationships).

Quantitative Operations assesses "counting and simple mathematical operations" (p. 8).

Copying is an optional subtest that requires the copying of a printed sentence.

SCORES

Two types of scores are offered: content-referenced and norm-referenced. Content-referenced scores consist of raw scores ("+" indicating that the student has learned the skills to proficiency, "/" indicating that the student is in the process of learning the skills, and "–" indicating that the student needs instruction) and performance ratings. Tables are used to obtain the performance ratings; however, no bases are provided to explain why a particular raw score should be considered to represent proficiency.

Norm-referenced scores combine subtests into four composites at Level 1 (Auditory Skill Area, Visual Skill Area, Language Skill Area, and Pre-Reading Composite) and five composites at Level 2 (the Quantitative Skill Area is added to the four composites at Level 1). Percentile ranks, stanines, scaled scores, and normal curve equivalents are provided for the composites. Neither means nor standard deviations of the standard scores are provided in the technical manual (Metropolitan Readiness Tests, Levels 1 and 2, Norms Booklet).

NORMS

For Level 1, separate norms are available for spring prekindergarten, fall kindergarten, and midyear kindergarten. For Level 2, norms are available for midyear kindergarten, spring kindergarten, and fall grade 1.

Stratified sampled of school districts were selected to represent the 1980 U.S. population for fall ($n = 180$ districts), midyear ($n = 140$), and spring ($n = 290$) standardizations. Whether the same school districts participated in more than one norming program is not reported. Stratification variables were size of school district, geographic region, socioeconomic status, and private or public school status. The sample varied by more than 10 percent from the U.S. population; however, the sample data were statistically adjusted so that the data used for the norm tables did approximate the census data.

RELIABILITY

KR-20 coefficients of internal consistency are provided for subtests and composites for fall, midyear, and spring norms. For the Pre-Reading Composite, coefficients exceed .90 for all norms. For the other composites, however, only two coefficients exceed .89 (Visual Skill Area, Level 2, midyear and spring kindergarten), and some are as low as .70 (Language Skill Area, Level 2, spring kindergarten). Stability coefficients (two-week interval) are presented for only two norm groups, Level 1, fall kindergarten; and Level 2, spring kindergarten. Only the stability of the Pre-Reading Compos-

ite for Level 1 exceeded .89; the stabilities of the remaining composites ranged from .74 (Language Skill Area, Level 2) to .88 (Auditory Skill Area, Level 1).

VALIDITY

The most important type of validity for a readiness test is predictive validity; educators want to know how students will fare in their various curricula. The results of two predictive-validity studies are presented in the technical manual. Level 2 was administered in the fall to first graders, and either the Metropolitan Achievement Tests or the Stanford Achievement Test Series was administered in the spring. For the Metropolitan, correlations ranged from .34 (Language Skill Area with total reading) to .65 (Pre-Reading with total achievement composite). The MRT was much more predictive of scores on the Stanford: coefficients ranged from .48 (Language Skill Area) to .83 (Pre-Reading Composite with the total basic battery and the total complete battery). However, for neither study were the curricula in which the students were enrolled described. The information presented is inadequate to establish either content or construct validity.

SUMMARY

The Metropolitan Readiness Tests is a group-administered device best suited for norm-referenced interpretation. Only the Pre-Reading Composite is sufficiently reliable for use in making important educational decisions. The test appears to be an unusually good predictor of achievement on the Stanford Achievement Test Series, but only a modest predictor of achievement on the Metropolitan

Achievement Tests. The MRT's predictive ability for particular curricula or other achievement tests is unknown, and therefore the test should not be used as a predictive device.

PRESCHOOL INVENTORY

The Preschool Inventory Revised Edition (Caldwell, 1970a, 1970b) is an individually administered, untimed device designed to assess the various skills deemed necessary for the school achievement of children 3 to 6 years of age. The first form of the device was known as the Preschool Achievement Test. After the first revision, it was known as the Preschool Inventory. The revised edition of the Preschool Inventory contains sixty-four items that can be administered in less than 15 minutes by anyone familiar with the device. The inventory assesses a child's knowledge of a variety of personal facts (such as name, age, and body parts), of social roles (mother,[5] teacher, and so on), of number concepts, of colors, and of geometric designs. The inventory also assesses whether a child follows instructions and copies various geometric forms.

SCORES

In the initial versions of the test, the author sampled items as though a criterion-referenced device were being developed. Subsequent revisions have followed more traditional norm-referenced psychometrics. It is difficult to consider the current revision as a criterion-referenced device for several reasons. First, many items tap multiple behaviors; for example, given the response blank with a circle,

5. Curiously, if a child responds to the question "What does a mother do?" with "Has babies," the response is not correct.

square, and triangle, the child is requested to color the circle yellow. Second, the items were selected on the basis of their correlations with total score and not on relative educational importance. Percentile ranks are provided for five age ranges: 3-0 to 3-11, 4-0 to 4-5, 4-6 to 4-11, 5-0 to 5-5, and 5-6 to 6-5.

NORMS

National norms are based solely on the performance of 1,531 children attending Head Start classes. Only the performance of children who were tested in English was included. No formal sampling plan is discussed. The ethnic and sex compositions of the norm sample for each of the five age ranges are presented. The age samples are about equally divided between boys and girls and are predominantly black (68.2 percent). Regional norms are based on the responses of at least 100 children, but in such cases neither sex nor ethnic breakdown is provided. In addition, specialized norms are provided separately for 246 4-year-old children in Louisville, Kentucky; for 133 children in Phoenix, Arizona; and for 317 children in North Carolina. Thus, the normative sample can, at best, be considered circumscribed and voluntary. And it is now out of date.

RELIABILITY

Two estimates of internal consistency, based on the performance of the standardization sample, are provided for each age group: KR-20 coefficients range from .86 to .92; split-half reliabilities (corrected by the Spearman-Brown formula) range from .84 to .93. Raw-score SEMs are also presented.

VALIDITY

The initial form of the device, the Preschool Achievement Test, could lay some claim to content validity by the procedures used to select items. The author drew on her personal observations of deficits exhibited by disadvantaged preschool children, on the observations of others who had worked with disadvantaged children, and on inspections of various kindergarten curricula. In subsequent revisions, the total number of items was reduced from 161 to 64. The deletion of items may have reduced the scope of the Inventory. Yet if the test user is interested in the behaviors sampled, there is still ample claim to content validity.

Empirical validity is generally lacking. Stanford-Binet IQs (Form L-M) were available for 1,476 children in the standardization sample; the correlation between the inventory and the Binet ranged from .39 (at 3 years) to .65 (at 5 years). In discussing the North Carolina norms, the author noted that in that sample the Inventory did not distinguish between children from high socioeconomic backgrounds and children from low socioeconomic backgrounds.

SUMMARY

The Preschool Inventory is a quickly administered device that can give a teacher a list of accomplishments for a pupil. The estimated reliability of the device is adequate for screening purposes, but the norms limit the interpretation of percentiles. Norms for this test are out of date.

TESTS OF BASIC EXPERIENCES 2

The Tests of Basic Experiences 2 (TOBE 2) (Moss, 1979) is a set of group-administered tests designed to assess important concepts that contribute to a child's preparedness for school and learning. The directions for testers are comprehensive and clear; best results are said to occur when group size is five or six. TOBE 2 has two levels, neither of which requires reading: level K (preschool and kindergarten) and level L (kindergarten and first grade). The battery consists of four tests of twenty-six items each: mathematics, language, science, and social studies. A practice examination is provided, and there are two demonstration items at the beginning of each test. Administration time is about 20 minutes for the practice test and about 45 minutes for TOBE 2.

The mathematics test assesses quantitative vocabulary and concepts, geometric shapes, and money. The language test assesses letter recognition, same-different, prepositions, letter-sound associations, and other vocabulary. The science test assesses basic facts of botany (for example, the one that grows in the driest place), physics (for example, falling objects, buoyancy), and zoology (for example, mark the bird's tracks). The social-studies test assesses social interactions, knowledge of occupations, and knowledge of tools, among other things.

SCORES

Scoring can be done by hand or by machine. Raw scores are summed for each subtest and the total; sums can be converted to percentile ranks, normal curve equivalents ($\bar{x} = 50$, $S \approx 21$), and stanines. A Class Evaluation Record is used to show for each child those concepts correctly identified as well as derived scores. The teacher can sum the columns for each concept to find the number of children in the class who correctly identify the concept.

NORMS

The standardization sample consisted of approximately 14,000 children. Since fall and spring testings were conducted in the same schools, the norms to some extent are longitudinal. Midyear norms are interpolated.

The children were intended to represent public school districts with enrollments over eleven in 1970 and the Catholic schools in 1975. Public school districts were stratified by geographic region, elementary school population, and relevant (but unspecified) demographic characteristics. Schools within districts were somehow selected, and all children in the target schools who were enrolled in kindergarten and first grade were tested. Catholic schools were stratified by geographic region and enrollment. Selection procedures for preschoolers were not discussed. Although voluminous data are presented, one cannot ascertain the extent to which the sample is representative. The general procedures followed should result in an adequate normative sample, however.

RELIABILITY

Internal-consistency estimates of reliability for each subtest and the total for each form are presented for both fall and spring scores. Reliability estimates range from .76 to .85 for subtests; estimates for total scores all exceed .9. Test-retest correlations, from fall to spring, for subtests range from .64 to .78; for the total scores the range is from .84 to .87. Thus, the reliability of the subtests appears adequate for screening purposes.

VALIDITY

Moss (1979) enumerates the components of each subtest and gives the number of items in each component. She also discusses the criteria used for including and excluding individual test items: effectively used in the first edition of TOBE, traditionally assessed on similar subtests, relevant, easily illustrated, free from ethnic-racial-sex bias, high item-total correlations (which are necessary for developing a reliable test), and item difficulties. Evidence for concurrent or predictive validity was not reported.

SUMMARY

The Tests of Basic Experiences 2 is a series of group-administered devices designed to assess pupil skill development in several areas. There are two levels of the test, with separate tests assessing development in mathematics, language, science, and social studies.

Although TOBE 2 was standardized on many children, it is difficult to ascertain from the data in the test manual how representative the sample was. Reliability data are adequate for screening. Users of the tests should be able to evaluate the content validity, since the necessary information is so clearly presented.

Coping with Dilemmas in Current Practice

There are three major dilemmas in assessing infants, toddlers and preschoolers. The first is that the performances of children who are very young are so variable that there is relatively little long-term prediction (for example, one year). This inability to predict precisely is particularly pronounced with shorter, quickly administered (and less reliable) measures. Since there is relatively poor predictive validity, most inferences must be drawn with great care. If individuals wish to use these measures to predict school success, they should recognize that the closer the predicted measure (that is, the criterion) is to the predictor measure (that is, the test), the greater the accuracy of the prediction. For example, language tests predict later language skills better than perpetual-motor tests do.

The second problem occurs when one uses tests of readiness and development as measures of current functioning and current attainment. When used in this way, the tests must be scrutinized. This is especially true when using developmental measures to document pupil progress at the preschool level. To use developmental measures in this way, one must make sure that there is appropriate linkage between the curriculum and the content of the test.

The third dilemma is the fact that students must be labeled to be eligible for preschool programs, but the act of labeling works to set up expectations for limited pupil performance.

Those who assess infants, toddlers, and preschool children need to assess within a context of situational specificity. There is much situational variability in performance, and this must be taken into account when making predictions or planning interventions.

Summary

Tests are used with preschoolers, infants, and toddlers for the purpose of screening. Focus generally is on identification of those children who would profit from early intervention. Assessment is based on the notions of prevention and developmental plasticity. It is assumed that it is a good idea to identify students early, intervene, change them, and prevent later problems. The impetus for preschool assessment is largely a legal one. The most recent major federal legislation to affect early assessment is Public Law 99-457.

There have been major advances in early assessment since the law was enacted in 1986. Educators now assess newborn infants, and that assessment typically involves neurobiological appraisal, consisting of assessment of neurological integrity, behavioral organization, needs, temperament, and state of consciousness. Increasingly, early childhood educators are engaged in planning interventions for medically high-risk infants and special needs infants and toddlers. They develop Individual Family Service Plans.

Readiness measures are a special form of preschool assessment. They are administered for the purposes of predicting who is not ready for formal school entry and predicting who will profit from remedial or compensatory intervention. Specific measures of school readiness were reviewed.

There are three major dilemmas in early assessment. Tests are administered for the purpose of predicting later performance, but at these young ages performance is so highly variable that prediction is very difficult. Second, it is dangerous to use preschool measures as indices of current standing. Third, provision of services is dependent on labeling children, but labeling works to set up expectations for limited pupil performance.

STUDY QUESTIONS

1. Differentiate between a *process orientation* and a *skill orientation* toward readiness.
2. In Chapter 2 we stated that a fundamental assumption in assessment was that only present behavior can be observed; any statement about future performance is an inference. Discuss the use of readiness measures in light of this assumption.
3. In assessing the validity of readiness tests, what considerations are important?
4. What are the four major areas assessed in neurobiological assessment?

ADDITIONAL READING

Bagnato, S., & Neisworth, J. (1979). Between assessment and intervention: Forging an assessment/curriculum linkage for the handicapped preschooler. *Child Care Quarterly, 8* (3), 179–195.

Bagnato, S. J., Neisworth, J. T., & Munson, S. M. (1989). *Linking developmental assessment and early intervention: Curriculum-based prescriptions.* Rockville, MD: Aspen.

Bailey, D. B., & Simeonsson, R. J. (1988). *Family assessment in early intervention.* Columbus, OH: Merrill.

Bailey, D. B., & Wolery, M. (Eds.). (1989). *Assessing infants and preschoolers with handicaps.* Columbus, OH: Merrill.

Bracken, B. A. (1988). Limitations of preschool instruments and standards for minimal levels of technical adequacy. *Journal of Psychoeducational Assessment, 5,* 313–326.

Conoley, J., & Kramer, J. J. (1989). *Buros tenth mental measurements yearbook.* Lincoln, NE: University of Nebraska Press.

Lewis, M., & Sullivan, M. W. (1985). Infant intelligence and its assessment. In B. B. Wolman (Ed.), *Handbook of intelligence: Theories, measurements, and applications.* New York: Wiley.

O'Donnell, K. J., & Oehler, J. M. (1989). Neurobehavioral assessment of the newborn infant. In D. Bailey & M. Wolery (Eds.), *Assessing infants and preschoolers with handicaps.* Columbus, OH: Merrill.

Paget, K., & Bracken, B. (1983). *The psychoeducational assessment of preschool children.* New York: Grune & Stratton.

Paget, K. D., & Barnett, D. W. Assessment of infants, toddlers, preschool children, and their families: Emergent trends. In T. B. Gutkin & C. R. Reynolds (Eds.), *The handbook of school psychology.* New York: Wiley.

Paget, K. D., & Nagle, R. J. (1986). A conceptual model of preschool assessment. *School Psychology Review, 15,* 154–165.

C·H·A·P·T·E·R 22

DIAGNOSTIC SYSTEMS

Earlier in this text we noted that tests are samples of behavior. Most tests sample behaviors from a single domain (for example, intelligence, achievement, or adaptive behavior). Two tests that sample behaviors from the same domain may actually differ significantly because they sample different behaviors from the same domain.

In the late 1970s test publishers began to develop measures that sample behaviors from several domains. Whereas other chapters in Parts 3 and 4 of this text are restricted to specific domains (although achievement is a multiple domain), the measures reviewed in this chapter are actually entire diagnostic systems.

WHY DO WE HAVE ASSESSMENT SYSTEMS?

Diagnostic systems offer two major advantages. The first is technical. The same normative sample provides derived scores for all measures in the various domains assessed in the diagnostic system. As you recall from Chapter 7, differences between test scores may be a function of differences in normative samples. Thus, if Sam's IQ is 115 and his standard score (mean = 100, standard deviation = 15) on an achievement test is 106, part of the difference between 115 and 106 may be attributed to differences in the norms of the two tests. Diagnostic systems provide more accurate comparisons of a person's performances in different domains because the derived scores in the different domains are based on the same norm group. The second advantage is that diagnostic systems may be more convenient for the assessor to use than several tests of single domains. For example, the time necessary to administer tests may be reduced since redundancies in several domains may be lessened. In addition, it may take assessors less time to put together the necessary materials for testing.

Specific Diagnostic Systems

Kaufman Assessment Battery for Children

The Kaufman Assessment Battery for Children (K-ABC) (Kaufman & Kaufman, 1983) is an individually administered norm-referenced battery intended to provide a comprehensive assessment of intelligence (learning potential and preferred learning style) and achievement for children between the ages of 2-5 and 12-5. Kaufman and Kaufman claim that the test is useful for several purposes: (1) psychological and clinical assessment (including projective interpretation of personality and inferences about impulsivity-reflectivity, perseverative behavior, rigidity-flexibility, and tolerance for frustration); (2) psychoeducational evaluation of exceptional children, particularly the learning disabled; (3) educational placement and planning; (4) assessment of minorities (especially blacks, Hispanics, and bilingual children); (5) preschool assessment; and (6) neuropsychological assessment.

Sixteen subtests are combined into three regularly administered scales and one supplementary scale. Intelligence is assessed on three scales: the Simultaneous Processing Scale, the Sequential Processing Scale, and the optional Nonverbal Scale. Simultaneous and Sequential Processing scales are combined to form the Mental Processing Scale. Achievement is assessed with the Achievement Scale.

The K-ABC draws heavily on the information-processing theories of Das (for example, Das, Kirby, & Jarman, 1975) and Luria (1966) as well as neuropsychological research of Cohen (1972). The processing of information is viewed dichotomously. One may act upon information sequentially or simultaneously. Many examples of tasks that are essentially sequential in nature are provided in the K-ABC manuals and include the following:

memorization of number facts, spelling, application of stepwise procedures in arithmetic (for example, the division algorithm), word-attack skills, and so on. The other method of acting on information is simultaneous processing. In many tasks separate elements are not handled sequentially; rather the elements are handled (processed) at once as a whole. For example, skilled readers seldom ponder individual letters in a word; they grasp the word as a whole.

Kaufman and Kaufman are also concerned with the assessment of culturally atypical children. The optional Nonverbal Scale combines subtests that can be administered gesturally and to which students can respond nonverbally. The Nonverbal Scale is believed to be "a good estimate of intellectual potential for . . . deaf, hearing-impaired, speech- or language-disordered, autistic, and non-English-speaking children" (1983, p. 35).

Achievement is conceptualized as "the ability to integrate the two types of mental processing and apply them to real-life situations" (Kaufman & Kaufman, 1983, p. 33). The "Achievement Scale is intended to assess factual knowledge and skills usually acquired in a school setting or through alertness to the environment" (Kaufman & Kaufman, 1983, p. 33).

Brief descriptions of each subtest, based on the descriptions provided by Kaufman and Kaufman between pages 36 and 57 of the Interpretative Manual, follow. Unless otherwise indicated, each subtest can be administered to children between 2-5 and 12-5.

Sequential Processing Scale

1. *Hand Movements* Requires a child to copy a sequence of taps made by the tester with the fist, palm, or side of the hand.

2. *Number Recall*   Requires a child to repeat a series of digits read by the tester.
3. *Word Order* (CA 4-0-12-5)   Requires a child to point to silhouettes of common objects in the order named by the tester.

Simultaneous Processing Scale

4. *Magic Window* (CA 2-6-4-11)   Requires a child to identify a picture that the tester rotates behind a narrow slit, exposing only a part of the picture at any one time.
5. *Face Recognition* (CA 2-6-4-11)   Requires a child to recall one or two faces that have been briefly presented by selecting the correct face(s), in a different pose, from a group photograph.
6. *Gestalt Closure*   Requires a child to complete an inkblot drawing and to name or describe it.
7. *Triangles* (CA 4-0-12-5)   Requires a child to assemble rubber triangles (one side blue, one side yellow) to match an abstract design.
8. *Matrix Analogies* (CA 5-0-12-5)   Requires a child to select the picture or design that completes a 2-by-2 visual analogy.
9. *Spatial Memory* (CA 5-0-12-5)   Requires a child to remember where pictures were arranged on a page.
10. *Photo Series* (CA 6-0-12-5)   Requires a child to organize photographs that illustrate an event and to place them in proper chronology.

Achievement Scale

11. *Expressive Vocabulary* (CA 2-6-4-11)   Requires a child to name objects from photographs.

12. *Faces & Places*   Requires a child to name famous persons, fictional characters, or places from pictures.
13. *Arithmetic* (CA 3-0-12-5)   Requires a child to name numbers, to count, to compute, and to understand mathematical concepts.
14. *Riddles* (CA 3-0-12-5)   Requires a child to name a concrete or abstract concept when given several of its characteristics.
15. *Reading/Decoding* (CA 5-0-12-5)   Requires a child to name letters and to read words orally.
16. *Reading/Understanding* (CA 7-0-12-5)   Requires children to act out commands given in sentences that they read.

Nonverbal Scale   The composition of the Nonverbal Scale varies with a child's age. For four-year-olds, the scale consists of Face Recognition, Hand Movements, and Triangles. For five-year-olds, the scale consists of Hand Movements, Triangles, Matrix Analogies, and Spatial Memory. For children 6 years and older, the scales consist of Hand Movements, Triangles, Matrix Analogies, Spatial Memory, and Photo Series.

SCORES

A variety of transformed scores are used. Scaled scores (mean = 10; $S = 3$) are available by chronological age for the Mental Processing subtests. Mental Processing subtests are combined into Sequential Processing, Simultaneous Processing, Mental Processing Composite, and Nonverbal scales (mean = 100; $S = 15$). Raw scores on the Achievement Scale yield standard scores with a mean of 100 and a standard deviation of 15. Percentile ranks are available for each subtest and scale. Age equivalents are available for each subtest of the Mental

Processing Scale, and grade equivalents are available for each of the Achievement subtests.

Norms

There are national norms and sociocultural norms available for comparisons. The *national norms* consist of 100 at each half year of age from 2-6 to 12-5. A representative sample was obtained by stratifying on sex, education of the parent, ethnic status (white, black, Hispanic, other), geographic considerations, and school placement. In addition, *sociocultural norms* are provided to compare a child to others of similar racial and ethnic background and socioeconomic status on the Mental Processing Scale and Achievement subtests (except Expressive Vocabulary).

Reliability

Both split-half and test-retest reliability coefficients, based on the standardization sample, are provided. Split-half coefficients, corrected with the Spearman-Brown formula, range from a high of .92 (Triangles at age 5) to a low of .62 (Gestalt Closure at age 7) on the Mental Processing *subtests*. Of the eighty coefficients reported, only one equaled or exceeded .90. Corrected split-half coefficients on the Mental Processing *Scale* (including the Nonverbal Scale) range from a high of .95 (several ages on the Composite Mental Processing Scale) to a low of .84 (ages 2 and 3 on the Simultaneous Processing Scale). As would be expected, the composites are more reliable than the subtests; of the forty-two coefficients, thirty equal or exceed .90. On the achievement *subtests*, corrected split-half reliabilities range from .97 (Reading/Decoding at age 6) to .70 (Faces & Places at age 3). Of the forty-eight age-subtest coefficients, twelve equal or exceed .90. The

reliability of the composite Achievement *Scale* exceeds .90 at all ages.

Test-retest reliabilities (two- to four-week interval between tests) were obtained by retesting 246 children from the standardization sample. The correlations were, however, based on several combined ages. Stabilities for the Mental Processing *subtests* range from .86 (Gestalt Closure at age range 9-0 through 12-5) to .59 (Hand Movements at age range 9-0 through 12-5). Of the 23 stability coefficients, none equals or exceeds .90. Stabilities for the Mental Processing *Scale* range from .93 (the Composite at age range 9-0 through 12-5) to .77 (Sequential Processing and Simultaneous Processing at age range 2-6 through 4-11). Of the twelve coefficients, two equal or exceed .90. Stabilities on the Achievement subtests range from .98 (Reading/Decoding at age range 5-0 through 8-11) to .72 (Riddles at age range 2-6 through 4-11). Of the fourteen age range-subtest coefficients, eight equal or exceed .90; the composite Achievement Scale exceeds .90 at the three age ranges.

Validity

Forty pages of the Interpretative Manual, describing numerous unpublished studies, are devoted to the validity of the K-ABC. To demonstrate construct validity, several types of evidence are presented. Scores on each subtest of K-ABC increase with age. The subtests are internally consistent (although this type of information is better considered as reliability). The results of several factor analyses that partially support the theorized factor structure of the K-ABC are also discussed. Convergent/discriminant validity is reported.

Criterion-related validity is also examined by correlating the K-ABC with several other tests. To support the contention that the K-ABC measures intelligence, correlations between the

K-ABC scales and various intelligence scales were examined. Correlation with the WISC-R full scale IQ and the Mental Processing Composite was .70. WISC-R full scale IQ and the Mental Processing Scale were moderately correlated: Simultaneous Processing and Nonverbal Scale, in the .60s; Sequential Processing, .47. Correlations with the Stanford-Binet using various samples of children ranged from .36 to .72 for the Mental Processing Composite, from .15 to .65 for the Simultaneous Processing Scale, from .27 to .63 for the Sequential Processing Scale, and from .31 to .70 for the Nonverbal Scale. Other tests of intelligence that were used as criteria include the McCarthy Scales, Cognitive Abilities Test, Woodcock-Johnson Cognitive Ability subtests, Columbia Mental Maturity Scale, and Slosson Intelligence Test. Finally, several studies examined the relationship of the K-ABC with the Peabody Picture Vocabulary Test. The sixty coefficients ranged from .21 (Sequential Processing) to .75 (Mental Processing Composite).

K-ABC scores were also used to predict achievement. Generally the correlations were unimpressive. For example, correlations between the PIAT subtests and the Sequential Processing Scale ranged from .12 (spelling) to .64 (math); with the Simultaneous Processing Scale, from .02 (reading recognition) to .62 (math); with the Nonverbal Scale, from .12 (reading recognition) to .51 (math). Correlations with various subtests from the Iowa Tests of Basic Skills, California Achievement Tests, and SRA Achievement Series are comparable to the PIAT correlations.

Validation of the Achievement Scale is less persuasive, largely because of the definition of achievement employed: "factual knowledge and skills usually acquired in a school setting or through alertness to the environment" (p. 33). (Achievement is more usually defined as the consequence of direct instruction.) The issue is further complicated by the way in which achievement subtests are described. For example, "Expressive vocabulary is a direct adaptation of the Stanford-Binet Picture Vocabulary task" (Kaufman & Kaufman, 1983, p. 51) or "Riddles probably comes closest to a Wechsler or Stanford-Binet Vocabulary subtest in terms of what it measures" (p. 54). The problem is that the Weschler scales and the Stanford-Binet are used by the Kaufmans to validate the *intelligence* components of their scale. This is not the same as proving that the scale measures achievement. In addition, the K-ABC provides no linkages to curricula; there is no table of specifications. Numerous correlations between the Achievement Scale and various achievement tests are presented. However, the composite achievement score is not meaningful because it mixes such disparate contents.

Although the manuals present considerable evidence to indicate the K-ABC assesses two different types of mental processing, there is little convincing evidence that the K-ABC can be substituted for more traditional measures of intelligence or achievement. No data are presented to validate the K-ABC as a measure of learning potential, for use in educational placement and planning, for clinical assessment, or for neurological assessment.

SUMMARY

The K-ABC is designed to assess the way children process information and the amount of information they have obtained compared to others of similar age and background. The battery was adequately standardized. The composite scales are generally reliable; the subtests are not. Although there is considerable indication that the battery measures different mental processes, the validity of the battery for the purposes for which it is intended is not established.

System of Multicultural Pluralistic Assessment

The System of Multicultural Pluralistic Assessment (SOMPA) (Mercer, 1979) is intended to provide comprehensive, nondiscriminatory assessment of public school pupils between the ages of 5 and 11. SOMPA provides data on children from three different viewpoints, called models: medical, social-system, and pluralistic. The medical model is intended to identify "biological anomalies, disease processes, sensory or motor impairment, or other pathological conditions in the organism" (Mercer, 1979, p. 42). The social-system model is intended to assess the extent to which the child meets the "expectations of the social systems in which he or she is participating" (p. 85). The pluralistic model is "essentially a redefinition of the traditional general intelligence model" (p. 52) and is intended to ascertain the child's "learning potential" or intelligence.

SOMPA offers two things. First, it contains a new scale, the Adaptive Behavior Inventory for Children (ABIC). Second, it offers a different score, the Estimated Learning Potential (ELP), that attempts to equalize the means of ethnic and social groups on the WISC-R. SOMPA stresses the requirement that, when intelligence is being assessed, a child should be compared only with children of comparable acculturation. This comparison is accomplished by locating the child's background in a two-dimensional matrix, ethnic group by sociocultural group. Three "ethnic" groups are included (black, Hispanic, and white). Sociocultural status is determined by administering the "Sociocultural Scales." Through multiple-regression techniques, separate norms are generated for each cell in the matrix. No group has a mean ELP of less than 100, although advantaged whites have means that are greater than 100.

Norms

There are eight different tests included in SOMPA, all standardized on the same sample of public school students. There are approximately 50 boys and 50 girls at each age from 5 to 11. The total sample consists of 2,085 children, with approximately equal numbers of blacks, Hispanics, and whites. A stratified cluster-sampling technique was used and appears to have provided a representative sample of *California* children. However, children from other states and regions were not included in the SOMPA norms. Therefore, great care should be exercised in using the norms in other areas of the country.

Sociocultural Scales

The sociocultural scales are of critical importance because they are used to (1) validate other measures within SOMPA and (2) transform WISC-R IQs into ELPs. The scales, administered to the child's mother in English or Spanish, are intended to measure the "extent to which the child's family background differs from the American core culture, and the socioeconomic status of the family within the ethnic group" (Mercer, 1979, p. 35). Although the concept of culture is a key one, little in the way of definition is offered: "language, values, customs, beliefs, and lifestyles" (p. 15). Current American core culture is never defined or described. Yet, the twenty-one questions on the sociocultural scales are supposed to pinpoint cultural differences. A description of the four scales follows.

Family Size

- Number of full siblings
- Number of persons living in household

Family Structure

- Biological relationship between child and head of household
- Biological relationship between child and respondent

Socioeconomic Status

- Occupation of head of household
- Sources of income

Urban Acculturation

- Sense of efficacy (an assessment of three beliefs)
- Community participation
- Anglicization (education of mother and head of household, geographic area in which mother and head of household were raised—deep South *or* foreign country versus the rest of the United States, and English usage of respondent)

SCORES

Raw scores are weighted. Separate tables for blacks, Hispanics, and whites are used to convert weighted sums to scaled scores ($\overline{X} = 50$, $S = 15$).

RELIABILITY

No reliability data are reported in the technical manuals.

VALIDITY

Since culture is never defined, judging the content validity of the scales is problematic. Originally all members of the standardization sample were asked thirty-eight "sociocultural" questions. Responses were factor-analyzed to reduce the question pool to twenty-one. The criteria by which the thirty-eight original questions were selected are not mentioned. No rationale was offered for factor-analyzing the sociocultural scales (especially since they are ordinal). Mercer does present a large number of significant differences among blacks, Hispanics, and whites on the means of the Sociocultural Scales. Apparently she believes that the presence of ethnic/racial differences implies that the scales are valid:

> From this analysis [mean comparisons] we reach this major conclusion: the Sociocultural Scales are measuring characteristics that do differentiate locations in sociocultural space. These locations differ sufficiently so that the white, black, and Hispanic children in our samples cannot be treated as a single population with a common lifestyle and a homogeneous cultural heritage. (1979, p. 37)

The conclusion that racial/ethnic differences must represent cultural differences is not logically valid. Finally, the Sociocultural Scales are supposed to "measure the extent to which the child's family background differs from the American core culture" (Mercer, p. 35). Yet, there was no reported effort to assess the responses of "core-culture Americans" unless *white* is taken to be synonymous with *core-culture* American. We conclude that these scales lack demonstrated validity for the purposes for which they were intended.

MEDICAL MODEL

In SOMPA the medical model consists of five measures:[1] Physical Dexterity Tests, Bender Visual Motor Gestalt Test, Weight by Height, Visual Acuity, and Health History Inventories. Mercer assumes that performance on these measures is "caused by biological conditions in the organism" (1979, p. 59).

Physical Dexterity Tests These consist of twenty-nine tasks clustered into six groups of activities.

1. *Ambulation* The child has to move up and down a 6-foot (by 2-inch) strip of masking tape stuck to the floor. The child is to heel-and-toe forward the length of the tape, then to return heel-to-toe backward. For each item, the number of errors (up to twenty) are counted; 0 indicates no errors.
2. *Equilibrium* The child is required to stand, with eyes closed and arms raised, and count to twenty. An error is scored if the child does not follow the directions, pauses during counting, changes the rate of counting, or fails to hold arms parallel to the floor, if the child's hands tremble or touch, or if the child grimaces.
3. *Placement* Two basic movements must be performed with eyes open, with eyes shut, with the right side of the body, and with the left side. The first movement is nose-touch, and the second is touching the shin with the heel of the foot. Up to three errors are scored on each of the eight tasks.
4. *Fine-Motor Sequencing* This timed tapping task is done with the index finger of first one hand, then the other, then with the toes of one foot (heel on floor), then with

the toes of the other foot. Up to three errors are scored per task.

5. *Finger-Tongue Dexterity* Four tasks are included in this group. The first two require the child to touch the thumb to each finger of the same hand, then to repeat the task with the other hand. The next task requires the child to open and close hands alternately. The last task requires the student to put the tongue in the left cheek, then the right cheek, and alternate between cheeks. Up to ten errors are scored.
6. *Involuntary Movement* This group includes six tasks, each of which requires that a position be maintained for 20 seconds. The first two tasks require the child to hold both arms straight from the shoulders with palms down. In the first task, the eyes are open, while in the second they are closed. The third and fourth tasks require that the child stand on one foot with hands at sides and eyes open. Standing on the left foot is one task; standing on the right foot, the other. The next task requires the child to stand with heels together, toes apart, hands at sides, and eyes closed. The last task requires the child to stand heel-to-toe with eyes closed and hands at sides. The scoring is based on the time the child holds each position: from 0 for 20 seconds to 3 for 9 seconds or less.

Bender Visual Motor Gestalt Test The Bender, with the Koppitz (1963) scoring system, is used. We have described this test in Chapter 14 and will not repeat it here except to note that the Bender cannot be considered a valid measure of organic pathology. SOMPA norms are used instead of Koppitz's.

Visual Acuity The Snellen Chart (see pp. 223 and 224 in this text) is used. For children

---

1. Although Auditory Acuity is listed as a "measure" within the medical model, no provision or requirement is made for collecting such information.

who wear corrective lenses, measures are taken with and without glasses or contact lenses. Children whose uncorrected vision is 20/40 or poorer are classified as "at risk" even if they wear glasses that correct their vision to 20/20.

Weight by Height   Each child is weighed and measured. Two scores are provided: (1) overweight or not, and (2) underweight or not.

Health History Inventories   The inventories consist of forty-five items: ten dealing with pre- and postnatal factors, six dealing with injuries, eighteen dealing with disease and illness, eight dealing with vision, and three dealing with hearing. Mercer and Lewis (1977) believe that this information is useful in identifying students who may "need further medical follow-up or specialized educational services" (p. 60).

SCORES

Mercer (1979) is particularly concerned with the shape of the distribution of scores within the medical perspective. Since she believes that measures within the medical model should not differentiate normal from superior status (and therefore should be negatively skewed), she developed scales with such characteristics, although such scales have undesirable statistical properties. On the Physical Dexterity Tests, the Bender Visual Motor Gestalt Test, and Weight by Height, raw scores at or below the mean are converted to scaled scores ($\overline{X} = 50$, $S = 15$); scores above the mean are given a score of 50. Percentile ranks of 16 or less and scaled scores of 35 or less are considered "at risk," while scores above those points are considered "not at risk." Children scoring "at risk" on the medical measures should receive "an in-depth

medical examination by a medical practitioner" (p. 44).

RELIABILITY

The various measures in the medical portion of SOMPA are clearly intended as screening devices. Reliabilities of the six physical-dexterity tasks at each age were estimated by internal-consistency (that is, odd-even split-half correlations corrected by the Spearman-Brown formula). The estimates range from .61 (finger-tongue dexterity at age 11) to a high of .94 (placement at age 5). Only twenty of the forty-two estimates equal or exceed .80, the desirable minimum standard for screening devices. The reliabilities for each age for each ethnic group are reported also.[2] They range from .65 to .74, unsatisfactory for a screening device. Reliability estimates for the other medical measures were not reported.

VALIDITY

Mercer claims that each model (that is, medical, social-system, and pluralistic) is validated differently and that it is inappropriate to extend validation procedures appropriate within one model to another.[3] For the medical model, Mercer admits two criteria for validity. First, "the validity of an instrument in the medical model will be determined by the extent to which it predicts scores on other biological measures" (Mercer, 1979, p. 44). Although the appropriate data are never summarized, they

2. Since Mercer (1979) insists that the medical measures are transcultural, we see no reason to report separate reliabilities for the three ethnic/racial groups.

3. We disagree.

are presented throughout the technical manual. Without considering average scores or scores at each age, there are fifteen separate scores in the medical model. Thus, there are 105 possible correlations. Of the 105, 42 are not significant, 55 are significant but account for less than 5 percent of the common variaation, and 8 are significant and account for between 5 and 10 percent of the common variation. Indicative of the inconsequential but statistically significant correlations is the one between the vision questions on the Health History Inventories and visual acuity assessed by the Snellen Chart: $r = .14$. Moreover, the logic of this criterion escapes us. For example, we see no reason for a valid measure of visual acuity to be correlated with being overweight.

The second criterion Mercer holds appropriate for judging the validity of medical-model measures is that there be nonsignificant correlations with sociocultural measures. There are sixty correlations of interest among the four sociocultural variables and the fifteen medical-model measures. Twenty-seven are statistically significant. Small correlations may be statistically significant because of the large N on which they are based. Therefore, Mercer "established the rule that a correlation must not only be statistically significant but must account for at least 5 percent of the variance in a measure before we would consider the relationship of substantive importance" (1979, p. 59). We can readily accept the 5 percent rule, but we wonder why it was not applied to intercorrelations among medical-model measures. If it were applied, only eight of the 105 correlations would have "substantive importance." Moreover, Mercer waffles on the same point later in the technical manual: "The Vision Inventory is an equally good predictor of difficulties. Eight of the eleven correlations are significant beyond the .01 level" (p. 83). Unfortunately, the greatest correlation accounts for less than 2

percent of the variance, and all the rest account for less than ½ of 1 percent of the variance. The logic of such a criterion again escapes us.

When "regular" logic is applied to SOMPA, many difficulties are apparent. The placement of the Bender Visual Motor Gestalt Test in the medical model is particularly troublesome. Mercer asserts, "standardized tests are measures of acculturation to the Anglo core culture and, as such, fit within the social system model" (1979, p. 20). The Bender is, of course, a standardized test. Its directions and the skills it assesses are no less culture-specific than WISC-R block design, coding, or maze subtests. Koppitz, whom Mercer cites as an authority on the Bender, claims it can be used as an intelligence test (although we disagree with that claim).

The content validity of the various subtests is suspect. The physical-dexterity tests are intended to provide tests of "the intactness and capability of the motor and sensory pathways." No evidence is offered that any of these measures are drawn from the appropriate domain. Some are very suspect (for example, follows directions, counts to 20). The weight-by-height measure is also of some interest. Medical tests are supposed to answer the question, "Is the child an intact organism?" or "to screen for biological abnormalities" or to find "pathological signs" (Mercer, 1979, p. 40). The relationship of the weight-by-height charts to these purposes is never specified.

One of the most severe shortcomings of the medical-model tests is that they are screening devices that have not been validated by further diagnosis. For example, the sixteenth percentile is the critical score selected by Mercer to indicate "at risk." There is no evidence offered that the sixteenth percentile isolates children determined by physicians to be at risk. Why should we believe that a child at, for example, the fifteenth percentile for underweight is at risk?

SOCIAL-SYSTEM MODEL

Within the social-system model a child's performance is evaluated in terms of the adequacy with which the child fills various social roles and "the extent to which the child is able to negotiate entry, establish interpersonal ties with other group members, learn the skills required to play social roles, and achieve an adaptive fit in each social system" (Mercer, 1979, p. 46). To assess role performance, two tests are given: (1) the WISC-R (as a measure of "academic role performance in the public schools") and (2) the Adaptive Behavior Inventory for Children (ABIC).

WISC-R   The WISC-R is reviewed in Chapter 10. Within SOMPA it is considered to be "a measure of how much the child has learned about the core culture of modern American society. . . . It is a measure of the child's adaptive fit to the student role" (Mercer, 1979, p. 114). The WISC-R is, moreover, an indirect measure of adaptive fit, and its validity within the SOMPA scheme is "determined by its 'predictive power.' Other forms of validity, such as construct validity, face validity,[4] and content validity, are not directly relevant and will not be considered further" (p. 116). Such a position is convenient, since there is a lack of content and construct validity for the WISC-R for this purpose. It was developed and validated as a test of intelligence and not as a measure of academic-role performance. It is unclear to us how block design, coding, digit span, or mazes measure learning of the core culture.

To establish the predictive validity of the WISC-R for the purposes of SOMPA, two studies of the correlations between WISC-R and grade-point averages are reported. These

correlations were generally .3 or less. Such correlations clearly indicate how poor the WISC-R is as a measure of academic-role performance. Several studies with the old WISC are also reported; generally, the results are the same: unacceptably low correlations.

Adaptive Behavior Inventory for Children
The Adaptive Behavior Inventory for Children (ABIC) contains 242 questions organized into six scales: family (52 questions), community (42 questions), peer relations (36 questions), nonacademic school roles (37 questions), earner/consumer (26 questions), and self-maintenance (49 questions). As with other measures of adaptive behavior, a respondent who is familiar with the child is interviewed. The interview may be conducted in English or Spanish. The first 35 questions are asked about all children; the last 207 use a basal and ceiling rule. "Questions were developed that would apply equally to both sexes, to all socioeconomic levels, and to all ethnic groups" (Mercer, 1979, p. 93). Other criteria used to include and exclude items are unclear. Subsequent analysis of the responses made by members of the standardization sample shows that questions favoring boys are approximately balanced by questions favoring girls, questions favoring high-status families by questions favoring low-status families. There are racial/ethnic differences.

SCORES

Responses to the ABIC receive one of five scores: latent role (child has not performed the activity), emergent role (child is beginning to perform the role), mastered role, no opportunity/not allowed, and respondent doesn't

---

4. Face validity is not generally considered as validity. It refers to the extent to which a test's content looks right on the face of it.

know. Raw scores for each of the six subtests of the ABIC are converted to standard scores ($\overline{X}$ = 50, S = 15). The average scale score is the mean of the six subscales.

RELIABILITY

Split-half estimates (with Spearman-Brown correction) were computed for each age level for each subscale of the ABIC. Reliabilities of the subscales are generally too low for use in making individual decisions (thirty-six of the forty-two estimates are less than .9). The reliabilities for the average scores are excellent, .97 or higher. Some evidence of interrater agreement is provided. The data are based on the responses of undescribed individuals completing training workshops. The standard deviations of scores are erroneously averaged;[5] this results in systematically underestimated variability. Nonetheless, it does appear that workshop completors score ABIC interviews consistently.

VALIDITY

Mercer asserts that for "proper" validation of the ABIC scales, one must distinguish between indirect measurement and direct measurement. Direct measurement is an evaluation that comes "from members of the system, . . . such as a peer evaluating a child's performance in the peer group" (Mercer, 1979, p. 107). Indirect measurements are evaluations by persons not members of the system. Indirect measurements are to be validated by predicting direct measurements. Direct measurements are to be validated by interrater agreement. Using Mercer's own criteria, the ABIC scales are unvalidated.

From a more usual perspective, the ABIC scales appear to be measuring adaptive behavior. However, the technical manual does not delineate the contents that ought to be sampled to assure content validity. Users of the scales will need to judge their validity for themselves.

PLURALISTIC MEASURE

The central tenet of SOMPA is that differences in measured intelligence among social classes and ethnic groups are the result of different opportunities to learn materials tested because "the genetic potential for acquiring the cognitive skills needed to perform as a student is essentially the same in all ethnic and cultural groups" (1979, p. 135). To turn this admirable social belief into a scientific fact, a statistical procedure is used to develop separate means and standard deviations for each racial/ethnic group at each sociocultural level. Specifically, a multiple regression equation is developed to predict WISC-R scores from the sociocultural scales for each racial/ethnic group. The predicted WISC-R score is assumed to be the mean for the group and is subtracted from the child's obtained WISC-R score; this difference is divided by the standard deviation of predicted scores.[6] The score produced is treated as a z-score and is then converted to an ELP (Estimated Learning Potential), a score with a mean equal to 100 and a standard deviation equal to 15.

---

5. Variances, not standard deviations, are additive.

6. The S of predicted scores is the standard error or estimate (S_{EE}). The S_{EE} can be computed by the formula $S_{EE} = S\sqrt{1-r^2}$.

RELIABILITY

The reliability of the ELP is not discussed in the SOMPA technical manuals. However, the ELP is essentially a difference score in which there is reliability associated with the estimated mean and with the obtained WISC-R score.

VALIDITY

Mercer asserts that the "appropriate test of the validity [of the ELP] is the amount of variance in WISC-R IQs accounted for by the sociocultural variables in the regression equation" (1979, p. 141). Indeed, the sociocultural scales do account for a modest proportion of the variation in WISC-R scores. Yet this seems a hollow criterion by which to judge a score as an indicator of a "child's probable potential for future learning" (p. 143). The unspoken criterion appears to be that the test must be considered a valid test of intelligence for members of the core culture. Its extension to other sociocultural groups is deemed permissible with "pluralistic" (that is, multiple) norms.

Two serious internal contradictions must also be noted. Mercer devotes four paragraphs to denying the appropriateness of correlating ELP scores with "social-system" measures. Six paragraphs later (p. 143) she urges that users focus their interpretations on Verbal ELPs "because it is more highly correlated . . . with both dimensions of the school role: academic performance and interpersonal relations." (Moreover, no correlations between ELPs and *any* measures are provided.) The second contradiction is most bothersome. Throughout the technical manuals, the SOMPA authors continually refer to discriminatory assessments as those that result in mean differences among ethnic/racial groups. After all the SOMPA ad-

justments are made, the mean for advantaged whites is still higher than the means for other groups. The reason is that SOMPA does not use the predicted WISC-R score as the mean when it is greater than 100. In these cases, ELP and WISC-R are interpreted to be the same. We believe that potential SOMPA users are deliberately misled into believing that racial/ethnic differences as well as social-class differences have been eliminated when in fact they have not been.

There are other fundamental problems with the validity of the ELP. SOMPA leads the reader to believe that once sociocultural factors are taken into account, genetic potential for learning will be assessed. Also, Mercer mistakenly calls the organism the genotype when she writes, "the genotype is modified by environmental factors such as the physical health and nutrition of the mother and, after birth, the nature of the physical environment" (1979, p. 52). Although the genotype is *not* altered,[7] the organism is indeed modified. However, the impact of this point was somehow missed: "inferences about a child's learning potential can be made *if* the child's performance is compared only with others who have come from similar sociocultural settings and presumably have had the same opportunity to learn the material in the test, the same motivation to learn that material, and the same test-taking experience" (Mercer, 1979, p. 53). Environment modifies learning potential, and to the extent that it does, SOMPA's ELPs are conceptually wrong. The most nurturing physical and psychological environments are not equally distributed among social groups (for example, the children of the rich do not usually suffer malnutrition). Another example of how the ELP may be in error involves rural and urban children. Mercer asserts that urban and rural children have equal

---

7. This thoroughly discredited theory is called the Lamarckian fallacy.

potential to learn. However, there is selective migration to cities. Children who move from rural areas to urban areas have higher IQs than the children who remain (Roberts, 1971). Obviously this will produce different means for urban and rural children. In short, SOMPA ignores a vast literature of the effects that environment can have on measured intelligence. There is much more than genotype and opportunity to learn the test materials.

Finally, it must be noted that the technical manual is most annoying. Factual errors are littered throughout. Critical information is absent (for example, intercorrelations of sociocultural scales). Standards for making decisions shift, so that the decision reached is consistent with dogma rather than data. Minor statistical misunderstandings crop up too often (for example, the WISC-R is called an ordinal scale

and then used in analyses that require equal-interval data).

SUMMARY

SOMPA is a system that attempts to provide data from multiple perspectives in order to understand a child's current level of functioning and potential for future learning. The norms are representative of public school students in California. Users outside of California should be extremely careful in using SOMPA's norms and regression equations. Except for the ABIC and WISC-R, reliabilities are either too low or unreported. Validities for various purposes are not established. At best, SOMPA should be considered experimental.

WOODCOCK-JOHNSON PSYCHOEDUCATIONAL BATTERY–REVISED (WJ-R)

The WJ-R (Woodcock & Johnson, 1989) is an individually admininistered, norm-referenced assessment system intended to assess the intellectual and academic development of individuals from preschool through adulthood.[8] In addition to the technical manuals that accompany the test, the WJ-R uses four easel kits for

presenting stimulus materials: one for the standard cognitive subtests, one for the supplementary cognitive subtests, one for the standard achievement subtests, and one for the supplementary achievement subtests.

The revision represents a substantial modification of the first edition. New features include ten new tests added to the cognitive battery, four new tests added to the achievement battery, alternate forms for the achievement tests, availability of computerized scoring, among others. The tests of interest have been dropped from the 1989 edition. The batteries require a skillful examiner to administer and score the subtests.

---

8. Basal and ceiling rules are used so that no subject is administered all of the items. These rules have been changed in the WJ-R. Some scoring criteria are not found in the easel used to present test stimuli. Thus, testers must refer to the examiner's manual during the administration to find the criteria.

TESTS OF COGNITIVE ABILITY

The Cognitive Battery is comprised of twenty-one cognitive tests and is based on the Horn-Cattell Gf-Gc theory of intelligence. To date, nine broad intellectual abilities have been identified in the work of Cattell, Horn, and others on Gf-Gc theory. The WJ-R measures eight of the nine abilities. The nine factors in the Horn-Cattell model are Comprehension-Knowledge (Gc), Fluid Reasoning (Gf), Visual Processing (Gv), Auditory Processing (Ga), Correct Decision Speed (CDS), Processing Speed (Gs), Short-term Memory (Gsm), Long-term Retrieval (Glr), and Quantitative Ability (Gq). The Standard Battery consists of the first seven subtests, each of which correspond to an hypothesized factor of intelligence.

Memory for Names   Consists of auditory visual tasks in which the individual learns the names of nine pictured space creatures.

Memory for Sentences   Consists of phrases and sentences that are presented individually on audiotape and that must be repeated by the individual.

Visual Matching   Consists of 70 sets of numbers; each set consists of six numbers that range from single digits to three-digit numbers. An individual's score is based on the number of correct matches in 3 minutes.

Incomplete Words   Consists of words with one or more missing phonemes that the individual is to identify.

Visual Closure   Consists of forty-nine visual stimuli that the individual must identify. The pictures are distorted, incomplete, or have patterns superimposed on them.

Picture Vocabulary   Consists of pictures of objects that the individual must name.

Analysis-Synthesis   A learning task that requires the individual to determine what components are missing from an incomplete logic puzzle.

The supplementary battery consists of the next fourteen subtests, which are designed to provide additional information about the factors measured by the standard intellectual battery.

Visual-Auditory Learning   Requires the individual to associate visual symbols with words and make sentences out of the symbols.

Memory for Words   Requires the individual to repeat lists of unrelated words; the lists range in length from one to eight words.

Cross Out   Consists of timed, match-to-sample tasks in which the individual must locate five drawings in a set of twenty that match the stimulus.

Sound Blending   Requires the individual to synthesize syllables into words.

Picture Recognition   Requires the individual to recognize a subset of pictures that have been presented with distracting pictures.

Oral Vocabulary   Requires the individual to give synonyms or antonyms in response to stimulus words read by the examiner.

Concept Formation   Requires the individual to specify concepts when given a set of materials that contains instances and noninstances of that concept.

Delayed Recall—Memory for Names Requires the individual to recall, after one to eight days, the names of the space creatures learned in the first test.

Delayed Recall—Visual-Auditory Learning Requires the individual to recall, after one to eight days, the symbols learned in the eighth test.

Numbers Reversed Requires the individual to repeat a series of digits backward.

Sound Patterns Requires the individual to listen to two complex sound patterns and tell if they are the same or different.

Spatial Relations Requires the individual to match shapes.

Listening Comprehension An oral cloze task in which an individual listens to a passage and supplies the last word.

Verbal Analogies Requires the individual to complete progressively more difficult analogies.

As shown in Figure 22.1, these tests can be combined into seven Cognitive Factor Clusters (Long-Term Retrieval, Short-Term Retrieval, Short-Term Memory, Processing Speed, Auditory Processing, Visual Processing, Comprehension-Knowledge, and Fluid Reasoning), four scholastic-aptitude clusters (Reading Aptitude, Mathematics Aptitude, Written Language Aptitude, and Knowledge Aptitude), two Oral Language Clusters (Oral Language and Oral Language Aptitude), and three total scores: Early Development Scale (using subtests appropriate for young children), Broad Cognitive Ability (based on the standard battery) and Broad Cognitive Ability (based on the extended battery).

TESTS OF ACHIEVEMENT

There are fourteen achievement subtests. The first nine make up the standard achievement battery.

Letter-Word Identification Assesses the identification of letters in isolation and in words.

Passage Comprehension Uses a modified cloze procedure to assess comprehension of short passages.

Calculation Assesses prowess in solving whole- and mixed-number problems involving

the basic operations as well as problems requiring higher mathematics (for example, trigonometry and calculus).

Applied Problems Assesses skill in solving practical mathematics problems.

Dictation Requires individuals to write answers to questions, to assess spelling, capitalization, punctuation, and word usage.

Writing Samples Require individuals to write answers to a variety of questions that range from very simple (for example, writing one's name) to more difficult (for example, writing a correct sentence describing a stimulus picture and using specified vocabulary).

Science Requires individuals to give oral answers to questions assessing knowledge in biology and physical science.

Social Studies Requires individuals to give oral answers to questions assessing knowledge in economics, history, geography, and so forth.

Humanities Requires individuals to give oral answers to questions assessing knowledge in art, music, and literature.

FIGURE 22.1 Relationship Between WJ-R Cognitive Tests and Composite Score

Selective Testing Table

TESTS OF COGNITIVE ABILITY	Early Development Scale	Standard Scale	Extended Scale	Long-Term Retrieval (Glr)	Short-Term Memory (Gsm)	Processing Speed (Gs)	Auditory Processing (Ga)	Visual Processing (Gv)	Comprehension-Knowledge (Gc)	Fluid Reasoning (Gf)	Oral Language	Reading	Mathematics	Written Language	Knowledge	Intra-Cognitive Discrepancies	Oral Language
STANDARD BATTERY																	
1. Memory for Names	●	●	●	●												●	
2. Memory for Sentences	●	●	●		●						●	●			●	●	
3. Visual Matching		●	●			●						●	●	●		●	
4. Incomplete Words	●	●	●				●									●	
5. Visual Closure	●	●	●					●							●	●	
6. Picture Vocabulary	●	●	●						●		●					●	
7. Analysis-Synthesis		●	●							●			●			●	
SUPPLEMENTAL BATTERY																	
8. Visual-Auditory Learning	○		●	●											●	●	
9. Memory for Words	○		●		●											●	
10. Cross Out			●			●										●	
11. Sound Blending	○		●				●					●		●	●	●	
12. Picture Recognition	○		●					●								●	●
13. Oral Vocabulary			●						●		●	●	●	●		●	●
14. Concept Formation			●							●			●		●	●	●
15. Delayed Recall — Memory for Names				○													
16. Delayed Recall — Visual-Auditory Learning				○													
17. Numbers Reversed					○											●	
18. Sound Patterns							○									●	
19. Spatial Relations								○		○							
20. Listening Comprehension									○		●						
21. Verbal Analogies									○	○	●						

● = Tests to administer for a cluster score
○ = Tests which can supply additional information

SOURCE: Reprinted from the *Woodcock-Johnson Tests of Cognitive Ability—Standard and Supplemental Batteries Examiner's Manual* (Woodcock & Mather, 1989a, p. 12). Used with permission of DLM.

The supplementary battery consists of the next five subtests that are designed to provide additional information about a student's achievement.

Word Attack Requires individuals to read orally low-frequency and nonsense words, to assess skill in applying rules of phonics and structural analysis.

Reading Vocabulary Requires individuals to read words and give synonyms or antonyms.

Quantitative Concepts Assesses knowledge of mathematical concepts and vocabulary.

Proofing Assesses individuals' ability to recognize and correct errors in capitalization, diction, punctuation, and spelling.

Writing Fluency Provides individuals with either stimulus pictures or three words and requires individuals to write appropriate responses. From this timed test, separate scores are obtained for punctuation and capitalization, spelling, usage, and handwriting.

As shown in Figure 22.2, these tests can be combined into five Achievement Clusters (Broad Reading, Broad Mathematics, Broad Written Language, Broad Knowledge, and Skills) and six skill areas (Basic Reading Skills, Reading Comprehension, Basic Mathematics Skills, Mathematics Reasoning, Basic Writing Skills, and Written Expression).

SCORES

Raw scores from the subtests are converted to *W*-scores, and *W*-scores are combined into cluster scores. *W*-scores, derived Rasch scores, are equal-interval scores with a mean of approximately 500 for fifth-graders. The psychometric basis for this score, item-response theory, is still not well understood by many practitioners. Thus, *W*-scores may not be readily interpretable.

Although conversion to age or grade equivalents[9] is easier than in the first edition, these scores have severe limitations. Percentiles and standard scores are readily understood and used by most practitioners and should be stressed. Conversions to these scores still appear to be tedious, time consuming, and so complex that they may be prone to error by examiners. In addition, the WJ-R uses Relative Mastery Indexes (RMIs). These scores predict success as a ratio; for example, a relative mastery index of 60/90 means that an individual will probably achieve 60 percent success on similar tasks while peers will achieve 90 percent. Finally, normative data for a variety of differences are available. Interpretation of a difference is based on the actual performance of individuals rather than being estimated mathematically. For example, in evaluating a difference between cognitive ability and achievement, the average achievement of individuals with the same cognitive ability is used to compare the obtained achievement of a student with the expected achievement.

NORMS

WJ-R norms are based on the performances of 6,359 individuals living in more than 100 communities. A stratified random sampling

---

9. The WJ-R uses an extended age- and grade-score scale that provides a hybrid of percentiles and equivalents. A superscript denotes the percentile rank for a person attaining the highest or lowest equivalent. For example, an age equivalent of 33[75] indicates that 33 is the highest age equivalent that can be determined and the raw score is at the 75th percentile for that age equivalent.

FIGURE 22.2 Relationship Between WJ-R Achievement Tests and Composite Score

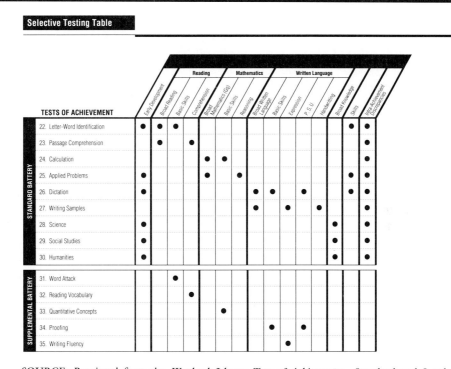

SOURCE: Reprinted from the *Woodcock-Johnson Tests of Achievement—Standard and Supplemental Batteries Examiner's Manual* (Woodcock & Mather, 1989a, p. 12). Used with permission of DLM.

plan was used to locate individuals. The sample was weighted, and the total sample corresponds closely (within 2 percent) to the most recent U.S. Census on relevant characteristics such as region, community size, sex, race, and so forth. Correspondence of the sample at specific ages to the census data is not presented.

RELIABILITY

Information about the WJ-R's reliability is incompletely reported. Except for the timed subtests, no data on score stability are reported.[10]

10. Neither the length of time between test and retest, nor the expected change in scores between retests is indicated.

The reliability information that is reported is for selected ages (2, 4, 6, 9, 13, 18) and age ranges (30–39, 50–59, and 70–79). Odd-even correlations, corrected by the Spearman-Brown formula, are used to estimate reliability for each untimed subtest, and test-retest correlations were used to estimate the stability of timed subtests. All the reliabilities for the Broad Cognitive and Achievement Clusters exceed .90, so it is probably a safe assumption that the Broad Clusters are also reliable enough at the missing ages to facilitate decision making for individual students. However, the same assumption should not be made for subtests and other cluster scores. The specific estimates of reliability are variable and often fall below the desirable minimum of .90. Moreover, we could not recognize consistent patterns of increasing or decreasing reliability by age within subtests and other clusters. Therefore, one should not presume the reliabilities of subtests and other clusters at missing ages are sufficient for making important educational and psychological decisions about individual students.

Cognitive Battery Of the 157 age-by-subtest reliabilities reported, 54 percent are less than .90, and 22 percent are less than .80. At only three ages did the stability of the two timed tests equal or exceed .80. Consequently, the subtests generally are not sufficiently reliable for making important decisions for individuals. On the extended scale, the scores for specific abilities are more reliable. Of the 56 age-by-subtest reliability coefficients reported, 16 are less than .90 and of these 16 only 3 are less than .80.

Achievement Battery All the reliability information is presented by age even though reliability by grade is usually more relevant. Of the 74 age-by-subtest reliabilities reported for the Standard Battery, 46 percent are less than .90, and 4 percent are less than .80. Of the 29 age-by-subtest reliabilities reported for the Supplementary Battery, 44 percent are less than .90, and 3 percent are less than .80. Of the 28 age-by-subtest stability coefficients, 75% are less than .90, and 21% are less than .80. Four of the 44 reliabilities for the clusters based on the Supplementary Battery are below .90.

VALIDITY

Careful item selection is consistent with claims for the content validity of both the Cognitive and Achievement[11] Battery. The items within subtests appear appropriate and carefully prepared.

The evidence of concurrent validity comes from studies using three-, nine-, and seventeen-year-olds. For the Cognitive Battery, scores on the WJ-R Broad Cognitive Clusters and performances on other intellectual measures appropriate for individuals at the ages tested were compared. For example, at age 3 the criterion measures included the Stanford-Binet (fourth edition), the Boehm Tests of Basic Concepts, and so forth. The correlations between the WJ-R and criterion measures were in the range of .46 to .73. For the Achievement Battery, their scores on the WJ-R Broad Achievement Clusters were also compared to their scores on appropriate achievement measures (for example, BASIS, KABC, KTEA, WRAT-R, and so forth). The pattern and magnitude of correlations suggest that the WJ-R is measuring skills similar to those measured by other achievement tests.

To establish the construct validity, the test authors examined the intercorrelations among subtests within each battery. As expected, subtests assessing the same broad cognitive ability or achievement area usually correlated more highly with each other than with subtests assessing different cognitive abilities or areas of achievement. Further evidence of construct validity comes from comparisons of groups of exceptional persons (that is, gifted, learning-disabled, and mentally retarded individuals) with nonexceptional persons. The means of each group of exceptional persons are arrayed as expected for the cognitive and achievement clusters: gifted individuals earn higher scores than normal individuals who, in turn, earn

11. As is the case for all commercially prepared achievement measures, test users must exercise great caution in applying test scores to specific curricula.

higher scores than learning-disabled individuals; learning-disabled individuals earn higher scores than mentally retarded individuals.

Summary

The WJ-R (Woodcock & Johnson, 1989) provides a comprehensive assessment of cognitive and academic ability throughout the life span. There are sixteen standard and twenty-nine supplementary subtests. A variety of scores are available although conversion is often awkward. WJ-R norms are based on a large and representative sample of the United States. No data on interscorer agreement are reported; except for the timed subtests, no data on score stability are reported. Internal consistencies are reported for selected ages, but not for grades. All the reliabilities for the Broad Cognitive and Broad Achievement Clusters exceed .90 so these scores are probably reliable at all ages. The reliabilities of subtests and other clusters are variable so these scores probably should not be used in educational decision making. For a new device, the WJ-R appears to have adequate validity.

Coping with Dilemmas in Current Practice

The general problems that are raised by diagnostic systems are often the same as those raised in the measurement of the domains that are included in the systems. Methods for coping with the problems are also the same. For example, when a diagnostic system examines achievement, the question of curriculum match must be addressed.

One problem is noteworthy. The theoretical constructs on which the diagnostic systems are based often force the assessor to interpret behavior samples in novel and unusual ways. For example, SOMPA uses the Bender Visual Motor Gestalt Test (with Koppitz's scoring procedures) as a measure of organic pathology. From SOMPA's perspective, there is a need for such a measure. From a more traditional measurement standpoint, the Bender cannot be used in this way. The K-ABC provides another example. Simultaneous and sequential processing are proposed as measures of intelligence. However, such an orientation to intellectual assessment is quite revolutionary. For many diagnosticians, acceptance of the K-ABC's orientation will require a considerably larger base of research support. We believe that the way to cope with novel theoretical orientations is to defer acceptance until a firm base of research indicates their validity. Until such research is available, patience and skepticism may serve the tester well.

Summary

Three diagnostic systems—assessment devices sampling behaviors in multiple domains—were reviewed: the K-ABC, SOMPA, and the revised Woodcock-

Johnson Psycho-Educational Battery. Each system offers the advantage of being standardized on the same sample. Therefore, differences between domains within a particular diagnostic system are unaffected by differences in standardization samples, and the examination of intra-individual differences is freed from a previously uncontrolled source of error. Other than sharing this common advantage, the diagnostic systems considered in this chapter differ sharply from each other.

The *Kaufman Assessment Battery for Children* has four components: a Sequential Processing Scale, a Simultaneous Processing Scale, an Achievement Scale, and an optional Nonverbal Scale. The first two scales are derived from a model of intellectual function that stresses how people process information; this model is different from the models on which many other measures of intelligence are based (i.e., a general intellectual factor, g).

The *System of Multicultural Pluralistic Assessment* (SOMPA) is intended to overcome potentially discriminatory testing of children from diverse cultural backgrounds. Although many elements of SOMPA resemble more traditional norm-referenced assessment devices, this diagnostic system is very untraditional in its interpretation of behavior samples. There are four key sources of information that make up SOMPA; Sociocultural Scales, Medical Model information, Social System Model, and Pluralistic information. Potential users should recognize that some interpretations lack validation and are controversial. For example, no empirical support for critical scores on measures used within the medical model is provided, and many would argue that the Bender Visual Motor Gestalt Test is not a measure of organic pathology and that the Wechsler Intelligence Scale for Children is not a measure of "academic role performance in the public schools."

The *Woodcock-Johnson Psycho-Educational Battery–Revised* (WJ–R) is a comprehensive assessment system designed to assess cognitive functioning and achievement. The cognitive battery is based on the Horn-Cattell theory of fluid and crystallized intelligence. While the domains assessed and their interpretations are well within the mainstream of modern testing, the methodology used to develop the test is quite different from the methods used to develop most other tests. The WJ–R uses Rasch's model of item-response theory. In this model, selection of test items and the development of norms are based on a set of assumptions and procedures that are quite different from the assumptions and methods used in the more traditional models discussed earlier in this book. Thus, much of the technical discussion of test development and some of the derived scores that are available may be unfamiliar to traditionally trained readers.

While each diagnostic system is intended by its authors to be used in its entirety, some practicing psychologists use only parts of a system. For example, it is not uncommon for a psychologist to use the *Wechsler Intelligence Scale for Children–Revised* in conjunction with the achievement battery from the *Woodcock-Johnson Psycho-Educational Battery–Revised* or the achievement scale from the *Kaufman Assessment Battery for Children*. Although such practices do not give a diagnostician the advantage of a shared normative sample, they do make sense; relevant domains are assessed in a way that provides the tester with technically adequate and meaningful information. In the final analysis, diagnostic systems provide additional ways and domains for assessment.

STUDY QUESTIONS

1. What instructional implications can you derive from the K-ABC?
2. To what extent does the SOMPA provide a nondiscriminatory assessment of students?
3. Identify three potential difficulties that users may face in using the SOMPA and the Woodcock-Johnson Psychoeducational Battery–Revised.
4. Earlier in this text we stated that one of the fundamental assumptions in assessment is that the student tested and the group on whom a test is standardized have comparable, although not necessarily identical, acculturation. The SOMPA employs multiple norm groups to address this assumption. To what extent does the SOMPA succeed?

ADDITIONAL READING

Journal of Special Education, Fall 1984 issue. (The entire issue is a symposium on the Kaufman Assessment Battery.)

School Psychology Review 8 (1) (1979). (The entire issue is a symposium on the SOMPA.)

CHAPTER 23

ASSESSING BEHAVIOR THROUGH OBSERVATION: AN OVERVIEW

In the general sense, the term *observation* refers to the process of gaining information through one's senses—visual, auditory, and so forth. Observation can be used to assess behavior, states, physical characteristics, and permanent products of behavior (such as a child's poem). In this chapter, we use the term *behavioral observation* to refer to observation of behavior *other* than behavior that has been elicited by a predetermined and standardized set of stimuli—that is, test behavior.

There are two basic approaches to observation—qualitative and quantitative observation. Qualitative observation is essentially descriptive. The observer begins without preconceived ideas about what will be observed and describes behavior that seems important. There are also two basic approaches to qualitative observation—ethnographic and participant-observer (see Suen & Ary, 1989). The difference between the two approaches lies in the behavior of the observer. In ethnographic observation, the observer maintains a role as someone who is watching what is occurring. In the participant-observer approach, the observer joins the target social group and participates in its activities. In either case, observation occurs over prolonged periods, and the observer tries to note all the activities and contexts. Although qualitative approaches may have intuitive appeal, they suffer from four limitations: (1) sophisticated and highly trained observers are required; (2) data collection requires a burdensome investment of time (sometimes years); (3) the observer's notes can be difficult to interpret and summarize; and (4) it is often difficult to maintain scientific objectivity (Suen & Ary, 1989).

Some qualitative observation often precedes quantitative observation. For example, an observer might watch students in specific situations to get a general feel for what is going on. Then that observer might set out to measure specific behaviors that are thought to be particularly important. This form of qualitative observation is sometimes referred to as "nonsystematic observation" or "monitoring" (that is, paying attention and noting important events). Probably the most common way of conducting nonsystematic observations is to keep anecdotal records of behaviors that seem important to the observer. These records should, at the minimum, contain a complete description of the behavior and context in which it occurred.

In this chapter, we stress quantitative approaches to observation. Quantitative observation is distinguished by five characteristics. First, the goal of observation is to measure (for example, count) specific behaviors. Second, these behaviors have been previously defined precisely. Third, before observation, the procedures are developed by which objective and replicable information about the behavior are gathered. Fourth, the times and places for observation are carefully selected and specified. Fifth, the ways in which behavior will be quantified are specified prior to observation.

The major criticism of quantitative approaches is that they may oversimplify the meaning and interpretation of behavior. Despite this criticism, quantitative analysis of behavior has proven to be very useful in developing theory and practice related to the modification of human behavior. Assessment based on quantitative behavioral observation is a topic suitable for an entire text, and only a general overview of good practices for those who develop and use behavioral observations can be treated in this chapter; interested readers are referred to texts by Boehm and Weinberg (1988), Alberto and Troutman (1990), or Salvia and Hughes (1990), among others. Readers interested in the statistical bases of measurement procedures used in systematic observation may consult the text by Suen and Ary (1989). Finally, the procedures and concepts discussed in detail in preceding chapters are not reexplained here.

WHY DO TEACHERS OBSERVE BEHAVIOR?

Humans are always monitoring external events, and the behavior of others is a primary target for our attention. Teachers are constantly monitoring themselves and their students. Sometimes they are just keeping an eye on things to make sure that their classrooms are safe and orderly, to anticipate disruptive or dangerous situations, or just to keep track of how things are going in a general sense. Often they notice behavior or situations that seem important and require their attention: the fire alarm has sounded, Harvey has a knife, Betty is asleep, Jo is wandering around the classroom, and so forth. In other situations—and often as a result of their general monitoring, teachers look for very specific behavior to observe: social behavior that should be reinforced, attention to task, performance of particular skills, and so forth. Information gained from observation can be used to make academic and social instructional decisions—for example, planning or evaluating instructional programs for individuals or groups of students.

GENERAL CONSIDERATIONS

Behavior that is to be analyzed quantitatively can be observed as it occurs (in real time), or at times after it has occurred, by devices such as video or audio recorders that can replay, slow down, or speed up records of behavior displays. Observation can be enhanced with equipment (for example, a telescope), or it can occur with only one's unaided senses. Observational systems can be classified along two dimensions: (1) obtrusive versus unobtrusive and (2) contrived versus naturalistic.

Obtrusive Versus Unobtrusive Observation

When antisocial, offensive, or highly personal or undesirable behaviors are targeted for assessment, observation often is conducted surreptitiously. Behaviors of these types tend not to occur if they are overtly monitored. For example, parents who hit their children privately may be very hesitant to do so publicly. For making observations of such behavior, observers can use hidden cameras that require minimum light or use extrasensitive recorders; or a human observer can become a trusted person around whom the target individual will act naturally.

Behavior that is not antisocial, immoral, or highly personal may also nonetheless be distorted by observation. For example, when a principal sits in the back of a probationary teacher's classroom for a periodic evaluation, both the teacher's and the students' behavior may be affected by the principal's presence. Often students are better behaved or respond more enthusiastically, in the mistaken belief that the principal is there to watch *them*. The teacher may write more frequently on the chalkboard, repeat directions more often, ask more questions of particular students, or give more positive reinforcement than usual, in the belief that the principal values those techniques. Moreover, a video camera, audio microphone, unusually bright light, or one-way mirrors can signal that someone is watching and, thus, become stimuli that set the occasion for atypical behavior.

Unobtrusive observations do not affect the way people behave. It is fortunate that most people quickly become desensitized to observers or observation equipment when the observers or equipment are part of their daily environment. A number of things can be done to hasten desensitization. Observers can sit behind or to the side of a classroom, and they can avoid eye contact and verbal interactions with students. Recording equipment that cannot be hidden can be left in operating position at all times. Moreover, any indication that the equipment is recording should be avoided. For example, if a red light comes on when a video camera is recording, students are likely to pay attention to the camera when the light is on; the red light should be disabled. Observation and recording can become part of the everyday classroom routine. In any event, assessment should not begin until persons to be observed are desensitized and are acting in their usual ways.

Contrived Versus Naturalistic Observation

Contrived observations occur in situations that have been set up before a student is introduced into the situation. For example, a playroom may be set up with toys that allow aggressive play (such as guns or punching-bag dolls) or with many desirable toys. The child may be given a book and told to go into the room and read or may simply be told to wait in the room. Other adults or children in the situation may be confederates of the observer and be instructed to behave in particular ways. For example, an older child might be told not to share toys with the child who is the target of the observation, or an adult might be told to initiate a conversation on a specific topic with the target child.

In contrast, naturalistic settings are not contrived. For example, specific toys are not added to or removed from a playroom; the furniture is arranged as it always is arranged.

DEFINING BEHAVIOR

It is worth repeating that behavior is observable. Moreover, behavior is always defined in terms of its observable attributes. Depending on the particular behavior and the reasons for observation, behavior can be described in several ways. Often the function that a behavior serves in the environment is described (for example, uses a pencil to write) and assessed. Sometimes, the topography of a behavior is assessed (for example, holds pencil at a 45-degree angle to the paper, grasping pencil between thumb and index finger with support from the middle finger).

The measurement of behavior—whether an individual behavior or a category of behavior—is based on four characteristics. These characteristics can be measured directly.

Duration   Behaviors that have discrete beginnings and endings may be assessed in terms of their duration—that is, the length of time a behavior lasts. The duration of a behavior is usually standardized two ways. First, the average duration of each occurrence may be computed. For example, Billy is out of his seat four times during a 30-minute activity, and the duration of each episode is 1 minute, 3 minutes, 7 minutes, and 5 minutes; then the average duration is 4 minutes [that is, $(1 + 3 + 7 + 5)/4$]. Second, the total duration may be computed. For example, Bill was out of his seat a total of 12 minutes. Often total duration is calculated as a rate by dividing the total occurrence by the length of an observation. This proportion of duration is often called the "prevalence" of the behavior. In the preceding example, Billy's prevalence is .60 (that is, 12/20).

Latency   The term *latency* refers to the length of time between a signal to perform and the beginning of the behavior. For example, a teacher might request that students take out their books. Sam's latency for that task is the length of time between the teacher's request and Sam placing his book on his desk. When latency is used, the behavior must have a discrete beginning.

Frequency   Behaviors that have discrete beginnings and endings may be counted. When the time periods in which the behavior is counted vary, frequencies are usually converted to rates. Using rate of behavior allows one to compare the occurrence of behavior across settings. For example, three episodes of out-of-seat behavior in 15 minutes may be converted to a rate of 12 per hour. However, Alberto and Troutman (1990) suggest that frequency should not be used under two conditions: (1) when the behavior occurs at such a high rate that it cannot be counted accurately (for example, many stereotypic behaviors, such as foot tapping, can occur almost constantly), and (2) when a behavior occurs over a prolonged period of time (for example, cooperative play during a game of monopoly).

Amplitude   The term *amplitude* refers to the intensity of the behavior. Amplitude can be measured precisely (for example, with noise meters) in many settings. However, in the classroom it is usually measured with less precision. Often, amplitude is estimated by rating the behavior on a scale that crudely calibrates amplitude in terms of the behavior itself (for example, crying might be scaled as "whimpering," "sobbing," "crying," and "screaming"). Amplitude may also be calibrated in terms of its objective or subjective impact on others. For example, the objective impact of hitting might be scaled as "without apparent physical damage," "blows that result in bruising," and "blows that cause bleeding." More subjective behavior ratings estimate the internal impact on others; for example, a student's humming could be scaled as "does not disturb others," "disturbs students seated nearby," "or disturbs students in the adjoining classroom."

   The characteristic of behavior to be assessed should make sense; we should assess the most relevant aspect of behavior in a particular situation. For example, if Billy is wandering around the classroom during the reading period, observing the duration of that behavior makes more sense than observing the frequency, latency, or amplitude of the behavior. If Minerva is always slow to follow directions, observing her latency makes more sense than assessing the frequency or amplitude of her behavior. For most behaviors, frequency and duration are the characteristics measured.

SAMPLING BEHAVIOR

As is the case for any assessment procedure, one can try to assess the entire domain of behavior or sample from it. And the sampling procedures assess the same aspects that were discussed in Chapters 7 and 8—contexts, items (in this case behaviors), and times.

Contexts

When specific behaviors become the targets of intervention, it is useful to measure the behavior in a variety of contexts. Usually the sampling of contexts is purposeful rather than random. We might want to know, for example, how Jesse's behavior in the resource room differs from his behavior in the regular classroom. Consistent or inconsistent performance across settings and contexts can provide useful information about what events might set the occasion for the behavior. Differences between the settings in which a behavior occurs and does not occur can provide potentially useful hypotheses about setting events (that is, environmental events that set the occasion for the performance of an action) and discriminative stimuli (that is, stimuli that are consistently present when a behavior is reinforced and come to elicit behavior even in the absence of the original reinforcer.[1] Bringing behavior under the control of a discriminative stimulus is often an effective way of modifying it.

Similarly, consistent or inconsistent performance across settings and contexts can provide useful information about what events could be consequating the behavior. (The consequences of a behavior maintain, increase, or decrease behavior.) Manipulating the consequences of a behavior can increase or decrease its occurrence. For example, if Joey's friends usually laugh and congratulate him when he makes a sexist remark, their reactions may be reinforcing his behavior. If the friends could be made to stop laughing and congratulating him, Joey's behavior might change.

Behaviors

Teachers and psychologists may be interested in measurement of and intervention on a particular behavior or a constellation of behaviors (for example, cooperation). When one views a target behavior as important in and of itself, other behaviors are not sampled, and only other contexts and times must be

---

1. Discriminative stimuli are not conditioned stimuli in the Pavlovian sense that they elicit reflexive behavior. Discriminative stimuli provide a signal to the individual to engage in a particular behavior because that behavior has been reinforced in the presence of that signal.

considered. For example, does Marc fail to take turns at the slide before school, during recess, and after school; does the behavior manifest itself at home and at his neighborhood playground as well as at school? When a specific behavior is of concern and when it can be modified across times and contexts, the problem is solved.

However, when one views a target behavior as part of a constellation of behavior, behavior sampling will be required in addition to sampling contexts and times. In such cases, the specific behaviors are aggregated into a total score much as subtests are aggregated into total scores although the statistical methods would be different. For example, Marc's failure to take turns using the slide on the playground may be viewed as representative of a whole class of behavior (that is, cooperation). Treating a single behavior as an element within a category of behavior requires that the content validity of the category be established. A variety of behaviors would have to be sampled (for example, taking turns on other equipment, following the rules of games, working with others to attain a common goal, and so forth). Then if the problem was found in other areas of cooperation, successful intervention on the class of behavior (with generalization to other times and contexts) would correct the behavior problem. In yet other instances, failure to take turns on the slide might be viewed as a symptom of a dysfunction in an hypothetical and internal process. For example, some might even argue that failure to take turns might indicate immaturity or even fixation at the anal stage of psychosocial development. In this orientation to the behavior, intervention would be aimed at the hypothesized internal cause rather than the surface behavior (taking turns on the slide). The success of the intervention would be judged by the same criteria used when a behavior is believed to be one of many included in a syndrome—modification across behaviors, times, and contexts.

Times

With the exception of some criminal acts, few behaviors are noteworthy unless they happen more than once. Behavioral recurrence over time is termed *stability* or *maintenance*. As explained in Chapter 7, there are almost an infinite number of times in a person's lifetime to exhibit a particular behavior. Moreover, it is probably impossible and certainly unnecessary to observe a person continuously during his or her entire life. Thus, temporal sampling is always performed, and any single observation is merely a sample from the domain.

Time sampling always requires the establishment of blocks of times (called *observation sessions*) in which observations will be made. A session might consist of a period of continuous times (for example, one school day). More often, sessions are discontinuous blocks of times (for example, every Monday for a semester).

Moreover, observers can record behavior continuously within sessions or they can sample within a session (that is, record discontinuously). Continuous observation requires the expenditure of more resources than discontinuous observation. When the observation session is long (for example, when it spans several days), continuous sampling can be very expensive and is often intrusive.

Two options are commonly used to estimate behavior in very long observation sessions. In the first option, rating scales can be used to obtain approximate estimates of the four characteristics of behavior.

Frequency   For example, a parent might be asked to rate the frequency of a behavior. How often does Patsy usually pick up her toys—always, frequently, seldom, never?

Duration   A parent might be asked to rate how much TV does Patsy typically watch each night—more than 3 hours, 2–3, 1–2, less than 1 hour?

Latency   A parent might be asked to rate how quickly Patsy usually responds to requests—immediately, quickly, slowly; ignores requests?

Amplitude   A parent might be asked to rate how much of a fuss does Patsy usually make at bedtime—screams, cries, begs to stay up, goes to bed without fuss?

In the second option, duration and frequency are sampled systematically during prolonged observation intervals. Three different sampling plans have been advocated: whole-interval recording, partial-interval recording, and momentary time sampling.

Whole-Interval Recording   In this sampling procedure, an observation session is subdivided into intervals. Usually observation intervals of equal length are spaced equally through the session, although recording and observation intervals need not be the same length. In whole-interval recording, a behavior is scored as having occurred only when it occurs throughout the entire interval. Thus, it is occurring when the interval begins and continues through the end of the interval.

Partial-Interval Recording   This sampling procedure is quite similar to whole-interval recording. An observation session is subdivided into intervals, and the intervals in which the behavior occurs are noted. The difference between the whole-interval and partial-interval procedures is that in partial-interval recording an occurrence is scored if it occurs during any part of the interval. Thus, if a behavior begins before the interval begins and ends within the interval, an occurrence is scored; if a behavior starts after the beginning of the interval, an occurrence is scored; if two or more episodes of behavior begin and end within the interval, an occurrence is scored.

Momentary Time Sampling   This is the most efficient sampling procedure. An observation session is subdivided into intervals. If a behavior is occurring at the last moment of the interval, an occurrence is recorded; if the behavior is not occurring at the last moment of the interval, a nonoccurrence is recorded.

Salvia and Hughes (1990) have summarized a number of studies investigating the accuracy of these time-sampling procedures. Both whole-interval and partial-interval sampling procedures provide inaccurate estimates of duration and frequency. Whole-interval recording overestimates the frequency and underestimates the prevalence of a behavior; partial-interval recording usually underestimates the frequency and overestimates the prevalence of a behavior.[2] Momentary time sampling provides an unbiased estimate of prevalence, but systematically underestimates the frequency of a behavior. Therefore, momentary time sampling can be used to estimate the prevalence of a behavior. The simplest way to estimate frequency seems to be continuous recording with shorter observation sessions.

TARGETING BEHAVIOR FOR OBSERVATION

Observations are usually conducted on behavior that may require modification or behavior that may indicate a handicapping condition. These behaviors are harmful, stereotypic, infrequent, or inappropriately exhibited.

Harmful Behavior

Behavior that is self-injurious or physically dangerous to others is almost always targeted for intervention. Self-injurious behavior includes such actions as head banging, eye gouging, self-biting or self-hitting, smoking, drug abuse, and so forth. Potentially harmful behavior can include leaning back in a desk or being careless with reagents in the chemistry experiment. Behavior harmful to others are those which directly inflict injury (for example, hitting or stabbing) or are likely to injure others (for example, pushing other students on stairs or subway platforms, bullying, or verbally instigating physical altercations). Unusually aggressive behavior may also be targeted for

---

2. Suen and Ary (1989) have provided procedures whereby the sampled frequencies can be adjusted to provide accurate frequency estimates, and the error associated with estimates of prevalence can be readily determined for each sampling plan.

intervention. Although most students will display aggressive behavior, some children go far beyond what can be considered typical or acceptable. These students may be described as hot-tempered, quick-tempered, or volatile. Overly aggressive behavior may also be physical or verbal. In addition to the possibility of causing physical harm to others, high rates of aggressive behavior may isolate the aggressor socially.

Stereotypic Behavior

Stereotypies (for example, hand flapping, rocking, and certain verbalizations such as inappropriate shrieks) are outside the realm of culturally normative behavior. Such behavior calls attention to students and marks them as abnormal to trained psychologists, or unusual to untrained observers. Stereotypic behaviors are often targeted for intervention.

Infrequent or Absent Desirable Behavior

Especially when behavior is related to physiological development (for example, walking), incompletely developed behavior is often targeted for intervention, especially when these behaviors enable desirable functional skills or social acceptance. Shaping is usually used to develop absent behavior while reinforcement is used to increase the frequency of behavior that is within a student's repertoire but exhibited at rates that are too low.

Normal Behavior Exhibited in Inappropriate Contexts

Many behaviors are appropriately exhibited in very specific contexts but are considered inappropriate or even abnormal when exhibited in other contexts. Usually, the problems caused by behavior in inappropriate contexts is attributed to lack of stimulus control. Behavior that is commonly termed *private* falls into this category; elimination and sexual activity are two ready examples. The goal of intervention should not be to eliminate these behaviors, but to confine them to socially appropriate conditions. Behavior that is often called *disruptive* also falls into this category. For example, running and yelling are very acceptable and normal when exhibited on the playground; they are disruptive in a classroom.

In selecting a behavior for intervention, a teacher may decide on the basis of logic and experience that a particular behavior should be modified. For example, harmful behavior should not be tolerated in a classroom or school; behavior that is a prerequisite for learning academic material must be developed.

In other cases, a teachers may seek the advice of a colleague, supervisor, or parent about the desirability of intervention. For example, a teacher might not know if certain behavior is typical of a culturally different student. How much flexibility does a teacher have in altering the goals in an academic area? Yet in other cases, a teacher might rely on the judgments of students or adults to see if particular behavior is troublesome or distracting for them. For example, does Bob's reading of problems aloud during arithmetic tests bother others? To ascertain if particular behavior bothers others, teachers can ask students directly, have them rate disturbing or distracting behavior, or perhaps complete sociograms to learn if a student is being rejected or isolated by his or her behavior.

For infrequent prosocial behavior or frequent disturbing behavior, a teacher may well wish to get a better idea of the magnitude and pervasiveness of the problem before initiating a comprehensive observational analysis. Casual observation can provide information about the frequency and amplitude of the behavior; carefully noting the antecedents, consequences, and contexts may provide useful information about possible interventions, if an intervention is warranted. If casual observations are made, anecdotal records of these casual observations should be maintained.

TARGETING THE EFFECTS OF ENVIRONMENTAL STIMULI FOR OBSERVATION

The term *ecobehavioral observation* is used in educational assessment to describe observations targeting the interactions among student behavior, teacher behavior, time allocated to instruction, physical grouping structures, the types of tasks being used, and instructional content. Ecobehavioral assessment thus enables educators to identify natural instructional conditions that are associated with academic success, behavioral competence, or problem behaviors. This approach is especially appealing because it recognizes the complex interrelationships between pupil behavior and environmental stimuli.

The CISSAR (Code for Instructional Structure and Student Academic Response) system is one approach to ecobehavioral assessment. This system was developed by personnel at the Juniper Gardens Children's Project in Kansas City, Kansas (Greenwood, Delquadri, & Hall, 1978). In the original system,[3] 19 student codes were defined, and these codes can be combined into three composite variables. (See Table 23.1.) CISSAR uses momentary time sampling (10-second intervals) over the entire school day. Observers record the instructional subject matter, curricular materials used, grouping structure

---

3. This system has been modified since 1978 by personnel at Juniper Gardens and at the University of Minnesota.

TABLE 23.1   Nineteen Student Response Codes for the Code for Instructional Structure and Student Academic Response (CISSAR)

Academic Engaged Time
Writing
Playing academic games
Oral reading
Silent reading
Talking appropriately
Answering academic questions
Asking academic questions
Passive responding

Inappropriate Behavior
Disruptive
Playing inappropriately
Inappropriate task
Talking inappropriately
Inappropriate locale
Looking around

Management Responses
Raising hand
Looking for materials
Moving
Playing appropriately
Waiting

teacher position, teacher behavior, academic responses, prerequisite or ena-bling responses, and competing responses. Once observational data have been recorded, the assessor can determine the frequency of occurrence of specific behaviors and the interactions among behaviors and environmental stimuli.

Another approach to ecobehavioral assessment is The Instructional Environment Scale or TIES (Ysseldyke & Christenson, 1987). TIES is designed to gather information and make judgments about the effectiveness of an instructional environment for individual students on twelve components that are grouped into four domains: instructional planning, classroom management, delivery of instruction, and monitoring/evaluating instruction. (These domains are described in Table 23.2.) TIES is a clinical instrument that enables users to make qualitative appraisals about the instruction that an individual student is receiving. Three methods are used to gather data: teacher interviews about target students, observation of target students in classroom settings, and student interviews. Moreover, students are observed at two times: when lessons are presented and when the student is engaging in practice. Data on ten of the twelve TIES components are gathered through observation and

TABLE 23.2   Components of Effective Instruction Assessed by Means of The Intructional Environment Scale

Planning Procedures

Instructional planning: The student's needs have been assessed accurately and instruction is matched appropriately to the results of the instructional diagnosis.

Teacher expectations: There are realistic yet high expectations for both the amount and accuracy of work to be completed, and these are communicated clearly to the student.

Management Procedures

Classroom environment: The classroom is controlled efficiently and effectively; there is a positive, supportive classroom atmosphere; time is used productively.

Teaching Procedures

Instructional presentation: Instruction is presented in a clear and effective manner; directions contain sufficient information for the student to understand what kinds of behaviors or skills are to be demonstrated; and the student's understanding is checked before independent practice.

Cognitive emphasis: Thinking skills used in completing assignments are communicated explicitly to the student.

Motivational strategies: The teacher has and uses effective strategies for heightening student interest and effort.

Informed feedback: The student receives relatively immediate and specific information on his/her performance or behavior; when the student makes mistakes, correction is provided.

Relevant practice: The student is given adequate opportunity to practice with appropriate materials. Classroom tasks are clearly important to achieving instructional goals.

Monitoring/Evaluation Procedures

Academic engaged time: The student is actively engaged in responding to academic content; the teacher monitors the extent to which the student is actively engaged and redirects the student when the student is unengaged.

Adaptive instruction: The curriculum is modified to accommodate the student's specific instructional needs.

Progress evaluation: There is direct, frequent measurement of the student's progress toward completion of instructional objectives; data on pupil performance and progress are used to plan future instruction.

Student understanding: The student demonstrates an accurate understanding of what is to be done in the classroom.

---

verified by teacher and student interviews. The observer must, in the end, make judgments about the extent to which the qualitative nature of instruction in the classroom is appropriate for the learner. Because the instructional environment differs for different students in the same setting, what is effective instruction for one student may not be effective for another.

CONDUCTING SYSTEMATIC OBSERVATIONS

Preparation

Careful preparation is essential in order for accurate and valid observational data to be obtained. Six steps should guide the preparation for systematic observation.

1. *Define target behaviors.* Target behaviors should be defined precisely in observable terms. Reference to internal processes (for example, understanding or appreciating) are avoided. It is also useful to include examples of instances and noninstances of the behavior. It is helpful to anticipate potentially difficult discriminations. Therefore, examples should include both subtle exhibitions of the target behavior, and noninstances should include related behaviors and behavior with similar topographies. The definition of the target behavior should include the characteristic of the behavior that will be measured (for example, frequency or latency).

2. *Select contexts.* The target behavior should be observed systematically in at least three contexts—the context in which the behavior was noted as troublesome (for example, in reading instruction), a similar context (for example, in math instruction), and a dissimilar context (for example, in physical education or recess).

3. *Select observation schedule.* Two choices must be made, and these choices are related to the contexts for observation. The first choice is the session length. In the schools, session length cannot exceed the period of time spanning a student's arrival and departure (including getting on and off the school bus, if appropriate). More often session length is related to instructional periods or blocks of time within instructional period (for example, 15 minutes in the middle of small-group reading instruction). The second choice to be made is for continuous versus discontinuous observation, and this choice will depend on the resources available and the specific behaviors that will be observed. When very-low-frequency behavior or behavior that must be stopped (for example, physical assaults) is observed, continuous recording is convenient and efficient. For other behavior, discontinuous observation is usually preferred, and momentary time sampling usually is the easiest and most accurate for teachers and psychologists to use. However, any discontinuous observation schedule requires some equipment to signal exactly when observation is to occur. The most common equipment is a portable audio cassette player and a tape with pure tones recorded at the desired intervals. One student or several students in sequence may be observed. For example, three students can each be observed at 5-second intervals. An audio tape would signal every 5 seconds. On the first signal, Henry would be observed; on the second

signal, Joyce would be observed; on the third signal, Bruce would be observed; on the fourth signal, Henry would be observed; and so forth.

4. *Develop recording procedures.*   The recording of observations must also be planned. When a few students are observed for the occurrence of relatively infrequent behaviors, relatively simple procedures can be used. Their behavior can be observed continuously and counted using a tally sheet or a wrist counter. When time sampling is used, observations must be recorded for each time interval; thus, some type of recording form is required. In the simplest form, the recording sheet contains identifying information (for example, name of target student, name of observer, date and time of observation session, observation-interval length, and so forth) and two columns. The first column shows the time interval, and the second column contains places for the observer to indicate whether or not the behavior occurred during each interval. More complicated recording forms may be used for multiple behaviors and students. When multiple behaviors are observed, they are often given code numbers. For example, "out of seat" might be coded as 1; "in seat but off task" might be coded as a 2; "in seat and on task" might be coded 3; and "no opportunity to observe" might be coded 4. Such codes should be included on the observation record form. Figure 23.1 shows a simple form on which to record multiple behaviors of students.

Complex observational systems tend to be less accurate than simple ones. Complexity increases as a function of the number of different behaviors that are assessed and the number of individuals who are observed. Moreover, both the proportion of target individuals to total individuals and the proportion of target behaviors that occur to the number of target behaviors to be recorded also have an impact on accuracy. The surest way to reduce inaccuracies in observations attributable to complexity is to keep things relatively simple.

5. *Select means of observation.*   First, the choice of human observers or electronic recorders will depend on the availability of resources. If electronic recorders are available and can be used in the desired environments and contexts, they can be used when continuous observation is warranted. If other personnel are available, they can be trained to observe and record the target behaviors accurately. Training should include didactic instruction in defining behavior, the use of time sampling (if it is to be used), how to record behavior, and practice using the observation system. Training is always continued until the desired level of accuracy is reached. Observers' accuracy is evaluated by comparing their responses to each other's or to a criterion rating (usually a previously scored videotape). Generally, very high agreement is required before one can assume that observers are ready to conduct observations independently. Ultimately, the decision of how to collect the data should also be based on efficiency. For

FIGURE 23.1   A Simple Recording Form for Three Students and Two Behaviors

Observer: _Mr. Jackson_

Date: _2/15/91_

Times of observation: _10:15 to 11:00_

Observation interval: _10 sec_

Instructional activity: _Oral reading_

Students observed:

S1 = _Henry J._

S2 = _Bruce H._

S3 = _Joyce W._

Codes:
1 = out of seat
2 = in seat but off task
3 = in seat, on task
4 = no opportunity to observe

	S1	S2	S3
1	_____	_____	_____
2	_____	_____	_____
3	_____	_____	_____
4	_____	_____	_____
5	_____	_____	_____
.			
.			
.			
179	_____	_____	_____
180	_____	_____	_____

example, if it takes longer to desensitize the students to an obtrusive video recorder than it takes to train observers, human observers are preferred.

Gathering Data

As with any type of assessment information, two general sources of error can reduce the accuracy of observation. First, random error can result in over- or underestimates of behavior. Second, systematic error biases the data in a consistent direction; for example, behavior is systematically overcounted or undercounted. Careful preparation and systematic monitoring of the observation process can head off trouble. Before observation begins, human observers should make sure that they have an extra supply of recording forms, spare pens or pencils, and something to write on (for example, a clipboard or table top). When electronic recording is used, it should be checked before every observation session to make sure it is in good working condition. When portable equipment is employed, the observer should have extra batteries, signal tapes, or recording tapes available. Before observation, a check list of equipment and materials that will be used during the observation can be prepared, and everything that is needed for the observation session can be assembled. Also, before the observation session, the observer should check out the setting to locate appropriate vantage points for equipment or furniture.

Random Error

Random errors in observation and recording usually affect observer agreement. Observers may change the criteria for the occurrence of a behavior, they may forget behavior codes, or they may use the recording forms incorrectly. Because changes in agreement can signal something is wrong, the accuracy of observational data should be checked periodically. The usual procedure is to have two observers who observe and record on the same schedule in the same session. The two records are then compared, and an index of agreement (for example, Kappa—see Chapter 7) is computed. Poor agreement suggests retraining or revision of the observation procedures. Periodic retraining and allowing observers to keep the definitions and codes for target behaviors with them can alleviate some of the problems. Finally, when observers know that their accuracy is being systematically checked, they are usually more accurate. Thus, observers might be led to believe that their observations are always being checked.

  One of the most vexing factors affecting the accuracy of observations is the incorrect recording of correctly observed behavior. Even when observers have applied the criterion for the occurrence of a behavior correctly, they may record their decision incorrectly. For example, if 1 is used to indicate occurrence and zero (0) is used to indicate nonoccurrence, the observer might accidentally record 0 for a behavior that has occurred. Inaccuracy can be attributed to three related factors.

1. *Lack of familiarity with the recording system.* Practice using a recording system is absolutely necessary when several behaviors or several students are observed. Practice is also called for when the target behaviors are difficult to define or when they are difficult to observe.

2. *Insufficient time to record.* Sufficient time must be allowed to record the occurrence of behavior. Problems can arise when using momentary time sampling if the observation intervals are spaced too closely (for example, 1- or 5-second intervals). Observers who are counting several different high-frequency behaviors may record inaccurately. Generally, inadequate opportunities for observers to record can be circumvented by electronic recording of the observation session; replaying and stopping gives observers unlimited time to observe and record.

3. *Lack of concentration.* It may be hard for observers to remain alert for long periods of time (for example, one hour), especially if the target behavior occurs infrequently and is difficult to detect. Using several observers who take turns, or recording sessions for later evaluation, can reduce the time that an observer must maintain vigilance. Similarly, when it is difficult to maintain vigilance because the observational context is noisy, busy, or otherwise distracting, electronic recording may be useful in focusing on target subjects and eliminating ambient noise.

Unusual events and departures from the observation plan (for example, a missed observation interval) can be noted directly on the observation form. Finally, observation should begin and end at the planned times.

Systematic Error

Systematic errors are difficult to detect. To minimize error, four steps can be taken:

1. *Guard Against Unintended Changes in the Observation Process.*[4] When assessment is carried out over extended periods of time, observers may talk to each other about the definitions that they are using or how they cope with difficult discriminations. Consequently, one observer's departure from standardized procedures may spread to other observers. When the observers change together, modifications of the standard procedures and definitions will not be detected by examining interobserver agreement. Techniques for reducing changes in observers over time include keeping the scoring criteria available to observers, meeting with the observers on a

---

4. Technically, general changes in the observation process over time are called *instrumentation problems*.

regular basis to discuss difficulties encountered during observation, and providing periodic retraining.

Like human observers, equipment can also change over time. Audio signal tapes (used to indicate the moment a student should be observed) may stretch after repeated uses; a 10-second interval may become an 11-second interval. Similarly, batteries that power audio playback units can lose power, and signal tapes may play slower. Therefore, equipment should be cleaned periodically, and signal tapes should be checked for accuracy.

2. *Desensitize students.*   Introducing equipment or new adults into a class-room as well as changes in teacher routines can signal students that observations are going on. Overt measurement can alter the target's behavior or the topography of the behavior. Usually the pupil change is temporary. For example, when Janey knows that she is being observed, she may be more accurate, deliberate, or compliant. However, as observation becomes a part of the daily routine, students' behavior usually returns to what is typical for them. This return to typical patterns of behavior defines desensitization functionally. The data generated from systematic observation should not be used until the students who are observed are no longer affected by the observation procedures and equipment or personnel. How-ever, sometimes the change in behavior is permanent. For example, if a teacher was watching for the extortion of lunch money, Billy might wait until no observers were present or demand the money in more subtle ways. In such cases, valid data will not be obtained through overt observation, and different procedures will have to be developed, or the observation will have to be abandoned.

3. *Minimize observer expectancies.*   Sometimes what an observer believes will happen affects what is seen and recorded. For example, an observer might expect an intervention to increase a behavior; that observer might uncon-sciously alter the criteria for evaluating that behavior or evaluate approxi-mations of the target behavior as having occurred. The more subtle or complex the target behavior is, the more susceptible it may be to expecta-tion. The easiest way to avoid expectations during observations is for the observer to be blind to the purpose of the assessment. When video or audio tapes are used to record behavior, the order in which they are evaluated can be randomized so that observers do not know what portion of an observation is being scored. When it is impossible or impractical to keep observers blind to the purpose, the importance of accurate observa-tion should be stressed and rewarded.

4. *Motivate observers.*   Inaccurate observation is sometimes attributed to lack of motivation on the part of an observer. Motivation can be increased by rewards, feedback, stressing the importance of the observations, reducing the length of observation sessions, and not allowing observation sessions to become routine.

Summarize Data

Depending on the particular characteristic of behavior being measured, observational data may be summarized in different ways. When duration or frequency is the characteristic of interest, observations are usually summarized as rates (that is, the prevalence or the number of occurrence per minute or hour). Latency and amplitude should be summarized statistically by the mean and standard deviation or median and range. All counts and calculations should be checked for accuracy.

CRITERIA FOR EVALUATING OBSERVED PERFORMANCES

Once accurate observational data are collected and summarized, they must be interpreted. Some behavior can be judged on *a priori* bases—for example, unsafe and harmful behavior. Most behavior is not evaluated simply by its presence. For example, knowing that the prevalence of Billy's out-of-seat behavior is 10 percent during instruction in content areas does not provide much information about whether or not that behavior should be decreased.

Evaluation of behavior rates can be evaluated in several ways. Normative data may be available for some behavior, or in some cases data from behavior rating scales and tests can provide general guidelines. In the absence of such data, social comparisons can be made. In *social comparison*, a peer whose behavior is considered appropriate is observed. The peer's rate of behavior is then used as the standard against which to evaluate the target student's rate of behavior. The *social tolerance* for a behavior can also be used as a criterion. For example, the degree to which different rates of out-of-seat behavior disturbs a teacher or peers can be assessed. Teachers and peers could be asked to rate how disturbing is the out-of-seat behavior of students exhibiting different rates of behavior. In a somewhat different vein, the contagion of the behavior can be a crucial consideration in teacher judgments of unacceptable behavior. Thus, the effects of different rates of behavior can be assessed to see if there is a threshold above which other students initiate undesirable behavior.

SUMMARY

Behavioral observation is the process of gaining information visually, auditorily, or through other senses. It can be used to assess any behavior or product of behavior; it cannot be used to assess events that are not observable (for example, thinking, feeling, or believing). Although behavior may be defined functionally or topographically, it is measured in terms of its duration, latency, frequency, and amplitude. Moreover, one can assess the entire domain of behavior or sample from the domain along three dimensions: contexts, behaviors, and times. Each dimension can provide important and useful information about the behavior and how it is maintained in the environment. Three different sampling plans have been advocated for measuring the duration and frequency of behavior: whole-interval recording, partial-interval recording, and momentary time sampling. Of these three methods, momentary time sampling is the most useful and in general the most accurate.

Observations are usually conducted on behavior that may require modification or behavior that may indicate a handicapping condition: harmful behavior, stereotypic behavior, infrequent or absent desirable behavior, and normal behavior shown in inappropriate contexts. However, observations may also be conducted to ascertain the effects of environment stimuli on behavior. Two ecobehavioral observation systems have been developed and used for this purpose: CISSAR (Code for Instructional Structure and Student Academic Response) and TIES (The Instructional Environment Scale).

Conducting systematic observations requires as much care and precision as testing during preparation, data gathering, and data summarization. When preparing to conduct systematic observations, (1) target behaviors must be carefully defined; (2) the contexts in which observations will be conducted and the observation schedule itself should be carefully selected; (3) the recording procedures must be thoughtfully developed; and (4) the means by which data will be collected must be decided (for example, using human observers). When gathering data, both random and systematic error should be minimized. Random error is usually attributed to lack of familiarity with the recording system, to insufficient time to record, or to lack of concentration. Systematic error is usually attributed to unintended changes in the observation process, to failure to desensitize target students, to observer expectancies, or to unmotivated observers. Finally, like all other assessment procedures, student performances must be evaluated. Some behavior can be judged on *a priori* bases—for example, unsafe and harmful behavior. Other behavior is based on normative data, social comparison, or social tolerance.

STUDY QUESTIONS

1. Explain each of the four types of behavior that are targeted for intervention.
2. What things should an observer consider when preparing to conduct systematic observations?
3. Name four types of systematic errors that can occur during observation. What can an observer do to minimize these types of errors?
4. Name three types of random errors that can occur during observation. What can an observer do to minimize these types of errors?

Additional Readings

Greenwood, C., Schulte, D., Dinwiddie, G., & Carta, J. (1986). Assessment and analysis of ecobehavioral interaction in school settings. In R. Prinz (Ed.), *Advances in behavioral assessment of children and families* (vol. 2). New York: JAI Press.

Salvia, J., and Hughes, C. (1990). *Curriculum-based assessment: Testing what is taught*. New York: Macmillan. (Chapter 9, Assessment of adaptive and social behavior).

C·H·A·P·T·E·R 24

TEACHER-MADE TESTS OF ACHIEVEMENT: AN OVERVIEW

Most evaluations of student achievement are conducted by teachers with materials that they have developed themselves, and the assessment practices that are actually used by teachers in classrooms are not well documented. This chapter provides a general overview of good practices for teachers who develop their own tests for classroom assessment in the core areas of reading, mathematics, spelling, and written language. Classroom assessment is a topic suitable for an entire text, and only a general overview of the formats used to test and the criteria by which pupil performance is evaluated can be treated in this general chapter. For more specific information on test construction, educational decision making, and managing assessment within the classroom, interested readers are referred to texts by Gronlund (1985) and Salvia and Hughes (1990), among others. Finally, procedures that have been discussed in detail in preceding chapters are not reexplained here.

WHY DO TEACHERS ASSESS ACHIEVEMENT?

Teachers regularly set aside time to assess their pupils for a variety of purposes. Most commonly, teachers make up tests to ascertain the extent to which their students have learned or are learning what has been taught or assigned. Knowledge about the extent to which children have mastered curricula allows teachers to make a variety of decisions—selection of current and future instructional objectives, placement of students in instructional groups, evaluation of the teachers' own instructional performances, and the necessity of referring students to other educational specialists for additional instructional services. Each of these decisions should be based on student achievement of instructional objectives. When students have met their instructional objectives, it is time to move on to new or related objectives. Students who meet objectives so rapidly that they are being held back by the progress of their slower peers can be grouped for enrichment activities or faster-paced instruction; slower students can be grouped so that necessary concepts can be learned to mastery without impeding the progress of their faster-learning peers. When many students in a classroom fail to learn material, teachers should suspect that something is wrong with their materials, techniques, or some other aspect of instruction. For example, the students may lack prerequisite concepts or skills, or the instruction may be too fast-paced, or poorly sequenced. Finally, when students lag far behind their peers in crucial curricular areas, teachers may seek outside help. For example, a student may receive Title I assistance, be placed in a slower educational track, or be referred to a child study team to determine eligibility to receive other special educational services.

ADVANTAGES OF TEACHER-MADE TESTS

Often teacher-made tests are not held in high regard. For example, some measurement specialists (such as Thorndike & Hagen, 1978) list carefully prepared test items as an advantage of norm-referenced achievement tests. By implication, careful preparation of questions may not be a characteristic of teacher-made tests. In addition, terms such as "informal" or "unstandardized" may be used to describe teacher-made tests. As a group, however, teacher-made tests cannot be considered informal, because they are not given haphazardly or casually. They also cannot be considered unstandardized, because students usually receive the same materials and directions, and the same criteria usually are used in correcting student answers. Perhaps a better characterization of teacher-made tests is that they are not usually subject to public scrutiny and may be more variable than commercial tests in terms of their technical adequacy (that is, reliability and validity). However, these characterizations are, themselves, speculative.

Teacher-made tests can be better suited to evaluation of student achievement than commercially prepared, norm-referenced achievement tests. The disadvantages of commercially prepared tests readily illustrate the two potential advantages of teacher-made tests: curriculum match and sensitivity.

First, commercially prepared tests are rarely designed to assess achievement within specific curricula. Rather, these tests are intentionally constructed to have general applicability so that they can be used with students in almost any curriculum. This intentional generality is in sharp contrast to the development of distinctive curricula. It has become increasingly clear that various curriculum series differ from one another in the particular educational objectives covered, the performance level expected of students, and the sequence of objectives; for example, DISTAR mathematics differs from Scott, Foresman mathematics (Shriner & Salvia, 1988). Even within the same curriculum series, teachers modify instruction to provide enrichment or remedial instruction. Thus, two teachers using the same curriculum series may offer different instruction. Although teachers may not construct tests that match curriculum, they are in the best position to know precisely what has been taught and what level of performance is expected from students. Consequently, they are the only ones who could match testing to instruction.

The second disadvantage of commercially prepared, norm-referenced tests is that the overwhelming majority are intended, first and foremost, to discriminate among test takers efficiently. In practice, developers of norm-referenced tests try to strike a balance between the minimum number of test items to allow reliable discrimination and enough items to imply content validity. This practice results in relatively insensitive tests that are unable to discriminate small changes in pupil performance. For example, to produce a reliable, norm-referenced test it may be unnecessary to discriminate among students who know the single-digit addition facts with 2's, 4's, and 6's from those who also know the 3's, 5's, and 7's. However, when instruction is provided in all single-digit addends, teachers likely would want to know, for example, which students have not yet mastered the 4's (and which of the 4's) so that they can provide further instruction. Moreover, once students have mastered the 4's, the change in their skill level should be observable from changed test performance.

In short, teachers need tests that are sensitive to small changes in knowledge. Teachers who are concerned with pupil mastery of specific concepts and skills usually test a narrow range of objectives directly and frequently. Norm-referenced tests are not well suited to this purpose not only because they contain relatively few relevant items but also because they seldom are published in multiple forms. Although teachers may not produce sensitive tests or test frequently, they are in a position to do so.

TESTING FORMATS USED BY TEACHERS

When a teacher wants to compare the performance of several students on a skill or set of skills or wants to assess pupil performance over time, the assessment must be standardized. Otherwise, observed differences could be reasonably attributed to differences in testing procedures. To be standardized, tests must use consistent directions, criteria for scoring, and procedures (for example, time allowed students to complete a test). Almost any test can be standardized if it results in observable behavior or a permanent product (for example, a student's written response).

Test formats can be classified along two dimensions. The first dimension is the modality through which the item is presented. Test items usually require a student to look at or to listen to the question although other modalities may be substituted depending on the particulars of a situation or on characteristics of students. The second dimension is the modality through which a student responds. Test items usually require an oral or written response, although pointing responses are frequently used with nonverbal students. Teachers may use the terms "see-write," "see-say," "hear-write," and "hear-say" to specify the testing dimensions.

In addition, "write" formats can be of two types. Select formats require students to indicate their choice from an array of the possible answers (usually called *response options*). True-false, multiple-choice, and matching are the three common select formats. However, these formats are not restricted to traditional test questions; for example, students may be required to circle incorrectly spelled words or words that should be capitalized in text. Formats requiring students to select the correct answer can be used to assess much more than the recognition of information, although they are certainly useful for that purpose. Select formats can also be used to assess understanding, the ability to draw inferences, and the correct application of principles. Select questions are not usually well suited for assessing achievement at the levels of analysis, synthesis, and evaluation. (See Chapter 8 for a discussion of Bloom's taxonomic levels.)

Supply formats require a student to produce a written or oral response. This response can be as restricted as the answer to a computation problem or a one-word response to a question such as "When did the potato famine begin in Ireland?" Often the response to supply questions is more involved and can require a student to produce a sentence, a paragraph, or several pages to answer the question satisfactorily.

As a general rule, supply questions can be prepared fairly quickly, but scoring them may be very time-consuming. Even when one-word responses or numbers are requested, teachers may have difficulty finding the response on a student's test paper, deciphering the handwriting, or correctly applying criteria for awarding points. In contrast, select formats usually require a considerable amount of time to prepare but, once prepared, they can be scored quickly and by almost anyone.

The particular formats teachers select are influenced by their purposes for testing and the characteristics of the test takers. Testing formats are essentially bottom-up or top-down. Bottom-up formats assess the mastery of specific objectives to allow generalizations about student competence in a particular domain. Top-down formats survey general competence in a domain and assess in greater depth those topics in which mastery is incomplete. For day-to-day monitoring of instruction and selecting short-term instructional objectives, we favor bottom-up assessments. With this type of assessment, teachers can be relatively sure that specific objectives have been mastered and that they are not spending needless instructional time teaching students what they already know. For determining starting places for instruction with new students and for assessing maintenance and generalization of previously learned material, we favor top-down assessments. Generally, this approach should be more efficient in terms of teachers' and students' time, because broader survey tests can cover a lot of material in a short period of time.

With students who are able to read and write independently, see-write formats are generally more efficient for both individual students and groups. When testing individual students, teachers or teacher aides can give the testing materials to the students and can proceed with other activities while the students are responding to them. Moreover, having students write their responses allows a teacher to defer correcting examinations until a convenient time.

See-say formats are also useful. Teacher aides or other students can listen to the test takers' responses and correct them on the spot or record them for later evaluation. Moreover, many teachers have access to various electronic equipment that can greatly facilitate see-say formats (for example, language masters).

Hear-write formats are especially useful with select formats when used with younger students and students who cannot read independently. This format can also be used for testing groups of students and is routinely used in the assessment of spelling when students are required to write words from dictation. With other content, teachers can give directions and read the test questions aloud, and students can mark their responses. The primary difficulty with a hear-write format with groups of students is the pacing of test items; teachers must allot sufficient time between items for slower responding students to make their selections.

Hear-say formats are most suitable for assessing individual students who do write independently or who write at such slow speeds that their written responses are unrepresentative of what they know. Even with this format, teachers need not preside over the assessment; other students or a teacher aide can administer, record, and perhaps evaluate the student's responses.

CONSIDERATIONS IN PREPARING TESTS

Different formats can be used within the same tests although it is generally a good idea to group questions prepared in the same format together. Regardless of the format used, the primary consideration is that the test questions are a fair sample of the material being assessed. When narrow skills are being assessed (for example, spelling words from dictation), either all the components of the domain should be tested (in this case, all the assigned spelling words), or a representative sample should be selected and assessed. The qualifier "representative" implies that an appropriate number of easy and difficult words as well as words from the beginning, middle, and end of the assignment will be selected. When more complex domains are assessed, teachers should concentrate on the more important facts or relationships and avoid the trivial. Moreover, they should ask a sufficient number of questions to allow valid inferences about students' mastery of all the material. Nothing offends test takers quite as much as a test's failure to question material they have studied and know, except perhaps their own failure to guess what content a teacher believes to be important enough to test. In addition, "fair" implies that the way in which the question is asked is familiar and expected by the student. For example, if students were to take a test on the addition of single-digit integers, it would be a bad idea to test them using a missing-addend format (for example, "4 + __ = 7") unless that format had been specifically taught and was expected by the students.

Regardless of question format, however, the directions should indicate clearly what a student is to do—for example, "Circle the correct option," "Choose the best answer," "Match each item in column b to one item in column a," and so forth. Also, teachers should explain what if any materials may be used by students, time limits, any unusual scoring procedures (for example, penalties for guessing), and point value when the students are mature enough to be given questions that have different point values.

SELECT FORMATS

Three types of select formats are commonly used: multiple-choice, matching, and true-false. Of the three, multiple-choice questions are clearly the most useful.

Multiple-Choice Questions

Multiple-choice questions are the most difficult to prepare. These questions have two parts: a stem that contains the question and a response set that contains the correct answer (that is, *keyed* response) and incorrect options called *distractors*. In preparing multiple-choice questions, teachers should generally follow these guidelines.

- Keep the options short and of approximately equal length. Students learn quickly that longer options tend to be correct.
- Keep in the stem the material that is common to all options. For example, a "the" appearing in each option should be put into the stem.
- Avoid grammatical tip-offs. Students can discard grammatically incorrect options. For example, when the correct answer must be plural, alert students will disregard singular options; when the correct answer must be a noun, students will disregard options that are verbs.
- Avoid implausible options. In the best questions, even distractors should be attractive to students who do not know the answer. Common errors and misconceptions are often good distractors.
- Make sure that one and only one option is correct. Students should not have to read their teachers' minds to guess which wrong answer is the least wrong or which right answer is the most correct.

- Avoid interdependent questions. Generally it is bad practice to make the selection of the correct option dependent on getting a prior question correct.
- Vary the position of the correct response in the options. Students will recognize patterns of correct options (for example, when the correct answers to a sequence of questions are a, b, c, d, a, b, c, d) or a teacher's preference for a specific position (for example, c).
- Avoid options that indicate multiple correct options (for example, "all of the above" or "both a and b are correct"). These options often simplify the question.
- Avoid similar incorrect options. Students who can eliminate one of the two similar options can readily dismiss the other one.
- Avoid using the same words and examples that were used in the students' texts or in class presentations.
- Make sure that one question does not provide information that can be used to answer another question. For example, teachers should not introduce one question with "In 1492 Columbus landed in the Western _____" and then ask another question requesting the year in which Columbus arrived in the Western Hemisphere.

When appropriate, teachers can make multiple-choice questions more challenging by asking students to recognize an instance of a rule or concept, by requiring students to recall and use material that is not present in the question, or by increasing the number of options.[1] In no case should teachers deliberately mislead or trick students.

Matching Questions

Matching questions are a variant of multiple-choice questions in which a set of stems are associated with a set of options simultaneously. Generally the content of matching questions is limited to simple factual associations (Gronlund, 1985). Usually teachers prepare matching questions so that there are as many options as stems and an option can be associated only once with a stem in the set. Although we do not recommend their use, there are other possibilities: more options than stems, selection of all correct options for one stem, and using an option more than once.[2] The latter possibilities increase the difficulty of the question set considerably.

1. For younger children, three options are generally difficult enough. Older students can be expected to answer questions with four or five options.

2. Scoring for these options is complicated. Generally separate errors are counted for selecting an incorrect option and failing to select a correct option. Thus the number of errors can be very large.

In general we prefer multiple-choice questions over matching questions. Almost any matching question can be written as a series of multiple-choice questions in which the same or similar options are used. Of course, the correct response will change. However, teachers wishing to use matching questions should consider the following guidelines.

- Each set of matching items should have some dimension in common. This makes preparation easier for the teacher and provides the student with some insight into the relationship required to select the correct option.
- Keep the length of stems approximately the same, and keep the length and grammar used in the options equivalent. At best, mixing grammatical forms will eliminate some options for some questions; at worst, it will provide the correct answer to a question.
- Make sure that one and only one option is correct for each stem.
- Vary the sequence of correct responses when more than one matching question is asked.
- Avoid using the same words and examples that were used in the students' texts or in class presentations.

It is easier for a student when questions and options are presented in two columns. When there is a difference in the length of the items in each column, the longer item should be used as the stem. Stems should be placed on the left and options on the right rather than placing all the options after all the questions. Moreover, all the elements of the question should be kept on one page. Finally, teachers often allow students to draw lines to connect questions and options. Although this has the obvious advantage of helping students keep track of where their answers should be placed, erasures or scratch-outs can be a headache to the person who corrects the test.

True-False Questions

In most cases, true-false questions should simply not be used. Their utility lies primarily in assessing factual information that can be better assessed with other formats, and effective true-false items are difficult to prepare. Because guessing the correct answer is so likely—50 percent—the reliability of true-false tests is generally low, and as a result they may well have limited validity. Nonetheless, if a teacher chooses to use this format, a few suggestions should be followed.

- Avoid specific determiners such as "all," "never," "always," and so on.
- Avoid sweeping generalizations. Such statements tend to be true, but students can often think of minor exceptions. Thus, there is a problem in the criterion for evaluating the truthfulness of the question. Attempts to avoid the problem by adding restrictive conditions (for example, "with minor ex-

ceptions") either renders the question obviously true or leaves a student trying to guess what the restrictive condition means.

- Avoid convoluted sentences. Tests should assess knowledge of content, not a student's ability to comprehend difficult prose.
- Keep true and false statements approximately the same length. As is the case with longer options being correct on multiple-choice questions, longer true-false questions tend to be true.
- Balance the number of true and false statements. If a student recognizes that there are more of one type of question than another, the odds of guessing the correct answer will exceed 50 percent.

SUPPLY FORMATS

It is useful to distinguish between items requiring a student to write one- or two-word responses (fill-in questions) and those requiring more extended responses (essay questions). Both types of items require careful delineation of what constitutes a correct response (that is, criteria for scoring). It is generally best for teachers to prepare criteria for a correct response at the time they prepare the question. In that way they can assure that the question is written in such a way as to elicit the correct type of answer—or at least not mislead students —and perhaps save time when correcting exams. (If teachers change criteria for a correct response after they have scored a few questions, they should rescore all previously scored questions with the revised criteria.)

Fill-in Questions

Aside from mathematics problems that require students to calculate an answer and writing spelling words from dictation, fill-in questions require a student to complete a statement by adding a concept or fact. For example, "_____ arrived in America in 1492." Fill-ins are useful in assessing objectives at the knowledge and comprehension levels; they are not useful in assessing objectives at the levels of application, analysis, synthesis, and evaluation. Teachers preparing fill-in questions should follow these guidelines.

- Keep each sentence short. Generally, the less superfluous information in an item, the clearer the question will be to the student and the less likely it will be for one question to cue another.
- If a two-word answer is required, teachers should use two blanks to indicate this in the sentence.
- Avoid sentences with multiple blanks. For example, the item, "In the year _____ , _____ discovered _____ " is so vague that practically any

date, name, and event can be inserted correctly, even ones that are content-irrelevant; for example, "In 1989, Henry discovered girls."

- Keep the size of all blanks consistent and large enough to accommodate the longest answer readily. The size of the blank should not provide a clue about the length of the correct word.

The most problematic aspect of fill-in questions is the necessity of developing an appropriate response bank of acceptable answers. Often some student errors may consist of a partially correct response; teachers must decide which answers will receive partial credit, full credit, and no credit. For example, a question may anticipate "Columbus" as the correct response, but a student might write "that Italian dude who was looking for the short-cut to India for the Spanish king and queen." In deciding how far afield to go in crediting unanticipated responses, teachers should carefully look over test questions to see if the student's answer comes from information presented in another question (for example, "The Spanish monarch employed an Italian sailor to find a shorter route to _____").

Extended Responses

Essay questions are most useful in assessing instructional objectives prepared at a comprehension level or higher. Two major problems are associated with extended response questions. First, teachers are generally able to sample only a limited amount of information because answers may take a long time for students to write. Second, responses to extended essays are the most difficult type of answer to score. To avoid subjectivity and inconsistency, teachers should use a scoring key that assigns specific point values for each element in the ideal or criterion answer. In most cases, spelling and grammatical errors should not be deducted from the point total. Moreover, bonus points should not be awarded for particularly detailed responses; many good students will provide a complete answer to one question and spend any extra time working on questions that are more difficult for them. Finally, teachers should be prepared to deal with responses in which a student tries to bluff a correct answer. Rather than leave a question unanswered, some students may answer a related question that was not asked, or they may structure their response so that they can omit important information that they cannot remember or never knew. Sometimes they will even write a poem or a treatise on why the question asked is unimportant or irrelevant. Therefore, teachers must be very specific about how they will award points, stick to their criteria unless they discover something is wrong with them, and not give credit to creative bluffs.

Teachers should also be very precise in the directions that they give so that students will not have to guess what responses their teachers will credit. Below are a number of verbs (and their meanings) that are commonly used in essay questions. It is often worthwhile to explain these terms in the test directions to make sure that students know what kind of answer is desired.

- "Describe," "define," and "identify" mean to give the meaning, essential characteristics, and/or place within a taxonomy.
- "List" means to enumerate and implies that complete sentences and paragraphs are not required unless specifically requested.
- "Discuss" requires more than a description, definition, or identification; a student is expected to draw implications and elucidate relationships.
- "Explain" means to analyze and make clear or comprehensible a concept, event, principle, relationship, or so forth; thus, "explain" requires going beyond a definition to describe the how's or why's.
- "Compare" means to identify and explain similarities among two or more things.
- "Contrast" means to identify and explain differences among two or more things.
- "Evaluate" means to give the value of something and implies an enumeration and explanation of assets and liabilities, pros and cons.

Finally, unless students know the questions in advance, teachers should allow students sufficient time for planning and rereading answers. For example, if teachers believe ten minutes are necessary to write an extended essay to answer a question that requires original thinking, they might allow twenty minutes for the question. The less fluent the students, the greater is the proportion of time that should be allotted.

DIRECT PERFORMANCE MEASURES

In many curricular areas, student achievement is expected to go beyond simple acquisition of skills and concepts; students are expected to become fluent in the performance of particular skills. For example, students may be expected to recognize sight vocabulary without having to use decoding strategies, give the multiplication facts without computation, or write letters without having to think about their formation. To assess skills of this sort, teachers often rely on direct performance: students are asked to read sight words, give multiplication facts, and so forth.

A *probe* is a special testing format that is especially well-suited to the assessment of direct performances. Probes first gained acceptance with the precision-teaching model (White & Liberty, 1980) but have since become more widely accepted. Probes are brief (usually three minutes or less), timed, frequently administered assessments that can be used for any purpose; a number of principles for making instructional decisions have been validated (Fuchs, 1986; Haring, Liberty, & White, 1980). Probes can assess single or multiple skills, and student performance is most often reported as the rate of correct responses per minute. However, when rate data are used, probes should contain more items than can be solved in the time allotted. Technically, having more questions than can be completed allows response rates to rise without reaching a ceiling; thus, the response is a *free operant*. Normative data are available for a number of standard tasks (for example, rate of oral reading) and have been summarized in various sources (for example, Mercer, Mercer, & Evans, 1982; Salvia & Hughes, 1990). The primary disadvantage of probes is that they are unsuitable for assessing sustained performance.

ASSESSMENT IN CORE ACHIEVEMENT AREAS

The assessment procedures used by teachers are a function of the content being taught, the criterion to which content is to be learned, and the characteristics of their students. With primary-level curricula in core areas, teachers usually want more than knowledge from their students—they want the material learned so well that correct responses are automatic. For example, teachers do not want their students to think about forming the letter *a*, sounding out the word *the*, or using number lines to solve simple addition problems such as "3 + 5 =____"; they want their students to respond immediately and correctly. Even in intermediate-level materials, teachers seek highly proficient responding from their students, whether that performance involves two-digit multiplication, reading short stories, writing short stories, or writing spelling words from dictation. However, teachers in all grades, but especially in secondary schools, are also interested in their students understanding vast amounts of information about their social, cultural, and physical worlds as well as their acquisition and application of critical thinking skills. The assessment of skills taught to high degrees of proficiency is quite different from the assessment of understanding and critical thinking skills.

In the sections that follow, core achievement areas are discussed in terms of three important attributes: the skills and information to be learned within the major strands of most curricula, the assessment of skills to be learned to proficiency, and the assessment of understanding of information and concepts. Critical thinking skills are usually embedded within content areas and are assessed in the same ways as understanding of information is assessed—with written multiple-choice and extended-essay questions.

Reading

Reading is usually divided into decoding skills and comprehension. The specific behaviors included in each of these subdomains will depend on the particular curriculum and its sequencing.

Beginning Skills

Beginning decoding can include letter recognition, letter-sound correspondences, sight vocabulary, phonics, and in some curricula, morphology. Automaticity is the end goal for the skills to be learned. See-say (for example, "What letter is this?") and hear-say (for example, "What sound does this letter make ____?") formats are regularly used for both instruction and assessment. During acquisition of specific skills, teachers should first stress the accuracy of student responses. Generally this concern translates into allowing a moment or two for students to think about their responses. A generally accepted criterion for the completion for early learning is 90 percent correct. As soon as accuracy has been attained (and sometimes before complete attainment), teachers change their criteria from accurate responses to fast and accurate responses. For see-say formats, fluent students will need no thinking time for simple material; for example, they should be able to respond as rapidly as teachers can change stimuli to questions such as "What is this letter?" For the most difficult content (for example, recognition of long or visually difficult words such as *through*), no more than a second or two should be needed by a student to verify the stimulus. However, when students have visual or articulation difficulties, these standards are unlikely to be appropriate.

For beginners, reading comprehension is usually assessed in one of three ways. The most direct method is to have students retell what they have read without access to the reading passage. Retold passages may be scored on the basis of the number of words recalled. Fuchs, Fuchs, and Maxwell (1988) have offered two relatively simple scoring procedures that appear to offer valid indications of comprehension. Retelling may be conducted orally or in writing. With students who have relatively undeveloped writing skills, retelling should be oral when it is used to assess comprehension, but may be in writing as a practice or drill activity. Teachers can listen to students retell, or students can retell using tape recorders so that their efforts can be evaluated later.

A second common method of assessing comprehension is to ask students questions about what they have read. Questions should address both main ideas, important relationships, and relevant details. Questions may be supply or select, and either hear-say or see-write formats can be used conveniently. As is the case with retelling, teachers should concentrate their efforts on the gist of the passage.

A third convenient, although indirect, method of assessing reading comprehension is to assess the rate of oral reading. Although this procedure may initially seem a bit strange, the rate of oral reading does appear empirically related to comprehension (Deno, 1985; Fuchs et al., 1988). Moreover, the relationship between rate and comprehension is logical: slow oral readers must expend their energy decoding words (for example, attending to letters, remembering letter-sound associations, or blending sounds) rather than concentrating on the meaning of what is written. Therefore, teachers probably should concentrate on the rate of oral reading regularly with beginning readers. To assess reading rate, teachers should have students read for two minutes from appropriate materials. The reading passage should be materials written with familiar vocabulary, syntax, and content; the passage must be longer than the amount any student can read in the two-minute period. Teachers have their own copy of the passage on which to note errors. The number of words correctly read and the number of errors made in two minutes are each divided by 2 to calculate the rate per minute. Mercer and Mercer (1985) suggest as desirable a rate of 80 words per minute (with two or fewer errors) as a goal for reading words from lists and a rate of 100 words per minute (with two or fewer errors) for words in text. See Chapter 17 for a fuller discussion of errors in oral reading.

More Advanced Students

Students who have already mastered basic sight vocabulary and decoding skills generally read silently. Emphasis for these students shifts, and new demands are made. Decoding moves from oral reading to silent reading with subvocalization (that is, saying the words and phrases to oneself) to visual scanning without subvocalization; thus, the reading rates of some students may exceed 1,000 words per minute. Scanning for main ideas and information may also be taught systematically. The demands for reading comprehension may go well beyond the literal comprehension of a passage; summarization, drawing inferences, recognizing and understanding symbolism, sarcasm, irony, and so forth may be systematically taught. For these advanced students, the gist of a passage is usually more important than the details. Teachers of more advanced students may wish to score retold passages on the basis of main ideas, important relationships, and details recalled correctly and the number of errors (that is, ideas, relationships, and details omitted plus the insertion of material not included in the passage). In such cases, the different types of information can be weighted differentially or the use of comprehension strategies encouraged (for example, summarization). However, it appears that read-write assessment formats using multiple-choice and extended-essay questions are more commonly used.

Informal Reading Inventories

When making decisions about referral or initial placement in a reading curriculum, teachers often develop informal reading inventories (IRIs). These inventories primarily assess decoding and reading comprehension over a wide range of skill levels within the specific reading curricula used in a classroom.[3] Thus, they are top-down assessments that span several levels of difficulty.

3. Some authors may include reading interest as a subdomain.

IRIs are given to locate the reading levels at which a student can read independently, requires instruction, and is frustrated. Techniques for developing IRIs and the criteria used to define independent, instructional, and frustration reading levels vary. Teachers should use a series of graded reading passages that range from below a student's actual placement to a year or two years above the actual placement. Using a reading series prepared for several grade levels, passages can be selected from the beginning, middle, and end of each grade. Students begin reading the easiest material and continue reading until they can decode less than 85 percent of words. Salvia and Hughes (1990) recommend an accuracy rate of 95 percent for independent reading and consider 85 to 95 percent accuracy as the level at which a student requires instruction.

Mathematics

Eight major components are usually considered in comprehensive mathematics curricula: readiness skills, vocabulary and concepts, numeration, whole-number operations, fractions and decimals, ratios and percents, measurement, and geometry (Salvia & Hughes, 1990). Mathematics curricula usually contain (1) problem sets in which only computations are performed and (2) word problems that require selection and application of the correct algorithm and computation. The difficulty of application problems goes well beyond the difficulty of the computation involved and is related to three factors: the number of steps involved in the solution; for example, a student might have to add and then multiply (Caldwell & Goldin, 1979), the amount of extraneous information (Englert, Cullata, & Horn, 1987), and whether or not the mathematical operation is directly implied by the vocabulary used in the problem; for example, words such as "and" or "more" imply addition while words such as "each" may imply division (see Bachor, Stacy, & Freeze, 1986). Although reading level is popularly believed to affect the difficulty of word problems, its effect is less clearly established (see Bachor, 1990; Paul, Nibbelink, & Hoover, 1986). At any grade level, the specific skills and concepts included in each of these subdomains will depend on the particular curriculum and its sequencing.

Beginning Skills

The whole-number operations of addition, subtraction, multiplication, and division are the core of the elementary mathematics curriculum. Readiness for beginning students includes such basics as classification, one-to-one correspondence, and counting. Vocabulary and concepts are generally restricted to quantitative words (for example, "same," "equal," "larger," and so forth) and spatial concepts (for example, left, above, next to, and so forth). Numeration deals with writing and identifying numbers, counting, ordering, and so forth.

See-write is probably the most frequently used format in the assessment of mathematical skills, although see-say formats are not uncommon. For content associated with readiness, vocabulary and concepts, numeration, and applications, matching formats are commonly used. Accuracy is stressed, and the ubiquitous 90 to 95 percent correct is commonly used as the criterion. For computation, accuracy and fluency are stressed in beginning mathematics; teachers do not stop their instruction when students respond accurately, but they continue instruction to build automaticity. Consequently, a teacher may accept somewhat lower rates of accuracy (that is, 80 percent). When working toward fluency, teachers usually use probes. Perhaps the most useful criterion for math probes assessing computation is the number of correct digits (in an answer) written per minute—and not the number of correct answers per minute. The actual criterion rate will depend on the operation, the type of material (for example, addition facts versus addition of two-digit numbers with regrouping), and the characteristics of the particular students. Students with motor difficulties may be held to a lower criterion or assessed with see-say formats. For see-write formats, students may be expected to write answers to addition and subtraction problems at rates between 50 and 80 digits per minute, and to simple multiplication and division problems at rates between 40 and 50 digits per minute (Salvia & Hughes, 1990).

Advanced Skills

The more advanced mathematical skills (that is, fractions, decimals, ratios, percents, and geometry) build on whole-number operations. These skills are taught to levels of comprehension and application. Unlike beginning skills, assessment formats are almost exclusively see-write, and accuracy is stressed over fluency except for a few facts such as "$1/2$ equals .5 equals 50 percent."

Spelling

Although spelling is considered by many as a component of written language, in elementary school it is generally taught as a separate subject. Therefore, it is treated separately in this chapter. Spelling is the production of letters in correct sequence to form a word. The specific words that are assigned as spelling words may come from several sources—spelling curricula, word lists, content areas, or a student's own written work. In high school and college, students are expected to use dictionaries and to spell correctly any word they use. Between that point and fourth grade or so, spelling words are typically assigned, and students are left to their own devices to learn them. In the first three grades, spelling is usually taught systematically using phonics, morphology, rote memorization, or some combination of the three approaches.

Teachers may assess mastery of the prespelling rules associated with the particular approach they are teaching. For example, when a phonics approach is used students may have to demonstrate mastery of writing the letters associated with specific vowels, consonants, consonant blends, diphthongs, and digraphs. Assessment formats are almost exclusively dictation—hear-write. Teachers provide the auditory stimuli themselves, or they may use aides or language masters. Although a criterion reflecting automaticity is intuitively appealing, emphasis is usually placed on accuracy.

Although teachers often give a spelling word and then use it in a sentence, students find the task easier if just the spelling word is given (Horn, 1967). Moreover, the findings from recent research suggest that a seven-second interval between words is sufficient (Shinn, Tindall, & Stein, 1988).

Written Language

Written language is no doubt the most complex and difficult domain for teachers to assess. Assessment differs widely for beginners and advanced students. Once the preliminary skills of letter formation and rudimentary spelling have been mastered, written-language curricula usually stress content and style (that is, grammar, mechanics, and diction).

Beginning Skills

The most basic instruction in written language is penmanship, in which the formation and spacing among uppercase (capital) and lowercase printed and cursive letters is taught. Early instruction stresses accuracy, and criteria are generally qualitative. After accuracy has been attained, teachers may provide extended practice to move students toward automaticity. If this is done, teachers will evaluate performance on the basis of students' rates of writing letters. Target rates are usually in the range of 80 to 100 letters per minute for students without motor handicaps.

Content generation for beginners is often reduced to generation of words in meaningful sequence. Teachers may use story starters (that is, pictures or a few words that act as stimuli) to prompt student writing. When the allotted time for writing is over, teachers count the number of words or divide the number of words by the time to obtain a measure of rate. Although this sounds relatively easy, decisions for what constitutes a word must be made. For example, one-letter words are seldom counted. Teachers also use the percentage of correct words to assess content production. To be considered correct, the word must be spelled correctly, be capitalized if appropriate, be grammatically correct, and be followed by the correct punctuation (Isaacson, 1988). Criteria for an acceptable percentage of correct words are still the subject of discussion. For now, social comparison, by which one student's writing output is compared to the output of students whose writing is judged acceptable, can provide teachers with rough approximations. Teaching style usually boils down to capitalization, simple punctuation, and basic grammar (for example, subject-verb agreement). Teachers may use multiple-choice or fill-in tests to assess comprehension of grammatical conventions or rules.

Advanced Skills

Comprehension and application of advanced grammar and mechanics can be tested readily with multiple-choice or fill-in questions. Thus, this aspect of written language can be assessed systematically and objectively. The evaluation of content generation by advanced students is far more difficult than counting correct words. Teachers may consider the quality of ideas, the sequencing of ideas, the coherence of ideas, and consideration of the reading audience. In practice, teachers use holistic judgments of content (Cooper, 1977). In addition, they may point out errors in style or indicate topics that might benefit from greater elaboration or clarification. Objectively scoring any of these attributes is very difficult, and extended scoring keys and practice are necessary to obtain reliable judgments, if they are ever attained. More objective scoring systems for content require computer analysis and at this time are beyond the resources of most classroom teachers.

POTENTIAL SOURCES OF DIFFICULTY IN TEACHER-MADE TESTS

In order to be useful, teacher-made tests must avoid three pitfalls. The first two are easily avoided; the third is more difficult.

First, teachers should not rely solely on a single summative assessment to evaluate student achievement after a course of instruction. Such assessments do not provide teachers with information to plan and modify sequences of instruction. Moreover, minor technical inadequacies can be magnified when a single summative measure is used. Rather, teachers should test progress toward educational objectives at least two or three times a week. Frequent testing is most important when instruction is aimed at developing automatic or fluent responses in students. Although fluency is most commonly associated with primary curricula, it is not restricted to reading, writing, and arithmetic. For example, instruction in foreign language, sports, and music often is aimed at automaticity.

Second, teachers should not use unstandardized testing procedures. In order to conduct frequent assessments that are meaningful, the tests that are used to assess the same objectives must be equivalent. Therefore, the content must be equivalent from test to test or probe to probe; moreover, test directions, kinds of cues or hints, testing formats, criteria for correct responses, and type of score (for example, rates or percentage correct) must be the same.

Third, teachers should develop technically adequate assessment procedures. Two aspects of this adequacy are especially important. First, the tests must have content validity. Seldom should there be problems with content validity when direct performances are used. For example, the materials used in finding a student's rate of oral reading should have content validity when they come from that student's reading materials; probes used to assess mastery of addition facts will have content validity because they assess the facts that have been taught. A problem with content validity is more probable when teachers use tests to assess achievement outside of the tool subjects. Although only teachers can develop tests that truly mirror instruction, teachers not only must know what has been taught but they must also prepare devices that test what has been taught. About the only way to guarantee that an assessment covers the content is to develop tables of specifications for the content of instruction and testing. However, test items geared to specific content may still be ineffective (see Chapter 8). Careful preparation in and of itself cannot guarantee the validity of one question or set of questions. The only way a teacher can know that the questions are good is to field-test the questions, and make revisions based on the results. Realistically speaking, teachers do not have the time for field-testing and revision prior to giving a test. Therefore, teachers must usually give a test and then delete or discount poor items. The poor items can be edited, and the revised questions used the next time the examination is needed. In this way, the responses from one group of students become a field test for a subsequent group of students. When teachers use this approach, they should not return tests to students because students may pass questions down from year to year.

The second aspect of technical adequacy is reliability. Interscorer agreement is a major concern for any test using a supply format, but is especially important when extended responses are evaluated. Agreement can be increased by developing precise scoring guides for all questions of this type and by sticking with the criteria. Interscorer agreement should not be a problem for tests using select or restricted fill-in formats. For select and fill-in tests, internal consistency is of primary concern. Unfortunately, very few people can prepare a set of homogeneous test questions the first time. However, at the same time that they revise poor items, teachers can delete or revise items to increase a test's homogeneity (that is, delete or revise items that have correlations with the total score of .25 or less). Additional items can also be prepared for the next test.

SUMMARY

Teachers assess during instruction in order to monitor pupil progress. Careful monitoring is necessary if instruction is to be modified, errors corrected early, and appropriate instructional pacing is to be maintained. Teachers also assess at the end of an instructional sequence to evaluate what their students have learned, assign grades, and select future instructional objectives. Because teacher-made tests are seldom subject to public scrutiny, many test theorists have doubts about their technical adequacy. However, teacher-made tests have several advantages over professionally prepared tests. Most important are (1) the capability of teachers to tailor their tests' content to the content of their teaching and (2) the potential to include many more pertinent test items, thereby ensuring the possibility of tests that allow teachers to make finer discriminations. Tests require students to select or supply responses to stimuli. The stimuli are usually auditory or visual, and student responses are usually vocal or written. When testing in core academic areas (that is, reading, mathematics, spelling, and written language) testing formats will vary, depending on the criteria that teachers use to evaluate learning and the level at which objectives are prepared. When fluent responses are sought by teachers, student performances in reading, math, and spelling are directly evaluated by supply tests. For example, students may complete math probes or read orally. Other objectives are assessed using more familiar testing methods. Select formats (that is, multiple-choice and matching) are useful in assessing instructional objectives prepared at the levels of knowledge, comprehension, and application. They are not well suited to higher-level objectives. Supply formats (that is, fill-in or extended essay) have varying utility. Fill-in questions can be used in much the same way as questions prepared in select formats. Extended essays can be used to assess objectives prepared at levels higher than knowledge although they are probably best reserved for objectives stressing analysis, synthesis, and evaluation. Teacher-made tests are most useful when they are administered during and after instruction, are carefully standardized, have content validity, and are reliable.

STUDY QUESTIONS

1. Explain the advantages and disadvantages of multiple-choice, matching, and true-false questions.
2. Explain how a probe differs from tests prepared in other formats.
3. Explain how teachers can use student-performance data gathered during instruction.
4. Explain the advantages of teacher-made tests.

ADDITIONAL READINGS

Gronlund, N. (1985). *Measurement and evaluation in teaching*, 5th ed. New York: Macmillan. (Part 2, Constructing classroom tests.)

Salvia, J., & Hughes, C. (1990). *Curriculum-based assessment: Testing what is taught*. New York: Macmillan. (Chapter 4, Development of appropriate assessment procedures: Collection and Summarization of Results.)

PART 5

APPLYING ASSESSMENT INFORMATION TO EDUCATIONAL DECISION MAKING

In the preceding portions of this text, we have provided basic information about the hows and whys of testing and assessment, discussed basic principles of reliability and validity, explained how norms and derived scores are obtained, and given our evaluations of many of the tests, from a variety of domains, that are used in today's schools. In this part of the book, we show how all of this information is applied to the process of making important decisions about students.

Assessment does not occur in a vacuum. Assessment is the process of collecting data for the purpose of making decisions about real people—decisions that are designed to enhance people's lives or life chances. The data that

have been collected do not stand alone but must be interpreted within the broader context of a person's development and current life circumstances. Knowing that Barry reads at the fourth percentile is a very useful bit of information. However, putting that score into a context gives it far more meaning. Suppose that Barry had attended organized educational programs since he was four years old; his first-grade teacher had tried numerous approaches to teaching him beginning skills in reading unsuccessfully; he was retained in first grade; his current second-grade teacher has also tried unsuccessfully to teach him beginning skills; and a recent, valid assessment places Barry in the moderately retarded range of intellectual functioning. Barry's lack of progress in reading in this scenario suggests something quite different than the same score in a different scenario. Suppose that Barry entered first grade without attending organized preschool or kindergarten; his parents were killed in a drive-by shooting midway through his first year in school; he moved across country to live with his maternal grandmother; his former school stressed sight vocabulary and contextual analysis in teaching of reading, while the second school began stressing phonics in kindergarten and first grade. In either scenario, Barry has not demonstrated a satisfactory level of skill development in reading. The interpretation of that performance differs.

In Part 5 we describe the ways in which assessment data are collected and used. Obviously, all of the possible contexts and all of the possible decisions cannot be illustrated. Instead, we focus on a series of decisions that can eventually lead to a student becoming eligible for special educational services—decisions about referral, classification, and instructional planning. We illustrate decision making with five students, each of whom has a different problem.

The activities described in this part of the book are examples of ways in which assessment information is collected and used in the schools. Frankly, the cases are simplified. For example, we have not discussed the basis on which a diagnostician selected particular tests, although in practice considerable time and energy may be expended in reviewing a student's specific curriculum and finding a technically adequate device that matches instruction; time and energy may be expended considering a specific student's sensory and physical limitations and selecting a technically adequate device to assess intellectual functioning in ways that do not penalize that student. Assessment in the schools is often likely to be far more complex than we portray in this section, and there is no substitute for hands-on experience.

C·H·A·P·T·E·R 25

MAKING REFERRAL DECISIONS

Technically speaking, a referral is a request for help. A teacher or parent calls a student to the attention of a specialist when assistance seems to be needed to provide the student with an appropriate educational program. There is, frankly, much confusion about the act of referral, and much of that confusion can be traced directly to misinformation that has been dispensed to teachers as part of their training. For years teachers were trained to look for specific kinds of problems that would indicate the need to refer a student to some other person. Teachers learned definitions of conditions and lists of characteristics associated with specific kinds of disorders. They learned those lists so that they could spot problems early and spot specific students who should be referred to others. This practice has contributed to some problems.

A cursory look at referral practices in today's schools reveals a mixture of practices. In some settings, practice is still pretty traditional, and teachers refer students to other professionals. In such settings, the act of referral is often one in which the teacher abdicates responsibility for a student. The teacher learns to give up or is reinforced for giving up on specific students and sending them to other professionals in the school. Such traditional practices are encouraged when those to whom students are referred (counselors, school psychologists, speech and language pathologists, social workers) respond by testing students and trying to find out "what is wrong with them."

In other settings referral is viewed as a request for help in providing an appropriate educational program for a student. There is considerable emphasis on prereferral assessment for the purpose of verifying and specifying the nature of academic, behavior, or physical problems. Some teachers have always engaged in significant prereferral assessment. Recently, the practice has become more prevalent. In part this is due to efforts, in response to Public Law 94-142, to educate students in least restrictive environments. In part, it is due to the fact that many states have written into their state rules and regulations the requirement that personnel engage in prereferral intervention as a part of the assessment process. Carter and Sugai (1989) reported that prereferral interventions are required in twenty-three states and recommended in eleven states.

THE PREREFERRAL ASSESSMENT PROCESS

We use the term *prereferral* to describe assessment activities that occur before formal assessment and consideration for placement. We do not assume that referral is an automatic activity subsequent to prereferral assessment or intervention. Under ideal circumstances, a great deal of prereferral assessment and prereferral intervention takes place before students are ever considered for special education placement. The goal of prereferral assessment and intervention is twofold: (1) verification and specification of the nature of a student's difficulties, and (2) provision of services in the least restrictive environment.

Graden, Casey, and Bonstrom (1983) describe five stages in prereferral assessment and intervention. We think it is important to review these stages, as they nicely illustrate ideal practice.

Stage 1: Request for Consultation   The first step in the process ought to be a request for consultation rather than a request for testing. The classroom teacher asks for help, either from a resource teacher or from some other specialist. A form similar to that shown in Figure 25.1 may be used to initiate the request.

Stage 2: Consultation   The resource teacher or other specialist works with the classroom teacher to verify the existence of a problem, to specify the nature of a problem, and to develop strategies that might relieve the problem. The following steps occur during this initial consultation.

a. The referring teacher is asked to specify, in observable terms, the reason(s) for referral. For example, the teacher may specify a problem by saying that "Heather does not recognize the letters of the alphabet" or that "Matthew does not complete homework assignments."
b. Reasons for referral are ranked in order of importance for action. This act helps the consultant to identify specific problems to be addressed. In the professional literature, this activity, along with the activity listed in step a above, are referred to as engaging in "problem clarification."
c. The referring teacher is asked to specify the ways in which the student's behavior affects the teacher and the extent to which the behavior is incongruent with the teacher's expectations. The focus is on the discrepancy between actual and desired performance.
d. An intervention is designed by the referring teacher. Graden, Casey, and Bonstrom (1983) find the form shown in Figure 25.2 useful in designing an intervention. In planning prereferral interventions, it is often helpful to involve the student, the parents, and other school personnel as appropriate.

FIGURE 25.1   Request for Consultation

Student _____ Sex _____ Date of birth _____

Referring teacher _____ Grade _____ School _____

_____

Describe specific educational/behavioral problems:

_____

_____

_____

_____

Current instructional level:

Reading _____ Math _____

What special services is the student receiving (e.g., speech, Title I, Reading Teacher)?

_____

_____

Results of vision, hearing, medical screening:

_____

_____

_____

Most convenient days/times to meet for consultation on referral:

_____

_____

THIS IS NOT A REFERRAL FOR TESTING

e. Interventions are implemented and evaluated. These interventions will either succeed in alleviating the problem or will lead to additional teaching modifications.

On completion of this stage, those who educate the child will have verified the existence of a problem, specified the nature of the problem, tried to intervene to remove the problem, and collected data on the effectiveness of those interventions.

Stage 3: Observation   Observation of pupil behavior in classroom settings makes it possible to document the specific nature of referral problems. It is one way to verify the existence of a problem or problems. The following kinds of activities may occur:

a. A designated person (resource teacher or school psychologist, for example) observes in relevant school settings, noting the frequency and duration of behaviors of concern and the extent to which the student's behavior differs from that of his or her classmates.
b. The observer describes (1) the curriculum being used with the student, the tasks the student is being asked to do, and the specific demands being placed on the student; (2) the way in which the teacher interacts with or responds to the student, specifically what the student does, grouping structure, and seating arrangements; (3) interactions between the student and his or her classmates; (4) causes and consequences of the student's behaviors.
c. The observer meets with the classroom teacher to provide feedback on what has been observed, and the two work together to verify the existence and specify the nature of the problem.
d. The observer and teacher develop prereferral interventions designed to address the problem. The form shown in Figure 25.3 can be used for this purpose.
e. Interventions are implemented and evaluated. Interventions will either alleviate the problem(s) or, perhaps, lead to additional instructional modifications.

The primary goals of stages 2 and 3 are the development of prereferral interventions and the evaluation of the extent to which those interventions alleviate problems that students show in classrooms. When interventions are implemented prior to formal referral and data are collected on the effectiveness of those interventions, school personnel develop a "track record." They can see the extent to which alternative instructional approaches work with a student. The form shown in Figure 25.4 can be used to document the effectiveness of interventions. When prereferral interventions are used, school personnel go through the following steps:

a. They plan several possible interventions based on data collected during consultation or observation.

b. For each intervention planned they specify (1) the behavior(s) to be changed (what); (2) the criterion for success; (3) the duration of intervention (how long); (4) the location of intervention (where); (5) the person(s) responsible for intervening (who); and (6) the methods to be used (how).

c. Intervention plans are ranked in terms of importance. They are then implemented, monitored, evaluated, and modified, continued, or terminated.

d. The process may end if interventions are successful. The process may continue until school personnel reach a limit of tolerance in attempts to intervene.

Stage 4: Conference   A conference may be held to review pupil progress and to decide whether formal referral is necessary. This meeting would involve appropriate school personnel and might also include the parents and/or the student. At this meeting, the following things occur:

a. Data on consultations, observations, and the effectiveness of interventions are shared.

b. Feedback from team members is solicited.

c. A decision is made to (1) continue interventions, (2) modify interventions, or (3) refer the student for formal psychoeducational assessment to consider her or his eligibility for special education services.

Stage 5: Formal Referral   A formal referral is made for psychoeducational intervention. The student enters the formal child study process and two kinds of assessment occur:

a. Data collected during the first four stages are evaluated.

b. Tests are administered or behaviors are sampled in an effort to gather information needed to plan a specific instructional program.

CASE STUDY EXAMPLES

Referral has two meanings. It is a request for help. It is also a request for evaluation. We now describe referral information on five different students. In each instance we assume the students are being formally referred for psychoeducational evaluation and that consultation, observation, and prereferral intervention have already occurred. We provide you with information on how problems were verified and specified. In Chapter 26 we will follow four of these students through the classification process. In Chapter 27 we will show how instructional interventions were developed for the students.

FIGURE 25.2 Consultation Contacts

Student _____ Sex _____ Date of birth _____

Teacher _____ Grade _____ School _____

Problem Identification Interview Date _____

Behavioral description of problem(s):

Conditions under which behavior occurs:

Performance to be measured:

What:

How:

By whom:

Teacher _____ Consultant _____

Next contact _____

FIGURE 25.2   Consultation Contacts (cont.)

Problem Analysis Interview   Date _____

Discrepancy between actual/desired performance:

Performance goals/objectives:

Strategies:

Teacher _____ Consultant _____

Next contact _____

_____

Implementation Contact   Date _____

_____ Implemented as planned

_____ Modifications to implementation plan (note): _____

_____

_____

Problem Evaluation Interview   Date _____

Evaluation of plan effectiveness:

_____ Follow-up contact to successful intervention.   Next contact _____

_____ Proceed to observation.   Next contact _____

Teacher _____ Consultant _____

FIGURE 25.3 Observation Contacts

Student _____ Sex _____ Date of birth _____

Teacher _____ Grade _____ School _____

_____

Report on Observation Date _____

Behavior observed:

Conditions of observed behavior:

Causes/consequences of observed behavior:

Teacher _____ Consultant _____

Next contact _____

FIGURE 25.3 Observation Contacts (cont.)

Observation Contact   Date _____

Feedback on observation:

Intervention plan based on observation:

Goals/objectives:

Strategies:

Teacher _____ Consultant _____

Next contact _____

Follow-up on Observation Interventions   Date _____

Evaluation of plan effectiveness:

_____ Follow-up contact to successful intervention.   Next contact _____

_____ Proceed to interventions.   Next contact _____

Teacher _____ Consultant _____

FIGURE 25.4 Intervention Contacts

Student _____ Sex _____ Date of birth _____

Referring teacher _____ Grade _____ School _____

_____

Intervention Plan Meeting   Date _____

Rank intervention objectives by priority:

Data needed to plan interventions:

Intervention goals/objectives:

  Behavior to be changed:

  Criterion for success:

  Duration of intervention:

  Context of intervention:

  Who will implement:

Strategies:

  Methods:

  Materials:

Teacher _____ Consultant _____

Next contact _____

FIGURE 25.4   Intervention Contacts (cont.)

Intervention Monitoring Meeting   Date _____

_____ Interventions implemented as planned.

_____ Modifications to intervention plan (note):

Teacher _____   Consultant _____

Next contact _____

Intervention Evaluation Meeting   Date _____

Outcomes of interventions:

_____ Follow-up on successful intervention plan.   Next contact _____

_____ Continued intervention.   Next contact _____

_____ Case referred to child study team.

Teacher _____   Consultant _____

Next contact _____

The cases illustrated are real, but students' names have, of course, been changed.

Phoebe

Phoebe was a 13-year-old eighth grader who was experiencing considerable difficulty with math problems. Phoebe came to the attention of school personnel when her parents asked the junior high school counselor to "have her tested for learning disabilities in mathematics." The counselor met with the eighth-grade math teacher (consultation) to discuss Phoebe's performance in math. The counselor was told that Phoebe could not do beginning algebra and that her performance in science was poor. The teacher reported that Phoebe was becoming truant, often skipped math class, and often talked about quitting school. The teacher reported that he had held two meetings with Phoebe's parents and that the parents seemed to be exerting a lot of pressure for Phoebe to succeed in math and science. The father, an engineer, had stated specifically that he wanted Phoebe to go to college and that he thought math and science were the two most important subjects in school.

The counselor reviewed Phoebe's previous school records. She could find no evidence of prior academic, behavior, or physical problems. The counselor noted that Phoebe's progress in school had been simply adequate. Most grades were B's and C's, with a D+ earned in seventh-grade science. Phoebe had taken a standardized achievement test, the California Achievement Test, in seventh grade and had scored at the 55th percentile in both math computation and math concepts and applications. The protocol was not available since it was machine scored.

In order to verify and specify the nature of Phoebe's math problems, the counselor decided to interview the teacher, the student, and the parents and to observe Phoebe's behavior in math and English classes.

Teacher Interview

The counselor discussed Phoebe's performance with the eighth-grade math teacher in an effort to specify the nature of her difficulties. The teacher reported that Phoebe's performance was very slow and that she seldom completed math tests. The teacher said Phoebe seemed overly concerned with the correctness of her performance, and overly concerned with errors. The teacher could not sort out any particular kind of math problem that was posing difficulty for Phoebe. He reported that Phoebe's record of turning in completed homework assignments was getting worse. When asked how Phoebe's performance compared to that of other eighth graders, the teacher reported that Phoebe was among the poorest students in Algebra I, but far better than students enrolled in Basic Math.

Student Interview

The counselor met with Phoebe to talk about her academic progress. Phoebe reported that it was taking more and more time to complete her math assignments and that her parents were increasingly "getting on her case" about performance in math. She stated that no matter how hard she tried, her parents "kept bugging her" about math. She said she wanted to give up, because no matter how hard she tried, her parents were always too busy to help her. She stated that her father repeatedly scolded her for spending more time on the phone than on math.

Parent Interview

The counselor met with the parents to discuss Phoebe's performance in math, and school in general. It was reported that the parents were highly success oriented and placed considerable emphasis on math achievement. The parents reported having purchased a microcomputer in response to an ad on television about students with math problems. They reported that Phoebe initially used the math software but now prefers to play games. The father indicated little understanding of or sympathy for Phoebe's difficulties, stating that math always came easily for him.

Classroom Observation

On three occasions the counselor tried to observe Phoebe in math class. Yet on only one of those occasions was Phoebe present. When Phoebe was observed, it was noted that she appeared to listen to instructions and worked very hard at completion of an in-class assignment. Phoebe seemed to be working harder than several other students in the class, yet about half of her work was completed incorrectly. Observation of her behavior in English class indicated little difference from her behavior in math.

Action

The counselor verified the existence of a problem in math by consulting with the math teacher, the parents, and Phoebe. The problem could not be specified beyond general, across-the-board difficulties in math and a developing negative attitude toward math. The counselor further verified the existence of a problem by direct observation in the classroom. A decision was made to forgo prereferral intervention for two reasons: (1) Phoebe's poor attendance in math class, and (2) the general rather than specific nature of her difficulties. Formal referral was made to the school psychologist who was asked to determine (1) the specific nature of Phoebe's difficulties in math and (2) whether or not Phoebe was eligible for special education services.

Bill

Bill was an 8-year-old black student whose third-grade teacher initially asked for help because Bill was having reading difficulties. The resource teacher, Mr. Will, responded to this referral by meeting with the third-grade teacher. The first step used by the resource teacher was one of clarifying and specifying the nature of the problems Bill was experiencing. The third-grade teacher informed Mr. Will that Bill was having difficulty in recognizing and decoding the very simplest words. In addition, Bill was beginning to withdraw from classroom interactions and to show behavior problems, especially as evidenced in scribbling on other students' worksheets.

Observation

The resource teacher observed Bill in class on two separate occasions, once for 45 minutes and once for 10 minutes. It was observed that Bill's performance in reading was at the very lowest level. During reading instruction he simply did not read. Bill was in the lowest reading group in his class, and clearly was the poorest reader in that group. Worksheets requiring him to match pictures with words were completed sloppily; performance was at a chance level.

Parent Interview

Mr. Will and the third-grade teacher met with Bill's parents. The parents both worked and were from a middle-class background. They stated that Bill's development had been pretty much normal and that he had had few physical illnesses. There was no history of vision or hearing problems. The parents said that Bill gets along "just fine" with other children in his neighborhood and that he spends most of his time playing with two 9-year-old neighborhood boys.

Prereferral Intervention

The resource teacher and classroom teacher together planned an intervention that involved Bill's going to a reading tutor three times a week for 45 minutes. The tutor selected 20 words that Bill did not know. She used flash cards and a word-picture association method to teach five words, a phonic approach to teach five others, a kinesthetic approach to teach five other words, and a combination of the three approaches to teach the remaining five words. The word-picture association approach worked best, but the overriding result was that Bill learned to recognize only two words under this approach. The tutor recommended that the teacher try using computer-assisted instruction (CAI) in which Bill had to match words with pictures.

A two-week intervention using CAI to teach word-picture association proved fruitless. Bill performed at random in efforts to match pictures to words. The teacher met with the resource teacher, and they recommended formal evaluation for potential special education placement.

Luis

Luis was a 7-year-old Hispanic student who was attending kindergarten at the time he was referred for psychoeducational evaluation. His parents had held him out of school until age 7 because so many developmental problems were indicated. Luis was referred by the kindergarten teacher during the first week in September. She asked for assistance, stating that "Luis shows developmental delays in all areas."

Teacher Interview

The school psychologist met with the kindergarten teacher to specify the nature of the difficulties shown by Luis. The teacher reported that Luis was extremely immature compared to other kindergarten children, that he had difficulty walking, had many toilet accidents, and spoke seldom and with little intelligibility. The teacher reported that Luis sometimes spoke in Spanish, but most often used English.

Parent Interview

The kindergarten teacher and school psychologist met with Luis's mother. They learned that Luis had shown considerable immaturity in all areas since he was an infant. The mother reported that Luis was much slower to walk and talk than her other children and that he had only begun to talk at age 5. The mother reported that both parents were bilingual, but that Luis's vocabulary in both Spanish and English was very limited.

Classroom Observation

The school psychologist observed Luis in the kindergarten classroom. Luis did not respond to teacher directions; he simply sat at a table and crumpled papers. He did not interact with other children and did not speak during the time he was observed.

Action

The school psychologist completed a formal referral for psychoeducational evaluation for consideration of eligibility for special education services.

Matt

Matt was a 13-year-old eighth grader whose teacher, Ms. Brooks, made a request for consultation. The request was received by the resource teacher, Ms. Edwards. Information on the form indicated that Matt was demonstrating serious behavior problems in English class and study hall, both conducted by Ms. Brooks.

The resource teacher met with Ms. Brooks to verify the existence of a problem and to specify the nature of the difficulties evidenced by Matt. Ms. Brooks reported that Matt was using frequent negative verbalizations. He teased other students and called them names. For example, he would say things like "You're ugly," "You're a jerk," or "You're stupid." Sometimes these statements were also made to the teacher. Often, the statements included obscenities. Ms. Brooks reported that she could not identify anything that triggered the negative verbal statements; they just occurred. She reported that teasing and name calling were more frequent during independent work time than during group instructional activities.

Ms. Edwards asked Ms. Brooks how she typically responded to Matt's teasing and negative verbal statements. Ms. Brooks said she usually told Matt his behavior was inappropriate, sometimes raised her voice in speaking with Matt, and often told him his behavior would not be tolerated. She said that on two occasions she had sent him to the vice principal's office but Matt had simply wandered around the school until the next class started. Ms. Brooks had not reported this to the vice principal. When Ms. Edwards asked how students who were picked on reacted to Matt, she was told that Matt was much bigger than the other students and they either ignored him or complained to the teacher. In addition, Matt did participate in class and was earning a grade of C.

Ms. Brooks stated that she wanted to decrease the number of instances of negative verbalizations *without* decreasing the number of positive verbalizations and contributions to class. She said she would like to find out if Matt had serious emotional problems and if he would be better off in a class for emotionally disturbed students. Ms. Edwards asked Ms. Brooks about the frequency of the teasing and name calling. Matt was said to have "good days" and "bad days." On good days the frequency of negative verbalizations ranged from 8 to 10 per hour. On bad days there were often as many as 40 to 50 in a one-hour class. Matt was said to have two or three "bad days" per week.

Observation

The resource teacher, Ms. Edwards, observed Matt's behavior in English class for three hours and in study hall for one hour. During three hours of observation in English class there were 90 negative verbalizations. During the one-hour observation in study hall, there were 41 negative verbalizations. Ms. Edwards kept track of ways in which Ms. Brooks responded to the negative verbalizations. Ms. Brooks responded inconsistently. Usually she would ignore two or three instances of negative behavior and then become loud and scolding on the next.

Teacher Meeting

Ms. Edwards met with Ms. Brooks to review the findings of her observation and to design an intervention. She reported the number of negative verbalizations per hour in English as 37, 8, and 45, and the number of negative verbalizations per hour in study hall as 41.

Intervention Plan

Ms. Edwards and Ms. Brooks designed an intervention for English class. If it worked, they would use it in study hall as well. Ms. Brooks first reviewed classroom rules with all students. She then met with Matt to explain to him that she would be keeping a record of his negative verbal statements by placing a tally mark on the chalkboard each time a negative verbalization was observed. Matt was allowed up to 15 verbalizations per day (Intervention A). For any day he did not exceed 15 negative verbalizations in English class, he would be allowed to listen to his radio in study hall for 10 minutes. To keep Matt from exceeding 15 negative verbalizations and then engaging in an excess number, a second condition was instituted. If Matt had no more than 5 negative verbalizations over the limit, he would receive 20 minutes of free time on Friday of the week.

  Ms. Brooks tallied negative verbalizations during English class for one week. During that time there was a steady decrease in negative verbalizations, and they averaged 9 per day (see Figure 25.5). Then, at Ms. Edwards's suggestion, the criterion was lowered to 10 negative verbalizations per day (Intervention B) and tallies were kept on a piece of graph paper at Ms. Brooks's desk. The record sheets were shared with Matt at the end of each day. After three more weeks, the frequency of negative verbalizations during English class decreased to an average of 3 per day. The intervention was then put in place in study hall (Intervention C) where, after three more weeks, negative verbalizations decreased to an average of 4 per day. (The number of instances of negative verbalizations was graphed. The graph for study hall and English class is shown in Figure 25.5.) The intervention was continued for the remainder of the school year and no formal referral for testing was made.

Marty

Marty was a 6½-year-old child who was coming to school for the first time. Although a preschool program for the handicapped and an integrated kindergarten were available within the district, Marty's parents had elected to hold him out of these programs.

FIGURE 25.5   Tally of Matt's Verbalizations in English Class and Study Hall

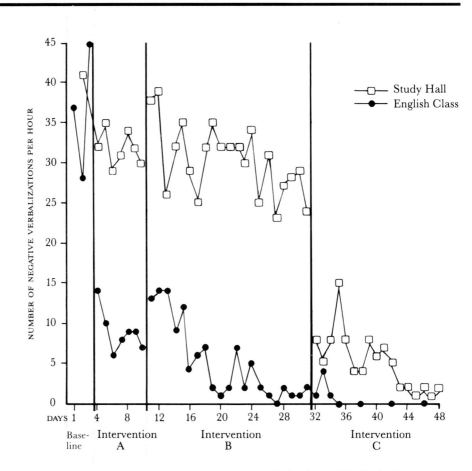

Intervention A = Tally of the negative verbalizations with a limit of 15 per day in English class only

Intervention B = Tally of the negative verbalizations with a limit of 10 per day in English class only

Intervention C = Tally of the negative verbalizations with a limit of 10 per day in both English class and study hall

Parent Interview

The school principal interviewed Marty's mother, Mrs. Webster, who brought Marty to school the first day. Marty is the only child of Mark and Danielle Webster. Mr. Webster is a loan officer at one of the local banks. Mrs. Webster works part-time in the editorial department of a small publishing company located in town.

Mrs. Webster informed the principal, Mr. Schmidt, that when Marty was almost 2 years old, she learned that he was legally blind and had been from birth. She understood that he would require special education services, and the physician had told her that Marty would never learn to read. Mrs. Webster presented the principal with an ophthalmological report that confirmed Marty's severe myopia (he had less than 20/200 vision in his better eye with the best correction) and nystagmus. Marty's mother wanted him to enroll in school and was quite fearful that he would have to go to the state school for the blind. Mr. Schmidt assured her that the school district would do its best to provide services for Marty right in their home community and that he would get Marty into the kindergarten where three other handicapped youngsters were enrolled on a trial basis.

Teacher Interview

Two days later Mr. Schmidt checked with the kindergarten teacher, Ms. Hampton. She reported that Marty accompanied his mother to the kinder-garten classroom each day. He appeared eager to come to school but was fearful that his mother would leave him. He talked freely with the other children but engaged in no gross motor activities; he expressed the fear that he would run into things. When the class lined up to go outside, Marty had trouble keeping in the line. On the playground, he was very hesitant to move away from the school building and stayed close to the school walls. When walking, Marty tended to shuffle his feet and had trouble when the surface on which he was walking changed from asphalt to grass.

Action

After observing Marty in the kindergarten for one week, Ms. Hampton prepared a referral. She noted that Marty was trying to use his vision. He did considerable head positioning—that is, tilting and turning his head to look indirectly at the chalkboard. She also noted that he pushed very close to her at story time. Ms. Hampton also mentioned that he became noticeably fa-tigued as the day wore on. He seemed a very agreeable child, but "a bit slow intellectually." Finally, she noted that the materials that were available in the classroom were just not suitable for Marty. Although the print size did not seem to be a major problem, all the printed materials were on glossy white paper.

Summary

Assessment information is used for the purpose of making referral decisions. Under ideal circumstances, a considerable amount of assessment and diagnostic teaching will take place prior to formal referral. We have used several case studies to illustrate how school personnel collect data, consult, interview, and observe to gather information necessary in deciding whether to refer a student.

Study Questions

1. Why might it be better to think of referral as a request for help rather than a request for testing?
2. Why would one want to develop interventions in regular classroom settings before testing students? What would be gained by doing so?
3. Identify at least four things that could be documented specifically by observing in classrooms.
4. Several prereferral interventions were attempted with Bill. Identify one other intervention that might have been tried.

Additional Reading

Algozzine, B., Christenson, S., & Ysseldyke, J. E. (1982). Probabilities associated with the referral to placement process. *Teacher Education and Special Education, 5,* 19–23.

Christenson, S., Ysseldyke, J. E., & Algozzine, B. (1982). Institutional and external pressures influencing referral decisions. *Psychology in the Schools, 19,* 341–345.

Christenson, S., Ysseldyke, J. E., Wang, J. J., & Algozzine, B. (1983). Teachers' attributions for problems that result in referral for psychoeducational evaluation. *Journal of Educational Research, 76,* 174–180.

Graden, J. L., Casey, A., & Bonstrom, O. (1985). Implementing a prereferral intervention system: Part II. The data. *Exceptional Children, 51,* 487–496.

Graden, J. L., Casey, A., & Christenson, S. L. (1985). Implementing a prereferral intervention system: Part I. The model. *Exceptional Children, 51,* 377–384.

Idol-Maestas, L. (1983). *Special educators' consultation handbook.* Gaithersburg, MD: Aspen.

Norby, J., Thurlow, M. L., Christenson, S. L., & Ysseldyke, J. E. (1990). *The challenge of complex school problems.* Austin, TX: Pro-Ed, Inc.

Ysseldyke, J. E., Christenson, S., Pianta, B., & Algozzine, B. (1983). An analysis of teachers' reasons and desired outcomes for students referred for psychoeducational evaluation. *Journal of Psychoeducational Assessment, 1,* 73–83.

C·H·A·P·T·E·R 26

MAKING
CLASSIFICATION DECISIONS

Assessment data are regularly used to make classification decisions about individuals. All of us are classified within several types of systems. Sociologists may assign us to particular social classes according to our education, occupation, and income. Individuals are classified in several ways under the legal systems of the federal and state governments: citizen or noncitizen, voter or nonvoter, felon, adjudicated delinquent, and so forth. When we are ill, our sickness may be classified by our physician: cold, sore throat, or herpes simplex. Psychiatrists may classify clients according to DSM-III-R *(Diagnostic and Statistical Manual of Mental Disorders–Revised)*.

One type of classification system is of particular importance—classification systems used to determine eligibility. Our society classifies individuals as eligible for various social services: social security benefits, food stamps, veterans' benefits, welfare, and so forth. Of importance for us is eligibility for special education services. One of the primary reasons for classifying students in the public schools is to ascertain their eligibility for special services.

There are several variables that can seriously affect a pupil's educational progress: chronic illness, ineffective instruction, lack of motivation, sensory or cognitive impairment, and so forth. It is very clear that society does not choose to help all students who fail to make adequate progress. Unmotivated students, students who receive inadequate or inappropriate instruction, and students living in a variety of disadvantageous conditions do not receive special help. Society has decided, when achievement is seriously impeded by a few select conditions, that government should come to the aid of the individuals affected. The federal and state governments extend special benefits to these individuals. For example, if Joey is mentally retarded, he may be excused from meeting certain educational requirements (for example, high school graduation requirements may be different); he may be taught by teachers who have had special coursework and practicum experiences and may have special certification; he may use special materials; he will probably be taught in smaller classes. These special services generally cost more than the educational services provided for most students in regular education. Part or all of the additional costs will be borne by state and federal government. Determining whether or not Joey is mentally retarded in essence determines whether or not part of his special education will be paid for under special provisions of federal and state law. Thus, in the schools, classification decisions usually are decisions about whether or not a child is eligible for additional help paid for by special funds earmarked for children with particular handicapping conditions.

DETERMINING ELIGIBILITY FOR SPECIAL SERVICES

Several classification systems are used in the United States today. As Table 1.1 in Chapter 1 shows, in different states, different terms are used to specify the handicapping conditions that are eligible for special education services. The most frequently used terms are those that are used for reporting under the regulations of PL 94-142.

Every definition of a handicapping condition requires that an assessment be made. (Many definitions or parts of definitions imply that testing be done; most state education codes *require* that testing be done.) When assessing for the purpose of classification, we gather information to clarify and to verify the relationship of a pupil's abilities and skills to the criteria for eligibility for special services used in a particular state. Sometimes school personnel do not gather the data; a physician or other professional may be required to perform the evaluation. In such cases, school personnel review the information and decide whether a pupil is eligible for services, and—if eligible—what services are to be provided. More often, school personnel themselves gather the information, decide about eligibility, and identify the particular services that will be delivered.

Classification Criteria

The process of classification begins with referral. Generally, a good referral contains some pertinent clues about the classification a student is likely to receive. All students who are classified as handicapped will probably demonstrate problem(s) in achievement unless some interventions have already been made.

Mentally retarded pupils are those who demonstrate "significantly subaverage intellectual functioning existing concurrently with deficits in adaptive behavior, and manifested during the developmental period" (Grossman, 1983). Students who are eventually labeled mentally retarded are often referred because of generalized slowness: they lag behind their agemates in most areas of academic achievement, social and emotional development, language ability, and perhaps physical development. This slowness must be demonstrated on an individually administered test of intelligence that is appropriate for the student being assessed. Thus, the test must be appropriate not only for the age of the student but also for the pupil's acculturation as well as physical and sensory abilities. However, a test of intelligence is not enough. The pupil must also demonstrate slowness in adaptive behavior. An assessment for mental retardation should always contain an assessment of achievement, intelligence, and adaptive behavior.

Learning-disabled pupils are those who demonstrate

> *a disorder in one or more of the basic psychological processes involved in understanding or in using language, spoken or written, which may manifest itself in the imperfect ability to listen, think, read, write, spell, or do mathematical calculations. The term* [learning disabilities] *includes such conditions as perceptual handicaps, brain injury, minimal brain dysfunction, dyslexia, and developmental aphasia. The term does not include children who have learning problems which are primarily the result of visual, hearing, or motor handicaps, of mental retardation, emotional disturbance, or environmental, cultural, or economic disadvantage. (U.S. Office of Education, 1977, p. 65083)*

Students who are eventually labeled learning-disabled are often referred because of inconsistent performance; they are likely to have pronounced patterns of academic and cognitive strengths and weaknesses. For example, Harry may grasp mathematics and social concepts quite well, but he may not learn to read no matter what his teacher tries; Joyce may be reading at grade level, be a good speller, have highly developed language skills, but not be able to master addition and subtraction facts. Criteria for eligibility for services for the learning-disabled vary considerably from state to state. Generally, a pupil must demonstrate normal (or at least nonretarded) general intellectual development on an individually administered test of intelligence. The student must also demonstrate, on an individually administered test of achievement, some areas that are within the normal range while demonstrating significantly delayed development in other areas of achievement, and demonstrate (corrected) hearing and vision within normal limits. Eligible pupils would not have significant emotional problems or cultural disadvantage. Finally, the basic process disorder that causes the learning disability may or may not have to be tested, depending on the particular state's education code. If assessed, measures of visual and auditory perception as well as measures of linguistic and psycholinguistic abilities would be administered.

Emotionally disturbed pupils exhibit

> *one or more of the following characteristics over a long period of time and to a marked degree, which adversely affects educational performance: (a) an inability to learn which cannot be explained by intellectual, sensory, or health factors; (b) an inability to build or maintain satisfactory interpersonal relationships with peers and teachers; (c) inappropriate types of behavior or feelings under*

normal circumstances; (d) a general pervasive mood of unhappiness or depression; or (e) a tendency to develop physical symptoms or fears associated with personal or school problems. (Education of Handicapped Children, Federal Register, Section 121a5, 1977)

Students who are eventually labeled emotionally disturbed are often referred for problems in interpersonal relations (for example, fighting or extreme noncompliance) and/or unusual behavior (for example, unexplained episodes of crying or extreme mood swings). Requirements for establishing a pupil's eligibility for special education services for the emotionally disturbed vary markedly among the states. Some or all of the following sources of information may be used in determining eligibility: observational data, behavior-rating scales, psychological evaluation, and examination by a board-certified psychiatrist or psychologist.

The standards applied to sensorily handicapped students are in some ways quite objective. A *blind person* has "visual acuity for distant vision of 20/200 or less in the better eye, with the best correction or visual acuity of more than 20/200 if the widest diameter of field of vision subtends an angle no greater than 20 degrees" (National Society for the Prevention of Blindness, 1966, p. 10). *Visually impaired students* have corrected visual acuity of 20/70 or less in the better eye. A *deaf person* has hearing acuity in the speech range of −90 decibels or less in the better ear while a *hard-of-hearing person* has hearing acuity of −35 decibels or less in the better ear. The standards applied to sensorily handicapped pupils can be complex and subjective, however, when one assesses sensorial functioning to decide about a particular placement and the extent to which vision or hearing may be used as a primary modality of instruction. Sensorily handicapped children often come to school already diagnosed. Sometimes they do not. Referrals for undiagnosed visually impaired students may indicate gross and fine motor problems, variable visual performance (for example, the size of print, amount of light, and fatigue all influence performance). Referrals for undiagnosed hearing-impaired students may indicate both expressive and receptive language problems, variable hearing performance, problems in attending to aural tasks, and perhaps problems in peer relationships. Assessment to establish eligibility for programs for sensorily impaired students is generally conducted by health professionals. Visual acuity and visual field are usually assessed by an ophthalmologist. Functional visual assessment is usually done by a specialist through systematic observation of a child's responses to various types of paper, print sizes, lighting conditions, and so forth. Assessment of hearing acuity is performed by an audiologist. Functional hearing assessment may be conducted by an audiologist or a teacher of the hearing-impaired.

The standards applied to *students with chronic physical and health problems* are seldom specified in state education codes. Rather, federal and state regulations typically require that the condition be so severe that education in the regular program is not possible and then enumerate the conditions that are eligible for special consideration (for example, spina bifida, muscular dystrophy, heart disease, and so forth). Physically handicapped pupils are generally identified prior to entering school. However, accidents and disease may impair a previously normal student. Medical diagnosis is necessary to establish the presence of the condition. The severity of the condition may be established in part by medical opinion and in part by systematic observation of the particular student.

Establishing Appropriate Classification

A word of caution is necessary. Sometimes the condition implied by the referral is *not* the handicapping condition. Those who are responsible for classification of pupils must adopt a point of view that is, in part, disconfirmatory—a point of view that looks to disprove the working hypothesis. Assessors must collect information that would allow them to reject the classification if a pupil proves not to be handicapped or to suffer from a different handicap. For example, if Harvey were referred for possible classification as a mentally retarded student, we would try to select tests of intelligence and adaptive behavior on which he would do well, in order to disconfirm the working hypothesis. As another example, if Tom were referred for inconsistent performance in expressive language even though his other skills—especially math and science—were average, we might infer that he could have a learning disability. What would it take to reject the hypothesis that he is learning disabled? If we could show that his problem was caused by a sensorineural hearing loss, he would not be learning disabled; if his problem arose because his primary language is a dialect of English, he would not be learning disabled; if he suffered from recurrent bouts of otitis media (middle-ear infections), he would not be learning disabled. Therefore, we should generate other possible causes of his behavior and collect data that would allow us to evaluate these other explanations.

Finally, in our attempt to establish that a student should be classified as handicapped, we often must choose among competing procedures and tests. There are different tests to *operationalize* the eligibility requirements. For example, to be mentally retarded in Pennsylvania, a pupil must earn a score of less than 80 on an individually administered test of intelligence. However, as we showed in Chapter 10, individual tests of intelligence are not interchangeable. They differ significantly in the behaviors they sample, significantly in the adequacy of their norms and reliability, and slightly in their standard deviations. A dull, but normal, person may earn an IQ of less than 80 on one or two tests of intelligence but earn scores greater than 80 on others. Thus, we can be caught in a terrible dilemma of conflicting information. The routes around and through the dilemma are easier to state than to accomplish. First, we should choose (and put the most faith in) objective, technically adequate (reliable and well-normed) procedures that have demonstrated validity for the particular purpose of classification. Second, we must consider the *specific* validity. For example, we must consider the culture in which the student grew up and how that culture interacts with the content of the test. Sometimes a test's technical manuals contain information about the wisdom of using the test with individuals of various cultures; sometimes the research literature has information for the particular cultural group to which a student belongs. Often theory can guide us in the absence of research. Sometimes it is just not possible to test validly, and we must also recognize that fact. Finally, when we find ourselves in a swamp of conflicting data, we must remember *why* we gathered the data. In this example, we gathered the data to learn if a student met the eligibility requirement of an IQ equal to or less than 80. (We did not give an intelligence test to see if the student needed help; we already knew that.)

Using Curriculum-Based Measurement to Make Eligibility Decisions

In practice, most classification, eligibility, and/or placement decisions are made using norm-referenced measures. Student performance is evaluated in reference to a normative standardization sample. Eligibility for services is determined by professionals who judge the behavior or performance of the student to be sufficiently abnormal relative to that of age or grade peers. Students are declared eligible for services for mentally retarded students when they perform at a low level relative to their agemates on measures of intelligence. They may be declared eligible for special education services when their vision, speech, or hearing is judged abnormal, or when they are said to evidence emotional disturbance.

There is one exception to this practice in the traditional model. Students who are declared learning-disabled do not necessarily have to perform poorly relative to their peers. Rather, in some states eligibility decisions are made using a discrepancy model. Students are shown to demonstrate a severe discrepancy between their ability and their achievement.

Eligibility decisions also can be made using curriculum-based measurement (CBM) procedures. Within a curriculum-based model, the focus is on demonstrating discrepancies between mainstream expectations and the performance of the individual pupil or a discrepancy between the achievement of typical peers and the performance of the typical pupil. Those who assess make normative peer comparisons, they make judgments about eligibility by examining pupil performance relative to others of the same age or grade, with little or no consideration of abilities, traits, or characteristics.

Deno (1985) describes how curriculum-based measures can be used in making eligibility decisions; he calls the process "peer referencing." In addition to repeatedly gathering direct data on the pupil's performance, the examiner gathers data on the performance of the pupil's classmates. An examiner might, for example, frequently and repeatedly assess the number of words per minute that the student reads aloud from the basal text used in the student's classroom. In order to have a basis for comparison, the examiner would also ask all students in the regular class to read aloud passages from the same basal text and would record the number of words each read correctly per minute. Figure 26.1 is an illustration of how such information might be recorded graphically. The graph shows the growth in reading performance over a fourteen-week time interval of a sixth-grade student named Rodney. Also illustrated on the graph is the average performance of Rodney's peers. The average peer read about 120 words per minute. Over time, Rodney's performance improved from about 30 words read correctly per minute to about 90 words read correctly per minute. Note that this comparison is expressed at the top of the graph as a normative peer comparison. Rodney's performance improved from reading 2.80 times slower than his peers to reading 2.49 times slower than his peers.

Germann and Tindal (1985) describe the use of curriculum-based measurement in making decisions about program continuance and continued placement in special education. They look at the discrepancy between a student's performance and the average performance of his or her peers. By monitoring pupil performance over time, they are able to use the kinds of procedures Deno (1985) recommends to examine the extent to which there are reductions in redundancies.

Marston and Magnusson (1985) similarly describe the use of direct and frequent measurement of pupil progress in both regular and special education settings. They also discuss ways in which curriculum-based measurement data can be used to make eligibility decisions. In order to use these procedures, the examiner must determine that level of discrepancy from peer performance that will qualify a student for special education. There are many opinions on this issue. Whereas some say a student should be performing at half the level of his or her peers, others believe only a 20 percent discrepancy is necessary. Marston and Magnusson describe a process by which placement team personnel "sample back" in the curriculum to determine how many years behind a student is. This process involves having students read words at increasingly easier grade levels, for example, and looking at the level of a pupil's performance. Marston and Magnusson recommend that students receive special education services when they are shown to be two years behind their peers.

Those who use curriculum-based eligibility declaration methods typically establish local norms for comparison. They examine the local curriculum to develop a list of the skills the students are to accomplish in the regular curriculum at given grade levels. Then they build measures consisting of samples of

FIGURE 26.1 Rodney's Performance in Reading Aloud from a Basal Reader

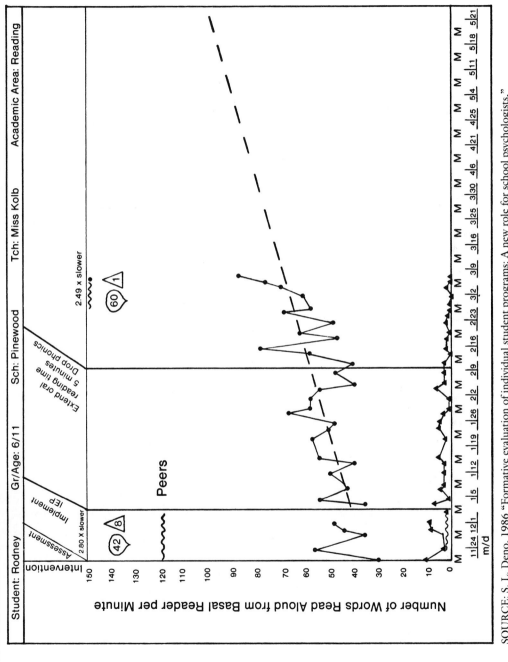

SOURCE: S. L. Deno, 1986 "Formative evaluation of individual student programs: A new role for school psychologists," *School Psychology Review, 15,* 358–374

skills from the larger domain. The measures are given to students in the local school system, and local norms are established. Shinn (1989) described two ways in which school personnel use CBM data to make screening and eligibility decisions. The first approach, called the *single-step approach,* is one in which CBM measures are given to referred students and eligibility decisions are made based on discrepancy from the typical performance of peers. The approach parallels the norm-referenced approach; the measures differ. The second method is one Shinn calls a "multiple-step identification model." Students must be shown to be discrepant from their agemates, they must perform outside the range of skills of their regular education peers, and they must perform outside the range of skills that could realistically be addressed in the mainstream classroom. Students are assessed on materials appropriate for their grade, and for each grade below them. The examiner computes percentile scores for each grade level, and examines that point in the curriculum at which the student is performing at an average level. If the level of average performance is two grades below current placement, the student is judged eligible for special education services.

Shinn (1989) identified a number of advantages to using curriculum-based measurement methods in making eligibility decisions. The decisions can be made in reference to what educators know best, namely, their own curriculum. The content of assessment is directly relevant to the content of instruction. Second, decisions about allocation of services are made in a less costly manner. Shinn similarly raises a number of cautions about CBM practices, specifically warning that they should not simply become "quick and dirty" ways of finding students eligible for services. The measures are best used within an ongoing instructional and measurement system.

CASE STUDY EXAMPLES

The remainder of this chapter provides four examples of classification. Here we will follow Phoebe, Bill, Luis, and Marty, who were discussed in the preceding chapter on referral. Please bear in mind that these cases are intended to illustrate the *process* of assessment for classification. The cases are very simple; in the schools, many will be far more complex.

Phoebe

Background

As you will recall, Phoebe's referral indicated that this thirteen-year-old was having problems in beginning algebra and science. She lived in a small midwestern college town. Ninety-two percent of the high school graduates not only attended college, they graduated; over the past ten years, 67 percent earned advanced degrees. The mean IQ (Otis-Lennon) of the students in her high school was 119. It was apparent that her academic problems were beginning to cause behavioral problems (truancy) and to cause her to rethink her future education plans.

From the referral data, Phoebe did not appear to have general academic problems, although the presence of behavior problems might have had implications. The initial impression was that a specific learning disability in math might be producing problems in science and conflict at home. On the other hand, if Phoebe were to be considered handicapped, her problems might be caused by a beginning emotional disturbance that was first manifesting itself in math and science.

An assessment plan was developed to verify the presence of a specific problem in math attainment and not in other academic areas. It was also decided to administer a measure of intellectual development to verify normal intelligence. These two tests would allow the disconfirmation of the label "learning-disabled." It was further decided to administer a diagnostic math test and to have the school psychologist interview Phoebe about her feelings toward school and her changed behavior. Three tests were selected. Since there were no indications of sensory or physical impairment and since there seemed nothing atypical in Phoebe's acculturation, the Wechsler Intelligence Scale for Children–Revised (WISC-R), Wide Range Achievement Test–Revised (WRAT-R), and the Test of Mathematical Abilities (TOMA) were administered. The test results are presented in Table 26.1.

Results

The test results indicated that Phoebe was of normal intelligence (FSIQ = 104). The ten-point difference between performance IQ and verbal IQ was neither reliable nor unusual. Her scores on the WRAT-R indicated above-average performances in reading and spelling and average performance in arithmetic computation. The TOMA results indicated a very poor attitude toward math, but average attainment of skills and concepts. Observations during testing indicated a slow and very careful approach to the test items. Moreover, she seemed anxious and unsure: she frequently asked if an answer was correct, said that she was dumb in math, said she hated math, and generally checked her work two or three times.

Decisions

In order to be classified as learning-disabled, Phoebe would have to demonstrate a significant discrepancy between achievement and ability not attribut-

TABLE 26.1   Summary of Phoebe's Test Performances

WISC-R standard scores ($\overline{X} = 100$, $S = 15$)	
FSIQ	101–107
VIQ	105–112
PIQ	94–104
WRAT-R standard scores ($\overline{X} = 100$, $S = 15$)	
Reading	122–128
Spelling	121–127
Arithmetic	93–100
TOMA (($\overline{X} = 10$, $S = 3$)	
Attitude Toward Math	4– 6
Vocabulary	10–12
Computation	8–10
General Information	10–12
Story Problems	9–11

NOTE: In 50 percent confidence intervals around her estimated true scores.

able to other handicapping conditions or to environmental deprivation. Phoebe's test performance confirmed that her math skills were not as well developed as other skills. However, they were well within the average range. Her intellectual ability appeared average. If anything, she earned higher scores in some areas of achievement than would be expected. There were no indications of severe emotional problems, although Phoebe was obviously stressed. Given the data collected, Phoebe did not meet the eligibility requirements for learning-disabled students. Furthermore, nothing in her records or from current assessment indicated any other handicapping conditions that would make her eligible for special education services. Phoebe was a normal student experiencing difficulties in math and science.

Recommendations

Several options within regular education were available for Phoebe. First, her math skills were adequate, and there did not appear to be any reason for her not to continue studying algebra. However, the pace of the instruction in the middle math track (regular algebra) did appear to be too fast for Phoebe. Therefore, it was recommended that Phoebe transfer to the slower (transitional) algebra track where first-year algebra is taught in two years. Next, the school counselor scheduled several conferences with Phoebe's father and mother in which the counselor tried to help the parents develop more reasonable expectations and better communication skills.

Bill

Background

Bill's referral—described in Chapter 25—indicated that this third grader was still having trouble with beginning reading and was experiencing some adjustment problems. He was now the poorest reader in the lowest reading group. In the referral information, there was no mention of generalized academic or intellectual problems. The behavior problems that were noted were just beginning to develop and were, therefore, considered a secondary problem, probably stemming from the reading problems. The initial impression was that Bill might have a specific learning disability (LD) in reading.

An assessment plan was developed that would provide data that could be used to decide whether Bill was eligible for services for LD students. To rule out sensory problems, the school nurse would use the Snellen Chart and the district hearing specialist would administer a pure-tone audiometric screening test. Since Bill was black and lived in a lower-class neighborhood, a home visit was scheduled to gather information on the family's acculturation prior to selecting standardized tests. (Intelligence and achievement testing would be the minimum testing required to determine eligibility for LD placement.)

Results

The results of the sensory screening tests indicated that Bill's vision and hearing were excellent. His parents were both interviewed at their home in the evening. Both parents worked, were high school graduates, and were native speakers of Standard American English. Nothing in the interview indicated that Bill's home environment could be considered culturally different. Bill's parents also indicated that he had had no recent illnesses and had an unremarkable developmental history. Both parents were very concerned about Bill's lack of reading skill.

After the parental interview and sensory screening, it was decided to test Bill with the achievement portions of the Woodcock-Johnson Psychoeducational Battery, the WISC-R, and the Developmental Test of Visual-Motor Integration (VMI). The results of these tests, in 50 percent confidence intervals, appear in Table 26.2. Bill's full-scale IQ was at the lowest end of the average range and well within the normal range. Subscale and subtest variation were also within the normal range. Bill's scores on the Woodcock-Johnson were quite varied. His math ability and general knowledge were within the low-average range. However, his score on the reading cluster was at the 1st percentile. Because of his poor performance on the reading cluster, the written language cluster was not administered. An analysis of Bill's performance on the subtests of the reading cluster indicated minimal letter recognition and no skill in letter-sound correspondences. Minor errors were noted on the VMI, but his performance was high average.

TABLE 26.2   Summary of Bill's Test Performances

WISC-R standard scores (50% confidence) ($\overline{X} = 100$, $S = 15$)	
FSIQ	89–95
VIQ	89–96
PIQ	91–100
Woodcock-Johnson percentile ranks (68% confidence)	
Reading	1
Mathematics	19–42
Written Expression	not administered
General Knowledge	23–48
VMI	age equivalent = 10-2

Finally, Bill was interviewed by the school psychologist. Of particular interest were Bill's feelings about school and his recent behavior problems. Bill was quite insightful. He said he had just given up. "They put me with the dumb kids. I just don't know how to read." When questioned about fighting and cursing, he said, "When they call me dumb, I punch 'em; they stop calling me dumb then." Bill expressed a willingness to try to learn to read again, and he promised that he would refrain from fighting unless "really provoked."

Decisions

Bill's normal intelligence precluded classification as mentally retarded. His behavior problems were too new and not severe enough to warrant classification as emotionally disturbed. His vision, hearing, and oral language skills all seemed quite normal. There were no signs of cultural deprivation. The only handicap that Bill could have had was a learning disability. He did have average intelligence; his reading skills were very discrepant. His teachers had tried (and had documented their efforts) to teach him to read. Bill met the eligibility requirements for LD.

Recommendations

There were several options available for Bill. The overriding concern was to improve his reading. Since he was already in the lowest reading group and was not making progress, it was decided to institute an intensive (40 minutes per day, five days per week) instructional program in an LD resource room. The rest of the day would be spent in the regular classroom.

TABLE 26.3   Summary of Luis's Test Performances

Stanford-Binet Intelligence Scale–Revised	41 (47)
Goodenough-Harris Drawing Test	62
ABIC ($\overline{X} = 50$; $S = 15$)	
Family	20
Community	18
Peer Relations	23
Nonacademic School Roles	10
Earner/Consumer	15
Self Maintenance	10
Boehm[a]	3rd percentile
Bender[a] (z-score)	−1.5 to −0.7

[a] Scores are given in 50 percent confidence intervals.

Luis

Background

As will be recalled, Luis was referred because of generally delayed perform-ance including preacademic skills, self-help skills (including toileting), and emotional development. Recent physical examinations indicated no physical or sensory impairments that might be causing his problems. Luis's parents are bilingual (Spanish and English); both languages are spoken in the home. The initial impression was that Luis was generally retarded and might be eligible for special services as a mentally retarded student.

An assessment plan was developed to gather data to see if Luis was, indeed, eligible for special education placement. However, his low level of functioning and bilingual background made it difficult to select appropriate standardized tests—especially tests of intelligence. Measuring his adaptive behavior would also require the recognition that his acculturation probably differed from that of most Anglo-Americans.

Results

It was decided to administer the Adaptive Behavior Inventory for Children (ABIC), the Stanford-Binet Intelligence Scale–Revised, the Goodenough-Harris Drawing Test, the Boehm Test of Basic Concepts, and the Bender Visual Motor Gestalt Test. Luis's scores on these tests are reported in Table 26.3 using 50 percent confidence intervals when possible.

The parental interview that formed the basis of the ABIC administration was conducted in both Spanish and English. The interviewer and mother flowed back and forth between the two languages. Luis earned scores that were significantly subaverage on all subtests. The directions for the Goodenough-Harris Drawing Test were given in English, then in Spanish. Luis's drawing of a man was 2.5 standard deviations below the mean. The Stanford-Binet was given in accordance with the standardized procedures and scored. Luis's responses were scored regardless of the language in which they were given; he earned an IQ of 41. The items that Luis missed between his basal and the last item in the ceiling were readministered in Spanish and re-scored. Luis earned an IQ of 47. Luis's performance on the Bender was also poor and was interpreted as exhibiting systematic immaturity. The Boehm produced similar results when given in Spanish and in English; Luis scored at the 3rd percentile.

Finally, the psychologist observed Luis in kindergarten and also engaged in diagnostic teaching. The kindergarten enrolled other bilingual Hispanic children. Luis did not engage in activities despite prompting by the teacher and the urging of other children. His spontaneous language consisted of one- and two-word utterances. He soiled himself just before lunch. Attempts to teach him three concepts from the Boehm were time-consuming; 17 five-minute sessions were necessary.

Decisions

Although Luis differed systematically in acculturation from the children in the norm group, English and Spanish administration of the tests of intelligence provided essentially the same results. Luis's intelligence test scores were clearly within the range of moderate mental retardation. Moreover, his adaptive behavior was significantly below what one would expect of a boy his age. Nothing in the systematic observations and parental interview contradicted these findings. Thus Luis met the two key criteria for classification as a mentally retarded student: significantly subaverage intellectual functioning and failure in adaptive behavior. Other measures (Boehm and Bender) implied the same conclusions: Luis was functioning at the very bottom of his age group. There was no evidence of severe emotional disturbance or physical/sensory problems that might account for his generalized development delays. Luis met the eligibility requirements for special education for the mentally retarded.

Recommendations

There were few options available for Luis. He lacked the self-help and pre-academic skills necessary for enrollment in a program for educable mentally retarded (EMR) students. His level of functioning indicated placement in a program for trainable mentally retarded students with provisions to monitor his progress. It was thought that he might later prove capable of work in the EMR curriculum.

Marty

Background

The classification of Marty as visually handicapped was straightforward. As will be recalled, Mrs. Webster brought an ophthalmological report indicating that Marty met the state's standards for special education for the visually impaired. Even a brief observation of Marty in the kindergarten class would validate the impression that Marty did, indeed, have a severe visual impairment.

Since the school was not equipped to provide special services if Marty was also handicapped in other ways, a thorough assessment was desired to rule out the possibility of multiple handicaps. First, as a precaution, Marty would be screened audiometrically to make sure his hearing was within the normal range. Marty's limited vision should not present a problem in assessing his hearing, so no special steps would be taken. Next, he would be tested to learn if he was developing cognitively at a normal rate, a rate that would allow the school to provide services on an itinerant basis. Clearly, Marty's vision was so poor that the use of many tests was ruled out. Any test requiring Marty to look at stimulus materials or write (or draw) a response would be inappropriate. However, several options were available since, except for his limited vision, he presented no special problems (such as inability to hear testing instructions or different acculturation). It was decided to administer the verbal scale of the Wechsler Intelligence Scale for Children–Revised. Finally, the school psychologist would observe Marty in kindergarten and interview him to form an impression of his freedom from emotional problems.

Results

Marty's hearing was well within the normal range in the speech frequencies. His obtained IQ was 115; a 50 percent confidence interval around his estimated true score was from 111 to 118. Clearly, his performance is within the normal range of intelligence. The interview by the school psychologist indicated no serious emotional problems, although there was a tendency for Marty to express more than usual feelings of dependency on his parents.

Decisions

From that data in the ophthalmological report and direct observation, it was clear that Marty was blind and therefore eligible for services for visually handicapped students. Furthermore, Marty did not appear handicapped in other ways and he did attempt to use his residual vision.

Recommendation

It was decided to provide itinerant services to Marty directly and to provide consultative services to his teacher, Ms. Hampton. Initially Marty would need to be provided with mobility training and instruction in the functional use of his residual vision. Because Marty did use his residual vision, it was also recommended that, at least at the start of instruction, the teacher would make use of Marty's visual as well as auditory abilities. Special, large-print materials were not likely to be needed initially since the kindergarten materials were in large print already.

SUMMARY

Assessment data are collected for the purpose of making classification decisions. Classification is an administrative act. Federal and most state special education laws contain provisions specifying that students must be classified before they can be declared eligible for services. Criteria for establishing the existence of handicapping conditions are specified in rules or guidelines and tests are used to ascertain the extent to which the criteria are met. Four cases (introduced in Chapter 25) show how assessment data are used in classifying students.

STUDY QUESTIONS

1. Why is it necessary for government to set standards for providing services to certain types of handicapped students?
2. List and explain three benefits of classification of handicapped students.
3. How would you go about selecting an assessment battery to see if a boy (age 8) should be eligible for special education classes?

ADDITIONAL READING

Cromwell, R. L., Blashfield, R. K., & Strauss, J. S. (1975). Criteria for classification systems. In N. Hobbs (Ed.), *Issues in the classification of children* (Vol. 1). San Francisco: Jossey-Bass.

Reschly, D. J. (1987). Learning characteristics of mildly handicapped students: Implications for classification, placement, and programming. In M. C. Wang, M. C. Reynolds, & H. J. Walberg (Eds.), *The handbook of special education: Research and practice.* Oxford, England: Pergamon Press.

Reynolds, M. C., & Lakin, K. C. (1987). Noncategorical special education: Models for research and practice. In M. C. Wang, M. C. Reynolds, & H. J. Walberg (Eds.), *The handbook of special education: Research and practice.* Oxford, England: Pergamon Press.

Shinn, M. R. (Ed.). (1989). *Curriculum-based measurement: Assessing special children.* New York: Guilford.

Ysseldyke, J. E. (1987). Classification. In M. C. Wang, M. C. Reynolds, & H. J. Walberg (Eds.), *The handbook of special education: Research and practice.* Oxford, England: Pergamon Press.

Ysseldyke, J. E., Algozzine, B., & Epps, S. (1983). A logical and empirical analysis of current practice in classifying students as handicapped. *Exceptional Children, 50,* 160–166.

C·H·A·P·T·E·R 27

MAKING INSTRUCTIONAL PLANNING DECISIONS

A major purpose of assessment is to provide for instructional planning. Unless differential treatment can be based on assessment data, assessment in the schools serves only two major purposes: research and evaluation of instruction. Pupils are treated differentially when individualized education programs are provided for them. Most people would agree that it is desirable to individualize programs for students in special and remedial education since the regular education programs have not proved beneficial to them. Assessment data can be important for such planning. Numerous books and hundreds of articles in professional and scientific journals discuss the importance of using assessment data to plan instructional programs for students. Public Law 94-142 requires a thorough assessment that results in an individualized education plan (IEP). However, beyond the general agreement about using information gained from assessment to plan education programs, there are sharp divisions within the education community about the way to assess. School personnel must make two different kinds of decisions in instructional planning. They must decide *what* to teach, and they must decide *how* to teach.

DECIDING WHAT TO TEACH

Decisions about what to teach include three major areas: selection of goals, selection of algorithms, and selection of objectives. Perhaps the most fundamental distinction between special and regular education is that we hold different goals for students completing the programs. We do not expect all handicapped students to achieve the same goals as nonhandicapped students: we do not expect deaf individuals to pass courses in music appreciation; we do not expect educable mentally retarded students to master calculus; we do not expect trainable mentally retarded students to pass American history; we do not expect quadraplegics to pass a swimming test. When we do hold the same goals for handicapped and nonhandicapped students, we may not expect handicapped students to achieve the goals at the same level of proficiency. Thus, we might require both normal and educable mentally retarded adolescents to take three years of high school mathematics in order to graduate. However, what is actually taught in the special education mathematics courses and in the lowest track of the regular mathematics courses may not be comparable. In social studies, we might require mentally retarded students to learn where and how to get help with paying their taxes, whereas nonhandicapped students might be asked to write an essay explaining how a constitutional amendment was necessary before an individual income tax could be levied by the federal government.

Next, we often use different algorithms (the way we teach or the way we try to achieve an instructional goal) to teach the same goal. The most obvious examples come from the education of sensorily handicapped students where a sensory loss precludes certain types of instruction. However, we often change algorithms for nonsensorily handicapped pupils. For example, we may wish educable mentally retarded and learning disabled students to compute long-division problems correctly. However, we might not use the typical "goes into" paradigm. We may instruct them in the correct use of a pocket calculator rather than the usual algorithm of long division. We might even use a cumulative subtraction algorithm. Thus, although the goal might be the same, the means by which we achieve the goal may differ considerably.

Finally, specific objectives may vary, although the goals and algorithms do not differ. For example, in teaching learning disabled adolescents who have problems with written language, we might have objectives that require the students to "tell" rather than to "write." We might also lower the level of mastery of the objective. For example, we may require students in a regular U.S. history class to *analyze* the causes of the Civil War, whereas students in special education may be required to explain "in their own words" how slavery was a cause of the war—a comprehension level of mastery.

Tests can be somewhat useful in helping parents and teachers agree on appropriate goals for handicapped students. When students are very far behind their peers, parents and teachers have two fundamental choices. The first choice might be to accelerate instruction in the retarded area—give more instruction—and pay less attention to a less important area. The second choice is to reduce substantially the importance of the goal in the area in which the pupil lags (in some cases, the area can actually be eliminated). In areas where instruction will continue, tests can be used to place pupils within the sequence of instruction. Curriculum-based measures are especially useful in helping us make decisions about what to teach. These tests assess the student's ongoing performance with respect to the curriculum the student is being taught. As such, they provide the assessor with a detailed analysis of the skills the student has and has not mastered. By learning what objectives the student has already mastered and knowing what objectives have yet to be mastered, teachers or caregivers can select the *next* objective in the sequence of objectives.

Thus, tests are useful for making decisions about what to teach in two ways: first, in specifying goal areas in which instruction should take place; second, in specifying appropriate short-term objectives to teach.

Deciding How to Teach

Several tests have been developed that are intended to tell teachers how to teach—for example, the Developmental Test of Visual Perception (Frostig, Maslow, Lefever, & Whittlesey, 1964), the Illinois Test of Psycholinguistic Abilities (Kirk, McCarthy, & Kirk, 1968), the Kaufman Assessment Battery for Children (Kaufman & Kaufman, 1983), and the Purdue Perceptual-Motor Survey (Roach & Kephart, 1966). These tests, while they are based on very different theories and have varying degrees of technical adequacy, have provided more publications and sales for their authors than innovations in effective teaching strategies for students in special and remedial education.

At present, the best way to teach handicapped learners is to rely on generally effective procedures. During acquisition, teachers can do several things to make it easier for their pupils to learn the material, skill, or behavior. They can model the desired behavior. They can break the terminal goal down into its component parts and teach each of the steps and their integration. They can teach the objective in a variety of contexts with a variety of materials to facilitate generalization. They can provide varying amounts of practice, and they can choose the schedule on which practice is done (in other words, distributed versus massed practice). Several techniques that are under the direct control of the teacher can be employed to teach any learner effectively. To help pupils recall information that has been taught, teachers have several strategies available. Organizing the material that a pupil is to learn is an effective strategy to facilitate recall. Providing rehearsal strategies is another effective way to help learners recall material. Overlearning facilitates recall of information that has been learned. Distributed practice also facilitates recall. There are also a number of things teachers can do to elicit responses that have already been acquired. Various reinforcers and punishers have been shown to be effective in the control of behavior.

Assessment personnel can help teachers identify specific areas in which instructional difficulties exist, and they can help teachers plan interventions in light of information gained from assessments. Recently developed procedures (Ysseldyke & Christenson, 1987) can aid assessment personnel in determining the nature of students' instructional environments. Procedures such as the Instructional Environment Scale (Ysseldyke & Christenson, 1987) may be used to pinpoint the extent to which a student's academic or behavioral problems are a function of factors in the instructional environment and to identify starting points for designing appropriate interventions for individual students. Yet there is just no way to decide ahead of time how best to teach a specific student. At present, we recommend that teachers first rely on general principles that are known and demonstrated to be effective in facilitating learning for handicapped students. However, we can seldom find validated translations of these principles into actual classroom activities and procedures. Moreover, even if we did find studies that demonstrated that a particular application of a learning principle "worked" for a research sample, we still could not be sure that it would work for the students in a specific classroom. The odds are that it will, but we cannot be sure. Consequently, we must treat our translation of these principles, known to be effective, as tentative. In a real sense, we *hypothesize* that our treatment will work, but we need to verify that it has worked. Deno and Mirkin (1977) make this point cogently:

> *At the present time we are unable to prescribe specific and effective changes in instruction for individual pupils with certainty. Therefore, changes in instructional programs which are arranged for an individual child can be treated only as hypotheses which must be empirically tested before a decision can be made whether they are effective for that child. (p. 11)*

Teaching is experimental in nature. Generally, there is no data base to guide our selection of specific tasks or materials. Decisions are made about particular strategies, methods, and materials to use in instruction, but these decisions must be tentative. The decision maker makes some good guesses about what will work and then implements an instructional program. We do not know the extent to which decisions are correct until we gather data on the extent to which the instructional programs actually work. We only know the program works *after* it has worked; we never know it will work until it has worked.

Tests do provide some very limited information about how to teach. Tests of intelligence, for example, yield information that gives a teacher some hints about teaching. Generally, the lower a pupil's intelligence, the more practice the student will require for mastery. A score of 55 on the WISC-R does not tell the teacher that a pupil needs 25 percent or 250 percent more practice. It does alert the teacher to the likelihood that the pupil will need more practice than the average child will. Other tenuous hints can be derived, but we feel that it is better to rely on direct observation of how a student learns in order to make adjustments in the learning program. Thus, we would observe Sally's recall of information to see if we had provided enough practice rather than looking at Sally's IQ to see that she would need a lot of practice. We cannot do anything about Sally's IQ, but we can do something about the amount of practice she gets.

FEASIBILITY CONSIDERATIONS

A major factor determining whether or not an intervention will be tried or implemented by teachers is feasibility. This is essentially a "hassle" dimension in intervention planning. Those who conduct assessments and make recommendations about teaching must consider the extent to which the interventions they recommend are feasible. Phillips (1990) identified eight major considerations in making decisions about feasibility. Using the dimensions she identified, we list below a number of specific questions assessors ought to ask.

Degree of Disruption   How much will the intervention I recommend disrupt school procedures or teacher routines?

Side Effects   To what extent are there undesirable side effects on the student (leading to social ostracism), peers, home and family, and faculty?

Support Services Required   To what extent are the support services required available and reasonable in terms of cost?

Prerequisite Competencies   To what extent does the teacher have the necessary knowledge and experiences to be able to pull off the intervention, and to what extent is the teacher motivated to implement the intervention? When teachers have a philosophic bias against the recommended intervention, they will not implement it.

Control   Does the teacher have control of the necessary variables to ensure the success of the intervention?

Immediacy of Results   Will student behavior change be quick enough that the teacher is reinforced for implementing the intervention?

Consequence of Nonintervention   What are the short- and long-term prognoses for the student if the behaviors are left uncorrected?

Potential for Transition   Is it reasonable to expect that the intervention will lead to student self-regulation and generalize to other settings, curriculum areas, or even to other students who are experiencing similar difficulty?

USE OF STAFF SUPPORT TEAMS

School districts increasingly are putting into place staff support teams called by a variety of different names. Most often they are called *teacher assistance teams* (Chalfant, Pysh, & Moultrie, 1979), though they may also be known as "mainstream assistance teams," "building-based teams," "intervention assistance teams," or "school-wide assistance teams." Stokes (1982) defines a staff support team as

> *A school-based problem-solving group whose purpose is to provide a vehicle for discussion of issues related to specific needs of teachers or students and to offer consultation and follow-up assistance to staff. The team can respond to staff needs in a variety of ways. It can provide immediate crisis intervention, short-term consultation, continuous support, or the securing of information, resources, or training for those who request its services. By providing problem-specific support and assistance to individuals and groups, the team can help teachers and other professionals to become more skillful, gain confidence, and feel more efficacious in their work with students. (p. 3)*

Staff support teams are different from child study teams. The focus of the team is on intervention planning, usually prior to referral and assessment, rather than on placement. Assessment data are gathered by staff support teams for purposes of planning or monitoring the effectiveness of interventions. Assessment data are used by child study teams for purposes of making placement and instructional planning decisions. Child study teams are typically multidisciplinary; staff support teams are typically comprised of regular class teachers. Yet in some settings staff support teams include representatives from multiple disciplines: psychologists, special education teachers, and so forth. Staff support teams increasingly are being used to try to avert placement of students in pullout programs, and to maintain their attendance in regular education.

CASE STUDY EXAMPLES

In previous chapters we have described the process of making referral and classification decisions about individual students. We now illustrate how instructional decisions might be made for four of the students.

Phoebe

Phoebe was a 13-year-old student referred because she was experiencing difficulties in mathematics. No interventions were tried prior to referral because of Phoebe's poor attendance and the general rather than specific nature of her problems. Several tests were administered in an effort to make a classification decision: the WISC-R, the WRAT-R and the TOMA. Phoebe was of normal intelligence and was functioning at an average level in mathematics. It was recommended that she be enrolled in the slower (transitional) algebra track.

No tests were administered in an effort to plan instruction. Rather, specific goals of the algebra curriculum were identified, and a system was set up by which Phoebe's teacher recorded the number of assignments she completed and the percentage of math problems she solved correctly on each assignment.

The counselor met with Phoebe to develop a contingency contract using the procedures of Homme (1969) in order to cut down on truancy. Phoebe earned points by attending all her classes in any school day. These points, in turn, could be exchanged for privileges. The privileges, therefore, were contingent on attending classes. Plans called for the contract to be rewritten over time so that criteria for class attendance increased.

Bill

Bill was referred because he was having difficulty in reading and was beginning to experience behavior problems. Several interventions were tried with Bill before referring him formally for evaluation. A tutor had tried several alternative approaches to reading instruction and had found that a word-picture association approach worked best. A two-week intervention using computer-assisted instruction to teach word-picture association proved fruitless.

Bill was classified as learning-disabled, and it was recommended that he receive intensive intervention (40 minutes per day, five days per week) in reading in a resource room setting. In an effort to plan an instructional program for Bill and to decide specifically what ought to be taught, the resource teacher used a criterion-referenced measure of skill development in reading. She used Diagnosis: An Instructional Aid in Reading (Shub, Carlin, Friedman, Kaplan & Katien, 1973) to pinpoint his skill development level.

Bill performed poorly on the survey measure of Diagnosis and all probes were administered. Bill demonstrated knowledge of letter names and letter sounds as long as the letters were at the beginning of words. He had considerable difficulty recognizing the sounds of consonants in the middle of words. Based on this knowledge, the resource teacher developed three short-term instructional objectives. For each objective the teacher used the Prescription Guide that accompanies the test to decide what instructional materials to use with Bill. Although the Lippincott Reading Series was used in Bill's school, the teacher decided to use a different series with Bill. The Lippincott series is a linguistic-phonics series, and data from the tutor who had intervened prior to referral indicated that Bill performed better when a "look-say" approach was used. The teacher decided to use the Scott, Foresman Open Highways Program. The following objectives and materials were specified:

1. "When Bill has worked through the materials prescribed, he will recognize the sound of the letter p in the middle of a word." To teach this the

teacher decided to use pages 60–62 of Teachers' Manual 3-2, page 11 of workbook 3-2, and page 7 of workbook 4. She used duplicating master 4 from set 4 to provide practice in recognition of the letter *p* in medial position.

2. "When Bill has worked through the materials prescribed, he will recognize the sound of the letter *m* in the middle of a word." To teach this the teacher decided to use pages 60–62 of Teachers' Manual 3-2, page 11 of workbook 3-2, and duplicating masters 12 from set 3-2 and 5 from set 4.

3. "When Bill has worked through the materials, he will recognize the sound of the letter *d* in the middle of a word." To teach this skill the teacher decided to use pages 60–62 of Teachers' Manual 3-2, page 6 of workbook 4, and duplicating master 5 from set 4.

You may ask how the teacher decided to use the specific materials identified in the objectives. The Prescription Guide in Diagnosis lists, for each skill assessed, the place in specific reading series where the skill is taught. The decision to use the Scott, Foresman series was based on knowledge about how Bill learns, which was obtained through actually teaching him (the prereferral intervention by the tutor). Only by monitoring Bill's progress and frequently testing the extent to which he accomplishes objectives will the teacher know whether the instructional choices she has made are appropriate.

Luis

Luis was referred because of generally delayed performance including preacademic skills, self-help skills, and emotional development. Assessment indicated that Luis was functioning as a trainable mentally retarded child. Special education was recommended to the parents, who agreed with the recommendation.

Initially, placement in a self-contained district classroom for trainable mentally retarded pupils was selected as the most appropriate (and least restrictive) environment for the boy. Luis's parents agreed to a program stressing language development, self-help skills, and play skills. However, they did not want the schools to work on toileting with Luis; they believed that was the responsibility of the parents. They were, however, willing to follow several suggestions offered by the school district. (The district recommended, essentially, that the parents follow the techniques of Foxx and Azrin.) Luis's parents also wanted to enroll in an evening program in behavior modification run by the school district for parents of handicapped students.

The school would stress social-emotional development (appropriate play and participation in small groups) and eating skills (Luis still could not use a fork or spoon). The school would also stress language. However, there was some concern about the language that Luis would learn. If Luis was expected to lead a semidependent life, he would not need the skills in English that he would need if he was expected to lead an independent life. The school district, however, was hesitant to agree to bilingual instruction in a class for trainable mentally retarded students. A compromise was struck whereby a bilingual teacher's aide would be employed in Luis's class. The aide would be responsible for repeating the language-enrichment exercises with Luis in Spanish.

As an aid in instructional planning, the AAMD Adaptive Behavior Scale was administered to Luis's mother. His mother checked the following behaviors:

1. "Feeds self with fingers, or must be fed"
2. "Does not drink from a glass or cup unassisted"
3. "Chews food with mouth open"
4. "Uses napkin incorrectly"

Also as an aid in instructional planning, Luis's behavior during free time (recess, unstructured playtime, and so on) was observed to ascertain the level of interaction with other children. Roberto, another Hispanic retarded child, was observed for comparison purposes. Over a three-day time span with fifteen observation periods, Luis did not initiate conversation or activities with other children; Roberto initiated seven brief interchanges and played next to other children during eleven intervals, but he did not play cooperatively with the other children in the class.

Based on these observations and test data (including the data obtained during classification), the following long-term objectives were established:

1. Luis will feed himself with a spoon at lunch with not more than one spill per minute of eating time.
2. Luis will initiate play activities with classmates.
3. Luis will initiate brief conversation with classmates.
4. Luis will increase his oral-language skills in both English and Spanish.

His teacher used a backward chaining paradigm to teach eating with a spoon. Initial observation indicated that Luis liked food (it was a natural reinforcer for him) and that he could (and would) hold a spoon. The teacher used a shaping program with a changing-criterion design to increase play and conversation with classmates. In addition, the teacher and the aide used the Peabody Language Development Kit with Luis.

Marty

Marty was referred for psychoeducational evaluation at the time of initial school entrance because he was legally blind. Despite his classification, primary placement in a regular class setting was recommended. Marty and his teacher were to receive the help of an itinerant teacher who specialized in working with blind and partially sighted students. Initially, Marty would be provided with mobility training and receive instruction in functional use of his residual vision.

Marty was assigned preferential seating for all classroom activities. Usually, he was seated in the first row center seat for routine activities but was allowed (and encouraged) to move closer for demonstrations. Because Marty could use residual vision, special care was taken in encouraging him to use his vision in learning. The teacher was instructed to speak as she wrote material on the board. Marty was always given the first copy of dittoed worksheets and was taught to put dittoes and other worksheets in yellow acetate folders to increase contrast and reduce glare.

Several other suggestions were made to the regular classroom teacher. She was reminded that activities requiring near vision and far vision should be alternated to reduce visual fatigue. She was reminded to take special precautions to reduce glare from the windows in the classroom. It was suggested that she reduce requirements for written drill for Marty because it would take him considerably longer than his classmates to complete such assignments.

Marty received the services of an itinerant vision specialist who worked with him on mobility training. The specialist designed a set of procedures to evaluate the extent to which a cane was necessary for mobility.

Since Marty was just beginning school, it was decided that, initially at least, all educational objectives appropriate for nonhandicapped students would be considered appropriate for Marty. Compensatory teaching methodologies would be used to help him accomplish these objectives. Objectives for Marty included development of prereading skills, alphabet learning, numerative learning, and learning social skills.

Summary

Assessment data are collected and used for the purpose of planning instructional programs. When teachers plan instructional programs, they must decide what to teach and how to teach. Tests are sometimes helpful in deciding what to teach. Experimentation with different methods is generally the best way to determine how to teach—the teacher selects and uses an approach that seems most suited to the student's needs and then gathers data on the effectiveness of the strategy. Adjustments are made or other approaches are tried until the teacher determines which strategy is most effective. We have followed cases introduced in earlier chapters to show how assessment data are used to make initial instructional decisions.

ADDITIONAL READING

Arter, J., & Jenkins, J. (1979). Differential diagnosis—prescriptive teaching: A critical appraisal. *Review of Educational Research, 49,* 517–559.

Christenson, S. L., & Ysseldyke, J. E. (1989). Assessing student performance . . . An important change is needed. *Journal of School Psychology, 27,* 409–429.

Deno, S. L., Marston, D., & Tindal, G. (1986). Direct and frequent curriculum-based measurement: An alternative for educational decision making. *Special Services in the Schools, 2,* 5–28.

Fuchs, L. S., & Fuchs, D. (1986). Linking assessment to instructional interventions: An overview. *School Psychology Review, 15,* 318–323.

Rosenfield, S. (1987). *Instructional consultation.* Hillsdale, NJ: Lawrence Erlbaum.

Stokes, S., (1982). School-based staff support teams: A blueprint for action. Reston, VA: Council for Exceptional Children.

Ysseldyke, J. E. (1986). The use of assessment information to make decisions about students. In R. J. Morris & B. Blatt (Eds.), *Perspectives in special education: The state of the art.* New York: Pergamon Press.

Ysseldyke, J. E., & Christenson, S. (1988). Linking assessment to intervention. In J. L. Graden, J. E. Zins, & M. J. Curtis (Eds.), *Alternative educational delivery systems: Enhancing instructional options for all students.* Washington, DC: National Association of School Psychologists.

Ysseldyke, J. E., & Marston, D. (1990). The use of assessment information to plan instructional interventions: A review of the research. In T. Gutkin & C. Reynolds (Eds.), *The handbook of school psychology.* New York: Wiley.

EPILOGUE

There are several ways of gathering the data we need to support the educational decisions we are called upon to make. Technically adequate norm-referenced devices have certain advantages over other assessment practices when we must make screening or placement decisions. Norm-referenced devices provide objective measurement, a method of comparing the performance of a particular student to the performance of similar students, and require no test-construction time of the user. They provide the teacher or diagnostic specialist with content created and evaluated by experts in an already usable format. When appropriately administered, scored, and interpreted, norm-referenced devices can serve to protect children from haphazard and capricious decision making. Historically, tests were constructed to compensate for the inadequacies of observation and decision making based on subjective feelings about a student. Norm-referenced assessment adds a perspective to the making of placement decisions, a perspective that allows educators to say that a child with an IQ of 90 is normal in a school district where the average IQ is 120—even though that child differs from the other children in the district.

Norm-referenced tests do have a place in educational decision making, provided they are used appropriately for the purposes for which they were designed. Two major difficulties confront both regular and special education: (1) the use of technically adequate devices for purposes other than those for which they were developed, and (2) the use of technically inadequate devices for any purpose. Reynolds (1975) describes the issue well.

> *Although there are legitimate and important uses for norm-referenced tests and institutionally-oriented decisions, it is argued . . . that they have been vastly overemphasized at levels of relatively early education where the orientation most properly should be to individual payoff. (p. 25)*

Criterion-referenced assessment, curriculum-based assessment, observation, and diagnostic teaching are the preferred techniques for determining appropriate educational interventions for individual students or when evaluating the extent to which they have profited from instruction. Criterion-referenced devices may be selected from commercially available systems, or they may be teacher constructed. Teacher-constructed tests are developed by constructing items that assess the extent to which specific instructional objectives have been attained. Gronlund (1976, 1982) has written several texts on teacher-constructed tests. As Hofmeister (1975) states, "Criterion-referenced testing can reach its full potential only when it is so integrated into the day-by-day functioning of the classroom that it cannot easily be separated out as a 'testing activity' " (pp. 77–78).

Curriculum-based tests may be selected from available devices (for example, Deno, 1986), or they may be developed to match specific locally used curricula. They are usually used in direct assessment of academic performance (Howell, 1986) or in functional assessment of the academic environment (Lentz & Shapiro, 1986).

Observation is an essential element of all classroom practices and, similarly, of all assessment practices. *Observation* is a generic term that can be applied to a range of activities from relatively informal observation of an individual to systematic counting of an individual's behaviors. Entire manuscripts have been written on observation (Boehm & Weinberg, 1977; Cartwright & Cartwright, 1974; Weinberg & Wood, 1975), and these outline the variety of systematic procedures that are used to observe students. Systematic observation is an integral component in the implementation of behavior modification in school settings. Kazdin (1973) has developed in detail the assessment strategies (frequency counting, duration counting, and interval recording) used when behavior-modification techniques are employed in school settings. Observation is both an integral part of other assessment procedures and a separate alternative to them.

Diagnostic teaching is not a new concept; it is a practice in which any effective teacher engages. Simply put, the concept refers to the practice of systematic trial and evaluation of a variety of instructional strategies (including materials, methods of presentation, and methods of feedback) with individual students as part of their everyday educational program. Other assessment procedures can be used and are used within diagnostic teaching. Teaching strategies are modified according to whether specified techniques used in particular educational settings result in success or failure for the student.

Assessment is an integral part of the educational process and is engaged in for many educational purposes. The main question in obtaining assessment information is not, How can we use tests? Rather, the fundamental question is, How can we obtain the information necessary to make certain educational decisions? The recent and significant revisions in public policy relating to the education of handicapped children are reflected in the intent and provisions of Public Law 94-142, the Education for All Handicapped Children Act of 1975. Public Law 94-142 mandates zero exclusion within educational settings, appropriate educational programming for all handicapped children, placement of all children in "least restrictive environments," assurance of extensive identification procedures, and maintenance of individual educational plans for all handicapped children. Assessment data are used in making important decisions to implement the law. Different decisions require different kinds of information. Many of the convictions expressed in this book now have the force of law.

We have presented detailed information about tests in an effort to facilitate their intelligent use. We have attempted to be objective and yet critical in our review of contemporary assessment practices and devices. Used appropriately, tests can and do provide extremely useful information to facilitate decision making; used inappropriately, tests are worthless. As professionals, we must be constantly aware of the fact that our first responsibility is to children and that test-based decisions directly and significantly affect them.

Assessment is a very important activity that often has lifelong consequences for the students who are assessed. Few educational practices have aroused so much controversy as assessment, and few educational activities are so carefully prescribed. Federal and state regulations prescribe what types of tests will be administered to make certain educational decisions. For example, individual tests of intelligence must be administered to determine eligibility for services for the mentally retarded. Regulations sometimes prescribe who will administer the tests. For example, certified school psychologists must administer certain types of tests within the schools. Certification, accreditation, and licensure requirements prescribe standards of training for testers. All of these prescriptions are designed to improve and guarantee high standards of assessment services.

Nonetheless, we are often overwhelmed with descriptions of abuses that occur in testing. There have been so many—in the scientific community, in policy, and in educational practice. In education, the abuses that have occurred are the result of ignorance and overzealousness. The most crucial uses—and consequently the most serious abuses—of tests are those that involve decisions about individual students: referral and screening, classification, program planning, and evaluation of individual pupil progress. Inappropriate testing for these purposes can, at best, result in wasted time and wasted money. At worst, assessment can result in inappropriate classification and labeling and inappropriate educational programming.

Several errors are worth noting. Using the wrong test is more common than we would like to admit. Tests are used in assessment to specify and to verify problems in several domains. This statement sounds so simple, and yet assessment is one of the most complicated of human endeavors. The most difficult tasks facing assessors are the selection and interpretation of appropriate assessment procedures. Testers usually have a choice among several devices that all ostensibly assess the same domain. However, the devices never work in the same way for the individual being assessed. Slight differences in norms and validity can produce variations in scores for a student. As a result, in many cases the selection of a particular test will produce one decision, whereas the selection of a different test would produce the opposite decision. Some tests are so poor that they should not be used for most purposes. Tests that inadequately reflect the domain to be assessed, that have unacceptable levels of reliability, and that are inadequately normed should not be used for making educational decisions. When inadequate tests are all that are available to verify or to specify problems in some domain, assessors will necessarily have to supplement their information with data from other forms of assessment (for example, systematic observation). They will also need to be far more tentative in their conclusions and recommendations since the data upon which they are relying are much less compelling.

Sometimes perfectly acceptable tests are used with children for whom those tests are inappropriate. Slight differences in acculturation and background experience can produce variations among students on scores on a test. If a pupil differs significantly in acculturation and background experience from the students for whom the test was developed and on whom the test was standardized, the test should not be used. Significant differences in age and language also preclude the use of an otherwise acceptable test with particular students.

Finally, test performances are sometimes misinterpreted. A good norm-referenced test, properly administered, scored, and interpreted, can only rank order students. That rank is a very limited piece of information. Even a good norm-referenced test cannot explain why students have performed as they have. A good criterion-referenced test, properly administered, scored, and interpreted can show the teacher only what skills and knowledge a student has acquired. It cannot explain why a student has or has not acquired those skills and concepts. Furthermore, we can only observe behavior on any test. We cannot observe mental retardation or giftedness on an intelligence test; we cannot see a deficit in auditory processing on the ITPA; we cannot see brain damage on a Bender protocol.

It easy to forget that the intentions of the testing establishment (testers and decision makers who use test data) are benevolent. However, we must not lose sight of the fact that good intentions are not enough.

Psychological and educational assessment is serious business. We've treated it that way in this textbook. It is serious business because the decisions professionals make about students have a significant effect on those students' life opportunities. We invite you to join us in the quest to improve the practice of assessing students.

APPENDIXES

Appendix 1 *Comparative Features of Major Cognitive Batteries*

TABLE 1 Content Features of Major Cognitive Batteries

Content Features	Stanford-Binets 1937 to 1972	Wechslers 1939 to 1981	McCarthy 1970
Includes a broad measure of intelligence	Yes IQ	Yes Full-scale IQ	Yes General cognitive
Includes measures of multiple intelligence	No	Yes 1. Verbal scale 2. Performance scale 1975 (Kaufman) 1. Verbal comprehension 2. Perceptual organization 3. Freedom from distractibility	Yes 1. Verbal 2. Perceptual-performance 3. Quantitative 4. Memory (short-term)
Age range of battery	2-0 to 18	WPPSI 4-0 to 6-6 WISC-R 6-0 to 16-6 WAIS-R 16 to 74	Age 2-6 to 8-6
Number of cognitive subtests	Numerous item types	WPPSI = 11 WISC-R = 12 WAIS-R = 11	15 total Age 2-6 to 4 = 14 Age 5 to 8-6 = 15
Allows longitudinal follow-up with the same measures (the same set of tests used for young subjects are also used for older subjects)	No	No	Yes (to age 8-6)
Special nonverbal administration instructions	No	No	No
Includes differential scholastic aptitude measures	No	No	No
Includes a measure of oral language ability	No	No	No
Includes controlled-learning test (with corrective feedback)	No	No	No

Woodcock-Johnson 1977	K-ABC 1983	Stanford-Binet IV 1986	Woodcock-Johnson– Revised 1989
Yes Broad cognitive ability	Yes Mental processing composite	Yes Composite score	Yes Broad cognitive ability
Yes 1. Verbal ability 2. Reasoning 3. Perceptual speed 4. Memory (short-term)	Yes 1. Sequential processing 2. Simultaneous processing	Yes 1. Verbal reasoning 2. Abstract/visual reasoning 3. Quantitative reasoning 4. Short-term memory 1988 (Sattler) 1. Verbal comprehension 2. Nonverbal reasoning/ visualization 3. Memory	Yes 1. Long-term retrieval 2. Short-term memory 3. Processing speed 4. Auditory processing 5. Visual processing 6. Comprehension-knowledge 7. Fluid reasoning 8. Quantitative ability (in WJ-R ACH)
Age 3-0 to 80+	Age 2-6 to 12-6	Age 2-0 to 23	Age 2-0 to 90+
12 total Age 3-0 to 5 = 6 Kdg to Age 80+ = 12	10 total Age 2-6 to 3 = 5 Age 4 = 7 Age 5 = 7 Age 6 to 12 = 8	15 total Age 2-0 to 6 = 8 Age 7 to 11 = 12 Age 12 to 13 = 15 Age 14 = 14 Age 15 to 23 = 13	21 total Age 2-0 to 90+ = 5 Age 4 to 90+ = 21
Yes	No	No	Yes
No	Yes (for 6 of the 10 subtests)	No	No
Yes 1. Reading aptitude 2. Mathematics aptitude 3. Written language aptitude 4. Knowledge aptitude	No	No	Yes 1. Oral language aptitude 2. Reading aptitude 3. Mathematics aptitude 4. Written language aptitude 5. Knowledge aptitude
Yes 1984	No	No	Yes
Yes 1. Visual-auditory learning 2. Analysis-synthesis 3. Concept formation	No	No	Yes 1. Memory for names 2. Analysis-synthesis 3. Visual-auditory learning 4. Concept formation

TABLE 1   Content Features of Major Cognitive Batteries (cont.)

Content Features	Stanford-Binets 1937 to 1972	Wechslers 1939 to 1981	McCarthy 1970
Spanish language version	No	Yes EIWN-R 1982 EIWA 1968 WISC-RM 1984	No
Source of Spanish norms	—	EIWN-R 1982: No norms EIWA 1968: Puerto Rico WISC-RM 1984: Mexico City public schools	—
Use of colorful pictures and materials	No	No	Yes

TABLE 2   Administration Features of Major Cognitive Batteries

Administration Features	Stanford-Binets 1937 to 1972	Wechslers 1939 to 1981	McCarthy 1970
Testing centered on subject's level of ability (basal and ceiling rules)	Yes	No	No
Auditory tests taped for standardized administration	No	No	No
Principle of selective testing by assessment purpose emphasized	No	No	No
Comprehensive manual includes examiner training activities	No	No	No

Woodcock-Johnson 1977	K-ABC 1983	Stanford-Binet IV 1986	Woodcock-Johnson– Revised 1989
Yes Bateria 1982	Yes (Nonverbal scale)	No	(In preparation)
1. Costa Rica 2. Mexico 3. Puerto Rico 4. Peru 5. Spain	No norms	—	(In preparation)
Some	Yes	Some	Yes

Woodcock-Johnson 1977	K-ABC 1983	Stanford-Binet IV 1986	Woodcock-Johnson– Revised 1989
Yes	No	Yes	Yes
Yes	No	No	Yes
Yes	No	No	Yes
Yes	No	No	Yes

TABLE 3 Interpretation Features of Major Cognitive Batteries

Interpretation Features	Stanford-Binets 1937 to 1972	Wechslers 1939 to 1981	McCarthy 1970
Norms provided for each cognitive subtest	No	No	No
University/college norms	No	No	No
Common norms provided with test of achievement	No	No	No
Sociocultural norms	No	Yes 1978 (SOMPA)	No
Error of measurement confidence bands available	No	Yes	Yes
Confidence bands are plotted on profile	No	No	No
Aptitude/achievement analysis based on discrepancy norms	No	No	No
Intracognitive analysis based on discrepancy norms	No	No	No
Intra-achievement analysis based on discrepancy norms	No	No	No
Types of derived scores:			
Developmental level scores	Yes 1. Mental age	Yes 1. Test age	Yes 1. Mental age
Mastery level scores (quality of performance)	Yes 1937 1. Ratio IQ No 1960, 1972	No	No
Peer Comparison Scores	No 1937 Yes 1960, 1972 1. IQ	Yes 1. IQ	Yes 1. Percentile rank 2. Standard score
Computer Scoring	No	Yes WISC-R: 1986 WAIS-R: 1986	No

Woodcock-Johnson 1977	K-ABC 1983	Stanford-Binet IV 1986	Woodcock-Johnson– Revised 1989
Yes 1980	Yes	Yes	Yes
No	No	No	Yes
Yes 1. Reading 2. Mathematics 3. Written language 4. Knowledge	Yes 1. Reading 2. Mathematics	No	Yes 1. Oral language 2. Reading 3. Mathematics 4. Written language 5. Knowledge
No	Yes	No	No
Yes	Yes	Yes	Yes
Yes	Yes	No	Yes
Yes	No	No	Yes
No	No	No	Yes
No	No	No	Yes
Yes 1. Age equivalent 2. Grade equivalent	Yes 1. Subtest age equivalent	Yes 1. Age equivalent	Yes 1. Age equivalent 2. Grade equivalent
Yes 1. Relative performance index (RPI) 2. Instructional range	No	No	Yes 1. Relative mastery index (RMI) 2. Developmental level band 3. Instructional range
Yes 1. Percentile 2. Standard score 3. T-score 4. Normal curve equivalent 5. Stanine	Yes 1. Percentile rank 2. Standard score 3. Stanine	Yes 1. Percentile rank 2. IQ	Yes 1. Percentile rank 2. Standard score 3. T-score 4. Normal curve equivalent 5. Stanine
Yes 1979	Yes 1985	No	Yes

TABLE 4   Technical Features of Major Cognitive Batteries

Technical Features	Stanford-Binets 1937 to 1972	Wechslers 1939 to 1981	McCarthy 1970
Extensive technical manual	No	No	No
Item analysis and scaling based on Rasch procedure (provides an equal-interval scale of growth across entire range of test)	No	No	No
Person variables in norming plan	1. Sex 2. Race (1937—all white; no mention of race for 1960 revision; no Hispanic origin variable)	1. Sex 2. Race (white, nonwhite) 3. Occupation 4. Education (no Hispanic origin variable)	1. Sex 2. Race (white, nonwhite) 3. Family SES (father's occupation; no Hispanic origin variable)
Community variables in norming plan	1. Location 2. Size	1. Location 2. Size	1. Location 2. Size
Size of norming sample	3484 (1937) 4498 (1960) 2351 (1972)	WPPSI = 1200 WISC-R = 2200 WAIS-R = 1880	1032
Comparative concurrent validity studies report a matrix of results among all major competitive tests	No	No	No
Precision of age norm tables	By month	WPPSI—By 3-month blocks WISC-R—by 4-month blocks WAIS-R—by 2-year blocks (age 16 to 19) By 5-year blocks (age 20 to 24; 65 to 74) By 10-year blocks (age 25 to 64)	By 6-month blocks (age 2-6 to 5-6) By 1-year blocks (age 5-6 to 8-6)
Precision of grade norm tables	None available	None available	None available

Woodcock-Johnson 1977	K-ABC 1983	Stanford-Binet IV 1986	Woodcock-Johnson– Revised 1989
Yes	Yes	Yes	Yes
Yes	No	No	Yes
1. Sex 2. Race (white, black, Indian, other, Hispanic) (Note: Hispanic origin confounded with race) 3. Occupation of adults 4. Education of adults	1. Sex 2. Race (white, black, Hispanic, Asian, Indian) (Note: Hispanic origin confounded with race) 3. Family SES (parental education)	1. Sex 2. Race (white, black, Hispanic, Indian, Asian/Pacific) (Note: Hispanic origin confounded with race) 3. Family SES (parental occupation and education)	1. Sex 2. Race (white, black, Indian, Asian/Pacific) 3. Hispanic origin 4. Occupation of adults 5. Education of adults
1. Location 2. Size 3. 13 community socioeconomic variables	1. Location 2. Size	1. Location 2. Size	1. Location 2. Size 3. 13 community socioeconomic variables
4732	2000	5013	6359
Yes	No	No	Yes
By 1-month blocks (age 3-0 to 18-11) By 1-year blocks (age 19 to 80+)	By 2-month blocks (age 2-6 to 5-11) By 3-month blocks (age 6-0 to 12-6)	By 4-month blocks (age 2-0 to 5-11 years) By 6-month blocks (age 6-0 to 10-11 years) By 1-year blocks (age 11 to 17 years) By a 6-year block (age 18 to 23 years)	By 1-month blocks (age 2-0 to 18-11) By 1-year blocks (age 19 to 90+)
By month (K.O to 12.9)	None available	None available	By month (K.0 to 16.9)

References

Kaufman, A. S. (1975). Factor analysis of the WISC-R at eleven age levels between 6 1/2 and 16 1/2 years. *Journal of Consulting and Clinical Psychology, 43,* 135–147.

Kaufman, A. S., & Kaufman, N. L. (1983a). *Administration and scoring manual for the Kaufman Assessment Battery for Children.* Circle Pines, MN: American Guidance Service.

Kaufman, A. S., & Kaufman, N. L. (1983b). *Interpretive manual for the Kaufman Assessment Battery for Children.* Circle Pines, MN: American Guidance Service.

McCarthy, D. (1972). *Manual for the McCarthy Scales of Children's Abilities.* San Antonio: The Psychological Corporation.

McGrew, K. S., Werder, J. K., & Woodcock, R. W. (1990, in press). *WJ-R technical manual.* Allen, TX: DLM.

Terman, L. M., & Merrill, M. A. (1960). *Stanford-Binet Intelligence Scale: Manual for third revision, Form L-M.* Boston: Houghton Mifflin.

Terman, L. M., & Merrill, M. A. (1973). *Stanford-Binet Intelligence Scale: Manual for third revision, Form L-M. 1972 norms edition.* Boston: Houghton Mifflin.

Terman, L. M., & Merrill, M. A. (1937). *Measuring intelligence.* Boston: Houghton Mifflin.

Thorndike, R. L., Hagen, E. P., & Sattler, J. M. (1986a). *Guide for administering and scoring the Stanford-Binet Intelligence Scale: Fourth Edition.* Chicago: Riverside.

Thorndike, R. L., Hagen, E. P., & Sattler, J. M. (1986b). *Technical Manual for the Stanford-Binet Intelligence Scale: Fourth Edition.* Chicago: Riverside.

Wechsler, D. (1967). *Manual for the Wechsler Preschool and Primary Scale of Intelligence (WPPSI).* San Antonio: The Psychological Corporation.

Wechsler, D. (1968). *Manual for the escala de inteligencia Wechsler para adultos (EIWA).* San Antonio: The Psychological Corporation.

Wechsler, D. (1974). *Manual for the Wechsler Intelligence Scale for Children–Revised (WISC-R).* San Antonio: The Psychological Corporation.

Wechsler, D. (1981). *Manual for the Wechsler Intelligence Scale–Revised (WAIS-R).* San Antonio: The Psychological Corporation.

Wechsler, D. (1982). *Manual for the escala de inteligencia Wechsler para ninos–Revisado (EIWN-R).* San Antonio: The Psychological Corporation.

Wechsler, D. (1984). *WISC-RM escala de inteligencia para nivel escolar Wechsler.* Mexico, DF: El Manual Moderno.

Woodcock, R. W. (1978). *Development and standardization of the Woodcock-Johnson Psycho-Educational Battery.* Allen, TX: DLM.

Woodcock, R. W., & Johnson, M. B. (1977). *Examiner's Manual for the Woodcock-Johnson Psycho-Educational Battery, Part One: Test of Cognitive Ability.* Allen, TX: DLM.

Woodcock, R. W., & Mather, N. (1989). WJ–R Tests of Cognitive Ability–Standard and Supplemental Batteries: Examiner's Manual. In R. W. Woodcock & M. B. Johnson, *Woodcock-Johnson Psycho-Educational Battery–Revised.* Allen, TX: DLM.

Appendix 2   Areas of the Normal Curve

Area equals the proportion of cases between the z-score and the mean; extreme area equals .5000 less the proportion of cases between the z-score and the mean.

z	.00	.01	.02	.03	.04	.05	.06	.07	.08	.09
0.0	.0000	.0040	.0080	.0120	.0160	.0199	.0239	.0279	.0319	.0359
0.1	.0398	.0438	.0478	.0517	.0557	.0596	.0636	.0675	.0714	.0753
0.2	.0793	.0832	.0871	.0910	.0948	.0987	.1026	.1064	.1103	.1141
0.3	.1179	.1217	.1255	.1293	.1331	.1368	.1406	.1443	.1480	.1517
0.4	.1554	.1591	.1628	.1664	.1700	.1736	.1772	.1808	.1844	.1879
0.5	.1915	.1950	.1985	.2019	.2054	.2088	.2123	.2157	.2190	.2224
0.6	.2257	.2291	.2324	.2357	.2389	.2422	.2454	.2486	.2517	.2549
0.7	.2580	.2611	.2642	.2673	.2704	.2734	.2764	.2794	.2823	.2852
0.8	.2881	.2910	.2939	.2967	.2995	.3023	.3051	.3078	.3106	.3133
0.9	.3159	.3186	.3212	.3238	.3264	.3289	.3315	.3340	.3365	.3389
1.0	.3413	.3438	.3461	.3485	.3508	.3531	.3554	.3577	.3599	.3621
1.1	.3643	.3665	.3686	.3708	.3729	.3749	.3770	.3790	.3810	.3830
1.2	.3849	.3869	.3888	.3907	.3925	.3944	.3962	.3980	.3997	.4015
1.3	.4032	.4049	.4066	.4082	.4099	.4115	.4131	.4147	.4162	.4177
1.4	.4192	.4207	.4222	.4236	.4251	.4265	.4279	.4292	.4306	.4319
1.5	.4332	.4345	.4357	.4370	.4382	.4394	.4406	.4418	.4429	.4441
1.6	.4452	.4463	.4474	.4484	.4495	.4505	.4515	.4525	.4535	.4545
1.7	.4554	.4564	.4573	.4582	.4591	.4599	.4608	.4616	.4625	.4633
1.8	.4641	.4649	.4656	.4664	.4671	.4678	.4686	.4693	.4699	.4706
1.9	.4713	.4719	.4726	.4732	.4738	.4744	.4750	.4756	.4761	.4767
2.0	.4772	.4778	.4783	.4788	.4793	.4798	.4803	.4808	.4812	.4817
2.1	.4821	.4826	.4830	.4834	.4838	.4842	.4846	.4850	.4854	.4857
2.2	.4861	.4864	.4868	.4871	.4875	.4878	.4881	.4884	.4887	.4890
2.3	.4893	.4896	.4898	.4901	.4904	.4906	.4909	.4911	.4913	.4916
2.4	.4918	.4920	.4922	.4925	.4927	.4929	.4931	.4932	.4934	.4936
2.5	.4938	.4940	.4941	.4943	.4945	.4946	.4948	.4949	.4951	.4952
2.6	.4953	.4955	.4956	.4957	.4959	.4960	.4961	.4962	.4963	.4964
2.7	.4965	.4966	.4967	.4968	.4969	.4970	.4971	.4972	.4973	.4974
2.8	.4974	.4975	.4976	.4977	.4977	.4978	.4979	.4979	.4980	.4981
2.9	.4981	.4982	.4982	.4983	.4984	.4984	.4985	.4985	.4986	.4986
3.0	.4987	.4987	.4987	.4988	.4988	.4989	.4989	.4989	.4990	.4990

SOURCE: Presentation of data used in the present volume is from *Statistics: An Intuitive Approach,* Third Edition, by G. H. Weinberg and J. A. Schumaker. Copyright © 1962, 1969, 1974 by Wadsworth Publishing Company, Inc. Reprinted by permission of the publisher, Brooks/Cole Publishing Company, Pacific Grove, California 93950.

Appendix 3 Percentile Ranks for z-Scores of Normal Curves

z	Area[a]	z	Area[a]	z	Area[a]
−4.0	.000	−1.0	.159	2.0	.977
−3.9	.000	−0.9	.184	2.1	.982
−3.8	.000	−0.8	.212	2.2	.986
−3.7	.000	−0.7	.242	2.3	.989
−3.6	.000	−0.6	.274	2.4	.992
−3.5	.000	−0.5	.308	2.5	.994
−3.4	.000	−0.4	.345	2.6	.995
−3.3	.001	−0.3	.382	2.7	.996
−3.2	.001	−0.2	.421	2.8	.997
−3.1	.001	−0.1	.460	2.9	.998
−3.0	.001	0.0	.500	3.0	.999
−2.9	.002	0.1	.540	3.1	.999
−2.8	.003	0.2	.579	3.2	.999
−2.7	.004	0.3	.618	3.3	.999
−2.6	.005	0.4	.655	3.4	1.000
−2.5	.006	0.5	.692	3.5	1.000
−2.4	.008	0.6	.726	3.6	1.000
−2.3	.011	0.7	.758	3.7	1.000
−2.2	.014	0.8	.788	3.8	1.000
−2.1	.018	0.9	.816	3.9	1.000
				4.0	1.000
−2.0	.023	1.0	.841		
−1.9	.029	1.1	.864		
−1.8	.036	1.2	.885		
−1.7	.045	1.3	.903		
−1.6	.055	1.4	.919		
−1.5	.067	1.5	.933		
−1.4	.081	1.6	.945		
−1.3	.097	1.7	.955		
−1.2	.115	1.8	.964		
−1.1	.136	1.9	.971		

[a]Move decimal two places to the right for the percentile rank. Values are rounded to three places.

SOURCE: Presentation of data used in the present volume is from *Statistics: An Intuitive Approach,* Third Edition, by G. H. Weinberg and J. A. Schumaker. Copyright © 1962, 1969, 1974 by Wadsworth Publishing Company, Inc. Reprinted by permission of the publisher, Brooks/Cole Publishing Company, Pacific Grove, California 93950.

Appendix 4   List of Equations Used in the Text

Location in Text	Term Defined	Equation
(4.1)	Mean	$\bar{X} = \dfrac{\Sigma X}{N}$
(4.2)	Variance	$S^2 = \dfrac{\Sigma(X - \bar{X})^2}{N}$ or $S^2 = \dfrac{\Sigma X^2}{N} - \left(\dfrac{\Sigma X}{N}\right)^2$
p. 74	Pearson product-moment correlation coefficient, where X and Y are scores on two tests	$r = \dfrac{N\Sigma XY - (\Sigma X)(\Sigma Y)}{\sqrt{N\Sigma X^2 - (\Sigma X)^2}\sqrt{N\Sigma Y^2 - (\Sigma Y)^2}}$ or $r = \dfrac{\Sigma Z_x Z_y}{n}$
p. 88	Percentile rank for a particular score	%ile = percent of people scoring below the score + ½ percent of people obtaining the score
(5.1)	z-score	$z = \dfrac{X - \bar{X}}{S}$
(5.2)	Any standard score	$SS = \bar{X}_{ss} + (S_{ss})(z)$
(7.2)	Coefficient alpha	$r_{aa} = \dfrac{k}{k - 1}\left(1 - \dfrac{\Sigma S^2_{items}}{S^2_{test}}\right)$
p. 116	Simple agreement	$\dfrac{100 \text{ (number of agreements)}}{\text{number of observations}}$
(7.3)	% agreement occurrence=	$\dfrac{100 \text{ (number of agreements on occurrence)}}{\text{number of observations} - \text{number of agreements on nonoccurrence}}$

Appendix 4 (cont.)

Location in Text	Term Defined	Equation
(7.4)	Spearman-Brown, correction for test length	$r_{xx} = \dfrac{2r_{(1/2)(1/2)}}{1 + r_{(1/2)(1/2)}}$
(7.5)	Standard error of measurement	$\text{SEM} = S\sqrt{1 - r_{xx}}$
(7.6)	Estimated true score	$X' = \bar{X} + (r_{xx})(X - \bar{X})$
(7.7)	Lower and upper limits of a confidence interval, where z-score determines level of confidence	$\text{Lower limit} = X' - (z)(\text{SEM})$ $\text{Upper limit} = X' + (z)(\text{SEM})$
(7.8)	Reliability of a predicted difference	$\hat{D} = \dfrac{r_{bb} + (r_{aa})(r_{ab}^2) - 2r_{ab}}{1 - r_{ab}^2}$
(7.9)	Standard deviation of a predicted difference	$S_{\text{dif}} = S_b\sqrt{1 - r_{ab}^2}$
(7.10)	Reliability of a difference	$r_{(\text{dif})} = \dfrac{\frac{1}{2}(r_{aa} + r_{bb}) - r_{ab}}{1 - r_{ab}}$
(7.11)	Standard deviation of a difference	$S_{\text{dif}} = \sqrt{S_a^2 + S_b^2 - 2r_{ab}S_aS_b}$
(7.12)	Standard error of measurement of a difference	$\text{SEM}_{\text{dif}} = \sqrt{S_a{}^2 + S_b{}^2 - 2r_{ab}S_aS_b} \times \sqrt{1 - \dfrac{\frac{1}{2}(r_{aa} + r_{bb}) - r_{ab}}{1 - r_{ab}}}$
(7.13)	Estimated true difference	$d' = (\text{obtained difference})(r_{xx(\text{dif})})$

Appendix 5 List of Tests Reviewed

AAMD Adaptive Behavior Scale, School Edition
AAMD Adaptive Behavior Scale for Children and Adults
Adaptive Behavior Inventory
AO H-R-R Pseudoisochromatic Plates
Arthur Adaptation of the Leiter International Performance Scale
Auditory Discrimination Test
Basic Achievement Skills Individual Screener
Battelle Developmental Inventory
Bender Visual Motor Gestalt Test
Blind Learning Aptitude Test
Boehm Test of Basic Concepts–Revised
BRIGANCE® Diagnostic Inventories
California Achievement Tests
Carrow Elicited Language Inventory
Cognitive Abilities Test
Columbia Mental Maturity Scale
Comprehensive Developmental Scale
Culture Fair Intelligence Tests
Denver Developmental Screening Test
Detroit Tests of Learning Aptitude–Primary
Detroit Test of Learning Aptitude–2
Developmental Indicators for the Assessment of Learning–Revised
Developmental Profile II
Developmental Test of Visual-Motor Integration
Developmental Test of Visual Perception
Diagnostic Mathematics Inventory/Mathematics Systems
Diagnostic Reading Scales
Durrell Analysis of Reading Difficulty
Dvorine Psuedo-isochromatic Plates
Educational Ability Series
Farnsworth Dichotomous Test for Color Blindness
Formal Reading Inventory
Full-Range Picture Vocabulary Test
Gates-MacGinitie Reading Tests
Gates-McKillop-Horowitz Reading Diagnostic Tests
Gilmore Oral Reading Test
Goldman-Fristoe Test of Articulation
Gray Oral Reading Tests–Revised
Henmon-Nelson Tests of Mental Ability
Illinois Test of Psycholinguistic Abilities
Iowa Tests of Basic Skills
Ishihara Color Blind Test
Kaufman Assessment Battery for Children
Kaufman Test of Educational Achievement

Appendix 6   List of Publishers

Individuals wishing to purchase test specimen kits or secure additional test materials can write to the test publisher. The following is a list of the publishers whose tests are reviewed in this book.

American Association on Mental Deficiency, 5101 Wisconsin Ave. N.W., Washington, DC 20016

American Guidance Service, Inc., Publishers' Building, Circle Pines, MN 55014

American Orthopsychiatric Association, 1775 Broadway, New York, NY 10019

American Printing House for the Blind, 1839 Frankfort Ave., P.O. Box 6085, Louisville, KY 40206–0085

American Psychological Association, Inc., 1200 17th St. N.W., Washington, DC 20036

Bausch & Lomb, Inc., Rochester, NY 14602

California Test Bureau/McGraw-Hill, Del Monte Research Park, Monterey, CA 93940

Campus Publishers, 713 West Ellsworth Rd., Ann Arbor, MI 48104

Childcraft Education Corporation, 20 Kilmer Rd., Edison, NJ 08818

Consulting Psychologists Press, Inc., 577 College Ave., P.O. Box 11636, Palo Alto, CA 94306

Counselor Recordings and Tests, Box 6184, Acklen Station, Nashville, TN 37212

C.P.S., Box 83, Larchmont, NY 10538

Curriculum Associates, Inc., 5 Esquire Rd., North Billerica, MA 01862

The Devereux Foundation Press, 19 South Waterloo Rd., Devon, PA 19333

Educational and Industrial Testing Service, P.O. Box 7234, San Diego, CA 92107

Educational Testing Service, Rosedale Rd., Princeton, NJ 08541

Grune & Stratton, Inc., 111 Fifth Ave., New York, NY 10003

Harvard University Press, 79 Garden St., Cambridge, MA 02138

Marshall S. Hiskey, 5640 Baldwin, Lincoln, NE 68507

Institute for Personality and Ability Testing, P.O. Box 188, Champaign, IL 61820–0188

Jastak Associates, 1526 Gilpin Ave., Wilmington, DE 19806

Learning Concepts, 2501 North Lamar, Austin, TX 78705

Charles E. Merrill Publishing Co., 1300 Alum Creek Drive, Box 508, Columbus, OH 43216

Modern Curriculum Press, 13900 Prospect Rd., Cleveland, OH 44136

T. Ernest Newland, 1004 Ross Dr., Champaign, IL 61820

NFER-Nelson Publishing Company Ltd., Darville House, 2 Oxford Rd. East, Windsor, Berkshire SL4 1DF, England

Northwestern University Press, 1735 Benson Ave., Evanston, IL 60201

Personnel Press, 20 Nassau St., Princeton, NJ 08540

Pro-Ed, 8700 Shoal Creek Blvd., Austin, TX 78758–6897

Psychodynamic Instruments, University of California, Santa Barbara, CA 93106

The Psychological Corporation, P.O. Box 9954, San Antonio, TX 78204

Psychological Test Specialists, Box 9229, Missoula, MT 59807

Psychologists and Educators Press, Inc., 211 West State St., Jacksonville, IL 62650

Random House, Inc., 201 East 50th St., New York, NY 10022

The Riverside Publishing Company, 8420 Bryn Mawr Ave., Chicago, IL 60631

Science Research Associates, 155 North Wacker Dr., Chicago, IL 60606

Slosson Educational Publications, 140 Pine St., P.O. Box 280, East Aurora, NY 14052

C. H. Stoelting Co., 1350 South Kostner Ave., Chicago IL 60623

Teachers College Press, 1234 Amsterdam Ave., New York, NY 10027

Teaching Resources Corporation, 50 Pond Park Rd., Hingham, MA 02043

The University of Illinois Press, 54 East Gregory Dr., Box 5081, Station A, Champaign, IL 61820

Western Psychological Services, 12031 Wilshire Blvd., Los Angles, CA 90025

Richard L. Zweig Associates, Inc., 20800 Beach Blvd., Huntington Beach, CA 92648.

Appendix 7 *How to Review a Test*

We have often been asked how we go about analyzing and reviewing tests for this book—and in general. So we have decided to include a how-to section. Before starting an analysis of a test, you must first assemble the materials. We find that it is best to order a specimen kit and any supplementary manuals available. Be prepared to experience difficulty obtaining material from some test publishers. When you request a specimen kit and supplementary materials, you will occasionally receive all materials. More often, when you review specimen sets, you'll learn that additional materials must be ordered separately. Sometimes, it takes a very long time to figure out just what is published where. Sometimes, it takes up to six months to acquire all the material on a test. Sometimes, you just never obtain materials. Patience and perseverance are almost always required.

When materials arrive, you must prepare yourself properly. The right setting is very important. A well-ventilated, well-lit room (preferably a bit on the chilly side) and a hard, straight-backed chair are essential.

Next, and more important, reviewers must adopt a "show me" attitude. Do not expect test authors to admit in the manuals that the test was poorly normed because there was no money to pay testers or that the test has inadequate reliability because they didn't develop enough test items. Test authors put the best possible face on their tests, as might be expected. You simply cannot accept the claims made by test authors and their colleagues who write the technical manuals. If you accepted them at their word, they would only have to say that they had a "good, reliable, valid, and well-normed test." Test authors must *demonstrate* that their tests are reliable, valid, and well-normed.

After assembling the relevant materials and finding a suitable place in which to ask "Where's the proof?" we usually follow these procedures. First, we skim through the material to get a general idea of what the test is intended to do and what is included in each document that accompanies it. We generally keep several separate sheets of paper—one for each topic that we consider: background and purposes, behavior sampled, scores, norms, reliability, and validity.

Then we reread the manuals. You might expect that test authors would organize test manuals neatly so that you could turn to the table of contents, find the section on, for example, reliability, and turn to the pages indicated for the proof. Sometimes, yes, more often, no. If manuals do not have section headings or chapters, we just begin reading and making notes under our headings. If the manuals are sectioned, we start with the behaviors sampled by the test. It doesn't matter too much where you start except that validity is best left until last. We often start with the behaviors sampled. Test manuals frequently contain a useful description of the behaviors sampled but more often they merely name the domains sampled. For example, a test may be said to assess reading, but that does not tell you if it assesses reading recognition, reading comprehension, or oral reading. Look at the test directions (especially directions on how to score student responses) and the protocol (the answer form). These sources generally give you a pretty good idea of what behaviors are actually measured. Then, try to describe the behavior in straightforward terms—avoiding psychological and educational jargon.

Next, we generally look at the section on norms. When evaluating a test's norms, first note the ages (or grades in the case of achievement tests) of the students on whom the test was normed. Next, look for statements describing the students. Also, anticipate quantification of the norm groups. For example, you should anticipate that the test author will tell you how many boys and how many girls and how many persons from various ethnic or racial groups were tested at each age or grade. Also expect geographic information. For example, what percentage of the sample lived in big cities? in the Northwest? Finally, expect socioeconomic information about the students: parents' occupations, parents' educational attainment, income of the household. Next, look for an explicit comparison of the characteristics of the norm group with the most recent census before publication of the test. Sometimes, test authors include all the data and all the comparisons in neat tabular form, but you may find substantial discrepancies between the norm sample and the population. Generally, we look for correspondence between the sample and the population within about 5 percent. Thus, if 31 percent of the sample lived in the Southwest and only 26 percent of the U.S. population lived in the Southwest, we would not be overly concerned about the discrepancy. We realize that this is an arbitrary margin of error. If you prefer a different one, that's fine.

Information on scores is apt to be located in many places: in the section on scoring the test, in the description of the norms, in a separate section on scores, in the section dealing with the interpretation of scores, or in the norm tables themselves. Generally, the best place to find information on the types of scores available is the norm tables. These tables allow the conversions of raw scores to derived scores and subtest scores to total scores. The next best place to look is in the section on scoring the test. There you find the directions for crediting responses and combining raw scores into derived scores. In the norms section, you may find phrases such as "percentile norms" or "grade-equivalent norms," sure tip-offs that percentiles and grade equivalents will be available. In the sections on interpretation, you may find information on the proper interpretation of derived scores. For example, many test authors will tell you the mean and standard deviation of standard scores and how they are to be interpreted. However, it pays to double check against the norm tables themselves because test authors occasionally err in their descriptions.

Finding reliability data may be more difficult. If there is a section on reliability, the task is fairly simple. You wish to see if there is evidence of each appropriate type of reliability. Demand numbers; do not settle for statements as to the test's reliability. Make the authors show you the proof. Read the tables. You should usually anticipate finding estimates of generalization across items (split-half, KR-20, coefficient alpha, alternate-form, and so on) and across time (test-retest reliability). If the scoring is difficult, you should also anticipate finding a section on interscorer agreement. (Data on the extent to which one can generalize across scores can often be found in the section on scoring.) You should expect to find reliability estimates for each subtest at each grade or age. In addition, tables giving the standard error of measurement for each subtest at each grade or age are occasionally provided.

The next step is very important: you must determine the scores that are to be interpreted, because those are the ones you must judge for adequacy. In the sections dealing with score interpretation, you will often find the scores that the test authors think are most important. Many tests have subtests that are combined into a total score. Sometimes the subtest scores are stressed over the total score (for example, the Illinois Test of Psycholinguistic Abilities), whereas other tests stress the total score or part scores over subtest scores (for example, the Wechsler Intelligence Scale for Children—Revised). The scores that are stressed as important and that are to be interpreted must meet the minimum desirable standards of reliability. Consequently, different test are held to different standards. For example, the subtests on the ITPA must meet a higher standard of reliability than the subtests of the WISC-R because we are urged to interpret the ITPA subtests but not the WISC-R subtests.

If there is no section on reliability, check the table of contents to see if there are tables for standard errors of measurement or reliability coefficients. You can usually find all the information that you need in the tables without reading the test. If there are no tables and no section on reliability, there may be no data on reliability in the manuals; it happens frequently. However, reliability information may be hidden in the section on validity or in the section on scores or in the section on interpretation. Keep a lookout for it as you skim and read.

The evaluation of a test's validity is the most difficult aspect of reviewing a test. You have already considered the adequacy of the norms and the reliability. If they are inadequate, there will be severe problems with validity. Even if they are adequate, the authors must still prove to you that the test is valid for each recommended use. This means that you must learn how the authors recommend using the test. Do not expect to find this information in a section labeled validity. More often you will find such statements in the beginning of the test manuals or in the promotional materials.

You will always find a statement to the effect that the test measures some domain. How do the test authors prove this? Data on content validity is often included in a section called "the development of the test" of "selection of items." In these sections, the authors will explain to you how they chose the items in the test. For other tests, the information will be buried in the manual. For still others, there will be no mention—no proof.

Depending on the particular type of test, you may also find information on concurrent and predictive validity and on construct validity. Again, you must remember that the purpose of presenting these data is to demonstrate to us that the test measures the domain its authors claim it measures. The data should logically bear on the issue of validity.

Beyond claims that the test assesses a particular domain, you may find assertions that the test can be used in particular ways. This is especially true for tests of achievement where we are often told the test can be used in program planning. When we see such assertions, we expect to find a large number of test items appropriate for each grade. We look at the test items, and we often look at the norm tables to get an idea of the difference in the number of test items at each grade. All you have to do is find the raw score at the 50th percentile at two adjacent grades. For example, suppose 17 points correct was the 50th percentile at the second grade and 21 points correct was the 50th percentile at the third grade. Then, only 4 raw-score points would separate second and third grade work. This is probably too few items on which to base an educational plan, although it may well discriminate among test takers. Sometimes we are told that scores can be used in particular ways. Such assertions are often found in the interpretation sections of the manuals. For example, you may find information on critical levels of performance; the authors may tell you that scores below a particular value are indicative of potential problems or that students earning such scores require special instructional interventions. Check out each assertion for the use of the test and expect to find proof.

Finally, we tend to be suspicious of strange formulations of reliability, validity, or scores. You should be, too. Remember, if you are an intended user of the test, the test author should provide all the necessary data in clear and usable form. If it isn't there, it isn't your fault.

REFERENCES

Achenbach, T. M. (1981). *Child Behavior Checklist for Ages 4–16*. San Antonio, TX: The Psychological Corporation.

Achenbach, T. M., & Edelbrock, C. (1986). *Child Behavior Checklist for Ages 2–3*. San Antonio, TX: The Psychological Corporation.

Adam, A., Doran, D., & Modan, R. (1967). Frequencies of protan and duetan alleles in some Israeli communities and a note on the selection of relaxation hypotheses. *American Journal of Physical Anthropology, 26*. 297–306.

Alberto, P., & Troutman, A. (1990). *Applied behavior analysis for teachers* (3rd ed.). Columbus, OH: Merrill.

Algozzine, B., Christenson, S., & Ysseldyke, J. E. (1982). Probabilities associated with the referral to placement process. *Teacher Education and Special Education, 5*, 19–23.

Alpern, G. D., Boll, T. J., & Shearer, M. (1986). *The Developmental Profile II (DP–II)*. Los Angeles: Western Psychological Services.

American Educational Research Association (AERA), American Psychological Association, & National Council on Measurement in Education. (1985). *Standards for educational and psychological testing*. Washington, DC: American Psychological Association.

American National Standards Institute. (1969). *Specifications for audiometers*. New York: American National Standards Institute, Inc.

American Psychological Association. (1979). *Ethical standards of psychologists*. Washington, DC: American Psychological Association.

American Psychological Association, American Educational Research Association, & National Council on Measurement in Education. (1974). *Standards for educational and psychological tests*. Washington, DC: American Psychological Association.

American Speech and Hearing Association. (1974). Guidelines for audiometric symbols. *American Speech and Hearing Association Journal, 16*, 260–263.

American Speech-Language-Hearing Association. (1980). *Guidelines for Audiometric Symbols*. *ASHA, 32 (Suppl. 2)*, 25–30.

Ames, W. (1965). A comparison of spelling textbooks. *Elementary English. 42*. 146–150, 214.

Ammons, R. B. & Ammons, C. H. (1948). *The Full Range Picture Vocabulary Test*. New Orleans: R. B. Ammons.

Ammons, R. B., & Ammons, C. H. (1962). The Quick Test (QT): Provisional manual. *Psychological Reports, 11*, 111–161.

Armstrong, R. J., & Jensen, J. A. (1981). *Slosson Intelligence Test: 1981 norms tables application and development*. East Aurora, NY: Slosson Educational Publications.

Arter, J. A., & Jenkins, J. R. (1979). Differential diagnosis-prescriptive teaching: A critical appraisal. *Review of Educational Research, 49*, 517–556.

Arthur, G. (1950). *The Arthur Adaption of the Leiter International Performance Scale*. Chicago, IL: C. H. Stoelting.

Bachor, D. (1990). The importance of shifts in language level and extraneous information in determining word-problem difficulty: steps toward individual assessment. *Diagnostique, 14*, 94–111.

Bachor, D., Stacy N., & Freeze, D. (1986). *A conceptual framework for word problems: Some preliminary results*. Paper presented at the conference of the Canadian Society for Studies in Education. Winnipeg, Manitoba.

Bailey, D. B., & Rouse, T. L. (1989). Procedural considerations in assessing infants and preschoolers with handicaps. In D. B. Bailey & M. Wolery (Eds.), *Assessing infants and preschoolers with handicaps*. Columbus, OH: Merrill.

Baker, H. J., & Leland, B. (1967). *Detroit Tests of Learning Aptitude (examiner's handbook)*. Indianapolis: Bobbs-Merrill.

Ballard, J., & Zettel, J. (1977). Public Law 94-142 and Sec. 504: What they say about rights and protections. *Exceptional Children, 44,* 177–185.

Balow, I. H., Hogan, T. P., Farr, R. C., & Prescott, G. A. (1986). *Metropolitan Achievement Test 6: Language Diagnostic Tests*. San Antonio: The Psychological Corporation.

Barraga, N. (1976). *Visual handicaps and learning: A developmental approach*. Belmont, CA: Wadsworth.

Batsche, G. M., & Peterson, D. W. (1983). School psychology and protective assessment: A growing incompatibility. *School Psychology Review, 12,* 440–445.

Beatty, L. S., Gardner, E. G., Madden, R., & Karlsen, B. (1985). *The Stanford Diagnostic Mathematics Test* (3rd ed.). San Antonio, TX: The Psychological Corporation.

Beery, K. E. (1982). *Revised administration, scoring, and teaching manual for the Developmental Test of Visual-Motor Integration*. Cleveland: Modern Curriculum Press.

Bellak, L., & Bellak, S. (1965). *Children's Apperception Test*. Cleveland: Modern Curriculum Press.

Bersoff, D. N. (1979). Regarding psychologists testily: Legal regulation of psychological assessment in the pubic schools. *Maryland Law Review, 39,* 27–120.

Bloom, B. (1956). *Taxonomy of educational objectives: The classification of educational goals. Handbook 1. Cognitive domain*. New York: McKay.

Bloom, B., Hastings, J., & Madaus, G. (1971). *Handbook of formative and summative evaluation of student learning*. New York: McGraw-Hill.

Bloom, L., & Lahey, M. (1978). *Language development and language disorders*. New York: Wiley.

Bloomfield, L. (1933). *Language*. New York: Holt, Rinehart, and Winston.

Blum, G. (1967). *Blacky Pictures: A technique for the exploration of personality dynamics*. Santa Barbara: Psychodynamic Instruments.

Boehm, A. E. (1986). *Boehm Test of Basic Concepts–Revised*. San Antonio: The Psychological Corporation.

Boehm, A. E., & Weinberg, R. A. (1988). *The classroom observer: A guide for developing observation skills* (2nd ed.). New York: Teachers College Press.

Box, G. (1953). Non-normality and tests on variance. *Biometrika, 40,* 318–335.

Bradbury, R. (1953). *Fahrenheit 451*. New York: Ballantine Books.

Brigance, A. (1977). *BRIGANCE® Diagnostic Inventory of Basic Skills*. North Billerica, MA: Curriculum Associates.

Brigance, A. (1978). *BRIGANCE® Diagnostic Inventory of Early Development*. North Billerica, MA: Curriculum Associates.

Brigance, A. (1980). *BRIGANCE® Diagnostic Inventory of Essential Skills*. North Billerica, MA: Curriculum Associates.

Brown, L., & Hammill, D. (1983). *Behavior Rating Profile*. Austin, TX: Pro-Ed.

Brown, L., & Leigh, J. (1986a). *Adaptive Behavior Inventory*. Austin, TX: Pro-Ed.

Brown, L., & Leigh, J. (1986b). *The Adaptive Behavior Inventory manual*. Austin, TX: Pro-Ed.

Brown, L., Sherbenou, R. J., & Dollar, S. J. (1982). *Test of Nonverbal Intelligence*. Austin, TX: Pro-Ed.

Brown, R. (1973). *A first language: the early stages*. Cambridge, MA: Harvard University Press.

Brown, R., & Bellugi, U. (1964). Three processes in the child's acquisition of syntax. *Harvard Educational Review, 34,* 133–151.

Brown, V. L., Hammill, D. D., & Wiederholt, L. (1986). *Test of Reading Comprehension: Revised Edition*. Austin, TX: Pro-Ed.

Brown, V., & McEntire, E. (1984). *Test of Mathematical Abilities*. Austin, TX: Pro-Ed.

Buck, J., & Jolles, I. (1966). *House-Tree-Person*. Los Angeles: Western Psychological Services.

Burgemeister, B. B., Blum, L. H., & Lorge, I. (1972). *Columbia Mental Maturity Scale* (3rd ed.). Cleveland: The Psychological Corporation.

Byrne, M. C. (1978). Appraisal of child language acquisition. In F. L. Darley & D. C. Spriestersbach, *Diagnostic methods in speech pathology* (2nd ed.). New York: Harper & Row.

Caldwell, B. (1970a). *Preschool Inventory Revised Edition*. Princeton, NJ: Educational Testing Service.

Caldwell, J., & Goldin, J. (1979). Variables affecting word problem difficulty in elementary school mathematics. *Journal of Research in Mathematics Education, 10,* 323–335.

Camarata, S., Hughes, C., & Ruhl, K. (1988). Mild/moderately behaviorally disordered students: A population at risk for language disorders. *Language, Speech, and Hearing Services in Schools, 19,* 191–200.

Campbell, D., & Fiske, D. (1959). Convergent and discriminate validation by the multi-trait-multi-method matrix. *Psychological Bulletin, 56,* 81–105.

Carrow, E. (1974). *Carrow Elicited Language Inventory,* Austin, TX: Learning Concepts.

Carrow-Wolfolk, E. (1985). *Test for Auditory Comprehension of Language, examiner's manual* (rev. ed.). Allen, TX: Developmental Learning Materials.

Carter, J., & Sugai, G. (1989). Survey on prereferral practices: Responses from state departments of education. *Exceptional children, 55,* 298–302.

Cartwright, C., & Cartwright, G. P. (1974). *Developing observation skills.* New York: McGraw-Hill.

Cattell, R., & IPAT Staff. (1986). *Sixteen Personality Factor Questionnaire.* Champaign, IL: Institute for Personality and Ability Testing.

Cattell, R. B. (1950). *Culture Fair Intelligence Test: Scale 1.* Champaign, IL: Institute for Personality and Ability Testing.

Cattell, R. B. (1962). *Handbook for Culture Fair Intelligence Test: Scale 1.* Champaign, IL: Institute for Personality and Ability Testing.

Cattell, R. B. (1973a). *Measuring intelligence with the Culture Fair Tests: Manual for scales 2 and 3.* Champaign, IL: Institute for Personality and Ability Testing.

Cattell, R. B. (1973b). *Technical supplement for the Culture Fair Intelligence Tests scales 2 and 3.* Champaign, IL: Institute for Personality and Ability Testing.

Cattell, R. B., & Cattell, A. K. S. (1960a). *Culture Fair Intelligence Test: Scale 2.* Champaign, IL: Institute for Personality and Ability Testing.

Cattell, R. B., & Cattell, A. K. S. (1960b). *Handbook for the individual or group Culture Fair Intelligence Test: Scale 2.* Champaign, IL: Institute for Personality and Ability Testing.

Cattell, R. B., & Cattell, A. K. S. (1963). *Culture Fair Intelligence Test: Scale 3.* Champaign, IL: Institute for Personality and Ability Testing.

Cattell, R. B., Cattell, M., & Johns, E. (1984). *High School Personality Questionnaire.* Champaign, IL: Institute for Personality and Ability Testing.

Chalfant, J., Pysh, M. V., & Moultrie, R. (1979). Teacher assistance teams: A model for within-building problem solving. *Learning Disability Quarterly, 2,* 85–96.

Chomsky, N. (1957). *Syntactic structures.* The Hague: Mouton.

Cohen, G. (1972). Hemispheric differences in a letter classification task. *Perception and Psychophysics, 11,* 139–142.

Coleman, J., Campbell, E., Hobson, C., McPartland, J., Mood, A., Weinfeld, F., & York, R. (1966). *Equality of educational opportunity.* Washington, DC: National Center for Education Statistics (F. S. 5.238: 380001)

Connolly, A., Nachtman, W., & Pritchett, E. (1976). *Manual for the KeyMath Diagnostic Arithmetic Test.* Circle Pines, MN: American Guidance Service.

Cooper, C. (1977). Holistic evaluation of writing. In C. Cooper & L. Odell (Eds.), *Evaluating writing: Describing, measuring, judging.* Buffalo, NY: National Council of Teachers of English.

Coopersmith, S. (1982). *Coopersmith Self Esteem Inventories.* Palo Alto, CA: Center for Self Esteem Development.

Cronbach, L. (1951). Coefficient alpha and the internal structure of tests. *Psychometrika, 16,* 297–334.

CTB/McGraw-Hill. (1985a). *California Achievement Test.* Monterey, CA: Author.

CTB/McGraw-Hill. (1985b). *Technical bulletin 1.* Monterey, CA: Author.

CTB/McGraw-Hill. (1986). *Technical bulletin 2.* Monterey, CA: Author.

CTB/McGraw-Hill. (1980). *Prescriptive Reading Inventory/Reading System.* Monterey, CA: Author.

Darley, F. L. (1961). Identification audiometry. *Journal of Speech and Hearing Disorders* (Monograph Supplement Number 9).

Das, J., Kirby, J., & Jarman, R. (1975). Simultaneous and successive syntheses: An alternative model for cognitive abilities. *Psychological Bulletin, 82,* 87–103.

Deno, S. (1985). Curriculum-based measurement: The emerging alternative. *Exceptional Children, 52,* 219–232.

Deno, S. L. (1985). Curriculum-based assessment: The emerging alternative. *Exceptional Children, 52,* 219–232.

Deno, S. L. (1986). Formative evaluation of individual student programs: A new role for school psychologists. *School Psychology Review, 15,* 358–374.

Deno, S., & Mirkin, P. (1977). *Data-based program modifiction: A manual.* Reston, VA: Council for Exceptional Children.

Dingman, H., & Tarjan, G. (1960). Mental retardation and the normal distribution curve. *American Journal of Mental Deficiency, 64,* 991–994.

Doll, E. A. (1965). *Vineland Social Maturity Scale,* Circle Pines, MN: American Guidance Service. (Originally published in 1953.)

Down, A. L. (1866/1969). Observations on an ethnic classification of idiots. In R. Vollman (Ed.), *Down's Syndrome (Mongolism), a reference bibliography.* Washington, DC: United States Department of Health, Education and Welfare.

Duffy, J. (1964). Hearing problems in school-age children. In *Maico Audiological Library Series I.* Minneapolis: Maico Electronics.

Dunn, L., & Dunn, L. (1981). *Peabody Picture Vocabulary Test–Revised.* Circle Pines, MN: American Guidance Service.

Dunn, L. M., & Markwardt, F. C. (1970). *Peabody Individual Achievement Test.* Circle Pines, MN: American Guidance Service.

Durrell, D., & Catterson, J. (1980). Durrell Analysis of Reading Difficulty. San Antonio, TX: The Psychological Corporation.

Dvorine, I. (1953). *Dvorine Pseudoisochromatic Plates* (2nd ed.). Baltimore: Waverly Press.

Edwards, A. (1966). *Edwards Personal Preference Schedule.* Cleveland: The Psychological Corporation.

Ekwall, E. E. (1970). *Locating and correcting reading difficulties.* Columbus, OH: Merrill.

Englemann, S., Granzin, A., & Severson, H. (1979). Diagnosing instruction. *Journal of Special Education, 13,* 355–365.

Englert, C., Cullata, B., & Horn, D. (1987). Influence of irrelevant information in addition word problems on problem solving. *Learning Disabilities Quarterly, 10,* 29–36.

Ervin, S. M. (1964). Imitation and structional change in children's language. In E. H. Lenneberg (Ed.), *New directions in the study of language.* Cambridge, MA: M.I.T. Press.

Exner, J. E. (1966). *Workbook in the Rorschach technique.* Springfield, IL: Charles C. Thomas.

Farber, B. (1968). *Mental retardation: Its social context and social consequences.* Boston: Houghton Mifflin

Farnsworth, D. (1947). *The Farnsworth Dichotomous Test for Color Blindness.* San Antonio, TX: The Psychological Corporation.

Farr, R. C., Prescott, G. A., Balow, I. H., & Hogan, T. P. (1986). *Metropolitan Achievement Tests 6: Reading Diagnostic Tests.* San Antonio, TX: The Psychological Corporation.

Fillmore, C. (1968). The case for case. In E. Bach & R. Harms (Eds.), *Universals in linguistic theory.* New York: Holt, Rinehart, and Winston.

Fitts, W. (1965). *Tennessee Self Concept Inventory.* Nashville: Counselor Recordings and Tests.

Frankenburg, W., Dodds, J., Fandal, A., Kazuk, E., & Cohrs, M. (1975). *Denver Developmental Screening Test, reference manual, revised 1975 edition.* Denver, CO: LA–DOCA Project and Publishing Foundation.

Frankenburg, W., Goldstein, A., & Camp, B. (1971). The revised Denver Developmental Screening Test: Its accuracy as a screening instrument. *Pediatrics, 79,* 988–995.

French, J. L. (1964). *Pictorial Test of Intelligence.* Chicago: The Riverside Publishing Company.

Fromkin, V., & Rodman, R. (1978). *An introduction to language.* New York: Holt, Rinehart, and Winston.

Frostig, M., Lefever, W., & Whittlesey, J. (1966). *Administration and scoring manual: Marianne Frostig Developmental Test of Visual Perception.* Palo Alto: Consulting Psychologists Press.

Frostig, M., Maslow, P., Lefever, D. W., & Whittlesey, J. R. (1964). *The Marianne Frostig Developmental Test of Visual Perception: 1963 standardization.* Palo Alto: Consulting Psychologists Press.

Fuchs, L. (1986). Monitoring progress among mildly handicapped pupils: Review of current practice and research. *Remedial and special education, 7,* 5–12.

Fuchs, L., Fuchs, D., & Maxwell, L. (1988). The validity of informal reading comprehension measures. *Remedial and special education, 9,* 20–28.

Fudala, J. (1970). *Arizona Articulation Proficiency Scale.* Los Angeles: Western Psychological Services.

Fulmer, S. (1980). *Pre-reading screening procedures and Slingerland Screening Tests for Identifying Children with Specific Language Disability, technical manual.* Los Angeles: Western Psychological Services.

Gardner, E. F., Callis, R., Merwin, J. C., & Rudman, H. C. (1983). *Test of Academic Skills* (2nd ed.). San Antonio, TX: The Psychological Corporation.

Gardner, E. F., Rudman, H. C., Karlsen, B., & Merwin, J. C. (1982). *Stanford Achievement Test* (7th ed.). San Antonio, TX: The Psychological Corporation.

Garrett, J. E., & Brazil, N. (1979). Categories used for identification and education of exceptional children. *Exceptional Children, 45,* 291–292.

Gates, A. I., & McKillop, A. S. (1962). *Gates-McKillop Reading Diagnostic Tests.* New York: Teachers College Press.

Gates, A. I., & McKillop, A. S., & Horowitz, R. (1981). *Gates-McKillop-Horowitz Reading Diagnostic Tests.* New York: Teachers College Press.

Germann, G., & Tindal, G. (1985). An application of curriculum-based assessment: The use of direct and frequent measurement. *Exceptional Children, 52,* 244–265.

Gessell, J. K. (1983). *Diagnostic Mathematics Inventory/Mathematics System.* Monterey, CA: CTB/McGraw-Hill.

Gilmore, J. V., & Gilmore, E. C. (1968). *Gilmore Oral Reading Test.* San Antonio, TX: The Psychological Corporation.

Ginzberg, E., & Bray, D. W. (1953). *The uneducated.* New York: Columbia University Press.

Goldman, R., & Fristoe, M. (1986). *Goldman-Fristoe Test of Articulation.* Circle Pines, MN: American Guidance Service.

Goldstein, K. (1927). *Die Lokalisation in der Grosshirnrinde.* In *Handb. Norm. Pathol. Physiologie.* Berlin: J. Springer.

Goldstein, K. (1936). The modification of behavior consequent to cerebral lesions. *Psychiatric Quarterly, 10,* 586–610.

Goldstein, K. (1939). *The organism.* New York: American Book.

Goodman, A. C., & Chasin, W. D. (1976). Hearing problems. In S. S. Gellis and B. M. Kagan (Eds.), *Current pediatric therapy 6.* Philadelphia: W. B. Saunders.

Goslin, D. A. (1969). *Guidelines for the collection, maintenance and dissemination of pupil records.* Troy, NY: Russell Sage Foundation.

Gottesman, I. (1968). Biogenics of race and class. In M. Deutsch, I. Katz, & A. Jensen (Eds.), *Social class, race, and psychological development.* New York: Holt, Rinehart and Winston.

Graden, J., Casey, A., & Bonstrom, O. (1983). *Pre-referral interventions: Effects on referral rates and teacher attitudes.* (Research Report No. 140). Minneapolis: Minnesota Institute for Research on Learning Disabilities.

Graham, F., & Kendall, B. K. (1960). Memory for Designs Test: Revised general manual. *Perceptual and Motor Skills, 11,* 147–188.

Gray, W. S., & Robinson, H. M. (1967). *Gray Oral Reading Test.* Austin, TX: Pro-Ed.

Greenwood, C. R., Delquadri, J., & Hall, R. V. (1989). Longitudinal effects of classwide peer tutoring. *Journal of Educational Psychology, 81,* 371–383.

Gresham, F., & Elliott, S. N. (1990). *Social Skills Rating System.* Circle Pines, MN: American Guidance Service.

Gronlund, N. (1985). *Measurement and evaluation in teaching* (5th ed.). New York: Macmillan.

Gronlund, N. E. (1976). *Measurement and evaluation in teaching* (3rd ed.). New York: Macmillan.

Gronlund, N. E. (1982). *Constructing achievement tests.* Englewood Cliffs, NJ: Prentice-Hall.

Grossman, H. (1983). *Manual of terminology and classification in mental retardation.* Washington, DC: American Association on Mental Deficiency.

Guarmaccia, V. (1976). Factor structure and correlates of adaptive behavior in noninstitutionalized retarded adults. *American Journal of Mental Deficiency, 80,* 543–547.

Guilford, J. (1954). *Psychometric methods.* New York: McGraw-Hill.

Guilford, J. P. (1967). *The nature of human intelligence.* New York: McGraw-Hill.

Hallahan, D., & Cruickshank, W. (1973). *Psychoeducational foundations of learning disabilities.* Englewood Cliffs, NJ: Prentice-Hall.

Hammill, D. D. (1985). *Detroit Tests of Learning Aptitude–2.* Austin, TX: Pro-Ed.

Hammill, D., Brown, L., Larsen, S., & Wiederholt, L. (1987). *Test of Adolescent Language: A multidimensional approach to assessment.* Austin, TX: Pro-Ed.

Hammill, D. D., & Bryant, B. (1986). *Detroit Tests of Learning Aptitude–Primary.* Austin, TX: Pro-Ed.

Hammill, D., & Larsen, S. (1983). *Test of Written Language.* Austin, TX: Pro-Ed.

Hammill, D., and Newcomer, P. (1982a). *Test of Language Development, Intermediate.* Austin, TX: Pro-Ed

Hammill, D., and Newcomer, P. (1982b). *Test of Language Development, Primary.* Austin, TX: Pro-Ed.

Hammill, D., & Wiederholt, J. L. (1973). Review of the Frostig Visual Perception Test and the related training program. In L. Mann and C. Sabatino

(Eds.), *The first review of special education* (pp. 33–48). Philadelphia: Buttonwood Farms.

Hardy, L. H., Rand, G., & Rittler, M. C. (1957). *AO H-R-R Pseudoisochromatic Plates.* Buffalo: American Optical Company, Instrument Division.

Haring, N., Liberty, K., & White, O. (1980). Rules for data-based strategy decisions in instructional programs. In W. Sailor, B. Wilcox, & L. Brown (Eds.), *Methods of instruction for severely handicapped students.* (pp. 159–192). Baltimore, MD: Brooks.

Harrison, P. (1985). *Vineland Adaptive Behavior Scales: Classroom Edition manual.* Circle Pines, MN: American Guidance Service.

Hieronymus, A. N., Hoover, H. D., & Lindquist, E. F. (1986). *Iowa Tests of Basic Skills.* Chicago: The Riverside Publishing Company.

Hiskey, M. (1966). *Hiskey-Nebraska Test of Learning Aptitude.* Lincoln, NE: Marshall S. Hiskey.

Hofmeister, A. (1975). Integrating criterion-referenced testing and instruction. In W. Hively and M. Reynolds (Eds.), *Domain-referenced testing in special education* (pp. 77–88). Minneapolis: University of Minnesota, Leadership Training Institute/Special Education.

Hogan, T. P., Farr, R. C., Prescott, G. A., & Balow, I. H. (1986). *Metropolitan Achievement Tests 6: Mathematics Diagnostic Tests.* San Antonio, TX: The Psychological Corporation.

Holtzman, W. (1966). *Holtzman Inkblot Technique.* San Antonio, TX: The Psychological Corporation.

Homme, L. (1969). *How to use contingency contracting in the classroom.* Champaign, IL: Research Press

Horn, E. (1967). *What research says to the teacher: Teaching spelling.* Washington, DC: National Education Association.

Howell, K. W. (1986). Direct assessment of academic performance. *School Psychology Review, 15,* 324–335.

Hresko, W., & Brown, L. (1984). *Test of Early Socioemotional Development.* Austin, TX: Pro-Ed.

Hurlin, R. G. (1962). Estimated prevalence of blindness in the U.S.—1960. *Sight Saving Review, 32,* 4–12.

Hutt, M. L., & Briskin, G. J. (1960). *The Hutt Adaptation of the Bender Gestalt Test.* New York: Grune & Stratton.

Ingram, D. (1976). *Phonological disability in children.* New York: American Elsevier.

Isaacson, S. (1988). Assessing the writing product: Qualitative and quantitative measures. *Exceptional children, 54,* 528–534.

Ishihara, S. (1970). *The Ishihara Color Blind Test book (children): 12 plates.* Tokyo: Kanehara Shuppan.

Jastak, S., & Wilkinson, G. (1984). *Wide Range Achievement Test–Revised.* Wilmington, DE: Jastak Assessment Systems.

Jenkins, J., & Pany, D. (1978). Standardized achievement tests: How useful for special education? *Exceptional Children, 44,* 448–453.

Jensen, J. A. & Armstrong, R. J. (1985). *Slosson Intelligence Test for Children and Adults: Expanded norms tables application and development.* East Aurora, NY: Slosson Educational Publications.

Kappauf, W. E. (1973). Studying the relationship of task performance to the variables of chronological age, mental age, and IQ. In N. Ellis (Ed.), *International review of research in mental retardation* (Vol. 6). New York: Academic Press.

Karlsen, B. & Gardner, E. (1985). *Stanford Diagnostic Reading Test* (3rd Ed.) San Antonio, TX: The Psychological Corporation.

Kaufman, A., & Kaufman, N. (1983). *Kaufman Assessment Battery for Children, interpretive manual.* Circle Pines, MN: American Guidance Service.

Kaufman, A., & Kaufman, N. (1985a). *Kaufman Test of Educational Achievement.* Circle Pines, MN: American Guidance Service.

Kaufman, A., & Kaufman, N. (1985b). *Kaufman Test of Educational Achievement, Brief Form manual.* Circle Pines, MN: American Guidance Service.

Kaufman, A. & Kaufman, N. (1985c). *Kaufman Test of Educational Achievement, Comprehensive Form manual.* Circle Pines, MN: American Guidance Service.

Kazdin, A. E. (1973). The effects of vicarious reinforcement in the classroom. *Journal of Applied Behavior Analysis, 6,* 71–78.

Kelley, M. F., & Surbeck, E. (1985). History of preschool assessment. In K. D. Paget & B. Bracken (Eds.), *The psychoeducational assessment of preschool children.* New York: Grune & Stratton.

Khan, L., & Lewis, N. (1983). *Khan-Lewis phonological analysis.* Circle Pines, MN: American Guidance Service.

Kirk, S. A., & Kirk, W. D. (1971). *Psycholinguistic learning disabilities: Diagnosis and remediation.* Champaign, IL: University of Illinois Press.

Kirk, S., McCarthy, J., & Kirk, W. (1968). *Illinois Test of Psycholinguistic Abilities*. Champaign, IL: University of Illinois Press.

Kohn, M. (1986). *Kohn Social Competence Scale*. San Antonio, TX: The Psychological Corporation.

Koppitz, E. M. (1963). *The Bender Gestalt Test for Young Children*. New York: Grune & Stratton.

Koppitz, E. M. (1968). *Human Figures Drawing Test*. New York: Grune & Stratton.

Koppitz, E. M. (1975). *The Bender Gestalt Test for Young Children: Volume II: Research and application, 1963–1973*. New York: Grune & Stratton.

Lahey, M., (1988). *Language disorders and language development*. New York: Macmillan.

Lambert, N. (1981). Diagnostic and technical manual. *AAMD Adaptive Behavior Scale–School Edition*. Monterey, CA: CTB/McGraw-Hill.

Lambert, N., & Nicoll, R. (1976). Dimensions of adaptive behavior of retarded and non-retarded public-school children. *American Journal of Mental Deficiency, 81,* 135–146.

Lambert, N., & Windmiller, M. (1981). *Diagnostic and technical manual, revised, AAMD Adaptive Behavior Scale–School Edition*. Monterey, CA: CTB/McGraw-Hill.

Lambert, N., Windmiller, M., Tharinger, D., & Cole, L. (1981). *Administration and instructional planning manual, AAMD Adaptive Behavior Scale–School Edition*. Monterey, CA: CTB/McGraw-Hill.

Lamke, T., Nelson, M., & French, J. (1973). *Henmon-Nelson Tests of Mental Ability*. Chicago: The Riverside Publishing Company.

Larsen, S., & Hammill, D. (1986). *Test of Written Spelling, 2*. Austin, TX: Pro-Ed.

Lashley, K. (1951). The problem of serial order in behavior. In L. Jeffress (Ed.), *Cerebral mechanisms in behavior*. New York: Wiley.

Lee, J., & Clark, W. (1962). *Manual Lee-Clark Reading Readiness Test*. Monterey, CA: CTB/McGraw-Hill.

Lee, L. (1969). *Northwestern Syntax Screening Test*. Evanston, IL: Northwestern University Press.

Lee, L. (1974). *Developmental sentence analysis*. Evanston, IL: Northwestern University Press.

Lee, L., & Canter, S. (1971). Developmental Sentence Scoring: A clinical procedure for estimating syntactic development in children's spontaneous speech. *Journal of Speech and Hearing Disorders, 36,* 315–340.

Lentz, F. E., & Shapiro, E. S. Functional assessment of the academic environment. *School Psychology Review, 15,* 346–358.

Levine, E. (1974). Psychological tests and practices with the deaf: A survey of the state of the art. *Volta Review, 76,* 298–319.

Lindquist, E. F., & Feldt, L. S. (1980). *Iowa Tests of Educational Development*. Chicago: Science Research Associates.

Luria, A. (1966). *Higher cortical functions in man*. New York: Basic Books.

MacGinitie, W. (1978). *Gates-MacGinitie Reading Tests*. Chicago: The Riverside Publishing Company.

Madden, R., Gardner, E. F., & Collins, C. S. (1983). *Stanford Early School Achievement Test* (2nd ed.). Cleveland: The Psychological Corporation.

Mann, L. (1971). Psychometric phrenology and the new faculty psychology: The case against ability assessment and training. *Journal of Special Education, 5,* 3–14.

Mardell-Czudnowski, C., & Goldenberg, D. (1983). *Developmental Indicators for the Assessment of Learning–Revised*. Edison, NJ: Childcraft Education Corp.

Mardell-Czudnowski, C., & Goldenberg, D. S. (1990). *Developmental Indicators for the Assessment of Learning–Revised*. Circle Pines, MN: American Guidance Service.

Marsh, H. W. (1988). *Self-Description Questionnaire I and II*. San Antonio, TX: The Psychological Corporation.

Marston, D., & Magnusson, D. (1985). Implementing curriculum-based measurement in special and regular education settings. *Exceptional Children, 52,* 266–276.

McCarthy, D. (1972). *Manual for the McCarthy Scales of Children's Abilities*. San Antonio, TX: The Psychological Corporation.

Mercer, C., & Mercer, A. (1985). *Teaching students with learning problems* (2nd ed.). Columbus, OH: Merrill.

Mercer, C., Mercer, A., & Evans, S. (1982). The use of frequency in establishing instructional aims. *Journal of Precision Teaching, 3,* 57–63.

Mercer, J. (1979). *System of Multicultual Pluralistic Assessment: Technical manual*. Cleveland: The Psychological Corporation.

Mercer, J., & Lewis, J. (1977). *SOMPA: Parent interview manual*. Cleveland: The Psychological Corporation.

Miller, G. (1951). *Language and communication*. New York: McGraw-Hill.

Miller, J. (1981). *Assessing language production in children*. Austin, TX: Pro-Ed.

Mischel, W. (1970). Sex typing and socialization. In J. M. Tanner (Ed.). *Carmichael's manual of child psychology*. New York: Wiley.

Moss, M. (1979). *Tests of Basic Experiences 2: Norms and Technical data book*. Monterey, CA: CTB/McGraw-Hill.

Mueller, M. (1965). *A comparison of the empirical validity of six tests of ability with young educable retardates* (IMRID Behavioral Science Monograph No. 1). Nashville: Institute on Mental Retardation and Intellectual Development.

Murray, H., and Bellak, L. (1973). *Thematic Apperception Test*. Cambridge, MA: Harvard University Press.

Naslund, R. A., Thorpe, L. P., & LeFever, D. W. (1978). *SRA Achievement Series*. Chicago: Science Research Associates.

National Society for the Prevention of Blindness. (1961). *Vision screening in the schools*. New York: Author.

National Society for the Prevention of Blindness. (1966). *Estimated statistics on blindness and vision problems*. New York: Author.

Neeper, R., Lahey, B. B., & Frick, P. J. (1990). *Comprehensive Behavior Rating Scale for Children*. San Antonio, TX: The Psychological Corporation.

Nelson, M., & French, J. (1974). *Henmon-Nelson Tests of Mental Ability: Primary Form 1*. Chicago: The Riverside Publishing Company.

Newborg, J., Stock, J. R., Wnek, L., Guidubaldi, J., & Svinicki, J. (1984). *The Battelle Developmental Inventory*. Allen, TX: DLM/Teaching Resources.

Newcomer, P. (1986). *Standardized Reading Inventory*. Austin, TX: Pro-Ed.

Newland, T. E. (1969). *Blind Learning Aptitude Test*. Champaign, IL: T. Ernest Newland.

Newland, T. E. (1973). Assumptions underlying psychological testing. *Journal of School Psychology, 11*, 316–322.

Nihira, K. (1969a). Factorial dimensions of adaptive behavior in adult retardates. *American Journal of Mental Deficiency, 73*, 868–878.

Nihira, K. (1969b). Factorial dimensions of adaptive behavior in mentally retarded children and adolescents. *American Journal of Mental Deficiency, 74*, 130–141.

Nihira, K., Foster, R., Shellhaas, M., & Leland, H. (1975). *AAMD Adaptive Behavior Scale for Children and Adults, 1974 Revision*. Washington, DC: American Association on Mental Deficiency.

Nunnally, J. (1967). *Psychometric theory*. New York: McGraw-Hill.

Nunnally, J. (1978). *Psychometric theory*. New York: McGraw-Hill.

Nurss, J. R., & McGauvran, M. E. (1986). *Metropolitan readiness tests*. San Antonio, TX: The Psychological Coproration.

Osgood, C. (1957). *Motivational dynamics of language behavior. Nebraska symposium on motivation*. Lincoln, NE: University of Nebraska Press.

Osgood, C. E. (1957a). A behavioristic analysis of perception and language as cognitive phenomena. In *Contemporary approaches to cognition* (pp. 75–118). Cambridge, MA: Harvard University Press. (Cited by Paraskevopoulos & Kirk, 1969.)

Osgood, C. E. (1957b). Motivational dynamics of language behavior. In M. R. Jones (Ed.), *Nebraska symposium on motivation* (pp. 348–424). Lincoln, NE: University of Nebraska Press. (Cited by Paraskevopoulos & Kirk, 1969.)

Otis, A. S., & Lennon, R. T. (1989). *Otis-Lennon School Ability test*. San Antonio, TX: The Psychological Corporation.

Paraskevopoulos, J. N., & Kirk, S. A. (1969). *The development and psychometric characteristics of the Revised Illinios Test of Psycholinguistic Abilities*. Champaign, IL: University of Illinois Press.

Paul, D., Nibbelink, W., & Hoover, H. (1986). The effects of adjusting readability on the difficulty of mathematics story problems. *Journal of Research in Mathematics Education, 17*, 163–171.

Phillips, K. (1990). *Factors that affect the feasibility of interventions*. Workshop presented at Mounds View Schools, unpublished.

Piaget, J. (1955). *The language and thought of the child*. Cleveland, OH: World.

Piers, E., & Harris, D. (1969). *The Piers-Harris Children's Self-Concept Scale*. Nashville: Counselor Recordings and Tests.

Piotrowski, Z. (1957). *Perceptanalysis*. New York: Macmillan.

Poole, I. (1934). Genetic development of articulation of consonant sounds in speech. *Elementary English Review, 11*, 159–161.

Porter, R. B., & Cattell, R. B. (1982). *Children's Personality Questionnaire*. Champaign, IL: Institute for Personality and Ability Testing.

Prechtl, H. F. (1974). The behavioral states of the newborn. *Brain Research, 6,* 185–212.

Prescott, G. A., Balow, I. H., Hogan, T. R., & Farr, R. C. (1984). *Metropolitan Achievement Tests 6: Survey Battery.* San Antonio, TX: The Psychological Corporation.

Prutting, C., & Kirshner, D. (1987). A clinical appraisal of the pragmatic aspects of language. *Journal of Speech and Hearing Disorders, 52,* 105–119.

Quay, H., & Peterson, D. (1987). *Revised Behavior Problem Checklist.* Coral Gables, FL: University of Miami.

Quick, A., Little, T., & Campbell, A. (1974). *Project MEMPHIS: Enhancing developmental progress in preschool exceptional childen.* Belmont, CA: Fearon.

Rees, N. S. (1973). Auditory processing factors in language disorders: The view from Procrustes' bed. *Journal of Speech and Hearing Disorders, 38,* 304–315.

Reynolds, C. R., & Richmond, B. O. (1985). *Revised Children's Manifest Anxiety Scale.* Los Angeles, CA: Western Psychological Services.

Reynolds, M. (1975). Trends in special education: Implications for measurement. In W. Hively and M. Reynolds (Eds.), *Domain-referenced testing in special education.* Minneapolis: University of Minnesota, Leadership Training Institute/Special Education.

Reynolds, W. M. (1987). *Reynolds Adolescent Depression Scale.* Palo Alto, CA: *Western Psychological Services.*

Roach, E. F., & Kephart, N. C. (1966). *The Purdue Perceptual-Motor Survey.* Columbus, OH: Merrill.

Roberts, J. (1971) *Intellectual development of children by demographic and socioeconomic factors.* (DHEW Publication No. HSM 72-1012). Washington, DC: U.S. Government Printing Office.

Robinson, N., & Robinson, H. (1976). *The mentally retarded child.* New York: McGraw-Hill.

Rorschach, H. (1966). *Rorschach Ink Blot Technique.* New York: Grune & Stratton.

Salvia, J., & Good, R. (1982). Significant discrepancies in the classification of pupils: Differentiating the concept. In J. T. Neisworth (Ed.), *Assessment in special eduction.* Rockville, MD: Aspen Systems.

Salvia, J., & Hughes, C. (1990). *Curriculum-based assessment: Testing what is taught.* New York: Macmillan.

Salvia, J., & Ysseldyke, J. E. (1972). Criterion validity of four tests for red-green color blindness.

American Journal of Mental Deficiency, 76, 418–422.

Salvia, J., & Ysseldyke, J. E. (1978). *Assessment in special and remedial education.* Boston: Houghton Mifflin.

Scannell, D. P. (1986). *Tests of Achievement and Proficiency.* Chicago: The Riverside Publishing Company.

Shinn, M. R. (Ed.). (1989). *Curriculum-based measurement: Assessing special children.* New York: Guilford.

Shinn, M., Tindall, G., & Stein, S. (1988). Curriculum-based measurement and the identification of mildly handicapped students: A review of research. *Professional School Psychology, 3,* 69–85.

Shriner, J., & Salvia, J. (1988). Content validity of two tests with two math curricula over three years: Another instance of chronic noncorrespondence. *Exceptional Children, 55,* 240–248.

Shub, A. N., Carlin, J. A., Friedman, R. L., Kaplan, J. M., & Katien, J. C. (1973). *Diagnosis: An instructional aid (reading).* Chicago: Science Research Associates.

Slingerland, B. (1970). *Teacher's manual to accompany Slingerland Screening Tests for Identifying Children with Specific Language Disability.* Los Angeles: Western Psychological Services.

Slingerland, B. (1974). *Slingerland Screening Tests for Identifying Children with Specific Language Disability. Form D for Grade V and Grade VI.* Cambridge, MA: Educators Publishing Service.

Slobin, D. I., & Welsh, C. A. (1973). Elicited imitation as a research tool in developmental psycholinguistics. In C. Ferguson and D. Slobin (Eds.), *Studies of child language development.* New York: Holt, Rinehart and Winston.

Slosson, R. L. (1971). *Slosson Intelligence Test.* East Aurora, NY: Slosson Educational Publications.

Solomon, I., & Starr, B. (1968). *School Apperception Method.* New York: Springer.

Sonnenschein, J. L. (1983). *Basic Achievement Skills Individual Screener.* Cleveland: The Psychological Corporation.

Spache, G. D. (1981). *Diagnostic Reading Scales.* Monterey, CA: CTB/McGraw-Hill.

Sparrow, S., Balla, D., & Cicchetti, D. (1984a). *Interview edition, expanded form manual, Vineland Adaptive Behavior Scales.* Circle Pines, MN: American Guidance Service.

Sparrow, S., Balla, D., & Cicchetti, D. (1984b). *Interview edition, survey form manual, Vineland*

Adaptive Behavior Scales. Circle Pines, MN: American Guidance Service.

Spivack, G., & Spotts, J. (1966). *Devereux Child Behavior Rating Scale.* Devon, PA: The Devereux Foundation Press.

Spivack, G., Spotts, J., & Haimes, P. (1967). *Devereux Adolescent Behavior Rating Scale.* Devon, PA: The Devereux Foundation Press.

Spivack, G., & Swift, M. (1967). *Devereux Elementary School Behavior Rating Scale.* Devon, PA: The Devereux Foundation Press.

Stake, R., & Wardrop, J. (1971). Gain score errors in performance contracting. *Research in the Teaching of English, 5,* 226–229.

Stevens, S. S. (1951). Mathematics, measurement, and psychophysics. In S. S. Stevens (Ed.), *Handbook of experimental psychology* (p. 23). New York: Wiley.

Stokes, S. (1982). *School-based staff support teams: A blueprint for action.* Reston, VA: Council for Exceptional Children.

Suen, H., & Ary, D. (1989). *Analyzing quantitative behavioral observation data.* Hillsdale, NJ: Lawrence Erlbaum.

Tanner, J. M. (1970). Biological bases of development. In J. M. Tanner (Ed.), *Carmichael's manual of child psychology.* New York: Wiley.

Terman, L., & Merrill, M. (1916). *Stanford-Binet Intelligence Scale.* Boston: Houghton Mifflin.

Terman, L., & Merrill, M. (1937). *Stanford-Binet Intelligence Scale.* Boston, MA: Houghton Mifflin.

Terman, L., & Merrill, M. (1973). *Stanford-Binet Intelligence Scale.* Chicago, IL: The Riverside Publishing Company.

Thorndike, R. (1963). *The concepts of over- and underachievement.* New York: Columbia University Press.

Thorndike, R., & Hagen, E. (1978). *Measurement and evaluation in psychology and education.* New York: Wiley.

Thorndike, R., & Hagen, E. (1986). *Cognitive Abilities Test.* Chicago, IL: The Riverside Publishing Company.

Thorndike, R. L., Hagen, E., & Sattler, J. (1985). *Stanford-Binet Intelligence Scale.* Chicago, IL: The Riverside Publishing Company.

Thorndike, R. L., Hagen, E., & Sattler, J. (1986). *Technical manual, The Stanford-Binet Intelligence Scale: Fourth edition.* Chicago, IL: The Riverside Publishing Co.

Thurstone, T. (1978). *Educational Ability Series.* Chicago: Science Research Associates.

Tucker, J. (1985). Curriculum-based assessment: An introduction. *Exceptional Children, 52,* 199–204.

Tyak, D., & Gottsleben, M. (1974). *Language sampling, analysis and training: A handbook for teachers and clinicians.* Palo Alto, CA: Consulting Psychologists Press.

U.S. Office of Education. (1977). Assistance to states for education of handicapped children: Procedures for evaluating specific learning disabilities. *Federal Register, 42,* December 29.

U.S. Public Health Service. (1971). *Vision screening of children* (PHS Document No. 2042). Washington, DC: Author.

Urban, W. (1963). *Draw-a-Person.* Los Angeles: Western Psychological Services.

Van Riper, C. (1939). *Speech correction.* Englewood Cliffs, NJ: Prentice-Hall.

Van Riper, C. (1963). *Speech correction: Principles and methods* (4th ed.). Englewood Cliffs, NJ: Prentice-Hall.

Vinter, R., Sarri, R., Vorwaller, D., & Schafer, E. (1966). *Pupil Behavior Inventory.* Ann Arbor: Campus Publishers.

Waksman, S. (1983). *Waksman Social Skills Rating Scale.* Brandon, VT: Clinical Psychology Publishing.

Waksman, S. (1984). *Portland Problem Behavior Checklist–1984 Revision.* Brandon, VT: Clinical Psychology Publishing.

Walker, D. K. (1973). *Socioemotional measures for preschool and kindergarten children.* San Francisco: Jossey-Bass.

Walker, H. (1983). *Walker Problem Behavior Identification Checklist.* Los Angeles: Western Psychological Services.

Walker, H. M., & McConnell, S. R. (1988). *Walker-McConnell Scale of Social Competence.* Austin, TX: Pro-Ed.

Wechsler, D. (1967). *Manual for the Wechsler Preschool and Primary Scale of Intelligence.* Cleveland: The Psychological Corporation.

Wechsler, D. (1974). *Manual for the Wechsler Intelligence Scale for Children–Revised.* Cleveland: The Psychological Corporation.

Wechsler, D. (1981). *Manual for the Wechsler Adult Intelligence Scale–Revised.* New York: The Psychological Corporation.

Weinberg, R., & Wood, R. (1975). *Observation of pupils and teachers in mainstream and special education settings: Alternative strategies.* Minneapolis:

University of Minnesota, Leadership Training Institute/Special Education.

Weiner, F. (1979). *Phonological process analysis*. Baltimore: University Park Press.

Wellman, B. L., Case, I. M., Mengert, I. G., & Bradbury, D. E. (1931). *Speech sounds of young children* (University of Iowa Studies in Child Welfare). Iowa City: University of Iowa Press.

Wepman, J. M. (1973). *Auditory Discrimination Test (rev. ed.)*. Chicago: Language Research Associates.

Werner, H., & Strauss, A. A. (1941). Pathology of figure-background relation in the child. *Journal of Abnormal and Social Psychology, 36*, 236–248.

White, O., & Liberty, K. (1980). Behavioral assessment and precise educational measurement. In N. Haring & R. Schiefelbusch (Eds.), *Teaching special children* (pp. 31–71). New York: McGraw-Hill.

Wiederholt, L. (1986). *Formal Reading Inventory*. Austin, TX: Pro-Ed.

Wiederholt, L., & Bryant, B. (1986). *Gray Oral Reading Test–Revised*. Austin, TX: Pro-Ed.

Wiley, J. (1971). A psychology of auditory impairment. In W. Cruickshank (Ed.), *Psychology of exceptional children and youth*. Englewood Cliffs, NJ: Prentice-Hall.

Williams, G. C., & McReynolds, L. V. (1975). The relationship between discrimination and articulation training in children with misarticulations. *Journal of Speech and Hearing Research, 18*, 401–412.

Winitz, H. (1975). *From syllable to conversation*. Baltimore: University Park Press.

Wirt, R. D., Lachar, D., Klinedinst, J. K., Seat, P. D., & Broen, W. E. (1984). *Personality Inventory for Children, Revised Format*. Los Angeles, CA: Western Psychological Services.

Wolery, M. (1989). Using direct observation in assessment. In D. B. Bailey & M. Wolery (Eds.), *Assessing infants and preschoolers with handicaps*. Columbus, OH: Merrill.

Wolfram, W. A. (1971). Social dialects from a linguistic perspective: Assumptions, current research and future directions. In R. Shuy (comp.), *Social dialects and interdisciplinary perspectives*. Washington, DC: Center for Applied Linguistics.

Woodcock, R. (1987). *Woodcock Reading Mastery Tests–Revised*. Circle Pines, MN: American Guidance Service.

Woodcock, R., & Mather, N. (1989a). *Woodcock-Johnson Tests of Cognitive Ability, Standard and Supplemental Batteries, examiner's manual*. Allen, TX: DLM.

Woodcock, R., & Mather, N. (1989b). *Woodcock-Johnson Tests of Achievement Standard and Supplemental Batteries, examiner's manual*. Allen, TX: DLM.

Woodcock, R. W., & Johnson, M. B. (1989). *Woodcock-Johnson Psycho-Educational Battery–Revised*. Allen, TX: DLM.

Ysseldyke, J. E. (1973). Diagnostic-prescriptive teaching: The search for aptitude-treatment interactions. In L. Mann and D. A. Sabatino (Eds.), *The first review of special education*. New York: Grune and Stratton.

Ysseldyke, J. E., & Christenson, S. L. (1987). *The Instructional Environment Scale*. Austin, TX: Pro-Ed.

Ysseldyke, J. E., & Marston, D. (1982). Gathering decision-making information through the use of non-test-based methods. *Measurement and Evaluation in Guidance, 15*, 58–69.

Ysseldyke, J. E., & Salvia, J. (1974). Diagnostic-prescriptive teaching: Two models. *Exceptional Children, 41*, 181–186.

GLOSSARY

Abscissa   The horizontal axis, or continuum on which individuals are measured.

Accommodative ability   The automatic adjustment of the eyes for seeing at different distances.

Acculturation   A child's particular set of background experiences and opportunities to learn in both formal and informal educational settings.

Achievement   What has been learned as a result of instruction.

Adaptive behavior   The extent to which individuals adapt themselves to the expectations of nature and society.

Age equivalent   A derived score that expresses a person's performance as the average (the median or mean) performance for that age group. Age equivalents are expressed in years and months; a hyphen is used in age scores (for example, 7-1). Age-equivalent scores are interpreted as a performance equal to the average of X-year-olds' performance.

Aid   An error in oral reading in which a student hesitates for more than 10 seconds and the word or words are supplied by the teacher.

Algorithms   The steps, processes, or procedures one goes through to solve a problem or reach a goal.

Alternate forms   Two tests that measure the same trait or skill to the same extent and are standardized on the same population. Alternate forms offer essentially equivalent tests; sometimes, in fact, they're called equivalent forms.

Amplitude   The intensity of a behavior.

Assessment   The process of collecting data for the purpose of (1) specifying and verifying problems and (2) making decisions about students.

Attainment   What an individual has learned, regardless of where it has been learned.

Audiogram   A graph of the results of the pure-tone threshold test.

Behavioral observation   Observation of behavior other than behavior that has been elicited by a predetermined and standardized set of stimuli—that is, test behavior.

Bimodal distributions   Distributions that have two modes.

Biserial correlation coefficient   An index of association between two variables when one has been forced into an arbitrary dichotomy (for example, smart/dull) and one is equal-interval (for example, grade-point average).

Cash validity   The notion that frequently used tests are valid tests.

Category A data   The basic, minimum information schools need to collect in order to operate an educational program, including identifying information as well as information about a student's educational progress.

Category B data   Test results and other verified information useful to the schools in planning a student's educational program or maintaining a student "safely" in school.

Category C data   Information that may be potentially useful to schools. This includes any unverified information, scores on personality tests, and so forth.

Classification   In the schools, a type of decision that concerns a pupil's eligibility for special services, special education services, remedial education services, speech services, and so forth.

Coefficient alpha   The average split-half correlation based on all possible divisions of a test into two parts. Coefficient alpha can be computed directly from the variances of individual test items and the variance of the total test score.

Concurrent criterion-related validity   How accurately a person's current test score can be used to estimate a score on a criterion measure.

Conductive hearing loss   Abnormal hearing sensitivity associated with poor air-conduction sensitivity but normal bone–conduction sensitivity.

Confidence interval   The range of scores within which the probability of a person's true score occurring is known.

Construct validity   The extent to which a test measures a theoretical trait or characteristic.

Consultation   A meeting between a resource teacher or other specialist and a classroom teacher to verify the existence of a problem, specify the nature of a problem, and develop strategies that might relieve the problem.

Content validity   The extent to which the test is an adequate measure of the content it is designed to cover. Content validity is established by examining three factors—the appropriateness of the types of items included, the completeness of the item sample, and the way in which the items assess the content.

Correlation   The degree of relationship between two or more variables. A correlation tells us the extent to which any two variables go together, the extent to which changes in one variable are reflected by changes in the second variable.

Correlation coefficient   Numerical index of the relationship between two or more variables.

Criterion-referenced tests Measure a person's development of particular skills in terms of absolute levels of mastery.

Criterion-related validity Refers to the extent to which a person's score on a criterion measure can be estimated from that person's test score on a test of unknown validity.

Curriculum-based assessment Use of assessment materials and procedures that mirror instruction in order to ascertain whether specific instructional objectives have been accomplished and to monitor progress directly in the curriculum being taught.

Deciles Bands of percentiles that are 10 percentile ranks in width; each decile contains 10 percent of the norm group.

Derived scores A general term for raw scores that are transformed to developmental scores or scores of relative standing.

Descriptive statistics Numerical values that describe a data set, such as mean, standard deviation, or correlation.

Developmental scores Raw scores that have been transformed into age equivalents (mental ages, for example), grade equivalents, or developmental quotients using the following formula: $100 * A.E./CA$.

Deviation IQs Standard scores with a mean of 100 and a standard deviation of 15 or 16 (depending on the test).

Deviation score The distance between an individual's score and the average score for the group, such as z-scores, T-scores, etc.

Discriminative stimuli Stimuli that are consistently present when a behavior is reinforced and occasion behavior even in the absence of the original reinforcer.

Disregard of punctuation An error in oral reading in which a student fails to inflect as a result of punctuation. For example, a student may not pause for a comma, stop for a period, or indicate voice inflection at a question mark or exclamation point.

Distractors Incorrect options contained in a response set.

Distributions The way in which scores in a set array themselves. Distributions may be graphed to demonstrate visually the relations among the scores in the group or set.

Duration The length of time a behavior lasts.

Ecobehavioral observation Observations targeting the interaction among student behavior, teacher behavior, time allocated to instruction, physical grouping structures, the types of tasks being used, and instructional content. Ecobehavioral assessment enables educators to identify natural instructional conditions that are associated with academic success, behavioral competence, or problem behaviors.

Equal-interval scales Scales on which the differences between adjacent values are equal but on which there is no absolute or logical zero.

Error Misrepresentation of a person's score as a result of failure to obtain a representative sample of times, items, or scorers.

Ethnographic observation   The observer maintains a role as someone who is watching what is occurring.

Etiology   Cause of a disorder.

Expressive language   The production of language.

Free operant   Having more problems than a student can answer in the given time period.

Frequency   The tabulation of behaviors that have discrete beginnings and endings. When the time periods in which the behavior is counted vary, frequencies are usually converted to rates.

Grade equivalent   A derived score that expresses a student's performance as the average (the median or mean) performance for a particular grade. Grade equivalents are expressed in grades and tenths of grades; a decimal point is used in grade scores (for example, 7.1).

Gross mispronunciation   An error in oral reading in which a student's pronunciation of a word is in no way similar to the word in the text.

Hesitation   An error in oral reading in which a student pauses for two or more seconds before pronouncing a word.

Historical information   Information that describes how that person has functioned in the past.

Individual consent   Consent by parent (or pupil) required for the collection of family information (religion, income, occupation, and so on), personality data, and other noneducational information.

Individualized education plan (IEP)   A document in which school personnel must specify the long-term and short-term goals of an instructional program, where the program will be delivered, who will deliver the program, and how progress will be evaluated.

Informal assessment   Any assessment that involves collection of data by anything other than a norm-referenced (standardized) test.

Informed consent   The parent (or pupil) is "reasonably competent to understand the nature and consequences of his decision" (Goslin, 1969, p. 17).

Insertion   An error in oral reading in which a student adds one or more words to the sentence being read.

Intelligence   An inferred ability, a term or construct used to explain differences in present behavior and to predict differences in future behavior.

Internal consistency   A measure of the extent to which items in a test correlate with one another.

Interscorer reliability   An estimate of the degree of agreement between two or more scores on the same test.

Inversion   An oral reading error in which a student says the words in an order different from the order in which they are written.

Keyed response   Correct answer in a response set.

Kurtosis   The "peakedness" of a curve or the rate at which a curve rises.

Language   A code for conveying ideas (cf. Bloom & Lahey, 1978; Fromkin & Rodman, 1978; Reich, 1986). Although there is some variation, language theorists also propose five basic components to describe the code—phonology, semantics, morphology, syntax, and pragmatics.

Leptokurtic curves   Fast-rising curves; tests that do not "spread out" (or discriminate among) those taking the test are typically leptokurtic.

Mean   Arithmetic average of scores in a distribution.

Median   Score that divides the top 50 percent of test takers from the bottom 50 percent. The point on a scale above which 50 percent of the cases (not the scores) occur and below which 50 percent of the cases occur.

Metalinguistic   This refers to the direct examination of the structural aspects of language.

Mixed hearing loss   Abnormal hearing sensitivity attributed to abnormal bone-conduction and even more abnormal air–conduction.

Mode   The most frequently obtained score in a distribution.

Momentary time sampling   A procedure used in systematic observation to determine when observations will occur. A behavior is scored as an occurrence if it is present at the last moment of an observation interval; if the behavior is not occurring at the last moment of the interval, a nonoccurrence is recorded.

Multiple-skill batteries   Tests that measure skill development in several achievement areas.

Negatively skewed distribution   An asymmetric distribution in which scores "tail off" to the low end; a distribution in which there are more scores above the mean than below.

Nominal scales   A scale of measurement in which variables and adjacent values have no inherent relationship among themselves.

Nonsystematic observation   Observations in which the observer notes behaviors, characteristics, and personal interactions that seem of significance.

Normal curve equivalents   Standard scores with a mean equal to 100 and a standard deviation equal to 21.06.

Normative sample or norm group   A group of subjects of known demographic characteristics (age, sex, grade in school, and so on) to whom a person's performance may be compared.

Norm-referenced devices   Tests that compare an individual's performance to the performance of his or her peers.

Objective-referenced assessment   Tests referenced to specific instructional objectives rather than to the performance of a peer group or norm group.

Observation   Refers to the process of gaining information through one's senses—visual, auditory, and so forth. Observation can be used to assess behavior, states, physical characteristics, and permanent products of behavior (e.g., a child's poem).

Omission   An error in oral reading in which a student skips a word or group of words.

Operationalize   Defining a behavior or event in terms of the operations used to measure it. For example, an operational definition of intelligence would be a score on a specific intelligence test.

Ordinal scales   Scales on which values of measurement are ordered from best to worst or from worst to best. On ordinal scales, the differences between adjacent values are unknown.

Ordinate   Vertical axis of a distribution showing the frequency (or the number) of individuals earning any given score.

Partial-interval recording   A procedure used in systematic observation in which an occurrence is scored if the behavior occurs during any part of the interval.

Partial mispronunciation   An error in oral reading in which a student may make one of several kinds of errors, including partial pronunciation, phonetic mispronunciation of part of the word, omission of part of the word, or inserting elements of words.

Participant-observer approach   The observer joins the target social group and participates in its activities.

Pearson product-moment correlation coefficient (r)   An index of the straight-line (linear) relationship between two or more variables measured on an equal-interval scale.

Percentile ranks (%iles)   Derived scores that indicate the percentage of people that occur at or below a given raw score. They are useful for both ordinal and equal-interval scales.

Phi coefficient   An index of linear correlation between two sets of naturally dichotomous variables (for example, male/female and dead/alive).

Phonology   Speech sounds.

Platykurtic curves   Distributions that are flat and slow rising.

Point biserial correlation   An index of linear correlation between one naturally occurring dichotomous variable (such as sex) and a continuous, equal-interval variable (height measured in inches).

Positively skewed distribution   Asymmetrical distribution in which scores tail off to the higher end of the continuum; a distribution in which there are more scores below the mean than above it.

Power tests   Untimed tests.

Pragmatics   The social context in which language appears.

Predictive validity   Using current test scores to estimate accurately what criterion scores will be at a later time.

Prereferral assessment   Activities that occur prior to formal referral, assessment, and consideration for placement. The goal of prereferral assessment and intervention is twofold—(1) verification and specification of the nature of a student's difficulties and (2) provision of services in the least restrictive environment.

Probe   A special testing format that is especially well-suited to the assessment of direct performances. Probes are brief (usually three minutes or less), timed, frequently administered assessments that can be used for any purpose.

Prognosis   A prediction of future performance.

Qualitative data   Information consisting of nonsystematic and unquantified observations.

Qualitative observation   A description of behavior, its function, and context. The observer begins without preconceived ideas about what will be observed and describes behavior that seems important.

Quantitative data   Observations that have been tabulated or otherwise given numerical values.

Quartiles   Bands of percentiles that are 25 percentile ranks in width; each quartile contains 25 percent of the norm group.

Random error   In measurement, the inability to generalize from an observation of a specific behavior observed at a specific time by a specific person to observations conducted on similar behavior, at different times or by different observers.

Range   The distance between the extremes in a set of scores, including those extremes; the highest score less the lowest score plus one.

Ratio IQ   A derived score based on mental age in which IQ equals $\dfrac{\text{MA (in months)} \times 100}{\text{CA (in months)}}$.

Ratio scales   Scales of measurement in which the difference between adjacent values is equal and in which there is a logical and absolute zero.

Readiness   Extent of preparation to participate in an activity. The term is used most often as an index of preparation to enter school but applies at all levels.

Receptive language   Refers to comprehension of language.

Referral   A request for help from a specialist. For example, a teacher or parent may call a student to the attention of a specialist to provide the student with an appropriate educational program.

Reliability   In measurement, the extent to which it is possible to generalize from an observation of a specific behavior observed at a specific time by a specific person to observations conducted on similar behavior, at different times, or by different observers.

Reliability coefficient   An index of the extent to which observations can be generalized. The square of the correlation between obtained scores and true scores on a measure r^2_{xt}.

Repetition   An error in oral reading in which a student repeats words or groups of words.

Representational consent   Consent to collect data given by appropriately elected officials, such as the state legislature.

Sample   The representative subset of the population.

Scotoma   A spot in the eye without vision.

Screening   An initial stage of assessment in which those who *may* evidence a particular problem, disorder, disability, or disease are discriminated from the general population.

Select formats   A method of presenting test questions in which students indicate their choice from an array of the possible test answers (usually called response options). True-false, multiple-choice, and matching are the three most common select formats.

Semantics   The study of word meanings. Although the scope of the term *semantics* can extend beyond individual words to include sentence meaning, the term generally applies to words.

Sensorineural hearing loss   Abnormal hearing sensitivity associated with poor bone and air conduction sensitivity usually occurring at about the same level.

Setting events   Environmental events that set the occasion for the performance of an action.

Single-skill tests   Tests that are designed to measure skill development in one specific content area (for example, reading).

Skew   An asymmetry of a distribution; the distribution of scores below the mean are not mirror images of scores above the mean.

Social comparisons   Observing a peer whose behavior is considered to be appropriate and using the peer's rate of behavior as the standard against which to evaluate the target student's rate of behavior.

Social tolerance   The threshold above which behaviors are viewed as undesirable by others.

Social validity   A consumer's reaction to an intervention or assessment.

Spearman rho   An index of correlation between two variables measured on an ordinal scale.

Speed tests   Timed tests.

Split-half reliability estimate   An estimate of internal consistency reliability derived by correlating people's scores on two halves of a test.

Standard deviation   A measure of the degree of dispersion in a distribution; the square root of the variance.

Standard error of measurement (SEM)   The standard deviation of error around a person's true score.

Standard score   The general name for derived scores that have been transformed to produce a distribution with a predetermined mean and standard deviation.

Stanines   Standard-score bands that divide a distribution into nine parts; the middle seven stanines are each 0.50 wide and the fifth stanine is centered on the X.

Stem   In select formats, the part of a problem that contains the question.

Substitution   An error in oral reading in which a student replaces one or more words in the passage with one or more meaningful words (synonyms).

Supply formats A method of presenting test questions in which a student is required to produce a written or oral response. This response can be as restricted as the answer to a computation problem or a one-word response or can require a student to produce a sentence, a paragraph, or several pages to answer the question satisfactorily.

Syntax Specific word order of sentences, which includes a description of the rules for arranging the words into a sentence.

Systematic error Consistent error that can be predicted; bias.

Systematic observations Observations in which an observer specifies or defines the behaviors to be observed and then typically counts or otherwise measures the frequency, duration, magnitude, or latency of the behaviors.

Test A predetermined set of questions or tasks to which predetermined types of behavioral responses are sought.

Testing Exposing a person to a particular set of questions in order to obtain a score.

Test-retest reliability An index of stability over time.

Tetrachoric correlation coefficient An index of correlation between two arbitrarily dichotomized variables (for example, tall/short, smart/dull).

True score The score that a student would earn if the entire domain of items were assessed.

T-scores A standard score with a mean of 50 and a standard deviation of 10.

Tunnel vision Normal central visual acuity with a restricted peripheral field.

Validity The extent to which a test measures what its authors or users claim it measures. Specifically, test validity concerns the appropriateness of the inferences that can be made on the basis of test results.

Validity coefficient A correlation coefficient between a test of unknown validity and an established criterion measure.

Variance A numerical index describing the dispersion of a set of scores around the mean of the distribution. Specifically, the variance is the average squared-distance of the scores from the mean.

Visual acuity The clarity or sharpness with which a person sees.

Whole-interval recording A procedure used in systematic observation in which an occurrence is scored if the behavior is present throughout the entire observation interval.

z-scores Standard scores with a mean of zero and a standard deviation of one.

INDEX

AN INVITATION TO RESPOND

We would like to find out a little about your background and about your reactions to the Fifth Edition of *Assessment*. Your evaluation of the book will help us to meet the interests and needs of students in future editions. We invite you to share your reactions by completing the questionnaire below and returning it to College Marketing, Houghton Mifflin Company, One Beacon Street, Boston, MA 02108.

1. How do you rate this textbook in the following areas?

	Excellent	Good	Adequate	Poor
a. Understandable style of writing	_____	_____	_____	_____
b. Physical appearance/readability	_____	_____	_____	_____
c. Fair coverage of topics	_____	_____	_____	_____
d. Comprehensiveness (covered issues and topics)	_____	_____	_____	_____
e. Examples and case studies	_____	_____	_____	_____
f. Appendixes	_____	_____	_____	_____
g. Organization of chapters	_____	_____	_____	_____

2. Can you comment on or illustrate your above ratings? _____

_____

3. What chapters or features did you particularly like? _____

_____

4. What chapters or features did you dislike or think should be changed? _____

_____

5. What material would you suggest adding or deleting? _____

_____

6. What was the title of the course in which you used this book? _____

   _____

7. What was your class standing at the time you took the course in assess-

   ment? Junior _____   Senior _____   Graduate _____   Other

   _____ (please explain) _____

8. Have you ever taught before? _____ If so, what courses have you

   taught? _____

   _____

9. What other courses in assessment or measurement and evaluation have you

   taken? _____

   _____

10. Will you be teaching in a regular classroom or in a special classroom? _____

11. Do you intend to keep this book for use during your teaching career? _____

12. We would appreciate any other comments or reactions you are willing to

   share. _____

   _____

   _____